T0367165

DAVID VICHNAR

THE AVANT-POSTMAN
EXPERIMENT IN ANGLOPHONE AND FRANCOPHONE FICTION IN THE WAKE OF JAMES JOYCE

CHARLES UNIVERSITY
KAROLINUM PRESS 2023

KAROLINUM PRESS
Karolinum Press is a publishing department of Charles University
Ovocný trh 560/5, 116 36 Prague 1, Czech Republic
www.karolinum.cz
© David Vichnar, 2023
Set and printed in the Czech Republic by Karolinum Press
Layout by Jan Šerých
First edition

A catalogue record for this book is available from the National Library of the Czech
Republic.

ISBN 978-80-246-4937-5
ISBN 978-80-246-4938-2 (pdf)
ISBN 978-80-246-5680-9 (epub)

The original manuscript was reviewed by Ladislav Nagy (University of South Bohemia in
České Budějovice) and Martin Procházka (Charles University in Prague).

ACKNOWLEDGMENTS

This manuscript grew out of a "cotutelle" PhD thesis written in 2011–14 between Charles University Prague, Université Sorbonne Nouvelle Paris-III, and Birkbeck College London, under the joint supervision of Louis Armand and Jean Bessière.

Fondly remembered is the useful feedback received from Derek Attridge, Martha Carpentier, Daniel Ferrer, William Rowe, Fritz Senn, and the late André Topia, who read and commented upon selected parts or aspects of the work. Joseph Brooker usefully supervised the research on the Anglophone part of the thesis during a scholarship stay at Birkbeck in 2011–12. Thanks are also due to Martin Procházka and Ladislav Nagy, the external readers at Karolinum Press, whose feedback was gracious and valuable. At Karolinum, the final-draft version was read by Lauren Lee and Karolína Klibániová, thanks to whose many useful edits the manuscript achieved its completion.

Research on the Francophone parts of the thesis during the research sojourn at the Paris-III in 2012–13 was endorsed by the Mobility Fund at Charles University Prague, and by James H. Ottaway, Jr., whose support went beyond monetary value.

In the years following the defence of the thesis in March 2014 and during its lengthy rewriting process, versions of individual sections, author studies, and passages from this book have seen the light of print in the following publications:

1. *Subtexts: Essays on Fiction* (Litteraria Pragensia Books, 2015) p. 120 (esp. sections on Kathy Acker, Christine Brooke-Rose, the Oulipo, Iain Sinclair, and Phillipe Sollers);
2. "Wars Waged With/Against Joyce: James Joyce and post-1984 British Fiction," *Joycean Legacies*, ed. Martha Carpentier (London: Palgrave Macmillan, 2015) pp. 150–71 (esp. parts of Chapter Five);
3. "Between the Pun and the Portmanteau: Multilingualism in and after Joyce's *Finnegans Wake*," *The Poetics of Multilingualism – La Poétique du plurilinguisme*, eds. Patrizia Noel & Levente Seláf (Cambridge Scholars: Newcastle upon Tyne, 2017) pp. 269–80 (esp. sections on Maurice Roche and Phillippe Sollers);

4. "Remediating Joyce's Techno-poetics: Mark Amerika, Kenneth Gold-smith, Mark Z. Danielewski," *Prague Journal of English Studies*, Vol. 8 No. 1 (September 2019) pp. 119–39 (esp. parts of Chapter Eight).

NOTE ON THE TEXT & DEDICATION

Wherever available, quotations from French fiction are provided in their English translation in the main text, and accompanied by the French original in corresponding footnotes. Where no English translation exists (or was not available), the relevant meaning of the French original is elucidated in the commentary. Both French originals and English translations are included in the chapter-by-chapter bibliography side by side.

I dedicate this book to its two spiritual fathers, Louis Armand and Jean Bessière. *Per aspera ad astra.*

TABLE OF CONTENTS

INTRODUCTION

JOYCE THE AVANT-

> We are still learning to be James Joyce's contemporaries,
> to understand our interpreter.
>
> Richard Ellmann, *James Joyce* (1983)

The famous opening of Richard Ellmann's monumental biography casts its subject matter—the life and work of James Joyce—in a peculiar double temporality. As if Joyce were somehow ahead of his fellow writers and us, his future readers; as if the actuality of his writing and life had somehow not yet exhausted their potential; as if Joyce's writing, in a messianic fashion, were dependent upon some second coming; as if its message, just as Sir Tristram in the second paragraph of *Finnegans Wake*, had "passencore rearrived" (*FW* 3.4-5). As if the novelty of Joyce's work, its "being ahead," its *avant-*, brought about certain belatedness within our reception of it, a *post--ness*.

The notion of being ahead, of being so novel as to seem to come from the future, is essential to the programmes of the movements of artistic avant-garde that have redefined 20th-century culture. Conversely, the notion of belatedness, of having one's present moment already defined by a past that somehow pre-programmes it, with little left to do for the present beyond re-enacting, repeating, or forging the past's originary actions and statements, resonates within the common detraction of post-war neo-avant-gardes in canonical criticism.[1] In a certain sense, the task set by Richard Ellmann—"to become Joyce's contemporary" (*JJ*, 3)—is reversed here: the present work covers the oeuvre of fifty post-war writers for whom Joyce was a contemporary, who consciously followed in the footsteps of Joyce's "revolution of the word," and took cue from his exploration of the materiality of language and the aesthetic autonomy of fiction.

Joyce's *Ulysses* and *Finnegans Wake* form a joint starting point from which genealogical lines of development are drawn and constellations of concepts are formed. The argument traces the many departures from Joyce's poetics in the post-war Anglo-American and Francophone novel, which came to be dubbed—by their adherents and detractors alike—"experimental" or

---

1   Also, one encounters this awareness of belatedness vis-à-vis Joyce everywhere in Joycean scholarship, which ever so often finds itself *already in the text*, coming not from the outside, but somehow generated from, solicited by, the Joyce text which always already includes, as it were, its own theory. Cf. my own *Joyce Against Theory* (Prague: Litteraria Pragensia Books, 2010), in view of whose overall argument, the criticism of Joyce appears as a discourse centred around a few governing notions and operations already "at work" in Joyce's text.

"avant-garde." The timeframe is, roughly speaking, the second half of the 20th century, with a coda on twelve writers active post-2000, bringing the entire genealogy into the present.

1. PRELIMINARY NOTES ON THE NOVEL, EXPERIMENT, AND THE AVANT-GARDE

The two adjectives used throughout—"experimental" and "avant-garde"—as well as the genre of the "novel" itself to which they apply in Joyce's case, are some of the most elusive terms of the critical discourse, their definitions as numerous as their definers, their own genealogies as complex and subjective as the present one of post-Joycean avant-garde experimentalism. Still, some preliminary notes on their understanding here, and application to *Ulysses* and *Finnegans Wake*, are in order.

In 1920, just when *The Little Review* was facing obscenity trial for publishing the masturbatory "Nausicaa" chapter and Joyce was already making "Nausicaa" pale in comparison with the chapter underway ("Circe"), Georg Lukács published his influential *Theory of the Novel*. In a not-so-rare instance of modernist telepathy (as *Ulysses*, *À la recherche du temps perdu*, and *Der Zauberberg* were still in the making, and *Finnegans Wake* was of course still a twinkle in Joyce's eye), Lukács immediately brought the genre of the novel into relation with the epic, by subtitling his study "A historico-philosophical essay on the forms of great epic literature." Yet the relation is one of contrast: to compare the modern novel with the ancient epic is like comparing a WWI tank with Achilles' shield – they "differ from one another not by their author's fundamental intentions but by the given historico-philosophical realities with which the authors were confronted."[2] Homer's epics are communal creations of a "concrete totality"; the modern novel is individualistic and made of "heterogeneous fragments." Whereas the modern novel has of necessity its beginning-middle-end,

> the way Homer's epics begin in the middle and do not finish at the end is a reflexion of the truly epic mentality's total indifference to any form of architectural construction [...] everything in the epic has a life of its own and derives its completeness from its own inner significance.[3]

If, in Homer's *Iliad*, "a rounded universe blossoms into all-embracing life," then the modern novel depicts a world where "the extensive totality of life

2   Georg Lukács, *The Theory of the Novel*, trans. Anna Bostock (orig. 1920; Cambridge: MIT, 1971) 56.
3   Lukács, *The Theory of the Novel*, 67–8.

is no longer directly given, in which the immanence of meaning in life has become a problem, yet which still thinks in totality." [4] So far so melancholy and nostalgic, but Lukács is perceptive enough to note that the very consummated character of Homer's epics was a hindrance to any further development of the Greek epic as a form. They were memorised for centuries and memorialised when written down—an unmovable boulder in the middle of the road. Whereas the sheer fragmentariness and incompletion of the novel as genre in the modern times is not only a crisis, but a chance: the genre remains open for constant innovation and redefinition, which is the only way of keeping it alive and relevant.

It is not difficult to see how Joyce's *Ulysses* and *Finnegans Wake* fit the bill of "a concrete totality" of a "rounded universe with no beginning and no end" of the epic while also composed of the modern-novelistic "heterogenous fragments" and busily engaging with the "immanence of meaning in life." And so it does not surprise that when surveying, from the opposite end of the century, the development of the modern novel that Lukács could only divine, Harold Bloom went so as far as to pronounce the *Wake* the central text of our (Viconian) "age of chaos," at least as regards its aesthetic merit: "The *Wake*, like Proust's *Search*, would be as close as our chaos could come to the heights of Shakespeare and Dante."[5] Where Bloom's *Western Canon* culminates and stops,[6] this book seeks to begin. Just as Lukács was hopeful about the fragmented novel's future potential, so will the genealogy mapped here of the post-war writing in the wake of Joyce's revolution of language show that for all its epic completeness, it provided experimentalists-to-come with enough stuff to dream on.

The adjective "experimental" will be understood here as pertaining to what, around the time Lukács was postulating his theory of the novel, philosopher John Dewey identified as the chief principle of the development of modern science:

The development of modern science began when there was recognized in certain technical fields a power to utilize variations as the starting points of new observations, hypotheses and experiments. The growth of the experimental as distinct from the dogmatic habit of mind is due to increased ability to utilize variations for constructive ends instead of suppressing them.[7]

---

4   Ibid, 56.
5   Harold Bloom, *The Western Canon—The Books and School of the Ages* (New York: Harcourt, 1994) 422.
6   "Joyce's Agon with Shakespeare" is Chapter 18 out of 23, accompanied by chapters on Woolf, Kafka, Borges, the only "follower" after Joyce (of sorts) in Bloom's genealogy being Beckett.
7   John Dewey, *Experience and Nature* (La Salle: Open Court, 1925) xiv.

Replacing the "modern science" in Dewey's argument with the concept of "revolution of language," an understanding of experimentalism arises that is conditioned by "a power to utilise variations as the starting points of new observations" and the "ability to utilize variations for constructive ends instead of suppressing them." Experimentation, thus, is less a question of programme than a "habit of mind," a mode of experiencing.

To say this is to commit an etymological pleonasm, as the word "experiment" came into English from the Old French *esperment, meaning "practical knowledge" and consequently "trial, proof, example, lesson," derived from the Latin experimentum* ("a trial, test, proof, experiment"), a verbal noun of action stemming from *experiri*, "to test, try." And out of this verbal root grows the word *experientia*, denoting "knowledge gained by repeated trials." In turn, the structure of the verb entails the prefix *ex-*, "out of," *peritus*, "tested, passed over."[8] Stemming from experience, thus experiment is the process of departing from what has been tested, of gaining knowledge by venturing beyond the known compass and toward the "testing ground of new literature." Hence the double focus, throughout the portraits of the writers included in this Joycean genealogy, on practice and theory of fiction as inseparable: *experimentation* always related to "bearing witness," to having "personal experience."

The meaning of "experimentalism" as conceived in this book will also come close to what, in the context of the visual arts, W. J. T. Mitchell has termed "irrealism." Departing from the conviction that all representations "are conventional in the sense that they depend upon symbol systems that might, in principle, be replaced by some other system" (and so "realism" might be nothing more than "simply the most conventional convention"),[9] the real difference between a "realist" tendency and its countertendency (by whatever name called) consists in their attitude to the cognitive and epistemological aspects of their representation. It is not, then, that realism is somehow the "standard," "familiar," or "habitual" mode of representation (were it so, no diachronic accounting for the many changes realism itself has undergone in just the last 200 years would be possible), but that it is "representation plus a belief system" regarding "the representational mode or what it represents."[10] This belief entails the following:

Truth, certainty, and knowledge are structurally connoted in realistic representation: they constitute the ideology or automatism necessary for it to construct a reality. That

---

8   Cf., e.g., James Douglas, *English Etymology – A Textbook of Derivatives* (London: Simpkin, Marshall & Co., 1872) 46.

9   W. J. T. Mitchell, "Realism, Irrealism, and Ideology: A Critique of Nelson Goodman," *Journal of Aesthetic Education* 25.1 (Spring 1991): 27.

10   Mitchell, "Realism, Irrealism, and Ideology," 30.

is why realism is such an apt vehicle for spreading lies, confusion, and disinformation, for wielding power over mass publics, or for projecting fantasy.[11]

Now, Mitchell of course is not as naïve as to posit "irrealism" as a simple binary opposite to realistic representation, for their commonalities are as important as differences. Still, "irrealism," in its three-part self-repre-sentation as "utopian ideal," "scientific fact," and "historical consensus," remains—in contrast with realism's "structural connotation" of its episte-mological certainties—"systematically ambivalent about its own 'certainty,' while relatively certain about its 'rightness.'"[12] Understood along the lines of Mitchell's irrealism, writing labelled experimental in this book is avant-gar-dist (a "utopian ideal"), invested in a non-realist mimesis of "the real" ("sci-entific fact"), and historically determined. This "chameleon status" of such writing, Mitchell continues, is not a weakness: on the contrary, it is precisely what gives this writing its rhetorical power as a positive, ahistorical—and yet historically determined—account of representational systems, [...] not as a philosophy that 'supplants' realism, but as a therapeutic thorn in its side, a way of keeping realism honest."[13]

This is where Mitchell's "irrealism" and this book's "experimentalism" dovetails into "avant-gardism." Writing described as "avant-garde" will here be understood—along the lines of Renato Poggioli's seminal study on *The Theory of the Avant-Garde*—as marked by its concentration on *linguistic creativity* as "a necessary reaction to the flat, opaque, and prosaic nature of our public speech, where the practical end of quantitative communication spoils the quality of expressive means," a reaction with an essentially social task in that it functions as "at once cathartic and therapeutic in respect to the degeneration afflicting common language through conventional habits."[14]

So, a therapeutic thorn in realism's side, again. Hence, avant-garde writing is one whose "cult of novelty and even of the strange" has definable historical and social causes in the "tensions of our bourgeois, capitalistic, and techno-logical society."[15] Informed by the aesthetic expressivism of such predecessors as Benedetto Croce, Poggioli's is a morphological, trans-historical analysis (in his account, the first avant-garde is not cubism or futurism, but romanticism), which serves him well in the effort to avoid losing sight of the avant-garde for-est for the idiosyncrasy of the individual movements' trees. Poggioli speaks of the avant-garde as "the dialectic of movements," a struggle for the "affir-

11   Ibid, 31.
12   Ibid, 33.
13   Ibid.
14   Renato Poggioli, *The Theory of the Avant-Garde,* trans. Gerald Fitzgerald (Cambridge, Mass.: Har-vard University Press, 1968) 37.
15   Poggioli, *The Theory of the Avant-Garde,* 80, 107.

mation of the avant-garde spirit in all cultural fields."[16] There are chiefly four "attitudes" informing this dialectics, two of which are "immanent" to the concept of a movement, and two of which "transcend" it. *Activism*, which springs from "the sheer joy of dynamism, a taste for action, a sportive enthusiasm, and the emotional fascination of adventure"; and *antagonism*, the formation of a movement in order to "agitate against something or someone," whether "the academy, tradition" or "a master" or more generally "the public," are the immanent ones.[17] The "transcendental" antagonism, which goes beyond specific targets by "beating down barriers, razing obstacles, destroying whatever stands in its way," Poggioli dubs *nihilism*; finally, activism pushed beyond any reachable goal, which "even welcomes and accepts this self-ruin as an obscure or unknown sacrifice to the success of future movements," is called *agonism*.

An "agonistic concept par excellence," then, is the idea of transition, the sense of belonging to an intermediate stage, to "a present already distinct from the past and to a future in potentiality which will be valid only when the future is actuality," and it is at this point that the name James Joyce first enters Poggioli's argument.[18] Poggioli's avant-garde, turned thusly into an aesthetic movement and stripped of its immediate socio-historical context, comes to resemble some of the more neutral, apolitical definitions of modernism. To take but Joyce's *A Portrait of the Artist*: Poggioli's tetrad of activism, antagonism, nihilism, and agonism can be found as underlying Stephen Dedalus' own rebellion against and gradual abandonment of family, Church, country, and embracing as his motto *Non serviam*, after Milton's Satan. Stephen's other creed, "the only arms I allow myself to use—silence, exile, and cunning" (*P*, 208), paves the way towards avant-garde marginality and purposeful obscurity. Futurism, however subtle, is present in Stephen's "desire to press in my arms the loveliness that has not yet come into the world" (*P*, 212); agonism underwrites his existential angst in his extrication from the strictures of religion, and courses through his most famous final invocation: "Welcome, O life! I go to encounter for the millionth time the reality of experience and to forge in the smithy of my soul the uncreated conscience of my race" (*P*, 213).[19]

In his famous re-contextualisation of Poggioli's argument within a broader historic-philosophical framework, Peter Bürger replaces Poggioli's vague

---

16 Ibid, 25.

17 Ibid, 25–6.

18 "That the avant-garde spirit was conscious of what this concept leads to is proved by the fact that a literary review, written in English, brought out for years in Paris the work of expatriate and cosmopolitan writers; it commends itself greatly to us for having published fragments of *Finnegans Wake* when James Joyce's extreme experiment was still 'work in progress.' The founder and director of this review, Eugene Jolas, chose to entitle it, paradoxically with an initial minuscule, *transition*" (Ibid, 25–6).

19 For a more detailed discussion, see Robert Langbaum, "Review of Poggioli's *Theory of the Avant-garde*" in *boundary 2*, 1.1 (Autumn 1972): 234–41.

trans-historicism with an insistence on the inherence of the historical avant-garde praxis to its proper historical context:

> In a changed context, the resumption of avant-garde intentions with the means of avant-gardism can no longer even have the limited effectiveness the historical avant-gardes achieved. To the extent that the means by which the avant-gardistes hoped to bring about the sublation of art have attained the status of works of art, the claim that the praxis of life is to be renewed can no longer be legitimately connected with their employment. To formulate more pointedly: the neo-avant-garde institutionalizes the *avant-garde as art* and thus negates genuinely *avant-gardiste* intentions.[20]

The dilemma throughout this book will be whether one can limit the function of the avant-garde to merely its linguistic creativity and collective impulse as anaesthetic markers (á la Poggioli) or whether its theory and praxis need to include a specific mode of political-critical engagement.

Bürger's *Theory of the Avant-Garde* construes modernism's non-instrumental aestheticism as signifying the artistic autonomy that makes modern art the institutional collaborator of modern bourgeois ideology. Bürger's political plotting of the art of modernity has direct repercussion for his detraction of post-war neo-avant-gardes. The shared intention, on the part of the many historical avant-gardes, of "returning art to the praxis of life," argues Bürger, falls flat when revived within a context where the avant-garde itself has become institutionalised as art, "the means of avant-gardism" no longer achieving "even the limited effectiveness" of the historical avant-gardes: "Neo-avant-gardiste art is autonomous art in the full sense of the term, which means that it negates the avant-gardiste intention of returning art to the praxis of life."[21]

As will become clear, one of the advantages of basing a "Joycean avant-garde" on Joyce's close alliance with the *transition* magazine consists in sidestepping the avant-garde/neo-avant-garde dichotomy in favour of a programme of writing which serves "cathartic and therapeutic" purposes in respect to "the degeneration afflicting common language through conventional habits" (à la Poggioli), while at the same time remaining "autonomous" and "anti-institutional" in its insistence on "the disintegration of words and their subsequent reconstruction on other planes," and in its ambivalent attitude to "the plain reader"[22] (à la Bürger).

20 Peter Bürger, *Theory of the Avant-Garde*, trans. Michael Shaw (Minneapolis: Minneapolis University Press, 1984) 58.
21 Bürger, *Theory of the Avant-Garde*, 59.
22 Eugene Jolas, "The Revolution of Language and James Joyce," *Our Exagmination Round His Factification for Incamination of Work in Progress: A Symposium*, ed. Samuel Beckett (New York: New Directions, 1929) 79–80.

2. JOYCE THE AVANT-GARDIST: THE *WAKE* IN *TRANSITION*

The *transition* magazine, during the eleven years of its activity (1927–38), published not only seventeen instalments from Joyce's "Work in Progress" (to become *Finnegans Wake* in 1939), as well as all the twelve essays that were to form the *Our Exagmination* collection, but also numerous theoretical analyses, polemics, proclamations, and defences of the work against its detractors. Its guiding spirits were Elliot Paul and especially Eugène Jolas (1894–1952), an American raised in Alsace, whose trilingual upbringing was reflected in the cosmopolitanism of the journal, arguably the last of the great vanguard vehicles of high modernism, and definitely the only one (at least of such scale and durability) explicitly devoted to the avant-garde.

In another instance of creative telepathy, Jolas himself echoed Dewey's observations on the development of modern science when conceiving of *transition* as a "documentary organ" dedicated to presenting what he referred to later as "pan-romanticism," and in retrospect, Jolas characterised *transition* as "a workshop of the intercontinental spirit, a proving ground of the new literature, a laboratory for poetic experiment."[23] Jolas' avant-garde undertaking, too, was marked by a certain belatedness: by the launch of its first number in 1927, the historical avant-garde had been on the wane if not defunct, and so *transition* gained another, retrogressive dimension: that of the archive. There is, thus, another sense in which *transition* proves a useful starting point for the genealogical lines charted in this book: its function of a documentary organ of the historical avant-garde is applicable to those post-war avant-garde groups, schools, or movements that chose to "perpetuate [Joyce's] creation," thereby becoming documentary organs of the effects of his poetics.

As a documentary organ, *transition*'s dedication to preserving the crucial documents of the historical avant-garde was impeccable: the list of the contributors to its first issues reads like an avant-garde who's who. With Dadaism, Tristan Tzara is present, e.g., in *transition* 19–20 (June 1930) right next to Joyce in the "Revolution of the Word" section. But that is just one of his occasional cameos: when it comes to Dada, Jolas had a clear editorial preference for the Zurich branch, and so *transition* 21 (1932), the one with the section, "HOMAGE TO JAMES JOYCE," comes with a cover-design by Hans Arp, and features the work of Richard Huelsenbeck, Hugo Ball, and Kurt Schwitters, among others. In 1936, *transition* 25 celebrates the twenty years of Dada by presenting the first English translations of Ball's "Fragments from a Dada Diary" and Huelsenbeck's "Dada Lives" manifesto. Surrealism is present—through the work of Louis Aragon, Robert Desnos, Philippe Soupault, and others—from *transition*

---

23   *Transition Workshop*, ed. Eugene Jolas (New York: The Vanguard Press, 1949) 13.

1 onward and throughout; André Breton's *Manifeste du surréalisme* is reprinted in *transition* 2 (May 1927), the opening chapter from his *Nadja*, in *transition* 12 (March 1928). But the same *transition* issue that celebrates the twenty years of Dada also features the first English translation of Franz Kafka's "Metamorphosis" and Alfred Döblin's *Berlin Alexanderplatz*, and German expressionism is present throughout, represented by Gottfried Benn and Georg Grosz, among others. A veritable avant-garde "funferall" (*FW* 13.15)![24] Last but not least, Jolas' *transition* was "a workshop of the intercontinental spirit"—its internationalism and threefold focus on America, Britain, and France is re-enacted in the present work; it acted also as "a laboratory for poetic experiment."

Although included in *transition* from its very start, it was not until *transition* 11 (Feb 1928) that Joyce's work was drafted as part of Jolas' revolutionary programme. In "The Revolution of Language and James Joyce," Jolas presents the first notes toward literature made genuinely "new":

The Real metaphysical problem today is the word. The epoch when the writer photographed the life about him, with the mechanics of words redolent of the daguerreotype, is happily drawing to its close. The new artist of the word has recognized the autonomy of language and, aware of the twentieth century current towards universality, attempts to hammer out a verbal vision that destroys time and space.[25]

Among other things, Jolas goes on to call for "the disintegration of words and their subsequent reconstruction on other planes," operations that "constitute some of the most important acts of our epoch."[26] This disintegration is made all the more necessary by progress in psychology and psychoanalysis, whose discovery of the subconscious "should have made it apparent that the instrument of language in its archaic condition could no longer be used."[27] And it is Joyce's "Work in Progress" on whose basis Jolas formulates the notion of aesthetic autonomy tied to the materiality of the word:

Modern life, with its changed mythos and transmuted concepts of beauty, makes it imperative that words be given new compositions and relationships. James Joyce, in his new work published serially in *transition*, has given a body blow to the traditionalists. As he subverts the orthodox meaning of words, the upholders of the norm are seized with panic, and all those who regard the English language as a static thing, sacrosanct

---

24 All three principal avant-garde groupings in the post-1960 British, American, and French fiction mapped here fulfilled this function. These were: B. S. Johnson's and his circle of neo-avant-gardists, the Surfictionist group around Raymond Federman, and the ensemble of literary theorists and practitioners around the *Tel Quel* magazine, respectively.
25 Jolas, "The Revolution of Language and James Joyce," 79.
26 Ibid, 79–80.
27 Ibid, 80.

in its position, and dogmatically defended by a crumbling hierarchy of philologists and pedagogues, are afraid.[28]

Jolas' reading of "Work in Progress" emphasises the materiality of the word as an agent of historical change and the necessity of the new aesthetics of "dec-reation." Axiomatic in Jolas' argument—and quite in tune with Joyce's own beliefs—is the conviction that the revolution of the word is one in which the new does not simply erase or replace the old, but where language is kept in a state of a constant flow of various sediments.

Jolas' revolution takes place not so much by replacing one regime with another, as by the new order surpassing and subsuming into itself the earlier one(s) – as Patricia Waugh has argued, Jolas espouses a kind of aesthetic Darwinism.[29] Despite the necessity of linguistic change, Joyce's creative deformation makes it easier to recover what persists through time. Jolas' version of the concept of autonomy, with its roots in Kantian ethical thought—tied with the modern idea of freedom, the capacity to follow self-determined, rationally formulated principles—was specifically intended to ease into history the linguistic macaronic of Joyce's work as a monument to the new cosmos of the scientists and philosophers. It was also meant to usher in the new self of psychoanalysis and anthropology; this concept of aesthetic autonomy, viewed by Jolas as the most radical effect of the revolution of the word, would soon become virtually definitive of cultural modernism.

However blatant in pursuing his own agenda at Joyce's expense, it is worth recalling that Jolas' theories were never disputed or opposed by Joyce.[30] On the contrary, in a few significant *Finnegans Wake* passages, Jolas is presented as Joyce's spokesman. A year after Jolas' conceptualisation of Joyce's linguistic autonomy, the June 1929 double-issue of *transition* 16/17 featured Samuel

---

28 Ibid, 81.
29 Patricia Waugh historicises Jolas' notion of linguistic autonomy as springing from "the 'magic idealism' of Novalis, the work of Jung and Freud, Bergsonian vitalism, and the French surrealists, abandonment of ordinary waking consciousness or of everyday language, of positivism and empiricism, as instruments of knowledge," going on to observe: "Jolas' idea of the revolutionary artistic word is borrowed from the new sciences of the mind which in turn depend upon a Darwinian understanding of evolution" (Waugh, "Introduction: Looking Back on the Modern Tradition," *Revolutions of the Word: Intellectual Contexts for the Study of Modern Literature*, ed. Patricia Waugh [London/New York: Arnold, 1997] 10–1).
30 Even Michael Finney's article in Hayman's collection, devoted to unmasking incongruities in Jolas' linguistic theory and literary practice and to stressing their foreignness to Joyce's project, ends on a lenient note: "Joyce agreed with some of the things Jolas had to say about reconstructing language, and he was indulgent of any philosophy or approach which would justify his linguistic and literary experiment. But whatever the truth, the fact remains that until its publication as *Finnegans Wake* in 1939, 'Work in Progress' was intimately associated with the Revolution of the Word—physically and ideologically—in the pages of *transition*" (Michael Finney, "Eugene Jolas, *transition*, and the Revolution of the Word," *In the Wake of the Wake*, 52).

Beckett's essay "Dante...Bruno.Vico..Joyce," which contains one of the most often-quoted observations about the language of the *Wake* in the whole critical canon:

> Here is direct expression – pages and pages of it. And if you don't understand it, Ladies and Gentlemen, it is because you are too decadent to receive it. You are not satisfied unless form is so strictly divorced from content that you can comprehend the one almost without bothering to read the other. [...] Here form *is* content, content *is* form. You complain that this stuff is not written in English. It is not written at all. It is not to be read – or rather it is not only to be read. It is to be looked at and listened to. His writing is not *about* something; *it is that something itself.*[31]

Beckett's concept of "direct expression" and his insistence on the conflation of content and form in Joyce's *Wake* were soon to become the guiding principles under which Joyce's materialist poetics would be enlisted by the various types of post-war concrete writing.

3. *TRANSITION* IN THE *WAKE*: JOYCE THE *TRANSITIONIST*

The history of "Work in Progress"/ *Finnegans Wake* in *transition* is known enough, but Joycean commentators sometimes underplay the reverse importance of Jolas for Joyce. As noted in Noel Riley Fitch's introduction to *In transition: A Paris Anthology*:

> Jolas not only helped Joyce with rewriting, revising and editing his "night world" before publication, he also provided a steady flow of essays explaining and defending the work. [...] The Jolases eventually became the major supporters and friends of the Joyce family. James Joyce reciprocated by making *transition* famous and by including in his *Work in Progress* numerous hidden references to the magazine.[32]

The history of *transition* in the *Wake*—of Joyce's "numerous hidden references to the magazine," mentioned but unspecified in Fitch's account—still remains to be told, and for obvious reasons cannot be told here.

As some dismissive commentators[33] keep stressing, there were some major differences between Joyce's project and Jolas' programme. To be sure, Jo-

---

31   Samuel Beckett, "Dante...Bruno. Vico..Joyce," *Our Exagmination Round His Factification for Incamination of Work in Progress: A Symposium*, ed. Samuel Beckett (New York: New Directions, 1929) 25–6.

32   Noel Riley Fitch, introduction to *In transition: A Paris Anthology – Writing and Art from transition Magazine 1927–30* (New York: Doubleday, 1990) 15.

33   See Michael Finney's article in David Hayman's collection, discussed below.

las' stress on collective subconscious and transcendental impersonalism, his notions of the "vertigral world," "chthonian mind," and various revivals of romanticism were anathema to Joyce's occupation with empirical linguistic material and history. One also wonders what Joyce could have made of some thinly veiled nationalism on Jolas' part as manifest, e.g., in his essay in *transition* 19–20, titled "The King's English is Dying—Long Live the Great American Language." It is also true that neither of Jolas' two fundamental manifestos, "The Revolution of the Word" and "Poetry is Vertical," was signed by Joyce (and there was no instalment of "Work in Progress" in the pivotal double-issue of *transition* 16–17), nor did he ever put his name down on any of Jolas' other proclamations. Still, their two major commonalities—the shared stress on the importance of linguistic experimentation and the use of dream material—as well as their lifelong friendship, collaboration, and the fact Joyce stuck with *transition* throughout its eleven-year production longer than with any other magazine, all this suggests more than just pragmatic non-involvement on Joyce's part. As none other than eye-witness Stuart Gilbert recalled:

> One sometimes hears it said that Work in Progress 'made' transition – but, in some respects, *the converse is equally true*. The fact that James Joyce's work appeared by instalments with a month's (later on, several month's) breathing space, so to speak, between them, gave the reader time to study, digest, and assimilate it to some extent.[34]

The one explicit acknowledgment of Jolas' personal and artistic importance directly from Joyce's pen is the "Versailles, 1933" limerick, marking the publication of Jolas' *Mots Déluge*, a book of poems in French:

> There's a genial young poetriarch Euge
> Who hollers with heartiness huge:
> Let sick souls sob for solace
> So the jeunes joy with Jolas!
> Book your berths! Après mot, le déluge! (Qtd. In *JJ*, 600)

"After the word, the flood." The closest historical-textual criticism has come to making sense of the sundry avant-garde references in the *Wake* on the basis of its scattered avant-garde references, to *transition* and others, is Dougald McMillan's magisterial *Transition 1927–38: The History of a Literary Era*, especially its two concluding chapters. For obvious reasons, the present account will constrict itself to highlighting McMillan's most salient points.

Joyce was always reserved and dismissive of the avant-garde movements of his time, especially the "mainstream" of futurism, Dadaism, and surreal-

---

34   Stuart Gilbert, *"transition Days," Transition Workshop*, 20 (my emphasis).

ism. Although, as always in the *Wake,* gossip and hearsay did their share in blurring Joyce's preferred dichotomies and division lines: in a famous letter to Stanislaus from September 1920, he complains of the rumour that he "founded in Zurich the Dadaist movement which is now exciting Paris" (*L* II, 22). He would parody the Dada Cabaret Voltaire in a "Salon de Espera" scene in the long "Yawn" episode of the *Wake* (III.3).

In this "salon of hopes," HCE finds himself in the company of "lodes of ores flocking fast to Mount Maximagnetic" (*FW* 497.16), a thinly veiled reference to *Les Champs Magnétiques,* Soupault and Breton's first collection of automatic writing, later on corroborated: "We are again in the magnetic field!" (*FW* 501.17). The salon is frequented, amid others, by "Merrionites," "Dumstdumbdrummers," "Cabraïsts," and " Ballymunites" (*FW* 497.17-20). As McMillan conjectures, these could very well be the followers of the futurist Marinetti, the rhythmical drummers of the Cabaret performances, and devotees of Hugo Ball, respectively, even though Ronald McHugh's authoritative *Annotations to Finnegans Wake* lists these as disguised pilgrims from the Dublin districts of Merrion, Dundrum, Cabra, and Ballybough. As usual, both are probably correct.[35] The surrealists also appear in the midst of HCE's trial in *FW* I.3, in an aside devoted to the sugar daddy: "Ack, ack, ack. With which *clap, trap,* and *soddenment, three to a loaf,* our mutual friends the fender and the bottle at the Bate seem to be implicitly in the same *bateau*" (*FW* 65.34-6, my italics), where "clap" is read by McMillan as referring to René Crevel's pronouncement—in the second edition of "La Révolution Surréaliste"—that everybody is more or less syphilitic; "soddenment," to Paul Claudel's statement that surrealism and Dada only mean one thing, "pederasty"; and "bateau" to Rimbaud's "Le Bateau ivre," considered an exemplary proto-surrealist text.[36]

To be sure, such derogatory cameos do not provide a steady rock on which to build the church of Joyce the avant-gardist. Still, although never a Dadaist or a surrealist, Joyce was decidedly a *transitionist.* From the numerous instances of either the magazine or Jolas himself receiving their respectful dues and honorary mentions, let us settle for a mere representative trio. In the *Wake*'s crucial chapter I.7, the "Shem" episode, a.k.a. "A Portrait of the Artist as an Old Man," we find Joyce's altered ego Shem living and creating, like some post-apocalyptic feral creature, in a "lair" with its "warpedflooring [...] persianly literature with" an endless (dis)array of objects real and imagined. These include:

telltale stories, stickyback snaps [...], alphybettyformed verbage [...], ompiter dictas [...], imeffible tries at speech unasyllabled [...], fluefoul smut [...], borrowed brogues

---

35   For more cf. McMillan, *Transition 1927-38: The History of a Literary Era,* 210-1.
36   Cf. Ibid, 212-3.

[...], once current puns, quashed quotatoes, messes of mottage [...], unused mill and stumpling stones [...], cans of Swiss condensed bilk [...]. (*FW* 183.11–30)

A list of items that, in the order of appearance as translated from *Wakese*, includes: fiction and photos, experimental writing, *obiter dicta* (critical pronouncements), modern poetry, erotica, literary borrowings, the *Wake* itself, pieces by Gertrude Stein, and some canned Dada from Zurich—a list that sounds very much like a table of contents of a *transition* issue.

For Shem's letter to be delivered, the figure of the postman, the letter-carrier, is required – and found in the character of Shem's brother Shaun. His eponymous chapter III.1 is replete with apostrophes directed at his many variant incarnations, such as: "Mine bruder, able Shaun [...], Winner of the gamings, primed at the studience, propredicted from the storybouts, the choice of ages wise! Spickspookspokesman of our specturesque silentiousness!" (*FW* 427.17–33). The epithet, "winner of the gamings," identifies Jolas as the Shaun figure via reference to his correct guess of the title (*Finnegans Wake*) of Joyce's book at the 1937 family Thanksgiving dinner. Here, Jolas is described as having been "propredicted from the storybouts," that is, predicted as the *Wake*'s propagator early on, a role which he fulfilled over the course of his lifelong friendship with Joyce, and as the "spickspookspokesman of our specturesque silentiousness," i.e., functioning as the spokesperson of Joyce's silence about his own work, with Joyce arguably "ghost/spook-writing" parts of Jolas' articles.[37]

As Joyce himself revealed in a letter to Harriet Weaver, "Shawn [...] is written in the form of a via crucis of 14 stations but in reality is only a barrel rolling down the river Liffey" (*L* I, 214), which Shaun the postman literally becomes in III.3 – a barrel of Guinness stout. In the final section of the *Wake*, Book Four, consisting of Anna Livia's banal and poignant leave-taking, this vehicle channelling Shem's letter receives the following invocation: "benedicted be the barrel; kilderkins, lids off; a roache, an oxmaster, a sort of heaps, a pamphilius, a vintivat niviceny, a hygiennic contrivance socalled from the editor" (FW, 596.17–9). Blessing here the barrel as a "hygiennic" contrivance of "its editor"—its off-spelling suggesting it is both salubrious and Eugenic—Joyce is gratefully saluting *transition* one final time.

And so, closer to the truth than Finney's glib dismissals of Jolas' programme as incompatible with Joyce's project is McMillan's nuanced estimation of the *Wake*'s pronouncements regarding *transition*'s instrumental role in delivering his message to the audience:

To be involved with *transition* was to be marked as part of the zealous avant-garde and to invite misunderstandings and hostility. But it was also to enjoy the benefits of

---

37   Cf. Ibid, 221–2.

a congenial, uniquely perceptive editor, open to radical experimentation and willing to provide the kind of context and explanation which defined the new modes of writing. Most of all it was to be a part of a significant literary revolution which produced some of the best literature of the century.[38]

4. JOYCEAN AVANT-GARDE: PARALLAX, METEMPSYCHOSIS, CONCRETISM, FORGERY, AND NEOLOGISM

Thus, the church of Joycean avant-garde can be erected on the rock of Joyce's lifelong preoccupation with language as material, partaking of Jolas' "revolution of the word" and the concept of aesthetic autonomy. In order to understand better Joyce's project in the *Wake*, a brief detour into *A Portrait* and especially *Ulysses* is in order, as it was on the back of the parodic subversion of the *Künstlerroman* in *A Portrait* and the ground-breaking critique of 19th-century realism in *Ulysses* that Joyce embarked on his final and most radically innovative experiment. *Finnegans Wake* also builds on *Ulysses'* structural parallax and narrative metempsychosis, and it was on the basis of the success of its 1922 publication with Shakespeare & Company and the *Ulysses* "cult" that Jolas took note of Joyce and invited him to join in *transition*. The following fast-forward through Joyce's three crucial texts is undertaken in concordance with a similar perception, on Hugh Kenner's part, of the unity in kind and variation in degree among these three:

> The progression from the *Portrait* through *Ulysses* into *Finnegans Wake* represents the dramatic action being transferred more and more thoroughly into the convolutions of the language itself. The liturgical implications are obvious; like the Mass, the linguistic actions in the later work are not merely analogous to another action: they *are* that action.[39]

Joyce's lifelong literary preoccupation was with systems of presentation. His development was toward the amplification of the verbal, the creation of autonomous forms in motion; toward the vitalised word of *Finnegans Wake*, the "collideorscape" (FW 143.28). To arrive there he was obliged to alter and recombine—destroy, according to his detractors—the existing expressive codes. En route, Joyce kept enhancing the tendency of the modernist "attention to the medium" to a principle governing the development of his oeuvre. His canon is thus marked—from the early floating signifiers of "paralysis," "gnomon," and "simony" in the first paragraph of "The Sisters" to the possibly

---

38   Ibid, 230.
39   Hugh Kenner, "The *Portrait* in Perspective," *The Kenyon Review* X.3 (Summer 1948): 368.

inexhaustible allusive potential of almost all "words" in *Finnegans Wake*—by a constant preoccupation with the materiality of language. Thus, the "scrupulous meanness" of the seemingly naturalist prose in *Dubliners* is complexified by means of Joyce's etymological recalls and syntactical manipulations conveying the idiosyncratic rhythms of Dubliners' speech.

In generic terms, *A Portrait of the Artist as a Young Man* exhausts and abandons the genre of the *Künstlerroman*, which had provided only "a tentative solution to the dilemma of Joyce's generation, by enabling writers to apply the methods of realism to the subject of art."[40] *A Portrait* achieves this by treating the very attitude of the novelist toward art as one of the critical questions of the novelist's subject—in other words, by staging the process of the writing of the novel as one of the subjects of the novel. That Stephen Dedalus gradually develops from Joyce's autobiographical *alter ego* into an increasingly *altered ego*, ironised, parodied, and observed from an increasingly critical distance, has been well-documented as one of *A Portrait*'s crucially innovative "perspectives." Joyce's "mythological method," though not yet as fully on display as in *Ulysses*, underwrites the theme of turning the artist's mind to "unknown arts" (as per Ovid's Daedalus), as well as the basic rhythm of the novel's five sections: flying—falling, soaring—plummeting, succeeding—failing, and such binaries as up/down, high/low, etc. In the famous final invocation, "Old father, old artificer, stand me now and ever in good stead" (P, 213), a series of fathers is appealed to and revoked—from the biological father to the Jesuit fathers to fatherland, all these are "nets to fly by" (P, 171) toward the one minotaur to be wrestled with: the mystery of becoming an artist.

One of the unifying leitmotifs of *A Portrait* is its increasing self-awareness of language as material and itself as linguistic construct. Its opening scene, with its multiple shifts in perspective, repetitiveness, and verbal deformation ("*O, the wild rose blossoms*" becoming "*O the geen wothe botheth*" [P, 7]), portrays the individual's entry into language as charged with sociosexual tension, famously subverting such naïve "realist" autobiographies as Dickens' *David Copperfield*. In various places throughout *A Portrait*, Stephen Dedalus perceives words "silently emptied of instantaneous sense," thereby forming "heaps of dead language" (P, 150). Language is conceived of as material foreign and mysterious to the human subjectivity, and yet affecting it profoundly: words like "suck" and "foetus" (described as "queer"), or, later on, *les jupes* and *mulier cantat*, evoke a bodily reaction of arousal and delirium.

40   Harry Levin, *James Joyce—A Critical Introduction* (1941), revised & augmented edition (New York: New Directions, 1960) 47.

Ulysses foregrounds linguistic materiality on many various macro-levels. First of all, by means of the famous mythological method—the "metempsychosis" (*U* 4.341) its Penelope asks its Ulysses about—the constant superimposition of multiple layers of narrative and the imposition of the Homeric and Shakespearean intertexts on its encyclopaedic rendering of 16 June 1904 in the Hibernian metropolis of Dublin. This encyclopaedism, intertextuality and narratological "parallax"—the word its Ulysses wonders about on his own (*U* 8.110)—was something publicised by Joyce himself post-publication, and captured in the pioneering criticism of Frank Budgen and Stuart Gilbert.

Yet its consequences for 20th-century storytelling and the genre of the "novel" are so momentous that T.S. Eliot's famous remark in "*Ulysses*, Order, and Myth" that it is "a book to which we are all indebted, and from which none of us can escape"[41] holds true for much of 20th-century fiction. As does Harry Levin's comment that *Ulysses* "is a novel to end all novels"[42]—though one must hasten to specify just what kind of novel it is that *Ulysses* smashes to a pulp. One of the many brilliant essays on Joyce of Hugh Kenner's, "The *Ulysses* Years," brings the structuralist narratology of *Ulysses* in direct relation to its deconstruction of the 19th-century "bourgeois realism." The "realism" of the opening "Telemachus" episode is shown in Kenner's perceptive reading as one far from evoking "reality" but rather "the mannerisms of a turn-of-the-century novel, once taken by readers for 'real,' in which nothing done by anybody goes unchaperoned by a helpful adverb."[43]

As long as Joyce had picked the *Odyssey* as *the* pioneer novel of the Western culture, in rewriting it *sub specie* 1904, Joyce surveyed the art of narrative in the twenty-seven intervening centuries, concluding that it "had done little more than contrive variations on Homer." Kenner continues: "We can penetrate its tricks once we reflect that the *Odyssey*'s fantastic wanderings are optional. Its node requires just four main characters: absent father, avenging son, beset wife, usurper, and many stories are the story of these four."[44] And so this structuralist grid of these four functions can be filled with the different sets of variables that form the backbone of the European tradition: Homer's "Ulysses—Telemachus—Penelope—Suitors" can become "The Ghost—Hamlet—Queen Gertrude—King Claudius" in Shakespeare's tragedy or "Il Commendatore—Don Ottavio—Donna Anna—Don Giovanni" of Mozart's opera.

The "narrative" of *Ulysses*, then, boils down to a juxtaposition of the two crucial tetrads of "Leopold—Little Rudy—Molly—Blazes Boylan," and "Si-

---

41   T. S. Eliot, "*Ulysses*, Order, and Myth" (1923), *Selected Prose of T. S. Eliot*, ed. Frank Kermode (London: Harvest, 1975) 175.
42   Levin, *James Joyce*, 207.
43   Hugh Kenner, *A Colder Eye - The Modern Irish Writers* (London: Allen Lane, 1983) 192.
44   Kenner, *A Colder Eye*, 196.

mon Dedalus—Stephen—Dead Mother—Mulligan," against the backdrop of 1904 Dublin subjugated by its "two masters: the imperial British state and the holy Roman catholic and apostolic church" (U 1.638), and in the grip of nationalist and antisemitic sentiments. Bloom's mourning for Rudy parallels Stephen's mourning for his mother parallels Ireland's mourning of its lost freedom parallels the Jewish diaspora's mourning for the lost Israel; Bloom's fear of Boylan's amorous usurpation of Molly parallels Stephen's alertness to Mulligan's clownish mischiefs parallels the Irish wariness of the British colonial rule parallels the Jewish fear of antisemitism infecting the European sensibility at the dawn of the 20th century; Bloom's alienation from his wife parallels Stephen's alienation from his father parallels the couple's alienation from the Irish national movement and from the Catholic dogma; Stephen's thwarted search for a spiritual father intersects with Bloom's vain search for a spiritual son, paralleling their precarious search for a national and religious identity, etc. etc. etc. The "many stories" of *Ulysses* are the stories of these four functions in the many permutations of their variables.

Ultimately, the "frustrating" dénouement of Joyce's narrative lies in the thwarting of the envisaged ideal tetrad, "Bloom—Stephen—Molly/Milly—Boylan/Bannon," by Stephen's refusal to stay the night at the Blooms'. This ideal quartet, notes Kenner, has a familiar shape: the shape of "the Picaresque Novel with a Happy Ending."[45] Bloom's schema would tie many of the loose ends of 16 June but *Ulysses* prefers to leave them undone. The ultimate "antagonistic" and "futuristic" traits of Joyce's novel (as per Poggioli) lie in how it completes and abolishes all the major conventions of the great urban novel in English. "Which is the end of an era," comments Kenner, "the English Novel so comprehensively, so consummately Done that there has been (at last) no need for it to be done again."[46]

In addition to its proto-structuralist treatment of the narrative as a parallactic constellation of perspectives, the ground-breaking ways in which *Ulysses* calls our attention to its medium of language by way of exploring the materiality of the word are legion. One is the multiplicity of its styles and parodies (e.g., the "Oxen of the Sun" episode at the maternity hospital,

---

45   Kenner continues: "In that novel, the bourgeois dream, many thousand times rewritten for 150 years, mankind is divided, like Quixote and Sancho, into two persons, the Picaro and the Benefactor. It is the bourgeois dream because it endows Sancho Panza with money and then brings him on stage to solve everything. Sancho Panza, it turns out, was all the time Ulysses in a clown's mask" (Ibid, 197).

46   Kenner concludes: "The great urban novel in English ought to have been set in London. It is set in Dublin. Its picaro ought to be a hearty spirited youth. He is morose and unwashed [...]. Its benefactor ought to be smiling, affluent, quietly top-drawer, [...]. He is Jewish, insecure, irregularly employed, cuckolded. It ought to end with an affirmation of universal rightness [...], it ends with a lonely man going to bed, and with the sleeplessness of his lonely wife. And the whole has [...] the encyclopedic finality of a sacred book" (Ibid, 198).

staging the evolution of the entire English language, from its Anglo-Saxon prehistory to its American evangelical futures), a multiplicity which foregrounds the relativity of literary style and its textual and linguistic "self-awareness." Another is the inclusion within its covers of a vast amount of "found" or "ready-made" linguistic material (cf. the "Eumaeus" chapter, stitched together from hundreds of recycled clichés, but, e.g., also the famous recursive "Plumtree's Potted Meat" advertisement [U 17.560] and the subject of "the influence of gaslight [...] on the growth of adjoining paraheliotropic trees" [U 17.13-14], lifted from the real-life edition of the *Evening Telegraph* of 16 June 1904, sighted at the cabman's shelter). Yet another is its exploration of the visual and graphic dimensions of typography and textuality (cf. the "Aeolus" episode at the newspaper room, but also the incident in which a "POST NO BILLS" wall inscription wears off into "POST 110 PILLS" [U 8.93]), but also on the micro-level of the word, the signifier, or even a single letter.

Examples on the micro-level abound: the very first sentence moves from "stately" to "crossed," from the "state" to the "cross" (symbolising the Church), but also alluding to the Biblical "stations of the cross" (U 1.1-3). Another notorious instance is Molly Bloom's translation of *metempsychosis* as "met him pike hoses" (U 4.343) whereby misheard Greek is turned into the speech of an Irish housewife, just as Joyce turns the Greek epic into an Anglo-Irish novel. Another exemplary instance is the opening of "The Sirens" episode, composed of 58 phrases (57 of which are repeated later on in the episode's text) which stage the interplay of letters and words as material that resists semantic interpretation, and foregrounds meaning as context-based. On the level of the letter, there is the letter *S* for "Stately" and "Stephen," opening the "Telemachiad"; there is the *M* for "Mr" and "Molly" opening the middle Bloom section; and finally the *P* for "Preparatory" and "Poldy" that opens the final *nostos* section: "S-M-P," the subject-middle-predicate of every proper syllogism, the concluding "Yes" circling back to the opening "Stately" (through which it runs backwards).[47] In the "official" journalist account of Paddy Dignam's funeral, Leopold Bloom becomes "L. Boom," with the missing "l" nettling him "not a little" (U 16.1260) – but perhaps this missing "l" has wandered off the page of *Evening Telegraph* into Martha Clifford's letter Bloom read earlier in his day, which misspelled "that other word" as "that other world" (U 5.245), because in the paperspace of *Ulysses*, the "word" and the "world" are one. And so on, and so, encyclopaedically and materially, forth.

If the "lesson" of *Ulysses* is that written language, when departing from the erstwhile rigid narrative standard on an "Odyssey of style," can create a world out of itself, then *Finnegans Wake* takes up where *Ulysses* checks off.

---

47   For more see Don Gifford, *Ulysses Annotated—Notes for James Joyce's Ulysses* (University of California Press, 2008) 12.

Where *Ulysses* was concerned with "representation" of the many super-structures of the modern microcosm, *Finnegans Wake* deals with the "pre-sentation" of the historical macrocosm, a point brought home through the contrast between the "Oxen of the Sun" episode of *Ulysses* (mentioned above) and "Anna Livia Plurabelle."[48] Over the eighty years of criticism regarding the *Wake*, few summaries of what the *Wake* can be said to be "about" have come close to the succinctness and precision of Harry Levin's fourfold, Dantesque list of its meanings: anagogical, allegorical, literal, and moral.[49]

Where *Ulyssean* superstructures are diachronic, in the *Wake*'s "present-ation" everything exists in the continual present of the act of writing, whose plethora of meanings exist contemporaneously, replacing any linear sense with the larger relationships of language to its own history. Or, in Ken-ner's witty reversal, the *Wake* differs from *Ulysses* chiefly in that "whereas in the earlier book Bloom occupies the foreground, re-enacting unawares Odysseus' adventures, in the latter book's universe it would be just as per-tinent to say that Odysseus was enacting the adventures of Bloom."[50] This contemporaneous present-ation in the present act of writing is informed by the philosophy behind the *Wake* – Giordano Bruno's doctrine of *coinciden-tia oppositorum*, the falling-together of opposites, the differential nature of the structuring of reality through human understanding. If in *Ulysses*, this coincidence is chiefly one of the mythological symbolic superstructure im-posed upon the naturalistic present-day content, then what fall together in the coincidence of *Finnegans Wake* are the universalised past of the myth and the particularised past of history, both diachronies exposed to the same syn-chronic, differential workings of language: "Universality, in so far as [Joyce] can be said to have attained it, is a mosaic of particulars."[51]

Where both these pasts merge is the most private and intimate, and si-multaneously the most universal and impersonal of human experiences: that of dreaming. Now, the *Wake* as text is a dream neither by narrating any single dream nor by involving any single dreamer, but by dreaming history, by subjecting historical material to the condensing and displacing

---

48   "When he sought words, in the hospital chapter of *Ulysses*, to reproduce the origins of life, he was foiled by the intervention of literary history, embryology, and other excrescences. Turning from representation to presentation, he allows nothing to intervene between the prose of *Finne-gans Wake* and the flow of the Liffey" (Levin, *James Joyce*, 162).

49   "Anagogically, it envisages nothing less than the development of civilization, according to Vico's conceptions. Allegorically, it celebrates the topography and atmosphere of the city of Dublin and its environs. Literally, it records the misadventures—or rather the nightmares—of H.C. Earwicker, as he and his wife and three children lie in their beds above his pub, and broken slumber reiterates the events of the day before. Morally, it fuses all three symbols into a central theme, which is incidentally Milton's—the problem of evil, of original sin" (Levin, *James Joyce*, 134).

50   Kenner, *A Colder Eye*, 230.

51   Levin, *James Joyce*, 161.

processes of the dreamwork, turning historical particulars into mythological universals, presenting the content of language as that which is also its
form.[52] For if words are the stuff the dreams of history in the Wake are made
of, then they, too, must undergo the processes of condensation (becoming
portmanteaus, e.g., "collideorscape") and displacement (performing paronomasia and punning). This is brought home in the *Wake*'s self-description,
quoted in the preceding section, as "once current puns, quashed quotatoes,
messes of mottage" (*FW* 183.22-3). Puns and paronomasia enact small linguistic versions of what *Ulysses* undertook on the level of narrative. Just as
Ulysses' parallactic narrativity brings home the point that no story exists
alone, but is part of a general narrative structure, then one of the larger
implications of the multilingual poetics of Joyce's *Finnegans Wake* is that no
language exists alone, but always in relation to others. We could think of
this as an implication of community – a community based on what David
Hayman has termed "the perpetuation of creation,"[53] of which the present
book functions as a record.

Regarding the *Wake*'s unity of form and content, spinning one more variation on Beckett's well-worn adage of the *Wake*'s linguistic autonomy, Levin
perceptively observes that its "drastic solution" to the dilemma of form and
content is "to subordinate content to form," and thereby "to reduce the plot
to a few platitudes that can be readily stylized, and confer complete autonomy upon words," which *"are now matter, not manner."*[54] The *Wake* explores
the materiality of language at the level of the signifier via the pun and the
portmanteau, foregrounding the indivisibility of meaning from its material
representation. Joyce's "whorld" (*FW* 100.29) order has the merit of being
based on and within language—which is human-made—rather than on incomprehensible cosmic events. Joyce thus simultaneously desacralises both
religion and language by means of signifiers that no longer refer to "something" signified but are objects in their own right, the Beckettian "something
itself."

Words become subjects of multiple intentions inviting different interpretations, their complexity making meaning not into something already accomplished, waiting to be expressed, but instead functioning as a performance
of semiotic production. Joyce's use of the portmanteau word and multilingual punning in *Wakese* can be seen as variously destabilising identity – of
language, history, nation, and last but not least, of its own existence as text,
within the potentially infinite rewritings imposed upon it in the reading pro-

---

52   "No writer, not Flaubert himself, has set a more conspicuous example of the cult of style.
Joyce's holy grail, la *dive bouteille*, is Shem's inkbottle" (Ibid, 146).

53   David Hayman, "Some Writers in the Wake of the *Wake*," *In the Wake of the Wake*, eds. David Hayman & Elliott Anderson (Madison: University of Wisconsin Press, 1978) 3-4.

54   Levin, *James Joyce*, 155, emphasis mine.

cess. In one of the many self-referential passages, the *Wake* describes itself as a "scherzarade of one's thousand one nightinesses" in which "that sword of certainty which would *indentifide* the body never falls" (*FW* 51.4–6, my italics). To *indentifide* is to identify with an "indentation" – for fiction functions and operates as a product of writing open to the operation of reading. Furthermore, the very same sentence indents *indentifide* as *idendifine*, performing one of the sundry internal variations and differentiations that run the whole gamut of the *Wakean* "indentity of undiscernibles" (*FW* 49.36–50.1) where the only (s)word that never falls is that of certain and unambiguous identity. The reader's identity, too, undergoes destabilisation in that every reading of the *Wake* becomes split between the eye that registers multiplicity and the voice which can sound only one text at a time.

Of the plethora of examples of the interplay between the ear and the eye let us pick one of the most obvious ones: the very last word of the Wake, which famously ends in mid-sentence with the definite article "the" (FW 628.16). However, the text of the *Wake's* last chapter repeatedly presents itself as a letter stained with tea, *thé* in French, and it may as well be that its sudden breakoff is due to a tea stain. For an example of multilingual paronomasia, one need only consider the very first word of the Wake: "riverrun" (FW 3.1). Literally, it is a reference to the river Liffey running through Dublin, but it is also a pun on Italian *riverrano*, "they will come again," referring to those Finnegans waking up in the title. In the religious context of the opening, "riverrun" also becomes paronomasia of "reverend" (the addressee of the letter), and in the dream context of the whole, of the French *rêverons*, "we will dream." The "riverrun" passage runs from English to Italian to French, all within one word, but only with the exertion of considerable interpretive effort. The important point about all these interpretive funfairs is that every one of the potentially inexhaustible readerly realisations *indents* the identity of the written: with the *Wake* more so than with any other text, to read is to rewrite, to countersign. Every reading is a performance with a difference of the textual material. *Indenting* stretches out into legal discourse not only via the contractual relation of *indenture*, but also in its denotation of *forging, duplicating* – and the voice's duplication, the performance of the written, is nowhere more forcefully limiting than when dealing with the *Wake*.

Finnegans Wake connects these concerns with the understanding of linguistic autonomy as its signature, the mark of its singularity. This is addressed in the famous rhetorical question, "why, pray, sign anything as long as every word, letter, penstroke, paperspace is a perfect signature of its own?" (*FW* 115.6–8). In the first of its interpretive investigations into the "original" trespass of HCE, a.k.a. Humphrey Chimpden Earwicker (*FW* 30.2), a.k.a. Here Comes Everybody (*FW* 32.18–9), one finds the following injunction: "Hesitency was clearly to be evitated. Execration as cleverly to be honnisoid" (*FW* 35.1-21). *Hesitency* as a mark of writing which over-means its own sound-realisation performs a number of functions. Most generally, it is a double figure for all reading and interpretation that forever re-realise its object, and for writing functioning as the subject's peculiarly alienated, original, and thus always to be forged, signature.[55] More specifically, Joyce uses it to refer to his own artistic *mark*, his own forgery of language in the *Wake* where so much revolves around a letter penned in order to wash away the blame sticking to HCE.

When elsewhere in the *Wake* Joyce's altered ego Shem mentions his "celebridging over the guilt of the gap in your hiscitendency" (*FW* 305.8-9), there is the unbridgeable "gap" out of which springs the notion of a "divided agency" behind any signature, behind all writing, but even more importantly, "hesitancy" becomes *hiscitendency*, the tendency toward citing. Forgery for Joyce is also a figure for literary writing, forged not only in the sense of writing as technology, but also in the sense of literature as "discourse" founded upon (mis)appropriation of the other's words, whether in the narrow sense of another writer's or in the widest sense of language itself. It is only rhetorically that Shem the penman raises the question: "Who can say how many pseudostylic shamiana, how few or how many of the most venerated public impostures, how very many piously forged palimpsests slipped in the first place by this morbid process from his pelagiarist pen?" (*FW* 181.36-182.3). Joyce's "pelagiarist pen" seems to insist, throughout his whole oeuvre but especially in the *Wake*, that literary authenticity is impossible without forgery: of the letter, of the word, of diction, of style.

Taken together, *Ulysses* and *Finnegans Wake* bring about a change in the conception of what literary writing can do, a change predicated on their sustained examination of language as material and their avant-garde conception of aesthetic autonomy. They launch a series of effects for which the post-war (neo-)avant-garde functions as a type of "documentary organ." These effects can be roughly divided into five groups:

1) *Narrative parallax*: story-telling as concatenation of functions and variables; narrative as *thema con variazioni* or *fuga per canonem* of motifs; "story" as parodic subversion of intertext; the "plot" as little more than "a series of verbal associations and numerical correspondences."[56]

55   David Spurr's knowledgeable account in "Fatal Signatures: Forgery and Colonization in *Finnegans Wake*," *European Joyce Studies, Vol. 8: Joyce – Feminism/Post/ Colonialism*, ed. Ellen Carol Jones (Amsterdam: Rodopi, 1998) ties "hesitency" to the infamous case of Richard Pigott's forgery of Charles Parnell's letters, meant to incriminate the latter in the 1882 Phoenix Park murders.
56   Levin, *James Joyce*, 126.

2) *Stylistic metempsychosis*: style as protean and always-already (self-)conscious and parodic; style as discourse, its mimicry or subversion aimed against ideology, hence style as always political; the Joycean "True Sentence"[57] always embedded in an ascertainable voice.

3) *Concrete writing*: typographical foregrounding of letters, words, even non-lexical signs as distinct objects; language as partaking of the world, "word become flesh"; the book as a material object existing in paperspace; a.k.a. "metatextuality"[58] and "liberature."[59]

4) *Writing as forgery*: Joyce's "pelagiarist pen" producing radically intertextual and citational texts; writing as an operation of emptying the "fullness" of speech through the depersonalising effects of writing; every "word, letter, penstroke" treated as a "perfect signature of its own."

5) *Neologising the logos*: plurality of meaning vs. univocity of sense; destabilisation of the conventional signifier as vehicle of univocal meaning; multilingual punning and the technique of the portmanteau; what Donald Theall has termed a Joycean "techno-poetics."[60]

These five formal traits would, then, constitute what throughout this book will be referred to as Joyce's "materialist poetics," since the common feature of all these five traits is a materialist treatment of language. Or, in other words, these five make up the Joycean avant-garde "signature" in solicitation

---

57   The conviction that reality "does not answer to the 'point of view,' the monocular vision, the single ascertainable tone. A tone, a voice, is somebody's, a person's, and people are confined to being themselves, are Evelines, are Croftons, are Stephens […] The True Sentence, in Joyce's opinion, had best settle for being true to the voice that utters it, and moreover had best acknowledge that when voices commence listening to themselves they turn into styles" (Hugh Kenner, *Joyce's Voices* [London: Faber and Faber, 1978] 16).

58   Michael Kaufmann uses the term *metatextuality* for works that "'show' themselves and comment physically on their material existence in the way that metafictional works comment on their fictiveness" and whose printed form "becomes a part of the narrative," so that ultimately, "the narrative occurs not only on the 'other side' of the page but directly in front of the readers' eyes on the surface of the page itself" (Michael Kaufmann, *Textual Bodies: Modernism, Postmodernism, and Print* [London/Toronto: Associated University Press, 1994] 14–5).

59   Katarzyna Bazarnik has coined the term *liberature* pertaining to works in which "the typography and shape of the book, or its bibliographic code, becomes a peculiar stylistic device deliberately used by authors […who] go beyond mere words, using typography, images, kind and colour of paper or other material they find more suitable for their purpose, sometimes even modifying the very form of the volume" (Katarzyna Bazarnik, *Joyce & Liberature* [Prague: Litteraria Pragensia Books, 2011] ii).

60   "Joyce wrote books that were pivotal for examining relationships between the body and poetic communication and for exploring aspects of such items on the contemporary intellectual agenda as orality and literacy; the importance of transverse communication in contemporary discourse; the role of transgression in communication; the role of practical consciousness in everyday life; and the relationship between the events of everyday life and their embodiment and materialization in the sensory nature of the contemporary interior monologue" (Donald F. Theall, *Beyond the Word: Reconstructing Sense in the Joyce Era of Technology, Culture and Communication* [Toronto: University of Toronto Press, 1995] 56).

of counter-signatures, of which this work will trace fifty most relevant in the history of post-war fiction. To be sure, this structuration of particular literary-historical narrative based on this rather *autotelic* model is a methodological fiction, but one which aims to deliver the critical mapping of the post-Joycean tradition from the sort of haphazardness and stagnation it has suffered from under the "postmodern" condition. The fifty avant-gardists covered in this book (38 in detail, 12 in a concluding survey) will be considered as both practitioners and theorists of fiction, as formulators of their own fiction programmes. Their critical work will therefore be examined as indicative of their attitude toward Joyce's materialist poetics. Explicit commentary on Joyce's treatment of language or his technical and stylistic advances will be taken as a starting point in evaluating the writers' positions within the lineage issuing from his writing.

Their fiction will be treated from two major viewpoints: the textual and the conceptual. By "textual" is meant both an overt acknowledgement of Joyce's writing in passing, an allusion or quotation, oftentimes of parodic purpose, as well as the more subtle link through a type of similarity, whether stylistic or thematic. From a "conceptual" perspective, symptomatic of a Joycean presence within the work of fiction under scrutiny will be the employment of a meta-narrative grid or scheme resulting in a multiplication of styles (as in *Ulysses*), and the enhancement of the expressive potential of language through verbal complexification, deformation, and recreation (à la *Finnegans Wake*). Throughout, however, *influence* will be understood not as mere borrowing or passive imitation, but as active transformation of the Joycean exploration of the materiality of language and the effects achieved through experimentation with the stylistic reservoir of language. A spectral Joycean presence will be found haunting a genealogy of post-war experimental writing that "countersigns Joyce's signature,"[61] of works that depart from *Ulysses* and *Finnegans Wake* by taking account of what is singular about their materialist poetics, and re-imagining what that singularity could become in the new contexts of post-war literary production, creating wholly new singularities.

---

61   In conversation with Derek Attridge, Jacques Derrida spoke of a "duel of singularities": "of writing and reading, in the course of which a countersignature comes both to confirm, repeat and respect the signature of the other, of the "original" work, and to *lead it off* elsewhere, so running the risk of *betraying* it, having to betray it in a certain way so as to respect it, through the invention of another signature just as singular" (Jacques Derrida, "'This Strange Institution Called Literature': An Interview with Jacques Derrida," *Acts of Literature*, ed. Derek Attridge [New York: Routledge, 1992] 69). For more on Derrida's notion of the countersignature, cf. the Conclusion.

5. JOYCEAN (?) TRADITIONS: HAYMAN, ADAMS, WERNER, LEVITT

The only real precursor to the present project, the only book-length treatise on literary response to *Ulysses* and *Finnegans Wake* attempting to conceptualise a tradition "in its wake," is Hayman and Anderson's co-edited work *In the Wake of the Wake*, combining critical essays with interviews and excerpts from the works representative of this tradition.

David Hayman's introduction starts by portraying how the reception of *Finnegans Wake* was also a belated one, for reasons of historical contingency: its 1939 publication on the eve of World War II, and the reaction—for most of the 1950s—against experiment in favour of a socially-oriented and politically-engaged cultural production, effectively turned Joyce's last work into a symbol of the end of an old era rather than an opening of a new one. As Hayman puts it, "after its 1939 publication, the *Wake* fell seemingly into a black hole," hiding in wait for its (belated) revisitation, calling upon future writers "to reshape the very tools of their craft, to say nothing of their means of perception." And Hayman is quick to add: "Not too many writers have answered the call, though a great many have responded and continue to respond to the less extreme challenge of *Ulysses*. Still, something else is now clear. The *Wake* belongs to a class (not a genre) of works which invite the reader to perpetuate creation."[62] In Hayman's introduction, the post-*Wake* tradition is conceptualised as "growing out of tendencies central to the *Wake* rather than directly out of the *Wake* itself," and Hayman is careful to limit his case for both influence and impact to "writers who have actually read and studied Joyce." Hence his two excellent interviews with Maurice Roche and Philippe Sollers, as well as inclusion of Haroldo de Campos' essay on "The *Wake* in Brazil and Hispanic America," documenting Hayman's conviction that "to date, most of the work in this 'tradition' has been done by writers in languages other than English."[63] Accordingly, Hayman's other examples include Hélène Cixous, Michel Butor, Raymond Queneau, the Brazilian Noigandres group of concrete poetry, and the German maverick experimentalist Arno Schmidt. Writers from the Anglo-American linguistic space include Christine Brooke-Rose, Anthony Burgess, Raymond Federman, and John Barth. Hayman's collection (and his introduction) is useful in systematising the possible modes of the *Wake*'s impact into four categories: the use of "language as a medium, the preoccupation with the process of saying as doing"; "the refusal of plot" in favour of approximating "a portable infinity" in which "meanings proliferate amid a welter of effects"; "the increased attention to

---

62   Hayman, "Some Writers in the Wake of the *Wake*," 3–4.
63   Ibid, 4–5.

universals, the generalizing or [...] 'epic' tendency"; and finally a tendency "to sublimate (not destroy) structure, harmony, and radiance in order to avoid the appearance, if not the fact, of aesthetic control."[64]

Despite its almost pioneering status within Joyce studies, there are issues with Hayman's collection and introduction. Hayman's book is a survey, and with the exception of its two interviews, it does not detail just how exactly these writers "have actually read and studied Joyce" – even though the degree of familiarity with Joyce's work varies greatly in such couplings as Burgess / Brooke-Rose or Butor / Federman. Moreover, Michael Finney's essay on "Eugene Jolas, *Transition* and the Revolution of the Word," fails to account for the essential points of connection between Jolas' revolutionary project and Joyce's *Wakean* poetics, settling instead for a philological critique of some of the more controversial of his linguistic theories. Failing to engage with the writers' own theories of fiction or pronouncements regarding the tradition that has come to inform their work, Hayman's tradition is one in which direct impact "inevitably mingles with fashions" and the question, "Would the same thing not have occurred without Joyce?"[65], remains unanswerable in his approach. Lastly and most importantly, Hayman's project in "The Wake of the *Wake*" entails a pinning-down of a Joycean "afterlife," in accordance with which he insists that "for a growing number of writers of 'experimental' fiction [...] Joyce's *Wake must* be a prime exemplar,"[66] presumably in order to be duly revered through emulation. Hayman's book is an exercise in "Joycean" scholarship projecting its self-image onto the "future of the novel," and in literary accountancy. But, to come back to Beckett: "literary criticism is not bookkeeping,"[67] and so this book will take a tack different from Hayman's.

Three more works of extant literary scholarship will be haunting—just as Joyce will be the writers under focus—my readings of post-war experimentalism that follow: Robert Martin Adams' *Afterjoyce: Studies in Fiction after Ulysses*, Craig Hansen Werner's *Paradoxical Resolutions: American Fiction since James Joyce*, and Morton P. Levitt's *Modernist Survivors: The Contemporary Novel in England, the United States, France, and Latin America.*

Adams is a historian of literary *influence* – and his study serves to show how "Joyce's influence worked either directly or indirectly in combination with many other influences."[68] His account is spot-on when pointing out how Joyce's idiosyncratic refashioning of extant literary techniques and

---

64   Ibid, 35–6.
65   Ibid, 36.
66   Ibid, 1, emphasis mine.
67   Samuel Beckett, "Dante... Bruno. Vico..Joyce," *Our Exagmination*, 19.
68   Robert Martin Adams, *Afterjoyce: Studies in Fiction after Ulysses* (New York: Oxford University Press, 1977) 3.

styles grew out of his equally personal take on literary history.[69] Useful are Adams' "three thematic interludes" in which he ekes out the peculiar traits of Joyce's heritage, treating it in terms of "the main devices-patterns-structures that he applied to prose fiction and that others applied after him."[70] These interludes deal, first, with "Paradigms and Grids" – Joyce's use of Homeric exoskeleton in *Ulysses* so highly influential among his contemporaries; second, in "Surfaces, Holes, Blurs, Smears," Adams describes Joyce's transformation of surfaces "from declaratives to interrogatives," turning Joyce into an advocate for "the rejection of representation in favour of overt artifice and the rejection of artifice in favour of vision"[71]; and last but not least, Adams deals with the broad theme of "Language," Joyce's chief operation performed thereon, and its "disintegration." Authors covered in Adams' study are variegated and his readings detailed: ranging from Joyce's contemporaries—both Anglophone (Virginia Woolf, William Faulkner, and Samuel Beckett) and German (Herrmann Broch, Alfred Döblin)—to Joyce's followers across linguistic and national traditions. Adams' "After-Joyce" tradition spans authors Anglo-American (Anthony Burgess, Lawrence Durrell, Vladimir Nabokov, Thomas Pynchon), Spanish (José Lezama Lima, Severo Sarduy), and Italian (Carlo Emilio Gadda, Italo Calvino). However, Adams' approach still remains restrictive and problematic in at least three respects. The *Wake*, for him, remains "a gigantic enigma, a labyrinth more inconceivably labyrinthine [...] than anything seen in literature [...], without transcending [...] the status of a curiosity"[72] – a scandalously gross simplification, especially given the broadly comparative approach and the time of publication of his study. Second, Adams remains preoccupied with documenting particular traces of Joyce's "influence" which he fails to define (insisting throughout on its "coincidental" nature) or document with meta-literary material; Adams has no recourse to the authors' works of criticism or public pronouncements, and thus provides no substantiation of actual Joycean links. Third, and consequent to the previous two, there is no attempt on Adams' part to conceive of Joyce's experimental heritage as a genealogy running across national and linguistic borders.

The subtitle of Werner's work delineates a specific field which is charted out with precision and consistency, exploring "the diverse ways in which the

---

69   As Adams points out, although Joyce studied novelists, both modern and traditional, the authors who had the most profound effect on his imagination were not writers of prose fiction, and (with the notable exception of Shakespeare) not English. Joyce's one chief acknowledged precursor—and the only novelist—was Flaubert; then there were poets (Homer or Dante), dramatists (Shakespeare or Ibsen), both (Goethe), and non-literary artists/theorists (Vico, Wagner).

70   Adams, *Afterjoyce*, 36.

71   Ibid, 57.

72   Ibid, 31.

current generation has created a post-Joycean tradition in American fiction."[73] Werner openly avows that his concern is "not so much to contribute to our understanding of Joyce as to study [...] the contemporary American novel."[74] Unlike Adams' carefully painted portrait of Joyce the stylistic innovator, Werner's Joyce is the momentous synthesiser between realist observance of detail and the romanticist elevation thereof onto the level of symbol – for him Joyce is a liberator, not so much of language or literature, as of experience.[75] From this nebulous and anachronistic picture emerges an equally blurry-eyed notion of the Joycean influence within the US post-war letters. Werner is certainly correct when he claims that "different writers read different Joyces—Dublin(er)'s Joyce, Stephen Joyce, Homer's Joyce, Humphrey Chimpden Joyce—and react accordingly," or when arguing that "Joyce had no one style, yet he has influenced nearly every stylistic development in contemporary fiction,"[76] although the disjunctive "yet" seems out of place. But Werner uses this "stylelessness" as license to pronounce "Joycean" every writer who supposedly shares with him however marginal a trait – personal, artistic, stylistic, aesthetic, ideological. In Werner's overview, Joyce becomes an equally relevant point of reference for writers as unlike as John Barth and Norman Mailer (who even appear coupled together as "writer-performers") or Saul Bellow and Gilbert Sorrentino. Moreover, questions remain why writers who "consolidate his advancement on traditional forms"—whatever that might entail—should matter equally to those who "extend Joyce's technical achievement," or indeed why writers who "participate directly in their works" (another vague notion) should be as relevant to his heritage as those who "emulate Joyce's control of biographical distance."[77] To his credit, Werner does strive to construct a Joycean tradition or genealogy – although only within the borders of one national literature. To his detriment, this is a tradition so inclusive and protean as to border on meaninglessness, the adjective "Joycean" emptied of any identifiable referent. Werner's concluding aquatic metaphor fits his impressionistic approach more than is desirable: "Joyce's shadow stipples the surface of the big two-hearted river, the mainstream of American fiction. The romantic and realistic currents flow on, whirling, eddying, never quite merging, pulsing in a single rhythm."[78]

---

73 Craig Hansen Werner, *Paradoxical Resolutions: American Fiction after James Joyce* (Urbana, Chicago, London: University of Illinois Press, 1982) 5.

74 Werner, *Paradoxical Resolutions*, 6.

75 "Joyce battles to liberate *experience*, to admit the full range of human life into the work of art. Joyce's most important weapon in this battle is [...] his "scrupulous meanness" of observation, his refusal either to raise or lower his eyes from the concrete experience, in both its real and its dream aspects" (Ibid, 4).

76 Ibid, 33.

77 Cf. Ibid, 7–8.

78 Ibid, 195.

Levitt's work, *Modernist Survivors*, differs from both Adams and Werner in using the example of Joyce to broach the broader implications of the historical periodisation of modernism, its "survival" well after its supposed demise (with World War II) and its influential presence in what is too simply referred to as "postmodernism." The generality of Levitt's treatment of Joyce is a self-acknowledged one[79] and unlike Adams, Levitt is unafraid to posit Joyce's centrality for the modernist era – and for the era following in its wake. However, Levitt fails to detail the specificities of the "Joycean" character of the Modernist Age beyond the vague notions of Joyce's "mythopoesis"—the "recognition that in myth we may test out not only our ties with societies of the past but the present status of our own society"—and Joyce's supposed "humanism," defined as "the diminished yet central vision of man surviving, of man persisting, a revised yet still powerful humanist vision."[80] It follows that Levitt's Joyce is not so much a source of genealogy as a persona, a symbolic figure: "It is the aura of Joyce that attracts me, just as I believe it compels all those novelists who follow him."[81] What is more, Levitt's "humanist" outlook and his literary historical focus leads him to effectively disparage critical theory (so instrumental in disseminating Joyce's legacy, particularly in France) and also to overlook several truly experimental, non-mainstream writers.[82] Levitt's argument is thus replete with shocking misjudgements, as when he makes the prediction that "Robbe-Grillet will surely be remembered more as footnote than as source, more for the implications of his theory than for its elaboration in fiction, and as far less significant novelist than his compatriots Butor and Simon."[83] Levitt's is a narrow focus on Joyce the mythmaker, delimiting Joyce's legacy to that of symbolical, mythical structure imposed upon detailed realism/naturalism, without any consistent attention to Joyce's manipulation of the linguistic medium, or indeed to that of his followers. Shared with Adams (and to some extent Werner) is also his avoidance of engagement with the heritage of Joyce's *Wake*.

So, this book will draw on the fortes of its three chief avant-texts while trying to evade their weaknesses: Adams' ad-hoc, isolated series of close

---

79 "I have been speaking of Joyce as if his art could stand for all Modernist art. This is not to deny the very real differences—artistic, philosophic, and human differences—which exist between Joyce and Mann, or Joyce and Proust, or Joyce and Kafka. [... But] it seems indisputable to me that this is the great age of the novel. And Joyce, despite his individuality, is its eponymous hero, symbol (in part because of his individuality) of its artistic and human commitment: the Modernist Age might as tellingly be labeled the Age of Joyce" (Morton P. Levitt, *Modernist Survivors* [Columbus: Ohio University Press, 1987] 9–10).

80 Levitt, *Modernist Survivors*, 10.

81 Ibid, 11.

82 Cf. Levitt's British chapter which takes extensive effort to deplore such mainstream figures as Margaret Drabble and Kingsley Amis while completely omitting experimentalists such as Christine Brooke-Rose or Brigid Brophy.

83 Ibid, 15.

readings will here be replaced with stress on a continuous genealogy; Werner's narrow monocultural focus will be pluralised here, his subjective impressionism superseded with as much "solid" evidence and data as is available; instead of Levitt's highly-reductive "humanist" outlook and his personal biases, the present work will aim for a more inclusive, "objective" approach.

6. POST-JOYCE

None of the conceptualisations of a post-Joycean writing detailed above deals with the obvious paradox entailed in positing the centrality of James Joyce for the literature of the post-war period: a challenge to most conceptualisations of what came to be called literary "postmodernism," which in its application as a period-marker is ever so often characterised as modernism's replacement or successor. The Conclusion will parallel the Introduction's construction of a Joycean avant-garde by formulating (and challenging) a Joycean postmodernity, uniting the "avant-" and the "post-" of the title, turning Joyce the avant-gardist into Joyce the avant-postmodernist.

The genealogy mapped here begins in France, with the so-called *nouveau roman* movement. French fiction was the first to respond to Joyce and (re-) construct itself post-WW2 in the wake of *transition*'s "workshop of the intercontinental spirit"—perhaps naturally so given that *Ulysses* saw the light of print in Paris and the last words of *Finnegans Wake* are "Paris, 1922–1939." Such writers as Nathalie Sarraute and Michel Butor were reclaiming and rethinking Joyce's heritage as early as the late 40s, within years from his death. And already by the mid-1950s, some of Alain Robbe-Grillet's theorisations of the New Novel, Claude Simon's novel constructions, Robert Pinget's public pronouncements, and Claude Mauriac's diary entries, all attest to the liveliness—even though not exclusiveness—of the Joycean poetics for the first post-war French avant-garde. Two more France-oriented chapters form the backbone of the present genealogy: the one in the middle (the Oulipo Chapter 4), and the other at the end (the *Tel Quel* Chapter 7). Oulipo, begun in 1960 and channelling the talents of such pronouncedly Joycean writers as Raymond Queneau and Georges Perec presents an aesthetic-type, post-war avant-garde. Concentrating the energies of writers-thinkers like Philippe Sollers, Hélène Cixous, and Maurice Roche, *Tel Quel* is the clearest instance of a successful co-opting of the Joycean avant-garde for an engaged writing praxis, a political-type avant-garde *par excellence*.

Interposed between these are four chapters charting the post-war developments in Anglo-American experimental fiction. The two British chapters detail the development of post-Joycean experimentation in the last forty years of the 20th century. The first chapter focuses on the circle of writers around B. S. Johnson, for whom Joyce's work provided a much-sought-after alternative to the various modes of post-Victorian or post-Edwardian novel. The other section details the careers of some of their sci-fi, feminist, post-colonial, and psychogeographic successors writing in the 1980s and 1990s, with the connecting bridge between the two being the remarkably long and variegated career of Christine Brooke-Rose, whose five decades of writing present an exceptionally productive "laboratory of the experimental spirit." The two American chapters present a reverse movement. The first one details the continuation of the Joycean impulse in the work of such maverick figures as William Burroughs, John Barth, and Donald Barthelme, in the 1950s and 60s. The other zooms in on the Joycean impulses driving the Language poetry movement and the Fiction Collective's "surfictionist" avant-garde, formed around such figures as Raymond Federman and Ronald Sukenick, in the 70s and 80s, as well as the explicitly political reworking of Joyce's legacy by such writers as Ishmael Reed and Kathy Acker. A final coda surveying the work of twelve authors writing post-2000 brings the entire genealogy into the present.

The originator of the genealogy of the fifty writers covered and mapped out in this book, Joyce is a writer whose continuous and ever-expanding examination of the materiality of language revolutionises the literary genre of the novel and challenges most of the dichotomies underlying literary vocabulary. His sublimation of structure was, in the last phase of his career, drafted in service of a specific avant-garde theory and programme, which in turn begat the following genealogy. It is within this genealogy that the avant-garde signature of Joyce's fiction (as countersigned by Jolas' theory) is preserved as valid and relevant, endowed with an importance that lingers on even in an age that claims to have succeeded modernism and postmodernism.

1.
JOYCE DE NOUVEAU: WITHIN OR BEHIND OR BEYOND OR ABOVE THE NEW NOVEL, 1947–67

Since this study is partly concerned with comparative cultural criticism, it might not be entirely inappropriate to open the account with an eye-witness report of a British poet visiting Paris in the immediate aftermath of WWII:

> France's intellectual vitality was as remarkable as ever, but it seemed to me to a large extent to be turning in a void. Whether it was the result of the shock of defeat and the humiliation of Nazi occupation, or of some deeper reason that went further back, the dominant spirit was, I thought, anti-humanistic, even nihilistic.[1]

This, to be sure, is a view of the French culture from the outside, and a British outside moreover, but what Lehman naively calls "anti-humanism" and "nihilism" might be symptoms of his amazement that the legacy of surrealism—not just its Bretonian orthodoxy but also its para- or proto-versions in the work of Raymond Roussel, Antonin Artaud, Blaise Cendrars, Jean Genet, and Raymond Queneau—was in the process of catching its second breath in France just at the time Britain's official culture was leaving modernism behind (see next chapter). Add to this the various and variable heritage of symbolism the nascent movement of the New Novel, with its critique of the notion of character, its shunning of the "myths of depth," and its promotion of literary "objectivity," and one understands why the Englishman abroad paints such a negative, bleak picture.

The first thing to make clear about the *nouveau roman* movement is that, just as the writers and artists associated with Jolas' *transition*, it is no group in any conventional sense of the term; in fact, part of the New Novelists' shared agenda was precisely to challenge the notions of literary grouping and group mentality as such. It has become a critical commonplace to stress the differences both on the basis of comparison between two or more New Novelists and within the development of their individual oeuvres. Critics oftentimes do little beyond making the usual acknowledgment that the New Novel, just as all literary-historical labels, is slippery and imprecise in terms of both the period described and authors referred to. Still, there are a few shared

---

1   John Lehman, *I Am My Brother* (London: Longman, 1960) 306.

traits discernible across a whole range of texts published simultaneously or within a couple of years of each other. As Laurent Le Sage observed as early as 1962, from the mid-1950s onward, the New Novel "attained a notoriety important enough to consecrate it as an authentic avant-garde phenomenon."[2] In fact, Le Sage's comment came just at the very peak of a five-year period which saw the publication of six novels by six still-unknown authors: *La Jalousie* (1957) by Alain Robbe-Grillet, *La Modification* (1957) by Michel Butor, Nathalie Sarraute's *Le Planétarium* (1959), Claude Simon's *La Route des Flandres* (1960), *La Marquise sortit à cinq heures* (1961) by Claude Mauriac, and Robert Pinget's *L'Inquisitoire* (1962). The period from 1957 to 1962 can be seen as a nucleus of the group's activity, with the preceding decade devoted to pioneering preparatory work and the subsequent two decades witnessing the group's transformations and gradual dissolution.

The term "New Novel" has its own genealogy and, just as so many other literary-historical terms, its problems. Its inception took place in the July 1958 special issue of the *Esprit* magazine devoted to novel-writing that featured the work of ten authors, including the authors discussed in this chapter (minus Claude Mauriac) plus the work of Jean Cayrol, Marguerite Duras, Kateb Yacine, and Jean Lagrolet. Although its *ad-hoc* character is best documented by the fact that the appellation of the New Novel post-dates the appearance of the first novels by no less than five years, still, the name—unlike the many other terms (Bernard Dort's 1955 *romans blancs*; Alain Bosquet re-application of Jean-Paul Sartre's notion of the *anti-roman* from 1947; Émile Henriot's notion of "École du regard"; or Ronald Barthes' *littérature objective*)[3]—did catch on and was sanctified at the beginning of the 1960s by Robbe-Grillet's *Pour un nouveau roman* (*For a New Novel*).

By the end of the 1960s, however, the troubles with its application to the above six authors (let alone the others) had begun to show. In one of the first book-length studies on the New Novel in English, John Sturrock observed in 1969 that although "responsible critics who show a keen and sympathetic understanding of the practices of the New Novelists have not abandoned the term," there have been "certain radical divergences in purpose and seriousness" between individual New Novelists (most notably Butor and Robbe-Grillet) which make it "perfectly understandable that the New Novelists themselves should have been outraged by the glib way in which their differences had been obscured."[4] Still, Sturrock's study—focusing on Robbe-Grillet, Simon, and Butor—argues for the viability and perti-

---

2   *The French New Novel: An Introduction*, ed. Laurent Le Sage (Pennsylvania State University Press, 1962) 1.

3   For more, see Le Sage's overview of the critical genealogy in *The French New Novel*, 2–3.

4   John Sturrock, *The French New Novel* (London: Oxford University Press, 1969) 1–3.

nence of the label, viewing the three novelists as proponents of "a central proposition about the *nouveau roman*: that these novels must *never* be read as exercises in naïve realism or naturalism, but as studied dramatizations of the creative process itself."[5] Despite its claim to "newness" and its outspokenly polemic character, Sturrock insists that the movement is "part of the tradition which insists that the novelist explain or reveal his principle of organization in the text itself" and has a point in showing that Robbe-Grillet, for all his brash exorcism of the past, "has always claimed that he was not overturning the past, but extending it in the only possible direction. His tradition of the novel extends back through Beckett, Faulkner, Kafka, Joyce, Proust, Roussel, and Flaubert, whom he values for their successive technical contributions to the form."[6]

Sturrock's study also launched the now broadly accepted periodisation of the New Novelist evolution as a movement, which it is useful to recall especially in the context of the next chapters (four and seven) detailing the development of other, subsequent groupings and movements, such as Oulipo or the group around the *Tel Quel* magazine, neither of which can be said to have supplanted or replaced the New Novel. All of the six *nouveaux romanciers* mentioned above went on to develop their novelistic output well into the 1980s and 1990s, and so the New Novel is "always there" within the context of post-World-War-II French novel. The common periodisation distinguishes three distinct phases. The first period, roughly from the mid-1950s to mid-1960s, saw Robbe-Grillet at the helm and the novelists he associated with by means of his editorial post at the Éditions de Minuit, publisher of Beckett's trilogy and *Les Gommes*, becoming the hub of the New Novel publishing. Sarraute, for her part, was committed to Gallimard (also the base for Raymond Queneau), and so markedly different were the agendas of the two publishing houses throughout the 1950s and 60s that for instance Butor's switch from Minuit to Gallimard in 1960 was meant to be taken as a gesture of active dissociation from Robbe-Grillet's New Novelist programme. Thus, the authors loosely connected by their publisher and critical proponents were oftentimes more alike in what they stood against than what they stood for.

The next decade, from the mid-1960s to the mid-1970s, saw the leadership of Jean Ricardou (Robbe-Grillet having withdrawn from theoretical polemics to cinema and artistic collaboration). It was Ricardou's organisation that sought to turn the New Novelists into a group of like-minded writers whose strategic participation in public events and conferences was meant to demonstrate their intent to collaborate in promoting the practice and theory of

---

5   Sturrock, *The French New Novel*, 3.
6   Ibid, 5.

the modern novel.[7] Ricardou's theory emphasised the self-reflexive nature of the novel and a critique of realism while limiting the active presence of writerly personality in favour of the productive power of language and critical reflection on the part of the reader.

The second phase—together with Ricardou's leading role—was brought to an end by Robbe-Grillet's return to the public forum at the 1975 Cerisy Colloquium, where he objected to the rigorously systematic character of Ricardou's analyses and interpretations which, to his mind, turned his novels into reassuringly comprehensible texts, a tendency at odds with his goal of producing meanings which were multiple and mobile. Thus, the third, post-1975 phase is marked by a turn against and away from Ricardou – its high point being the 1982 New York Colloquium, where Robbe-Grillet, Pinget, Sarraute, and Simon celebrated Ricardou's absence and placed a renewed emphasis on the novelist's expression of their personality.

The members of Robbe-Grillet's generation were deeply scarred by France's humiliating wartime occupation—in fact most of the New Novelists experienced the occupation in highly personal and sometimes traumatic terms—which had shaken the grounds of their belief in the commitment to the philosophy and ideology of literature as preached by intellectuals of the preceding generation, particularly Jean-Paul Sartre and Simone de Beauvoir. Robbe-Grillet spoke for many when calling, in *Pour un nouveau roman*, such concepts as meaning, identity, story, and history "obsolete," positing instead the necessity of acknowledging the instability, relativity, and indeterminacy in individual perceptual and conceptual consciousness of the surrounding world.

Sarraute dubbed this tendency toward indeterminacy "suspicion" and, quoting Stendhal, turned it into the guiding principle of the post-war era. Suspicion, to her mind, was particularly directed toward the self-unity and self-identity of the staple ingredient of the traditional novel – the character:

The character today is reduced to a shadow of his former self. Only reluctantly does the novelist endow him with attributes that could make him too easily distinguishable: his physical aspect, gestures, actions, sensations, everyday emotions, studied and understood for so long, which contribute to giving him, at the cost of so little effort, an appearance of life, and present such a convenient hold for the reader. (AS, 69)[8]

---

7   Sturrock rightly observes that "the idea of the Nouveau roman as a group of novelists served all its members by promoting interest in their work. Their novels became well-known to generations of foreign university students [...] the French Ministry of Culture sent New Novelists abroad to represent the French novel; no comparable movement arose to take its place" (Ibid, 6–7).

8   "[L]e personnage n'est plus aujourd'hui que l'ombre de lui-même. C'est à contrecœur que le romancier lui accorde tout ce qui peut le rendre trop facilement repérable : aspect physique,

Robbe-Grillet's conception of the New Novel can be viewed as a phenomeno-logical revision of Sartre's existentialism. His early work posits the pheno-menological view of consciousness, in which the world is confronted without pre-existing ordering notions, marked by what Husserl terms "intentiona-lity": an orientation toward the world. Le Sage was among the first critics to tease out the implications of Husserl's philosophy for the practice of the New Novelists, paralleling their rejection of the analytical method of presenting characters with Husserl's rejection of ideality.[9]

In literary terms, the New Novel can best be understood as a revolt against the realist tenet of objectivity, regarding it as an illusion to be discarded to-gether with what Robbe-Grillet calls "old myths of profundity": myths on which the novel used to be based. To be discarded together with the illusion of objectivity is Sartre's programme posited in his 1948 work, *Qu'est-ce que la littérature?*, and commonly denoted as *littérature engagée*. In his *For a New Novel*, Robbe-Grillet treats "engagement" as precisely one of the "obsolete no-tions" to be discarded. He rejects Sartre's call for a *moral* literature as a uto-pian fantasy and insists with a Jolas-like emphasis on literary "purity" that as soon as one "expresses something outside literature," literature itself "begins to disappear."[10] In the same breath, Robbe-Grillet calls for engagement to be restored to "its only sense possible for us," that is, "the full consciousness of the current problems of one's own language, the conviction of its extreme importance, and the willingness to resolve them from the inside."[11] The only engagement possible for a New Novelist, Robbe-Grillet insists elsewhere in the book, is literature rather than politics, since "political life obliges us

---

gestes, actions, sensations, sentiments courants, depuis longtemps étudiés et connus, qui con-tribuent à lui donner à si bon compte l'apparence de la vie et offrent une prise si commode au lecteur" (*ES*, 74).

9   "The new novelists' rejection of the analytical method of presenting characters is postulated upon the same philosophic rejection of ideality that motivated Edmund Husserl in the first years of this century to reject neo-Kantism. Husserl, before Sartre or any of the new writers, had said that the world is there before it is anything. But the world to be there is not to be fully autonomous. The world is there only because it is perceived by human consciousness, which gives it its significance and its reality" (*The French New Novel*, 16).

10 "Then what remains of commitment? Sartre, who had seen the danger of this moralizing litera-ture, advocated a moral literature, which claimed only to awaken political awareness by stating the problems of our society, but which would escape the spirit of propaganda by returning the reader to his liberty. Experience has shown that this too was a Utopia: once there appears the concern to signify something (something external to art), literature begins to retreat, to disap-pear" (*FNN*, 41).

11 "Let us, then, restore to the notion of commitment the only meaning it can have for us. Instead of being of a political nature, commitment is, for the writer, the full awareness of the present problems of his own language, the conviction of their extreme importance, the desire to solve them from within. Here, for him, is the only chance of remaining an artist and, doubtless too, by means of an obscure and remote consequence, of some day serving something—perhaps even the Revolution" (*FNN*, 41).

incessantly to suppose known significations," whereas art is "more modest—or more ambitious," as in it, "nothing is ever known in advance" (*NFF*, 141). It is, however, not only on the political level that Sartre's programme is to be rebuffed, from Robbe-Grillet's perspective. Despite the occasional nod of approval toward *La Nausée*'s protagonist Roquentin—in a sense a blueprint for so many New Novelist anti-heroes—Robbe-Grillet rejects the novel's perceived adherence to a "Balzacian" order of realism, i.e., the subservience of form to content or message in so much of existentialist writing. But more on Balzacian rejections later.

That the New Novelist tradition as invoked by Sarraute and Robbe-Grillet should primarily include Kafka the Prague German, Faulkner the Southern American, and the two Irishmen, Joyce and Beckett (with a 19th-century enjambment of Flaubert, in Robbe-Grillet's case, and of Dostoevsky, in Sarraute's) is symptomatic of their revolt against the so-called "Balzacian" tradition of the French novel, whose repercussions they viewed as stretching far beyond the demise of 19th-century mentality in the trenches of World War I. By comparison with these six writers, the importance of French modernists like Proust or Roussel is acknowledged much less readily, and still less so in the case of stylistically more conservative writers like Gide or Valéry.

The one major attempt at claiming the central position within the New Novelistic canon for Joyce as *the* "great predecessor" of the nouveau roman—Vivian Mercier's monumental study *The New Novel: From Queneau to Pinget*—posits as the primary impulse for the New Novel not so much Husserl as "a deep dissatisfaction with an art form now paying the penalty for the high degree of development it had achieved in the nineteenth century," which meant that a hundred years later, "it badly needed to 'retool,' following the lead of such English-language masters as Joyce, Faulkner, and Virginia Woolf."[12] It seems that in their blank refusal of the French novelistic tradition, Robbe-Grillet and Sarraute had thrown out the baby with the bath water. Proust they accepted with reservations and Roussel they valued primarily as a theorist of *Comment j'ai écrit certains de mes livres*, Gide's *Les Faux-Monnayeurs* receives an occasional nod of approval, but other modernists like Paul Valéry and surrealists like André Breton were largely ignored. What the New Novelists, at least Robbe-Grillet and Sarraute, seem to not only disavow but revolt against, is existentialism as practiced by Jean-Paul Sartre and Albert Camus, novelists committed to humanist causes.

Given the New Novel's eclectic formation of tradition and their overt alliance with figures like Faulkner, Kafka, and Joyce, and the necessary confusion evoked by such labels as "modernism" or "postmodernism" vis-à-vis the New Novel, theorist Stephen Heath prefers to exclude these lables from

---

12   Mercier, *The New Novel From Queneau To Pinget* (New York: Farrar, Strauss & Giroux, 1971) 3.

his criticism of the New Novel altogether and to focus instead on the issue of its "new realism." For, if Robbe-Grillet famously claimed that "Flaubert wrote the new novel of 1860, Proust the new novel of 1910," (*FNN*, 10), then what he meant by "new" was not so much their formal or stylistic innovations as what Roland Barthes called "la connaissance du langage" and what Heath calls the "practice of writing," defined as "a radical experience of language."[13] Heath's Joycean training leads him to consider the *Wake* as precisely a text in which such a radical experience of language takes place, offering "the *space* of a work always '*in progress*,' the scene of a play of language and not, as in realist writing, the (intended) linear progression of a process of notation."[14] In this respect, Heath argues, the "situation of the nouveau roman is post-Joycean: Joyce, that is, is a major element in its situation."[15]

In its conception of constantly reworked tradition and what Heath terms "a radical experience of language," the New Novel is firmly embedded in the genealogy stretching from Stendhal and Flaubert to Joyce and Beckett. Here is perhaps as opportune a moment as any to substantiate the glaring omission of Samuel Beckett from the genealogy covered in this book. The reasons for this are chiefly twofold: its rather idiosyncratic nature and its status as one of the best-documented if contested literary intertexts in the entire Anglophone canon. The sheer fact of his singularly personal closeness to Joyce and the well-documented lifelong fascination with his acknowledged master turns Samuel Beckett into a most usual suspect of Joyce's influence in post-WWII fiction. Apart from a plethora of essays and papers, there are no fewer than four major monographs and essay collections to date devoted just to the Joyce/Beckett personal relationship and artistic intertext[16] However, his problematic personal relationship to Joyce, the multiple fresh starts and breaks with the past throughout his writing career (from English to French and from poetry to prose to drama), and last but not least the very singularity of Beckett's own poetics, all these have made the seemingly "natural" influence into something of a minefield for criticism, vastly exceeding the scope and interest of the present monograph.[17]

---

13   Stephen Heath, *The Nouveau Roman: A Study in the Practice of Writing* (London: Elek Books, 1972) 24.
14   Heath, *The Nouveau Roman*, 26.
15   Ibid, 29.
16   Cf. Barbara Gluck, Beckett & Joyce (New Jersey: Associated University Press, 1979); Re: Joyce 'n' Beckett, eds. Phyllis Carey & Ed Jewinski (New York: Fordham University Press, 1992); In Principle, Beckett is Joyce, ed. Friedhelm Rathjen (Norwich: Page Bros, 1994); P. J. Murphy, Beckett's Dedalus: Dialogical Engagements with Joyce in Beckett's Fiction (Toronto, Buffalo, London: Toronto University Press, 2009).
17   For a more detailed discussion and overview of extant critical work on the Joyce/Beckett intertext, cf. my own "Coincidental Opposites: A Portrait of Samuel Beckett as a Young Joyce," *Tradition and Modernity – New Essays in Irish Studies*, eds. Radvan Markus et al. (Prague: Charles University, 2014), pp. 13–25.

Just as in the following chapters, the avant-garde status of the New Novel will be examined through the prism of the avant-garde heritage of James Joyce. The ordering of the following six authors is one of progressive Joyce-involvement, from minimum to maximum, starting from those who imply or acknowledge his influence, but write decidedly "after" him, and moving towards those who tackle his legacy directly, writing "through" or "with" him.

1.1 "EQUIVALENT IMAGES, ANALOGOUS SENSATIONS": NATHALIE SARRAUTE

Nathalie Sarraute was the first *nouveau romancier* to begin her career as a writer – her earliest text, an unusual series of short sketches in prose entitled *Tropismes*, was written in 1932 and published—just like the *Wake*—on the eve of the WWII; her first novel, *Portrait d'un inconnu*, was written during the war (which she, as a Russian-born Jew, spent in hiding) and published in 1948; and her first essayistic work on the theory of the novel came out in 1956 as *L'Ère du soupçon* (*Age of Suspicion*). Her oeuvre, completed as late as 1997 with her last novel *Ouvrez*, would comprise a dozen novels, seven theatre pieces, and several volumes of essays. In all its genres Sarraute's work preceded her fellow New Novelists' by more than a decade. This is an important consideration for reading *L'Ère du soupçon*, later on recognised as a sort of New-Novelist manifesto, but written before the notion itself came into circulation.

L'Ère du soupçon comprises four long essays, of which the eponymous one turns out the shortest. The first essay, "De Dostoïevski à Kafka," sets out to defend the psychological novel (as written by Dostoevsky and Kafka) against the onslaught of the existentialist novel of the absurd as practiced by Camus. On the basis of *L'Étranger*, Sarraute shows that despite his programmatic proclamations to the contrary, Camus' writing is not devoid of conventional, realist psychologising. The title essay has already been quoted above – its thesis is that Stendhal's diagnosis of the "age of suspicion" sounded the death knell for the "Balzacian" era of character verisimilitude and "liveliness." Crucial for the disbelief in and suspicion of "character" is psychoanalysis and its discovery of the unconscious – particularly the Jungian "collective unconscious," which reveals any claim to human individuality as a problematic construct. The psychoanalytic discovery goes hand in hand with developments in literary modernism. As Sarraute notes, "[e]ven a name, which is an absolutely necessary feature of his accoutrement, is a source of embarrassment to the novelist," and her examples include Joyce's *Wake*: "Gide (without the patronyms), Kafka (an initial), Joyce designates by the initials, H.C.E., of multiple interpretations, the protean hero of *Finnegans Wake*" (*AS*, 70). This anti-realist vein is taken up in the fourth and last essay, "What the birds see," which critiques the trompe-l'oeil realism in the novel as a rhetorical construct and style far removed from any lived "reality." The well-structured novel with its plot, subplots, realistic dialogue, refined character study, setting, and descriptions is not, for Sarraute, destined to produce an "objective" study of the outer and inner worlds of man, but rather a formalistic deformation of them.

In the collection's third and longest essay, "Conversation et sous-conversation," Sarraute opens with what appears a dismissal of Virginia Woolf and her claim of the "dark spaces of psychology" as the modern novelist's chief point of interest: "Who today would dream of taking seriously, or even reading, the articles that Virginia Woolf wrote shortly after the First World War on the art of the novel?" (AS, 97) Sarraute continues with a presage of an era in which Joyce and Proust would not be revisited unless guided and in "respectful silence" pertinent to "historical monuments":

> The works of Joyce and Proust already rise up in the distance like witnesses of a past epoch, and the day will soon come when no one will visit these historical monuments otherwise than with a guide, along with groups of school children, in respectful silence and somewhat dreary admiration. For several years now interest in "the dark places of psychology" has waned. (AS, 97)[18]

She goes on to dismiss "the great blinding truths" of the "literature of the absurd," claiming that to her generation, these seem no longer credible, and she observes that Joyce—with the implied reference to the "Penelope" episode of *Ulysses*—failed to draw out of these "dark depths" anything more than "an uninterrupted sequence of words." However, only after these preliminary dismissals does the true difficulty posed by the moderns for Sarraute appear:

> And it is true that we cannot repeat what Joyce or Proust did, even though Stendhal and Tolstoy are repeated every day to everybody's satisfaction. But isn't this, first of all, because the moderns displaced the essential interest of the novel? For them it ceased to lie in the enumeration of situations and characters or in the portrayal of manners and customs, but in the revelation of a new psychological subject-matter. (AS, 104)[19]

---

18 "[L]es œuvres de Joyce et de Proust se dressent déjà dans le lointain comme les témoins d'une époque révolue. Le temps n'est pas éloigné où l'on ne visitera plus que sous la conduite d'un guide, parmi les groupes d'enfants des écoles, dans un silence respectueux et avec une admiration un peu morne, ces monuments historiques. Voilà quelques années déjà qu'on est revenu des « endroits obscurs de la psychologie »" (ES, 84).

19 "Et il est bien vrai qu'on ne peut refaire du Joyce ou du Proust, alors qu'on refait chaque jour à la satisfaction générale du Stendhal ou du Tolstoï. Mais n'est-ce pas d'abord parce que les modernes ont transporté ailleurs l'intérêt essentiel du roman ? Il ne se trouve plus pour eux dans le dénombrement des situations et des caractères ou dans la peinture des mœurs, mais dans la mise au jour d'une matière psychologique nouvelle" (ES, 95).

In a sense, this remark turns an explicit critique into an implicit praise – Joyce and Proust cannot be "repeated" with the same ease as Stendhal or Tolstoy because they have "displaced the essential interest of the novel" and imposed upon it the necessity of revealing a "new psychological subject-matter." It slowly becomes apparent that what Sarraute is denouncing is precisely her day and age in which it is more convenient for authors to repeat Stendhal and Tolstoy rather than to take seriously the challenge posed by modernists:

> Indeed, as soon as a writer renounces the legacy of those whom, thirty years ago, Virginia Woolf called "moderns" and, disdaining the liberties (the "facilities," he would say) that they conquered, succeeds in capturing a few soul reactions couched in the pure, simple, elegant lines that characterise the classical style, he is praised to the skies. (AS, 81)[20]

If there is a critical point to be made about the modernists, for Sarraute, it lies in the fact that the modernist subject still falls prey to the trap of individual completion, that their characters have a finished absoluteness about them and that their presentation is by and large inward. Portrayed in opposition to the "sub-conversational" Proust or Joyce, and ultimately praised more highly, is Ivy Compton-Burnett and her "absolutely original solution, which has both distinction and power," making her "one of the greatest novelists that England has ever had." Compton-Burnett's method of character presentation is dialogical, exterior, and yet decidedly "written": "These long, stilted sentences, which are at once stiff and sinuous, do not recall any conversations we ever heard" (AS, 119).

What emerges from Sarraute's essays are reservations about the particular ends to which the modernist experiment had been brought—by Proust, Woolf, or Joyce—but also her unambiguous pledge toward taking it further. As long as the well-structured realist novel is to be refused as a deformation of reality, then the modernist exploration of unbiased subjectivity is to be supplemented with an equally unbiased objectivity. Sarraute situates her work within a tradition of psychological realism, while simultaneously proposing to take the genre to its logical conclusion and to surpass any individual psychology. As Mercier has elegantly summarised: "No doubt Madame Sarraute was not entirely satisfied with the achievements of Proust, Joyce, and Virginia Woolf, but she was certain that the French novelists of 1956 had not yet learned the lessons taught by this trio well enough to go beyond them."[21]

---

20   "Aussi, dès qu'un auteur, renonçant à l'héritage que lui ont légué ceux de Virginia Woolf appelait il y a trente ans les modernes, dédaignant les libertés [...] qu'ils ont conquises, parvient à capter quelques mouvements de l'âme dans ces lignes pures, simples, élégantes et légères qui caractérisent le style classique, aussitôt on le porte aux nues" (ES, 86–7).

21   Mercier goes on to say: "The newness of the New Novel, one may say, lies in the attempt of its authors to begin where these three great experimenters (Proust, Joyce, Virginia Woolf) had left

The widespread misreading of Sarraute as a critic of modernism is also in stark contrast to her own pronouncements regarding her attachment to Joyce and the moderns. She repeatedly stated that her early reading had convinced her, if not how to write, then definitely how *not* to: "As for me, after reading Proust and Joyce, which I did between 1922 and 1924, and then reading Virginia Woolf, I felt that it was no longer possible to write as people had done previously."[22]

The extensive "Art of Fiction" interview with Sarraute in the Spring 1990 issue of *The Paris Review* revisited her novelistic beginnings and charted the same genealogy:

> The traditional novel, with its plot and characters, etcetera, didn't interest me. I had received the shock of Proust in 1924, the revelation of a whole mental universe, and I thought that after Proust one could not go back to the Balzacian novel. Then I read Joyce, Virginia Woolf, etcetera . . . I thought *Mrs. Dalloway* was a masterpiece; Joyce's interior monologue was a revelation.[23]

Last but not least, *L'Ère du soupçon* is also noteworthy for including Sarraute's creed as a writer, her "Comment j'ai écrit" confession regarding her first book, *Tropismes*. In what has become one of the most-cited passages in all of her canon, Sarraute speaks of her texts as "spontaneous expressions of highly lively impressions," produced by what she terms "movements [...] interior actions on which I've long fixed my attention." In her preface to the collection, Sarraute defines them as follows:

> These movements, of which we are hardly cognizant, slip through us on the frontiers of consciousness in the form of undefinable, extremely rapid sensations. They hide behind our gestures, beneath the words we speak, the feelings we manifest, are aware of experiencing, and able to define. They seemed, and still seem to me to constitute the secret source of our existence. (*Tr*, vi)[24]

As Mercier points out, Maria Jolas' 1967 translation of *mouvements* as simply "movements" is inadequate, and his suggested surrogate makes for a better

off, instead of reverting to the classical tradition of the French novel or following what Sarraute calls the 'behaviorist' approach of American novelists like Hemingway" (*The New Novel*, 138).

22 Germaine Brée, "Interview with Nathalie Sarraute," *Contemporary Literature* (Spring 1973): 138.

23 "The Art of Fiction CXV. Nathalie Sarraute," trans. Jason Weiss & Susha Guppy, *The Paris Review*, 114 (Spring 1990): 150.

24 "Ces sont des mouvements indéfinissables, qui glissent très rapidement aux limites de notre conscience ; ils sont à l'origine de nos gestes, de nos paroles, des sentiments que nous manifestons, que nous croyons éprouver et qu'il est possible de définir. Ils me paraissaient et me paraissent encore constituer la source secrète de notre existence" (*ES*, 8).

approximation: "emotional stirring."[25] This passage resonates with echoes of *Stephen Hero*'s notorious definition of the epiphany as "sudden spiritual manifestation, whether in the vulgarity of speech or of gesture or in a memorable phase of the mind itself" (*SH*, 211).[26] The resemblance is striking – Sarraute says "mouvements" where Joyce says "moments," but both draw parallels between word, gesture, and emotion ("sentiments" in Sarraute and "phase of the mind" in Joyce) and both agree that such "mouvements" / moments represent the writer's point of departure. However, any direct influence of Joyce's epiphany upon a text composed between 1932 and 1939 can be ruled out, as *Stephen Hero* was not published until 1944 and *The Workshop of Dedalus*, a first complete edition of the epiphanies and the early drafts of *A Portrait*, only in 1965. However coincidental, the affiliation is still remarkable.

Upon closer inspection, dissimilarities between *Tropismes* and Joyce's epiphanies begin to surface. In her foreword to the English translation, Sarraute claims that while these movements/stirrings are performed, "no words express them, not even those of the interior monologue" and thus it is "not possible to communicate them to the reader otherwise than by means of equivalent images that would make him experience analogous sensations."[27] Where Joyce records or reconstructs, Sarraute constructs "analogous sensations." Thus, none of the textual snippets collected in *Tropismes* achieves the total, unmediated (as much as can be), scrupulous objectivity of a Joycean epiphany – it is Sarraute's choice of "equivalent images" that turns her *Tropismes* as well as her *Portrait d'un Inconnu* into studied and contrived contrasts between the banal sphere of characters (whether in action or conversation) and the narrative's "analogous" imagery and metaphors.

Nevertheless, closely analogous to Joyce's is Sarraute's methodology, following which both developed their first novelistic endeavours as elaborations upon these respective snippets of text – as Sarraute observes, "this first book contains *in nuce* all the raw material that I have continued to develop in my later works."[28] Mercier notes that at least half of the items in *Tropismes*—Nos. II, IV, V, VII, VIII, IX, XIV, XV, XVII, XX, XXII, XXIII—suggest one or more of the three main characters in the later *Portrait*: the domineering old man, the patriarch's shrinking daughter, and the hypersensitive young man. His example is the following extract from Tropism No. XV and a correspond-

25   Mercier, *The New Novel*, 104.
26   Cf. the full passage: "This triviality made him think of collecting many such moments together in a book of epiphanies. By an epiphany he meant a sudden spiritual manifestation, whether in the vulgarity of speech or of gesture or in a memorable phase of the mind itself. He believed that it was for the man of letters to record these epiphanies with extreme care, seeing that they themselves are the most delicate and evanescent of moments" (*SH*, 211).
27   Nathalie Sarraute, foreword to *Tropisms*, trans. Maria Jolas (New York: Grove Press, 1967) vi–vii.
28   Qtd. in Mercier, *The New Novel*, 113.

ing passage from Sarraute's *Portrait*: "Dover, Dover, Dover? Eh? Eh? Dover? Thackeray? England? Dickens? Shakespeare? Eh? Eh? Dover?" (*T*, 95). A novelistic rendering of this passage in *Portrait* looks as follows: "'Biarritz? hein? hein? Ustarritz? Vous savez ce que c'est? Vous connaissez? Ustarritz?' Il roule les r très fort. 'Biarritz? La Bidassoa? hein? hein? Chocoa?'" (*PI*, 137).

Upon comparison between Joyce's and Sarraute's *Portraits*, differences proliferate: where Joyce's text presents the gestation and development of an individuality with the goal—whether achieved or not—of becoming an artist, Sarraute's text examines the very possibilities and general qualities of such a presentation in the first place. Through this, she was formulating not only the programme for her own career as writer, but a general ambition of the New Novelistic movement as a whole – as attested to by Sarah Barbour, who spoke of a "changing notion of the literary text itself."[29] This novel's examination of its own novelistic procedures led Jean-Paul Sartre, in his famous 1947 preface, to call it an "anti-novel" and define it as "le roman en train de réfléchir sur lui-même" (*PI*, 8). If there is a relation between Sarraute's and Joyce's *Portraits*, it consists not in allusions or references, whether direct or indirect, but in what Sarraute herself believed her task as a post-Joyce writer to be: to write where he "left off."

This continuation is present on a very literal basis: the novel opens with the first-person narrator "encountering life," the two subjects/objects of his art: "Une fois de plus je n'ai pas pu me retenir, ç'a été plus fort que moi, je me suis avancé un peu trop, tenté, sachant pourtant que c'était imprudent et que je risquais d'être rabroué" (*PI*, 15). Just as Joyce's, Sarraute's *Portrait* describes the narrator's search for reality as expressed and constituted through the medium of language. However, Joyce concerns himself with an aesthetical establishment of ironic distance between Stephen's would-be-artistic interiority and the drab everyday outside whose poetic potential is beyond his grasp, whereas Sarraute remains stubbornly non-theoretical and external. The focal point of the narrator's attention lies on the outside: in his attempts to discover the truth about the relationship between an old man and his daughter. Like a detective, he spies on them and even imagines scenes between them at which he is not present – his method of exploration consists of perceiving and imagining precisely the above-defined "tropisms." However, the Joycean ironic distance is still palpably there, found almost on

---

29   The problematization of linearity found in the works of the *nouveau roman* issues from a changing notion of the literary text itself, which represents an investigation of what has been considered literature's mimetic relationship to lived reality. The innovations in form enacted by these works constitute a reflection on the act of creation and of making meaning as it effects a more reciprocal perception of the relationship between art and reality" (Sarah Barbour, *Nathalie Sarraute and the Feminist Reader – Identities in Process* [London/Toronto: Associated University Press, 1993] 16).

every page, even if transposed onto another level: that between "conversation" and "sub-conversation."[30] A case in point would be the longest and most important scene of the novel, presumably imagined, in which the daughter and the father—compared to two dung beetles—lock horns in an epic battle whose rhetorical and metaphorical bombast is undercut by the banality of the reason for their brawl: hassle over money for the daughter's medical care.

Even though Sarraute would continue, after *Portrait* and *L'Ère du soupçon*, writing highly influential novels for another four decades, the aesthetic principles formulated in her early fiction and mid-1950s essayistic work would undergo surprisingly little change. Unlike Joyce who would, to a large extent, repudiate the scrupulous objectivity of *Dubliners* and abandon his youthful alter ego Stephen Dedalus by the end of *Ulysses*, Sarraute devoted the best of her works to analysing tropisms and moving away from the representation of interiority. In the former, she remained faithful to her first work of fiction; in the latter, to her first book of essays and her tribute to Ivy Compton-Burnett. Never, however, did Sarraute direct her exploration of tropisms and psychology to the linguistic possibilities of articulating these aspects, never did she attempt to match these novel and complex conceptions of identity to an equally novel and complex language, and so, despite acknowledging him as a shaping influence, her fiction stayed very much her own.

1.2 "THE ADDITIONAL STEP IN SUBVERTING THE SYSTEM": ALAIN ROBBE-GRILLET

As said before, Alain Robbe-Grillet did more than any other novelist to theorise and practise the *nouveau roman*, and was—whether self-appointed or not—the generally acknowledged leader of the group. The most interesting biographical fact about this, according to many, "most influential French writer of his generation"[31] is that he was not educated in the humanities but in agronomy, which he also pursued as his vocation. Employed by the Institut des Fruits et Agrumes Coloniaux, between 1948 and 1951, he travelled to Morocco and farther to Guinea, Guadeloupe, and Martinique, but on account of ill-health had to be repatriated. He never returned to his career of agricultural science, using the period of convalescence to focus on his writing and,

---

30   As Mercier notes, whether "slight enough at times" or "very often breath-taking," the contrast between "the banal conversation or action" and the "imagery used to define the underlying 'movements'" is essentially comic and not without ironic overtones (Mercier, *The French New Novel*, 106).

31   Cf. John Fletcher, "Alain Robbe-Grillet," *Dictionary of Literary Biography, Volume 83: French Novelists Since 1960*, ed. Catharine Savage Brosman (Tulane University, Detroit: The Gale Group, 1989) 197–211.

with the 1953 publication of *Les Gommes*, became a full-time writer/editor at the Éditions de Minuit instead.

Just as the name of the New Novel movement itself came after the fact (i.e., the publication of Sarraute's and Robbe-Grillet's novels), so did its theoretical articulation. The publication of his famous essay collection, *Pour un nouveau roman*, postdates his first novels by nearly a decade and its primary impulse is reactive: Robbe-Grillet's surprise at how critical response to his first novels was guided by "an implicit—or even explicit—reference to the great novels of the past, which were always held up as the model on which the young writer should keep his eyes fixed" (*FNN*, 8). Robbe-Grillet argues for a turn-away from the past great novelist (Balzacian) tradition and posits the necessity of following Flaubert and Proust in search of "a new realism" (*FNN*, 14). Robbe-Grillet's own theory begins by declaring that the surface of things must no longer be thought of as a mask for reality, but as the only reality we can grasp. According to one his often-repeated tenets, the world is neither significant nor is it absurd – it simply *is*, and it is to this simple existence that the new realism must stick, postulating nothing about what may or may not lie behind phenomena.

The new realism entails a redefinition of what Robbe-Grillet famously terms "obsolete notions," such as character, plotline, the literary treatment of time, or form and content as separate entities – obsolete not as such but in the way they were treated in realist novelistic tradition and its critical discourse. Repeatedly, Robbe-Grillet insists on the parochialism of French critics who have not taken into account the achievements of Joyce, or Kafka, or Faulkner,[32] and stubbornly refuses to apply the notion of "avant-garde" to the New Novel, because the word has come to denote a mere aberration from the standard. Of the seven defining traits of the movement collected in "Nouveau Roman, Homme Nouveau" ("New Novel, New Man"), the only avant-garde goal lies in the very heading of the essay: the New Novel both responds to the new reality of its contemporaneity and reshapes it so as to address and possibly help to generate—a new man. Apart from this, the seven postulates are again reactive: opposed to the "absurd notions" that have marked the critical response to the New Novel.

---

32   "*Ulysses* and *The Castle* are already over thirty. *The Sound and the Fury* was translated into French over twenty years ago. Many others have followed. In order not to see them, our good critics have, each time, pronounced one or another of their magic words: 'avant-garde,' 'laboratory,' 'anti-novel' . . . in other words: 'Let's close our eyes and go back to the sane values of the French tradition'" (*FNN*, 26). ["*Ulysse* et *le Château* ont déjà dépassé la trentaine. *Le Bruit et la Fureur* est paru en français depuis vingt ans. Bien d'autres ont suivi. Pour ne pas le voir, nos bons critiques ont, chaque fois, prononcé quelques-uns de leurs mots magiques : « avant-garde », « laboratoire ," « anti-roman » ... c'est-à-dire : « fermons les yeux et revenons aux saines valeurs de la tradition française »" (*PNR*, 26).]

The seven tenets are as follows:

The New Novel is not a theory, it is an exploration.
The New Novel is merely pursuing a constant evolution of the genre.
The New Novel is interested only in man and in his situation in the world.
The New Novel aims only at a total subjectivity.
The New Novel is addressed to all men of good faith.
The New Novel does not propose a ready-made signification.
The only possible commitment for the writer is literature.
(FNN, 134–42)[33]

Two points deserve to be zoomed-in on: Robbe-Grillet's "total subjectivity," which counters the early critical claims that the New Novel represented an objective literature of "chosisme," oftentimes denoting cold neutrality and aloof impartiality. This, Robbe-Grillet insists, is a harsh misunderstanding, as not only is it always "a man" who "describes everything," it is "the least neutral, the least impartial of men."[34] The other point concerns the New Novelist proposition of an incomplete signification: here, Robbe-Grillet argues that realist object-descriptions in., e.g., Balzac are reassuring because "they belonged to a world of which man was the master; such objects were chattels, properties, which it was merely a question of possessing, or retaining, or acquiring" (FNN, 140).[35]

Le Voyageur collects Robbe-Grillet's essays on literature and cinema from chiefly the 1980s and 90s. With the hindsight of the many years that have elapsed since *Pour un nouveau roman*, Robbe-Grillet repeatedly restates the claim implied in his early criticism; i.e., that the 1950s New Novel could seem a revolutionary undertaking only to a "curiously illiterate" group of critics in the major periodicals of the times.[36] This point, cited here from the 1976

33 "*Le nouveau roman n'est pas une théorie, c'est une recherche. / Le nouveau roman ne fait que poursuivre une évolution constante du genre romanesque. / Le nouveau roman ne s'intéresse qu'à l'homme et à sa situation dans le monde. / Le nouveau roman ne vise qu'à une subjectivité totale. / Le nouveau roman s'adresse à tous les hommes de bonne foi. / Le nouveau roman ne propose pas de signification toute faite. / Le seul engagement possible, pour l'écrivain, c'est la littérature*" (PNR, 114–20).

34 "Not only is it a man who, in my novels for instance, describes everything, but it is the least neutral, the least impartial of men: always engaged, on the contrary, in an emotional adventure of the most obsessive kind, to the point of often distorting his vision and of producing imaginings close to delirium" (FNN, 138). "Non seulement c'est un homme qui, dans mes romans par exemple, décrit toute chose, mais c'est le moins neutre, le moins impartial des hommes : engagé au contraire toujours dans une aventure passionnelle des plus obsédantes, au point de déformer souvent sa vision et de produire chez lui des imaginations proches du délire" (PNR, 117–8).

35 "ils appartenaient à un monde dont l'homme était le maître ; ces objets étaient des biens, des propriétés, qu'il ne s'agissait que de posséder, de conserver ou d'acquérir" (PNR, 119).

36 "On a beaucoup dit que le nouveau roman des années 50 représentait une révolution totale par rapport au roman tel qu'il était avant nous. Si cela a été dit, c'est parce que les gens qui avaient

essay "Cinéma et l'idéologie," is repeated on another four occasions throughout the collection. In a 1978 tribute piece to Roland Barthes, "Pourquoi j'aime
Barthes," Robbe-Grillet goes further in his analogy between the New Novel
and its predecessors in positing as a constant of the development of the novel
genre its tendency toward reaching an impasse. The novel as *genre*, contends
Robbe-Grillet, is predicated upon the constant need of being in an impasse,
on the brim of violating the rule constitutive of its creation – just as there had
been a Joyce impasse, so there was, later on, an impasse of the *nouveau roman*.

In the opening interview, which acts as a preface to his last collection
of essays, *Préface à une vie d'écrivain*—in many senses his "last word" on the
many subjects of his interest—Robbe-Grillet connects the notion of a shared
impasse to his lifelong refusal of the term "avant-garde" and speaks of the
exemplary importance of the "dazzling path" taken by Joyce's work, with its
peak in *Ulysses*.[37] In an essay entitled "On raconte toujours la même histoire"
("One is always telling the same story"), Robbe-Grillet presents his most
complete account of his personal fascination with Joyce's *Ulysses*, "one of the
founding books of contemporary modernity."[38]

This fascination came to inform the first of Robbe-Grillet's novels. In
a late interview included in the *Voyageur* collection, Robbe-Grillet notes on
the subject of *Les Gommes* (1953) that its "attitude to Sophocles" still remains
an unanswered question to him: "How did the presence of this text come to
be?" And he avows that the "deformed" motto from Sophocles in *Les Gommes*

---

la parole à l'époque étaient curieusement illettrés. [...] Ils n'avaient pas lu Proust, ils n'avaient
pas lu Dostoïevski, ni Kafka, ni Faulkner, ni Joyce bien sûr, etc.; si bien que ce roman, le nôtre,
qui pour nous était simplement la suite, le pas supplémentaire dans la subversion du système,
ce roman paraissait, pour eux, une chose parfaitement aberrante; ils étaient les victimes de ce
mythe de la naturalité du roman de type balzacien, c'est-à-dire d'un système d'ordre reposant
sur la chronologie, la continuité causale et la non-contradiction" (LV, 144).

37   "Pas du tout. On pourrait même presque dire que chaque carrière d'écrivain est une sorte
d'impasse. C'est Blanchot qui dit que chaque écrivain s'achemine vers son propre silence, et
effectivement, on ne voit pas très bien ce que Joyce pourrait écrire après *Finnegans Wake*, que
nous-mêmes, vous et moi, avons beaucoup de mal à lire, surtout dans les traductions françaises !
Le très fulgurant parcours fait par Joyce, depuis les *Dubliners* jusqu'à *Finnegans Wake*, avec ce qui
pour moi est le sommet, *Ulysses*, ce très bref parcours est allé au bout de son impasse, c'est-à-dire
que ça n'a pas été l'avant-garde de quoi que ce soit" (PVE, 13).

38   "Joyce avait une grande culture, très supérieure à la mienne dans de nombreux domaines. Une
culture grecque d'une part, chrétienne d'autre part, qui m'a complètement manqué, et aussi
une très grande connaissance de Shakespeare. Dès lors, comment se fait-il qu'*Ulysse* me pas-
sionne alors que je suis à peu près sûr de n'y percevoir, au mieux, qu'un petit quart de ce que
l'auteur y a mis ? Parce que les choses que je ne décrypte pas, je les sens malgré tout comme
cryptogrammes. Cela crée une sorte d'épaisseur énigmatique du monde qui fait que je lis ce
livre, *Ulysse*, avec passion. Il est très facile d'accès, contrairement à ce que les gens disent. Après,
Joyce a écrit des livres très difficile, comme *Finnegans Wake*, qui est presque illisible, ou en tout
cas intraduisible, or comme je ne connais pas l'anglais, cela revient pour moi à la même chose.
Tandis qu'*Ulysse* est un récit à peu près cohérent, seulement tout ce qui s'y passe à son double
ailleurs" (PVE, 99).

was meant to function identically to the title of Joyce's novel – as a "key" to its mythical inter- or subtext.[39] Just as in *Ulysses*, the mythological framework in *Les Gommes*—the Theban myth of Oedipus—becomes quickly juxtaposed with many other intertextual parallels, chiefly generic: *Les Gommes* embraces and transforms the genre of the thriller/detective novel as developed by Raymond Chandler. Critic John Fletcher quotes Robbe-Grillet's claim that *Les Gommes* is faithful to the mystery genre, having a murderer, a sleuth, and a body: "indeed, the traditional functions are respected insofar as a killer fires a fatal shot, a victim dies, and a detective solves the crime to everyone's satisfaction," with the important corrective that "the relationship among these functions is far from straightforward."[40] Just as Joyce's deployment of the myth entailed certain structural aberrations from Homer, so too does Robbe-Grillet's treatment of the structure of the thriller genre: chiefly the notorious fact that the protagonist Wallas—during the "vingt-quatre heures en trop," or the superfluous twenty-four hours of the action, throughout which his watch stands still—turns from the murder's investigator into the murder's perpetrator, fulfilling the fated Oedipal crime of patricide. The somewhat mysterious title refers to Wallas' purchase of erasers from (unbeknownst to him) his stepmother for whom he experiences a tinge of desire. The text is structured like an ancient tragedy, with a prologue, five sections, and an epilogue.

The title of *Le Voyeur* (1955) underwent erasure already as an avant-texte, for originally Robbe-Grillet had planned to call it *Le Voyageur*: Mathias the protagonist is a travelling watch salesman, visiting the island of his birth on a trip from the mainland. The criminal plotting is provided by the motif of a girl of questionable reputation called Jacqueline, who disappears during the day and whose photograph conjures up in Mathias the memories of Violette, with whom he was evidently once involved. His interior perception merges the two women, a confusion important on account of the French *viol* meaning rape. After Jacqueline's body is washed ashore, it is commonly assumed—and officially stated—that she had become a victim of an accident. Mathias eventually leaves the island. As long as *Les Gommes* was structured by means of a reference to an (absent) myth, early on it becomes evident that *Le Voyeur* also circles around a gap, a hole, within the text: something has been left out in the account of Mathias' sojourn on the island, a period of time dur-

---

39 "Lisant *Ulysse*, j'étais très frappé de m'apercevoir que, ma culture étant insuffisante, je n'aurais très probablement pas vu, sans la préface de Valery Larbaud, que le voyage de Leopold Bloom à l'intérieur de la ville de Dublin reproduisait le circuit *d'Ulysse* en Méditerranée. J'étais donc intéressé de savoir si le texte ancien était caché, ou exhibé, dans le nouveau texte. [...] Je croyais donc être aussi honnête en insérant la citation de Sophocle, déformée, en tête des *Gommes*. Aucun des critiques qui ont écrit sur le roman n'a détecté ce texte caché à l'intérieur de mon texte, ce qui m'a énormément troublé. [...] Parmi mes proches, seul un lecteur l'avait immédiatement remarqué, c'était Samuel Beckett" (*LV*, 262).

40 Fletcher, "Alain Robbe-Grillet," *Dictionary of Literary Biography*, 198.

ing his first day is missing from his schedule and goes unaccounted for. Out of the various hints and obsessive fantasies haunting Mathias' mind emerges the strong suggestion that he attacked, tortured, raped, and killed the girl, the scene observed all the while by a certain Julien Marek and his accusatory eyes – perhaps the "voyeur" of the title. As critics (Jean Ricardou, Ben Stolzfus) have noted, *Le Voyeur* is organised into series of eight juxtaposed circles, the figure *8* acting as what Robbe-Grillet would later call a "signe générateur" ("a generating sign"), a point of departure for multiple figures "eight" on the island: on the jetty, on doors, in the newspaper, and so on. For instance, Mathias covers the same itinerary twice, thus running two identical circular courses; the voyeur's eyes are described as two adjacent circles; etc.

La Jalousie (1957) perhaps best encapsulates Robbe-Grillet's tenets of "total subjectivity" in his fiction, despite its frequent misunderstanding as its very opposite. It takes up where *Le Voyeur* has left off, by making the voyeur and the narrator into one. The title plays on the double meaning of "jealousy" and "venetian blind" – through which so much of the jealousy-driven observation takes place. Set in an unspecified plantation colony, the narrative involves closely scrutinised descriptions of a budding affair between the voyeur's wife, designated simply as A, and Franck, the owner of a nearby plantation. The narrator's namelessness, his absence, and the constructed "objectivity" of his account are so extensive as to completely eradicate him from the narrative. There is not a single "je" in his narration, his verbal participation in the action narrated (e.g., in the evening soirées on the terrace) is limited to such impersonal constructions as "The moment has come to inquire..." and "the question comes up..." The very word "description" becomes inadequate here, as Robbe-Grillet's narrative *enacts* the workings and processes of the husband's jealousy-driven, obsessive mind undertaking a morbid scrutiny of the presumed lovers' slightest utterance or gesture.

Sometimes his presence is even more subtle, and just as the tuned-down presence of Joyce's "arranger" in the early chapters of *Ulysses*, it is reduced to the use of adverbs as in: "She rests her other hand on the arm of the chair and bends over him, so close that their heads touch. He murmurs a few words: probably thanking her" (*TN*, 48).[41] In passages like the following, his presence is disguised behind an impersonal syntactic construction:

"Don't you think that's better?" A asks, turning toward him. "Certainly more *intime*," Franck answers. He drinks his soup in rapid spoonfuls. Although he makes no excessive gestures, although he holds his spoon quite properly and swallows the liquid

41 "Elle s'appuie de l'autre main au bras du fauteuil et se penche vers lui, si près que leurs têtes sont l'une contre l'autre. Il murmure quelques mots : un remerciement, sans doute" (*J*, 18). N.B. that Robbe-Grillet's "sans doute" is much emotionally stronger than Howard's "probably."

without making any noise, he seems to display, in this modest task, a disproportionate energy and zest. It would be difficult to specify exactly in what way he is neglecting some essential rule, at what particular point he is lacking in discretion. (*TN*, 34–5)[42]

Although "it would be difficult to specify where exactly" Franck "lacks discretion," such exactitude is not necessary: the very hint points to how, to the narrator's mind, Franck is already suspicious. Elsewhere still, jealousy motivates a hypothetical conditional and one of the many stray observations: "If Franck wanted to leave, he would have a good excuse: his wife and child who are alone in the house. But he mentions only the hour he must get up the next morning, without making any reference to Christiane" (*TN*, 37).[43]

In a sense, Robbe-Grillet expands upon what Hugh Kenner has described in Joyce as the "Uncle Charles Principle."[44] Later on in the narrative, Franck and A spend the night away in a hotel – after their return the next day, a punctured tyre of their truck is blamed and no further sign is given as to what the night might have involved. Once left alone, however, the husband becomes haunted by increasingly detailed and derailed visions involving sexual intercourse between his wife and Franck, all products of the powers of his erotic imagination. The already blurry line between the narrator's foggy memory and obsessive imagination becomes almost non-existent: at one point, Robbe-Grillet heightens the confusion through a double meaning of the word *serviette*, meaning both "napkin" and "towel." Thus, Franck's "real-life" gesture of crushing a centipede crawling upon the wall with his napkin wadded into a ball after the first dinner *chez* A becomes confounded with his "imagined" repetition of the same action in the hotel room shared with A – only this time, with a wadded towel.

The imperceptible transitions from serviette as napkin to serviette as towel momentarily disguise the fact that the narrative has slipped from the remembered into the imaginary, indeed into erotic fantasy, in which the

---

42   « Vous ne trouvez pas que c'est mieux ? » demande A..., en se tournant vers lui. « Plus intime, bien sûr, » répond Franck. Il absorbe son potage avec rapidité. Bien qu'il ne se livre à aucun geste excessif, bien qu'il tienne sa cuillère de façon convenable et avale le liquide sans faire de bruit, il semble mettre en œuvre, pour cette modeste besogne, une énergie et un entrain démesurés. Il serait difficile de préciser où, exactement, il néglige quelque règle essentielle, sur quel point particulier il manque de discrétion" (J, 23).

43   "Si Franck avait envie de partir, il aurait une bonne raison à donner : sa femme et son enfant qui sont seuls à la maison. Mais il parle seulement de l'heure matinale à laquelle il doit se lever le lendemain, sans faire aucune allusion à Christiane" (J, 30).

44   The conviction that reality "does not answer to the 'point of view,' the monocular vision, the single ascertainable tone. A tone, a voice, is somebody's, a person's, and people are confined to being themselves, are Evelines, are Croftons, are Stephens... The True Sentence, in Joyce's opinion, had best settle for being true to the voice that utters it, and moreover had best acknowledge that when voices commence listening to themselves they turn into styles" (Hugh Kenner, *Joyce's Voices* [London: Faber and Faber, 1978] 16).

wife, excited by Franck's manly action against the insect, closes her fingers in a grip on the sheet of the bed. After this climactic scene of emotional turmoil, the narrative turns to—yet again—a mathematically precise description of the geometry of the banana plantations and concludes by a recapitulative summary of the elements occupying its opening pages. This is an appropriately cyclical ending for a narrative in which temporal linearity is constantly undermined. So, rather than aiming to abolish the psychological novel—as so many critics misinterpreted his real goal in fiction—Robbe-Grillet's project in *La Jalousie* is an ironic juxtaposition between extreme emotional involvement and pseudo-objectivism.[45]

Dans le labyrinthe (1959) has an even thicker storyline to extract and paraphrase: following a major military defeat, a soldier wanders around a town snowbound by harsh winter, searching for a man to whom he has, it appears, undertaken to give a parcel containing the personal effects of a dead comrade. When the advance guard of the enemy troops arrives to occupy the abandoned town, the soldier is wounded in trying to escape, and eventually he dies in the flat of a young woman whose small son had befriended him, as surrogate father while her husband was at the front. Critical consensus is that this is Robbe-Grillet at his most Kafkaesque, his most anxious, and his most inward: c.f., e.g., the accounts of the soldier's nightmares or the paroxysm preceding his death, which are among the most emotionally loaded pages in all of Robbe-Grillet. *Dans le labyrinthe* is thus the most character-based and driven, and in a sense the most conventional of his novels.

Critics were quick to establish a sort of a template of the New Novelistic writing on the basis of the four Robbe-Grillet novels published over the course of the 1950s. Yet, especially in the number of derogatory criticisms directed against him and the New Novel, many of Robbe-Grillet's theories were misunderstood as pertaining to his fiction and often in a garbled form misapplied to them.[46] As critic George Szanto has also pointed out, "to no small extent Robbe-Grillet himself has contributed to the rampant misunderstanding about his fiction." Szanto explains how Robbe-Grillet manifested

---

45 He takes "psychological analysis a stage further than great predecessors such as Stendhal and Proust: he makes the jealous character an observer recounting the whole business in the third person as if it were of no direct personal concern to himself. But it is, of course: from this inherent contradiction between the hero's emotional involvement and his pseudo-objective stance Robbe-Grillet derives fine effects of irony—ones which Stendhal and Proust would have appreciated" (Fletcher, "Alain Robbe-Grillet," 203).

46 Critic George Szanto was among the first to notice that "Robbe-Grillet's first three novels, *The Erasers, The Voyeur, and Jealousy* are told in the third person, yet the importance of each novel lies in its capacity to produce the immediate presence of a narrator. In each novel the narrator exists at every point only within the character relevant to that particular narrative. There is no gratuitous description, no gratuitous object; everything is linked to the central character" (George H. Szanto, *Narrative Consciousness: Structure and Perception in the Fiction of Kafka, Beckett, and Robbe-Grillet* [Austin: University of Texas Press, 1972] 134).

this: first, by investing his critical interest more into "considering the nature of the external world" than into "discussing the techniques he utilized in viewing that world." Second, by too easily dismissing the mimeticism of Balzacian realism and the psychologism of existentialist fiction as somehow already superseded; far from it, Robbe-Grillet's novels "display a relevant realism that keeps them in the tradition of that fiction which is altogether descriptive of human experience." Finally, and in consequence to the previous two points, "in his enthusiasm to formulate the boundaries of a New Novel, Robbe-Grillet attempted to begin with too much of a clean slate, and, for the earlier critics, everything was erased."[47] Thus, any sensitive reading beyond some of the more sweeping generalisations must discover that Robbe-Grillet's argument was always far more nuanced than his first critics would allow.

The first half of the 1960s saw Robbe-Grillet at work on his essays and in the realm of cinema (in collaboration with, e.g., Alain Resnais), and so his next novel, *La Maison de rendez-vous* (1965), appeared six years after *Dans le labyrinthe*, heralding a new departure in his fiction. Its place-specific setting in Hong Kong is immediately a striking innovation compared to the general, unspecified locales of his previous texts. However, it soon becomes clear that here, Hong Kong is the city of the popular imagination, replete with clichés identifying it as ridden with opium traffic, sexual indulgence, and gang warfare – it is the Hong Kong of the early British colonial rule. Another stereotype is the setting of a high-class brothel, the "house of assignation" of the title, with its madam, Lady Ava, and Lauren, its most expensive girl. The storyline is again cyclical, with scenes and sentences repeated in unbroken sequence, and actions often recurring at intervals.[48] Thus, in *La Maison* Robbe-Grillet can be seen to move from his exploitation of the clichés of particular literary genres in his early fiction toward systematic deployment of the pop-cultural myths of the collective unconscious.[49] *La Maison de rendez-vous* demonstrates the New Novelist lesson *par excellence* that for anything like consistency to

---

47   Szanto, *Narrative Consciousness*, 124–5.

48   The plot centres around a Victorian-pornographic-novel-type character: a blasé Englishman called Sir Ralph, alias Johnson, who kills a certain Manneret, his associate in shady business, and consequently is in need of leaving Hong Kong in a hurry. Wishing to take Lauren with him, he applies to his associate Manneret for the necessary money, and upon being refused, decides to murder him. Consequently, he needs to leave Hong Kong in a hurry, etc. Finally, he makes the mistake of returning to the brothel to elope with Lauren, only to find the British police lying in wait for him, betrayed by his *femme fatale*.

49   As Christopher Butler has observed, "this is a kind of Jung updated, modified by a Pop-art acceptance of the urban environment, and a Barthesian treatment of the thing as a sign (but without any attempt to say what or how significant their underlying codes may be, for Robbe-Grillet's codes are the codes of his own writing) [...] The point that it does have, once we turn to the novels that are supposed to exemplify the theory, is to suggest that the 'subconscious' of society is an irredeemably banal mixture of sadomasochistic fantasies" (Christopher Butler, *After the Wake: An Essay on the Contemporary Avant-Garde* [Oxford: Clarendon Press, 1980] 47).

emerge, a narrative has to resist or eliminate a number of contradictory elements.[50]

Projet pour une révolution à New York (1970) presents the city as the home of violence, the stereotypical setting of the gangster story and the mythical site of American urban violence. The genre exploited in the book is pornography, particularly sadistic erotica, so that Robbe-Grillet's city of subways, sky-scrapers, narrow straight streets, and ubiquitous fire escapes is no more (or less) like the real New York than the Hong Kong of *La Maison de rendez-vous* is like the British colony in southern China. Violence here is trivialised and repeated *ad nauseam*, used as little more than narrative material upon which to display possible permutations in structuring. Critic Christopher Butler has connected this structuralist bent to Saussure, in that here, "extreme stylistic simplicity in description goes hand in hand with a very complex ordering."[51] It is, thus, in his late fiction that Robbe-Grillet—unlike the early proponent of a literature of *désengagement* — begins to write socially, if not politically engaged texts, his method connected to a further ideological concern, a move away from "emotional concerns."[52] Bruce Morrissette argued along similar lines when observing about the section of *Projet pour une révolution à New York* written in the form of an interrogation that its referent needs to be sought in the social realm. The precedents of this technique are less Joyce or Pinget than "the innumerable interviews that Robbe-Grillet himself has given."[53]

After *Projet pour une révolution à New York*, Robbe-Grillet engaged with other popular genres—such as dystopian or apocalyptic science-fiction in *Topologie d'une cité fantôme* or *Souvenirs du triangle d'or*—whilst sticking to his predilec-tion for the hardcore pornographic. Critical evaluation, whilst unanimously positive as regards his earlier output, becomes increasingly ambiguous and negative as one moves in time across Robbe-Grillet's canon. For instance, John

---

50   "In Robbe-Grillet's works from *La Maison de rendez-vous* onward, Butler argues, "the notion of the even freer, 'ludic' novel has become central to his thinking. This deliberately exploits the narrative and thematic clichés in his work," with central emphasis put "on their structural in-terrelations, which demonstrate the free creativity of the author" (Butler, *After the Wake*, 45).
51   Butler, 49.
52   "This can be expressed in the claim that the breaking away from emotional involvement with persons, and that sequential type of narrative which is tied to bourgeois assumptions concern-ing the social order is in *itself* revolutionary or liberating. This has become a commonplace amongst many French writers and critics, reflecting an alliance between the two attacks on the nineteenth-century narrative led by Roland Barthes and Robbe-Grillet" (Ibid, 50).
53   "Interrogation itself is a new technique with Robbe-Grillet, and he gives it, as may be supposed, unforeseen twists. The basis or precedent for these passages is perhaps less literary than one would at first think. We are reminded less of the question-and-answer chapter of Joyce's *Ulysses*, or of Robert Pinget's *L'Inquisitoire* (despite undeniable resemblances), than of the form taken by the innumerable interviews that Robbe-Grillet himself has given to reporters and reviewers, a large number of which are printed in the format of an interrogation" (Bruce Morrissette, *The Novels of Robbe-Grillet* [Ithaca/London: Cornell University Press, 1975] 283).

Fletcher's highly admiring account of Robbe-Grillet's career ends on the grim note that "the novels published since *La Maison de rendez-vous* are mechanical and disappointing affairs, peddling an increasingly suspect form of near-pornography."[54] Butler, while sharing Fletcher's disgust and boredom, offers a holistic perspective from which Robbe-Grillet's later move into pornographic pastiche might entail more than the "inability to repeat the achievement" of his early work — a move into the sphere of untrammelled "écriture."[55] And although doubts remain as to the permanent effects of such "revolutionary" writing, constantly under the threat of functioning as little more than the demonstration of its own methods, it is precisely in this later work that Robbe-Grillet moves beyond redefining the modernist mythical framework and approximates the kind of conceptual écriture that critics like Stephen Heath perceive as the lasting heritage of Joyce's *Finnegans Wake* and Ben Stolzfus discerns as underlying the later stages of Robbe-Grillet's career.[56]

Although by no means the sole or most important presence in his canon, it is clear that Robbe-Grillet did turn to Joyce as to an ancestor and source of a type of inspiration during both distinctive phases of his career. Their parallels need to be conceived of on the conceptual plane: in their shared exploration of contemporary and ancient social mythology, and the pursuit of a fiction whose subversive character (recasting, however temporarily, the whole of the past tradition of novel-writing) could inscribe itself within this social mythology and bring about a much-needed change in the status quo.

1.3 "FOREVER ADVANCING ON SHIFTING SANDS": CLAUDE SIMON

Claude Simon's biography, unlike the other New Novelists', encompasses active engagement with politics and involvement in major historical events of the first half of the 20th century, much of which informed

---

54 Fletcher, "Alain Robbe-Grillet," *Dictionary of Literary Biography*, 211.

55 "The new realism of Robbe-Grillet and others was thus as much philosophical stance as new technique. It was also a recasting of tradition, an attack on the straw man of nineteenth-century narrative. Robbe-Grillet's later move into the free play of structures, or 'écriture,' can be seen as a logical development from his earlier belief in the free play of the mind upon things. [...] It is in the later ludic novels that the theory of creation and of imaginative freedom begins to get a grip on the equally theory-dominated narrative procedures. The point of these is [...] to liberate the reader from bourgeois ways of seeing the world in the play of the text" (Butler, *After the Wake*, 51–2).

56 "This dramatization of language and its productive or generative capacities, by stressing the internal reflexive activity of language and narration, is of seminal importance for the New New Novel [after *La Maison de rendez-vous*]" (Ben Stoltzfus, *Alain Robbe-Grillet – the Body of the Text* [London/New Jersey: Associated University Press, 1985] 25–6).

his fiction works.[57] Simon's place in literary history seems to have been secured by the 1985 decision of the Swedish Academy to award him the Nobel Prize in Literature, even though the circumstances of this crowning recognition of his work attest to his life-long obscurity.[58] His alliance with the New Novel was as problematic as his claim to literary fame; so much so that critics dealing with his work customarily begin by singling his oeuvre out from the New Novelist canon and insisting on its difference.[59] Simon himself voiced similar reservations in his contribution to the 1982 New York Colloquium entitled "Reflections on the Novel." He sets off by remembering that at the time he joined the Éditions de Minuit, he had read none of the writers published there with the sole exception of Beckett, and that no conspicuous sense of affiliation stood out "all that clearly to me when I became acquainted with their works, unless, just as in my case, the period of a certain form of novel seemed to them to have come and gone, a form that had become unbearable even, and that like me they were seeking to do 'something else.'"[60] His own work follows no precepts or programme, but continually reverts to the work of several of his predecessors:

> I used to work, and still work, in a totally empirical way, taking—to begin with—what suited me, and rejecting what did not suit me in one or other of the authors I liked to read, such as Dostoevsky, Conrad [...], Joyce, Proust, Faulkner, and I made my way

---

57   Simon was born in Tananarive, Madagascar, then a French colony. Shortly after the outbreak of World War I (in which his father died) his family returned to southern France to their ancestral home, where he was raised by his mother, whose death left him to the care of his maternal uncle. His studies of mathematics were followed by his military service after which, in 1935, he joined the Spanish Civil War on the Republican side. He then served again as a cavalryman in the French army, before being captured and transferred to a POW camp in southwest France in October 1940. Having escaped from the camp, he went to Perpignan and participated in the Resistance movement. In 1944, under the threat of possible denunciation, he fled to Paris where he stayed until the end of the War. For more see Doris Y. Kadish, "Claude Simon," *Dictionary of Literary Biography, Volume 332: Nobel Prize Laureates in Literature, Part 4*, ed. Catharine Savage Brosman (Tulane University, Detroit: The Gale Group, 2007) 261–83.

58   In his acceptance speech, the laureate himself alluded to the fact that Parisian journalists had searched frantically for information on the new winner, which *The New York Times* (18 October 1985) echoed in their report, detailing the perplexity of New York literati, few of whom were acquainted with Simon's name.

59   Most recently, critic Alastair Duncan has argued that Simon "always made it clear that he is a novelist, not a writer with theories about the novel" and even though historically, "Simon's work can be related to the New Novel and shows traces of the New Novelists' common history," still, "as a dominant perspective in which to view Simon's work as a whole the New Novel is too limiting: it omits too much of what is specific to Simon and sets him in too narrow a framework" (Alastair Duncan, *Claude Simon: Adventures in Words* [Manchester and New York: Manchester University Press, 1994] 7–8).

60   Claude Simon, "Reflections on the Novel," trans. Anthony Cheal Pugh, *Review of Contemporary Fiction* 5.1 (Spring 1985): 16.

forward (and still do so) like a blind man, never knowing when I start a text what it will be like at the end of the day.[61]

Simon goes on to show that, twenty years after Robbe-Grillet's defence of the New Novel against "traditional" criticism, the critical response to his then--latest novel *The Georgics* still operated with criteria such as the "reality" of characters, "fragmentation" of narrative or "frustration of narration," which he counters with the assertion that *discontinuity* should form the basic mode of perception and experience and that "realism" is discontinuity "concealed from the reader's eyes by the assurance given by the writer that he is reporting there 'the essentials.'"[62]

    The crucial break in the literary tradition of discontinuity is located round the year 1913 "because at the same moment Proust and (although to a lesser extent) Joyce (for *Ulysses* still wants to load itself with more or less esoteric meanings) undertake to construct texts in which [...] considerations of quality will govern the linking, or, if you prefer, the confrontation of elements." The decisive and differential element is, once again, verisimilitude and "faithfulness" vis-à-vis reality. This break, and reaction against it, brought about two dangers or "maximalisms." Just as the world—according to Valéry's famous quip—is menaced by two dangers, i.e., order and disorder, language is also jeopardised by two dangers: "on the one hand, that of being considered only a vehicle for meaning; and on the other, as only a structure, for it is always *at the same time* one and the other."[63] Simon concludes on an unambiguous note of affiliation with the New Novel on the basis of their shared principle of epistemic uncertainty: within the material processed and presented in the novel, "too many unknowns remain, too many contradictions, too many doubts":

And it is doubtless this uncertainty, over and beyond our divergent views, which creates the solidarity existing between myself and my friends in the New Novel movement, [...] a common feeling brings us together, a feeling that one is never quite sure of anything and that we are forever advancing on shifting sands.[64]

---

61   Simon, "Reflections on the Novel," 16–7.
62   Ibid, 17.
63   "Proust, Joyce, or Faulkner erect constructions whose solidity trustworthiness, and *continuity* seem to be far more determining, if one can use such a word, than a fortuitous encounter of two characters or two animals in a fable, for these other kinds of meetings, if they are dictated by associations between impressions or images, are also [...] inseparable from the raw material" (Ibid, 20).
64   Ibid, 23.

Following the earlier critical divisions of Simon's career, one can now speak of five distinct phases in the development of his oeuvre.[65] *L'Herbe* (1958) is marked by what critics have described as a baroque, proliferating Faulknerian style, combining lengthy sentences oftentimes running for many pages, including many subordinate constructions set off by parentheses or dashes. Recurring grammatical constructions within that style include such participle forms such as *"se rappelant"* ("remembering"), *"se demandant"* ("wondering"), *"se voyant"* ("seeing him/herself"), etc. Syntactically, Simon makes use of conjunctive constructions, which oftentimes posit alternative or mutually exclusive meanings ("soit... soit..." ["whether... or whether..."]; "sans doute... ou peut-être..." ["probably... or perhaps"]; "mais peut-être même pas" ["but perhaps not even that"]), and his regular sentence thus becomes crammed with actions, images, hypotheses, and recollections that seldom yield an unambiguous, coherent picture. The narrative of *L'Herbe* launches Simon's regional family saga in a fashion not unlike Faulkner's imaginative mapping of the Yoknapatawpha County. *L'Herbe*'s muddled storyline concerns the personal ramifications of World War II as they mark a group of family members living in the South of France.

In *La Route des Flanders* (1960), again, the narrative concern with personal memory points to Proust; its occupation with group and place identity (further development from *L'Herbe*) in the time of war, to Faulkner, both of whom are present in the enormous length and sinuousness of Simon's syntax. Although the character of the down-to-earth, cynical Jew Blum—a counterpoint to Georges the protagonist with whom he fights in combat and later becomes reunited with in the prisoner-of-war camp—has been seen by, e.g., Levitt as a nod toward *Ulysses*, it is Simon's stylistic and linguistic experiments in *La Route* that yield more conclusive evidence of a Joycean presence. Mercier cites the first of the many instances of Simon's description of female genitals ("cette chose au nom de bête, de terme d'histoire naturelle—moule poulpe pulpe vulve—faisant penser à ces organismes marins et carnivores aveugles mais pourvus de lèvres, de cils..." [*RF*, 39]), where *moule* means both

---

65   1945-1957, the early period from *Le Tricheur* to *Le Vent*, first published by Minuit; 1958-1967, the decade from *L'Herbe* via *La Route des Flandres* to *L'Histoire*, where all the novels are "based on Simon's experiences or on the lives of members of his family and question what we can know about others or the past since all knowledge is partial, memories fragmentary;" 1969-1976, a period of a novel tetralogy comprising *La Bataille de Pharsale*, *Les Corps conducteurs*, *Triptyque* and *Leçon de choses*, which all seem to follow similar formal and compositional procedures (typically featuring the use of present tense, elaboration of the associations of key words and situations, interweaving of parallel stories, multiple point of view and streams of more than one single consciousness); 1981-1989, in which the three novels—*Les Géorgiques*, *L'Invitation* and *L'Acacia*—are all conceived on a grand scale and combine the features of the two main earlier phases of his work; 1997-2001, where the last two works, *Le jardin des plantes* and *Le tramway*, revisit and play variations upon Simon's favourite themes of microcosmic personal memory and macrocosmic history.

"mussel" and "mould," and it is this second meaning—by which the vulva becomes the mould into which man is pressed and from which he issues— that is played on a few lines later: "ces moules dans lesquels enfant il avait appris à estamper soldats et cavaliers" (*RF*, 39). This "moule" becomes one of Simon's leitmotifs to which he returns throughout the text (e.g., "moule humide d'où sortaient où j'avais appris à estamper en pressant l'argile du pouce les soldats fantassins cavaliers et cuirassiers se répandant de la boîte de Pandore..." [*RF*, 238]) and which he weaves into a series of scenes.

Punctuating these and other reminiscences is the constant phrase "co-mment savoir?" or "comment appeler?" ("how do you know?" "what do you call?"), both pointing to the central theme of the novel: the elusiveness, if not impossibility, of any understanding of the past. This impossibility is furthe-red by the narrative practice of calling into question the narrator's identity. The "I" who narrates and the Georges, or "he," whose actions are narrated, appear as two separate characters whose voices are discordantly juxtaposed. When, however, after some fifteen pages narrated in the first person, the novel abruptly changes to the third one, with similar shifts occurring throu-ghout the novel, one discovers the two perspectives to be interrelated. It is this oscillation that, to Stephen Heath's mind, generates the strongest parallel between *La Route des Flanders* and the *Wake*, both texts deeply invested in the questioning and destabilising of identity.[66] Simon himself contributed to critical parallels with Joyce by describing his novel's geometrical design and its compositional procedure,[67] having been quoted to the effect that during the final stages of writing the novel, he used "coloured threads and strips of paper marked with coloured pencils to represent the different themes and visualize their interweaving."[68]

The title of *Histoire* (1967) means either "history" or "story"; and in Si-mon's blend of personal memory with collective history, the two become conflated. The narrative begins at night, as the narrator's perceptions of the

---

66   "In the writing of *Finnegans Wake* Joyce demonstrated clearly that the question of 'who speaks?', of the origin of expression, avoids the recognition of the real problematic. No one speaks in *Finnegans Wake*: the drama is played *between* Joyce as subject and language (personal, cultural, historical, social, etc.) and in its attention to that drama Joyce's book realizes its scene, reads itself as 'polyhedron of scripture.' For all that it conceals the scene of its production, a semiotic analysis could, in fact reconstitute this scriptural scene of a realist text. To pose the question: 'who speaks?' with regard to Simon's text (a text that is post-Joycean) is to pose that problem-atic the consciousness of which is at the heart of Simon's *practice* of writing" (Stephen Heath, "Claude Simon," *Claude Simon*, ed. Celia Britton [London/New York: Longman, 1993] 192).

67   Mercier quotes Simon likening the form of *La Route des Flanders* to the shape of ace of clubs, which one cannot draw "without lifting pencil from paper except by passing three times over the same point [...], the dead horse toward which, in their wanderings, the cavalrymen return three times" (Mercier, *The French New Novel*, 29).

68   Simon's outlines and maps can be consulted in an appendix to the 2006 *Pléiade* edition of his *Oeuvres*. See more in Kadish, "Claude Simon," 270.

fragmented forms and movements of a tree give rise to recollections about members of his family (with many characters recurring from *La Route*). The second chapter presents the narrator in the morning of the single day recounted in the novel, again recalling the past as he goes about his mundane daily routine. The motifs most frequently reverted to include, again, the Spanish Civil War, memories from World War I, Simon's dead father, and the narrator's obsession with his family's postcards. Simon's reuse of the myth has been commented upon by various critics.[69]

A more relevant theme is *Histoire*'s treatment of Christianity used, in Mary Orr's understanding, "to explore and create language associations, but in order to bypass the *mystical* elements of such vocabulary."[70] Here, perhaps the most explicit Joycean borrowing in all of Simon occurs in the form of the character Lambert, who in *Histoire* perverts the words of the Kyrie to produce pornographic statements, a direct echo of Joyce's Ned Lambert who also, in *Ulysses* (particularly in the "Aeolus" episode), introduces pastiches of literary style, especially bombastic and pretentious language. Simon's Lambert provokes pastiche, but of a more sacrilegious kind: "Arsenal de calembours et de contrepèteries censé d'affranchir par la magie du verbe des croyances maternelles et des leçons du catéchisme. Donc je suppose quelque chose comme *Introibo in lavabo*" (*H*, 43). Here, Simon incorporates the famous parody of the mass ritual as performed by Buck Mulligan on the first page of *Ulysses*. Critic J. A. E. Loubère has noted how this particular sentence also reinforces the connection between the Latin and the eroticism of the novel, while simultaneously foregrounding the fragility of the link between sense and sound in the most solemn circumstances: "A word is never sacred, says the pun, it can be subverted by the tripping tongue, and once we have ceased to give it credence, it can only reveal our preoccupation with ourselves."[71] By deploying Joyce's vocabulary and style, Simon's "non-mystical language" inflates both the Latin and eroticism to exaggerated proportions, as in Lambert's Kyrie:

69 Levitt has regarded *Histoire* as the "culmination of Simon's modernist novel series" marked by a style "built upon a continual and perilous accretion of language and detail, on rhythms which are seductive and endlessly involving [...] a style which in itself is emotionally, as well as intellectually, demanding" (Levitt, *Modernist Survivors*, 158). Orr has argued that *Histoire* "undoubtedly comes closest to *Ulysses*, it being Simon's most epic novel, with many classical references embedded in it, but not according to any elaborate scheme like that to the be detected in *Ulysses*." Not only is there no overarching mythological framework, but to Orr's mind, Simon inverts references to classical mythology through almost crass deflation, "pushing this anti-mythic use of language to the point of gently mocking Joyce's practice of presenting Bloom as contemporary Ulysses" – an example being the exaggerated recreation of a Theseus figure, not in the labyrinth killing Minotaur, but in a boiler-room, to show the incongruity of such mythical comparisons (Mary Orr, *Claude Simon: The Intertextual Dimension* [Glasgow: University of Glasgow, 1993] 149).
70 Orr, *Claude Simon*, 149.
71 J. A. E. Loubère, "The Generative Function of Translation," *Orion Blinded - Essays on Claude Simon*, eds. Randi Birn & Karen Gould (Lewisburg: Bucknell University Press, 1981) 190–1.

"Qui riez et les frissons ou j'ai z eu ta bite si gloire il y a au lieu de Kyrie Eleis-son ou de Jésu tibi sit gloria" (*H*, 336).

Similarly Joycean is also Simon's demystification of the INRI inscrip-tion, reminiscent of Bloom's musings on the subject in "Lotus Eaters," or his presentation of ritual and ritualistic language as banal, even ridiculous – for example through the repetition of "Miséricorde" (*H*, 27). However, Orr is correct to point out the limitations of Simon's Joycean borrowings.[72] The les-sons Simon appears to have learned from Joyce centre on verbal association and wordplay as structuring devices, and it is the epic project of *Histoire* that permits him the "one-off" collision with Joycean avant-garde writing, even though on a reduced scale. In Orr's estimation, for Simon, being a revolution-ary entails "a different thematic way to Joyce," and later on Simon "expur-gates Joycean tendencies of language usage in *Histoire* and indeed from his subsequent novels."[73]

As ever so often, part of Simon's "Joycean tendencies" reside in the eye of the beholder, as at least two other of his novels take a few steps further than *Histoire*. *La Bataille de Pharsale* (1969) betrays a conceptual rather than textual Joycean influence through its concern with multiple viewpoints, the writing of history, and historical cyclicality.[74] The radical departure from the use of a single point of view occurs when the narrator and other characters come to be designated as O, *l'oeil* ("the eye") or "observer" who serves as the narrative focalisation. Just as with the Joycean HCE or ALP, O can be anyone, anywhere, at any time. But O is also the phoneme in the first word of the novel, *jaune* ("Jaune et puis noir temps d'un battement de paupières et puis jaune de nouveau" [*BP*, 9]), and the repetition of the opening sentence (only this time introduced by "O. écrit:" [*BP*, 271]) also brings home the point of O functioning as the emblem of the circular form of the novel.

Part One—"Achille immobile a grands pas"—foregrounds, via a quote from Valéry on the arrested flight of Zeno's arrow, the transtemporal arrange-ment of verbal images, which become paired up, interwoven, and linked to-gether in a synchronic arrangement. Part Two, "Lexique," explores the poetic

---

72   "By encompassing Joyce, however, Simon fails to supersede him. This is partly due to a vocabu-lary consisting of mythical and mystical components, but constructed so as to demythologize and demysticize them in a new banal context. In part also, it is the erotic associativeness of Joyce that holds sway in *Histoire* at the expense of other elements from *Ulysses*. The biggest hurdle to further Joycean intertextual activity on Simon is the erudite density of the English which is quite beyond Simon in ways which Proust's is not" (Orr, *Claude Simon*, 151).

73   Ibid, 152.

74   In Levitt's estimation, this novel presents "the turning point" between distinctive phases of Si-mon's writing, marked by "a new dynamic operating: the author's own self-conscious involve-ment with the process of writing as process, with the literary text as a manifestation of a reality ostensibly more basic than that of love or politics or betrayal, with the reconstitution of a text as if it were life" (Levitt, *Modernist Survivors*, 161).

qualities of seven words presented as unrelated units in a lexicon – thus, the first entry, "Bataille," presents discontinuous fragments of battle scenes as depicted in various artworks, and "Machine" entails a meticulous description of an abandoned MacCormick harvester gone from a functioning system to a collection of dysfunctional bits and pieces. Part Three, "Chronologie des Événements," establishes still other narrative patterns, switching into the present tense, impersonal narration, and simple style, no longer reminiscent of Faulkner or Proust but far more in alignment with Robbe-Grillet's 1950s style – even though Simon's is a style which, just as in Proust, ultimately enables the central narrative consciousness to generate the text in front of us, as it were.

The last of Simon's novels surveyed here, *Triptyque* (1973), is marked by the deployment of so-called "generating images" designed to determine the content and narrative coherence of the novel, in the absence of a preconceived narrative design. The tripartite structure highlighted in the title—inspired, as is so often the case with Simon's writing, by a parallel with the visual arts (this time, a painting by Francis Bacon)—maintains equality among the various three-part arrangements in the novel. The three sections are of three different spatiotemporal settings (a country village, a northern industrial city, and a southern resort city) and of three main types of artistic representations (postcards, posters, and films) – triangular images of all sorts, including geometrical figures, run the length of all three:

> « Connaissant la valeur de l'angle ABC, démontrer : 1) que le rapport des surfaces des triangles ABC et A'B'C' est proportionnel à... » Pénétrant par la fenêtre ouverte le soleil projette dans la chambre un parallélogramme de lumière dont l'un des côtés coupe en oblique l'angle supérieur droit de la feuille où est tracée la figure, délimitant un triangle rectangle éblouissant. (T, 24)

The narrative concerns a series of implied events to do with such archetypical situations as sexual intercourse (voyeuristically spied upon), wedding, infidelity, death, and betrayal. What connects the three sequences is the central issue of how reality is represented, with emphasis on angles of vision and lighting, generating an acute awareness of the mediated nature of the narrated situations. Loubère has linked *Triptyque*'s "excessive emphasis on abrupt alterations in the language structures," which calls attention to "the process of textual fabrication," to similar processes at work in the "Oxen of the Sun" episode of *Ulysses*.[75] Shifts occur also in the very medium of the representation: Simon's frequent use of a *mise en abîme* technique is designed to blur further any distinction between the narrated reality and its "representation."

---

75   J. A. E. Loubère, *The Novels of Claude Simon* (Ithaca/London: Cornell University Press, 1975) 222.

Another common theme in Simon is eroticism, treated in a startlingly graphic way in *Triptyque* – explicit descriptions of genitalia and sexual acts become longer and more prominent as the novel progresses, with the close association of certain recurrent colours (pink, yellow, purple), forms (triangles, vertical lines, openings), and words (such as "lips"). These colours, forms, and words are the basis of the passages from one sequence to another. Especially the first sexual encounter between a chaperone and a farmworker at a barn (introduced by the passage quoted above) has all the geometrical precision and clinical language of, e.g., the "Ithacan" description of Bloom's semi-pornographic photograph. Christopher Butler praises *Triptyque* for how it "beautifully adapts the techniques of the New Novel to make up" for "one of the chief conventional constraints upon the narrative artist as opposed to the painter," that is, the impossibility of going back "to the same subject, as the painter can, and produc[ing] variants."[76]

Simon's technique of redescription with variations and recombinations is based on his virtuoso control of point of view in quite the *literal* sense. This visual metamorphosis, as Butler has observed, is deftly combined with "that play of language that constitutes 'écriture,' and frees it, not of course from narrative as such, but from any dependence upon spatio-temporal continuity, and from that moral significance which arises from seeing characters in a book as continuously 'real' persons."[77] Correspondences between the stories are brought about by means of metaphors, tropes, associations, oppositions, etc., and it is this contrast between linguistic patterning and narrative arbitrariness that defeats any search for a single underlying narrative unity. One of the crucial *mise-en-abîme* motifs entails a late scene in which a completion of a jigsaw puzzle by one of the characters yields an image which turns out to be the very same hamlet, river cascade, and so on, of the novel's opening description, which brings home the point, as Butler's analysis points out, how "the act of assembling the puzzle is analogous to that of reading the novel; the pieces do not correspond with whole objects, any more than do the partial descriptions of the text correspond to completed sentences."[78] Thus, more significant than the rather superficial echoes of *Ulysses* noted earlier are parallels between Simon's later output and the *Wake*. In this respect, Simon is rightly regarded as working and playing "on various levels of sense and sound, reality and myth, rhythm and structure, granting to no one element precedence over the rest, but constantly establishing new ties between all the details, however minute,

---

76   Butler, *After the Wake*, 150–1.
77   Ibid, 151.
78   Ibid, 153.

that go to make up a continually renewable text."[79] Not least of these ties is circularity or cyclicality.[80]

However implicit and understated, Simon's lifelong interest in and passion for Joyce—combining his refusal of the *Wake*'s engagement in "the incommunicable" with his embrace of its underlying structural and narrative principles, as well as textual conception of history—stands as testimony to the *Wake*'s (and Joyce's) unclassifiability vis-à-vis the modern/postmodern dichotomy.

1.4 "ANAMNESIS OF LEITMOTIFS": ROBERT PINGET

Apart from Simon, Robert Pinget is the only New Novelist without any essayistic, critical, or theoretical body of work expressive of his poetics and novelist practice. In fact, he made a point of evading publicity, refusing interviews, and shunning any sort of self-promotion. Had it not been for Robbe-Grillet's interest in his early-1950s novels, which he republished with Minuit, Pinget is highly unlikely to ever have made an effort on his part to associate himself with the New Novelists at all. Toward the end of his life, he even embarked on systematically destroying his papers, notes, and correspondence; a gesture of purposeful self-eradication from history, particularly poignant in the context of his work.[81] Of the little that is known about his obscure personal life, the following outline can be reconstructed.[82] His novelistic output took the form of an expanding, cyclical novel, with recurrent characters, themes, topics, situations, stylistic devices, and turns of phrase, all set in Agapa, Pinget's version of Faulkner's Yoknapatawpha County. Pinget's novels are exercises in

---

79   Ibid, 241–2.
80   "Like Joyce, Simon brings us along Vico's circular road from the end to the beginning. [...] Simon's writing is about writing. [...] Joyce is the Master of the Games from which derive so many of the manoeuvres in the texts we are now considering." (Ibid, 242).
81   Cf. Robert M. Henkels, "Robert Pinget," *Dictionary of Literary Biography, Volume 83: French Novelists Since 1960*, ed. Catharine Savage Brosman (Tulane University, Detroit: The Gale Group, 1989) 177–8, which the present overview loosely follows.
82   Pinget was born into a comfortable Catholic middle-class family in Geneva, studied at the Collège de Genève and at the school of law, where he took a licence. After his law studies he moved to Paris in order to take up painting as a pupil of Souverbie and acquired certain renown as an artist. His gradual shift to writing occurred in the early 1950s, when, following the rather modest reception of his first two novels, his third novel, *Le Renard et la boussole* (1953), caught Robbe-Grillet's attention and earned Pinget the stable publication platform with the Éditions de Minuit. His long travels took him on an extended sojourn at a kibbutz in Israel. His work, like that of the other New Novelists, covers multiple genres including theatre – here, his life-long friendship with Samuel Beckett gains in importance. Their collaboration was mutual: among other things, Pinget translated *All That Fall* into French, a favour Beckett returned by transposing Pinget's *La Manivelle* ("The Crank") into English as *The Old Tune*. (For more information, see Robert M. Henkels, *Robert Pinget – The Novel as Quest* [The University of Alabama Press, 1979], esp. "Introduction" & "Part Four: Taking Stock.")

sequential coherence and incoherence, which endows them with potential for intertextual connection and thematic variation.

It was not until 1993 that the first book-length interview with Pinget was published, conducted by Madeleine Renouard. Here, apart from shunning political questions and dismissing the notion of postmodernity as "absurd," Pinget's most interesting self-revelation concerns his attitude toward Beckett. They were "friends," and of Beckett's oeuvre, Pinget singles out three plays (*Waiting for Godot, Endgame,* and *Happy Days*) and the novel trilogy as works that have "marked him the most" – especially by what he pinpoints as Beckett's most admirable quality, "le combat qu'il a mené contre toute facilité."[83] Pinget goes on to claim that very early on, Beckett perceived a "similarity" between Pinget's and his own work, which facilitated their rapprochement. Twice he mentions the subjects of their many talks: "Il me parlait de Joyce, Dante, de son propre travail, de ses hésitations," and, even more revealingly, "il me parlait souvent de Joyce également, avec beaucoup d'admiration toujours."[84] Still, Pinget insists that, for all their proximity, "il n'y a pas de rapport entre mon écriture et la sienne," and that the only major influence Beckett ever had on him consisted in "la conscience même que l'on met à son travail."[85] The few other times Pinget broke his silence and appeared in public always made for a memorable event, especially his appearances at the New Novel Colloquia, at Cerisy in 1975 and New York in 1982, with the latter coming closest to an artistic creed.

He opens his "Address to the NYU Conference" with a polite critique of the "scientificality" of contemporary literary criticism (particularly, if also anachronistically, "New Criticism"), whose attempt at rational grasp of literary work as text displaces, to Pinget's mind, such traditional features— examined by, e.g., Poe or Baudelaire—as "innateness, spontaneity, inspiration." Immaterial and immeasurable though these may be, they all belong to the unconscious components of the creative process and as such should be reflected in the critical process, for it is "not solely in the light of pure deductive reasoning that my books should be approached, for insofar as it is possible I allow them to be activated by the irrational, particularly in their sequences." This, Pinget insists, is not to argue for some kind of "psychological" primacy in the creative process over the aesthetic significance of the product, but instead to "avert the error people may fall into if they consider that once my book has been closed, nothing should remain but the pleasure—or boredom—of having read it. Something more, something indefinable, fortunately, is intended to be its distinguishing characteristic."

---

83   *Robert Pinget à la lettre – Entretiens avec Madeleine Renouard* (Paris: Belfond, 1993) 32.
84   Ibid, 33, 244.
85   Ibid, 243.

Here, Pinget broaches the topic of his technique – the structure of his novels is described as "built on recurrences," essentially of four kinds: 1) complete recurrence or repetition of the first part of the text in the second – what he calls "a bipartite structure" and describes as ridden with "modifications, distortions, variations, transfigurations, which finally destroy, or at least shake, the certainties that the reader may have fastened on in the first part"; 2) partial and progressive recurrence of certain parts of the text, at certain points – a recap of sorts, what Pinget terms "unipartite" structure; 3) complete but reversed recurrence, starting from the middle – a bipartite structure "disguised as unipartite," what Pinget also calls *anamnesis*; 4) pure and simple repetition of certain key-phrases or *leitmotifs*.[86] Taken as a whole, these structures of recurrence have all in common certain self-negation, self-contradiction, illogicality – but as Pinget argues, his writing is founded not upon logic but upon exploration of *potentiality*. A necessary ramification of this technique is "the intermingling of themes and variations," that is, treatment of motifs and topics as particles of a musical form – throughout the interview with Renouard, Pinget expresses his admiration for baroque music. More specifically, Pinget emphasises the sound-property of his writing, "linked to oral expression."[87]

Pinget's declared intention, from his very first book, is "to extend the limits of the written word by replenishing it with the spoken word." His novels, Pinget repeats, belong in the realm of art in that they are artificial, composed of "every artifice of language," among which contradiction is Pinget's preferred semantic gesture, accompanied with all the possible "suggestions, refutations, prolongations and metamorphoses of fragments of speech" that could be taken stock of. Examination of these possibilities, then, points back to Pinget's earlier emphasis on the unconscious in creativity: he speaks of approaching "the dark face of language, in order to make it easier for unconscious values to break through and thus enlarge the field of my conscious activity." Pinget concludes by stressing that his thirty years of publication with Les Éditions de Minuit have been a conscious gesture expressing his "affiliat[ion] to the New Novel" and his support of "its efforts and discoveries, which are of great diversity and undeniable present-day significance."[88]

---

86 Robert Pinget, "Address to the NYU Conference," trans. Barbara Wright, *Review of Contemporary Fiction* 3.2 (Summer 1983): 102.

87 "For thirty years I have devoted myself to a kind of experimental writing that is intimately linked to oral expression. My exercises in vocabulary, syntax, rhythm, punctuation, have always been aimed at trying to match this writing to the voice that inspires it. My ear catches something that my pen endeavours to transcribe. My books are to be listened to, rather than to be read" (Ibid, 103).

88 Ibid, 104.

Perhaps the decisive traits that set Pinget off from the rest of the *nouveaux romanciers* is the levity of his diction, verbal humour, and what Robert Henkels—author of *Robert Pinget: The Novel as Quest*, the sole book-length study on Pinget in English to date—calls the "atmosphere of practical jokery" that "lingers over Pinget's world" – a feature which, particularly in the engaged 1950s, gave Pinget the unfashionable semblance of "a light-fingered Harlequin."[89] John Updike, prefacing the English edition of three of Pinget's early texts, pitches his poetics as navigating the uneasy ground between the Scylla of Beckett and the Charybdis of Joyce.[90] However genuine Pinget's desire "to blow conventionalized wisdom sky-high," his early novels went almost unnoticed by the reading public, making "stimulating, if difficult, fare because of the originality of both what he says and the way in which he says it."[91] His first work of prose, *Entre Fantoine et Agapa* (1951), already sketches out the basic map for his subsequent novel series by introducing two urban areas—the city of Agapa and the two interchangeable villages, Fantoine and Sirancy—their geographical dispositions, historical determinants, and present-day inhabitants.

While seemingly taking over the format of the realist, Balzacian small-town novelistic sociology, Pinget stands many of the genre's staples on their heads, revelling in parody and invention, ridiculing constraint and enlarging the scope of verbal expression. The text, generically resembling a collection of loosely and vaguely interconnected short stories, is divided into two parts, composed of some twenty surrealistic flights, connected through some very loosely associative principles, and all based on the generative power of language. For instance, Henkels quotes a passage describing the steeple at Fantoine, where *clocher* ("steeple") suddenly becomes *"cocher"* ("coachman") – a possible misprint. However, it is a property and achievement of Pinget's "polysemous writing" that in the particular context, "the resulting sentence is no more satisfying than the original. The author plays with both words in order to create a polyvalent context in which neither of them makes conventional sense."[92] The eponymous story, "Between Fantoine and Agapa," is a five-page meditation on a notice spotted by the narrator's wife, "Alopecia-impetrating prohibited" (T, 54). Another story is about a parrot enunciating mysterious prophecies, yet another is about the well-being of

---

89   Henkels, *Robert Pinget – The Novel as Quest*, 4, 12.
90   "Unlike Beckett, he has not turned his back on the seethe of circumstance, or, like the mature Joyce, taken refuge in nostalgic reconstruction. For all his flouting of conventional expectations and all the sly comedy of his rambling village talebearers, Pinget strikes one as free of any basically distorting mannerism or aesthetic pose. His recourse remains to the real, without irony" (T, 13).
91   Ibid, 12-3.
92   Ibid, 16.

pumpkins. Already in his first text, Pinget's later remarks about his fusion of the rational and irrational, conscious and unconscious seem palpably present. Pinget also furnished the English edition with a short preface, in which he pronounced the allegiance of his first book—not to the *nouveau roman*, but surrealism:

> I was still very much under the influence of the surrealists, of attempts to approach the unconscious; in short, of experiments made on language in what might be called its nascent state, that's to say: independent of any rational order. A gratuitous game with the vocabulary—that was my passion. [...] And so it was a fascination with the possibilities, the absolute freedom of creation, an intense desire to abolish all the constraints of classical writing, that made me produce these exercises which [...] neither the philosopher, nor the moralist, will find to his taste. (*T*, 25)

Le renard et la boussole (1953) directs its parodic onslaught against the voyage--story genre, continuing also the freewheeling experiments in verbal association and the dissolution of character unity. Its novelty lies in the employment of the story-within-a-story device, or a novel-within-a-novel, which would, from then on, form an indissociable part of basically all Pinget's prose works. Thus, an account of the journey to the Middle East of two characters, David and Renard, is counterpointed by a description of how the would-be narrator (of the patently ridiculous name John Tintouin Porridge) struggles and fails to squeeze that story into adequate expression in words, again rendering the limits of linguistic representation within the literary convention into the novel's subject and object. Henkels notes how another departure is presented by Pinget's turn "away from merely spoofing nineteenth-century narrative," toward a more direct engagement "with serious questions of writing and what writing means."[93] As the tension between the two narrative lines escalates, so does the increasingly episodic nature of the "narrative" and the fanciful associations of sound and image linking one projected story with a next one.

The most Joycean scene is the novel's surreal climax at a medical amphitheatre, in which a surgeon is calmly dissecting the cadaver of Joan of Arc. With an evident nod to the medical examination of Bloom's body in the "Circe" episode of *Ulysses*, the doctor discovers male organs upon her body, and the spectator's choppy commentary sputters into verbal fireworks similar the dialogues of absurd theatre or Joycean mock-catalogues. In Henkels' translation:

---

93 Ibid, 28.

Mercy on us, says the priest. – Heavens Above, says the schoolmistress. Mein Gott, says the Balance-Sheet. – What the Hell, says the general's wife. – The dirty rats, says Cecile and Michonne. – Superb, says Poppie, – Faulty drafting, say the jurors. – Good enough to eat, says the sewer rat. – Outlandish, says the tailor . . . – Bed-hopper. – Horse's Ass. – Aspen. – Crab Apple. – Poppycock. – Fricasseed . . . – Instigator. – Mouse-trap. – Scrounger. – Fowler. – Asshole. – Cooked-butt. – Monkey prick. – Feather of goose. – One balled asparagus. – Hot cock. – Soil the Virgin. – Pierce the Noodle. (*R&B*, 211–2)

Wordplay is even more prominent in Pinget's next novel, *Graal Flibuste* (1956), which broadens the parody of conventions associated with the voyage motif and thus extends the experimentation in the previous text. Here, the explorer is an alcoholic teetering between drunken delusions and no-less delusional, hung-over glimpses of reality. The novel opens with a cautionary introduction that transcribes the blurry impressions of a drunkard, presaging the jumbled journey to follow in the form of diary notes. The journey takes the narrator and his coachman through a region of fantasy, peopled by bizarre beings and replete with mystery, crime, legends, and quests. Again, the movement is from (at least attempted) incipit "objectivism" and "realism" toward an increasing level of sureality. The title is richly suggestive of the two key generic intertexts, combining overtones of the Grail Quest ("graal") and piratical adventures (*"flibuste"* / *"flibustier"* ["buccaneer"]), in accordance with which "the novel moves back and forth between the known and the unknown, trundling on to the next mystery once the last one has been more or less elucidated."[94] The pseudo-scientific objectivity and historicity is first undermined by a Joycean device *par excellence* – the parodic catalogue. Here is one enumerating Graal Flibuste's family tree:

Affaful begat Boot-Boot.
Boot-Boot begat Lapa.
Lapa begat Yumsk.
Yumsk begat Pawt.
Pawt begat Pawt-Pawt.[95]

As Henkels notes, just as in Rabelais' genealogies, so here "the wheezes, sneezes, puns, and multilingual puns produced by the list of names casts doubt on the accuracy of the very process of naming, and if read aloud, the genealogy sounds like a vintage motor car being started after a long rest in the garage."[96]

94   Henkels, "Robert Pinget," *Dictionary of Literary Biography*, 180.
95   "Affaful enfanta Boute-Boute. / Boute-Boute enfanta Lapa. / Lapa enfanta Miamsk. / Miamsk enfanta Loin. / Loin enfanta Peute. / Peute enfanta Peute-Peute" (*GF*, 73).
96   Ibid, 181.

Indeed, all erudition and pretext of mastering reality through knowledge is ridiculed via the mocking names Pinget devises for the authors of the learned treatises studied by the protagonist: "Ida's Mishaps" by a certain W. H. Sampeek (*"ça me pique,"* "it's itching me") and a treatise on erotic dreams by one "S. Blanculz" (*"blanc cul,"* "white arse"). Together with the verbal pyrotechnics (the similar sound and reversed vowels of the words *"céramiste"* and *"camériste"* provide the one tenuous link between two chapters; at another point, Pinget puns on the slang expression for girlfriend, *Nana,* by playing with the sounds of *"Maman," "Anna,"* and *"Ex-Nana"*)[97] what comes to a head is the gradual trailing off of any coherent narrative line, which yields to longer and longer non-sequiturs, digressions, and increasingly detailed accounts. *Graal Flibuste* marked Pinget's entry into the Éditions Minuit circle of authors, connecting him with the poetics and politics of the *nouveaux romanciers.*

The first group of novels, affiliated by their shared parodic impulse and linguistic complexity, culminated in *Baga* (1958), another work whose narrative centres on a voyage of self-discovery in which the narrator makes repeated and inconclusive efforts to write his memoirs. The voyage, here, is introspective, and features the protagonist, King Architruc (a mispronunciation or *Archiduc,* in Henkels' translation, King "Super-thingamajig"), a man questioning his own dignity in the flickering light of his life's major events. Again, the memoirs develop coherently only up to a certain point, after which the narrative branches off into a labyrinth of self-contradictory hypotheses, Architruc projecting himself into a succession of avatars (warrior-king, adoptive parent, hermit, postulant nun), a metempsychosis that provides him, however, with no ultimate discovery. In Henkels' well-wrought formulation, Pinget's first novelistic tetralogy foregrounds a paradox central to his understanding of language and literary statement: language as "open to multiple associations" and at the same time "inadequate to express anything completely."[98]

Pinget's second tetralogy is undertaken as a parodic rewriting of the detective-story genre, based on either letter/document-writing or an interrogation that generates various distortions and deformations of the narrated "reality" outside. Importantly, their linguistic makeup undergoes similar distortions and deformations, and so Pinget's *Le Fiston* (1959) is narrated through what seems a series of successive drafts of a letter from a Monsieur Levert (his name being the title of the book's 1961 US translation) to his runaway son, trying

---

97   Ibid, 52–3.
98   "[T]hat language is at the same time open to multiple associations and inadequate to express anything completely. When a word is bound by narrow dictionary definitions, it becomes a dead cipher. And yet when a word or phrase can trigger so many associations that it seems without limit, it means nothing [...] that every affirmation implies its own contradiction-whence the lack of closure in his novels and the reappearance of material from one book to the next" (Ibid, 182).

to convince him to return home. However, about half-way through the text, Pinget introduces "a technical device for which it is difficult to recall a precedent in the history of the novel"[99] by letting the impersonal narrative break off, and restart in the first person. Each of Levert's drafts starts off by an increasingly blurry description of a funeral of the daughter of a certain Madame Chinze, with whom Levert may have been amorously involved, which has in turn a potentially incestuous implication for his son's possible affair with her now-dead daughter. Each of these hypotheses, however, is carefully undone or deconstructed by Pinget's use (described in his NYU address) of repetition with variation bordering on outright contradiction. What remains beyond all contradiction is an urge to confess, but the contents of the confession remain insubstantial. The first edition of the book even came out unpaginated, a gesture eliminating the conventional and convenient points of reference within the text's "progression"—even though in this text, there is practically none.

Linguistically, this novel is Pinget at his most Joycean, for the variations upon the first-draft letter bring to mind the late-*Ulysses* self-referential deformations and the *Wakean* paronomasia of guilt and confession. The narrator's initial statements seem straightforward: "La fille du cordonnier est morte. L'enterrement a eu lieu jeudi dernier. Il y avait la famille et quelques personnes. Madame Chinze, la mère, était recouverte d'un crêpe noir, on ne voyait rien d'elle et c'était tant mieux. Le père avait un chapeau melon à la main" (*LF*, 7). Later on, the narrator rewrites his letter at a bar, hoping that alcohol may help to clear up his powers of recollection. But what it does instead is hamper his linguistic abilities and the tipsy narrator's words glide furrily into unintended puns, giving voice to admissions that he is trying to repress. So, eighty-one pages later, the opening paragraph is cited almost verbatim, but the form it takes is the following: "la fille du nier du la fille à nier. Aveugle. A nier. La nier du mordofille est corte. L'enterdi eu a jeu linier derment. La Chinzille et pelquame ersonnes. Famère étout recremoire un pauverte von nelloyait mientant nieuxvelle cherpinze lostait coirume oireau echon memain lonla fetit plusemme" (*LF*, 88).

As Henkels observes, "the resulting gibberish sends English readers of French sputtering to the dictionary repeatedly until they realize that Pinget is holding language up to a distorting mirror."[100] Particularly revealing is the dislocation of the last syllable of *cordonnier* ("cobbler"), which gives rise to the verb "*nier*" ("to deny"), a Freudian slip that brings Levert's repressed paternity to the surface: "The fatherhood he struggles to deny finds its way, willy-nilly, into words."[101] Throughout *Le Fiston*, Pinget insists on the linguistic foun-

99 Mercier, *The French New Novel*, 394.
100 Henkels, *Robert Pinget*, 78.
101 Ibid.

dation of reality, according to which what lies outside words is nonbeing. The novel's last sentence concerning Levert's perpetually unfinished letter ("En dehors de ce qui est écrit c'est la mort") posits the paradoxical prevalence of the written, despite its many flaws and insufficiencies, over the lived spoken.

Clope au dossier (1961) is even more elusive and ambiguous as to what "actually happens" and "how to make sense of it." It dramatises a failed experiment, a novel that turns out not to get written, after all. The narrator, Clope, sets out to compose a dossier of recorded conversations with witnesses regarding a single act: the firing of a shot, which he determines to focus on rather than the interlocking reactions to the death of Marie Chinze. Again, Pinget's interlocking of Clope's rather venial sin—of firing a shot from his garden in a fairly thickly inhabited area which brought down a wild goose passing overhead—with overtones of a person's death, suggests a possible (however irrational) connection between these two incidents. The novel's episodes unfold in a spiralling, snail-shell pattern that pivots around the axis of that precise moment. There are no sections as such, only six enormous paragraphs, various characters' accounts of their actions at the time of the shooting, their day-to-day routine, etc. The narrative impersonality is breached in various special places and situations; for example, in the second paragraph, devoted to Simone née Brize, and her daily routine as a young mother of a small boy, there is a detailed shower scene during which her naked body is examined with voyeuristic precision. This occasions a sudden eruption of the first-person singular (in a form reminiscent of a stream of consciousness) in what poses as an impersonal narrative:

> Le cul à Simone. Rose grassouillet fondant que le Pierrot qu'il aime tant ça qu'il a même essayé mais oui ce cochon essayé aïe tu me fais mal gros dévergondé et tant trituré tout dur lui allons c'est bon gueule pas là tu vois là ça va mieux oui. Rinçage. Ensuite pauvre Simone les pieds. Elle pose la cuvette par terre et les met dedans et se baisse continuons et les savonne pauvre Simone merde toute la vie comme ça se laver les pieds. Attends sois sage qu'elle dit attends voilà je viens c'est fini. (CD, 52)

However, again, when it comes to dealing with Simone's intimacy, the narrative undergoes some excitement-induced disturbances: "La fièvre. Prise de fièvre. Flambe. L'image de sa queue partout grossie grossie partout bouche ventre cul là là oui viens oui ça rrrrrrr ensemble ça cá rrrrrrr ensemble rrrrrrraaaaaaa" (CD, 112). This feverishness is also what marks Clope's concluding soliloquy as he puts the finishing touches to the dossier that he faintly hopes will prove his innocence. Such disturbances give rise to a juxtaposition of multiple conflicting versions of the gunshot and the narrative ostensibly intended to explain it – and the text closes on a note of ultimate indeterminacy and self-inconsistency.

But these disruptive outbursts also mark certain other instances through-out the text which have the air of impersonality, bringing home the point that below the surface-objectivity lies an organising—and disturbed—sub-jectivity. Throughout, Pinget uses an intrusive phrase, "eardrum damaged," to puncture the narrative flow, suggesting the narrative subject's proximity to the scene of the shooting. The first appearance of this phrase also leads to a disintegration of congruent syntax à la Beckett or Joyce:

> Eh oui le temps villain temps villain temps villain temps de mon temps voyez-vous, eh bien oui quoi le temps passé il y a beau temps je dis bien tout ce temps tout ce temps passé et quel passé ah là là un temps pour tout un temps un sale temps ne trouvez-vous pas le temps d'aimer et le temps de mourir alors qu'est-ce que vous croyez bien pire bien pire on a le temps de croyez-moi mourir pas d'aimer il est bien temps grand temps vous m'entendez et tenez tout ce temps qu'on perd à vouloir en gagner mais oui à tant le temps qu'on a mis à ne pas le perdre vous m'entendez mais allez leur faire entendre allez donc leur faire entendre allez donc. (CD, 27–8)

But there are linguistic sleights of hand more subtle than such outbursts. Henkels usefully exemplifies these on the basis of Simone Brize's expres-sions, twisted in transmission from English to French, which provides them with a hit-or-miss quality: for example, "*ouisqui,*" "*ouell boy,*" and a "*djip.*" The narrator achieves a similar effect by giving different names to the same cha-racter. The cinematic cut between scenes is oftentimes made on the basis of a double-meaning within single words that perform the shift. For example, "*tirer*" in French means both "to pull" and "to shoot," which enables Pinget to make the sudden cut from a scene of shooting to a housewife and her maid making the beds: "Elle voulait dire qu'Anne Dothoit avait tiré sur son mari. Tirez moins fort dit-elle vous me tuez. Elles tiraient toutes les deux sur les draps" (CD, 16). Puns appear in parallel scenes describing the same action performed by different characters. Thus, in an account of the housecleaning in the Bille family: "Mme Bille cherchait un pendant d'oreille sous le piano, elle disait *ce pendant* n'a pourtant pas pu s'envoler, tu perds tout dit Bille." And then: "*Cependant* que Julie Pommard pliant l'avant dernier drap ou était-ce le dernier..." (CD, 18, my emphasis).[102]

Widely regarded as his masterpiece, on account more of its scope and breadth (the only Pinget novel to run up to almost 400 pages) than its aes-thetic merits, Pinget's *L'Inquisitoire /The Inquisitory* (1962) has invited the most

---

102 Such overlapping scenes, argues Henkels, "invite the reader to intervene actively," by offering him to "rearrange the garbled syntax as he pleases. The punctuation of the text and the division of blocks of experience and of run-on sentences are left open for him to explore" (Henkels, *Robert Pinget*, 96).

numerous (if also superficial) Joycean parallels springing from its question-answer form reminiscent of Joyce's "New Novelistic" *Ulysses* episode, "Ithaca." The inquiry concerns an old, nearly-deaf servant who is subjected to an interrogation regarding his previous employment (and employers) at a local chateau. In the course of the novel-spanning Q&A, the servant's answers—by turns heated, impassive, engaged, evasive, funny, and boring—hint at a whole number of seedy events, including drug dealing, tax evasion, illicit orgies, even murder. To quote the back-cover of the English edition: "In trying to convince the inquisitor of his innocence, the servant creates a web of half-truths, vague references, and glaring inconsistencies amid 'forgotten' details, indicating that he may know more than he's letting on."

"Yes or no answer" (I, 5) is the first of more than two thousand questions posed, beginning with those concerning the daily routine at the chateau, the location of rooms and staircases, and the general tone of the parties held there. In these early passages—when the old man is asked to provide a detailed inventory of the furniture in virtually every room of the chateau—Pinget's cataloguing and enumeration does achieve the exhaustiveness and personal dimension of Joyce's "Ithacan" lists.[103] But already the answer to the first question has a certain free-flowing, torrential quality about it closer to "Penelope" or "Cyclops" than "Ithaca":

> Yes or no yes or no for all I know about it you know, I mean I was only in service to them a man of all work you might say and what I can say about it, anyway I don't know anything people don't confide in a servant, my work all right my work then but how could I have foreseen, every day the same the daily round no I mean to say you'd better ask my gentlemen not me there must be some mistake, when I think that after ten years of loyal service he never said a word to me worse than a dog, you pack up and go you wash your hands of it let other people get on with it after all I mean to say, man of all work yes but who never knew a thing it's enough to turn you sour isn't it... (I, 5)

The lengthy quotation—apart from giving a taste of the novel's rambling, colloquial, frustratingly circumlocutional oral style—is also meant to bring home a point about the one typographical oddity peculiar to *The Inquisitory*: the total absence, from all its pages, of a single full-stop, question mark, or exclamation mark. Even on the last page, in the final circling back to the novel's opening, a repetition of the incipient question—"Yes or no answer / I'm tired" (I, 399)—is left hanging open without a period.

---

103   As Mercier has rightly observed, the fact that all of the old man's answers are permeated by "indirect self-revelations" makes the numerous inventories "far from tedious, for he cannot help offering his personal associations with this or that piece of furniture, work of art, or building" (Mercier, *The French New Novel*, 369).

In the course of the interrogation, the questions become increasingly detailed and personal, probing into the old man's dim past – his air of a confirmed old bachelor is shattered upon the discovery of his past marriage and present widowerhood of ten years, the persistent prodding of the unidentified questioner also reveals his heavy drinking habit, his personal quirks, etc. Finally, an admission is dragged out of the old servant that a certain M. Pierre lives in one of the chateau's towers, takes his meals alone, receives few visitors, and observes the stars. The questioner's interest in other members of the staff, the relationships among them, and their acquaintances in town, becomes an opportunity for Pinget to recast dozens of his characters from practically all his previous novels. Reference is occasionally made to the central events of both *Le Fiston* and *Clope au dossier*, but instead of casting some light upon them, the examination obscures them further by piling up more hearsay.

In a sense, Pinget takes the New-Novelistic generic interest in the detective genre and thematic concern with alienatingly detailed descriptions of the physical surroundings and turns the "content" of the New Novel into the very form of his narrative, which consists entirely of inquiring into facts and fictions about outward reality:

> Go on with the description of your room / That's all / Is it a good bed / Yes / How is it fitted up / Fitted up with what / Blankets and so on / One woollen blanket beige and a padded quilted coverlet / Colour / Red / And that's all / For the winter an eiderdown as well / Good one / Very heavy / The sheets / She changes them for me once a month / No pillow / One pillow and a bolster I slip under the bottom sheet / Go on / That's all / Nothing to decorate the room, no picture / Over the bed a sort of carpet a small blue one to protect the wall / Plain blue / There are cats on it / Go on / At the head of the bed a First Communion picture belonging to their son / What does it represent / The Child Jesus (*I*, 395)

And so infinitely on, and so maddeningly forth. The stylistic effect is remarkable in how the purely descriptive sequences of question-and-answer ultimately produce the alienating effect of an objective emptiness in which all that remains are words.

This is also why *The Inquisitory* can be regarded as different in degree, not in kind, as a synthetic work that summarises Pinget's previous interests and concerns. Language achieves some level of Joycean playfulness by means of speech distortions caused by the old servant's deafness. The act of overhearing becomes the generator of some trivial and less trivial spoonerisms such as (Henkels' list): "clergyman" becoming "kleptomane"; "nymphomane" – "nymphatique"; "misanthrope" – "misancroque"; "somnifères" – "somnifèvres" ("sleeping pills" and "sleeping bills"); "Menerve" is domesticated into "M'énerve"; "Venus Aphrodite" becomes "Venus

Amphibite"; études de seminaires become the very opposite, "études d'inseminaires"; cottes de maille turn into "crottes de maille" ("sheath of armor" and "shit of armor"); etc.[104] Another Joycean parallel has been brought up by Mercier, that of the circular form wherein the last question is a repetition of the first: "The opening implies that the questioning has already gone on for some time and the close does not necessarily imply that the questioning is over. In spite of the hint of cyclic form, life does not fit into a neat pattern even here."[105]

However superficially, *L'Inquisitoire* is Pinget at his most Joycean, if not at his most formally and linguistically experimental. His next novel, *Quelqu'un* (1965), returns to an examination of writing, featuring another hunt for a missing manuscript. It also features the writer-figure by the name of Mortin, who would become Pinget's alter ego in a few novels to come – in, e.g., *Le Libera* (1968). What has been observed of Robbe-Grillet and other *nouveaux romanciers* counts in Pinget's case as well: after the culmination of the New Novelist style in his early-1950s to mid-1960s works, he embarked on an increasingly individualised (and autobiographical) style, less in common with the New Novelist aesthetics as well as Joyce.

1.5 "TO FAIL THIS WAY, IN A SUPERHUMAN ATTEMPT": CLAUDE MAURIAC

Claude Mauriac's coinage of the term *"alittérature"* (in 1958) was motivated by the perceived "pejorative" sense into which *littérature* had fallen, and formed through the use of the same morphological process by which the negation of "morality" is "amorality" by means of the private prefix *a-*. In his conception, *aliterature* is literature pruned of precisely those aspects that have rendered it a pejorative term – though Mauriac does not bother with enumerating them, it is supposed that one of them is the above-mentioned "morality." The point of the essay collection, Mauriac holds, is to present "alittérature contemporaine" as practised by some of its most significant representatives, whether essayists, poets, or novelists. Aliterature, he states, "n'évite de se dégrader en littérature que pour tomber dans l'excès contraire. Appel au secours chez Kafka, mais appel rédigé en clair, même si nous ne sommes pas toujours surs de le comprendre, elle glisse chez d'autres

---

104 In Henkels' summary: "In short, the preliminary hearing leads nowhere. The interrogation never comes up with the key question. The grand synthesis obscures everything. Individual words release Roman-candle showers of meanings, and the scrambling of titles of famous works of art suggests that the sacrosanct humanistic tradition itself is vulnerable to chaos, and confusion, and derision" (Henkels, *Robert Pinget*, 109).

105 Mercier, *The French New Novel*, 375.

dans l'incohérence" (*AC*, 9). It is this vague conception of incoherence that Mauriac sees as culminating, from silence in Rimbaud, via the blank page in Mallarmé or the inarticulate cry in Artaud, in the "l'alittérature en allitérations" that takes place in Joyce:

> L'auteur de *Finnegan's* [sic] *Wake* crée en effet de toutes pièces des mots chargés de tant de significations différentes qu'ils en sont occultés. Pour Beckett au contraire, les mots disent toujours la même chose. À la limite, c'est en écrivant n'importe quoi que cet auteur exprime le mieux ce qui lui tient à cœur. Le résultat est le même. (*AC*, 10)

However radical and subversive, even aliterature stops short of Joyce's experiment – apparently, "coherence" is not a concept as easily discardable as "morality." And yet, both Artaud and Beckett (as well as Bataille, Borges, Ionesco, and many others) are each awarded a lengthy, appreciative essay, with pride of place accorded to Kafka as the epicentre of the aliterary activity – Joyce's presence is reduced to this one fleeting remark. Still, Mauriac's was an epoch-making book, whose whole third was devoted to the yet undefined group including Butor, Pinget, Robbe-Grillet, Sarraute, Simon, Jean Cayrol, and Philippe Sollers.

Le Temps immobile is a monumental diarist endeavour, whose composition was begun shortly after Mauriac's *père*'s passing in 1970 and whose first volume saw the light of day in 1974. It combines excerpts from his diary begun as far back as the 1930s with observations contemporary with their recombination and reworking over the course of the second half of the 1970s and the 1980s; a work, as he termed it, of a "montage romanesque." The project came to comprise ten volumes published over the course of fourteen years, from *Le Temps immobile* (1974) to *L'Oncle Marcel* (1988). The first volume covers the period from 1958 to 1975, focusing mostly on three men who played a dominant role in Mauriac's life during those years: General de Gaulle, André Malraux, and Michel Foucault. Joyce starts appearing very early on:

> Paris, mardi 19 juin 1973 : Cas exemplaire de « work in progress » que *Le Temps immobile*. Joyce, justement, eut une influence décisive sur moi dès avril 1938, au lendemain même de ma libération, après dix-huit mois de service militaire. Le roman que je commençai alors, comme ceux que j'écrivis et publiai enfin, tant d'années après, naquirent de lui. (*LTI*, 33)

Not only is Mauriac's own opus magnum likened to that of Joyce's, but ever since his first novelistic attempts in 1938, Joyce is described as having had "a decisive influence" on him, and all of Mauriac's later novels "issued forth from him." However, Mauriac's attitude toward Joyce is not one of uncritical admiration and unconditional acceptance of his aesthetics. In a diary snippet from 1938, Mauriac speaks of Joyce's "errors" and "omissions."[106]

Joyce's "error," as Mauriac sees it, lies in his reduction of the human experience to all but its "least animalistic" aspect – there is more to human experience, insists Mauriac, than Joyce allows. Still, what Joyce detects is of "capital" importance to Mauriac, and to "founder in this way, in an attempt at the superhuman, is a remarkable success" in his estimation. Even though, as his reading proceeds, he likes *Ulysses* "less and less," it enables Mauriac to discover a way of writing whose existence has hitherto been unknown to him.[107] Not only does a reaction to Joyce evoke Mauriac's first novelist attempt, but Joyce remains a steady point of reference throughout Mauriac's further diary entries and volumes detailing his subsequent writing career.

Joyce is a steady presence in any discussion of literary style, particularly interior monologue and stream of consciousness – as Mauriac's reading experience of *Ulysses* shows, his admiration pertains largely to the early style and gradually diminishes during the later parodic episodes. This becomes increasingly conspicuous during Mauriac's composition of his novel tetralogy entitled *La dialogue intérieur*,[108] when sundry random recollections of early *Ulysses* and *A Portrait* seem to dovetail with his own novelistic exploration. Two entries are of particular significance, both à propos Mauriac's 1961 novel, *La Marquise sortit à cinq heures*.[109] The tetralogy Mauriac published in

---

106 "*Vémars, vendredi 8 avril 1938*: J'ai continué à feuilleter l'*Ulysse* de James Joyce. Tentative ratée mais passionnante. Je transpose, grace aux leçons de ma propre vie, et c'est la découverte de possibilités prodigieuses. Les erreurs de Joyce m'apparaissent et je les sens évitables. Plus que ses erreurs, ses omissions. Car il méprise, me semble-t-il, toute une partie de la vie intérieure, la plus belle peut-être, la moins animale. Je ne veux pas dire qu'il faille instaurer une hiérarchie dans nos sensations. Il faut voir ce qui est. Or, il y a plus que ce que Joyce y voit. Ce qu'il y décèle est pourtant capital. Echouer de cette façon, dans une tentative aussi surhumaine, est une remarquable réussite" (*LTI*, 36).

107 "Cela vous plaira, j'en suis persuadé ," me dit Chadourne de sa voix douce. Non, cela ne m'a pas plu. Cela me plaît de moins en moins. Mais cela me montre une voie dont je ne soupçonnais pas l'existence. Une voie merveilleuse. Comme Joyce a peu profité, a mal profité, de cet extraordinaire instrument dont il percevait si bien pourtant la valeur ! Je ne puis m'empêcher de commences dès ce soir *Le Cœur battant*, mon roman. J'écris de dix heures à minuit. Timide essai. Première prise de contact, passionnante" (*LTI*, 37-8).

108 As Mercier notes, Mauriac's original intention was to name the tetralogy *Le Temps immobile*, only later on deciding to reserve that particular title to his diary series.

109 In the one (Paris, lundi 17 juin 1963), Mauriac quotes Stephen's metaphor of history as a nightmare from which to awake as an "*illumination d'où sont nées tant d'œuvres d'aujourd'hui et celle-ci*" (*LTI*, 98). The other is evoked by Mauriac's rereading of Jean-Jacques Mayoux's work on Joyce and a quote from *A Portrait* ("So timeless seemed the grey warm air, so fluid and impersonal his own mood, that all ages were as one to him" [*P*, 153].), in which he finds, to both his sadness and joy, an encapsulation of what he attempted in *La Marquise*: "Je pense fugitivement, tristement, avec une joie vague pourtant : c'est ce que j'ai moi-même tenté d'exprimer dans *La Marquise*, sans savoir que Joyce . . . Ou l'ayant oublié . . . Nous essayons tous indéfiniment de dire le même secret. C'est donc qu'il y a un secret. Cela pour la joie. Ceci pour la tristesse : mais à quoi bon, après Joyce, après Proust . . ." (*LTI*, 164).

the prime of the New Novelist movement, between 1957 and 1963, and entitled *La dialogue intérieur* will also present the focal point of this exposé, since his engagement with Joyce there achieves its most explicit form.

Toutes les femmes sont fatales (1957) introduces the protagonist of the whole tetralogy, Bertrand Carnéjoux, by means of the most straightforward and least experimental of the methods deployed in the novel series – that of a single-character stream of consciousness. The text is divided into four sections ("La plage de Rio ou les incertitudes du désir," "Une soirée dans le monde ou le sérieux de la séduction," "La promenade à New York ou les vérités de l'amour," and "Une nuit d'amour ou la solitude du plaisir"), four separate interior monologues, each covering a brief period of time, but the entire set spans about fifteen years, and the narrative follows the protagonist's amorous conquests and reminiscences of conquests past. Apart from a womaniser (his surname literally means "flesh and games"), Bertrand is also a would-be novelist, planning on writing an *essai romanesque*, tentatively and pretentiously entitled *Phenomenology of Physical Love*; so a staple New Novelist motif of novel-within-a-novel is played upon, even though not as fully developed as for instance in Pinget.

The interior monologue, into which the reader plunges at the very start, approximates the immediacy and camera-like montage quality of the modernist/Joycean stream of consciousness:

> Deux trous d'ombre à la place des yeux, Mathilde est étendue non loin de moi. Avec ses seins lourds, sa taille mince, ses jambes longues, sa peau surtout, fruitée, veloutée, dorée, elle serait une des plus jolies filles que j'ai connues si elle ne manquait à ce point d'expression. Elle se tait. J'ai toujours aimé les femmes silencieuses. Le sable est doux à mon corps presque nu. Il s'affaisse sous mon entre et tout à la fois se tasse, m'enserrant dans une gangue souple. Élasticité électrisée. Tiédeur. Il suffirait d'une pensée et de l'ébauche d'un mouvement pour ce que ce plaisir se précisât. (*TFSF*, 9)

Le Dîner en ville (1959) is composed of the conversation and unspoken thoughts of eight characters seated around a dinner table, with characters recurrent from the previous novel. The book opens with the guests' arrival at the dining room and closes as they leave the table to go back to the salon for coffee. The plot is characteristically non-existent. The apartment is that of Bertrand Carnéjoux, now married to Martine, the daughter of one of his former mistresses. While no major formal innovation or progress is made compared to the previous narrative, it is peppered with some of the first instances of Mauriac's *dialogue intérieur* – those rare moments when one character's unspoken thoughts answer those of another with a coherence seldom found even in spoken dialogue. An example is a passage (*LDV*, 99–100) where two characters, Gilles and Gigi, exchange memories of their long-gone love affair without a word spoken aloud. What is developed to some extent is the intratextual thematisation of Bertrand's book, meditations on whose contents and form permeate his stream of consciousness.

The obvious effect of the interior monologue and stream of consciousness is to suggest a kind of equality of all the elements of the novel and of previous writings (imaginary or not), where interior monologue and stream of consciousness ensure a continuity of writing.

However, it is only in *La Marquise sortit à cinq heures* (1961) that Mauriac embarks on a genuinely innovative novelistic text. The time span of a single evening in *Le Dîner* is further reduced to one hour, and the private interior location is replaced with a public urban one: the Carrefour de Buci, a five-street intersection in central Paris. Bertrand Carnéjoux is still the central character and spends the hour watching the street scene from his balcony, now separated from his wife and resigned from his editorial positions, fully devoting himself to the writing of his next book, which is the one we are reading. The title refers to Paul Valéry's famous remark to André Breton (cited in his *Surrealist manifesto*), refusing novel-writing on the basis of an aversion to ever beginning a text with a phrase as trite and shallow as "The marquise went out at five" – Mauriac reverts to this statement and attempts to write an experimental poetic text that would still issue from this banal opening: "La marquise sortit à cinq heures. Reposée. Bichonnée. Pomponnée. Ballonnée. Ça, c'est moins bien. Ce ventre, il faut vraiment que je m'en occupe sérieusement. A part cela, en forme. D'attaque, quoi. Ne parlons pas de malheur ! Chère marquise. Traîner dans les rues, à son âge" (*MSCH*, 11).

Mauriac's stream of consciousness is here enforced by the matrix of haphazard sensations and fleeting impressions that is the modern urban space. What is novel, however, and goes beyond Joyce's early *Ulysses* style, is Mauriac's attempt to present the eight centuries of recorded history of the place, by means of insertions from authentic historical documents. He foregrounds these by means of Carnéjoux's alter ego Desprez, an erudite historian, who is watching from a balcony on the other side of the intersection, assuming the part of commentator (his name, in turn, echoes the famous local church of St-Germain-des-Prés). In a gesture reminiscent of Pinget's *La Fiston*, half-way through the novel, the marquise is replaced by another imagined character:

Rose. Avais-je déjà eu une fille de ce nom ? Pas tout à fait idiote, mais un peu dérangée. J'aimerais la mettre dans mon livre, mais alors il faut que je change de sujet, la marquise ne peut la connaître. Ce carrefour, mon carrefour, en voilà un beau thème et que m'importe la marquise, je renonce à la marquise, mais j'introduirai Rose, avec mes autres voisins, dans mon roman... (*MSCH*, 165)

What is more, this is followed by the elevation of Carnéjoux into the author of the book in front of us. Now that he has become the omniscient narrator and Mauriac's surrogate, Mauriac enters the text's conclusion, as it were, *in propria persona*: and in a theatrical fashion of a "master of ceremony" of sorts, showing how the series of narrative removes have turned his protagonist into

> personnage triple, puisqu'il est supposé écrire les livres où il joue lui-même en tant que héros un rôle. Romancier animé par un romancier que romancier moi-même j'ai mis dans un roman où rien pourtant ne fut inventé, un jeu de miroir y prenant à ses pièges, des sensations, des sentiments et des pensées vécues [...]. Mon livre, je l'ai imaginé, écrit, achevé sans idée préconçue autre que celle de ce thème : la réalité du temps à la fois exacerbée et niée par cette foule qui de jour en jour, d'année en année, de siècle en siècle, n'a cessé de traverser un même carrefour de ma ville. (*MSCH*, 311)

After the personal intervention of the authorial voice, the novel quickly dissipates into a series of statements about writing, language, and literature, with the final sentence, "La marquise ne sortit pas à cinq heures," negating the novel's opening premise and, as Leon Roudiez has powerfully argued, challenging the notion of fiction's self-importance.[110]

Finally, *L'Agrandissement* (1963) continues the project of immobilising time, now reduced to an interval of barely two minutes. As the title suggests, this text is an enlargement of a detail of the preceding work, consisting of a long stream of Carnéjoux's consciousness that takes place in the length of time required by the Carrefour de Buci traffic light to turn amber to red, green, and amber again. In these two minutes, Carnéjoux/Mauriac presents a commentary on the preceding three novels, and offers his thoughts on a planned fourth one – apparently, the one we are in the process of reading: at one point, the observation is made that "Ce livre est l'histoire d'un monsieur qui se demande comment il va écrire un roman que j'ai déjà écrit" (*A*, 197). *L'Agrandissement* is thus not only a reprise and a blow-up of several of the details of the previous books, it is also an afterword to the series. It explicitly features, most notably, the notion of *dialogue intérieur*: "Notons dès maintenant qu'il existe une forme de dialogue intérieur voisine du mono-

---

110   "He undoubtedly shared the apprehensiveness of many older novelists when faced with Valéry's dictum. Even though he used the anathematized statement to show that the poet had been mistaken, his last sentence, 'The marquise did not go out at five,' is an unwitting justification of Valéry's distrust. In emphasizing the reality that lies at the source of his fiction, he not only refuses to recognize the creative power of language but, by laying bare the mechanisms of his work, he has in one sense retreated from the position assumed by traditional novelists, who, like Balzac, might have considered their fiction more important than reality" (Leon S. Roudiez, *French Fiction Today – A New Direction* [New Brunswick: Rutgers University Press, 1972] 147).

logue intérieur, si même elle ne s'y ramène pas" (A, 14), which, at a later stage, becomes "a dialogue, but with oneself": "Pourquoi ne pas choisir cette technique pour mon roman: du dialogue, mais avec soi-même" (A, 172). Thus, Carnéjoux's monologue is periodically interrupted by his interior dialogue with the imagined professor-character from *La Marquise* – the majority of the text may be viewed as mainly a combination of this type of interior dialogue, consisting of an author's dialogue with characters already seen in previous texts. Most importantly, the Carnéjoux/Mauriac exchanges concern literature and questions of technique and artistic ancestry. Joyce looms high in these discussions, particularly as an acknowledged antecedent of Mauriac's (re)discovery of the interior dialogue:

> qu'en 1903 James Joyce, de passage, découvrit sur un rayon, parmi d'autres invendus, un livre abandonné là depuis une quinzaine d'années, *Les Lauriers sont coupés*, d'Édouard Dujardin, où il devait trouver l'idée du monologue intérieur. Émotion de penser au hasard qui fit tomber ce roman inconnu dans les mains d'un obscur Irlandais, le seul homme au monde à pouvoir en comprendre l'importance et y prendre ce qui devait, grâce à lui, devenir plus important encore, le monologue intérieur, que nous avons réemployé à sa suite et qui nous a permis de (re)découvrir le dialogue intérieur. (A, 52)

Interior monologue is, then, linked to the notion of simultaneity and spatial representation. Here, Mauriac notes: "*On pourrait dire : chez Joyce simultanéité pratiquement alternée ; chez Dos Passos, simultanéité émiettée ; chez Carnéjoux, simultanéité aussi instantanée que peut le rendre ce non-simultané qu'est l'écriture. Mais je ne le dirai pas, n'ayant pas relu Joyce et Dos Passos récemment*" (A, 92). Joyce also makes an appearance in a discussion of literary description and "key sentences":

> Mais à qui bon, à quoi bon, puisqu'il existe deux phrases-clefs. Joyce, probablement. Joyce, sûrement : *Face hargneuse de gargouille qui me provoquait dans la rue Saint-André--des Arts au-dessus de notre gargote et de ses hachis de boyaux. Des mots et des mots pour des mots, palabras.* Les deux phrases y sont. Il faudrait retrouver le passage original dans *Ulysse*. [...] Des mots et des mots pour des mots, palabras. Words, words. *On ne s'attendait guère à voir Ulysse en cette affaire.* (A, 61-2)

The sentence quoted in italics is a translation from the "Scylla and Charybdis" episode of *Ulysses* (U 9.576-7) detailing Joyce/Stephen's recall of meeting Synge in Paris. At a later stage, the sentence is quoted in the original: "*Harsh gargoyle face that warred against me over our mess of hash of lights in rue Saint--André-des-Arts. In words of words for words, palabras*" (A, 107). Throughout, however, Joyce remains an object of deliberation rather than a formal or linguistic source of inspiration; Mauriac has little interest in following Joyce in terms of his linguistic complexity, and his formal experiments with the narrative point of view are decidedly his own.

Again, Mauriac's authorial voice intervenes on the last-but-two page, and the final cadenza of the book presents us with the narrative subject staring, as so often throughout the text, at his own hand, and—in what seems another, perhaps unwitting Joycean/Daedalian echo—sticking to "the simple, incontestable words":

> Ce n'est que moi, à mon balcon, soir, été : rien que de certain et de rassurant. Des mots dans lesquels je peux avoir confiance. Feu orange. Bientôt feu rouge. La sonnerie du téléphone s'interrompt. La mouche se pose sur une feuille de lierre. Des mots simples, incontestables, pour des choses vraies, irrécusables... (A, 200)

L'Agrandissement marks the high Joycean point of Mauriac's writing, the culmination of his tetralogy, as well as a point beyond which the Carnéjoux series could not logically be continued.

Mauriac's next work *L'Oubli* (1966) marks the beginning of another series of seven more novels, grouped under the title *Les Infiltrations de l'invisible*, and worked on until early 1990s. *L'Oubli* is markedly different from the preceding tetralogy in that it is at once a parody of and a tribute to the New Novelist aesthetics and movement. *L'Oubli*'s mock detective-story genre combines Robbe-Grillet's *cinéroman* and Arsène Lupin stories. Its action takes place over the course of a single night and centres on a clique of novelists termed "Les Treize," without however providing any comprehensive account of its thirteen members. The ending presents an incomplete catalogue of five of its members, including some thinly disguised authors of the present selection, also entailing a tribute to Beckett and via him, to Joyce, portraying "Sam" as "même le premier de nôtres depuis que James est mort" (O, 228). On this note of Mauriac's high recognition of Joyce as the *primus inter pares* among the New Novelists, the present survey exhausts the Joycean focus on Mauriac's work, which makes for an interesting case of denial/dismissal mixed with admiration/acceptance.

1.6 "DO WHATEVER YOU CAN TO GET THE MOST OUT OF IT": MICHEL BUTOR

In comparison with Pinget's tangential involvement with the group, Michel Butor's association with the *nouveaux romanciers* is even more tenuous – in fact, his 1960 switch in publisher from Minuit to Gallimard was meant as a signal of his active dissociation from Robbe-Grillet's movement. The two most

significant biographical traits shared with Butor's[111] "master" Joyce are his
devoutly Catholic family background and Jesuit upbringing—with subsequent
abandonment thereof and rebellion against it—as well as a highly nomadic
existence.[112] A general overview of Butor's multifarious and extremely prolific
output should include four early novels, a dozen other book-length works of
unique genres, half-a-dozen volumes of essays, an equal number of volumes
of literary criticism, a three-volume collection of interviews, books of collaborations with visual artists (such as Jacques Monory, Pierre Alechinsky, and
Czechoslovak artist Jiří Kolář), and numerous poetry collections.

Butor's novelistic creed was formulated in his 1955 essay, "Le roman
comme recherche," which maintains a loosely phenomenological viewpoint
in which the novel appears as a particular form of *récit*, understood more
broadly than its conventional sense of "story," approaching the status of "discourse" or "narrativity" as such. For Butor, it is a phenomenon surpassing the
domain of fiction as "un des constituants essentiels de notre appréhension
de la réalité." He broadens the notion of *récit* to include all discursive structures that determine any individual's behaviour or knowledge acquisition.
These he terms "récits véridiques," as their common trait is their verifiabil-
ity – however, unlike all these, the novelistic *récit* is marked by its "deliberate
invented" nature (*R1, 7*). The very word *roman* signals, in Butor's phrase, "qu'il
est vain de chercher [...] confirmation" – and thus does not have to rely on
external evidence, but generates its own production of reality, becoming an
"ideal phenomenological domain."[113]

Butor then turns to the question of form – and basically voices a sentiment identical to the one Sarraute and Robbe-Grillet would (later) express:
that only a new form can reveal "new things and relations in reality" and that
"traditional techniques are incapable of integrating the new conditions" of

---

111 Butor's lycée years were marked by the German occupation, which his family weathered in its
very heart – the Nazi-occupied Paris. In 1945 he enrolled in the School of Letters at the Sorbonne,
and in 1949 he defended his thesis on "Les Mathématiques et l'idée de nécessité" under the direction of philosopher Gaston Bachelard. Shortly after his graduation, Butor accepted a position of
French teacher abroad, which took him to Egypt for a year, during which time he also explored
Tunisia and Algeria. Between 1951 and 1953, he held the same position at the University of Manchester, then, from mid- to late-50s, in Greece, Turkey and other destinations. In 1960, Butor relocated to USA, where he held various academic positions at various institutions until the early
1970s, during which time he also visited Japan or Australia for considerable periods of time.
112 Critic Michael Spencer went as far as to consider the basis of his writing as consisting in "a violent personal reaction to what he sees as the *malaise* of the Western world, stemming from the
imposition of Christianity on a way of life in direct contrast to it – with the blame falling on the
religion rather than on the society it has invaded" (Michael Spencer, *Michel Butor* [New York:
Twayne Publishers, 1974] 16).
113 "C'est pourquoi il est le domaine phénoménologique par excellence, le lieu par excellence où
étudier de quelle façon la réalité nous apparaît ou peut nous apparaître ; c'est pourquoi le roman
est le laboratoire du récit" (*R1, 8*).

the contemporary era. This search for new forms, however (again, a point Robbe-Grillet would agree with), is "bien loin de s'opposer au réalisme comme l'imagine trop souvent une critique à courte vue, est la condition *sine qua non* d'un réalisme plus poussé" (R1, 9). Such "realism pushed further" reveals that any application of the novel to "reality" is an endeavour of "extreme complexity," as it appears that realism within the novel (what Butor also terms its "theme or sujet"), forms a unity with "formalism and symbolism." For Butor, this unity—when pushed forward—results in a transformation of the very genre and its approximation of the condition of poetry.[114]

Butor's 1948 "Petite croisière préliminaire à une reconnaissance de l'archipel Joyce" is an expository guide piece. Appreciative of *Dubliners'* achievements of being "on par with reality," and slightly deprecating *A Portrait* and *Exiles* as "works whose interest lies in what their author wrote afterward," he devotes most attention to *Ulysses*, which, "before being anything else, is a novel" (R1, 199). The diversity of Joycean style renders the genre "un instrument d'une étonnante variété, explorant souplement les uns après les autres tous les niveaux de ses personnages," but Joyce does not stop here: "On a dit que le principal personnage d'*Ulysses*, c'était le langage, et il y a là quelque chose de profondément vrai" (R1, 201). As regards the novel's theme, Butor identifies as its "central problem" the relation between father and son, which binds the novel's "entire dialectic" – in its early stage, via the question of *Hamlet*.[115]

In the opening of Butor's discussion of the *Wake*, *Ulysses* is itself viewed as a "transitional" text: "de même que le *Portrait* conduisait de *Dubliners* à *Ulysses*, *Ulysses* forme le passage nécessaire entre le monde de *Dubliners*, inséré dans la tradition anglaise, et celui de *Finnegans Wake*" (R1, 208). In the *Wake*, Butor argues, Joyce expands the breadth of the stylistic variety of the English language as explored in *Ulysses*, not primarily by opening it up to the verbal material of dozens of other languages, but by integrating "tous les provincialismes et tous les défauts de prononciation," multiplying "les néologismes et les formations argotiques," and employing verbal deformation which produces "une vertigineuse densité d'expression." This density of expression, or what Butor claims Joyce himself called "word fermentation," renders this work one whose essence is "de n'être lisible et intelligible que graduellement."

114 "Il résulte de tout ceci que toute véritable transformation de la forme romanesque, toute féconde recherche dans ce domaine, ne peut que se situer à l'intérieur d'une transformation de la notion même de roman, qui évolue très lentement mais inévitablement [...] vers une espèce nouvelle de poésie à la fois épique et didactique, à l'intérieur d'une transformation de la notion même de littérature qui se met à apparaître non plus comme simple délassement ou luxe, mais dans son rôle essentiel à l'intérieur du fonctionnement social, et comme expérience méthodique" (R1, 11).

115 It is here that Butor's observation surfaces about how even though "Stephen est la peinture et le porte-parole de Joyce lui-même," in reality, "Bloom l'est tout autant et, dans l'existence, il faut bien que le fils devienne père à son tour" (R1, 205).

The first instance of the to-be-famous concept of *illisibilité* is, for Butor, in accord with the nature of the project and actually empowers the reader rather than incapacitating them.[116]

Now, it is true that Butor subscribes to the then-popular reading, furthered by Joyce himself, of the *Wake* as a dream-book, that his claim of the *Wake's* musicality is supported by the drastically overblown and incorrect biographical information according to which "Joyce had gone completely blind" during the *Wake's* composition, and that his four-page overview of the "histoire" is largely derived from the famous *Skeleton Key*. However, Butor's is an exceptionally informed and well-written account of the *Wake's* chief characteristics, and his admiration for Joyce's achievement is particularly striking especially given the essay's very early timing.[117]

Nine years after this first probe, Butor returned to the problematic notion of the *Wake* as a "language of the dream" in his "Esquisse d'un seuil pour Finnegan," where he subjects it to further elaboration and refinement. There are at least six conceptual areas to which Butor contributes with fresh insight. The first is the notion of the *Wake's* (un)readability, Butor's avowal that—even now, nine years after his first piece—he cannot claim to have read the *Wake* "au sens où vous entendiez le mot lire ; non, certes, je n'ai jamais réussi, moi non plus, l'ayant attaqué à la première ligne, à le suivre jusqu'à la dernière sans en sauter un seul mot, évidemment, ni même une seule phrase, évidemment, ni même des pages entières." Nevertheless, this fact "ne m'empêche, certes, nullement d'avoir eu *lots of fun at « Finnegans Wake »*. [...] Je m'y suis amusé et plus qu'amusé, j'en ai bien profité et il n'y a pas d'autre façon de le lire" (*R1*, 219).[118]

The second insight concerns the *Wake's* succession to *Ulysses*: where *Ulysses* oftentimes juxtaposes two or more "mots primitifs," the *Wake* will contract and mould them together. It is at this point that Butor introduces Lewis Carroll's concept of the portmanteau word – Joyce's achievement lies in his transformation of the concept onto a whole new level, again challenging his own authority as the text's creator. The third point pertains to the differ-

---

116 "C'est une apparence de chaos et chacun peut entrer à l'intérieur de son organisation per des voies qui lui sont propres. [...] *Finnegans Wake* est avant tout une symphonie. Le langage y est traité d'un bout à l'autre comme une matière musicale à l'intérieur de laquelle se déroulent thèmes et variations" (*R1*, 209–10).

117 "Le langage de *Finnegans Wake* est certes le plus grand effort jamais tenté par un homme pour transcender le langage à partir de lui-même, mais le poids du langage n'est qu'une expression du poids même de l'histoire sur nous, et le mythe de *Finnegans Wake* est certes un des plus grands essais de transcender l'histoire à travers l'histoire même" (*R1*, 212).

118 A re-take on the notion of *illisibilité*, here developed into the claim that the *Wake* dispels the illusion of an "integral reading" – in accordance with his earlier remarks on the *récit* of the novel, Butor expands the concept of "reading" to include "les autres, que nous ne réussissons jamais à lire aussi intégralement que nous l'imaginons, passant souvent des pages, relâchant notre attention" (*R1*, 220).

ence between the prosaic and the poetic functions of Joyce's word-contrac-tions.[119] It is here that Butor's concept of "the dream of language" surfaces – in a neatly Joycean twist, the genitive is both objective and subjective: the *Wake* becomes "cet état vers lequel nous désirons que le langage tende. Il est un rêve sur le langage" (*R1*, 223).

Fourthly, in a striking anticipation of David Hayman's concept of "no-dality," Butor notes how Joycean deformations gradually begin to serve the function of "topoi," or "lieux communs" – and urges the reader to commence "reconnaître les lieux communs joyciens classiques." These *lieux communs* have one aspect in common: their formal status as "calembours" and their thematic connection with the notion of *lapsus*:

> Toutes les différences peuvent être interprétées comme des lapsus significatifs consci-ents ou inconscients exprimant la personnalité de Joyce, projetant son rêve à travers sa lecture de cette seconde phase. Mais prenons bien garde que cette réduction à l'anglais normal est arbitraire. (*R1*, 224–5)

In one of Butor's memorable phrases, this turns the *Wake* into "a treasury of the possible slips of tongue in the English language."

Butor's fifth intriguing remark concerns his intimation of Joyce's com-positional method, which in the mid-1950s was still largely unexplored: Joyce's overwriting and writing-through of other texts.[120] Last but not least, Butor returns to the notion of *lapsus* and unreadability to claim that *lapsus* is not only the constitutive element of the text's composition, but also of its reading and interpretation. Even though reading the *Wake* "out loud" is the best way about it, there are inherent problems: not only "il nous faut néces-sairement prendre de nombreux mots autrement qu'ils sont écrits, abandon-ner une partie de leurs lettres et leurs significations possibles," but also: "le lecteur est obligé de faire un choix, d'adopter une prononciation, et peu à peu, entraîné par le rythme et le ton du texte, il se met à l'animer et en quelque sorte à le jouer" (*R1*, 225-6). It is only in this sense and context that Butor's remark about the *Wake* as "a machine to provoke and facilitate my own dreams," often trivialised in its garbled form, actually makes sense and stands as testimony to

---

119   "Joyce dans *Finnegans Wake* va faire de ces mots contractés un emploi soit prosaïque, lorsque leurs significations ne fonctionnent qu'alternativement, soit poétique lorsqu'elles fonctionnent simultanément, lorsque la formation du mot lui-même par conséquent apparaît comme immé-diatement justifiée. [...] D'autre part, pour que la contraction puisse avoir lieu, il est nécessaire qu'il y ait entre les deux ou trois mots primitifs quelques lettres ou syllabes communes. Le mot contracté est donc toujours une allitération contractée" (*R1*, 223).

120   "Joyce prend un texte, on pourrait presque dire n'importe lequel, il rêve sur lui, il déchiffre à tra-vers lui un autre texte, qu'il y intègre et qui devient aussi important que le premier, qui joue exactement le même rôle que lui" (*R1*, 225).

his sensitive understanding of the *Wake*.[121] Butor's essays make for a fascinating read especially given the time and circumstances of their composition. As Butor himself remarked much later, his first article took shape through his readings, at the Sainte-Geneviève library, of *Ulysses* and the *Stèle pour James Joyce* by Louis Gillet, back when Joyce was "practically unknown" in France.[122]

Naturally, Butor's novelistic output could not have gone unmarked by such a thorough and early exposure to Joyce's late work. However, were one to look for direct allusions to Joyce à la Mauriac or quotations from Joyce à la Simon, one would search in vain. Yet, the reason for discussing the two essays in such a detail is their value as interpretive tools for the poetics of Butor's own fiction.

The three-volume, monumental edition of Butor's *Entretiens*, containing his interviews over the four decades from 1956 to 1996, includes plenty of name-dropping and references to Joyce, mostly pertaining to Butor's own work. When prompted, Butor is also willing to identify very loose, conceptual rather than textual connections between his novels and Joyce's work: for instance, in an interview from December 1957 for *Le Figaro littéraire*, he discusses how the Joycean / Proustian heritage of "the long sentence" was all the encouragement he needed to write *L'Emploi du temps* and *La Modification* in the particular fashion he did: "Si j'ai osé me lancer dans des phrases longues, c'est parce que Proust, Joyce en avaient fait avant moi. Sinon je ne sais pas si j'aurais osé."[123]

Almost all further parallels are both reverential and interesting, but also rather immaterial and impressionistic. It is only much later—in the 1980s and 1990s interviews—that Butor elaborates at some length on the slow and complex process by which he both absorbed and consciously resisted Joyce's influence. In a March 1983 interview for *Esprit*, Butor is posed a question regarding the very heart of the matter: "Is it possible to be truly 'post-Joycean'? Is it possible to escape [...] repetition?" Butor begins, as is his wont, with the general,[124] and proceeds with the particular:

---

121 "*Finnegans Wake* est ainsi pour chacun de nous un instrument de connaissance intime, car ce portrait de moi-même que j'y discerne, ce n'est pas celui que j'aurais dessiné avant la lecture. Ces phrases dont l'orthographie ambiguë me contraint de les interpréter au moyen d'innombrables lapsus servent de catalyseurs à ma conscience, rongent et minent peu à peu les étages de ma censure. Ce n'est donc pas, comme on le dit souvent, la simple description d'un rêve, mais une machine à provoquer et faciliter mes propres rêves" (R1, 226).

122 "Quand j'ai écrit mon premier article sur Joyce, en 1948, il était presque inconnu en France. On en avait beaucoup parlé à une certaine époque, puis la vague de l'Occupation l'avait recouvert, comme tant d'autres choses. Ce qui m'a influencé chez lui, c'est l'utilisation de grilles, le fait d'écrire non pas au fil de la plume, au long du texte, mais en quelque sorte perpendiculairement à lui" (*Michel Butor - Rencontre avec Roger-Michel Allemand* [Paris: Argol, 2009] 57).

123 *Michel Butor - Entretiens, Vol. 1 (1956–68)*, 53.

124 "Effectivement il y a beaucoup de choses en littérature contemporaine actuelle qui sont des exploitations de détails de l'œuvre de certains grands écrivains du début du XXe siècle et en particulier de l'œuvre de Joyce : cela est tout à fait normal... C'est un phénomène très courant

En ce qui me concerne, j'ai fait tout ce que j'ai pu pour tirer le maximum de leçons de Joyce, je n'ai pas fini, j'aurais encore bien des choses à lui prendre. Pendant un certain temps, je me suis efforcé d'éviter ce qui aurait été des emprunts trop voyants ; par exemple je me suis longtemps interdit d'inventer des mots. Aujourd'hui je n'hésiterais plus parce que j'ai établi des distances telles que ça n'a plus d'importance. Lorsque j'étais plus jeune je ne pouvais pas, justement pour tirer le meilleur profit de Joyce.[125]

Here, Butor confesses to an interesting dialectic at work in his absorption of Joycean influence: in order to "make the best profit" out of Joyce's lessons, he concedes that for a certain time he "forced himself to avoid the most obvious borrowings" of his influence, so that, for example, he "forbade" himself "to invent words." Now that he had established "a distance" between himself and Joyce, he "would no longer hesitate" to let his texts be marked by Joycean borrowings. On another occasion, in an interview for the Winter 1994 issue of *Otrante*, Butor gives an early example of such "borrowing at a distance" in *L'Emploi du temps*.[126]

Butor repeatedly posits his re-appropriation of Joyce's invention of "an external grid" as an organising principle of the novelistic material as his most overt Joycean debt – even though here he insists that the uses to which he puts his mythic patterns in *L'Emploi du temps* differ markedly from those of Joycean Homeric parallels. The presence of temporal patterns in Butor's work was implied by himself on numerous occasions and most successfully elaborated in Dean McWilliams' book-length study of Butor:

	DAY	YEAR
1. *PASSAGE DE MILAN*	7:00 PM-7:00 AM	
2. *L'EMPLOI DU TEMPS*	Revel writes a journal at night	1 Oct. to 30 Sept.
3. *LA MODIFICATION*	8:10 AM – 5:45 AM	15–16 Nov.
4. *DEGRÉS*		Oct. 1954 – Nov. 1955
5. *DESCRIPTION DE SAN MARCO* AND *PORTRAIT D'ARTISTE*	Begins at midday ends at sunset	

---

et qui ne permet pas du tout de dire qu'il soit particulièrement difficile de faire quelque chose après Joyce ; au contraire, c'est plus facile. Il y a chez Joyce une telle dose de nouveauté que c'est contagieux."

125   *Michel Butor – Entretiens, Vol. 3 (1979–96)*, 127.

126   "Évidemment, beaucoup de choses dans ce livre viennent d'une réflexion sur Joyce. Mais il y a une différence profonde entre *Ulysses* et un livre comme *L'Emploi*. Dans *Ulysses*, le mythe sert de grille et de thème, mais il n'est pas raconté à l'intérieur du livre. Il est à l'extérieur, seulement dans le titre. Ce sont les commentateurs qui vont donner des titres aux chapitres. Tandis qu'à l'intérieur de *L'Emploi*, les histoires de Caïn et de Thésée sont racontées. L'histoire de Dédalus et Bloom reproduit l'histoire de Télémaque et Ulysse, mais sans qu'ils le sachent et sans qu'ils y fassent quoi en ce soit" (Ibid, 334).

EN JEUNE SINGE	Central section: 8 days and 7 nights	Covers seven weeks
6 MOBILE	3:00 AM EST to 12:00PM MST	Vernal equinox
7 6.810.000 LITRES D'EAU PAR SECONDE		April to March

The existence, in Butor, of temporal patterns, of cycles, the ritual "of withdrawal, initiation, and return"[127] identified by McWilliams needs no further belabouring. The point, as has been argued, of utilising these grids and patterns is, for Butor, similar to Joyce's: "Just as it is possible to discover the universality of the *Odyssey* in the heart of the twentieth-century Dublin, similarly Butor's novels make considerable use of dreams and mythological symbolism in order to uncover some kind of pattern or structure underlying our acts."[128]

In Butor's first novel, *Passage de Milan*—published in 1954 by Éditions de Minuit—the temporal grid is further enhanced by spatial arrangement: Butor uses the device of the apartment-house setting. The novel's organisation is symmetrical and neat. The action of *Passage de Milan* takes place within twelve hours, from seven in the evening until seven in the morning, at an apartment house divided into seven stories. There is a marked vertical segmentation, from the highest level with lofty characters such as Abbé Jean—who in the opening scene contemplates the sky, observing the flight of an airplane or perhaps a hawk—to the lowest level, beset by the incessant din of Paris metro and inhabited by the working class.

The complicated, story-driven narrative is composed as an almost musical counterpoint of motifs and character actions that get repeated, with variations, floor after floor. Various commentators have also noted the double-meaning of the title, which can refer to both the street where the novel is set, and the "passage" of the Kite, the savage bird of prey connected with Abbé Jean's Egyptian studies. Butor employs the interior monologue technique to examine the psychic interiority of many of the sixty-six characters that people the apartment house. Curiously, no critic[129] so far has commented on Butor's observation, printed on the back cover of the book, according to which "Les événements futurs projettent déjà leur ombre sur nous," which is almost a literal translation of a sentence from *Ulysses*: "Coming events *cast their shadows before*" (*U* 8.526). Another Joycean allusion is provided by one of the subplots involving a group of writers attempting a collective work, an imaginary book entitled *Les Faubourgs de Trieste*, the first long-term locale of

127 Dean McWilliams, *The Narratives of Michel Butor: The Writer as Janus* (Columbus: Ohio University Press, 1978) 10.

128 Spencer, *Michel Butor*, 25.

129 Not even F. C. St. Aubyn in his excellent entry on Michel Butor in *Dictionary of Literary Biography, Volume 83*, 13–29, where this fact is mentioned and briefly analysed.

Joyce's exile from Dublin. On a more general level, another modernist trait of *Passage de Milan* is its simultaneous presentation of the consciousness of people in motion: Butor's enactment of their dreams, desires, and ambitions reveals them as hopelessly isolated, non-communicative entities.

Butor's observations on the structuring of *Ulysses* and the language of the *Wake* can be taken as insights into his own creative procedure within his first novel. For instance, his insistence on *Ulysses* being, first and foremost, a novel, expresses the intention of his own first four novels to partake of the most elastic of forms; his reading of the *Wake* as structured around *lieux communs* in turn reveals his own activity in *Passage* as closely corresponding to this description.[130] In *Passage*, the *lieux communs* are formed by numerous colloquial phrases and clichés that circulate in the characters' consciousnesses (e.g., "entre chien et loup," "faire le pied de grue," "on ne les connaît ni Eve ni d'Adam," "les vannes sont ouvertes") and although these commonplaces are not deformed or "fermented," Butor does achieve some punning orchestration with them. For instance, as Lydon notes, the phrase "faire le pied de grue" (lit. "to make the foot of the crane," to stand motionlessly and expectantly in one place) becomes echoed when the female protagonist, Angèle Vertigues, who is just about to be shot dead, is mentally dismissed by another character as "une petite grue," slang for "slut" or "whore," but literally a "crane" in English, which in the French (*crâne*) means "skull." Such incidents, although relatively scarce, point to Butor's Joycean preoccupation, attested to throughout his interview, with "les moments où, tiens, quelque chose que nous ne comprenions pas se met à se révéler à nous, quelque chose nous devient clair"[131] – one need not fetch the analogy too far to link such pronouncements to Joyce's epiphany.

In fact, the very title of Butor's book is precisely such an instance of epiphanic double-coding: the showing forth of Horus, the hawk-like sky god, of whom each of the Pharaohs is held to have been a reincarnation, which is a palpable echo of the "hawklike man" Daedalus within the Joycean mythology surrounding *A Portrait*. Among the other broader themes and concepts identifiable as Joycean is Butor's preoccupation with paternity (the *Hamlet* theme), fraternity (three brothers of the Mogne family refer to "la tête d'Essau" [*PM*, 149] and speak of "ta main et la sienne" [*PM*, 160], echoing the Biblical allusion to Esau and Jacob from the *Wake*'s opening), and the family at large. Last but not least, *Passage de Milan* is an encyclopaedic work, testifying to Butor's proclaimed ambition of "trying to put everything in it." The question, for Lydon, remains whether the Joycean (and Balzacian) analogies

---

130 Cf. Mary Lydon, *Perpetuum Mobile – A Study of the Novels and Aesthetics of Michel Butor* (Edmonton: The University of Alberta Press, 1980) 54–5.

131 *Michel Butor – Entretiens*, Vol. 1, 27–8.

provoked by the text "detract from the novel's originality." It is here that the strongest, essential parallel between Butor's *Passage de Milan* and Joyce's *Portrait* arises.[132] Thus, Lydon concludes, as long as Pater and Newman are "discernible in the background of *Portrait*," then equally one can say that "*Ulysses* could not have been written if *Portrait* had not first been produced." And in the context of Butor's oeuvre, *Passage de Milan* fulfils the same function, even giving rise to the notion that "his first novel is the matrix of his *oeuvre*."[133]

As long as his first book had come and gone without causing much of a stir, Butor's second novel, *L'Emploi du temps*, fared much better, effectively launching his career as a writer. Where *Passage* deals with the time span of twelve hours, *L'Emploi* spans twelve months, detailing the hardships of a young French newcomer to a large industrial city of the English Midlands – evidently based on (and written during) Butor's own sojourn in Manchester, fictionalised as the city of Bleston in the novel. Apart from Butor's New-Novelistic experiment with the detective story genre, a few metatextual devices (diary-keeping, novel-writing characters), and a staple mythological intertext with the Theseus myth, discussed above by Butor himself, this novel presents little by way of the formal design or linguistic innovation of Butor's first book, and need not be treated in much detail. Its most markedly intertextual gesture beckons toward Proust's examination of time and memory, its chief ambition, expressed in the phrase "donner une durée au langage" (*ET*, 88), to Proust's philosophical bedrock, Henri Bergson.

Butor's third novel, *La Modification*, is formally experimental and has combined both critical acclaim and popular success. Divided into three sections of three chapters each, *La Modification* presents the same mathematical precision as the previous novels, while recounting in meticulous detail a train trip from Paris to Rome with close attention to the stations along the way. Its most idiosyncratic stylistic trait is its form of the second-person verbal address, Butor's use of *vous* throughout the text, and the unprecedented degree of identification with the novel's hero evoked in the reader. If *Passage* traces the differences and parallels among multiple consciousness(es), *Modification* focuses on its protagonist, Léon Delmont, who embarks on a train journey from Paris to Rome in order to leave his family and begin a new life with his mistress, only to undergo a "modification" and end up determined to return to his family.

---

132 "No doubt all artists are indebted to other artists, a fact which has led to the conclusion that every artist's career begins with the pastiche. This term might seem a little strong, but if it is accepted, for the sake of argument, the ambivalent nature of this initial pastiche must be emphasized. It is at once an effort at absorption and expurgation (at least in the case of the great artist), and on its success depends the emergence of his mature works. This is the essential difference between such pastiche and the activity of those who take the famous book of days gone by and tart them up" (Lydon, *Perpetuum Mobile*, 64).

133 Ibid.

Here, Butor's *lieux communs* include a series of questions originating in the chief character's dreams during his all-night trip, raised by the haunting spectre of the Grand Veneur, in fact a ghost of his wife. The questions are "M'entendez-vous?" ("Do you hear me?"), "Qu'attendezvous?" ("What are you waiting for?"), "Où êtes-vous?" ("Where are you?"), "Êtes-vous fou?" ("Are you crazy?"), "Qui êtes-vous?" ("Who are you?"), and they function as leit-motifs haunting the narrative subject throughout, not least in the scene of a similar questioning at the French-Italian border. The occasional wordplay, though muted, does achieve some comic effect, e.g., in the sentence about the train's loudspeaker ("Alors une bouffée d'air frais entre dans le compartiment et l'on entend la voix raque d'un haut-parleur qui profère des syllabes mécon-naissables" [M, 40]) which evokes the apparition of a sibyl in Léon's dream via the euphony of "*syllabe*" and "*sibylle*" – a word "fermentation" of precisely the kind identified by Butor in Joyce. Most frequently, and appropriately for the train setting, Butor seems to delight in the phrase "être en train de faire" (M, 83, 85, 120, 196, 205), be in the process, lit. "on the train," of doing. Another of Butor's *lieux communs* includes having his protagonist determined to effec-tuate his liberation from his past and present by writing a book; presumably, the book that is *La Modification*. Ultimately, the "you" address is an appeal upon the reader to undergo their own "modification" into a mental state con-ducive to creativity.

Butor's fourth novel, *Degrés*, has a pivotal status in his oeuvre in that it stands as the last in his so-called "Romanesque" period, the last book to bear the subtitle *roman*, in a sense condensing and combining the methodol-ogy of the previous three while also anticipating Butor's post-novel period, which breaks with the poetics established in the four novels. Also, its 1960 publication with Gallimard marks the end of Butor's most explicit allegiance with the New Novel. Again, the title is ambiguous and rich in meanings. The central narrative situation concerns the various degrees of relationship in a Parisian lycée among thirty-one students and their eleven professors, and the students' academic degrees. However, their studies of geography, physics, or geometry also involve the degrees of longitude and latitude, of heat, and of the circle; their private lives raise questions of degrees of drunkenness; and last but not least, several of the important characters come down with the grippe, which ineluctably necessitates a thermometer.

Structural symmetry is here taken to a whole new level of complexity: there are three parts, each narrated by a different subject and divided into seven sections. The three parts are in a sense variations on the same struc-ture. In the first part the characters are taken up three by three, in the sec-ond, two by two, and in the third, one by one. In each of the triads of the first part, three characters are introduced in each of the seven sections, either two professors and one student or two students and one professor, thus gradually introducing all thirty-one students and all eleven professors. The chief meta-literary project involves the professor of history writing down notes toward a true phenomenological description ("une description littérale, sans intervention de mon imagination, un simple enregistrement de faits exacts" [D, 22]) which would enable his nephew to attempt a total recall of a single day, his fifteenth birthday. However, embarking upon this modernist ency-clopaedic project turns out an impossible undertaking for the professor: not only is it impossible to represent reality in language without "intervening" in it himself, he also needs the intervention of his nephew, the addressee of his account – a shift in viewpoint also brings about a change in pronominal designation, the "I" suddenly usurped by the nephew, the professor becoming a "you." The project exhausts the uncle to the point of reducing him to bed, at which point another professor takes over the third part. He becomes the "I" of the narrative, the "you" denotes the nephew, and the uncle becomes reduced to a "he" – a veritable confusion of pronouns, so that the uncle's final question which also concludes the text, "Qui parle?," is one repeatedly raised by the text itself. And so *Degrés* shows the totalising novel to be impossible, insisting that no writing can effectively reach the world: although this world has been extensively "said" and described by too many novels.

Having completed his novelistic tetralogy, Butor went on to produce texts of highly idiosyncratic character, each with a genre, as it were, of its own making. Only two years after *Degrés*, Butor published perhaps his most radical experi-ment, *Mobile* (1962). Printed on unusually large pages, the text is typeset in what appears to be a highly idiosyncratic manner. Use is made of five different types of margins—the leftmost concerning the state whose chapter this is, and the others denoting the neighbouring states progressively more removed from it—and several type-faces. The text is divided into fifty "chapters," one for each state taken in the alphabetic order, the time-span of the narrative stretching across forty-eight hours over the spring equinox: the sections for the "daylight" states begin with a "Welcome to—" road sign, which is omitted at "night"; some pages are covered with print, others are so-called *aéré*.

Lydon has stressed the connection between *Mobile* and what Butor called (and theorised as) the "book-object," in which use is made of the spatial pos-sibilities of print distribution and its visual properties, and which challenges the so-called "book-idea." The form, as is so often the case with concrete textual objects, is mimetic, expressive of its content. It is determined by Butor's per-ception of the United States and serves as means of making that country, as he perceived it, present to the reader.[134] Also noted by Lydon is the work's sub-

---

134 "Few countries could rival America in the sweep and complexity of its links between differ-ent times, places, and persons. What conjunctions are possible between the statements one

tle attempt at circularity: the first page opens with "nuit noire à CORDOUE, ALABAMA, le profond Sud" (suggesting the blackness and segregation of the South and also potentially referring to the Moors of Cordoba), a peculiar beginning in an alphabetically organised text which seems to omit the letters *A* and *B*. However, the last two cities to be mentioned are ALBANY and BUFFALO, and thus "the series A, B, C links the end of the book with the beginning, just as the last word in *Finnegans Wake* points backwards to the first.[135]

Now, the evident difference between Butor's treatment of language in *Mobile* and Joyce's *Wake* is that there is no "fermentation," no deliberate distortion, of words. The similarity with Joyce's procedure, however, lies in the incessant mutability and fluctuation of the meaning of everyday words: Butor takes special care to pick those US place names that are based on their European predecessors or analogies; and the specifically American keywords, such as Washington or Lincoln, designate now men, now mountains, now cities, now rivers, etc. *Mobile* is the rare case in Butor's oeuvre of a *lieu commun* made into both matter and manner, thereby, to Lydon's mind, "neutralizing the tendency to consider *Mobile* either as a literary work or as a representation of the U.S. – to divide it into form and content."[136] Butler notes that the basic syntactic form is the list, "echoing that of the sales catalogue, quotations from which also have a large part to play in the text and seem to symbolize American consumerism and diversity."[137]

Shortly after *Mobile*, Butor went on to produce a "texte radiophonique" and an "étude stéréophonique" – Réseau aérien (1962) and 6 810 000 litres d'eau par seconde (1962), respectively. The former is a description of ten aeroplanes flying in tandem around the globe, none of which completes the circuit. The latter is a typographical and linguistic conveyance of the mass of water in the Niagara Falls. Réseau aérien is prefaced by a "note technique," a body of instructions regarding the "realisation of the text:"

Le texte est conçu pour être réalisé par 10 acteurs : / 5 hommes : A B C D E / 5 femmes : f g h i j. / Les acteurs sont toujours traités par couples auxquelles est donné chaque

---

could make about this New World; what conjunctions connect it with the Old, link together the man-made states of the Union? Among those proposed by Butor are the homonyms among place names that are found in state after state, often echoing the names of European cities, the catalogues of the giant mail-order companies of Sears and Montgomery Ward, and the four time zones that testify to the vastness of the country" (Lydon, *Perpetuum Mobile*, 163).

135 Ibid, 167.

136 Ibid, 170.

137 "A fascinating tension is thus set up between the fragmentation of any particular sequence (this supposedly representing the discontinuity of reality and the way in which we are daily bombarded from all sides by information whose truth or falsity we cannot possibly assess) and our growing awareness that the fragments do fall into thematic groups and thus implicitly at least encourage us to make judgements" (Butler, *After the Wake*, 84–5).

fois un petit fragment de dialogue comportant six répliques. Les italiques indiquent la nuit, enregistrement sourd avec réverbation. Le signe [aéroplane] indique un bruit d'avion. Le signe [visage] un bruit de foule. Le signe [tunnel] une percussion sourde. Les chiffres qui suivent [les signes] indiquent le numéro de l'avion (il y en a 10). Ils peuvent être réalisés en prenant deux enregistrements du premier prélude du *Clavecin bien tempéré*, clavecin pour le jour, piano pour la nuit, et en donnant sur le fond du bruit le nombre de notes correspondant ; mais on peut rêver d'une musique faite pour le texte. (*RA*, 7)

In addition to these symbols, two type-faces and four kinds of margins are employed, the text punctuated by technical instructions, the "narrative" constantly switching among the actors, planes, symbols, etc. The route of the text is, ultimately, cyclical, beginning and ending at the Orly airport. *6 810 000 litres* is prefaced by a similar note, only this time concerning the reading procedure:

Les lecteurs pressés prendront la voie courte en sautant toutes les parenthèses et tous les préludes. Les lecteurs moins pressés prendront la voie longue sans rien sauter. Mais les lecteurs de ce livre s'amuseront à suivre les indications sur le fonctionnement des parenthèses et à explorer peu à peu les huit voies intermédiaires pour entendre comment, dans ce monument liquide, le changement de l'éclairage fait apparaître nouvelles formes et aspects. Deux voix au centre, celle du speaker, fort, celle du lecteur, assez fort. (*6 810*, unpaginated)

Echoes of Butor's notions of the *Wake*'s "unreadability" and his procedure of reading it resonate here.

Finally, Butor's most explicitly textual reference to a Joycean avant-texte was realised in his 1967 work, *Portrait d'artiste en jeune singe*. Joycean already by its allusive title, as Butor explained in an April 1967 interview for *Les Lettres françaises*, its parody works on multiple levels.[138] Not only does Butor "do for Joyce what he himself has done already" (there is also the intercepting

---

138 "Parodie du titre d'un livre fameux de Joyce, qui lui-même était parodique par rapport non pas au titre d'un livre, mais à celui de très nombreux tableaux. Donc ce que je fais pour Joyce, c'est ce que Joyce lui-même avait fait. D'où le titre *Portrait* mais non *en jeune homme : en jeune singe*. Dans le mot *singe*, ce qui est souligné d'abord, c'est la notion d'imitation, de singerie, si vous voulez : dans ce titre, je montre que je suis le singe de Joyce (et bien d'autres) mais je rappelle que Joyce lui-même était le singe des peintres (ce que d'ailleurs je suis moi-même à certains égards). D'autre part, entre ma parodie et celle de Joyce vient s'inscrire une parodie intermédiaire qui est celle de Dylan Thomas. Le poète gallois a publié un recueil de nouvelles sous le titre *Portrait de l'artiste en jeune chien*. C'était déjà une parodie, avec un certain sarcasme, à l'égard de Joyce. Eh bien, dans *Portrait de l'artiste en jeune singe*, il y a une portée qui est au moins quadruple, dans l'ironie : il y a une ironie à l'égard des peintres, une ironie à l'égard Joyce, puis de Dylan Thomas, enfin : de moi-même" (*Michel Butor – Entretiens, Vol. 1*, 320).

presence of Dylan Thomas), but Butor's choice of a "young ape" has its own agenda independent of the two. As he makes clear in the book's back-cover quotation: "Dans le titre, sous l'hommage à James Joyce et Dylan Thomas, on reconnaîtra la représentation médiévale de cette éminente espèce d'artiste qu'était l'alchimiste comme 'singe de Nature.'" So, underlying his homage to Joyce and Thomas is the figure of the alchemist, that medieval artist whose ambition it was to "ape" nature. The conceptual connection between the two *Portraits*, then, is metamorphosis: in Joyce via the reference to the Dedalian myth in Ovid, in Butor via the theme of alchemy as the art of matter transformation.

There are some more textually specific parallels, too: there is the character of Père "Uriel" Athanase Kircher of the Jesuit order, which played such an important part in the formation of both Joyce and Butor. Lydon also finds "Stephen Dedalus' lapse into the seven deadly sins and his valiant effort to practice the seen virtues in their stead, with the help of the seven gifts of the Holy Ghost, as well as his status as a student of the seven liberal arts" paralleled in Butor's *Portrait* where the insistence on the magic number 7 is "even more pronounced."[139] Critic Jennifer Waelti-Walters has drawn attention to the importance, in both texts, of the symbolic presence of Thoth, the Egyptian god of writing, who, as Butor's *Portrait* notes, was "*souvent représenté par un singe,*" and later on, as Hermes Trismegistus, came to represent the god of alchemy.

Stylistically, a tentative parallel may be drawn between their treatment of the materiality of language – e.g., in the "Mineralogy" section, a whole page is laid out as follows:

> (un moulage en plâtre d'un squelette d'ichtyosaure derrière une vitre brisée),
> « mais il y a surtout cette immense collection de minéraux »
> (zircons jaune gris traversant des monazites, aragonites en zigzag)
> « poussiéreuse, en désordre, nous n'avons pas encore eu le temps d'arranger tout cela »
> (il soufflait sur des argentites arborescentes, [...]),
> « qui n'est pas bien spectaculaire, les spécimens dépassent rarement la taille d'une noix »
> (il époussetait barytines en livre ouvert, cinabres en efflorescences, dolomites rhomboédriques, vivianites bleues)
> « mais certains sont, paraît-il, fort précieux »
> (P, 97)

Thus, written almost entirely in a vocabulary foreign to all but mineralogists, the spatial arrangement of this page seems to treat words both literally and

---

139   Lydon, *Perpetuum Mobile*, 221.

metaphorically as pieces of stone in a mosaic-type arrangement. However, both Lydon and Waelti-Walters are correct in pointing out some equally significant differences between the texts.[140] There is, on the one hand, a broadly conceived, yet fundamentally important, parallel between Butor's oeuvre and Joyce's or Pound's modernist project. Modernism's conception of time and history follows from its rejection of the diachronic form for the diachronic age of realism, meeting "terror of history" with various modes of description for the human experience in time.[141]

The desire, shared by most if not all modernists, to frame a portrait of the modern world as a holistic situation, is essentially an epic ambition. And as long as Butor repeatedly described himself as a writer for whom "the great novels of the twentieth century have existed," then his work shares with the modernist masters the similarly epic "general area of historical and cultural interest" – Butor's cultural inventory/"repertory" is of striking depth and breath. The two modernist figures that come closest to this scale are Joyce and Pound – yet any comparison with their poetics yields Butor's fundamental difference.[142] Butor also imagines the past in a way fundamentally different from that of his modernist ancestors: if, for Joyce, the Homeric Golden Age occurred some three thousand years distant from the Dublin day in 1904 described in *Ulysses*, and if the echoes and similarities that have survived from that long-dead epoch must necessarily be ironic fragments, then Butor, on the other hand, "discovered on his first fateful voyage to the cradle of civilization that ancient Egypt was not irretrievably lost in the third millennium BC where the historians had placed it but is alive today."[143] Alive today from the point of view of a description—the genius in Butor is the genius of a place.

---

140 Whereas Butor's is "a product of the writer's maturity," as such it "does not suffer from the rather uncontrolled lyricism of Joyce's book" and actually is "more in the line of *Ulysses*" – even though much shorter and less ambitious, "its range of reference and impulse toward a totalization of experience, if not on the same scale as Joyce's masterpiece, at least may be measured by the same standard" (Jennifer Waelti-Walters, *Michel Butor – A Study of His View of the World and a Panorama of His Work 1954-1974* [Victoria: Sono Nis Press, 1977] 119-20). Lydon, in turn, argues that even though both Joyce's and Butor's poetics evokes a kind of reading that "allows all the elements in it to combine and recombine in constantly evocative patterns," their means to this end differ: whereas Joyce uses linguistic material, "Butor juxtaposes works of art, historical eras and objects to attain the same end" (Lydon, *Perpetuum Mobile*, 228).

141 McWilliams singles out two of these modes of replacing or supplementing the historical model of a horizontal line: "by a vertical line (subjective interior experience of temporal depth) and a circle (circular rhythms of the day or the year)" (McWilliams, *The Narratives of Michel Butor*, 109).

142 "Greece, Rome, and the Renaissance come to us in *Finnegans Wake* and the *Cantos* in broken, often barely recognizable fragments, brilliant and beautiful, but dead. Butor, on the other hand, has painstakingly separated each layer, joined broken shards, and attempted to resurrect the essential genius of each of these cultures" (Ibid, 112).

143 Ibid, 113.

Butor was a programmatically post-Joycean writer who continued in the linguistic and formal experimentation of the avant-garde tradition of "making it new." It would be reductive to constrain the Joycean presence in Butor's writings to his early essays and first novels: Joyce, for Butor, represented much more than a youthful master-figure to be overcome in maturity; rather, he was a paradigm to be constantly returned to and re-applied.

2.
"BUT HOW MANY HAVE FOLLOWED HIM?" JOYCE IN BRITAIN (1955–75)

One of the possible case studies by which to exemplify the turning of the tide between the cultural and literary climate of the 1950s and that of the mid- to late-1960s is the reception of James Joyce in the British fiction of the two decades. As explicitly stated by the title of Rubin Rabinovitz's influential study on the literature of the period, the 1950s in the English novel were marked by a reaction "against" experiment.[1] Paralleling their contemporaries in poetry, the novelists emerging in the 1950s re-visited the chief interests (class and society) and methods (the realist novel sequence) of Victorian/Edwardian fiction. The shift in artistic ideology also evoked a change in "the canon" of the time, and homage was paid to the social engagement and realistic style of H. G. Wells and Arnold Bennett, authors whom once upon a time Virginia Woolf famously rejected. Now, the tables had turned and it was Woolf who was literally the odd one out. Speaking with a virulence and hostility emblematic of the whole Zeitgeist was Kingsley Amis in 1955:

> The idea about experiment being the life-blood of the English novel is one that dies hard. "Experiment," in this context, boils down pretty regularly to "obtruded oddity," whether in construction—multiple viewpoints and such—or in style; it is not felt that adventurousness in subject matter or attitude or tone really counts. Shift from one scene to the next in midsentence, cut down on verbs or definite articles, and you are putting yourself right up in the forefront, at any rate in the eyes of those who were reared on Joyce and Woolf and take a jaundiced view of more recent developments.[2]

With the grotesquely caricatured literary experiment narrowed down to "multiple viewpoints and such," Joyce and Woolf had become a literary disease, of which the "more recent developments" are now curing the British tradition. Further examples of both novel-sequence writers and public detractors of Joyce (*ad hominem*) and experimentalism (*ad rem*) are C. P. Snow and William Cooper. There is, for instance, Snow's statement recorded in *Times Literary Supplement* on 15 August 1958 to the effect that "Joyce's way is at best

---

1   Rubin Rabinovitz, *The Reaction against Experiment* (New York: Columbia University Press, 1967).
2   Qtd. in Rabinovitz, *The Reaction*, 40–1.

a cul-de-sac."[3] Cooper is alleged to have stated that "the Experimental Novel" had to be "brushed out of the way before we could get a proper hearing."[4] More relevantly still, Levitt's *Modernist Survivors* quotes Cooper explicitly tying his generation's distaste for experiment with nationalist concerns:

> Aren't the French wonderful! Who else in these days could present a literary *avant--garde* so irredeemably *derrière*? *Avant-garde*—and they're still trying to get something out of Experimental Writing, which was fading away here at the end of the thirties and finally got the push at the beginning of the fifties. What a *garde*! [...] The point not to miss is this: not only are these anxious, suspicious, despairing French writers nulli-fying the novel, but they are weakening the intellectual world as a whole, by bringing one part of it into disrepute.[5]

The hostility against Woolf's and Joyce's experimentalism is here doubled with nationalist chauvinism and projected on the French *nouveaux romanciers* and those who readily embrace their heritage. Speaking as late as 1963, John Wain, another Angry Young Man, still had reasons enough to observe plainly that the "experimental novel" had "died with Joyce" and that since *Ulysses*, "there has been little experimental writing that strikes one as serious, or motivated by anything more than faddishness or the irritable search for new gimmicks."[6]

Joyce's ghost haunts not only the Angry Young Men's critical pronounce-ments, but also their fiction – and to only slightly lesser derogation. Garnet Bowen in Kingsley Amis' *I Like it Here* compares his two months abroad to "making a determined start on *Finnegan's* [sic] *Wake* – an experience bound in itself to be arduous and irritating, but one which could conceivably ren-der available rich variety of further experiences."[7] The "lucky" Jim Dixon is also portrayed as a reader of Joyce, remembering a "sentence in a book he'd once read" which turns out to be from the "Cyclops" episode of *Ulysses*. John Wain's parody of the *Wake* in *Hurry On Down* reaches almost poetic heights: "Clout bell, shout well, pell-mell about a tout, get the hell out. About nowt."[8] As Levitt has argued, hand in hand with this misconception in practice comes a similar incomprehension on the part of theory and criticism, which seems almost a case in point of a Freudian repression: "Some quality in the fiction of Joyce and Woolf is evidently so threatening to the British sense of

---

3   Qtd. in Randall Stevenson, *The Last of England?* (Oxford: Oxford University Press, 2004) 406.

4   Qtd. in Rabinovitz, *The Reaction*, 6.

5   Qtd. in Morton P. Levitt, *Modernist Survivors* (Columbus: Ohio State University Press, 1987) 37.

6   Qtd. in Rabinovitz, *The Reaction*, 8.

7   Qtd. in Stuart Laing, "Novels and the Novel," *Society and Literature 1945–1970*, ed. Alan Sinfield (London: Methuen & Co., 1983) 251.

8   John Wain, *Hurry on Down* (London: Secker & Warburg, 1953) 53.

tradition that it must be denied regardless of logic or the evidence of their work."[9]

No wonder, then, that the early-1970s accounts of the state-of-the-art British novel sound the death knell to experimentalism in Britain. Bernard Bergonzi's highly influential *The Situation of the Novel* (1970) observed that whereas "the French and many Americans feel compelled to strive for novelty," the English "seem to have settled for the predictable pleasures of genre fiction"[10] – and let this evaluation stand even in a second edition from 1979. Malcolm Bradbury's account of "The Post-war English Novel" in his 1973 *Possibilities* went so far as to pit England and America against each other as binary oppositions:

> The novel is not dead but fled; it is alive and well and living in America. It is the English novel only that bears the marks of exhaustion, provincialism, of "reaction against experiment" [...]. In these assumptions we have an interesting antithesis and a view of it: a contrast between realism and experiment, and a proposal that realism is a feature of moribundity and English, and experiment a feature of growth and American.[11]

In such generalisations, the question always becomes one of definitions and their (mis)application in a transcultural dialogue, and as this chapter will show, there was a lively—even though obviously not enough for these critics—strand of experimentalism flourishing around the time of their writing. But statements such as Bergonzi's and Bradbury's are too numerous to ignore, and even more thorny and disquieting when explanations are sought for.

Nevertheless, Laing's and other more historically and empirically oriented accounts of the period indicate that the 1950s had not fully succeeded in exorcising Joyce's ghost:

> In the sixties Joyce was allowed to come down from the bookshelves. The competition of visual media [...], a new openness to European and, particularly, American influences, the sociological and literary rediscovery of the working class, the post-*Chatterley* trial atmosphere and a reawakened interest in novels' formal properties [...] – all created space for active appropriation of Joycean techniques.[12]

---

9   Levitt, *Modernist Survivors*, 28.
10   Bernard Bergonzi, *The Situation of the Novel* (London: MacMillan, 1970/1979) 20.
11   Malcolm Bradbury, "The Post-war English Novel," *Possibilities* (Oxford: Oxford University Press, 1973) 167.
12   Laing, "Novels and the Novel," 252.

In addition, 1959 was also the year in which John Calder published a complete English translation of Beckett's *Trilogy*. Calder's importance for the 1960s British experimentalism is difficult to overstate in this context, as Giles Gordon reminisced, in his introduction to the 2001 re-edition of Ann Quin's *Berg*,

> The British literary establishment was much turned on, after the Second World War and Churchillian patriotism, by the irreverence and anti-intellectualism of the Angry Young Men. [...] To those of us resenting this parochialism, the publications of John Calder were a breath of fresh air. He introduced us to Beckett, Burroughs, Creeley, Duras, Claude Mauriac, Henry Miller, Pinget, Robbe-Grillet, Sarraute [...]. We felt fiction mattered again.[13]

1960 then saw a reprint (with MacGibbon & Kee) of Flann O'Brien's *At Swim-Two-Birds,* as well as the Bodley Head re-edition of *Ulysses*. It was this (re-) entry of Irish experimental prose into the literary circulation and consciousness at the dawn of the 1960s that invigorated fictional innovation. Later on, it would also make it possible for B. S. Johnson to claim himself "besotted by Irish writers like Sam Beckett, James Joyce and Flann O'Brien,"[14] to begin his first novel with a reference to O'Brien's *At Swim-Two-Birds*, to preface his third novel with a motto from Beckett's *Unnameable,* and to devote his last critical text to pledging his allegiance to Joyce.

In the introduction to his last work, the 1973 collection of shorter fiction *Aren't You Rather Young to Be Writing Your Memoirs?*, Johnson argues that in Britain, the cultural dominance of the conservative, Victorian/Edwardian, realist novelistic story-telling was by no means restricted to the 1950s decade of the Angry Young Men movement. Johnson opens his argument by positing Joyce's centrality for contemporary writing – he is "the Einstein of the novel," whose "theory of relativity" materialises in the plurality of the styles of *Ulysses* which relativise any one attempt at a unified vision:

> For the style alone, *Ulysses* would have been a revolution. Or, rather, styles. For Joyce saw that such a huge range of subject matter could not be conveyed in one style, and accordingly used many. Just in this one innovation (and there are many others) lie a great advance and freedom offered to subsequent generations of writers. (*ARY*, 11)

However, when addressing the current British literary scene, Johnson avows that there are indeed "very few" writers who have followed Joyce's *Ulysses* revolution; their fewness is especially palpable in comparison with the

---

13   Giles Gordon, "Reading Ann Quin's *Berg*," *Berg* (Chicago: Dalkey Archive, 2001) viii.
14   Qtd. in Stevenson, *The Last of England?*, 410.

legion of writers writing "as though the revolution that was *Ulysses* had never happened" and relying on "the crutch of storytelling" (*ARY*, 15). Still, Johnson concludes by providing the following list:

> Samuel Beckett (of course), John Berger, Christine Brooke-Rose, Brigid Brophy, Anthony Burgess, Alan Burns, Angela Carter, Eva Figes, Giles Gordon, Wilson Harris, Rayner Heppenstall, even hasty, muddled Robert Nye, Ann Quin, Penelope Shuttle, Alan Sillitoe [...], Stefan Themerson, [...] John Wheway, [...] and Heathcote Williams [...]. (*ARY*, 28–9).

This rather over-inclusive list of no fewer than nineteen (including himself) writers defines not so much a common poetics, programme, let alone a movement, but a vanguard of Johnson's fellow warriors who are "writing as though it matters," enlisted to stand beside Johnson in his war waged against the "anachronistic, invalid, irrelevant, and perverse" (*ARY*, 13) realist mode of the nineteenth-century novel.

There are quite a few writers whose inclusion within the experimental vein seems problematic. For instance, both Rayner Heppenstall's and Stephan Themerson's novelistic prime significantly predates the present moment of Johnson's introduction, having occurred between the late 1930s and the early 1950s. Heppenstall's *Blaze of Noon* (1939) is a story told from the perspective of a blind man taken as a constraint with which to experiment with what the literary narrative form can do: in Heppenstall's view, now that "the cinema had taken over the story-telling functions of the exteriorised novel," literature ought to "become more lyrical, more inward."[15] In doing so Heppenstall's book revisits and upgrades such staple modernist tropes as narrative parallax, interior monologue, and stream of consciousness, in ways directly anticipatory of the French *nouveau roman*, as attested to by Hélène Cixous' hailing it as "the novel which had inaugurated the *nouveau roman*,"[16] and her point had a certain validity and influence. But neither *The Connecting Door* (1962) nor *Two Moons* (1972) attempted anything nearly as daring or innovative as even a "standard" French *nouveau roman*. Heppenstall himself felt "somewhat typecast"[17] by Johnson's inclusion of his name in the list, and much of his criticism is written out of deeply traditionalist, anti-modernist convictions.

Themerson's claim to fame or influence in the sixties is even more tenuous: apart from his publishing activity in his progressive Gaberbocchus Press,

---

15   Rayner Heppenstall, "Introduction," *Blaze of Noon* (Sphere: London, 1967) 6.
16   Hélène Cixous, "Langage et regard dans le roman expérimental: Grand-Bretagne," *Le Monde* (6959.viia, 18 May 1967): 16.
17   For more, see G. J. Bucknell, *Rayner Heppenstall – A Critical Study* (London: Champaign, 2007) 77.

his major novel, *Professor Mmaa's Lecture* (written during the troubled 1940s and published in 1953)—portraying a termite world in order to expose and deride the various socio-political conventions and constraints of the human world—is even older news, hardly more experimental than a "standard" Jonathan Swift, yet another satire on human conformism in face of "progress" and absolute government. Although hailed as an early attempt as "xenofiction," *Professor Mmaa's Lecture* is now chiefly (half-)remembered for the preface of Bertrand Russell (appearing himself in the text as "Errtrand Bussell"), who encapsulates the main "message" of Professor Mmaa's Lecture in terms of its critique of religion: "The world contains too many people believing too many things, and the less we believe, the less harm we do."[18]

Just as Heppenstall and Themerson, so do John Berger and Angela Carter seem "radical" and "innovative" in their ideological intent rather than experimentation with style or method: Johnson wrote his list in the aftermath of the 1972 Booker Prize, awarded to Berger's *G.*, which, for all its sexual explicitness and modicum of narrative fragmentation, traces a fairly linear tale of the protagonist's journey across class consciousness. Carter's early novels, e.g., *The Magic Toyshop* (1967), did little by way of innovation beyond focusing on female sexuality and drawing on the then-fashionable South-American magic realism. Thus, one must pick cautiously and selectively from the list of Johnson's conscripts, for they are indeed legion.

In comparison and contrast, Francis Booth's magisterial panorama of "*The British Experimental Novel, 1940–1980*," called—in homage to Johnson's last unfinished novel—*Amongst those Left*, devotes the bulk of its 700+ pages to detailed portraits of thirteen writers (Anna Kavan, Stefan Themerson, Rayner Heppenstall, Nicholas Mosley, Christine Brooke-Rose, Alexander Trocchi, Alan Burns, Eva Figes, B. S. Johnson, Jeff Nuttall, Ann Quin, Penelope Shuttle, and Rosalind Belben) and shorter miniatures of another fourteen (among others, Emma Tennant, Giles Gordon, and most notably, the "New Wave Science Fiction" duo, Brian Aldiss and J.G. Ballard). Booth's list of British experimental novelists is, thus, both a reduction (thirteen to Johnson's nineteen "nuclear" writers) and an expansion of Johnson's list, compiled with the benefit of another ten years of development. Just why, then, the British situation should be so markedly different from the "post-humanist" French New Novel (see previous chapter) and the "comic-apocalyptic" American innovative fiction (see next chapter), is competently tackled in Booth's preface to his opus magnum.

It is, first of all, due to the "predominantly liberal humanist base" from which it "seemed to claim to provide truths about society, morals and char-

---

18   Bertrand Russell, "Preface" to Stephan Themerson, *Professor Mmaa's Lecture* (New York: Overlook Press, 1984) ii.

acter," and for which "not only humanism but realism were seen [...] to be an indispensable part of the novel."[19] This general consensus, despite the occasional polemic (like Johnson's), has been so widespread as to preclude any "serious and sustained public debate on the role and nature of fiction in this country [...], plenty of random sniping but no full-scale engagement."[20] Due to this built-in conservatism, experiment with literary form and liberal humanist novel have come to seem almost antithetical. Permeating the liberal humanism of the English novel (and just about any- and everything English, really) is class-awareness: the rise of the English novel is the rise of the bourgeoisie, and so, for the last two hundred years, "the British novel has been remarkably homogeneous both in its concerns and in the backgrounds of its authors."[21] The British novel has been written *by* the bourgeois *for* the bourgeois, and so "realism"—except for the radically international and heterogenous modernist detour—is its almost default setting. Apart from these broad socio-historical roots, there are also some contemporary and "practical" ones:

> It seems to be characteristic of the British literary scene that there is much less cross-influence among novelists than in France or America. French avant-garde novelists tend to write criticism (of each other's work sometimes) and theory and [...] to be far more influenced in non-literary theory. American novelists tended to be academics [...] or at least taught on creative writing courses, and this must have made them more aware both of the tradition in which they work, and of formal problems.[22]

The point about academia (perhaps less about creative writing) is valid in that pedagogical activity and academic curricula have ensured—even enforced—an immediate serious and sizeable audience for works of fiction that in Britain would hardly ever find a reader. Added to this is John Sutherland's point linking the conservatism of the British novel to the economics of the literary market—British books sold, usually as hardbacks, at far higher prices than French paperbacks—and connected with it, the far stronger presence of the institution of the public library on the British market, acting as the major purchaser of all new fiction and its mediator to the British public that, consequently, buys far fewer books than the French.[23] Perhaps the clearest indication of the sorry state of the British publishing industry with regards to all things experimental is the fact that Booth's magisterial opus

---

19   Francis Booth, *Among Those Left—The British Experimental Novel 1940–1980* (self-published, 2012) 28–9.

20   Booth, *Among Those Left*, 32.

21   Ibid, 43.

22   Ibid, 45.

23   For more, see J.A. Sutherland, *Fiction and the Fiction Industry* (London: Athlone, 1978) 21–2.

remained, for almost forty years after its composition, self-published via Amazon's print-on-demand.[24]

Following cue from both Johnson's and Booth's lists, the present chapter selects six authors who can be considered as symptomatic of some of the strands of innovative writing of the period. Brigid Brophy, Alan Burns, Johnson himself, and Ann Quin are generally regarded as forming the nucleus of the loose avant-garde "grouping" that came to the fore in the early 1960s and for the next decade-and-half produced some of the most experimental work in the entire post-war British fiction. Christine Brooke-Rose was a maverick figure who, though affiliated with the Johnson circle, soon diverged on a personal trajectory, forming—by both her life and fiction—a bridge between British experimentalism and the French *nouveau roman*. Finally, although a writer of commercial success and a nearly mainstream status, Anthony Burgess most explicitly of all post-war British writers based his experimentalism on his lifelong preoccupation with Joyce's work. In 1975 (two years after Johnson's memoirs), his last novel, *See the Old Lady Decently*, plus Christine Brooke-Rose's last piece of her first tetralogy, *Thru*, plus a volume edited by Giles Gordon and entitled *Beyond the Words: Eleven Writers in Search of a New Fiction*, would see the dusk of the period. With Johnson and Quin already dead, Brophy no longer active as novelist, Burns gone to Australia and then the USA, Brooke-Rose already in France, Burgess firmly settled in Monaco, and each on their own, markedly different course altogether, it is safe to say that by 1975, the Johnsonian circle had reached both its fulfilment and vanishing point.

2.1 "A HORROSHOW CRACK ON THE OOKO OR EARHOLE": ANTHONY BURGESS

Anthony Burgess seems the oddest member of the grouping discussed here since, with the exception of Beckett, he stands out as arguably the only canonical author on Johnson's list, and definitely the only commercially successful writer. Burgess' output is prolific and multifarious, comprising thirty-three novels, twenty-five works of non-fiction, two volumes of autobiography, three symphonies, more than a hundred-and-fifty other musical works, and scores of journalist criticism. His work is surrounded by a solid body of exegetical, biographical, and critical material, and his major novels are steadily in print, adorning university syllabi and reading curricula. He is at the same time, and without exception or parallel, the one post-war British writer who programmatically conceived of his literary career as a follow-up on Joy-

---

24   Until, in 2020, it finally received the imprimatur of the one and only Dalkey Archive Press.

ce's heritage. However, the Joycean legacy will be shown as acting not only as an enabling influence on Burgess' work and its canonical underpinning, but also as a yardstick of its critical appreciation, frequently to Burgess' own detriment.

Burgess' critical—or rather promotional—engagement with Joyce has suffered a no less contradictory reception, and this for sound reasons, since some of its basic premises are open to criticism. The intention and overall tenor of his 1965 *Here Comes Everybody* (reedited and republished the following year as *ReJoyce*) is quite apparent from its opening gambit: due to "the amount of research that already fences them around," *Ulysses* and *Finnegans Wake* are found "more and more regarded as mystical codices and less and less as masterly novels intended to entertain" (*RJ*, 9). Hence the purpose of Burgess' book to "rescue" Joyce from "the professors" and the initial premise of *ReJoyce* that "the appearance of difficulty is part of Joyce's big joke; the profundities are always expressed in good round Dublin terms; Joyce's heroes are humble men;" in short: "If ever there was a writer for the people, Joyce was that writer" (*RJ*, 9). However honourable the intention to bring Joyce closer to the "common reader" (whoever that might be), Burgess' foray against Joyce scholarship is absurd and ultimately self-refuting. His next paragraph opens with the admission that "naturally, I could not have written [this book] without help from the scholars" (*RJ*, 9), after which comes a lengthy list of everybody who was somebody in the earliest Joyce criticism, and finally Burgess' flimsy attempt to salvage himself and the present study from the enemy camp by calling it "commentary rather than criticism" (*RJ*, 10).

Apart from this rather peculiar entrée, Burgess' pilot-commentary on Joyce's entire canon (though the main focus is on *Ulysses* and *Finnegans Wake*) is undertaken with wit and competence, even if especially the chapter-by-chapter summary of *Ulysses* is delivered in so much detail and lengthy textual quotation as to seem almost a reading "substitute" rather than "stimulus" for critical engagement. More interestingly perhaps, the part on *Finnegans Wake* opens with a quasi-genetic approach, Burgess laying bare Joyce's method behind the construction of his text by showing the progressive complexification of a paragraph from the ALP chapter. Joyce, throughout the book, is portrayed as the superb modernist, a master builder of structures, parallels, networks of references, an author invested in juxtaposing multiple orders of reality, and also an author of an essentially Catholic outlook. Given that "the fundamental purpose of any work of art is to impose order on the chaos of life as it comes to us," then Joyce's attempt to "build for himself an order" is to Burgess' mind "a substitute for the order he abandoned when he abandoned the church" (*RJ*, 83; 87). As for the moral of the mythical superstructure, the following statement encapsulates Burgess' outlook on Joyce as a whole: "*Ulysses* is a story, and a simple story at that. It is a story about the need of people for each other, and Joyce regards this theme as so important that he has to borrow an epic form in which to tell it" (*RJ*, 87). For Burgess, Joyce is not in essence the high priest of difficulty, but a "democratic" and "humanist" writer cognisant of the fundamental and the essential.

Joysprick (1973) further elaborates on this conviction. The last chapter, "Language of the People," opens with the observation that "for the last time in literary history, the novels of Joyce celebrate the confluence of curious erudition and the language of the streets" (*J*, 162). Burgess' second Joyce book is structured far more loosely as a series of forays into the various Joycean themes and motifs. Instead of structures and intertexts, the focus is now on language (in such chapters as "Signs on Paper," "The Joyce Sentence," and "The Language of Gestation"), on style ("Musicalisation" and "Borrowed Style") and on topics peculiar to Joyce ("Onomastics" and "Oneiroparonomastics"). Burgess' own multilingualism and a composer's outlook make his expedition into the seldom-mapped interzone between linguistics and stylistics a highly personal, but mostly competent undertaking. New is also his stress on phonetics, especially in "The Dublin Sound" chapter where Stephen's meditations on the difference between "his" English and the dean's language in the "tundish" episode of *A Portrait* are read in terms of differences in pronunciation between Hiberno- and Queen's English. The opening chapter makes a broader claim to position Joyce within the distinction between "class 1 novelist," for whom "language is a zero quality, transparent, unseductive, the overtones of connotation and ambiguity totally damped," and "class 2 novelist," for whom it is important that "the opacity of language be exploited, so that ambiguities, puns and centrifugal connotations are to be enjoyed rather than regretted" (*J*, 15). Even though some of Burgess' observations are not as original as he believes them and there is a hefty (and largely unacknowledged) debt to newer Joyce criticism (particularly to Hugh Kenner's *Dublin's Joyce* and *Stoic Comedians*), the looser structure of individualised forays makes for a far more successful "popularisation" piece than the sometimes slavish commentary of *ReJoyce*.

Various biographers have recorded the manner in which Burgess fashioned "his" Joyce (just as Stephen Dedalus did with Shakespeare) in order to most strongly resemble his own life and ideological inclinations. Burgess' connection with Joyce emerges from his critical writings as chiefly twofold: one, an almost religious adoration for (and almost sexual pleasure derived from) the miscegenation of languages in search of *le mot juste*; and two, the belief in the necessity of grander mythological frames of reference by which to shape his fictional narratives.[25] In 1959, having spent the past decade in Ma-

---

25   Aggeler quotes Burgess to the effect that "I tend to write from a Catholic point of view—either from the point of view of a believing Catholic, or a renegade Catholic, which is I think Joyce's po-

laysia and Brunei as an English teacher in the British Colonial Service, Burgess was diagnosed with a brain tumour and given the (fortunately erroneous) prognosis of one year of life left, which compelled him to write five novels in the twelve months given by his doctors, a rare feat of literary productiveness: *Inside Mr Enderby, The Wanting Seed, The Doctor is Sick, The Worm and the Ring,* and *One Hand Clapping* (published between 1960–62), where the outlines of a Joycean comic-epic quest are conspicuously present. However, it was only in the aftermath of his critical engagement with Joyce that Burgess wrote four of his formally most innovative works: *A Clockwork Orange* (1962), *Nothing Like the Sun* (1964), *M/F* (1971), and *Napoleon Symphony* (1974).

The first, particularly following the scandalous and controversial 1971 film version by Stanley Kubrick, gained Burgess worldwide notoriety, but also obscured most of his other, equally challenging works. The indebtedness of the language of *A Clockwork Orange* to Joyce's *Finnegans Wake* is a refrain of much of the criticism of the Joyce/Burgess intertext,[26] though fewer critics seem to stress the obvious differences between Burgess' *Nadsat* and Joyce's *Wakean* project. There is, for instance, the far clearer location of the former between English and Russian, as opposed to Joyce's far broader multilingualism. The ideological implications of these two linguistic experiments are also vastly different: Burgess' is a Cold-War dystopian outlook on English "invaded" by the language of the enemy in subservience to the "morale" of his tale; Joyce's is an ultimately humanist, democratic, Babelian project with which to unmask and resist nationalist ideology. In fact, the most direct "Joycean moment" of *A Clockwork Orange* is the opening mock-heroic performative gesture of rejection:

The chelloveck sitting next to me […] was well away with his glazzies glazed and sort of burbling slovos like "Aristotle wishy washy works outing cyclamen get forficulate smartish." He was in the land all right, well away, in orbit, and I knew what it was like, having tried it like everybody else had done, but at this time I'd got to thinking it was a cowardly sort of a veshch, O my brothers. […] I could feel the knives in the old moloko starting to prick, and now I was ready for a bit of twenty-to-one. So I yelped: "Out out out out!" like a doggie, and then I cracked this veck who was sitting next to me and well away and burbling a horroshow crack on the ooko or earhole, but he didn't feel it and went on with his "Telephonic hardware and when the farfarculule gets rubadubdub." He'd feel it all right when he came to, out of the land. (*CO,* 4–5)

---

sition. Reading *Ulysses,* you are aware of this conflict within a man who knows the Church thoroughly and yet has totally rejected it with a blasphemous kind of vigor" (Qtd. in Geoffrey Aggeler, *Anthony Burgess – The Artist as Novelist* [University of Alabama Press, 1979] 28).

26   See, e.g., Beryl Schlossman, "Burgess/Kubrick/*A Clockwork Orange* (twenty-to-one)," *Anthony Burgess and Modernity,* ed. Alan R. Roughley (Manchester: Manchester University Press, 2008).

The whole passage abounds in Joycean references. To name but a few: "forficulate" refers to *forficula auricularia*, Latin for the common earwig, a *Wakean* leitmotif; "twenty-to-one" alludes to the betting odds of the Throwaway horse in *Ulysses*; the description of the "chelloveck" features references to Joyce's bespectacled face ("glazzies glazed"), the seemingly meaningless string of words featuring "Aristotle" and "telephonic hardware," both Joycean themes par excellence. Alex puts an abrupt end to this solipsistic performance, which has been regarded as symptomatic of Burgess' "breaking away" from the "modernists' abstract deconstruction of language."[27] However, it should be noted that this repudiation is a rather symbolic one and Burgess is careful to stage this scene as a parody of Stephen's skirmish with Private Carr at the end of the "Circe" episode of *Ulysses*. What is more, it has been suggested[28] that one of Burgess' most famous neologisms—"horrorshow" as the Anglicisation of the Russian хорошо—can be traced back to the *Wake*'s "horrasure" (*FW* 346.34). Joyce's influence, then, is not so much abnegated as transformed.

Of all Burgess' novels, in *M/F* the modernist mythopoetic method is put to most effect by most independent means. Already the acrostic in the title invites several readings: the protagonist's initials, male/female, mother/father, and via the novel's chief preoccupation with the topic of incest, *mother/ fucker*. The narrative is composed of archetypical motifs, featuring Miles Faber's quest for his mysterious origins that takes him to an island shrine in pursuit of ancient mystical scrolls. Burgess' conflation of the Biblical story of Jonah with Classical Greek Oedipal and Algonquin Indian myths surrounding the incest taboo derives from Claude Lévi-Strauss' *The Scope of Anthropology*, and Burgess is on record as admiring Lévi-Strauss' study, whose pioneering structuralist viewpoint he translates into his own Catholic terms: "Structuralism is the scientific confirmation of a certain theological conviction—that life is binary, that this is a duoverse [...] The notion of essential opposition— not God/Devil but just x/y—is the fundamental one."[29] Lévi-Strauss proves useful to Burgess' purposes especially by providing the link between riddling and incest, both representing frustrations of "natural" expectation. One passage from *M/F* in particular stands out as both Burgess' nod to the *Wake* and his warning against exegesis:

> Don't try distilling a message from it, not even an expresso cupful of meaningful epitome or a sambuca glass of abridgement, *con la mosca*. Communication has been the

27   Carla Sassi, "Lost in Babel: the search for the perfect language in Anthony Burgess' *A Clockwork Orange*," *Anthony Burgess and Modernity*, 257–8.

28   See David Hayman, "Some Writers in the Wake of the Wake," *In the Wake of the Wake*, eds. David Hayman & Elliott Anderson (Madison: University of Wisconsin Press, 1978) 17.

29   "Anthony Burgess – The Art of Fiction," *The Paris* Review 56 (Spring 1973); reprinted in *Writers at Work: Paris Review Interviews*, ed. Malcolm Cowley (New York: Viking, 1976) 354.

whatness of the communication. For separable meanings go to the professors, whose job it is to make a meaning out of anything. Professor Keteki, for instance, with his *Volitional Solecisms in Melville*. (MF, 240–1)

Melville, here, alludes to the whale of Jonah, and the "whatness" of communication harks back to Beckett's notorious observation regarding the language of the *Wake* – and Burgess' slapstick Professor Keteki (Sanskrit for "riddle") to Joyce's "Brotfressor Prenderguest" from the *Wake* (FW 124.15). However, behind the structure and the punning lies a moral impetus, in this particular instance refreshingly original, viewing racism as atavism of incestuous tendencies.[30] Burgess' *M/F* elevates incest into a symptom of universal malaise, one also to do with perhaps the doom of the modern age: the pathologically racialised and nationalised conceptions of human identity. *M/F* thus clearly ranks as one of Burgess' most socially-minded works of experimentation.

Nothing Like the Sun, the fictionalised love-life of Shakespeare told by a tipsy Professor Burgess to his Malayan students, together with *Napoleon Symphony*, the musicalised epic of Napoleon's career patterned on Beethoven's *Eroica*, rank among Burgess' "most celebrated achievements" according to most commentators, this mainly due to "their Joycean intertext, their experimental form, their popular appeal balanced by their demanding aesthetics."[31] Burgess' composition journal on *Nothing Like the Sun*—published as the essay "Genesis and Headache"—cites Stephen's Shakespeare theory from *Ulysses* as the source of an important plot element in which Shakespeare is cuckolded by his younger brother Richard.[32] Debt to Joyce is owed and paid both on the micro- and macro-levels: the novel's interior monologues bear the mark of those in *Ulysses*, and Burgess' exploration of Shakespeare's sexual life derives to a considerable extent from the theory propounded in the "Scylla and Charybdis" episode.[33]

Were one to stop here, *Nothing Like the Sun* would be little more than another obvious, and rather unexciting, Joycean intertext in the Burgess canon.

---

30 As Aggeler points out: "The whole pattern of Western culture, as Burgess sees it, is incestuous. Race consciousness in particular, which has in no way diminished in recent years, is symptomatic of an incestuous pull. In Burgess' view, 'the time has come for the big miscegenation.' All of the races must overcome their morbid preoccupation with color identity and face the merger that is inevitable in any event" (Aggeler, *The Artist as Novelist*, 221).

31 Aude Haffen, "Anthony Burgess's Fictional Biographies: Romantic Sympathy, Tradition-Oriented Modernism, Postmodern Vampirism?," *Anthony Burgess and Modernity*, 137.

32 Burgess, "Genesis and Headache," *Afterwords*, ed. Thomas McCormack (London: Harper & Row, 1968) 42.

33 John Stinson's careful exposé reveals practically all the major and minor traits of Stephen's theory (including, e.g., his "proof" that Shakespeare was a Jew) reflected in Burgess' novel – an all-inclusiveness which, "given the relative oddity of Stephen's theory [...], is all the more remarkable" (Stinson, "*Nothing Like the Sun*: Faces in Bella Cohen's Mirror," *Critical Essays on Anthony Burgess*, ed. Geoffrey Aggeler [Boston: G. K. Hall & Co., 1986] 93).

However, these neat identifications obscure the more subversive and interesting features of Burgess' doubly plagiarist undertaking: his play on his own
real name, John Anthony Burgess Wilson. There are two distinct bearers of
this name in *Nothing Like the Sun*, and both are relevant in their more and
less veiled reference to "Will's son." In identifying himself with Will's son,
Burgess claims his creative paternity to spring from Shakespeare rather than
Joyce. Moreover, as critic John Stinson notes, in a scene redolent of symbolic relevance, the first John Wilson character (a clerk) records the birth
of the twins Hamnet and Judith, and when recording the name of the father,
the "WS" initials blot the name actually transcribed, WILSON. Burgess, as
son of Will, is thus identified with Hamnet the son. In a scene alluding to the
opening of *Ulysses*, the other Wilson character—actor John Wilson—baptises
the newly opened Globe Theatre with the formula "Ego te baptizo, in nomine
Kyddi et Marlovii et Shakespearii" (*NLS*, 206).[34] Thus, *Nothing Like the Sun* is
more than a hackneyed spoof of a popularised "Scylla and Charybdis," for
Burgess' achievement takes stock of the *Ulyssean* interplay between fiction
and history, and its subversion of literary tradition.

In *Napoleon Symphony*, to draw upon and follow Joyce means for Burgess
to challenge him, to think through and possibly beyond him, perhaps more
markedly than anywhere else in his output. Again, the textual references and
storyline motifs are so obvious as to border on pastiche. From the breakfast
kidneys via the archaic villanelle in celebration of Napoleon's return from
Egypt down to the last word of the novel, "rejoice," Burgess displays his familiarity with the trivium of his Joyce schooling. However, examples from
the quadrivium are equally numerous:[35] as Burgess notes in his *Joysprick* (on
which he worked simultaneously with *Napoleon Symphony*), Joyce's *siglum*
for the ALP *Wake* character was the Greek letter delta. So, Burgess has his
Napoleon write to his Josephine, "Oh, how I hunger [...] to munch your delta
of silk in the valley of bliss," and elsewhere has Josephine's lawyer reflect on
Napoleon's Italian campaign, "And did not the way to the Alps lie [...] between
her legs?" (*NS*, 3, v). Burgess thus develops Joyce's *Wakean* scaffolding into
a rich, punning metaphor which combines the military with the erotic in the
geography of Napoleon's exploits. Burgess is also careful to draw upon the
Joycean archetypes: Josephine is water and fluidity, Napoleon is earth and

---

34   Stinson is spot-on when refining the *Ulysses* intertext informing *Nothing Like the Sun* in the following, less straightforward terms: "With *Ulysses* serving *Nothing Like the Sun* something in the
way that the *Odyssey* does *Ulysses* [...], it seems apparent that Burgess wants us to see himself,
Bloom, and Stephen returning the gaze of Shakespeare on the other side of that mirror. Expect-
ing, then, that his readers will see his WS refracted in the Joycean mirror, Burgess creates a hall-
of-mirrors effect that is, like so much in *Ulysses* itself, either mock-ironic or serious, dependent
upon one's precise angle of vision" (Stinson, "Faces in Bella Cohen's Mirror," 96).

35   The following account is indebted to John Mowat's article, "Joyce's Contemporary: A Study of
Anthony Burgess's *Napoleon Symphony*," *Critical Essays on Anthony Burgess*, pp. 185–97.

solidity. Consequently, his aquaphobia is sterile and the cause of his undo-ing both symbolic and historical: illustrated by not only his naval defeat at Trafalgar, but also his fiascos at the Berezina River, at Waterloo, and by his imprisonment on St. Helena surrounded by the oppressive Atlantic.

The "art" of *Napoleon Symphony* is music and the chief structuring in-tertext for Burgess' novel is Beethoven's *Eroica*, so much so that throughout the four-part novel, a ratio is observed between the amount of text and the number of bars in the corresponding passage from Beethoven's score. Typical of Burgess' use of the acoustic properties of language tied to gender-ideology is a song from Part II, the funeral march:

There he lies
Ensanguinated tyrant
O bloody bloody tyrant
See
How the sin within
Doth incarnadine
His skin
From the shin to the chin.
(*NS*, 125)

Burgess also provides a "female version" of this song: "Rowers row in rows. / Posied roses interpose / Twixt the rows and the rose," etc. (*NS*, 142). As noted by Mowat, the phallic *I* that marks Napoleon's song turns into the vaginal "o" of its female counterpart. The use of these vowels as physical, sexual/proc-reative symbols in Joyce's *Wake* has been noted by Burgess in *Joysprick*: "The All-Father is I and his consort is O [...]. Introduce the dart to the egg, or the phallus to the Elizabethan 'thing of nought,' and we have IO, symbol of crea-tion" (*J*, 20). Accordingly, *Napoleon Symphony* offers precisely such union by printing these parallel letters side by side (*NS*, 152).[36] Explicitly *Wakean* is also Burgess' use of typography, again departing from his *Joysprick* observations about the *Wake's* use of italics to represent the "obliquity" of the artist (Shem) and capitalisation, the "loud uprightness" of the man of action (Shaun). Accordingly, Napoleon speaks in capitals, Josephine in lower-case romans, and Eugène and Hortense in italics, as for instance in the following passage:

36 Of the overall musicality of the novel, Mowat is right in drawing an important division line be-tween Joyce's approach in the "Sirens" episode of *Ulysses* and Burgess' in *Napoleon Symphony*: "On the whole, there is less direct mimicry of music than there is duplication and transformation of detail in an attempt at musical "musicalisation" in *Ulysses* but to the dreamlike multiplication of duplication in *Finnegans Wake* [...] Images split and coalesce or are superimposed as they enter into patterns of duplication, recurrence, and inversion [...] there is a mirror at the center of the dream which is history" (Mowat, "Joyce's Contemporary," 192-3).

"oh you are breaking out AND LOVE they wish to break all our AND A FAMILY OF LOVING *hearts* hearts HEARTS" (*NS*, 60). Even more so than in *Nothing Like the Sun*, Burgess' re-use of Joycean techniques (including the acrostic, anagram, onomatopoeia, etc.) in *Napoleon Symphony* achieves a considerable degree of complexification and independence.

The 1973 publication of *Joysprick* was by no means an end to Burgess' occupation with Joyce. In numerous interviews and articles, he went on to broach the issue of parallels and differences between himself and Joyce. In "Joyce Can't Really Be Imitated," he averred: "Unfortunately I've had to earn my living writing books – no priestly vocation like Hopkins, no munificent patroness like Harriet Shaw Weaver who helped to support Joyce. This means that I've had to compromise, avoiding overmuch word play and verbal oddity."[37] Though together with Joyce the institution of patronage might have become passé and defunct, Burgess never tired of stressing the liveliness of Joyce's heritage for the literature of his day: "We should all now be writing novels like *Finnegans Wake*, not necessarily so obscure or so large, but starting on the way Joyce has shown in exploring the resources of the language," he insisted in 1964.[38] Many years later, his view was quite the same: "We've got a hell of a long way to go with modernism. Some people think *Finnegans Wake* is the end of modernism [... but] I think we're still in a modernist phase."[39]

However, it is one thing to conceive programmatically one's literary career as based on Joyce's legacy (to write about, and sometimes with, Joyce), and something wholly other to become an experimentalist and innovator in one's own right (to write *after*, but also *beyond* Joyce). Cases like *M/F*, *Nothing Like the Sun*, and *Napoleon Symphony* succeed in the latter, but as far as the vast Burgess oeuvre is concerned, these remain exceptions – as opined by such critics as Levitt,[40] Adams,[41] and Hayman.[42] It is revealing that none of these

---

37   Burgess, "Joyce Can't Really Be Imitated," *Books and Bookmen* 15 (July 1970): 9.

38   Burgess, "Speaking of Writing—VIII," *The Times* (16 January 1964): 13.

39   Samuel Coale, "An Interview with Anthony Burgess," *Modern Fiction Studies* 27 (Autumn, 1981): 444.

40   "The writer most commonly linked with the Modernists, and particularly with Joyce, is actually not very Joycean at all. [...] The misleading public image of Anthony Burgess [...is] further proof of the rule that Modernist influence in Britain has been terribly tenuous and that fiction has suffered as a result" (Levitt, *Modernist Survivors*, 52).

41   Regarding *The Clockwork Orange* and *Tremor of Intent* as "Joycean" novels, R.M. Adams observes that the former, when stripped of its dialect, "would be not only a sparse but a muddled book, with its bare bones in evident disarray," and that the latter's sole curiosity lies in an "even more marked application of Joycean prose in pure entertainment" (Adams, *Afterjoyce*, 166–8).

42   Hayman is less dismissive when describing Burgess as "a gifted, facile, witty novelist in the relatively unadventurous British vein." Still, focusing on *A Clockwork Orange* and the *Enderby* novels, he terms Burgess' Joyce-indebted works as nothing more than "clever adaptations" which for him "should not stand as examples of what to do after the *Wake*," and goes on to criticise Burgess' (mis)reading of the *Wake* as "about guilt" (Hayman, "Some Writers," 18).

three derogatory exposés of Burgess' supposed secondary superficiality vis-à-vis Joyce deals with *Nothing Like the Sun* or *Napoleon Symphony*, the two works where Burgess does indeed *rework* rather than *imitate* Joyce. It would thus seem that, comparisons with Joyce aside, Burgess' work is best viewed within the context of the early-to-mid-1960s restoration of the modernist heritage within English fiction. So long as most of the writers of his generation tended to blame their own reactionary conservatism and ideological constraints on the widely-regarded exhaustion of the possibilities of technical innovation (with Joyce's *Wake* as its infamous summa), Burgess deserves credit for the vigour with which he insisted on the necessity of reverting to Joyce's materialist poetics and departing from them in new directions.

2.2 "THE EINSTEIN OF THE NOVEL": B. S. JOHNSON

Jonathan Coe opens his monumental biography of B. S. Johnson with the following statement, whose grandiosity the rest of *Like a Fiery Elephant* seeks to prove:

> B. S. Johnson was, if you like, Britain's one-man literary avant-garde of the 1960s. Yes, of course there were other avant-garde writers around at the time (Alan Burns, Eva Figes, Ann Quin, Christine Brooke-Rose spring immediately to mind). But they were not as famous as he was, they were not as good at putting their names about, they did not appear on television as often as he did, they did not argue their case as passionately or fight their corners as toughly as he did [...]. B. S. Johnson was different. B. S. Johnson was special.[43]

Substantiating this claim, the dust jacket of the 2004 Picador *Omnibus* edition of B. S. Johnson's *Albert Angelo, Trawl,* and *House Mother Normal* is adorned with Samuel Beckett's and Anthony Burgess' appraisals of Johnson as "a most gifted writer" and "the only British author with the guts to reassess the novel form, extend its scope and still work in a recognisable fictional tradition," respectively.

Yet similar pronouncements, during the lifetime of the notoriously sensitive and irascible Johnson, were few and far between. Upon their appearance, practically all of his novels met with critical response that was lukewarm at best. Moreover, even the more critically savvy accounts of the Joycean roots of Johnson's techniques seem to have been largely detrimental to his reputation. Philip Tew, author of the first book-length study on Johnson's work, has shown that most Johnson criticism is marked by "remarks upon similarities

---

43   Jonathan Coe, *Like a Fiery Elephant* (London: Picador, 2004) 3.

to Joyce, Samuel Beckett and John Fowles" which merely "cast doubt upon his originality." Tew's study, instead, shows that "if Johnson admits, uses and incorporates the lessons of Joyce, he does so without any desire to imitate or replicate slavishly."[44] An overview of Johnson's seven completed novels substantiates Tew's argument that Johnson's "use" of Joyce was one of "creative intuition" and "methodological uncertainty as development," and enables a more nuanced critique than that of such literary historians as Levitt who take Johnson's late expression of admiration for Joyce's achievement as a sign of his life-long artistic vassalage.

Travelling People (1963), a work whose juvenile mishmash of styles and mixture of facts with fiction Johnson came to regret later on in his career (even refusing its republication), is a novel steeped in the Joycean stylistic experiments of Ulysses—each of its chapters is written in a different mode (first-person, third-person, film script, epistolary, stream of consciousness, etc.)—as well as in typographical innovation à la Sterne (e.g., the advertisements seen on an escalator in the London Underground presented in a descending diagonal sequence or the imitation of the black pages in Tristram Shandy indicating death, randomly scattered grey dots signifying unconsciousness, or regularly ordered dots signifying sleep). Joyce's Ulysses even makes a cameo, its mention taken to be a reference to the eponymous Hollywood epic. What lies underneath the formal extravagance, however, is a conventional Bildungsroman with a social-realist dimension not unlike those of the Angry Young Men. Travelling People suffers from a discrepancy between its excessive attention to form and the thinness of its narrative material. The stylistic self-consciousness is overshadowed by the book's emotional centre, "a celebration of human warmth in the social journey on which we are all fellow travellers," which in Dominic Head's judgment has no obvious link with the formal playfulness, and so Johnson's stylistic richness in Travelling People seems "an over-elaboration in what is in essence a conventional picaresque novel of self-discovery."[45]

In Albert Angelo (1964) Johnson launches his doctrine encapsulated in the well-worn formula that "telling stories is telling lies." A hundred-and-

---

44   Tew offers a deeper reading of Johnson's Joyce/Einstein simile in the following terms: "To understand the comparison fully it is essential to recall that Einstein argued for intuitive leaps of understanding for scientific advance, and therefore Johnson uses Joyce to indicate the possibilities of a complex relationality of fiction, a mapping of life experience on to the adaptable and mobile features of language as communicative device. [...] Einstein insisted famously on intuitive, sympathetic understanding where there exists an interplay between experience and [...] 'methodological uncertainty.' I suggest that Johnson admires less the specificity of Joyce's adaptations of the novel form as if such adaptations were set in stone, but more convincingly he was inspired by Joyce as the literary exemplar of such methodological uncertainty as development" (Philip Tew, B. S. Johnson: A Critical Reading [Manchester, New York: Manchester University Press, 2001] 134).

45   Dominic Head, The Cambridge Introduction to Modern British Fiction, 1950-2000 (Cambridge: Cambridge University Press, 2002) 228.

sixty out of its hundred-and-eighty pages trace, in a rather fragmentary and episodic manner (fusing narrations in multiple personal forms), a narrative drawn from Johnson's experiences working as a supply teacher in the early 1960s. New typographical oddities emerge as dictated by necessity. In *Albert Angelo*, as Johnson writes in the introduction to *Aren't You Rather Young*,

> I broke through the English disease of the objective correlative to speak truth directly if solipsistically in the novel form, and heard my own small voice. When Albert finds a fortune-teller's card in the street it is further from the truth to describe it than simply to reproduce it. And when a future event must be revealed, I could (and can; can you?) think of no way nearer to the truth and more effective than to cut a section through those pages intervening so that the event may be read in its place but before the reader reaches that place. (*ARY*, 22-3)

These gimmicks aside, the real breakthrough of *Albert Angelo*—contrary to the earliest reviews that praised its "realist" narrative at the expense of its "experimental oddity"—is what Johnson does to "realistic" mimesis. For instance, the double-column passages are meant to represent the interplay between external dialogue and internal "thoughts," exposing the sheer conventionality of the "realistic" mimesis that separates them through the use of quotation marks. The most notable instance of Johnson's reworking "realistic" mimesis occurs on the five pages of the novel filled with the full call of the register of Albert's class (*AA*, 34-9). As Johnson confided to Alan Burns, "[a] list implies that you are including everything, it's an absolute, an attempt to impose pattern on the chaos, it's all sorts of things. [...] A straightforward novelist would have written: He called the register."[46]

The narrative is famously disrupted by the authorial aposiopesis of the fictional illusion: "OH, FUCK ALL THIS LYING!" (*AA*, 163) at the beginning of the "Disintegration" section, written in an unpunctuated stream of consciousness – again, however, an "aposiopesis" clearly signalled as such and thus mediated as yet another convention. Moreover, since the section's style of fragmentation, erratic capitalisation, and punctuation bears striking resemblance to the pupils' discourse, "Disintegration," taken as an attempt to break through the interplay of styles, turns out self-subverting. It itself disintegrates under the weight of its own problems and contradictions, giving way to the final paragraph of the "Coda" that brings Albert's life to a ghastly end at the hands of his infuriated pupils—in a discourse which again is markedly theirs.

As will be the case of all his novels, including the "directly autobiographical" *Trawl* (1966) and *The Unfortunates* (1969), the only "truth" Johnson's texts

---

46   *Imagination on Trial*, eds. Alan Burns & Charles Sugnet (London: Allison & Busby, 1981) 92.

tell is the truth of "fiction," of how narrative and discourse construct the extra-textual "real." Both of Johnson's autobiographical novels abandon the stylistic plurality of *Albert Angelo* and pursue a motto taken from Beckett's *The Unnamable*, the imperative to write about "nothing else but what happens to me" (*T*, 1). However vastly different the modes employed by the two, both have been described as continuing in Johnson's formal experiments. The title *Trawl* derives from the setting of the narrative on a fishing trawler and the protagonist's determination "to shoot the narrow trawl of my mind into the vast sea of my past" (*T*, 3). In Johnson's own characterisation, the narrative is "a representation of the inside of my mind but at one stage removed; the closest one can come in writing" (*ARY*, 22) and as such, it comes rather as a disappointment that the remove, the mediation through writing, is nowhere foregrounded. The only real textually mimetic problem here, for Johnson, was the representation of "breaks in the mind's workings," a problem solved by a stylised scheme of 3–em, 6–em, 9–em spaces, punctuated by dots at decimal point level "in order not to have a break which ran-on at the end of a line looking like a paragraph" (*ARY*, 23). As all the other typographical or formal innovations employed by Johnson, this gadget fulfils some strictly mimetic purposes. Still, for all its narrative conventionality, *Trawl* ranks among the most aesthetically accomplished texts in Johnson's whole oeuvre, its prose at his most lyrical and charged and, its concluding note of "I, always with I......one always starts with I.....And ends with I" (*T*, 183), clearly pointing to a Beckettian intertext.

The Unfortunates is Johnson's most notorious novel, presented and produced in 27 unbound sections collected in a small box, to be shuffled and read at random, with the exception of the first and last. The mimesis of randomness serves a twofold purpose. It enacts the rambling workings of the mind, where present perceptions (coverage of a football match) evoke and interact with memories of the past (in this case, of Tony Tillinghast, a close friend who died in 1964 at the age of twenty-nine). Secondly, this textual randomness conceptually refers to the haphazard process of carcinogenic cell growth that had caused Tony's death. Here, the "remove" of writing is more pronounced than in *Trawl*, and many passages read not as a written record of consciousness, but rather as a diary of a writer's dilemma of how to compose such a record. "Randomness" itself is a difficult concept to sustain, since Johnson's decision to bind individually the 27 sections undermines the overarching resolution to do away with linearity. As it is, *The Unfortunates* presents a good many 12-page sections of perfectly linear narrative. This issue was also raised by Christine Brooke-Rose in her only, and rather dismissive, remark on B. S. Johnson in her vast body of criticism and literary theory. To her mind, for all its experimental coating, *The Unfortunates* is "still a realistic and dreary novel of a football player returning to his Midlands home-town."[47] This objection is hard to dismiss: critique of *The Unfortunates'* stylistic simplicity and self-contradictory experimentation has only been challenged recently by Nicolas Tredell's appraisal of the novel as an ironic subversion of the conventions of the *Bildungsroman*. In paying homage to his dead friend (to whom the promise, "I'll get it all down, mate," is regularly recalled), Johnson is consciously writing an "autobiography" and thus cannot escape textual play with his own name and subjectivity. This is brought home by an amusing piece of trivia recurrent throughout the text: Tony had been an academic authority on Boswell, the amanuensis of Samuel Johnson, whose combined initials yield—B. S. Johnson.[48] Furthermore, *The Unfortunates* paints an ironic "portrait of the artist" in the age of mass media entertainment.[49] Still, the incongruity between typographical and textual experimentalism vis-à-vis "drearily realist" narrative strategies and content has proven self-defeating. For realist and experimentalist detractors alike, *The Unfortunates* remains a dead end, a reified fetish of a novel-in-a-box, a singularity never to be repeated, which of course is a rather questionable achievement for a writer aiming to wield the baton of innovation. In view of this, it was not just out of escapism that Jonathan Coe's introduction to the 1999 re-issue of the text tried to reclaim *The Unfortunates* as "a contribution to the enduring tradition of confession writing," which was to resurface in the 1990s (partly also in Coe's own fiction) – it was a real attempt to rescue the text from its reputation of "a quirky offshoot of sixties experimentalism."[50]

House Mother Normal abandons once more the Beckettian imperative of "truthfulness" – only at the beginning and end is there a reminder of the fictitiousness of the material presented, and again the idiosyncratic narrative layout serves a peculiar mimetic purpose. The narrative centres around an evening in an old people's home, constructed as a stream-of-consciousness representation of the simultaneous perception of one sequence of events as experienced by the eight inmates and their House Mother. Johnson explained that the text was typeset so that every distinct moment in each of the 21-page monologues got allotted a specific page and line number, so that the final text was a narrative polyphony recorded in a text organised on the principles of a music score, to be read horizontally as well as vertically.

---

47   Christine Brooke-Rose, *Rhetoric of the Unreal* (Cambridge: Cambridge University Press, 1981) 358.

48   For more, see John Sturrock, "'Shake Well Before Use' – Review of B. S. Johnson's *The Unfortunates*," *Times Literary Supplement* (February 20 1969): 175.

49   "*The Unfortunates* does in fact contain an ironic "portrait of the artist" on its first level of illusion, when it shows the narrator trying to write a report on the football match. This portrayal functions as a satirical commentary on representations of the "serious author" which it both resembles and departs from; this writer is, after all, concerned with applying the conventions of a field of discourse, with arranging sentences and paragraphs" (Tredell, "Telling Life," 36).

50   Coe, introduction to B. S. Johnson, *The Unfortunates* (London: Picador, 1999) xiv-v.

House Mother Normal critiques the dominant mode of realism through its engagement with issues of mental decay as thematised by its introduction of each of its eight inmates and, of course, House Mother herself. Prefacing each of its increasingly fragmentary streams of consciousness is a list of personal, psychic-physical coordinates, such as the opening one:

Sarah Lamson

age	74
marital status	widow
sight	60%
hearing	75%
touch	70%
taste	85%
smell	50%
movement	85%
CQ count 10	
Pathology	contractures; incipient hallux valgus; osteo-arthritis; suspected late paraphrenia; among others.

(*HMN*, 8)

Following these are a series of recorded responses to the goings-on of one social evening at an old people's home, involving such disgusting and demeaning activities as the game of "pass the parcel" (which turns out to include dogshit) and the spectacle of House Mother letting her dog perform cunnilingus on her ("*Here, Ralphie! Up on the table with Mummy!* That's it, you know what to do with your long probing red Borzoi tongue, don't you, Ralphie!" [*HMN*, 172]).

The sequence of the individual speakers is one in which their minds gradually deteriorate in their outward perceptions as well as their textual transmission, which is mimetically rendered by dwindling typography, disintegration of paragraphs, sentences, and even individual words, until the final monologue (of one Rosetta Stanton) breaks off five pages too early, leaving the remaining paper space blank. The eight inmates' monologues, in their differing ways, revolve around world-war memories and experiences: whether those of fighting in the trenches of France, or of civic engagement back at home. These are all lives that dedicated their best years to sorting out the state's ugly business, Johnson implies, and this is how the state repays them when it has no more "use" for them—by locking them away in the hands of sadistic psychopaths. In this respect, the concluding "refrain" of six of the inmates' monologues—"Listen to her! No, doesn't matter" (*HMN*, 24, 41, 58, 74, 91, 109)—suggests a last-ditch attempt at an escape: in an environment of systematic outward oppression, the last relief is to be experienced inwardly, away inside one's mental world.

The final, extra, twenty-second page of the concluding monologue of House Mother involves a similar "alienation effect" to that of *Albert Angelo*. House Mother is allowed to step out of character, addressing the reader directly: "Thus you see I too am the puppet or concoction of a writer (you always knew there was a writer behind it all? Ah there's no fooling you readers!)" (*HMN*, 173). A note of weariness, observes Coe, "the sound of a writer beginning to give up on his own art; becoming bored by it; ceasing to believe [...] that it might somehow compensate him for the pain of living."[51] This is a rather bleak and reductive view, however, as *House Mother Normal* is also Johnson at his most viciously funny and socially critical. Neither can one view Johnson's critique of "realism" as a simple clash of competing discourses: the inner monologues of the inmates' psychic worlds contrasting with the "normalising" voice of the House Mother as authority figure. For indeed, there is nothing "normal" about House Mother: her incipient list of psychic-physical data includes the sense of "taste" reduced to "40%" and her pathology as "mild clap; incipient influenza; dandruff; malignant cerebral carcinoma (dormant)" (*HMN*, 156). In *House Mother Normal*, the doctor herself is a sick, STD- and brain-tumour-ridden individual, and so the world she is meant to treat is itself sick at heart.

Christie Malry's Own Double-Entry (1973) was the last novel Johnson saw published, and though not without its intriguing peculiarities, presents his most straightforward narrative with strong elements of social critique. The eponymous protagonist applies double-entry bookkeeping to grievances against him (debits) and favours in his benefit (credits) from the outside world. Several "Reckonings" interrupt the narrative, during which the dual columns are tallied. The Christian doctrine of apocalypse, final-reckoning redemption and doom, is thus parodied in a very down-to-earth fashion. Here, Johnson's belief in the chaos of lived experience and its prevalence over, if not incompatibility with, any rational or narrative ordering is voiced with an eschatological urgency:

> It seems that enough accidents happen for it to be a hope or even an expectation for most of us, the day of reckoning. But we shall die untidily, when we did not properly expect it, in a mess, most things unresolved, unreckoned, reflecting that it is all chaos. Even if we understand that all is chaos, the understanding itself represents a denial of chaos, and must be therefore an illusion. (*CMODE*, 30)

Later that year Johnson would—this time writing *in propria persona*—voice almost an identical conviction in his aforementioned introduction to his memoirs: "What characterises our reality is the probability that chaos is the

51   Coe, *Like a Fiery Elephant*, 25.

most likely explanation; while at the same time recognising that even to seek an explanation represents a denial of chaos." A new type of art form is sought which "will be of such a type that it admits the chaos, and does not try to say that the chaos is really something else [...] To find a form that accommodates the mess, that is the task of the artist now" (*ARY*, 6–7).

This call for an artistic form capable of accommodating chaos is heeded in Johnson's last project, *See the Old Lady Decently* (1975), by far his most formally ambitious work. This novel-memorial for his deceased mother was written as the first volume of an envisaged trilogy, which was to include *See the Old Lady Decently, Buried Although, Among Those Left Are You*, with the titles running the length of the three volumes' spines to form a single sentence. Michael Bakewell's introduction implies that Johnson had a complex design in mind, aiming to combine the death of his mother with "the decay of the mother country" and "the renewal aspect of motherhood" (*ST*, 8). Thus, the project was simultaneously personal, socio-political, and spiritual: the first part was to cover the period from his mother's birth in 1908 until his own birth in 1933, the second was to carry the theme through until the end of World War II, with focus on the evacuation he himself experienced, and on his father's visit to Ypres, where his wife's father had been buried during World War I. Finally, the third was to address his mother's death in 1971, "paralleling the decline of Britain and the Empire/Commonwealth during this time, a third visit to Ypres by himself and his father," and the conclusion, "the inevitability of regeneration in all three themes," was to bring the *Matrix Trilogy* full circle (*ST*, 8).

Always the meticulous categoriser, Johnson devised a system of textual markers to distinguish between fiction, half-fiction/half-truth, and All Truth – and also to demarcate the source / purpose / form of other material used. The fiction is marked V, set in a kitchen where his mother worked, dominated by a monstrous chef named Virrels:

V2

Now then. I have to invent some more Virrels scenes. (*ST*, 26)

I shall eat now, the manuscript stained on purpose with the melting butter. What a pity it is not possible for you all to read the ms! Where was I again? (*ST*, 28)

Half-truth is marked by date and age of mother (e.g., "16 (8)" means "1916, mother 8 years old") and consists of material assembled from tape-recorded memories of eye-witnesses, her letters, and documents pertinent to her life that were to hand. This material is introduced without amendment.

The section on Great Britain is written in the manner of a guided tour of Britain's growth across the centuries and its decay during the period of the three novels (which according to Johnson began at Ypres). What is essentially a transcript of some extant historical discourse is estranged by the elision of actual names, Johnson's intention being "to give generality, if not universality"; the section is marked by the signs GB and BB (for Broader Britain):

GB1
When Sir was marching from Shrewsbury to relieve he stayed two nights at, for the other Sir was a stout.   It was called in Domesday, being architecturally somewhat poor in character.

It is partly old and partly.   The ground it stands on was given by for advising the use of calthrops in the Battle of in. Hence the motto GANG WARRILY which appears upon the family. It is fitted up as an armoury at present and contains much of specimens of ancient and other.

(*ST*, 20)

BB7
The natives are very low down in the scale of humanity, and yet they use a which has puzzled the wisest mathematicians of.

      The is not such a mysterious engine as the, but the skill with which they use it is astonishing. The fix the butt-end of their into this, grasping the other which they thus give a great impetus to and can with astonishing accuracy as far as fifty.

(*ST*, 81)

The Mother Goddess section is composed of a series of quotations from Erich Neumann's *The Great Mother*, whose anthropology of the cult of the mother derives from the basic premise that every child experiences his/her mother as the Great Mother; these extracts are marked as N in the text.

Then there are Poems which form an essential part of the structure of the work; there is a concrete visual one (*ST*, 128) in which the shape of a female breast is textually achieved by means of the repeated single word "breast," with the intrusive letters of "n" and "c" gradually forming the word "cancer." Then there are other sequences: fictionalised ideas, personal statements about the novel itself, allocated smaller signs, seemingly random, but following a complex system. Finally, two more symbols: *H* for Field Marshal Lord Haig (whom Johnson hated with a passion):

H1
holocaust   atrocity   injury   grievance
(*ST*, 35)

H2

haemorrhage	abort	insane	gore

(*ST*, 63)

H3

hatred	anguish	indescribable	grieving

(*ST*, 95)

And O for birth, death and regeneration, the great round, which fuses the beginning and the end:

O¹

O let me open as though there were a beginning, though all there can be is the Great Round, uroboros, container of opposites, within which we war, laugh, and are silent (*ST*, 17)

O²

They gave her no drugs, just a whiff of chloroform towards the later stages.
Which were over by about half past one in the morning.
So: it began with the Great Round, and everything had to follow:
   from them
   from Em

       from
       embryo
       to embryan
     from Em,
      Me

(*ST*, 138–9)

One final time, then, does Johnson "write himself" into his text via a textual montage – not only by reversing "em" (short for Emily, his mother) into the concluding "Me," but also through fusing "em" with "bryan" in order to form "embryan."

 Johnson's final project in *See the Old Lady Decently* draws upon a vast array of various material sources, presenting his most sustained attempt at merging the individual and the social, truth and fiction, the particular and the archetypical, in what is his most overtly cyclical and linguistically complex text. The time of its creation coincided with Johnson's work on his declaration of dependence upon Joyce's revolution, in whose introduction he defined the project of "writing as though it matters" as follows:

It is not a question of influence, of writing like Joyce. It is a matter of realising that the novel is an evolving form, not a static one, of accepting that for practical purposes where Joyce left off should ever since have been regarded as the starting point. (*ARY*, 12)

See the Old Lady Decently, then, might be seen as Johnson's most "realised" text in which "where Joyce left off" is regarded as "a starting point." As a whole, Johnson's variegated, innovative—if uneven and sometimes formulaic—oeuvre heeds well the necessity of not only following, but also departing, from the Joycean materialist revolution of language, particularly as far as the exploration of concrete writing and visual typography are concerned.

2.3 "THIS DISTANCED TECHNIQUE OF WRITING FROM THE UNCONSCIOUS": ALAN BURNS

The writing career of barrister Alan Burns began with a case in point of epiphany:

I saw a silver frame for sale [in a jeweller's window] and in the frame a photograph of a youngish couple kissing, embracing. It was a sweet photo, rather old-fashioned, [...] and it rang a bell because I'd seen a similar photo in the family album, of my father and mother kissing on their honeymoon in Monte Carlo [...] I had long wanted to write about my parents and the love between them and the not-love between them but I didn't know where to start. At that moment I realized I needn't tackle their psychology or their histories, I could start with a picture. [...] And that became the starting point of my first book, *Buster*.[52]

An epiphany, of course, with a difference: what for Joyce is the power of the word becomes the power of the image for Burns. *Buster* (1961) is still rather traditional, even in its "imagery," but *Europe after the Rain* (1965), taking its title from a Max Ernst painting, is a conscious attempt at taking fiction in the direction of a surrealist painting.

Its complexity is rather conceptual and narrative than linguistic and mimetic. Also, Burns' method of composition is an early presage of his later formal experiments; in a piece included in *Beyond the Words*, Burns confided that its basis derived from a journalistic report on life in Poland after the war:

This last provided most of my background material. I had this badly-written guidebook on my desk and I typed from it in semi-trance. My eyes glazed and in the blur only the sharpest and strongest words, mainly nouns, emerged. I picked them out and wrote them down and made my own sense of them later. [...] Perhaps some of *Europe After*

52 . *Imagination on Trial*, eds. Burns & Sugnet, 161–3.

Rain's "numbness" derives from this distanced technique of writing from the uncon-scious.[53]

Burns was to find the formal procedure underlying his most experimental works, *Babel* (1969) and *Dreamerika!* (1972), in the "cut-up" method of com-position (invented by Brion Gysin and popularised by William Burroughs, cf. Chapter Three), in which odd fragments of material were cut, divided, and reassembled into new verbal arrangements.

In a letter Burns describes his mosaic method through reference to Baudelaire's "Ragpicker" and to Schwitters' incorporation, within his paint-ings, of such concrete textual objects as tram tickets. Like the Dadaists and *poètes maudits* before them, however, he went beyond his sources of inspi-ration in working not only on the macro-level of narrative, but also on the micro-level of syntax. Burns' "Essay" explains: "The quality I wanted was that not only the narrative but also the sentences were fragmented. I used the cut-up method to join the subject from one sentence to the object from another, with the verb hovering uncertainly between."[54]

The text, as is implied by its title, is formed of a melange of voices and characters, "all demanding their place in the narrative, struggling to enun-ciate their uniqueness, yet together overwhelming the reader and leading to a sense of cacophony and confusion."[55] To take an example of a typical *Babelian* sequence, here is one from early on in the text:

> THE FATHER RAPES HIS DAUGHTER, which is something she shouldn't see. The fe-llow is knuckling down and getting in further. It is hard behaviour from a man with religious grounding. And he expects his son to turn out really bad. [...] After a time he knifed her in the kitchen, between the counter and the machine, as the fork water turned dreadful, the noise from the machine as from eight women, trays on dregs of purplish colour full of the whirring fan continually in fever. (B, 6–7)

Again, the radical formal disjuncture holds together by means of an under-lying conceptual unity, and the medium, as ever, is the message, and form expresses content. Even though *Babel* itself speaks of "some sort of social and political fragmentation, some sort of dissolution sooner than you anticipate" in which "families are falling apart, falling away from the natural pattern, the intimate parental relationship" (B, 20), Burns' "Essay" in Gordon's collection is even more explicit:

---

53   Alan Burns, "Essay," *Beyond the Words*, ed. Giles Gordon (London: Hutchinson, 1975) 65.
54   Burns, "Essay," *Beyond the Words*, 66.
55   Ibid.

It was about the power of the State. How in every street, every room, every shop, every workplace, every school, every institution, and particularly in every family, the essential pattern of power relations is dictated by the underlying rules, assumptions and moral principles of the State. [...]
Babel described not the obvious apparatus of dictatorship but the hints nods assents implications agreements and conspiracies, the network of manipulations that envelops the citizens and makes them unaware accomplices in the theft of their liberty.[56]

Unlike for William Burroughs, then, the aleatory for Burns is primarily not just mechanical randomness; there is selection and further processing of material at work. In a 1982 article entitled "Writing by Chance," Burns differentiates himself from Burroughs and, in the opinion of his colleague Charles Sugnet, rightly so.[57] Also, next to Burroughs' tape recorders and steamer trunks, Burns sets a much homier image of his own way of working: "Four of my own novels were written this way – I leave slivers of paper on my desk with the window open, or a cat or a three year old allowed in to further the random order."[58]

After *Babel* and *Dreamerika!*, in a sense a formal and conceptual sequel to *Babel*, Burns "gave up writing from the subconscious, making a mosaic of found pieces," for having "written four books that way," the excitement "had gone out of it."[59] Instead, he turned to the tape recorder, exploring the possibilities of creating a collage of multiple (semi-)fictional narrations in *The Angry Brigade* (1973). In 1975, Burns left England for Australia, then relocated to the USA, co-edited the *Imagination on Trial* collection with Sugnet, and went on to revisit his earlier, less radical explorations of surrealist imagery and relation between fiction and history (in, e.g., *The Day Daddy Died*, 1981).

Even though Joyce's method is a far cry from the aleatory Dada, Burns has repeatedly acknowledged the importance of his precedence, in ways more significant than through the brief Joyce cameo in *Babel*:

THE GENIUS THREW SCRIBBLES ACROSS A PAGE. Increasingly fragmentary construction is a solitary occupation. The accidental imagination passionately battles, the blind man guides the black ink on silk, the desperate man is a work of art.
JAMES JOYCE IS A FAMILY BUSINESS. The people have heard of him. Ulysses takes a taxi back from where he was going.
(B, 82)

---

56   Ibid, 66–7.
57   Sugnet writes: "There's a bit of boundary-minding going on here, as Burroughs has received so much publicity for inventing the 'cut-up method,' and Burns has sometimes unfairly been seen as following him" (Sugnet, "Burns' Aleatoric Celebrations: Smashing Hegemony at the Sentence Level," *Review of Contemporary Fiction* 17.2 [Summer 1997]: 194).
58   Sugnet, "Burns' Aleatoric Celebrations, 195.
59   Burns, "Essay," 66.

Throughout the interviews Burns himself conducted in *Imagination on Trial* with both American and British writers, his questions keep returning to Joyce's writing as one which managed to forge its own literary idiom, thereby achieving "the evocation of the past and present together," and to Joyce as an author who has become synonymous with a certain kind of "complexity."[60] In an interview with David W. Madden, editor of the *Review of Contemporary Fiction* issue, Burns was explicit about the matter:

> Joyce changed everything, made everything possible. Master of all styles, all genres, all languages, all cultures . . . beyond that mere puffery, I'm wary of commenting on Joyce, overwhelmed not only by him as poet and novelist but by his mighty intellect. However, his influence on me was not intellectual but instinctive, which is to say, his achievement seemed to give me permission to follow my instinct wherever it led. Word-coinage is an obvious example, but it goes beyond that to, say, the structure of *Babel*, and much more.[61]

Burns is on par with Johnson in terms of regarding Joyce as a liberator, as an author who "made new things possible," even things at odds with their own methods and techniques. In Burns' case, this "instinctive" influence, however difficult to pin down, has allowed for a development of an idiosyncratic technique, different from the Joycean one in kind, though similarly radical in degree.

2.4 "THE VOYCE CRYING IN THE WILDERNESS, REJOICE WITH ME": BRIGID BROPHY

Writing just a few weeks after her death in a special issue of *Review of Contemporary Fiction* devoted to her literary legacy, Steven Moore reviewed the reputation of Brigid Brophy in some highly bleak terms: "[M]ost of her books are out of print on both sides of the Atlantic and few readers under forty recognize her name."[62] The reasons provided by Moore for this, however, had to do with the vicissitudes of Brophy's life and idiosyncrasies of her fiction. Her fifteen-year-long struggle with multiple sclerosis had drastically reduced her writing output after 1980, and she also seems to have been writing "too far ahead of her time" of topics and in styles that would only later gain broader social relevance, an example of which is her 1953 juvenilia novel

---

60   *Imagination on Trial*, eds. Burns & Sugnet, 33, 57, 154.
61   Madden, "An Interview with Alan Burns," 122.
62   Steven Moore, "Brigid Brophy: An Introduction and Checklist," *Review of Contemporary Fiction* 15.3 (Fall 1995): 7.

Hackenfeller's Ape, dealing with the issues of animal rights, experiments, and vivisection, well before the cause gained public attention. These reasons notwithstanding, Moore insists that

> any informed reckoning of twentieth-century literature must take Brophy's work into account: not only her nine books of fiction, but a career's worth of sharp, intelligent essays (most gathered into three collections), books on Mozart, Freud, and Beardsley, and a 600-page tour de force "defence of fiction in the form of a critical biography of Ronald Firbank," *Prancing Novelist*.[63]

Mozart and musical, particularly operatic, form is often used as a structuring device in Brophy's earlier output: her second novel, *The King of a Rainy Country* (1956) relies on Mozart's *Le Nozze di Figaro*, just as her fifth novel, *The Snow Ball* (1964), a satirical comedy of manners, borrows its storyline from *Don Giovanni*. Interspersed among her music novels were texts dealing with a variety of other topics: her non-fiction, *Black Ship to Hell* (1962), is a Freudian analysis of the human proclivity to violence; her most elliptical fiction work, *The Finishing Touch* (1963), an important step in the history of lesbian and, more broadly, anti-homophobic literature; or indeed her purposefully provocative, co-authored *Fifty Works of English and American Literature We Could Do Without* (1967), into which she famously included *Hamlet*, *Alice in Wonderland*, and works by Coleridge or Whitman.

For Brophy, the 1960s were to culminate with a work widely regarded as her masterpiece, *In Transit* (1969). Together with the 1960s culminated also Brophy's career as novelist, as most of the decade leading up to the breakout of her incapacitating and ultimately terminal illness was spent on her massive and again pioneering biography of Ronald Firbank (1973), around whom she built a whole theory of creative fiction; her critical assessment of the painter Aubrey Beardsley (1976); and her final, fairy-tale novel, *Palace without Chairs*. Given the magnitude, and the timely and timeless relevance of Brophy's career as writer and public activist, Moore's concluding note of exasperation seems apposite: "The neglect of this brilliant woman's work and contributions to contemporary aesthetics is scandalous."[64]

Fearless iconoclasm is what marks Brophy's crucial text, "A Heroi-Cyclical Poem," *In Transit* (1969). In terms of critical classification and characterisation, *In Transit* is an oddity: when describing the text, even a critic as perceptive and skilful as Frank Kermode had to settle for the indeterminate metaphor of "a kit of symbols" that can be "fit together in an indeterminate

---

63   Moore, "Brigid Brophy," 7.
64   Ibid.

number of ways."[65] His description echoed one of the text's many self-defi-
nitions as "less a book than a box of trick tools, its title DO IT YOURSELF KID"
(*IT*, 14), a Joycean instance of the text "reading itself."

The novel's opening offers a reflexion on the linguistic, or indeed textual,
representation of consciousness and the issue of authorial authority and
presence:

> Ce qui m'étonnait c'était qu'it was my French that disintegrated first.
>
> Thus I expounded my affliction, an instant after I noticed its onset. My words went, of
> course, unvoiced. A comic-strippist would balloon them under the heading THINKS –
> a pretty convention, but a convention just the same. For instance, is the 'THINKS' part
> of the thought, implying the thinker is aware of thinking?
>
> (*IT*, 11)

Following this is a meditation on time and tense function in literature, as well
as the distinction between history and fiction: "History is in the shit tense.
You have left it behind you. Fiction is a piss: a stream of past events but not
behind you, because they never really happened" (*IT*, 13).

The four-section narrative is set in an airport transit lounge and famously
centred on the protagonist Evelyn Hilary "Pat" O'Rooley's plight of "no longer remember[ing] which sex I was" (*IT*, 69). Its progression can indeed be
characterised as a concatenation of disintegrations of many of the central
concerns of the 1960s. From language and communication (the very first sentence is also a first symptom of the narrative subject's "linguistic leprosy") to
sexuality and gender (the main storyline, but also the many quips like "we
shall soon reach a point where the questionnaire item 'sex' gets filled as 'yes,
thrice weekly'" [*IT*, 74]). From modernist artistic styles ("our century prefers function to style" [*IT*, 22]) to cosmopolitan internationalism ("no one is
native. We're all transients" [*IT*, 29]). From history "in the shit tense" to the
currently fashionable liberation movements: the two precepts of the female
uprising are "WOMEN OF THE WORLD UNITE. / YOU HAVE NOTHING TO
LOSE / BUT YOUR LABOUR PAINS" and "WOMEN OF THE WORLD UNITE.
/ YOU HAVE EVERYTHING TO / GAIN – IN PARTICULAR, / YOUR DAISY
CHAINS" [*IT*, 130]).[66] Conversing with Leslie Dock in 1976, Brophy herself
stressed disintegration as the leitmotif of her novel:

> *In Transit* is about a series of disintegrations of rulebooks, including the sexual stereo-
> types, ending with the question of whether Aristotelian logic might disintegrate [...]

---

65   Frank Kermode, "Sterne Measures – Review of *In Transit*," *The Listener* (25 September 1969): 414.
66   For more, see, e.g., Brooke Horvath, "Brigid Brophy's It's-All-Right-I'm-Only-Dying Comedy of
     Modern Manners: ,Notes on *In Transit*," *Review of Contemporary Fiction* 15.3 (Fall 1995): 46.

I mean that what is being questioned is, do [the rules of the logic] reflect any necessary truths, or are they entirely arbitrary?[67]

In fact, the protagonist's loss of awareness, or indeed visibility, of gender, is foreshadowed by an early mediation on its linguistic roots:

They're sly, though, these romance languages, in this matter of sex. Sly rather than shy, I shurmise; for they sometimes do, sometimes won't, the girlish things. Sometimes the adjectives don't change. Vous êtes triste? Tick:— masc.▫ fem.▫. Strik(e) out whichever does not apsly. J'en suis content(e). And o that so demurely flirtatious mute *e* that may be appended to *ami*, where, dimpling, it can be seen but not heard. That's why my French is literary. I am so sex-obsessive *I must know*. They're sexsessive, too, the languages: but unsophisticatedly. I shed them in sheer impatience at the infantility of their sexual curiosity. *I do not want to be told the sex of inanimate objects.* (*IT*, 41)

The technique which the text itself terms "masophistication" (*IT*, 51)—one in which commonly held distinctions and binary oppositions are brought to interact with and collapse upon one another—is revealed as a direct corollary to what Brophy perceives as the aesthetic principle of her time:

What's the nearest to a twentieth-century style? Why, that sort-of-pop-brutalistic tabbying, those curds of canned plum-juice declining to integrate with custard, bits of a jigsaw free-drifting weightless in space: an amateur method of do-it-yourself exterior house-painting, developed out of military camouflage, whose purpose is, precisely, camouflage: to disguise the silhouettes of Victwardian buildings, to break up the outlines of their structure or pseudo-structure. (*IT*, 23)

However, it is one of the transitory features of the text that Brophy not only preaches against the twentieth-century "pop-brutalistic tabbying," but also joins in the game. She has her "he/she-Pat" narrator take part in a TV show *What's My Kink?* ("devised by Brigid Brophy"), one of whose panellists is "the well-known Irish-German writer, Thomas Mahon" (*IT*, 131; 136). Parts of her narrative are recast in the form of an opera libretto (called *Alitalia*, featuring male sopranos and female baritones). In one of her "Interlewds" (*IT*, 98), vast portions of the text quote from a fictitious pornographic novel *L'Histoire de la Langue d'Oc* (a parody of *The Story of O*). Finally, her whole narrative is flipped into a cliché thriller featuring Pat in the role of Slim O'Rooley, "dead-beat dick; weeper peeper, down-at-the-heel heel" (*IT*, 153).

The associative link connecting these overblown burlesque slapstick scenes is largely wordplay and punning: Pat's briefcase, carried through the

---

entire mock-quest, gives rise to his/her detective reincarnation being deter-mined to make a "brief case" of the goings-on (*IT*, 163); the transportation belt workers' uprising evokes a response from a mob with a bar counter used as headquarters – a veritable "counter-revolution" (*IT*, 202). In a late "alienating interlude" Brophy makes it clear that "at least one of the hero(in)es immolated throughout these pages is language" and together with that, "the work's sub-title is: "Or *The Autobiography of Sappho's Penis*" (*IT*, 214). Brophy's "misprinted mistranslated oversestimated sadomasturbatory pornofantasy-narrative" (*IT*, 143) is a "juicifixion" (*IT*, 217) that repeatedly stages a failure to nail down the body in and through language; together with lapse in gender awareness the multilingual narrator is stricken with "linguistic leprosy": "My languages gave their first dowser's-twig twitch and I conceived they might be going to fall off" (*IT*, 12).[68]

Brophy clearly aligns her experimentation, however mock-seriously, with what she recognises as Joyce's anti-imperialist, de-colonising linguistic project. In the conclusion, Pat is killed off twice in two textual columns, first as a she, then as a he, yet the final-page images of St. Theresa "expir[ing] in a smile of orgasmic ecstasy" and Aphrodite ("re-sea-born of the sperm and spume bubble-and-squeaking about her da's off-torn, projectiled, sea-crashed virile member") suggest a rebirth and rejuvenation. The text con-cludes with a fish-ideogram, the French word for end, FIN, written over its lower "fin," harking back to the "Ce qui m'étonnait" of the opening premise (*IT*, 230). *In Transit* is a fundamentally Joycean text.[69]

"How" *In Transit* is both Joycean and very much its own has been noted by critic Chris Hopkins, who points out that although Joycean, *In Transit* is independent of its precursor through the complete absence of its protago-nist's identity.[70] Hopkins is not entirely correct, here, for Pat O'Rooley's "I,"

68   Critic Karen Lawrence has noted how the narrative switching between gender identifications (and Pat switching back and forth between a *he* and a *she*), enables Brophy to launch "a fantastic, punning linguistic journey," a "wild ride of the signifier" through which Brophy "parodies the myth of the phallus as transcendental signifier, the myth that props up all the paradigms of the journey underwriting Western culture" (Karen Lawrence, *Penelope Voyages: Women and Travel in the British Literary Tradition* [Ithaca/London: Cornell University Press, 1994] 233).

69   As Lawrence has suggested, Pat's final suicide suggests the painful position of Pat, the Irish or-phan, who "feels both a kinship with her Joycean heritage and the sense of an ending, the possi-bility that that heritage no longer sustains her circulations" (Lawrence, "*In Transit*: From James Joyce to Brigid Brophy," 42).

70   Hopkins argues: "Here the model is clearly James Joyce [...], but the text has games of its own to play, in particular with gender. For while *In Transit* is as interested as any Joyce text in multilin-gual punning, its most striking feature is that its first-person narrator has no idea of her own identity. The speaking "I" knows that it is in an airport [...] and hence "in transit" and seems to have a capacity for generating language, but that is all. Thus the voice has a great consciousness of the culture embodied in language, but no knowledge of how it relates to the discourses it refers to so promiscuously" (Chris Hopkins, "The Neglect of Brigid Brophy," *Review of Contempo-rary Fiction* 15.3 [Fall 1995]: 16).

though notoriously ephemeral, does have one explicit anchoring: its Irish heritage of an orphan whose two sets of parents (natural and foster) have been killed in plane crashes, a harsh contrast with some early idyllic reminiscences from a childhood spent in Dalkey. The theme of Irishness is functionally employed in service to Brophy's chief project of the "immolation of language": "We speak English as a foreign language, even when we have no other (This is my foster-mother-tongue, since when I have used no other)" (*IT*, 34). Irishness is also used as a backdrop for several irresistible puns, such as "What name shall we coin for the natives of Erin? Erinyes," or "We are all Greek heroes, we Irish – O'Dysseus (whom Joyce disguised under the vocative form You-Lysses), O'Edipus, and most cogently of all, with not a syllable displaced, O'Rion – [...] O'Restes" (*IT*, 47, 56).

In a more serious vein, Irishness is presented both generally and specifically as linked to other colonial groups and their experience of "transculturation" as "disculturation" but also as a special case of the colonial legacy:

> We Irish had the right word on the tip of our tongue, but the imperialist got at that. [...] What begins as endemic lapsus linguae we peddle as precious lapis, with which we illuminate our Book of Sells (an early Book of Ours). We are never knowingly underbold. We are in the grips of compunsion.
> Youlysses have fore-suffered all. Before the Jew wandered, jew did.
> Is that another of your dog-headed Irish slips?
> (Pardon me, ma'am, your mollibloomers is shewin'.)
> Cynoscephalae, ladies, sigh no tom-moore.
> (We lost Thermopylae, the double pom-pom Bloom.)
> (*IT*, 35)

Indeed, it is the legacy of Joyce that Brophy most explicitly invokes as the precursor of the linguistic side of her experiment; a precursor fondly acknowledged, but later outgrown. Near the very end of the novel Pat apostrophises Joyce through Finnegan: "O, it's *thou*. Old Father Finnegan Go-and-don'tsinagain. Father Irefish Finn. Well, I saw through you, you old pro-façade, before I was out of my boyhood or girlhood. [...] I can't hear you, ex-father. I've switched me deaf-aid off" (*IT*, 228). Despite the irreverent linkage between influence and "deaf-aid," it is clear that Brophy's imaginative "revolution of language" is based on that of Joyce. This is evident in how mentions of Joyce are tied with evocations of Odysseus, "the hero who can never accomplish the return of the native, because he isn't one" (*IT*, 35).

At one point, the hero/ine of *In Transit* identifies with "Oruleus (latinised as Ulrix and thence rather quaintly englished as Unruly)" (*IT*, 175). Early on in the text, the "I" admits that his/her "fantasy steps tiptoed up on that ever-tempting serpent, my compatriot, mike" and wonders, should he/

she "snatch it and announce to all In Transit my tribute to my great Tries-tine compalien, the comedi-chameleon, the old pun gent himself?" (*IT*, 36). A rhetorical question, of course, for the text itself *is* a tribute to Joyce, but if the novel names Joyce as a forefather, it nevertheless also treats him as father who must be outgrown. For the "Triestine compalien" blends together *compatriot* and *alien*. Karen Lawrence has shown that Brophy, through her exploration of a postgendered position for her protagonist, takes issue with Joyce whose "revolution of the word works its disruptions still within a cer-tain phallic framework," and that through her central metaphors of circula-tion and transit, Brophy attempts "to figure more radical indeterminacies of sexual identity, even as they pay homage to Joycean (and, by way of Joyce, Odyssean) exile."[71]

In doing so, Brophy posits the narrative's own ancestry as a problematic one. Even the metaphor of parentage, with its secure roles for male and fe-male, does not suffice to represent the foster, mixed, and transcultural ances-try of the sex-changing narrative. Still, *In Transit* is one of the most explicit proofs that Joyce's voice, within the context of the British fiction writing of the 1960s, was not of one crying in the wilderness, but found listeners who carried its message further: "I could loose on the Lounge his obituary: I am the voyce of one crying in the wilderness; rejoice with me" (*IT*, 36).

2.5 "A DEATH WISH AND A SENSE OF SIN": ANN QUIN

Ann Quin emerged from her troubled childhood (marked by her father's aban-donment of the family and the highly traumatic experience of receiving her upbringing, despite her atheism, at a Roman Catholic convent) with a seve-rely impaired mental health which, following a series of nervous breakdowns from which she periodically suffered throughout her life, arguably also brou-ght about her death by drowning at age thirty-six in 1973.[72] She spoke of her Catholic upbringing as of "a ritualistic culture that gave me a conscience. A death wish and a sense of sin. Also a great lust to find out, experience what evil really was."[73]

---

71   Lawrence, "*In Transit*: From James Joyce to Brigid Brophy," 40.
72   The most valuable sources in the otherwise scarce biographical material on Quin used in the present account are Nicolas Tredell's entry on Quin in *Dictionary of Literary Biography, Volume 231: British Novelists Since 1960*, ed. Merritt Moseley (Farmington Hills: The Gale Group, 2000) 230–8; Giles Gordon, "Reading Ann Quin's *Berg*" reprinted in the 2001 Dalkey Archive re-edition of *Berg*; Brian Evenson, "Introduction," Ann Quin, *Three* (also with Dalkey, 2001); Lee Rourke, "Who cares about Ann Quin?," *The Guardian* (May 2007); and the excellent website dedicated to Quin's work, run by Nonia Williams: http://annquin.com/
73   Qtd. in Evenson, "Introduction," Ann Quin, *Three* (Chicago, Illinois: Dalkey Archive, 2001) vii-viii.

In her fiction, Quin developed an idiomatic style blending non-linear fragmentary narration, multiple viewpoints, and stream of consciousness, marked by poetic lyricism, fantasy-embedded, at-times hallucinogenic registration, to explore such topical themes as the search for identity, the influence of the past on the present, and intergenerational pressures.[74] Her oeuvre, comprising four novels and drafts and notes for a fifth one, is marked by a unique kind of development, an aesthetic progression of increasingly extreme experimentation with language and form – a progression paralleled with her fall from grace with its critical reception.

Philip Stevick offers a fitting encapsulation of the poetics of Quin's fictional spaces by pinpointing their four cardinal points: first, "the characters are never at home [...] physical surroundings tend to be perceived in the way in which one sees them on a trip"; second, "the whole of experience in Quin's fiction tends to be eroticized [...], the phenomenal world tends to appear as if charged with sexual energy"; third, "wholes, perhaps more properly gestalts, tend to be fragmented [...] in a way related but roughly opposite, the whole of anything threatens always to erode, split, merge into another thing"; and finally, Quin's fiction "takes place at several levels of discourse simultaneously, alternately, contrapuntally."[75]

Unlike her first two texts, both of which were rejected by publishers (and never appeared in print), *Berg* (1964) was published by John Calder[76] and was met with critical success, this despite its explicit indebtedness to the *nouveau roman* movement. Set in Quin's native town of Brighton (although never specified as such), *Berg*'s narrative is, in a monomaniacal fashion, determined by one sole intention stated already in the very first sentence: "A man called Berg, who changed his name to Greb, came to a seaside town intending to kill his father" (*B*, 1).

However, the intended parricide never takes place. Instead of killing him, Alistair Berg embarks on a Hamletian series of deferrals, substitutions, and repetitions. He becomes involved with his father's mistress Judith, goes on to kill her cat as well as his father's caged budgerigar, and winds up strangling

---

74   Tredell paints a picture of Quin as a follower of the modernist project of "developing style and structure in an attempt to achieve a closer fidelity to the moment-by-moment texture of lived experience" (Tredell, "Ann Quin," 230).

75   Phillip Stevick, "Voices in the Head: Style and Consciousness in the Fiction of Ann Quin," *Breaking the Sequence – Women's Experimental Fiction*, eds. Ellen Friedman & Miriam Fuchs (Princeton: Princeton University Press, 1989) 234–6.

76   Giles Gordon pointed to the prestige attached to Quin's having her first book pubslihed with Calder: "Calder, and his partner Marion Boyars, published only a few British novelists, and thus when *Berg* was published it was something to be read. Here was a working-class voice from England quite unlike any other, which had absorbed the theatrical influences of John Osborne and employed the technical advances of the nouveau roman. *Berg*, to use shorthand, is a Graham Greene thriller as if reworked by a somewhat romantic Burroughs" (Gordon, "Reading Ann Quin's *Berg*," ix).

a vaudeville-act dummy made in his father's image. Following that, Berg consciously misidentifies a body washed up on the beach as his father's and returns to Judith, taking his father's place. Thus, instead of killing him, Berg gradually comes to resemble, even displace, his father. At the end of the novel, a man resembling Berg's father has moved into the adjacent—formerly his own—room, the cycle returning to its beginning, ready to restart.

This is coupled with extensive animal parallelism underwriting and accompanying the crucial Oedipal triads: Nathy's budgie Berty always endangered by Judith's cat Seby – until both are dispatched as surrogate sacrificial animals by Berg. Quin constructs the sexual identities of her characters through animal tropes. Dead or alive, these animal allusions form alienated images of gender and sexuality, leaving the characters in the novel void of any meaningful relationship. Berg's "sexual rebellion"[77] consists in its reworking of the Western meta-narrative of the Oedipus complex, but Quin modifies this traditional structure by inserting animals, alive and dead, as well as living-dead (stuffed), further complicating her parody of Freud's Oedipus with the uncanny, in which the dead live on, as Judith's room is a taxidermic museum, stuffed animals giving Berg the evil eye even in death.

Berg's own body on page one is in turn rendered amphibian, "white-scaled [...] with curled-webbed toes," continuously identified as a "fish without fins," and he repeatedly imagines "birds waiting... outside to tear me to shreds" (B, 60). Again, the cyclicality and essential stasis of the whole process is brought home on the penultimate page where Berg is informed that Judith has ordered herself a cat, while a stuffed budgie flutters on the periphery (B, 160). Judith's body, too, is pushed into subhuman alienation: "Her fingers that had played with a button between her breasts, now flew, dived into a thin gold net which encased her yellow bush of hair" (B, 25). Judith's "fingers" and "breasts" seem to exist as separate entities, as well as "her yellow bush of hair'" where Quin's adjective "yellow" sits uncomfortably as a replacement of "blonde," and perhaps equates Judith's body to that of the yellow bird on the table.

Immediately after killing Judith's cat, Berg is made aware of the "bits of fur clinging" to his hands (B, 26), and although he never mentions the incident again, as shown by critic Jennifer Komorowski, "the rest of the novel is filled with references to fur."[78] Freud's notion of the involuntary repetition is at play here, and when Berg enters Judith's flat he is "confronted by warmth, smell of wet fur" (B, 54), which neatly echoes his feeling "something like wet fur against his face" (B, 37) when he falls after the incident. The un-

---

77   Loraine Morley, "The Love Affair(s) of Ann Quin," *Hungarian Journal of English and American Studies* 5.2 (1999): 128.

78   Jennifer Komorowski, "Dead Animals: Uncanny and Abject Imagery in Ann Quin's *Berg*," *Liberated Arts* 1.1 (2015): 2.

canny prevalence of wet fur echoes the murder, as when he wipes his hands he notices, again, "bits of fur clinging to them" (B, 35). As Komorowski suggests, "the uncanny presence of wet fur is both indicative of Berg's guilt as a result of killing the cat, and the fact that he cannot escape his unresolved Oedipus complex."[79]

Despite the strictly familial storyline, *Berg* features a series of breaks and flows in the protagonist's search both for stable subjectivity and freedom from it:

> I must recall the precise feelings that have nurtured the present circumstances, when nothing at all from outside interfered, not even thoughts of time past, present, or time future. Isn't there a moment caught between two moods, that space within, separated form life, as well as death, when the sun is faced without blinking, when eternity lies here inside; no divisions whatsoever, simply a series of circular motivations? [...] Definitely the supreme action is to dispose of the mind, bring reality into something vital, felt, seen, even smelt. (B, 31–2)

Quin's protagonist perceives continuity—in the form of "feelings that have nurtured the present circumstances"—as a series of interferences, but is still pinned down to the notion of subjectivity achieving the point of no "divisions." Such desire in turn is frustrated by "a series of circular motivations," hence revealing its innately antagonistic nature vis-à-vis the mind: "the supreme action" being "to dispose of the mind," with the goal of superseding perception with "vital, felt, seen, even smelt" reality. Thus, despite his presumably triangulated subjectivity, Berg is not unaware of the machinic processes of production and counter-production.

Quin's achievement lies in marrying this mechanical plotting based on cross-dressings, mixed gender-roles, and blurred identity boundaries with a style generative of precisely this central narrative ambiguity:

> Window blurred by out of season spray. Above the sea, overlooking the town, a body rolls upon a creaking bed: fish without fins, flat-headed, white-scaled, bound by a corridor room—dimensions rarely touched by the sun—Alistair Berg, hair-restorer, curled by webbed toes, strung between heart and clock, nibbles in the half light, and laughter from the dance hall opposite. [...] A week spent in an alien town, yet no further progress—the old man not even approached [...]. Oh yes I have seen you with her—she who shares your life now, fondles you, laughs or cries because of you. Meeting on the stairs, at first the hostile looks, third day: acknowledgement. A new lodger, let's show him the best side. [...] Rummaging under the mattress Berg pulled out the beer-stained piece of newspaper, peered at the small photograph.

---

79   Komorowski, "Dead Animals," 3.

> Oh it's him, Aly, no mistaking your poor father. How my heart turned, fancy after all
> this time, and not a word, and there he is, as though risen from the dead. That Woman
> next to him, Aly, who do you suppose she is?
>
> (B,1)

Quin's narrative technique blends first-person and third-person descriptions
of one character's experience with words or sensations uttered or registered
by other speaking subjects and consciousnesses (and thus either experienced,
remembered, or hallucinated) without setting them off as dialogue by quotation marks or other means. In so doing, the style reinforces the key narrative
theme: Berg's failure to develop an independent identity. Only the words of
Berg's mother, indented and set in smaller type, are differentiated from Ber-
g's – through these interpolations Quin manages to introduce into her narrative
a style and sensibility markedly different from that of her protagonist's. But
ambiguity persists: are these interpolations remembered and recited, read and
reproduced (through letters), or ventriloquised and hallucinated? Quin's narrative methods create a highly unsettling, frighteningly volatile sense of identity:
in this respect, Stevick argues, her interior monologue surpasses even its modernist precursors.[80] In her evaluation of Quin's narrative strategies, Christine Brooke-Rose qualified Stevick's emphasis on originality by tying Quin's methods to
Beckett – and Joyce: "In fact Quin uses either straight narrative sentences [...] or,
as more often in *Berg*, direct speech, straight from Beckett and ultimately from
Molly Bloom's monologue in *Ulysses*. These are formal remarks, not intended to
detract from Quin's originality in other ways."[81]

   Indeed, *Berg*'s originality is not only stylistic but also of the political kind:
it is a tug-of-war against the Oedipal code, and patriarchal construction of
masculinity. The "intention to kill" that opens the novel is akin to a machinic
desire producing the ripples of flows and breaks which signify that Oedipus
is but another break. An early reflection on his course has Berg experiencing
a rare occasion of insight:

> But this was hopeless, far worse being the border-line case, brewing on tit-bits made
> up from the antidotes of artificial respiration upon the imagination; the survival of
> those who preferred remaining halfway, never accepting, or rejecting, aware only of

---

80   "It is not the inner monologue of a character in Virginia Woolf, registering sensation, conflating
     past and present, musing on other people, all in a kind of watercolor voice. It is not the inner
     talk of Joyce, as Bloom or Stephen observe the phenomenal world and interrogate themselves.
     Berg's talk scarcely seems "inner" at all, seems rather actual speech, acted out in the theater of
     the mind, and one imagines Berg talking aloud to himself, at least shaping his words with his
     lips." (Stevick, "Voices in the Head," 232)
81   Christine Brooke-Rose, *Stories, Theories and Things* (Cambridge: Cambridge University Press,
     1991) 78.

the urge to defeat boredom. I take, I see, I subject my own mediocre self into something big. Berg walked away from the reflection that threw a superficial slant on the growth that had formed inside. (B, 34)

Berg's creed here expresses his internal libidinal split into two conflicting forces set into action by Oedipalisation. One half of it is his acknowledgment of "higher formations," an Oedipus personified ("I subject myself as a partial object to the global person who is someone big"), and the other part is his awareness of the existence of the "transcendent laws" ("my own mediocre self tends to align itself with someone big").

Underlying Quin's narrative is a certain schematic grid that renders the entire narrative action mechanical, uncannily automatic, like a round of switching in a game of trading places. No change has taken place; Berg has not escaped his prison, but merely re-shuffled the roles of prisoners and prison-keepers, the mechanism ready for another repeat. And this because he has not cut himself free of, or at least transformed, the only chain link immune to change, the entire storyline's unmoved mover and the crux of all of Berg's problems: the all-excusing, all-forgiving, yet all-pervading mother. It is her incessant pleas that set her son on his futile mission, and her constant carping and nagging, communicated through her letters, holds him back from developing a fully independent persona.

As shown by Francis Booth in his section of *Amongst Those Left* on Quin, "it is his mother from whom Berg needs to be free and not his father" as it turns out "she is the one who is holding him back from a fully independent life if anyone is,"[82] the Oedipal mother of whom the son never lets go. Despite all the split and recoupled doublings and psychoanalytic dynamics of her narrative, Quin in *Berg* creates a story of stuck stasis, of mechanical proceduralism, a narrative of schematisation that at one and the same time parodies and pays homage to the grand narratives of psychoanalysis. The book's warm reception inaugurated Quin's career[83] and won Quin two fellowships which took her on exotic travels from which her subsequent three novels were to draw inspiration.

Quin's second novel, *Three* (1966), was completed during time spent in America on an academic scholarship. *Three* moves a step further than *Berg* in presenting a triangulation of characters matched by a triple narrative mode. The character triangle is composed of Leonard and Ruth, a well-off

---

82   Booth, *Among Those Left*, 501.
83   The *Times Literary Supplement* reviewer called Berg "a most impressive debut" and although not resisting the temptation to align Quin with "such French novelists as Nathalie Sarraute" and the "nouvelle vague (New Wave) movement in the cinema," the review did affirm that *Berg* was "something of a breakthrough in the sense that, for the first time, these techniques have been used to produce a novel that is both wholly English in atmosphere and quite unpretentious" (*Times Literary Supplement* [25 June 1964]: 552).

middle-aged married couple, and "S," a temporary refugee seeking shelter at their house while recovering from an abortion, who disappears (at both the novel's beginning and end), leaving a note that suggests that she may have drowned herself. The three narrative modes (marked as variously typeset blocks) in *Three* are the following: accounts of Leonard and Ruth that detail their actions and conversations in camera-eye, *nouveau romanesque* fashion; transcripts of tape-recordings by S, presented in discontinuous lines akin to free verse; and extracts from Leonard's, Ruth's, and S's journals. The narrative is presented as a process of unveiling, and yet the documents employed that claim to reveal the past end up raising more questions than they resolve. From the very start, ambiguities also arise concerning Leonard and Ruth's possible implication in S's disappearance:

> *A man fell to his death from a sixth-floor window of Peskett House, an office-block in Sellway Square today. He was a messenger employed by a soap manufacturing firm.*
>
> Ruth startled from the newspaper by Leonard framed in the doorway. Against the white-washed wall. A wicker arm-chair opposite the Japanese table. Screen. Sliding doors. Rush matting. A mirror extended the window. Gardens. A bronzed cockerel faced the house.
>
> What's the latest? Fellow thrown himself out of a window. Ghastly way to choose. But Leon hers wasn't like that—I mean we can't really be so sure could so easily have been an accident the note just a melodramatic touch. No one can be blamed Ruth we must understand that least of all ourselves.
>
> (*Th*, 1)

Here, Quin's clinical, objective narrative tone renders a reality perhaps less pathogenic than in *Berg*, but a no less oppressive one: the reality of a dysfunctional childless marriage replete with petty bickering, mutual estrangement, and highly traumatic sexuality. An obsessive accumulation of detail pertains to descriptions both of the physical surroundings and of character action: "The hotel. A room. Three beds. Cupboards that never close. Turn about. Green wallpaper. An old man bears hot chocolate on a silver tray" (*Th*, 22); "Leonard leaned forward, legs apart, body suspended in an enclosed area" (*Th*, 40). In both cases, the most common effect of Quin's camera-eye technique is defamiliarisation. S' diaries—deciphered by both Leonard and Ruth—are less about preserving facts than about asserting a self, and providing a world to go with it. This world is highly autobiographical, as reminiscences of childhood spent at a Catholic convent, often accompanied with punning Joycean blasphemy, suggest:

> Corpus Christ processions.
> Wearing white. Petals thrown.

Kneeling on hot tennis courts. Tarmac clinging. Hymns chanted.
Hell Mary full of grapes. Our Father who farts in Heaven.
(*Th*, 36)

Three's prime interest lies in the tension between the married couple's inner lives and their outer reality, and the disintegrating effect of the absence, from that reality, of the third, silenced member. As Brian Evenson notes, *Three* is a text "whose function is not primarily representational; instead, it is affective, and refuses to stay at a comfortable distance."[84] Quin resists any kind of resolution, preserving ambiguity till the end, which is the narrative's most intriguing, if also frustrating, feature: a frustration that was reflected in the novel's critical reception, far less enthusiastic than with *Berg*.

Passages (1969) forms the third stage of Quin's gradual attenuation of the narrative conventions of plot, temporal continuity, and characters, taking further the process of merging identity with the poetic properties of her prose style. Here, the plotline becomes extremely diffuse, featuring a man and a woman travelling in an unnamed, probably Mediterranean, country beset with political tension, bringing about the couple's suspicions of being under surveillance. Commentators speculate that Quin's travels in Greece and the 1967 military coup might have formed the backdrop. The main driving force of the narrative is, again, established in the opening sentence and sequence; the woman is on the quest after her disappeared brother, whose status is unknown:

> Not that I've dismissed the possibility my brother is dead. We have discussed what is possible, and what is not. They say there's every chance. No chance at all. Over a thousand displaced persons in these parts, perhaps more. So we move on. Towards. Away. Claiming another to take his place, as I place him in profile. Shapes suiting my fancy. Rooms with or without connecting doors. He watches when she isn't around. A perverse protection he knows she needs. From this need
>
> he takes notes. For a book. Journal. Report in some hotel. I no longer question. Parts of him I want to know, others he tells me of. Trips he has made here before. The sea. [...] Light in parts of skin. Movement so near, by stretching my hand into the open
>
> I heard cicadas, wind colliding with trees. Sounding an ocean in the long room. I opened the shutters. Town huddled above the sea. Thin shadows of cypresses.
> (*P*, 5)

Quin once again employs block-form in the narrative, dividing the text into four sections: the first and third can be attributed to the woman, and the

---

84 Evenson, "Introduction," *Three*, xiii.

second and fourth to the man. As is clear from the quote above, the first and third parts consist of paragraphs separated by multiple line spaces, with paragraphs breaking off before a sentence is completed, and the opening words of the following paragraphs completing the sentence, though every now and then the course of the sentence is diverted from its expected track.

The second and fourth segments are composed of the man's notes, possibly for a book, journal, or report, stylistically a pell-mell of aphorisms, definitions of words, mythological allusions, bits of dialogue, notes on the woman's fantasies, descriptions of (or fantasies about) her, and "cut-up dreams" in which elements of two dream-accounts are spliced together. The use of parallel columns adds to the disorienting effect of these passages. The left-hand column includes entries in small type, whereas the entries in the right-hand column are in standard type. A note at the front of *Passages* describes the items written in the left column as the thoughts that provoked the entries in the right column, but the link between the two is open to arbitrary realisation differing from one reading to another.

There are several mythical references in the man's text, especially to Greek mythology. Thus, *Passages* presents a first conscious deployment in Quin's fiction of intertextual linkages.[85] More importantly, they also provide some disquieting linkages between the seemingly separate man's/woman's passages, and these uncanny echoes of the mythical within the everyday mark the emergence of the ancient and the pristine within drab contemporaneity. The novel's final passage, set in the diary-form, ends on a note unresolved to the point of offering a new beginning, a new opening, which resists the final full-stop:

Saturday
So let us begin another journey. Change the setting. Everything is changing, the country, the climate. There is no compromise now. No country we can return to. She still has her obsession to follow through and her fantasies to live out. For myself there is less of an argument. I am for the moment committed to this moment. This train. The distance behind and ahead. And that soon perhaps we will cross
(*P*, 111–2)

Despite both refining the style of Quin's previous novels and deploying hitherto unused techniques, *Passages* was met with an even more lukewarm critical response. For instance, The *TLS* reviewer, even though among the most positive, still complained that "a good deal" of the text was "irritatingly opaque and elliptical" and judged its sole merit to lie in exploring "the con-

---

85 As Nicolas Tredell has observed, many of the Greek references are slightly adapted brief extracts from Jane Harrison's 1903 *Prolegomena to the Study of Greek Religion*, which examines Greek ritual as preliminary to a scientific understanding of Greek religion.

trast between those passages which use words to elucidate and those which attempt to bypass language in search of some expressive manner more comprehensive and simpler than prose."[86]

Quin's last novel *Tripticks* (1972), which draws on her American experience, is her most fragmented text, endowed with a graphic dimension provided by Carol Annand's pop-art style illustrations. The narrative is at its thinnest here, attributed to a male narrator whose opening sentence foregrounds his own multiplicity: "I have many names. Many faces" (*Tr*, 7). The narrator is being pursued by his first "X-wife" and her lover (or possibly he is pursuing them). The pursuit involves car chases, a sojourn in a motel room next to the room occupied by his former wife and her lover, a stay at a CENTRE FOR STUDIES OF THE BODY AND THE SOUL, and finally, a visit to an Indian reservation. Identities further dissolve and disseminate themselves as the chase becomes interspersed with monstrous, comic, and erotic images and anecdotes of the narrator's relationships with his many wives, his mother and stepfather, and with other relatives and prominent strangers.

Sexual explicitness, graphic directness, and the franticness of presentation of the concerns of Quin's earlier novels positions *Tripticks* vis-à-vis her oeuvre in the position assumed by the "Circe" episode in *Ulysses*. Familiar themes are magnified and carnivalised – the narrator again resents and wants to kill his father and, at times, his first X-wife and her lover. Eavesdropping and voyeurism are also prominent, as when the narrator overhears and looks through a keyhole at the lovemaking between his first X-wife and her lover. Finally, he also witnesses the primal scene during which he suffers through "every move, every moan my mother made from my room next to theirs" (*Tr*, 57). *Tripticks* offers a variety of styles and images, operating according to principles of collage which continue to lessen the importance of narrative progression and plot. Linguistically, increasing portions of narrative are occupied with lists – here is the narrator's "statement of personality":

smart, well-educated	Lack of respect for authority
ambitious	lack of spiritual and moral
deep concern for social	fibre
problems	lack of responsibility
good values, character	lack of manners
communicate	lack of dialogue with elders
independent thinker	values ill-defined
poised personality	lack of good study habits
vocal, will speak up	lack of love for fellow men
mature, prepared for	lack of self-respect

---

86   *Times Literary Supplement*, 3 April 1969 (Qtd. in Tredell, "Ann Quin," 236).

life	too impetuous
versatile, able	too introspective
intellectually curious	too introspective
well-groomed	nothing missing
care about community	
(*Tr*, 16)	

A similar cataloguing impetus drives the novel's fetishist depiction of sexuality:

Waitresses clad in bikini bottoms and pasties serve noon-time Bloody Marys and roast-beef sandwiches. We even dressed up for these scenes, and had all the necessary equipment:

Prostitute	half-bra of shimmering satin the sensational lift supported the under bust urging her up and out and leaving her excitingly bare but fully supported.
Lesbian	a penis-aid to assist, non-toxic, flesh-like material with LIFE-LIKE VEINS
Nymphet	grease-resistant – easy to clean. Soft. Pliable.
Flagellist	a raised clitoral stimulator. Comes in three colours.
	EBONY. BROWN. FLESH-COLOUR.

(*Tr*, 40–1)

Quin's critique of the consumerism of contemporary American culture is manifest in her overuse of meaningless acronyms, commodities made of letters that serve a specific ideological purpose:

don't forget to practise Enthusiasm daily APRPBWPRAA (Affirmative Prayers Release Powers By Which Positive Results Are Accomplished). (*Tr*, 35)

Man's wanderlust conquering time. Who's helping to increase his mobility? The R. D. (Re-frocked Diplomat); the M.A. (Mythmaker Allies); D. Gs. (dependent Generals); the N.I.M.H. (National Institute of Mental Health); the D.S.I.A. (Diaper Service Industry Association); S.D.S.A. (State Department Security Agent); and HEW. (*Tr*, 45)

Having abandoned her own version of interior monologue and the polyphony of lyrical narrative voices, Quin's last text is a surprisingly ironic and parodic pastiche targeting some of America's most acute historical-social traumas, especially the ongoing wars in Vietnam. It is not only identities and selves that are in danger of collapsing into each other, it is the very possibility of articulating any self without immediately entangling it in the emptied language of systems of power, ideology, and commodification. In the conclusion, the narrator symbolically—in view of Quin's own impending self-silencing—abjures this power by ceasing to speak: "I opened my mouth, but no words. Only the words of others I saw, like ads, texts, psalms, from those who had attempted to persuade me into their systems. A power I did not want to possess. The Inquisition" (*Tr*, 192).

While the back cover hailed it as a work "prefiguring the formal inventiveness of Kathy Acker" and *Books and Bookmen* praised its exploration of "a verbal continuum somewhere between ambidextrous punpricks, Joycean parody and sub-Burrovian cut-uppery," the reception of the British press was at its chilliest, the *TLS* deploring its "fatal attention to the powerful underlying humourlessness of the whole thing."[87] Soon after completing *Tripticks*, Quin suffered another mental breakdown and spent a month in a London hospital, unable to speak. While at work on her fifth novel, "The Unmapped Country," and compensating for her lack of formal education by enrolling in University of East Anglia to read English, in August 1973, Quin drowned in the sea off her native town of Brighton. Suicide is the unofficial but likely cause.

According to more recent critical estimates, like Giles Gordon's in 2002, Quin's was a unique voice combining a "working-class" sensibility and agenda with "the technical advances of the nouveau roman"[88], a point made even more pronouncedly by Jennifer Hodgson in her preface to *The Unmapped Country*: "Quin was a rare breed in British writing: radically experimental, working class and a woman [...] on a search for the spiritual antipodes of her homeland, which she depicts in her writing as buttoned-up, repressed, and mildewed around the edges."[89] Quin's experimental novels exhibit a profound sensitiveness to the workings of the mind and consciousness as always determined by language and perceptual processes. Stevick recounts an anecdote in which Quin's psychiatrist, treating her in 1970, requested for copies of her novels as therapeutic material. A request which might be viewed as naïve, yet appears "perceptive and compassionate," for in Stevick's conclusion, Quin's novels "do give a record of a mind that is, at once, artful, distanced, dispassionate and raw, immediate, its tensions unresolved."[90]

Quin's idiosyncratic combination of themes and techniques gave rise to a style unique in its powerful energy and disorienting effects, gradually abandoning depiction of consciousness for the sake of exploring the workings of language and the possibilities of their typographic representation.

---

87 *Times Literary Supplement* (5 May 1972), qtd. in Tredell, "Ann Quin," 237.

88 Giles Gordon, "Reading Ann Quin's *Berg*." Introduction to Ann Quin, *Berg* (Chicago: Dalkey Archive, 2001) ix.

89 Jennifer Hodgson, "Introduction," *The Unmapped Country: Stories & Fragments* (London: And Other Stories, 2018) 7–8.

90 Stevick continues: "And that is what makes those four novels so powerful and so unusual. They take the self and others, one's voice, the voice of the nonself into areas not quite occupied before. "I opened my mouth, but no words," reads the end of Quin's last novel, *Tripticks*, with an accent that, even now, startles" ("Voices in the Head," 239).

The recent resurgence of academic interest in the long-forgotten work of Ann Quin is well-deserved, for hers is an uncanny ability to lampoon psychoanalysis and other authoritative discourses of the late 1960s, and to ventriloquise high literary experiment while employing the popular genre of the thriller, in order to deal with the stark reality of 1960s working class.

2.6 "WHO'S SHE WHEN SHE'S (NOT) AT HOME": CHRISTINE BROOKE-ROSE (1964–1975)

"The Great British Experimentalist You've Never Heard of" was the title of Natalie Ferris' obituary, published in *The Guardian* two days after Christine Brooke-Rose's death on March 21, 2012. Apart from other issues, Ferris' graceful review of her life and work raised the (unanswered) question of whether "Brooke-Rose ever was really with us."[91] Tracing Brooke-Rose's lifelong engagement with verbal lipogrammatic experimentation, Stuart Jeffries—also of *The Guardian*—wrote in a similar vein of Brooke-Rose's estrangement from Britain: "As if to continue the theme of erasure, Britain has all but airbrushed one of its most radical exponents of experimental fiction. When Brooke-Rose published a volume of criticism in 2002, it was not, perhaps, entirely devotion to Roland Barthes' death of the author thesis that led her to call it *Invisible Author*."[92]

Christine Brooke-Rose[93] escapes easy compartmentalisation on many levels – first and foremost, by standing in between the French *nouveau ro-*

---

91   Natalie Ferris, "The Great British Experimentalist You've Never Heard Of," *The Guardian* (23 Mar 2012). Online: https://www.theguardian.com/books/2012/mar/23/christine-brooke-rose.

92   Stuart Jeffries, "Christine Brooke-Rose Obituary," *The Guardian* (23 Mar 2012). Online: https://www.theguardian.com/books/2012/mar/23/christine-brooke-rose1.

93   Born in Geneva to a Swiss-American mother and a British father, Brooke-Rose (whose combined surnames attest to the double parentage) grew up speaking French, English and German. It was not until after the separation of her parents (in 1929) and the death of her father (in 1934) that she moved with her mother to Brussels, and two years later (in 1936) to Britain. Her polyglotism stood her in good stead during World War II and her work for Bletchley Park, assessing intercepted German communications. After the War, she pursued an academic career, gaining a PhD in Middle English from University College London in 1954. Having defended her dissertation on medieval French and English literature and already written a few early novels in the "traditional" vein (e.g., her first novel, *Languages of Love*, 1956), in 1962 she herself suffered a serious illness during which she was convinced she would die. After recovery she achieved a new level of consciousness which she has described as "a sense of being in touch with something else – death perhaps." In 1968, Brooke-Rose left her husband and accepted a post at the newly created Université de Paris VIII at Vincennes, where she taught for twenty years before retiring in 1988 to the south of France to concentrate on her novel-writing. Brooke-Rose died on 21 March 2012, aged 89. For a more detailed overview of Brooke-Rose's life and work, cf. David Vichnar, "Whose Afrayed of Christine Brooke-Rose; Or, Tribute to the Great British Enigma," *Subtexts* (Prague: Litteraria Pragensia Books, 2015) 85–103.

man and British experimental fiction of the 1960s/1970s and after. As Frank
Kermode observed in his evaluation of Brooke-Rose's *Thru* on the back
cover of the 1986 Carcanet *Brooke-Rose Omnibus*, "if we are to experience
in English the serious *practice* of narrative as the French have developed it
over the last few years, we shall have to attend to Christine Brooke-Rose."
Sarah Birch, author of the pioneering and highly useful critical study on
Brooke-Rose's fiction, takes this remark by the author herself as a key to
understanding her fiction:

> I deal in discourses, in the discourses of the world, political, technological, scientific,
> psychoanalytical, philosophical, ideological, social, emotional, and all the rest, so that
> knowledge to me is not an extraneous element I can put in or withhold at will, it *is*
> discourse, it *is* language [...] the source of most of my comic effects is the grafting to-
> gether, or onto each other, of all these different discourses [...] Discourse comes from
> Latin *discurrere, to run here and there*. It has today become whole sets of rigid uses, and
> I am trying to make it run here and there again.[94]

According to Birch, what this key opens is access to "the common denomina-
tor of all Brooke-Rose's fiction, [...] the prismatic effect of viewing one field
of knowledge, one language, or one culture through the discursive lens of
another, and the idea of crossing between cultural domains is manifest in
her novels as a structural principle." It is in this sense that, paradoxically,
"her novels are more realistic, if not more realist, than those of many of her
contemporaries."[95]

Brooke-Rose's criticism constitutes in itself an admirable body of work,
comprising *The Grammar of Metaphor* (1958), *A ZBC of Ezra Pound* (1971), and
most notably, *A Rhetoric of the Unreal: Studies in Narrative and Structure* (1981)
as well as *Stories, Theories, and Things* (1991). Almost symbiotically, her critical
work deals with the intellectual sources and theoretical preoccupations of
her fiction: contemporary science; post-Saussurean theories of language and
discourse (particularly Derridean, Lacanian, and Foucauldian); the technical achievements of Ezra Pound, Samuel Beckett, and the *nouveaux romanciers*; feminist and gender theory; and Mikhail Bakhtin's theory of the novel.
Underwriting all these concerns is Brooke-Rose's "passionate concern with
language" which she claims to share with "Pound and Beckett."[96] In terms of
his importance for Brooke-Rose as a writer, Joyce receives repeated mentions
as a significant precursor to the anti-novelistic explorations of the present-

---

94   Brooke-Rose, "Ill wit and good humour: women's comedy and the canon," *Comparative Criticism*,
     Vol. 10, ed. E. S. Shaffer (Cambridge: Cambridge University Press, 1988) 129.
95   Birch, *Christine Brooke-Rose*, 3.
96   Ibid, 9–10.

tense narrative sentence—notably, more as the author of *Finnegans Wake* than of *Ulysses*. In *A Rhetoric of the Unreal*, Brooke-Rose writes:

> The use of the present tense throughout, first by Dujardin, then by Gertrude Stein, then by Joyce in *Finnegans Wake*, and later by Robbe-Grillet and others, clearly flattens out all such clear markings in a perpetual present. "A continuous present is a continuous present," wrote Gertrude Stein as if it were a rose. (*RU*, 313)

Ten years later, only the focus shifts, but the viewpoint remains the same:

> Robbe-Grillet (1962) loudly dismissed the *passé simple* as the hallmark of the traditional novel, and adopted (after Dujardin and Joyce in *Finnegans Wake*) the present tense, which he used in a brilliantly unsettling manner (since time-shifts are necessarily unmarked), though this was soon more weakly imitated. (*STT*, 78)[97]

Opening her first tetralogy of experimental texts with *Out*, a futuristic tale set in Africa, Brooke-Rose launched her lifelong exploration of one crucial literary constraint: the present-tense narrative sentence which in a lipogrammatic structure replaces traditional past tense narration, traced by Brooke-Rose herself in her essay "The Author is Dead: Long Live the Author" to the context of the French *nouveau roman*.[98] The narrative of *Out* microscopically depicts a sick and unemployed white male who spends most of his time being tended to by his wife in their small shack, inhabiting a post-apocalyptic world which bears the effects of a radical reversal of black on white, "negative" on positive. Of crucial concern, then, are issues of racial inequality through a reversal in the values historically (i.e., colonially) attached to the white/black binary: "Through all the false identities that we build, the love-making, the trauma-seeking, the alchemising of anecdote to legend, of episode to myth, what really happened to us?" (*O*, 120). Thus, already at the outset of her career, Brooke-Rose dealt with the macroscopic themes of history, identity-building, trauma, and "alchemising" mythopoesis reminiscent of the concerns of Joyce's alter-ego, Shem the "last alshemist," in *Finnegans Wake* (FW 185.34).

Such uses a similar subversive strategy to deconstruct the psychoanalytic discourse by means of astrophysics. Featured in its first half under the name of "Someone," psychiatrist Larry comes back in the second half from a state of clinical death, after a prolonged coma and a period of next-to-zero mental activity. His convalescence features an extended lecture on the prin-

---

97   For a more detailed discussion of Brooke-Rose's criticism, see Chapter Five.
98   Brooke-Rose, *Invisible Author: Last Essays* (Columbus: The Ohio State University Press, 2002) 130–56.

ciples of astrophysics, paired with an indirect critique of the discourse of psychoanalysis in which it becomes apparent, as Birch has observed, that "reconstruction or aetiology of a patient's illness is impossible," since the analytic process itself "would alter the unconscious memories and fantasies that constitute traces of the origin of an illness."[99] From the narratological viewpoint, *Such* is the beginning of a series of Brooke-Rose's novels exploring the expressive form in which form conveys content. Staging the death of her white, male protagonist, Brooke-Rose simultaneously stages the death of traditional realistic narrative. Or, more accurately, she "stages the life and death of narrative in the fits and starts of the story."[100] More interestingly still, *Such* is an early instance of Brooke-Rose's link to the Joycean poetics, in particular, the aesthetics of cinematic phantasmagoria that informs the "Circe" chapter of *Ulysses*.[101]

Larry's first ordeal in the otherworld is suffering a heavy woman to squat on his chest, "her huge buttocks in my face" (*S*, 203), just as in Nighttown, Bella/Bello Cohen squats on Bloom's upturned face. Larry's otherworldly hallucination procreates five children (who are also planets) with the names of classic blues songs—Dippermouth Blues, Gut Bucket Blues, Potato Head Blues, Tin Roof Blues, Really the Blues; a motif bearing striking resemblance to Bloom's fantasy of giving birth to eight miraculous children (Nasodoro, Goldfinger, Chrysostomos, Maindorée, Silversmile, Silberselber, Vifargent, and Panargyros).[102] As far as possible experimental inspirations informing *Such* are concerned, the much less tenuous (and author-corroborated) link is the title's obvious reference to the *Tel Quel*, however much played down by Brooke-Rose herself: "I got it from *Tel Quel*, which I was reading. And it's not easy because I say once or twice, 'interested in things as such.'"[103]

While *Out* and *Such* explore the discursive limitations and inherent or mutual incompatibilities between "science" and "fiction"—the science of fiction and fictionality of science—while their hybridity remains largely on

---

99   Birch, *Christine Brooke-Rose*, 66.
100 Lawrence, *Techniques for Living*, 53.
101 For more see Brian McHale, "'I draw the line as a rule between one solar system and another': The Postmodernism(s) of Christine Brooke-Rose," *Utterly Other Discourse: the Texts of Christine Brooke-Rose*, eds. Ellen G. Friedman & Richard Martin (Chicago: Dalkey Archive Press, 1995) 195.
102 According to McHale, the reason these and other examples cannot be straightforwardly treated as explicit references to Joyce, is that in November 1990, Brooke-Rose avowed to him in personal communication that she had been "a latecomer to Joyce" and denied having read *Ulysses* prior to the publication of *Such*. Here is McHale on the matter: "More to the point, perhaps, is the peculiar character of the 'Circe' chapter itself, which makes it all but immune to postmodernist parody. For 'Circe' is itself already a parody of modernism; it already stands in a parodic relation to the modernist poetics of the earlier chapters of *Ulysses*. 'Circe,' that is, is one of those chapters of Joyce's text [...] in which Joyce seems already to have outstripped modernist poetics [...] and to anticipate modernism" (McHale, "The Postmodernism(s) of Christine Brooke-Rose," 195).
103 Qtd. in Lawrence, *Techniques for Living*, 214.

the conceptual level, *Between* (1969) deals with a complexity of the linguistic kind. The employment of the expressive form in *Between* presents both a narrative *of* and narrative *as* a journey. The narrative traces a nameless protagonist ("A woman of uncertain age uncertain loyalties" [B, 445]) whose life story locates her on the boundary between France (her French mother, dead), Germany (her German father, disappeared), and England (her husband, divorced). Her vocation only enhances her transitional state – a simultaneous translator (French to German) who is always "between conferences."

The principle of narrative organisation, then, is formed in the verbal consciousness of the protagonist, as it traces two overlapping lines: the saga of the protagonist's marriage annulment, and a series of love-letters written in medieval French, eventually discovered to be from an ageing Frenchman and terminated after the first tryst and the realisation that "fornication by airmail" is more enjoyable than the real thing. The metaphoric networks that bind together *Between*'s thematic sequences are centred on two chief images: enclosure (her body afloat in the bellies of countless airplanes or huddled between the sheets in countless hotel rooms) and intercourse (her mind a crossroad where languages meet, a locus of multilingualism). A sustained metaphor parallels the blending of linguistic and cultural codes with sexual act:

> As if languages loved each other behind their own façades, despite alles was man denkt darüber davon dazu. As if words fraternised silently beneath the syntax, finding each other funny and delicious in a Misch-Masch of tender fornication, inside the bombed out hallowed structures and the rigid steel glass modern edifices of the brain. Du, do you love me? (B, 445)

Or later, at the disappointing tryst with her French *amour* épistolaire:

> E allora the languages fraternise a little as he sips his mineral water without the ice under the staring southern eyes that well yes burn. Why do you speak in English? To remind me of the old days and my youth as a simultaneous interpreter of ideas nobody ever acts upon? Vous n'aimez pas ma langue? La langue de mes lettres? La langue—and the tip of his tongue peers out, moves slowly round his open lips, then in, then slowly out again, and in, and out in a dumb show pour éveiller en vous tous les désirs mais si. (B, 548)

Besides the implications of linguistic intercourse (fraternisation) as essentially incestuous, Brooke-Rose's experiment in *Between* goes further than trivial macaronics. Destabilisation of signification occurs on both single-word and discursive levels. In sentences such as "the words prevent any true EXCHANGE caught in the late afternoon sun that stripes the airport hall between the slats of the venetian blinds on the vast wall of glass" (B, 399), the word "EXCHANGE" starts operating performatively, changing the course of the sentence. In a passage like "Have you anything to declare such as love desire ambition or a glimpse that in this air-conditioning and other circumstantial emptiness freedom has its sudden attractions as the body floats in willing suspension of responsibility to anyone" (B, 422), customs declaration turns into a declaration of love. Apart from interlinguistic intercourse, Brooke-Rose also uses syntax to enhance the expressive form of her text, a syntax which engages in transgression, in that sentences often wander along unpredictable trajectories, replete with metonymic slides that produce a sense of the random movement of the protagonist.

As critics (e.g., Birch) have noted, *Between* is "a verbal lipogram" in that it avoids the use of the verb "to be" in any of its forms, performing its insistence on the need to "be" "tween," that is to say, "be two," a becoming that resists unity and identity by remaining twofold. Just as the identity of meaning (which any one language imposes upon an object by calling it its name) disappears in confrontation with any other language and such identity, so should, Brooke-Rose implies, all other identities (mistakenly) believed to be non-linguistic: "We live in an age of transition wouldn't you agree and must cope as best we can" (B, 476). However, it would be an oversimplification to regard the narrative of *Between* as somehow devoid of distinct temporal/spatial/linguistic coordinates. Despite all the rush, mobility, and in-betweenness of both the style and the traveller, Brooke-Rose does provide checkpoints in the fluid movement across boundaries; despite its use of the present tense and abandonment of temporal sequence, *Between* still does relate its "present" moment to a specific European geography and history: particularly, the Germany in (the immediate aftermath of) World War II. This aspect presents *Between* at its most personal: Brooke-Rose herself characterised it as based on "two non-experiences of the author (simultaneous interpretation, woman as passive transmitter) fused with genuine experiences of worldviews (stories, etc.) to produce an imaginative experience that rang true, at least to the author" (STT, 7).

Unlike the case of *Tel Quel*, Brooke-Rose is rather sceptical as regards her own ties with the Oulipo group. The lipogrammatic technique in Brooke-Rose's use is primarily concerned with lexicon, grammar, or syntax, and not letters as in the French "Workshop of potential literature." In a late interview, Brooke-Rose dismissed Lawrence's parallel between her work and Georges Perec's by claiming that "one has to keep in control with the constraints. And with some constraints, one doesn't really see the point. I've never understood the point of writing a novel without the letter *e*," and specifies her own attitude to the technique:

To me, a constraint must be a grammatical or a syntactical constraint, part of the syntax, not a letter. But that may be a prejudice, about form. Because that becomes going through dictionaries and looking for words. I mean, like him. But I don't see the point. [... Perec] announced it loud and long, so it was known. I didn't say anything about no verb 'to be' until much later. And then it did get repeated, but without further comment.[104]

As Chapter Four of this book will show, Perec's omission of the letter *e* from *La Disparition / A Void* has some specific—and poignantly personal as well as historically tragic—reasons. Thus, Brooke-Rose's dismissal of Perec and the constraint-based experimentation of the Oulipo group might have more to do with her tastes or indeed "prejudices about form," her own personal need for distinction and distancing, rather than with substantial differences between the two lipogramatic approaches.

Taking yet another direction in the last part of her tetralogy, Brooke-Rose's *Thru* carries the parodic tactics of *Between* a step further by turning away from the discourse of culture in the wide sense towards the discourse of the self-reflexive plane of metafiction, used here in reference to its definition in Waugh as "a tendency *within* the novel which operates through exaggeration of the tensions and oppositions inherent in all novels: of frame and frame-break, of technique and counter-technique, of construction and deconstruction of illusion."[105] It is perhaps this overt self-reflexivity and verbal innovativeness that links Brooke-Rose's text to Joyce's final opus, though to call it "an offshoot of *Finnegans Wake*,"[106] like Levitt does, would be an overstatement disregarding its individual concerns which are markedly different from those of the *Wake*.

Departing from the opening reference to a rear-view mirror ("le rétro viseur [...] some languages more visible than others" [*T*, 579]), critic Hanjo Berressem is more spot-on in likening *Thru* to Carroll's *Through the Looking Glass*, showing how "the text immediately begins to reflect not only faces but other texts," largely from linguistics, literature as well as structuralist and post-structuralist theory, and links the opening question "Who speaks?" to Lacan's essay on desire in the Freudian Unconscious, rendered here as "Qui parle?," reflected in *Thru* by the otherwise unaccountable slide into French.[107] If individual parodies challenge specific theories and texts by Derrida, Lacan, and French poststructuralist feminists, *Thru* takes as its guiding narrative tool Propp's anatomy of folk-tales, its characters turned into variables with

---

104   Ibid, 206–7.

105   Patricia Waugh, *Metafiction: The Theory and Practice of Conscious Fiction* (London: Methuen, 1984) 14.

106   Levitt, *Modernist Survivors*, 24.

107   Berressem continues: "The shift into French facilitates the metamorphosis of an object (driving mirror) into a subject (le viseur). It links the spatial image of a subject caught between images originating from behind which are projected forward by the mirror to Lacan's notion of a decentered, barred subject which can recognize itself only by projecting its past into the future" (Hanjo Berressem, "*Thru* the Looking Glass: A Journey into the Universe of Discourse," *Review of Contemporary Fiction* 9.3 [Fall 1989]: 128).

constant functions. The dynamics of reflection finds its morphological enactment in the names of principal characters, generated from within the text:

> I am in fact dead, Jacques. Oh, he's asleep. What a pity. Everything becoming clear at
> last. God! No! Yes! Quick, pen and paper.
> ARMEL SANTORES
> LARISSA TOREN
> Yes! It figures. So that's why she said about Armel not finding his ME in her and she
> not finding her I. Why the names are anagrams. Except for Me in hers and I in his. Am
> I going mad? Help!
> (*T*, 647)

The obsession on the part of Brooke-Rose's narrative subjects with decoding
and unveiling is also manifest in one of the strategies that the text employs
in order to—as it were—read itself: mesostics, the technique famously
employed in John Cage's "Roaratorio," which followed the letters "JAME-
SJOYCE" through the text of the *Wake*. For example, the question on page 583,
"Who's she when she's at home?" is answered on the next page as:

> fan**G**s
>   c**R**uel
>   bo**A**rish
> bea**M**
>   **M**oat
>   **E**tc
>   alrea**D**y   (all read eyes)
>
>   na**I**ls
>   **N**ails
>
> upon **T**hese
> eyes of t**H**ine I'll
>   s**E**t
>
> the re**M**ote s**T**one
> **W**ide   **E**yes w**E**t?
> p**A**rch **M**ent wa**X**
> ar**X**i   st**O**ne   **T**race
>   d**R**y
>   pap**Y**rus
>   eye'**S**
>
> (*T*, 584)

That is, "grammed in the wax memory's text." Mesostics give way to reams of interior monologue devoted to punning and paronomasia, as when Larissa puns: "Are adagia functions? arbitrary? obituary? a bit awry? a bit aware?" (*T*, 632). While it would be reductive to claim an exclusively Joycean heritage for these and other textual effects, it is easy to see how they take shape in the multifarious discourses of French poststructuralism, which originated, explicitly and consciously, within the sphere of Joyce's influence—cf., e.g., the "Lacanian" pun that renders syntagmatics as "SIN TAG MA TICKS" (*T*, 581), linking its 'SINful TAGging' to its obsession with the mother figure ("MA TICKS").

Significantly, Brooke-Rose avails herself of a strategy whose genealogy stretches as far back as Freud (even though, in *Thru*, Lacan is a far more pervasive presence) and whose potential for literature has been best exploited by Joyce's materialist poetics: the pun. As Brooke-Rose explicitly states in the text, "the pun is free, anarchic, a powerful instrument to explode the civilization of the sign and all its stable, reassuring definitions, to open up its static, monstrous logic of expectation into a different dialectic with the reader" (*T*, 607). Hence, again, the aims and uses of Brooke-Rose's employment of the technique are decidedly her own and not derivative from Joyce's. She is far more concerned with how the workings of the pun undermine scientific, theoretic discourse, or indeed the claims of univocity of discourse as such. While destabilising and dissolving the realist idea of "character," Brooke-Rose novelises the supposedly distanced and logical position of "theory" and shows it to be a function of desire, an endless, for circular, dissemination of meaning:

> Revolution is not an institution. We demand the abolishing of all idylls and a complete reorganisation of generating structures. Truth is an outmoded institution. Precisely. Words imply the absence of things just as desire implies the absence of its object. [...] Words seeking to be true become false and inversely, words seeking to be false become true. We end up experiencing the feelings that we pretend, one can't speak, or write, with impunity. (*T*, 725–6)

Brooke-Rose herself considered this "novel about the theory of the novel, that is, a narrative about narrativity, a fiction about fictionality, a text about intertextuality" as "her best and most daring book in the self-reflexive genre," even though "the external harm this book did to her reputation as incomprehensible and pretentious was lasting and profound."[108] The charge of pretension is surely more misguided than that of incomprehensibility, for issues of meaning, comprehension, their limits as well as limitations, are

---

108 Brooke-Rose, *Stories, Theories and Things*, 8.

precisely what Brooke-Rose's exploration of the unconscious must address by necessity. Brooke-Rose's chief concern is, as always, representation and representability.[109] *Thru*, then, ends as it must do: within the dissemination of possible endings, the story finally "tells itself," and the final words of the narrator are written acrostically into the narration: "exeunt narrators with a swift switch of signifiers no more I superimposing" (*T*, 735). The final sentence, then, takes up the initial mirror image and shows again the subject gliding on its lonely night-ride journey.

Despite *Thru*'s circularity, extreme self-reflexivity, and deep immersion in the French theory of the 1960s to mid-70s, Joyce's name does not feature in the concluding five-page list of "sem(id)Idiotic irrecoverable narrators gone" (*T*, 737)—but this might be simply because he *is* recoverable and *not* "gone," for a linguistically materialist and neologistically innovative poetics following in the footsteps of Joyce's revolution of language was yet to develop in Brooke-Rose's second novel tetralogy written and published in the course of the 1980s. First, however, the argument digresses into a comparative discussion of 1960s literary experiment in American fiction.

---

109 "How does one hold up a mirror to the unconscious? How adjust the mirror to represent that which is missing from view? And how to do so, particularly when the unnamed male driver at the beginning of the novel seems to control the 'intensity of illusion' in the driving mirror?" (Lawrence, *Techniques for Living*, 85).

3.
MAKING JOYCE
"PART OF THE LANDSCAPE":
THE AMERICAN LITERARY EXPERIMENT,
1953–1973

Just as its British counterpart, the American fiction of the conservative 1950s was one generally opposed to formal innovation. Ronald Sukenick, one of the key writers of the 1970s who opposed literary conservatism, characterised the decade as "august and self-confident" in its pursuit of "the tradition of the 'great novel'," in which writing even as radical as Joyce's came to be neutralised:

> The important thing about *Ulysses* was not that it called into question the very fictive tradition it epitomized, but that it was a "great novel," one in a series. Only that could explain the awe in which it was held and the totality with which it was ignored by fiction in the fifties. Fiction at that time paid a great deal of lip service to Joyce, Kafka, Lawrence, Proust, Faulkner and literary modernism, but somehow all that had very little to do with us, with fiction in America.[1]

Although presenting a rough generalisation about the American 1950s—whose conservatism and reactionism also produced the Beats, Burroughs, and Gaddis—Sukenick's chief point is valid: two very different lessons are learned if *Ulysses* is taken as yet another "great novel" whose cultural status is to be capitalised upon, or as a subversive text undermining the very possibility of novelistic tradition. These two lessons also yield a very different kind of knowledge and creative practice.

Donald Barthelme's observation (recorded by Jerome Klinkowitz) to the effect that Joyce should be "taken as part of the landscape, around which the reader's life could be slowly appreciated, like one's home or neighborhood"[2] is particularly noteworthy in that here, a short-story writer acknowledges the importance of Joyce *not* as the writer of *Dubliners*, but of *Finnegans Wake*. Although part of the landscape, Joyce was by no means the sole landmark or centre around which the scene would revolve.

Apart from his Modernist co-pioneers (Kafka and Proust), as well as his American colleagues and Paris acquaintances, there were at least two other

1   Ronald Sukenick, "Fiction in the Seventies," *In Form: Digressions on the Act of Fiction* (Carbondale/Edwardsville: Southern Illinois University Press, 1985) 35. For more on Sukenick, cf. Chapter Six.
2   *The New Fiction – Interviews with Innovative American Writers*, ed. Joe David Bellamy (Urbana/Chicago/London: University of Illinois Press, 1974) 45.

writers whose influence was almost universal in the American fiction of the 1960s: the Argentinian Jorge Luis Borges and the Russian émigré Vladimir Nabokov. Both acknowledged Joyce as a shaping influence, both conducted lifelong "infinite conversations"[3] with Joyce. Borges' stretched from his early admiration for and support of *Ulysses* in the mid-1920s to his attendance of the centennial 1982 Dublin Joyce Symposium; Nabokov's took place in his lectures on Joyce's *Ulysses* presented at Harvard in 1951–52, and throughout his two decades of academic tenure at Wellesley and Cornell University. Both Borges' and Nabokov's lifelong preoccupations with Joyce have been the subject of much critical work, which highlights their ill-ease with specific phases or facets of his work (particularly, the *Wake*), their own artistic programmes, and other influences: in a word, their profound *dissimilarity* from Joyce.[4]

Still, for the generation of American writers coming of age in the 1960s, James Joyce is a stable reference point in their creative remapping of the landscape of the literary tradition. Given their shared engagement in multinational, cross-cultural redefining of contemporary fiction, it is legitimate to raise questions about their national specificity – how to construct their "Americanness." Bernard Bergonzi, whose derogatory remarks addressed at the British novel were quoted already in the introduction to the previous chapter, singled out the triad of "the tragic, the violent, and the comic" as underlying the specifically American novel and ensuring it would not quite fall into the straight-jacket of British conventionalism:

> The conventions of the realist novel may be upheld, but only for as long as it suits the author; at any moment they may be undermined by some unashamedly fantastic or surrealist device. The characters are in no sense "rounded" or "substantial" [...]. The author is a whole-hearted manipulator, whose consciousness of what he is doing dominates the whole novel. And his powers of manipulation frequently extend to the reader, who is likely to be involved in every kind of trap and mystification.[5]

Bergonzi's diagnosis is a mere elaboration on John Hawkes' creed, famously expressed in a 1965 interview, that "I began to write fiction on the assumption that the true enemies of the novel were plot, character, setting and theme,"[6]

---

3   Cf. Patricia Novillo-Corvalán, *Borges and Joyce – An Infinite Conversation* (Leeds: Maney Publishing, 2011) for a detailed discussion of the Borges-Joyce relationship.

4   For more, see the overviews of Borges' and Nabokov's relationships with Joyce in César Augusto Salgado's "Barroco Joyce: Jorge Luis Borges' and José Lezama Lima's Antagonistic Readings," *Transcultural Joyce*, ed. Karen Lawrence (Cambridge: Cambridge University Press, 1998) 63–93, as well as the above-mentioned study by Patricia Novillo-Corvalán, and Julian Moynahan's article, "Nabokov and Joyce," *Garland Companion to Vladimir Nabokov*, ed. Vladimir Alexandrov (New York: Routledge, 1995) 433–44.

5   Bernard Bergonzi, *The Situation of the Novel* (London: Macmillan, 1970/1979) 82–3.

6   John Hawkes, "An Interview," *Wisconsin Studies in Contemporary Literature* (Summer 1965): 149.

and his notions of narrative manipulation, of the mixture of realism "as long as it suits" with the fantastic and surrealist, apply to Hawkes as well as all the six writers covered in this chapter.

The reasons for this American "progressivism" are as numerous and complex as those for the comparative reactionism of the English novel: it has been pointed out that unlike in Britain, America "never had a bourgeois class with homogeneous reading habits,"[7] and so the realist novel never took as deep a root within its fiction, always preceded and dominated by the Puritan heritage of the religious mode of allegory and by the romantic mode of symbolism, as argued by English critic Walter Allen: "Indeed, symbolism seems to be the specifically American way of apprehending and rendering experience in literature. It is not the English way. And allegory and symbolism are ingrained in the American sensibility for good reasons: they are part of the heritage of Puritanism."[8] In searching for "internal" reasons, some critics like Bergonzi took aboard the Americans' relation to the English language, going so far as to speak of a sense of linguistic estrangement akin to that of Joyce's Stephen Dedalus: "The American writer will take nothing for granted; he has to forge his own style as a basic act of self-definition [...] Whereas young American writers think that novels must be written, with a full concentration of resources, young English writers seem merely to exude them."[9]

These sentiments are echoed in the introduction to Tony Tanner's epochal account of the post-war era, the appropriately titled *City of Words – American Fiction 1950–1970*, which starts by juxtaposes the dream and nightmare of American literature: the dream that "an unpatterned, unconditioned life is possible, in which your movements and stillnesses, choices and repudiations are all your own" with the dread that "someone else is patterning your life, that there all sorts of invisible plots afoot to rob you of your autonomy of thought and action, that conditioning is ubiquitous."[10] Tanner traces this dialectics all the way back to the great American romantics, especially Hawthorne, Melville, and Poe, making a case for conceiving of this bipolarity as an American cultural constant by engaging, in the three Appendices to his volume, with the discourses of social anthropology, behavioural psychology, and linguistics. According to Tanner, the paradox peculiar to the post-war writer is of a distinctly linguistic nature:

If he wants to write in any communicable form he must traffic in a language which may at every turn be limiting, directing and perhaps controlling his responses and for-

---

7   Per Gedin, *Literature in the Market Place* (London 1977) 186.
8   Walter Allen, *Tradition and Dream* (London: Dent, 1966) xvi.
9   Bergonzi, *The Situation of the Novel*, 67–9.
10   Tony Tanner, *City of Words – American Fiction 1950–1970* (London: Jonathan Cape, 1971) 15.

mulations. If he feels that the given structuring of reality of the available language is imprisoning or iniquitous, he may abandon language altogether; or he may seek to use the existing language in such a way that he demonstrates to himself and other people that he does not accept nor wholly conform to the structures built into the common tongue [...] Any writer has to struggle with existing language which is perpetually tending to rigidify in old formulations, and he must constantly assert his own patterning powers without at the same time becoming imprisoned in *them*.[11]

On top of these can be added the existing languages of the writer's predecessors: As the paradigms of Borges and Nabokov show, Joyce's influence was hardly ever unanimously accepted in post-war US literature, especially as regards the related questions of the usefulness and (in)imitability of his example, or indeed the possibility of going beyond it. In comparison with the UK, there were no Kingsley Amises or C. P. Snows in the US letters to react against modernist experiment and consider Joyce a "cul-de-sac." However, nor was there an Anthony Burgess or a B. S. Johnson to argue for Joyce's essential import for their writing. Tanner's comparison with the English novel of manners stretches along the following lines:

The American writer has much less sense of a stable society which his hero encounters and enters – the process by which the European hero usually gains an identity. The institutions, even the buildings, of American society have never had this stability [...] hence the perpetually dissolving cityscapes, and the sense of moving among insubstantial ephemera, to be found throughout contemporary American fiction. This is one reason [...] why there is much less interest in conventional character study and analysis in it than in contemporary English fiction.[12]

In order to map and make sense of the development of American experimental fiction written post-war and in the wake of Joyce, this chapter will be devoted to revisiting the heritage of William S. Burroughs, William Gaddis, John Barth, William H. Gass, Donald Barthelme, and Thomas Pynchon.

3.1 "A NEW MYTHOLOGY FOR THE SPACE AGE": WILLIAM S. BURROUGHS

As many of his biographers record, an early promoter of psychedelic drugs, William Seward Burroughs had to flee the States for Mexico in 1949 in order to escape impending detention at the Angola state prison. He would later

---

11   Tanner, *City of Words*, 16.
12   Ibid, 151.

recall the accidental killing, in 1951, of his wife Joan Vollmer as an event which "motivated and formulated my writing" since "the death of Joan brought me in contact with the invader, the Ugly Spirit, and manoeuvred me into a lifelong struggle, in which I have had no choice except to write my way out" (Q, xxiii).

Many have documented (most authoritatively, Barry Miles' seminal biography)[13] how Burroughs' nickname, *el hombre invisible*—earned with Spanish street kids in Tangier in the late 1950s, complimenting his skill at slipping untraceably through narrow alleys to score a drug fix—was symbolically apposite for the tortuous life of a figure notoriously ambiguous and difficult to pin down. American by origin and nationality and an exile during his formative years as a writer; a Harvard English literature graduate from a well-to-do family, yet for most of his life an underdog and never-to-do-well; both an associate and close friend of many of the Beatniks, yet always apart and different from them; a husband and father turned into an open and misogynist homosexual; both a lifelong drug user and a staunch instigator against addiction of any kind; both an outcast and outlaw, as well as a pop-cultural icon. More pertinently still, Burroughs' textual existence is as dubious and open to critical conjecture: so many of his works have remained in an indefinite, non-definitive, "flawed," or otherwise doubtful state, or exist in multiple editions and variants, this from his earliest novel *Junkie/Junky* with a variation in its very title to the late re-editions and re-writes of many of his juvenilia. This is largely due to Burroughs' practice of constant revision of even published material, as well as to his reliance on outside advice concerning the final organisation of his material.

This invisibility also shrouded Burroughs in a spectral omnipresence as character, dedicatee, or honorary mention in much of the work of his contemporaries, particularly of the Beat generation whose éminence grise he had become. Oliver Harris' study presents a list of the Beats' works marked by Burroughs' presence,[14] and while conceding that Burroughs has always been "tangential to the movement – its elder statesman, godfather, mentor, or tutelary spook," Harris insists that "those who think that Burroughs' early texts can now be read outside the Beat context, taken out like a picture from an old frame, should think again" since all four of his 1950s texts come "framed in some way by Beat reference, none of which actually dates from that decade," most markedly in the case of *Junky*, which features Allen Gins-

---

13   Barry Miles, *William Burroughs: El Hombre Invisible* (New York: Hyperion, 1994).

14   Prominent among these are Kerouac's *The Town and the City*, John Clellon Holmes' *Go*, Gregory Corso's *The American Express*, Ginsberg's dedication of "Howl" (1956) to Burroughs (with the promise of the forthcoming *Naked Lunch* as the "endless novel which will drive everybody mad"), and Kerouac's *On the Road* (where "Old Bull Lee" is endowed with "phenomenal fires and mysteries") – these are works where Burroughs' presence is particularly palpable.

berg's 1977 introduction. What this "intrusion of such an array of accessory texts" ultimately means to Harris' mind is that "Burroughs remains bound by and to the Beats"[15] and conversely, for the Beats, Burroughs' invisibility exercises a spectral presence and a haunting effect reminiscent of that of Joyce's vis-à-vis the avant-gardists.

However, Burroughs' literary alliances stretch much further than the Beat group. When in early 1963, publisher John Calder—by way of introducing Burroughs' work to England—put out *Dead Finger Talk* (an amalgam of *Naked Lunch, The Soft Machine,* and *The Ticket that Exploded*), the book received a long, hostile review in the *Times Literary Supplement,* sparking off a 14-week, heated correspondence often running up to four pages per issue. Burroughs' defence was actively taken by Eric Mottram, professor of English at London University. Mottram quotes Burroughs' account of the interior logic of his experimental quartet, according to which

> in *Naked Lunch* and *The Soft Machine* I have diagnosed an illness, and in *The Ticket that Exploded* and *Nova Express* suggested remedy. In this work I am attempting to create a new mythology for the space age. I feel that the old mythologies are definitely broken down and not adequate at the present time.[16]

Burroughs goes on to ally himself with the tradition of the "verbal innovators and experimenters" of the 1920s—Gertrude Stein and James Joyce—but his verbal investigations are directed toward discovering "what words actually are, and exactly what is their relationship to the human nervous system."[17]

Throughout the many interviews given over the course of his long career, Burroughs repeatedly credits Joyce as an important precursor in chiefly two respects. One, Joyce as an expander of awareness;[18] and two, Joyce as an explicitly sexual, "erotic," and "pornographic" writer.[19] However, apart from acknowledging him, Burroughs also repeatedly distances himself from Joyce's radical linguistic experimentation in the *Wake.* His argument, again

---

15 Oliver Harris, *William Burroughs and the Secret of Fascination* (Carbondale/Edwardsville: Southern Illinois University Press, 2003) 3-4.

16 William Burroughs, "The Algebra of Need," ed. Eric Mottram, *Burroughs Live: The Collected Interviews of William S. Burroughs 1960-1997* (Los Angeles/New York: Semiotext(e), 2001) 55.

17 "Algebra of Need," ed. Mottram, 55-6.

18 As in a 1986 interview: "One very important aspect of art is that it makes people aware of what they know and don't know that they know [...] Joyce made people aware of their stream of consciousness, at least on a verbal level. He was at first accused of being unintelligible. So the artist then expands awareness" ("Writing in the Future," ed. Jürgen Ploog, *Burroughs Live,* 621).

19 "I'd simply refer to writers who've written more or less explicitly or frankly about sexual matters. [...] Certainly Joyce, Miller, and D. H. Lawrence were very important as pioneers and made some very important breakthroughs, so that now virtually anything can be published" ("A New Frog," *The Job - Interviews with William Burroughs,* ed. Daniel Odier [London/New York: Penguin, 2008] 55).

rehearsed in multiple variations in different places and at different times, was most eloquently put forth in a 1973 London interview with Daniel Odier, where the *Wake* for Burroughs represented "a trap into which experimental writing can fall when it becomes purely experimental."[20] And in Paris, 1978, Burroughs explicitly tied his turn toward more traditional and straightforward narrative with rejection of experimentation à la the *Wake*, and the need to "make a living."[21] For Burroughs, then, the Joyce to admire is the Joyce of "The Dead," whose famous ending he reportedly memorised, oftentimes quoted and praised as "one of the famous scenes in English prose."[22] It is also this passage that Burroughs cuts up into his own prose in various places.

In the tetralogy of novels which followed after *Junkie*—from *Naked Lunch* to *Nova Express*—Burroughs finds the form in which to convey his drug experiences: the celebrated method of the cut-up, for whose discovery Burroughs painstakingly credited the American painter Brion Gysin, whom he had befriended during his Beat Hotel years in Paris. Published in Paris in 1959 (and in 1962 in an American edition), *Naked Lunch* was assembled from the thousand-odd pages of notes taken during Burroughs' worst period of addiction in Tangier. In a 1968 postscript to his surrealist novella *The Beat Hotel*, Harold Norse presents his eye-witness account of the discovery and earliest stages of the method's development. The first cut-ups appeared when

> Brion Gysin took several articles from *The Paris Herald Tribune*, *The London Observer*, *The London Daily Mail* and *Life Magazine* advertisements, sliced them down the middle and re-assorted them in collage form, about forty years after Tristan Tzara had picked out single words, also at random, snipped from newspapers, to form Dadaist poems.[23]

Like Gysin, Norse conceives of the method as a mode of literary "catching-up" with other art forms; moreover, he stresses the importance of "exceptions" like Joyce for the hope and belief shared by the experimentalist circle around Burroughs that "Victorian standards" could be done away with.[24] Gysin

---

20   Burroughs continues: "I would go so far with any given experiment and then come back; that is, I am coming back now to write purely conventional straightforward narrative. But applying what I have learned from the cut-up and the other techniques to the problem of conventional writing. It's simply if you go too far in one direction, you can never get back, and you're out there in complete isolation" ("From Eden to Watergate," *The Job*, 55).

21   "If your objective is to have people read your books, then there has to be at least a line of narrative they can follow. Take the case of Joyce who spent 20 or 30 years writing *Finnegans Wake*, a book no one can really read. I can't let that happen. For one thing, I have to make a living" (Gérard-Georges Lemaire, "Terrorism, Utopia and Fiction," *Burroughs Live*, 420).

22   Alan Bold, "No Future," *Burroughs Live*, 582.

23   Harold Norse, *The Beat Hotel* (San Diego: Atticus Press, 1983) 65.

24   "Painters and composers were 50 years ahead of writers. The blank canvass and silence have already preceded the blank page. The English language, in the face of increasing absurdity, persisted in its Victorian standards, with exceptions such as James Joyce and Gertrude Stein, adher-

himself more explicitly tied his cut-up method with the Dada and surrealist avant-garde: "The cut up method brings to writers the collage which has been used by painters for fifty years. And used by the moving and still camera . . . You cannot will spontaneity. But you can introduce the unpredictable spontaneous factor with a pair of scissors."[25]

In a 1964 BBC broadcast, Burroughs described the cut-up as a process in which "pages of text are cut and rearranged to form new combinations of word and image, that is, the page is actually cut with scissors, usually into four sections, and the order rearranged." To this, Burroughs added his own contribution, a second step of sorts, what he referred to as the "fold-in":

> A page of text, my own or someone else's, is folded down the middle and placed on another page, the composite text is then read across, half one text and half the other. The fold-in method extends to writing the flashback used in films, enabling the writer to move backwards and forwards on the time track by repetition and rearrangements of musical themes . . . [...] What I would like to emphasize is that this is a technique [...] and in any case it is a matter of experimentation, not argument.[26]

As critic Robin Lydenberg points out, one should think of the Gysin-Burroughs relation less as one of influence than confluence of independent energies: Burroughs did not encounter Gysin's *Minutes To Go* until 1959, by which time "he had already served an unconscious cut-up apprenticeship in editing and rearranging the voluminous material that finally yielded the published version of *Naked Lunch*."[27]

Naked Lunch can be read as a novelisation of the documentary material presented in *Junkie*, a series of sketches arranged in random order. Tanner describes the text's structure as having "no narrative continuity, and no sustained point of view; the separate episodes are not interrelated, they coexist in a particular field of force brought together by the mind of Burroughs which then abandons them."[28] The disorienting effect of what makes for a relatively straightforward narrative is the random ordering in which its sections are presented. The prose is a tissue of hospital, political, and other jingoistic jargons fused, as Mottram has put it, into "the spluttering language

---

ing to the false pretense that, somehow, in the face of all evidence to the contrary, life still made sense, in spite of alienation and state-controlled double-talk on both sides of the Iron Curtain" (Norse, *The Beat Hotel*, 68).

25   Eric Mottram, *William Burroughs – The Algebra of Need* (London: Marion Boyars Ltd, 1977) 37.

26   Qtd. in Mottram, *The Algebra of Need*, 39.

27   Lydenberg has also noted how the modernist heritage present in Eliot's phrase, "Who is the third who walks always beside you?," was adopted by Burroughs and Gysin "to designate the collaborative consciousness which could be generated by the cut-up method: a third mind free of the restrictions of context, culture, and subjectivity" (Lydenberg, *Word Cultures*, 44–5).

28   Tanner, *City of Words*, 111.

of nationalism and diplomatic hypocrisy, a mixture which finally blows the state control panel."[29]

Burroughs' aesthetic method is in full service to the overriding ideology of his writing. As long as the cure for the human historical urge to addiction is anarchist self-regulation, an act of individuality, then in writing, it can begin with cut-up methods developed explicitly as a revolutionary gesture against mass togetherness and the deterioration of language. The point is to create texts whose reading will replicate the writing process, texts which will lend themselves to cutting up by means of reading, so that in every reading every reader will assert their individuality. Cut-ups are ultimately meant to serve as new connections between extant images and texts, thus resisting the control exerted by the previously extant ones. As Burroughs stated himself,

> you can cut into *Naked Lunch* at any intersection point . . . *Naked Lunch* is a blue-print, a How-To Book . . . How-To extend levels of experience by opening the door at the end of a long hall . . . Doors that only open in Silence . . . *Naked Lunch* demands Silence from The Reader. Otherwise he is taking his own pulse . . .[30]

As is so often the case with modernist writing, the perceived difficulty of Burroughs' texts stems from the method and style rather than from theme or content.[31]

The Soft Machine[32] presents Burroughs' first attempt to incorporate the technique in a full-length narrative, constructing a literary mythology through which to show the destruction of love and individuality by power and corrupt sexual energy. Also for the first time, in *The Soft Machine*, Burroughs ventures into the science-fiction genre and, in addition to Gysin's cut-up method, fragments continuous images. The title—with explicit reference to the human body—indicates the innate biological device which allows the virus to enter the human body, and a thematic unity connecting the disparate scenes is need and its transmutations: the need for sex, drugs, and power to dominate and/or kill. Cut-ups usually follow after the use of drugs, or are

---

29   Mottram, *Wiliam Burroughs*, 52.
30   Qtd. in Mottram, *Algebra of Need*, 64.
31   Timothy Murphy has explicitly connected Burroughs' and Joyce's innovations when he observed: "Once its fundamental strategies are understood, the *Nova* trilogy is no more difficult to read than Gertrude Stein's *Tender Buttons* or Joyce's *Finnegans Wake*, two "unreadable" works which have experienced popular and scholarly revivals of interest in recent years. Like the pun that serves as the basis of *Finnegans Wake*, the basic cut-up technique is very simple: one takes at least one printed text, physically cuts it up into fragments, and reassembles the fragments in random order" (Murphy, *Wising Up the Marks*, 104).
32   Published in 1961 in Paris by Olympia Press, and in a revised form in 1966 in the U.S. (with Grove Press) and in 1968 in England (at Calder and Boyars).

produced as effects of the confusion of drug withdrawal, or the more natural blurred and jumbled workings of memory, or the utmost natural perception of motion. Lydenberg records Burroughs arguing that "any film of a street scene, any moving film of *anything* is a cut-up."[33]

The Ticket that Exploded was originally published in 1962, but its final version did not appear until 1967, in which interval Burroughs enhanced the cut-up method to include experiments with tapes and film. As a consequence of these advances, the cut-up effects here seem more controlled and less hallucinatory or psychedelic. Burroughs continues his exploration of the interface between the human machine and the machinic human. The focus, here, is on how the victims of vampirism themselves become addicts in a chain or organised predatory lust and loss of identity. The characters of Burroughs' mythology make their reappearance as science-fiction mutants from other planets – a fictional recycling akin to what *Ulysses* performs on *Dubliners*, e.g. As his stock character, Inspector Lee, explains:

> The basic nova technique is very simple: Always create as many insoluble conflicts as possible and always aggravate existing conflicts—This is done by dumping on the same planet life forms with incompatible conditions of existence—Their conditions of life are basically incompatible in present time form and it is precisely the work of the mob to see that they remain in present time form, to create and aggravate the conflicts that lead to the explosion of a planet, that is to nova (*TTE*, 54–5)

One word-effect explored in particular in *The Ticket that Exploded* is the effect of simultaneity, or the "*déjà vu* phenomenon," as Burroughs called it, which can be "produced to order" by folding page one into page one hundred and then inserting the composite in the text as page ten.[34] The ticket is to be exploded and reassembled – the total resistance called for in Burroughs' text demands more violent methods than alienation or estrangement. The word must be not only released from the predetermined patterns set by habit and routine, but more thoroughly obliterated. However, Burroughs insists—thereby implying the limits of his indebtedness to, e.g., Joyce's radical aesthetics—that this obliteration must not surpass the level of communicability: "I don't believe in being obscure; I feel that a writer should be comprehensible to any intelligent reader."[35]

---

33   Lydenberg, *Word Cultures*, 61.
34   Thus, Robin Lydenberg observes, "even a first reading of *The Ticket that Exploded* will have the haunting quality of a rereading, of a return to mysteriously familiar terrain," a quality akin to the reading experience of Joyce's *Wake*: "An initial reading of this fragmented narrative is disorienting, frustrating, almost physically unpleasant. Each chapter promises a particular focus, but it is rarely maintained" (Ibid, 72–3).
35   Qtd. in Mottram, *Algebra of Need*, 98.

Burroughs' conservatism vis-à-vis Joyce is best manifested in *Nova Express* (1964, 1966), the last part of his cut-up series. It opens with a "Foreward [sic] Note," stating that "an extension of Brion Gysin's cut-up method which I call the fold-in method has been used in this book which is consequently a composite of many writers living and dead" (*NE*, 7). The open didacticism of *Nova Express*, springing from the rejection of Burroughs' earlier work at the hands of the public, marks it off as different from the preceding cut-ups. In fact, the incipit section, entitled "Last Words," takes the form of a direct address to the reader from Burroughs' alter ego, signed as "Inspector J. Lee, Nova Police." Its apostrophe to the reader runs as follows:

> What scared you all into time? Into body? Into shit? I will tell you: *"the word."* Alien Word *"the." "The"* word of Alien Enemy imprisons *"thee"* in Time. In Body. In Shit. Prisoner, come out. The great skies are open. I Hassan i Sabbah *rub out the word forever*. If you I cancel all your words forever. And the words of Hassan i Sabbah as also cancel. Cross all your skies see the silent writing of Brion Gysin Hassan i Sabbah: drew September 17, 1899 over New York. (*NE*, 10)

The ultimate purpose of *Nova Express*, Lee reveals, is

> to expose and arrest Nova Criminals. In *Naked Lunch, The Soft Machine* and *Nova Express* I show who they are and what they are doing and what they will do if they are not arrested. Minutes to go. Souls rotten from their orgasm drugs, flesh sundering from their nova ovens, prisoners of the earth to *come out*. With your help we can occupy The Reality Studio and retake their universe of Fear Death and Monopoly—" (*NE*, 12)

Fold-ins from earlier works appear. For example, here is a passage already quoted from *The Ticket*:

> The basic nova mechanism is very simple: Always create as many insoluble conflicts as possible and always aggravate existing conflicts—This is done by dumping life forms with incompatible conditions of existence on the same planet—There is of course nothing "wrong" about any given life form since "wrong" only has reference to conflicts with other life forms—The point is these forms should not be on the same planet. (*NE*, 50)

Clearly, Burroughs' repetition is one with a difference: while previously presenting a simple description of a status quo, now he engages in ethical discourse, pointing out the "wrong" and suggesting a remedy. Cut-up passages, such as the one below, seem still more structured and compact, usually revolving around a series of associations and image parallelisms:

The grey smoke drifted the grey that stops shift   cut   tangle they breathe
medium the word cut shift   patterns   words   cut   the insect tangle
cut   shift   that coats word cut   breath   silence shift   abdominal.
cut   tangle stop word holes.
(*NE*, 57)

Burroughs' own relation to his writing is highly ambivalent throughout *Nova Express*, and what takes centre stage is the crucial ambiguity of Burroughs' "message," of waging a war on the word *by means of* the word, where the same medium by which the writer transcends his own solitude and solipsism is in danger of becoming an addiction which restricts his freedom. The problem, for Burroughs, is how to make contact and communication effective without giving up the freedom from restraint achieved by the cut-up and fold-in methods.

His solution is to increase the incorporation of found texts into his narratives: there are quotations from *Newsweek*, e.g., on the theory of "supernova or exploding star," there is an extended citation from Kafka's *Trial*, but Burroughs goes further. In the "Smorbrot" section, he explores the interdependence and intersection between footnote and main text; his footnotes deal, in a quasi-scholarly discourse, with the theories and experiments of Wilhelm Reich, crucial for his purposes. Burroughs' own suggested antidote for the word-addiction is, (not so) simply, silence:

So leave the recorders running and get your heavy metal ass in a space ship – Did it – Nothing there now but the recordings – Shut the whole thing off – *Silence* – When you answer the machine you provide it with more recordings to be played back to your "enemies" keep the whole nova machine running – The Chinese character for "enemy" means to be similar to or to answer – Don't answer the machine – Shut it off (*NE*, 155)

The final paragraph from "The Dead" becomes present in the final paragraph of *Nova Express* itself:

The great wind revolving turrets towers palaces – Insubstantial sound and image *flakes fall* – *Through* all the streets time for him to forbear – Blest be he on walls and windows people and sky – On every part of your dust *falling softly* – *falling* in the dark mutinous "No more" […] Melted into air – You are yourself "Mr. Bradly Mr. Martin –" *all the living and the dead* – You are yourself – There be – (*NE*, 156, my emphasis)

With the hindsight knowledge of this passage, one might be tempted to trace the motif of "flakes falling" throughout the rest of *Nova Express* and to identify it as Burroughs' cut-ups of Joyce, as, e.g., here, with echoes of Eliot's *The Wasteland* interspersed:

Now hazard *flakes fall* – A huge wave rolled treatment "pay back the red you stole" [...] Dreams are made of might be just what I am look: Prerecorded warning in a woman's voice – Scio is pulling a figure out of logos – A huge wave bowled a married couple off what you could have [...] *Hurry up please its* accounts – Empty thing police they *fading out* – Dusk through narrow streets, toilet paper, and there is *no light in the window* – April wind revolving illness of dead sun – Woman with red hair is *a handful of dust* (NE, 143, my emphasis)

But the point is that the sources of cut-ups should be by and large unidentifiable unless intended otherwise, only then will the addiction of authorship as proprietorship over words be overcome. Norse quotes Gysin to the effect that "words belong to everybody," that "nobody owns words," that "there's nothing sacred" about them, and so the writer's task is to "break the word habit."[36] As Lydenberg notes, for Burroughs the verb "to write" carries "the connotation it has in junky's jargon – to write a prescription for drugs," and so when Burroughs' "writing arm is paralyzed," this is to him "no failure of creativity or imagination but rather a reflection of the author's courage to kick the habit, the refusal to feed the monkey that straddles his back and that of his reader."[37] It is despite his deep distrust of language that Burroughs continued to write, publish, and even perform his work.

The 1980s trilogy *Cities of the Red Night*, *The Place of Dead Roads*, and *The Western Lands* (1981–7) continues the destructive task of disassembling and reassembling the word (on the syntactical level, at least), but it also offers affirmative models for reorganising society in order to avoid the powerful dialectics of social and linguistic control. The last part of the trilogy, *The Western Lands*, has been read as Burroughs' elegy for Gysin (to whose memory it is dedicated) and also his farewell to the medium of language: "He had reached the end of words, the end of what can be done with words. And then?" (WL, 258). Here, Burroughs seems to suggest that the labour of eliminating language, capital, and the human subject must transpose the writer's medium into different realms. Accordingly, Burroughs goes on to extend his literary project to include film and recording. However, as has already been argued, Burroughs now forsakes his project of disassembling words, and becomes equally conservative in his treatment of quotation. There is the trademark self-repetition with a difference, e.g., when he sets the tone of the final section of the novel, "The Wishing Machine," with a paraphrase of the opening sequence:

The old writer lived in a boxcar by the river. This was fill land that had once been a dump heap, but it was not used anymore: five acres along the river which he had inherited from his father, who had been a wrecker and scrap metal dealer. (WL, 1)

---

36   Norse, *Beat Hotel*, 62.
37   Lydenberg, *Word Culture*, 115.

The old writer lived in a converted boxcar in a junk heap on the river. The junk heap was owned by a wrecking company, and he was the caretaker. Commander of a junk heap. Sometimes he sported a yachting cap. The writer didn't write anymore. Blocked. It happens. (*WL*, 246)

However, Burroughs' favourite Joyce passage appears no longer as a scrambled part of a complexly woven texture, but as conventionally as can be: "Snow was coming down in great soft flakes, falling like the descent of their last end on all the living and the dead, the writer remembered" (*WL*, 246-7).

Thus, Burroughs' late renunciation of his cut-up method entails accepting his favourite Joycean passage in its almost intact form into his writing. And, as Ward records, it was ultimately less the cut-up method than his personal status that proved Burroughs' most lasting influence—which in any case turned out to be more momentous in poetry. While "most writers of fiction have found the cut-ups [...] hard going," their influence on poets "has been immense."[38] As J.G. Ballard put it in his obituary notice for *The Guardian* from 4 August 1997, "now that William Burroughs has gone, all we are left with are the career novelists."[39]

3.2 "THE SELF WHO COULD DO MORE": WILLIAM GADDIS

It is a curious coincidence that a version of William Gaddis' first novel, *The Recognitions*, was begun in Mexico City in 1947, a mere three years before another Harvard English literature major, William Burroughs, was to reside there and launch his very different writerly career. This version was temporarily abandoned as Gaddis continued on his journeys across Panama, the Caribbean, North Africa, back and forth between Madrid and Paris, and the book was finished after his return to New York in 1953.

Curiously enough, the history the critical reception of Gaddis' work had until very late in his life and career (1990s) taken place in the shadow of one particularly detailed—and, Gaddis would insist, misguided—comparative reading of *The Recognitions* alongside Joyce's work. Bernard Benstock's "On William Gaddis: In Recognition of James Joyce" was a pioneering essay in two respects: as the first critical piece on Gaddis' novel (to appear with a shocking delay of ten years after its publication) and as an early attempt to chart

---

38 Ward, "The Mutations of William Burroughs," 120.

39 Although the post-1970 period was not as innovative or radical as "that in which early novels like *Naked Lunch* were written," it was still the period in which "they passed beyond their initial shock-value and became influential." Among "the novelists who have pushed further into territories first explored by Burroughs," Ward mentions "cyberpunk maestro William Gibson, Angela Carter, Kathy Acker, Iain Sinclair, Irvine Welsh and Alan Warner" (Ibid, 122).

Joyce's legacy for subsequent writers from the purview of so-called "Joyce Studies." Taking its cue from a blurb on *The Recognitions* by none other than Stuart Gilbert, Benstock's examination of the Joyce / Gaddis intertext is based on loosely conceived conceptual and thematic affinities rather than on empirical textual evidence. More bluntly, some highly nebulous and tangential textual evidence from within Gaddis' text is used to make bold claims as regards direct influence.[40]

The parallels between *The Recognitions* and *A Portrait* listed by Benstock are numerous, and it is on their basis that Benstock begins to draw parallels with Joyce's novelistic project of similar magnitude, *Ulysses*, noting how Wyatt's "wanderings, gropings and demon-driven fantasies relate essentially to the all-important search for the transsubstantial father which underlies *Ulysses*," even if Gaddis' approach here is "more parody than parallel." Benstock catalogues possible references to *Ulysses*, from the more obvious—if still rather ambiguous—such as Wyatt's description of his Spanish sojourn: "In this country, without ever leaving Spain, a whole Odyssey within its boundaries, a whole Odyssey without Ulysses" (*TR*, 816), to the most obscure ones, such as the motif of Molly Bloom's habit of drying her handkerchiefs over a mirror, echoed in one of the characters' similar custom. Finally, Benstock draws attention to a mention of the Viconian theory of the origin of religion and civilisation (*TR*, 417), suggesting its use toward a formulation of "a definitive theory of imitation and conscious borrowing, even though such a theory is never spelled out."[41]

There are, Benstock concedes, significant differences between Gaddis' novel and Joyce's writings: except for one single scene (*TR*, 391–5), Gaddis "generally avoids using the interior monologue so often associated with Joyce," yet the speculative reasons against its use are traced back to Joyce with whom "such a device as the interior monologue may have run its course." Despite these differences, Benstock conclusion emphasises Gaddis' "indebtedness" to Joyce, and the consequent retrospective, rather than prospective, quality of his novel: although crediting Gaddis with "having created a rare and unusual book," it nonetheless remains one which "still pays respectful homage to James Joyce."[42]

---

40   For instance, when dealing with Mr. Sinisterra's apostrophy of a dead artist as "a real craftsman, like Johnny, or Jim the Penman" (*TR*, 519), Benstock at first concedes that "it is the fictional character, the facsimile, that Gaddis uses," but then goes on to state that "it is to Joyce that the real allusion refers," a statement for which no further evidence is adduced.

41   Bernard Benstock, "On William Gaddis - in Recognition of James Joyce," *Wisconsin Studies in Comparative Literature* 6.2 (Summer 1965): 182–3.

42   Benstock, "On William Gaddis," 188–9.

Shortly after its publication, Benstock's article received much scorn from Gaddis critics and even Gaddis himself.[43] Still, so convincing was Benstock's Joycean reading and so pervasive the critical impression of a Joycean Gaddis that ten years after, in a letter to Grace Eckley dated 3 June 1975, Gaddis desperately and exasperatedly denied any sort of Joycean inspiration.[44] However, the fact remains that Gaddis was a Harvard drop-out in English literature and his erudition on even the most abstruse subjects (such as alchemy or the Kabala) has become the stuff of many critical legends, and that, however sweeping, inaccurate, and ultimately irrelevant Benstock's Joycean parallels, his was a pioneering piece breaking the silence and neglect surrounding Gaddis' work at the time. Despite Gaddis' insistence to the contrary, Stephen Moore's guide to *The Recognitions* discovers a few more parallels with *Ulysses*, while also setting straight Gaddis' pronouncements about never having read Joyce."[45]

Only with the publication of his second novel, *J R* (1975)—twenty years after his first book—did the critical industry begin to take notice of Gaddis.[46]

---

43 In a 27 Sept 1963 letter to the Joyce scholar Jack Dalton, Gaddis had this to say: "I found [...] the original reviews frustrating in their generally invidious comparisons between *The Recognitions* and the work of Joyce, not then having read any more of him than *Exiles*, the *Dubliners* stories, about 40 pages of *Ulysses* & 10 of *Finnegans Wake*, and still unconvinced of the osmosis theory of literary influence in which the reviewers take refuge." *Letters of William Gaddis*, ed. Stephen Moore (Champaign / London / Dublin: Dalkey Archive Press, 2013) 912.

44 "I appreciate your interest in *The Recognitions* & have to tell you I've reached the end of the line on questions about what I did or didn't read of Joyce's 30 years ago. All I read of *Ulysses* was Molly Bloom at the end which was being circulated for salacious rather than literary merits; No I did not read *Finnegans Wake* though I think a phrase about 'psychoanaloosing' one's self from it is in *The Recognitions*; Yes I read some of *Dubliners* but don't recall how many & remember only a story called 'Counterparts'; Yes I read a play called *Exiles* which at the time I found highly unsuccessful; Yes I believe I read *A Portrait* but also think I may not have finished it; No I did not read commentary on Joyce's work & absorb details without reading the original [...], anyone seeking Joyce finds Joyce even if both Joyce & the victim found the item in Shakespeare, read right past whole lines lifted bodily from Eliot & c, all of which will probably go on so long as Joyce remains an academic cottage industry" (Qtd. in Stephen Moore, *William Gaddis* [Boston: G. K. Hall & Co., 1989] 7).

45 Moore notes how Gaddis went on to specify his 1975 statements by claiming never to have read *Ulysses* apart from the "Penelope" episode, and even this comes to be challenged when tracing the apostrophe of the sea as "the mother, last lover" (*TR*, 845) to *Ulysses* – here, Moore recalls Gaddis' surprising avowal to Green of having "indeed read the first forty pages of Joyce's *Ulysses*" and so toys with the possibility that "he may have remembered Buck Mulligan's query in the first chapter on Algy and grey sweet mother" (Moore, *A Reader's Guide*, 275).

46 Reasons for this "invisibility" have been aptly summarised in John Aldridge's review of *J R*: "As is usually the case with abrasively original work, there had to be a certain passage of time before an audience could begin to be educated to accept *The Recognitions*. [...] even the sophisticated reading public of the mid-Fifties was not yet accustomed to the kind of fiction it represented. Curiously enough, even though the most radical experimentation had by then been made respectable by the great modernist masters, there was still a resistance to it when attempted by living novelists" (John Aldridge, "The Ongoing Situation [A Review of *JR*]," *Saturday Review* [4 October 1975]: 27).

The surge in critical interest prodded by *J R* did yield occasional applications of Benstock's comparative reading to other Gaddis novels. In *J R*, the long meandering sentences, so typical of *The Recognitions*, are no more – in fact, all the usual narrative scaffolding is gone. Gaddis' self-elimination from the text as narrative presence is consummated: there is virtually no narrator to indicate the saying and the doing of the characters. Narrating the story of the eponymous 11-year-old boy who obscures his identity through payphone calls and postal money orders in order to parlay penny stockholdings into a fortune on paper, the novel broadly satirises what Gaddis, in a rare 1987 interview for the *Paris Review*, called "the American dream turned inside out."[47] The novel's form is almost entirely conversational or dialogical, sometimes with little indication—other than the conversational context—regarding which character is speaking – a narrative conceit tied by Gaddis, in the same interview, to the purpose of turning the reader into a collaborator in the process of creating the characters. Despite the fragmentary and discontinuous narration, the text appears as a continuous flow with no chapter or section breaks, with transitions between scenes occurring through shifts in focalisation reminiscent of the panning or tracking shot in cinema. This disorienting effect is enhanced by Gaddis' substitution of quotation marks with em-dashes as signposts for direct speech—and this is a mark of Joyce's writing from *Dubliners* to *Finnegans Wake*. Characters constantly interrupt each other or themselves, or are besieged by relentless distractions, speaking in sentences that mutilate grammar and syntax, replete with clichés, euphemisms, insults, mangling up bits of high and popular culture into nearly incomprehensible fragments. Gaddis' "message" here seems to be that language in the service of money, ideology, and art becomes garbage: *J R* is "what America's all about, waste disposal and all" (*J R*, 27). Entropy is omnipresent and frequently foregrounded in its various guises – most markedly, in the form of the "paper empire" built on one single muffled pay-phone transaction. Although not exactly linguistically materialist or neologistic, even *J R* does exhibit the use of some Joycean motifs (if not techniques or styles).[48] In the wake of *J R*—which despite its immense length and demands on the reader won its author the National Book Award,

---

47   William Gaddis, "The Art of Fiction," *The Paris Review Interviews II* (London: Picador, 2007) 287.

48   Joyce scholar Tim Conley has drawn parallels between *J R* and *A Portrait* beyond their generic affiliation as *Bildungsromans*. There are similarities in their conclusions, where "both monologues exude raw, even rapturous ambition at the same time that they register the isolation of the speaker: no one but the reader is 'listening' to *J R*, no other character has access to Stephen's diary." But even though "both want to write a book," functioning as would-be artists, there are ultimately more differences than similarities: "Stephen craves independence, flight, and the power to create; *J R* wants none of these things" (Tim Conley, "This Little Prodigy Went to Market: The Education of *J R*," *William Gaddis, "The Last of Something": Critical Essays*, eds. Crystal Alberts, Christopher Leise & Birger Vanwesenbeeck [London: McFarland & Co., 2010] 127).

a Guggenheim Fellowship (1981), a MacArthur Foundation Fellowship (1982), and his election into the American Academy of Arts and Letters—Gaddis' reputation was on the mend.

Following two of Gaddis' less ambitious and complex books, *Agapē Agape* (2002), a posthumously published manuscript found in Gaddis' bequest, is composed of a 96-page stream of prose uninterrupted by paragraph-breaks, which thematically traces the "secret history of the player piano," to whose research Gaddis devoted a substantial part of his life and efforts. At the same time, *Agapē Agape* deals with an artist who is mindful of his impending death and strives to put his work and his life in some semblance of order. *Agapē Agape* assumes from the very start the semblance of a free-flowing discourse reminiscent of *J R*:

> No but you see I've got to explain all this because I don't, we don't know how much time there is left and I have to work on the, to finish this work of mine while I, why I've brought in this whole pile of books notes pages clippings and God knows what, get it all sorted and organized when I get this property divided up and the business and worries that go with it while they keep me here to be cut up and scraped and stapled and cut up again my damn leg look at it... (*AA*, 1)

That the parallel with Joyce—Gaddis opens his monologue with a "No" just as Joyce opened and closed Molly Bloom's with a "Yes"—is far from haphazard becomes clear early on via a direct reference to Joyce:

> O God, O God, O God, Chi m'a tolto a me stesso that's Michelangelo, that's from my book, Ch'a me fusse più presso O più me potessi that's in my book, who has taken from me that self who could do more, and what is your book about Mister Joyce? It's not about something Madam, it is something and goodbye to that hidden talent, those ghostly fingers hard as petrified wood look at mine. (*AA*, 17–8)

Although pertaining to Beckett's famous statement about the *Wake* rather than to Joyce proper, the reference appears in a particularly important context of a quote from Michelangelo, "The self who could do more," a phrase which appears in every one of Gaddis' books and recurs throughout *Agapē Agape*, also forming its haunting conclusion. Is this a late acknowledgment on Gaddis' part of a lifelong anxiety of influence vis-à-vis Joyce, who "has taken from me that self who could do more" but did not manage to do so, obfuscated as it was by Joyce's shadow?

Gaddis organises his thoughts on the subject of the history of the piano player into a series of imaginary conversations—Walter Benjamin (and his seminal essay on the aura vis-à-vis technological reproduction) in dialogue with Johan Huizinga, Friedrich Nietzsche communing with himself in final days spent madly improvising on the piano, and the man on the bed—undisguised as none other than Gaddis himself—in direct conversation with various characters from fiction such as E. T. A. Hoffmann (from Offenbach's posthumously published *Tales*) and Pózdnyshev (from *The Kreutzer Sonata*).[49] Instead of opposing an artistic individualism against an impersonal, collectivist technology, Gaddis lays bare their common historical roots as creative collaborations.

From Vaucanson's mechanical loom for figured silks to Jacquard to the drum roll on the player piano to the punched data card in the first computers: in part, the digital age owes its existence to the arts. What the two spheres also share is a creation of "detachable selves." Just as technology produces the McLuhanesque extensions of man, then so does fictional creation of voices, subjectivities, personae and characters. Both technology and fiction, thus, give rise to the "self who can do more":

> Finally yes that, where it's all been going from the start, that cry from Michelangelo, O Dio, o Dio, o Dio, Chi m'a tolto a me stesso Ch'a me fusse più presso O più di me potessi, che poss'io? O Dio, o Dio, who has taken the one closest to me who could do more than no, no it's not that pedestrian it's fifteenth, sixteenth century Italian nearer poetry [...] O Dio, o Dio, odious, repugnant, from odium, hatred, odisse to hate God the bedmaker [...] That was youth with its reckless exuberance when all things were possible pursued by Age where we are now, looking back at what we destroyed, what we tore away from that self who could do more, and its work that's become my enemy because that's what I can tell you about, that Youth who could do anything. (*AA*, 95-6)

As Tabbi has observed, "everything depends on the language, on the living author's struggle with a past artist's words and on the future reader's ability to hold in mind two opposed meanings—*O Dio* and odium, repugnance" (*AA*, 109).

And so, against all forgeries, simulations, and wastes of the world, Gaddis' oeuvre, marked by a peremptory resistance to any simplistic notion of Joyce's influence, nevertheless engages in a lifelong dialogue with its precursor, culminating with a text at once most personal as well as *Wakean* in its multilingual survey of history and its cultural "message."

---

49 In the neat formulation of Joseph Tabbi's "Afterword" to the novel, Gaddis' last work details how "*Agapē*—the community of brotherly love celebrated by early Christian writers—has come apart (agape) through mechanization and a technological democracy that reduces art to the level of light entertainment, a spectacle for the gaze of the masses" (*AA*, 108).

3.3 "THAT STYLE WHICH DELIBERATELY EXHAUSTS ITS POSSIBILITIES": JOHN BARTH

Few essays left a larger impact upon the literary thought and theory of the US 1960s and 1970s, and few have continued to cause more controversy, than John Barth's essays, "The Literature of Exhaustion" (1967) and "The Literature of Replenishment" (1980). However, as Barth reminisces in his 1984 preface to the former essay in his *Friday Book*, more often than not, the two met with misunderstanding.[50]

Barth opens his essay by pitting—against "a good many current novelists [who] write turn-of-the-century-type novels, only in more or less mid-twentieth-century language and about contemporary people and topics"—the more interesting group of the "excellent writers who are also technically contemporary: Joyce and Kafka, for instance, in their time, and in ours, Samuel Beckett and Jorge Luis Borges" (*FB*, 66). Given that at the time of the writing, the twentieth century is "more than two-thirds done," it is for Barth "dismaying to see so many of our writers following Dostoevsky or Tolstoy or Balzac, when the question seems to me to be how to succeed not even Joyce and Kafka, but those who *succeeded* Joyce and Kafka and are now in the evenings of their own careers." The kind of writers clearly of Barth's preference consists of "the few people whose artistic thinking is as *au courant* as any French New Novelist's, but who manage nonetheless to speak eloquently and memorably to our human hearts and conditions, as the great artists have always done" (*FB*, 67–8).

One of the clearest signs that Barth's essay is not yet another "death-of-the-novel" elegy is its positive treatment of the extreme experimentation of Joyce's *Wake*, considered as an exercise in fictional exploration of an "ultimacy." What is "modern" about Beckett or Borges is that "in an age of ultimacies and 'final solutions,'" their work in separate ways "reflects and deals with ultimacy, both technically and thematically, as for example *Finnegans Wake* does in its different manner." A "contamination of reality by dream," as Barth himself calls it, is found to be one of Joyce's "pet themes" in that it "turns the artist's mode or form into a metaphor for his concerns, as does the diary-

---

50 "The Literature of Exhaustion" arose in mid-sixties, a period leading up to, as Barth recollects, "the American High Sixties: The Vietnam War was in overdrive through most of the period; the U.S. economy was fat and bloody; academic imperialism was as popular as the political kind" In 1967, Barth took a sabbatical from teaching and—after the long novels *The Sot-Weed Factor* (1960) and *Giles Goat-Boy* (1966)—a break from long novels in order to write *Lost in the Funhouse*, a text of hybrid genre describable as a *Bildungsroman* narrated in the form of a loose short-story collection. Coinciding with Barth's work on *Lost in the Funhouse* was the writing of the essay, in which, Barth remembers, "I set down my mixed feelings about the avant-gardism of the time," a piece which "has been frequently reprinted and as frequently misread as one more Death of the Novel or Swan-Song of Literature piece" (*FB*, 62–4).

ending of *A Portrait* or the cyclical construction of *Finnegans Wake*." One of Barth's exemplary ultimacies is the feeling that "the novel, if not narrative literature generally, if not the printed word altogether, has by this hour of the world just about shot its bolt" (*FB*, 70–1).

Barth's own response to this ultimacy were *The Sot-Weed Factor* and *Giles Goat-Boy*, "novels which imitate the form of the Novel, by an author who imitates the role of Author." The sort of fiction that slowly emerges from Barth's account as the preferred species is what has subsequently come to be referred to as "metafiction," only here Barth conceives of its different nature as one of "engagement in imitation":

> This is the difference between a proper, "naïve" novel and a deliberate imitation of a novel, or a novel imitative of other kinds of documents. The first sort attempts [...] to imitate actions more or less directly, and its conventional devices [...] have been objected to as obsolete notions, or metaphors for obsolete notions. (*FB*, 72)

What is "exhaustive" about this kind of literature championed by Barth is not some kind of death-of-the-novel eschatology, but—with reference to Borges' definition of the Baroque—as "that style which deliberately exhausts (or tries to exhaust) its possibilities and borders upon its own caricature." Borges' image of "the infinite library," then, is the resource to be exhausted, and "the labyrinth" presents a place in which, ideally, "all the possibilities of choice (or direction, in this case) are embodied, and [...] must be exhausted before one reaches the heart" (*FB*, 75).

The 1980 essay, "Literature of Replenishment," was written as "a companion and corrective" to the 1967 piece. Its most striking difference is its engagement with critical theorisations of so-called postmodernism, a term viewed by Barth, as by so many fellow novelists, as useless and ridiculous:

> while some of the writers labeled as postmodernists, myself included, may happen to take the label with some seriousness, a principal activity of postmodernist critics [...], writing in postmodernist journal or speaking at postmodernist symposia, consists in disagreeing about what postmodernism is or ought to be, and thus about who should be admitted to the club—or clubbed into admission. (*FB*, 194)

The term itself is found by Barth "awkward and faintly epigonic," suggestive, "like 'post-impressionism,'" less of a "vigorous or even interesting new direction in the old art of storytelling" than of "something anticlimactic, feebly following a very hard act to follow."[51] This inferiority of postmodernism

---

51   Barth approaches the modernist/postmodernist relation via a consciously Joycean simile: "One is reminded of the early James Joyce's fascination with the word *gnomon* in its negative geomet-

vis-à-vis modernism, in turn, calls for a (re)definition of modernism itself, for the "post-"ness implies that modernism is somehow consummated and estimable. On the one hand, Barth agrees that the "adversary reaction called modernist art," aimed against "the rigidities and other limitations of nineteenth-century bourgeois realism," is one which nowadays has nothing to react against as "these nineteenth-century rigidities are virtually no more." However, Barth adds a peremptory "but":

> BUT I deplore the artistic and critical cast of mind that repudiates the whole modernist enterprise as an aberration and sets to work as if it hadn't happened [...] It *did* happen: Freud and Einstein and two world wars and the Russian and sexual revolutions and automobiles and airplanes [...] and except as readers there's no going back to Tolstoy and Dickens. (FB, 202)

Barth calls for a programme attempting "the synthesis or transcension of these antitheses, which may be summed up as premodernist and modernist modes of writing" and that the ideal postmodernist should "neither merely repudiate nor merely imitate either his twentieth-century modernist parents or his nineteenth-century premodernist grandparents." The "exhaustion" of present-day literature, Barth repeats, is neither one of language nor one of literature, but of "the aesthetic of high modernism: that admirable, not--to-be-repudiated, but essentially completed 'program' of what Hugh Kenner has dubbed 'the Pound era.'" In this context, Barth concludes, the first post--war generation of American writers should be seen as "working out, not of the next-best thing after modernism, but of the *best next* thing: what is gropingly now called postmodernist fiction" and what Barth proposes to call "a literature of replenishment" (FB, 206).

How, then, does Barth's own fiction answer this call for replenishment in view of the exhaustion of modernism? To adopt Barth's terms, his earliest output was a reaction against modernism of a distinctly premodernist nature, a return to the well-crafted nineteenth-century plot. After his juvenilia, *Floating Opera* (1956) and *The End of the Road* (1958), both of which nested securely within the then-mainstream of realistic novels with contemporary settings, came a first decisive break with the contemporaneity of the novelistic setting—which was to influence a few of his other novels—in his book *The Sot-Weed Factor* (1960). In an interview with J. D. Bellamy, Barth observed of his early period crowned with *The Sot-Weed Factor* the following:

---

ric sense: the figure that remains when a parallelogram has been removed from a similar but larger parallelogram with which it shares a common corner" (FB, 196).

The possibility of constructing a fantastically baroque plot appealed to me most: the idea of turning vigorously against the modernist notion that plot is an anachronistic element in contemporary fiction. I've never found that a congenial notion; it seemed to me that there were ways to be quite contemporary and yet go at the art in a fashion that would allow you to tell complicated stories simply for the aesthetic pleasure of complexity, of complication and unravelment, suspense, and the rest.[52]

Barth's *Giles Goat-Boy* (1966) uses the structure of the heroic myth as the organisational principle for this comic picaresque novel, producing a text that is as much about literature and literary analysis, and its own status as fiction as it is about the extra-textual "real." There are two fictitious prefatory quasi-documents in which Barth undermines his own authority: a "Publisher's Disclaimer" by "The Editor-in-Chief," composed of four editors' reports on the novel (two vote against publishing the book, one in favour, and the fourth resigns his position as a result of having read the manuscript) and a "Cover-Letter to the Editors and Publishers," signed "J. B.," in which a struggling academic writer explains how Giles Stoker's book, *The Revised New Syllabus*, was delivered to him by a mysterious young man.

The plot invites readings on multiple levels and deals with a dizzying array of topics: from a political allegory of the Cold War and a mystical allegory of spiritual enlightenment to its admonitory foregrounding of the role of computers in society; from its preoccupation with the mythology surrounding contemporary American popular culture to its elaborate and sustained parody of world myths, especially the Bible and medieval saints' lives. Talking to Bellamy, Barth pointed out the subversive element to his treatment of myth as structure. However important the Joycean heritage in this parodic undertaking, Barth was also careful to distance himself from Joyce's treatment of myth, proposing to write from "the right end of the mythopoetic stick."[53]

Despite his apparent dismissal of Joyce as an "already-succeeded" writer (a dismissal he came to regret and revise later on), it is in *Lost in the Funhouse* (1968) that Barth explicitly draws upon the Joyce canon.[54] The opening mi-

---

52   *The New Fiction*, ed. Bellamy, 7.
53   "Much as one may admire those novels (Updike's *Centaur*, Joyce's *Ulysses*), their authors have hold of the wrong end of the mythopoetic stick. The myths themselves are produced by the collective narrative imagination (or whatever), partly to point down at our daily reality; and so to write about our daily experiences in order to point up to the myths seems to me mythopoetically retrograde. I think it's a more interesting thing to do, if you find yourself preoccupied with mythic archetypes of what have you, to address them directly" (Ibid, 13).
54   Critic Michael Hinden has even gone so far as to argue that "in an attempt to exhaust the possibilities of its own tradition, *Lost in the Funhouse* begins as an elaborate parody, revival and refutation of Joyce's masterpiece, *A Portrait of the Artist as a Young Man*" (Michael Hinden, "*Lost in the Funhouse*: Barth's Use of the Recent Past," *Twentieth Century Literature* [April 1973]: 108).

cro-story, "Frame-Tale," consists of the phrase "ONCE UPON A TIME THERE" on the right-hand margin of the recto, and the phrase "WAS A STORY THAT BEGAN" on the left-hand margin of the verso of the same leaf, the idea being for the top of the leaf to be cut out, twisted, and the ends glued together to form a Möbius strip that would read "Once upon a time there was a story that began once upon a time . . .," *ad infinitum*. In a 1988 foreword to the paperback edition, Barth explicitly ties this circularity to Joyce's *Wake*, describing *Lost in the Funhouse* as

> a book of short stories: a sequence or series rather than a mere assortment [...] strung [...] together on a few echoed and developed themes and [...] circl[ing] back upon itself: not to close a simple circuit like that of Joyce's *Finnegans Wake*, emblematic of Viconian eternal return, but to make a circuit with a twist to it, like a Möbius strip. (*LF*, vii)

This piece can be (and has been) taken as a figure for many aspects of the book, including its emphasis on paradox, self-reflexive content, and circular structure. The title story provides another unifying metaphor for the book, that of literature as a maze of distorting mirrors and echo chambers, an alternate reality constructed by writers within which readers can find themselves by temporarily—and productively—disorienting themselves. At times, Barth takes the mode of self-conscious fiction to another level, letting his fiction make the case against itself: "Another story about writing a story! Another *regressus in infinitum*! Who doesn't prefer art that at least overtly imitates something other than its own processes? That doesn't continually proclaim 'Don't forget I'm an artifice!'?" (*LF*, 112).

The protagonist is one Ambrose, a boy who is literally lost in a funhouse but knows that he will become a writer. The third-person narrator, who sometimes seems to be Ambrose writing as an adult, underscores the parallel between constructing fun houses and fiction, parodying Daedalus the labyrinth-builder: "Therefore he will construct funhouses for others and be their secret operator--though he would rather be among the lovers for whom funhouses are designed" (*LF*, 94). Barth also indulges in the use of such metafictional techniques as reproducing a drawing of Freitag's Triangle (*LF*, 91), a diagram traditionally used to represent the narrative stages of development, climax, and resolution, as he attempts to figure out how to construct his own narrative.

Hints to Joyce are explicit: Ambrose recalls that "the Irish author James Joyce, in his unusual novel entitled *Ulysses*, now available in this country, uses the adjectives *snot-green* and *scrotum-tightening* to describe the sea. Visual, auditory, tactile, olfactory, gustatory" (*LF*, 71). The penultimate story in the collection, "Menelaiad," finds a form to represent both the Möbius strip and the funhouse in its intricate embedding of eight narrative levels, each paralleling and intersecting with the others and reaching a formal climax when the

word """""""Love!""""""" (*LF*, 150) is uttered simultaneously by all eight narrators. Two sections, "Autobiography: A Self-Recorded Fiction" and "Title,"
end in mid-sentence without a comma. The "Glossolalia" section features six
rhythmical parodies of the Lord's Prayer, spoken by six different characters.
The blasphemous parody technique of the sacred is, of course, an essentially
Joycean trait (below are first two lines of each):

> Still breathless from fending Phoebus, suddenly I see all—and all in vain. A horse
> excreting Greeks will devour my city. [...]
> Dear Procne: your wretched sister--she it is weaves this robe. Regard it well: it hides
> her painful tale in its pointless patterns. [...]
> I, Crispus, a man of Corinth, yesterday looked on God. Today I rave. What things my
> eyes have seen can't be scribed or spoken. [...]
> Sweet Sheba, beloved highness: Solomon craves your throne! Beware his craft; he mis-
> translates my pain into cunning counsel. [...]
> Ed' pélut, kondó nedóde, ímba imbá imbá. Singé erú. Orúmo ímbo ímpe ruté sceléte.
> [...]
> Ill fortune, constraint and terror, generate guileful art; despair inspires. The laureled
> clairvoyants tell our doom in riddles.
> (*LF*, 111–2)

Barth followed his first venture outside of the form of the novel with its
"twin," *Chimera* (1972), a collection of three related novellas (the tripartite
mythical beast had the head of a lion, body of a goat, and tail of a serpent) that
continues the rewriting of classical stories through the parodic language and
formal devices that Barth used with "Menelaiad" and "Anonymiad" in *Lost in
the Funhouse*.

    It was in his seventh work of fiction, *LETTERS* (1979), that Barth took
another step further in going backward. He revisited his six previous books
and recast them within a framework in which he fused the epistolary novel
form à la Richardson with the full-blown metafictional, discursive, and narrative play à la Borges or Joyce. Barth composed his seventh novel out of
letters from seven correspondents writing in seven different styles, six of
whom were drawn from his first six books: Todd Andrews from *The Floating
Opera*; Jacob Horner from *The End of The Road*; Andrew Burlingame Cook VI,
a descendant of Ebenezer Cooke of *The Sot-Weed Factor*; Jerome Bray from
Giles Goat-Boy; Ambrose Mensch, featured in three of the stories in *Lost in
the Funhouse*; and John Barth, who made an appearance (albeit unnamed) in
the "Dunyazadiad" section of *Chimera* and who has published under his own
name the works that were really written by his "characters." Interestingly
enough, despite his earlier reservations regarding modernism, Barth now refers to his fictional alter ego as the "last-ditch provincial Modernist" (*L*, 767).

Each writer continues with his original story more or less where it left off and extends it forward and backward into complex interrelationships with the stories of all the other writers. The novel's self-reflexiveness reaches its climax in a late epistolary exchange between "The Author" and Ambrose Mensch. In his final "Letter to the Author," Ambrose outlines for his friend and writing mentor a projected "old-time epistolary novel by seven fictitious drolls & dreamers" (L, 769), an epistolary recapitulation of the novel "The Author" has just completed *by that novel*. In a precise numerological touch, Ambrose's letter consists of seven paragraph clusters, with each cluster summarising the "traditional letter-symbolism" of one of the first seven letters of the alphabet (L, 768).

As Werner and others have noted, *LETTERS* brims with references to Joyce, most having to do with the only "new" character, Lady Amherst, a middle-aged British academic who represents the strong modernist version of the delicate damsel in distress by becoming romantically involved with most of the other characters (and impregnated—in the allegorical union of the experimental and the traditional—by Ambrose Mensch). To name but a few: Lady Amherst's first letter ends with an invocation of the reader to "like Molly Bloom at the close of *her* great soliloquy (whose author was, yes, a friend of your friend's friend—say to us *yes*, to the Litt. D. *yes*, to MSU *yes,* and *yes* Dorchester, *yes* Tidewater, Maryland *yes yes yes*!" (L, 11–2); her friendly terms with Joyce are further elaborated as "my rebellious adolescent enthusiasm for the author of *Ulysses* and *Work in Progress*, to sit at whose feet [...] I went to Paris" (L, 72). On a more abstract level, emphasis is put on how "James Joyce was terribly interested in cinema, and had a hand in opening the first movie-house in Dublin" (L, 40), later rephrased as "blind Joyce's interest in the cinema" (L, 354). The letter *S*, the only one missing from "the standard typewriter-testing sentence stripped of its redundant characters—THE QUICK BROWN FX JMPD V LAZY G—is referred to as "the one hallowed by [...] James Joyce as the first in the scandalous novel he'd just begun serializing in *The Little Review*" (L, 418).

Sometimes, Joycean allusions have an amusingly parodic effect, e.g., Jacob Horner's "list of cuckolds" parodying the list of Molly's suitors in "Ithaca":

Cuckold	Wife	Lover(s)	Remarks
Mensch, Hector	King, Andrea	a. Erdmann, Willy (?)	
		b. Mensch, Karl (?)	issue: Mensch, Peter (?) &/or
		c. Mensch, Konrad (?)	Ambrose (?)
[...]			
Mensch, Peter	Guilianova, Magda	Mensch, Ambrose	a. May 12, 1947
			b. 1967–69 no issue

(L, 428)

At one point, the opening of the *Wake* is quoted at length (*L*, 68), and again Joyce is present in spirit if not in letter in the many blasphemous parodies, as in Jerome Bray's last epistle in *LETTERS*, with an incipit containing an incantation to his "Grandama," parodying the lyrics of the American anthem:

O see, kin, "G. III's" bottled dumps--oily shite!--which he squalidly hauled from his toilet's last gleanings, 5 broads stripped and, bride-starred, screwed their pearly ass right on our rampart! You watched? Heard our growls and their screamings? Now Bea Golden ("G's" heir)'s Honey-Dusted 4-square: grave food for her bright hatch of maggots next year! Our females are all seeded: our enemies are not alive: so, dear Grandama, take me to the hum of your hive! (*L*, 755)

But Werner is right in pointing out that more importantly Joycean than these allusions—witty and clever though they are—is Barth's preoccupation with "generational patterns," as when Jerome Bray, descendant of the Harold Bray of *Giles Goat-Boy*, concludes a letter with an invocation directed to his "Lost Mother, articifrix" (*L* 427). Also of note as a Joycean strategy is how Barth writes his name/initials into the text, an acrostic technique adapted from the *Wake*: Barth reminds us of the continual presence of John Barth by repeating the initials J. B. in the names of Jerome Bray, Jean Blanque (*L*, 110), Joseph Brant (*L*, 135), Jerome Bonaparte (*L*, 240), Joseph Bacri (*L*, 288), and many others.[55] *LETTERS* presents the summa of Barth's development over the previous two decades, and is a work of marvellous, and substantially Joycean, innovation.

What is more importantly *Wakean* about *LETTERS* goes beyond borrowings and wordplay: its concern with the fictional ultimacy of metafiction, i.e., self-conscious fiction. The problem with such infinitely regressive texts as *LETTERS* is that, as argued by Marjorie Godlin Roemer, texts incorporating their own critical postures ("Surely no author has gone further than he in supplying all the possible analyses of his own texts")[56] are clearly engaged in an effort to pre-empt and neutralise any conceivable critical attack. The problem Barth wrestles with here—the "ultimate value and commitment in the world of the self-conscious, infinitely regressive text"—is that of postmodern academic discourse, also largely at a loss vis-à-vis the categorical imperative to take a moral position, however involuted and sophisticated the manipulations of the cultural superstructure in which we operate. Roemer usefully zooms in on a late quote from *LETTERS*—its call for "the transcension of paralyzing self-consciousness to productive self-awareness" (*L*, 652)—in order to raise the question of whether "Barth succeeds in the hoped-for transcension

55   For more see Werner, *Paradoxical Resolutions*, 153.
56   Marjorie G. Roemer, "The Paradigmatic Mind: John Barth's *Letters*," *Twentieth Century Literature* (33.1, Spring 1987): 47.

to productive self-awareness; the question still remains open whether or not full human commitment is jeopardized by the sustained hedging of dialogized speech."[57] But even in Roemer's critical account, faulting Barth for his excesses and extremes, *LETTERS* is praised for its Dantesque "commitment to pursue the implications of his themes to their ultimate ends" and Barth for his "bearing witness with his own consciousness to the 'hard and perilous track' of late-twentieth-century self-reflexivity, and thus telling once again in our time the 'terror that cannot be told.'"[58]

With *Sabbatical: A Romance* (1982) Barth circles back toward the realistic mode (and more modest length) of his first two novels. Within this relatively realistic narrative framework, Barth has continued his trademark experimentation with point of view and inclusion of metafictional commentary and speculation to very much the present day. *Sabbatical* also marks the beginning of a new cycle of narratives, where, e.g., Barth's eleventh book, *Once upon a Time: A Floating Opera* (1994) is another self-retrospective, this time revisiting all of the ten books that have gone before it; *The Book of Ten Nights and Night* (2004) uses gadgets similar to those utilised in *Lost in the Funhouse*; and the following work, *Where the Roads Meet* (2005), presents three interlinked novellas, very much in the fashion of *Chimera*.

The gist of Barth's contribution to American novelistic experimentation, however, lies fully expressed in his seventh novel, ensconced in a retrospective evaluation (from the vantage point of the late 1970s) of the still-unexhausted potential of 1960s spirit of rebellion and innovation.

3.4 "NEVER CUT WHEN YOU CAN PASTE": WILLIAM H. GASS

The only writer whose influence upon the US fiction of the 1970s and 80s as a literary thinker and theorist can match Barth's is William Gass. In fact, so prolific was he as a theorist that the number of his non-fiction works far outnumbers his five volumes of fiction. From *Fiction and the Figures of Life* (1971) via *On Being Blue: A Philosophical Inquiry* (1976), *The World Within the Word* (1978) and *Finding a Form* (1997) to the recent *A Temple of Texts* (2006) and *Life Sentences* (2012), Gass produced a significant body of literary theory and criticism important far beyond its coinage of the term "metafiction." Although much sparser, Gass' fictional output—especially *Willie Master's Lonesome Wife* (1968) and his opus magnum *The Tunnel* (1995)—formed a remarkably holistic canon of stylistically innovative fiction informed, if not explicitly by Joyce, then by his modernist companions and antipodes, Gertrude Stein and Ezra Pound.

---

57   Ibid.
58   Ibid, 49.

To call Gass' opinion on fiction a "theory" is perhaps to overstep the bounds of his intentions, for he repeatedly refuses to write according to a doctrine, stressing that fictions should constitute their own worlds of words. Rather than attempting to represent some external reality, fictional texts should generate and maximise their own linguistic existence. Already the opening piece of his ground-breaking 1971 essay collection, *Fiction and the Figures of Life,* "Philosophy and the Form of Fiction," aims to emphasise the fictionality of the philosophical discourse by juxtaposing it with—and linking it to—Joyce's *Wake*:

> So much of philosophy is fiction. Dreams, doubts, fears, ambitions, ecstasies . . . if phi-losophy were a stream, they would stock it like fishes. [...] And how thin and unlaced the forms of *Finnegans Wake* are beside any of the *Critiques*; how sunlit Joyce's darkness, how few his parallels, how loose his correspondences. With what emotion do we watch the flight of the Alone to the Alone, or discover that *"der Welt ist alles, was der Fall ist."* (*FFL,* 3)

The parallel between fiction and philosophy, for Gass, is their obsession with language, their conceptual self-makeup, their creation of worlds: "Worlds? But the worlds of the novelist, I hear you say, do not exist. Indeed. As for that—they exist more often than the philosopher's" (*FFL,* 4). The following statement can be taken as encapsulating Gass' aesthetic creed:

> The esthetic aim of any fiction is the creation of a verbal world, or a significant part of such world, alive through every order of its Being. [...] The artist's task is therefore twofold. He must show or exhibit his world, and to do this he must actually make so-mething, not merely describe something that might be made. (*FFL,* 3–5)

Hence, any philosophical analysis of fictional texts should not concern itself with teasing out some overriding thesis or argument—should not, in other words, focus on the content—but should examine their status *as fictions*, understood not as "ways of viewing reality," but as "additions to it" (*FFL,* 24–25). Gass coins the term "metafiction" for those literary texts "in which the forms of fiction serve as the material upon which further forms may be imposed," whose fictionality is foregrounded within themselves (*FFL,* 25). Literature is, first and foremost, language, and "stories and the pla-ces and the people in them are merely made of words as chairs are made of smoothed sticks and sometimes of cloth or metal tubes" (*FFL,* 27). Gass' main point is that their use in literature is different.[59] Turning to the novel, Gass

---

59   "But the use of language in fiction only mimics its use in life. A sign like GENTS, for instance, tells me where to pee. It conveys information; it produces feelings of glad relief. I use the sign,

accords Joyce's two final works special places in the tradition of the genre as *Ulysses*, for him, is an example of a book of "all trivialities, items which could never find their way into any serious history" (FFL, 56), whereas the *Wake* is "a work of learning. It can be penetrated by stages. It can be elucidated by degrees. It is a complex, but familiar, compound. One can hear at any distance the teeth of the dogs as they feed on its limbs" (FFL, 87).

In the last two essays of *The World Within the Word* (1978), Gass linked this tendency toward inclusion and recycling to the method of the modernist collage and its undermining of the notion of "metadiscourse."[60] Metadiscourse is to be rejected for the sake of engaging with the text's fictionality – this includes the biographical one. Thus, with due reference to Aquinas, Gass observes of Joyce's final text that "the causes of the composition of *Finnegans Wake* might mount into the millions, matching the misprints, but only its own inner constitution (its radiance, wholeness, clarity) will guarantee its right to be read, to be repeated, praised, and pondered" (WWW, 302). In the final essay, "The Ontology of the Sentence, or How to Make a World of Words," Gass revisits, after Bruno and Vico, the principle of *coincidentia oppositorum* in a lyrical meditation.[61] Joyce's next step from these considerations, as Gass tells it, was the decision that "these metahistorical transformations were consequently circular," that "the minimum of one contrary takes its motion from the maximum of another; that we die by living; that corruption is generation, that the Upward and Downward Paths [...] are the same; that the concave creates the convex, sin the saved, etcetera the series etcetera continues by concluding?" (WWW, 310-1). Joyce's ultimate achievement, in Gass' view, lies in how he managed to conflate his literary method with the structure and purpose of the world as such, the word capturing the world: "The River Liffey swiftly overflows its banks to become Woman (i.e., History, i.e., Time), and shortly the cycle

---

but I dare not dawdle under it. It might have read MEN or borne a moustache. This kind of sign passes out of consciousness, is extinguished by its use. In literature, however, the sign remains; it sings; and we return to it again and again" (FFL, 30-1).

60   "Half of the novels we encounter are made from diaries and journals, left-over lifetimes and stale aperçus. A theory of fiction looms large in the Counterfeiters; every third hop in Hopscotch finds your shoe coming down in a pile of it; [...] Rilke threw into Malte huge chunks of his Paris letters—what the hell—and Finnegans Wake contains all its explanations. Let nothing be lost. Waste not even waste. Thus collage is the blessed method: never cut when you can paste" (WWW, 282).

61   "Vico concluded from these arcane observations that not only were the maxima and minima of particular contraries identical, the maxima had to be identical as well. Which is unquestionably the long and the short of it, inasmuch as God, for Bruno, is both the ultimate minimum (since everything is external to Him), and the ultimate maximum (since all things are contained in Him). [...] External to Him but contained . . . Is your fancy in fine fettle? God is a bubble of soap then—infinitely thin, infinitely large, infinitely hued. The outer rim of reality—its rubberous skin—is all that's real" (WWW, 310).

of evaporation, cloud formation, rain and run-off, is serving Vico's system of historical renewal and decay as if the world, and not the *Wake*, had been planned that way" (*WWW*, 312).

Gass' central points about the relationship between fiction, history, and reality were perhaps most clearly expressed in his interviews. The summative *Conversations with William H. Gass* volume, edited by Theodore G. Ammon, provides insight into Gass' thinking on the subject. In a *Contemporary Literature* interview, Gass agrees with the view that "Huckleberry Finn is more 'real' than, say, Alexander the Great because he is more fully realized in language," and in an interview with the *Chicago Review*, he develops this by claiming that "a sentence can contain more being than a town" where "more being" is rhetorical and designed to set the idea in motion against the opposition, and where the division that is commonly made "between life on the one hand and literature on the other isn't tenable." Ammon comments upon this maxim that for Gass, "the war for reality is a war of texts, and some texts turn out more interesting, more important, more influential, and more real than many people and also true than historical events."[62]

Combined with this emphasis on autonomy of the literary text is Gass' conviction as to the nature of the writer's vocation. In a 1976 interview for *The Iowa Review*, Gass insists that "as a writer I have only one responsibility, and that's to the language I'm using and to the thing I'm trying to make. Now as a person I have a lot of other responsibilities."[63] Joyce figures in Gass' meditations chiefly as the originator of a profound change in the author-reader relationship: "The myth is that Joyce tried to indicate that the speed passages in *Finnegans Wake* should be taken by variously spacing the words. In the novel I'm working on now, I want, for instance, a certain word to sound like a bell the whole time the reader is reading certain lines. I want this bong going bong all the bonging time." But ultimately, Gass is not a specific reader-group oriented writer: "I don't think much about the reader. Ways of reading are adversaries—those theoretical ways. As far as writing something is concerned, the reader really doesn't exist."[64] Echoing a version of Jolas' tenet of Joyce's linguistic autonomy, Gass posits that words do not principally serve as vehicles transporting the reading subject to some external reality, but rather constitute a reality themselves – the punny Joycean "world within the word." Analogously, fiction is not merely to be understood as a depiction of experience but as a competitive addition to experience, another new thing that stands in a peculiar relation to the world – and engaged in this process of addition is also Gass' own fiction.

---

62   *Conversations with William H. Gass*, ed. Ammon, xii.
63   Ibid, ix.
64   Ibid, 25.

Gass' first novel, *Omensetter's Luck* (1966), and the novella/short story collection *In the Heart of the Heart of the Country* (1968), are both fairly conventional in terms of their typographic presentation, style, and narrative strategies. In *Willie Masters' Lonesome Wife*—Gass' most formally experimental work—the innovation lies in the typographical interaction of various types of fonts that complement or clash with one another: there is a recto page typeset as a mirror version of the preceding verso, there are signs of physical damage to the page, including coffee-cup rings that blot out or encircle the most disparate textual segments. A collage of divergent elements arises, in which the narrative is consistently broken until it vanishes completely, giving rise to an almost abstract textual object. Also, the text is constantly in dialogue with images: photographs, usually of the naked female body in provocative postures, as, e.g., on the very first page which has the first letter "S" magnified—in a manner reminiscent of the 1922 *Ulysses* edition—and actually embedded in an image of a woman's hand carrying the letter to her open mouth. In terms of argument, as long as there is one to be extracted, the text is a monologue of one Babs Masters, the wife, a former stripper and prostitute, which takes place while she is having sex with her lover Phil Gelvin. So explicit is the text's sexual content and so contagious its generic promiscuousness that, as Ammon records, "Gass wanted a condom included with his novel [...] so that one could enter the text properly and safely."[65]

Although amusing as a gadget in a vaguely machoistic fashion, this gesture expresses *Willie Master's Lonesome Wife*'s deeper concern with the theme of the textual representation of femininity and, conversely, in conceptualising language and textuality as a form of *jouissance*, sexual pleasure. Molly Bloom-like discourse, peppered with Joycean neologisms, is to be found in many places, as for example in a passage in bold type on the second page of the (unpaginated) text: "**Suppose, for instance, a stranger were to—oh, say you're laughing uproariously, and that's the occasion for it—spit in your mouth, god forbid. [...] You don't go hithering and thithering, do you? moaning, do you? God, my god, my head is leaking, lord, my head is leaking through my mouth**" (*WMLF*, unpaginated). The acknowledged predecessor is Flaubert: "I dream like Madame Bovary. Only I don't die during endings. I never die. They fall asleep on me and shrivel up. I write the *finis* for them, close the covers, shelf the book." The physicality of the abject bodily excretions contemplated by Gass' heroine goes well beyond Molly's flow or wind:

> It's called the wine of love because, when drunk, it signifies acceptance. That's my theory. There's no woman who's not, deep inside her, theoretical. That's why we

---

65 Ibid, 10.

> love, in men, not them, but place and reputation—money, honor, age, effects, and
> aura—radiation; not them, but their love, we love—our idea and transubstan-
> tiating notion of them. That's my theory. Most people are distressed, honestly
> enough, by their own dirt. Imagine the shit of a lifetime packed in tubs. It would
> be small comfort knowing it was yours. Still, the dirt of others is even more dis-
> tressing. Pick another's nose, for instance. Proof enough? Well, that's my theory.
> (*WMLF*)

Like D. H. Lawrence, Gass also struggles with terminology, in the effort to
evade words that are either obscene or clinical; like Joyce, he oftentimes
resorts to punning and innuendoes: intercourse becomes "oomfy whoozis on
the sofa," a skinny girl is called an "udder disappointment" by her beau, to
which she retorts, "I pricktickily don't like you either" (*WMLF*).

Appropriately for Gass' more serious concerns, central among Babs' many
aliases in the book is that of "language" or "text" Herself, a sinuous, sensuous
mistress: "I'm only a string of noises, after all—nothing more really—an arrangement, a column of air moving up and down, a queer growth like a gall on
a tree, a mimic of movement in silent readers maybe, a brief beating of wings
and cooing of a peaceful kind, an empty swing still warm from young bloom-
ers" (*WMLF*). However, this view is not consistent: Gass also foregrounds the
medium, the remove, of language/print/paper, claiming that

> The muddy circle you see just before you and below you represents the ring left on
> a leaf of the manuscript by my coffee cup. Represents, I say, because, as you must su-
> rely realize, this book is many removes from anything I've set pen, hand, or cup to. For
> example, suppose there were imprinted here, as in letters of love, a pair of lips; could
> you, by kissing them, let the paper pander between us? (*WMLF*)

At other times, Gass insists that the book is a woman – toward the end, the
narrative subject observes that "I am that lady language chose to make her
playhouse of, and if you do not like me, if you find me dewlapped, scabby,
wrinkled, old (and I've admittedly as many pages as my age), well sir, I'm not,
like you, a loud rude noise and fart upon the town" – and surely enough, there
are thirty sheets of paper within which the thirty-year-old female textual
consciousness is constructed. Ultimately, however, the emphasis falls on the
distance in linguistic mediation, and in the last coffee-cup ring there is the
concluding message: YOU HAVE / FALLEN / INTO ART / —RETURN TO /
LIFE. Recognised by critics as the crucial work of what Gass himself would
call metafiction, *Willie Masters' Lonesome Wife* examines the nature of fiction-
-making and of the reading process, endowing such commonplace, indeed
invisible, entities as pagination, typographical setup, paragraph, sentence,
and the word with unusual density, intensity, and strangeness.

After 1968, Gass as fiction writer fell silent for another twenty-five years, turning to philosophy, essays, and criticism, but also to writing his opus magnum, *The Tunnel*. He began the novel in 1966, publishing excerpts in a number of literary journals such as the *Review of Contemporary Fiction*. Almost thirty years in the making, *The Tunnel*'s pre-publication history created the type of anxious anticipation among critics and Gass' readership similar to the one that accompanied the 17 years of the composition of *Finnegans Wake*. Its critical reception was no less divided: on the one hand, there were critics agreeing with Robert Alter's complaint that the work exhibits "sheer adipose verbosity and an unremitting condition of moral and intellectual flatulence," and what is more, that the work reduces "the enormity of genocide [...] into the nickel-and-dime nastiness that people perpetrate in everyday life."[66] In other words, as Robert Kelly concluded in *The New York Times Book Review*, to say that one has known "bedrooms bad as Belsen"[67] shows alliteration running away with proportion. On the other hand, many reviewers side with Steven Moore's assessment in *The Review of Contemporary Fiction* that Gass has produced "truly one of the great books of our time," in which "rhetorical energy and excess redeem personal failure and emptiness,"[68] or Michael Dirda's in *Washington Post Book World* (February 1995) that "for 650 pages one of the consummate magicians of English prose pulls rabbits out of sentences and creates shimmering metaphors before your very eyes."[69] However divided, the critical reaction of the time agrees on one point: that *The Tunnel*, again similarly to the *Wake*, is a belated aftermath of the era of its conception in the mid-1960s, the high point of the American post-war epic, on par with Gaddis' *The Recognitions* and Barth's *LETTERS*.

As is evident from the reviews above, *The Tunnel*'s thematic challenge (its style an expansion on the typographical eccentricities of *Willie Masters' Lonesome Wife*) lies in Gass' deployment of his linguistic innovations in the context, or at the expense, of the greatest trauma of modern history, the Holocaust. The protagonist of this novel on "the frustrations of private life in an age of historical enormities"[70] is William Frederick Kohler, a historian teaching at a Midwestern university during the 1960s, who has nearly finished with his academic masterpiece, *Guilt and Innocence in Hitler's Germany*. While devising the introduction, he becomes side-tracked into relating all

---

66   Robert Alter, "The Levelling Wind," *The New Republic* (27 March 1995). Online: https://newrepublic.com/article/146163/leveling-wind
67   Robert Kelly, "A Repulsively Lonely Man," *The New York Times Book Review* (26 February 1995): 17.
68   Stephen Moore, "A Review of *The Tunnel*," *Review of Contemporary Fiction*, Vol. 15, No. 1 (Spring, 1995): 159.
69   Michael Dirda, "In the Dark Chambers of the Soul," *Washington Post Book World* (12 March 1995): 10.
70   Alter, "The Levelling Wind."

manner of scandalous confessions about his colleagues, his frustrating family relationships, his dirty secrets and squalid affairs, and his aesthetic and philosophical reflections, until these added pages, all inserted within the pages of his historical project proper, overwhelm his original intention. As Gass himself observed, the challenge was "to bring grandeur to a shit," and so Kohler might very well be the least likeable in the long line of Gass' lonesome, maniacal, misanthropic eccentrics. Kohler's tunnel—both metaphorical, the one he digs through the mass of historical data and through his own history of his private grudges, evil thoughts and deeds; as well as literal, the tunnel he digs in the basement of his house—might be the most complexly elaborated withdrawal in all fiction. A recurring theme is his idea to found the Party of Disappointed People—the PdP; Gass has Kohler doodle designs for the PdP logo throughout the text, including proposed flags, insignias, banners, and a "Medal for ingratitude." The last page of the book is a picture of the PdP logo.

Two of Gass' lifelong concerns—with the language of history and with history *as* language—are foregrounded in ways informed by his demonstrated knowledge of Joyce. For example, Gass repeatedly uses the *Wakean* metaphor of history as a midden heap:

> The study of history is essentially the study of symbols and markers, of verbal remains—symbol middens, shall we say?—and tombs. Our study, gentlemen, the study of history, is really a study of language. Only words speak past the present; only words have any kind of honest constant visual life. (*TT*, 5)

And every now and then, Gass has Kohler meditate on the (r)usefulness of language vis-à-vis reality:

> Language is always honest. Language does not lie, only its users. I think barrel suckers say that about guns. Notice how 'lover' is mostly spelled by 'over' and 'sex' is two-thirds 'ex'. If fucking were pretty it would have a pretty name, like 'meadow', like 'gazelle, or 'paramour'. If fucking were so fundamental, then it would bind us more dearly and devotedly together, as its gestures pretend, instead of driving us away from one another, into our own close satisfactions or the sullen distance of our discontents. (*TT*, 560)

The answer to the question of whether *The Tunnel* garners rhetorical capital out of the death camps and trivialises the Holocaust by reducing it to sheer wordplay, or not, ultimately depends on whether the reader grants Gass his prioritisation of language in its materiality, its rhythm, its evocative powers over its referential function. Gass' lifelong creed was that

> the artist's fundamental loyalty must be to form, and his energy employed in the activity of making. Every other diddly desire can find expression; every crackpot idea or

local obsession, every bias and graciousness and mark of malice, may have an hour; but it must never be allowed to carry the day (*FF*, 35).

That his stories "are malevolently anti-narrative," that his "essays are maliciously anti-expository," is all due to his "ideology of opposition" springing from the belief that "life was meaningless, since life was not a sign; that novels were meaningful, because signs were the very materials of their composition" (*FF*, 46). Joyce makes a few interesting cameos in *The Tunnel*, whether in the letter, as in this passage combining a reference to the "snotgreen sea" from *Ulysses* with the *Wake*'s "museyroom":

> Here we have a meaningless moment no doubt, memorialized by the camera, and now placed in this small unvisited museyroom where time lies in a stagnancy of nothing to report, and a snot-green film blown from the nose of James Joyce has hankied about its holy gloom. Martha keeps the place dusted, but I still sneeze. It's as if a little fish had jumped. (*TT*, 451)

Or in the spirit of the many punning sacrilege and obscenity, like in the following limerick:

> I once went to bed with a nun,
> who had screwed every nation but one.
> I don't want to Russia,
> but your Pole feels like Prussia—
> far too Chile—to Finnish the pun.
> (*TT*, 157)

A constant concern of the text, if not of its protagonist, are the limits of human history as linearity vs. the natural world of the constant present and recycling. *The Tunnel* does for Mississippi what the *Wake* does for the Liffey:

> Do rivers. Do. I did. I did them. Long after they were rivers, really, when they were only lines forefingered on Lou's back and flank and beautiful bottom. The pretense was painful. What could the Mississippi be now that not even its lovely name was whisted, and its many locks counted, its great bluffs passed, the long broad line drawn gradually yet grandly down to the slowly spreading delta and the river's cessation in the gulf? Humbly dumbly only to wash up. Washed up. Beached. But there were mostly banks to rivers. Where Anna Livia flopped her sheets upon the rocks. (*TT*, 555)

At this stage of remembering Joyce, Gaddis has his protagonist reflect on a well-worn modernist technique, and even the scatological pun entailed in the title of Joyce's *Chamber Music*: "is that really The Stream of Consciousness we've heard so much about? The bladder's music? What a relief it is to piss after a beery day" (*TT*, 555). *The Tunnel* also ends on a *Wakean* note of wistfulness, self-recrimination, death, and renovation, with Kohler's farewell ruminations highly reminiscent of ALP's:

> I've got to decide. Clean up. Get on? Make my wrong right. [...] Takes a signature. Resignation. With decency subside. [...] In short, to abide. In the last hamlet of feeling. I'm inclined to say why not? Sure. Or dump every dirty drawer onto my desk [...] till the desk's hid, [...], covering the pages of my History as my History sheeted me; there to let my words wait, like the disappointed people bide, before they try *life again*. Meanwhile carry on without complaining. No arm with armband raised on high. No more booming bands, no searchlit skies. *Or shall I, like the rivers, rise?* Ah. Well. Is rising wise? Revolver like the Führer near an ear. Or lay my mind down by sorrow's side. (*TT*, 652, my emphasis)

Controversial due to its stylistic aestheticism overriding its problematic politics, *The Tunnel* remains a late masterpiece in the 1960s-70s tradition of the great American novel, a book that has the increasingly scarce ability to shock, provoke, and affront, all to a notable degree resulting from its coming to terms with Joyce's materialist poetics.

3.5 "THE BOOK REMAINS PROBLEMATIC, UNEXHAUSTED": DONALD BARTHELME

More than any other major American writer of the 1960s, Donald Barthelme took to heart Borges' lifelong dedication to short fiction and his suspicion of grand fictional narratives, a dedication which is rather rare in experimental writers.[71] At the beginning of Barthelme's career there was a critical engagement, not so much with Borges as with his Irish precursor and antipode. In an essay entitled "After Joyce" from 1964 (collected in the posthumously published collection *Not-Knowing*), Barthelme takes issue with Kenneth Burke's view of the writers of the *transition* school as political recluses and aesthetic deserters. Barthelme notes that such a view raises "the sticky question of what art is 'about' and the mysterious shift that takes place as soon as one says that art is not about something but is something" (*N-K*, 3). With Joyce, argues Barthelme, "fiction altered its placement in the world in a movement

---

71   As Morris Dickstein's "Fiction at the Crossroads" observes, "the short story, even in the hands of Chekhov and Joyce, had always been the most conservative of all literary genres, the most tied to nineteenth-century conventions of incident and character, the least given to formal or technical innovation" (Morris Dickstein, "Fiction at the Crossroads," *Critical Essays on Donald Barthelme*, ed. Richard F. Patteson [New York: G.K. Hall & Co., 1992] 59).

so radical that its consequences have yet to be assimilated." Departing from the well-known dictum of Beckett's essay on the "Work in Progress," Barthelme notes that the consequences of creating literary "objects" as "worlds" in themselves present a "stunning strategic gain for the writer. He has in fact removed himself from the work, just as Joyce instructed him to do." What is further characteristic of the literary object is

> that it does not declare itself at once, in a rush of pleasant naiveté. Joyce enforces the way in which *Finnegans Wake* is to be read. He conceived the reading to be a lifetime project, the book remaining always *there*, like the landscape surrounding the reader's home or the buildings bounding the reader's apartment. The book remains problematic, unexhausted. (*N-K*, 4)

Barthelme singles out a number of Joycean writers, of a chiefly twofold tendency. The first group is called the "aggression" group, including such writers who "respond to the world by adding to it constructs which are hostile to life, and Burroughs, most in debt to Joyce, makes the deepest wounds" (*N-K*, 8). The other group is marked by "playfulness" and is represented by writers like Kenneth Koch, J. P. Donleavy, and Henry Green, all of whom "demonstrat[e] a consciousness of the word as object, of the medium as message" (*N-K*, 9). Against these writers of interest, Barthelme indiscriminatingly pits French New Novelists (Butor, Sarraute, Robbe-Grillet, Simon, and Sollers) who

> have on the other hand succeeded in making objects of their books without reaping any of the strategic benefits of the maneuver – a triumph of misplaced intelligence. Their work seems leaden, self-conscious in the wrong way. Painfully slow-paced, with no leaps of the imagination, concentrating on the minutiae of consciousness, these novels scrupulously, in deadly earnest, parse out what can safely be said. [...] they arrive at inconsequence, carrying on that traditional French war against the bourgeois which ends by flattering him: what a monster! (*N-K*, 10)

Linguistic playfulness, in Barthelme's critical estimation, is ultimately what emerges as the most valuable part of the legacy of Joyce's textual objects, as well as wicked humour—blending the haphazard and the grotesque with the absurd—a marker of much of Barthelme's own fiction.[72]

Barthelme's familiarity with the *Wake* came to fruition in his novels. For his first, *Snow White* (1967), Barthelme turned to a familiar myth rather than

---

72   Michael Hudgens perceptively described his relation to Joyce when he said that "Barthelme was no Joycean scholar, but he knew the work and viewed it as an obstacle course to be crossed" (Michael Thomas Hudgens, *Donald Barthelme - Postmodernist American Writer* [Lewiston: The Edwin Mellen Press, 2001] 48).

to "reality" to provide a basic framework for his tale, although the "material" which he places into the framework is drawn from a wide range of literary and cultural sources. Larry McCaffery observed that its fragmented character owes to its reworking of the modernist legacy.[73] The novel, doing without such literary devices as plot or characters, mainly limits itself to fragmentary take-offs on a huge variety of rhetorical styles and verbal trash. Barthelme's satire revolves around the friction of diverse languages—e.g. in "The Report" section contrasting the jargons of hardware and software, technology, and the humanities—and the disjunctive tension between narcotised consciousness and the explosive object. In *Snow White*, Jane's letter to Mr. Quistgaard—whose name she has picked at random from the telephone book—is an epitome of Barthelme's relationship to his reader. Jane's letter opens with a description of a "threatening situation":

> You and I, Mr. Quistgaard, are not in the same universe of discourse. You may not have been aware of it previously, but the fact of the matter is, that we are not. We exist in different universes of discourse. [...] You may have, in a commonsense way, regarded your own u. of d. as a plenum, filled to the brim with discourse. You may have felt that what already existed was a sufficiency. People like you often do. That is certainly one way of regarding it, if fat self-satisfied complacency is your aim. But I say unto you, Mr. Quistgaard, that even a plenum can leak. (*SW*, 44–5)

Passages such as this one suggest that for Barthelme, analytic literary vocabulary itself can become as stale as any other language when not exposed to discursive variety, becoming rigidified in its use.

The myth tackled in Barthelme's second novel *The Dead Father* concerns the Oedipal dynamics. It abandons the satiric language of *Snow White* in favour of Rabelaisian catalogues and word-heaps. The opening lines of the prologue begin a detailed description of the father, a colossus toppled to earth, who is being pulled by nineteen men to a trench where he will be covered by bulldozers. Curiously enough, the eponymous hero is alive and kicking throughout the text. In fact, as he gradually assumes increasingly abstract properties, the Dead Father comes to embody any hegemonic belief system, representing all the major systems of authority nestled by Western civilisation: God, King, Reason, History, State.

---

73   "As in *Ulysses* and works by other writers of encyclopedic tendencies [...] *Snow White* presents us with a profusion of bits and pieces drawn from books and other literary storehouses such as folktales, movies, newspapers, advertisements and scholarly journals. [...] Even more often, however, these fragments are drawn from clichés of learning and literature. We find, for instance, parodies of specific literary styles and conventions, pseudo-learned digressions about history, sociology, and psychology, mock presentations of Freudian and existentialist patterns, and inane concrete poems" (McCaffery, *The Metafictional Muse*, 138).

The Dead Father is both creative (having fathered multitudes) and destructive: for instance, when exasperated at being excluded from sex with Julie—the central female character of the novel—he escapes to a grove where he slays a large number of musicians. Thomas, the filial character, sets out on a quest to inter the Dead Father and also to bring about a transfer of authority. Upon meeting, the couple tell each other stories – high among these, for reasons obvious in due course, is the story of The Great Father Serpent, narrated by Thomas: "a serpent of huge bigness which held in its mouth a sheet of tin on which something was written, the roars rattled the tin and I was unable to make out the message" (*DF*, 44).

The Great Father Serpent is described as dressed in "fine smallclothes of softwhispering blushcolored changeable taffeta," his "upper or more headward length" covered with "a light jacket of white silk embroidered with a thread nutmeg in color and a thread goose-turd in color, these intertwined, and trimmed with fine whipped lace" (*DF*, 44). After another whole page devoted to the details of the serpent's attire the description arrives at "a doublet, a great cloak, a girdle, and a French hat" (*DF*, 44-5) – the Great Father Serpent is dressed in an emblematically Joycean attire. The Serpent's riddle posed to Thomas is "*What do you really feel?*" (*DF*, 45-6) and Thomas' answer is "Like murderinging," revealing that behind the façade of an obedient son, Thomas is driven by murderous wishes. The Serpent gives Thomas "A Manual for Sons," so self-sufficient as to have been published as an independent work by Barthelme. It is here that fatherhood is exposed as the source of the grand narratives which "make men so unhappy," proposing as a solution:

> to reproduce every one of the enormities touched upon in this manual, but in an attenuated form. You must become your father, but a paler, weaker version of him [...] Fatherhood can be, if not conquered, at least "turned down" in this generation – by the combined efforts of all of us together. (*DF*, 145)

The Serpent's Joycean lesson is that parricide—just as the symbolic slaying of the suitors toward the end of *Ulysses*—should be performed mentally and spiritually, that fatherhood should be conquered on the inside, repudiated from within, as when Stephen Dedalus, "tap[ping] his brow," observes, "But in here it is I must kill the priest and the king" (*U* 15.4436-7). And, just when the Dead Father is to be put to rest by his son, the famous *Wakean* interior monologue spells out his own uncertainties, his own filial dependence:

> AndI. EndI. Great endifarce teeterteeterteetertottering. Willit urt. I reiterate. Don't be cenacle. Conscientia mille testes. And having made them, where now? what now? [...] Thegreatestgoodofthegreatestnumber was a Princeapple of mine. I was compassiona-

te, insofarasitwaspossleto-beso. Best I cud I did! Absolutely! No dubitation about it! Don't like! Don't want! Pitterpatter oh please pitterpatter (*DF*, 171–3)

Here, the monologue ends, without a period, an obvious *Wakean* parallel which did not elude Werner, who reads *The Dead Father* as an (unsuccessful) parody of Joyce.[74] However, as Richard Walsh has observed, parody is a notion whose applicability—to Barthelme's text and in general—is fraught with inherent inconsistencies, arguing that the Dead Father's monologue is "not exactly parody, since it does not function as an implicit critique of the manner or author parodied."[75] Actually, the very notion of parody, with such two authors as Barthelme and Joyce, becomes problematic: "But what exactly would a "real parody" of Joyce consist of? With language already so self--conscious and ironic, the self-critical function of parodic language has been largely pre-empted. This is more mimicry than parody, an appropriation of style to a different end, the nature and rationale of which is the burden of the novel's argument. Barthelme's formal innovation is not an irresponsible aestheticism, but the means to a more sophisticated engagement with life." Furthermore, one of Barthelme's departures from the modernist Joycean structure is his deflation of numerological and conceptual symbolism, his parallels and correspondences existing without eventually adding up to some ultimate overarching resolution. Carl Malmgren's examples of "signifiers that float freely or cancel each other out" are instructive.[76] Whether a parody or a pastiche, *The Dead Father* is a markedly Joycean text, featuring an allegorical impersonation of his very person and an adaptation and reuse of his *Wakean* portmanteau technique.

A short-story writer turned novelist, Barthelme was an author whose writing, although original and self-sufficient in its own right, took Joyce's avant-garde exploration of the materiality of language and creation of literary objects as a source for some of its most experimental moments.

---

74   "Whatever its intent, the passage lacks the diverse frames of reference of even the most crystal-line *Wake* passages. It degenerates into a dictionary game for the glossing of collapsing card-board characters, leaving the reader with the feeling that he has confronted a very un-Bar-thelmean allegorical failure or a parody which has failed to find its target" (Werner, *Paradoxical Resolutions*, 101).

75   Richard Walsh, *Novel Arguments – Reading Innovative American Fiction* [Cambridge: Cambridge University Press, 1995] 45.

76   "A case in point in *The Dead Father* is the signifier 23. There are twenty-three characters in the troupe, twenty-three chapters in the novel, twenty-three sections in "The Manual for Sons," twenty-three types of fathers (including the dead father). The number seems loaded with sig-nificance but finally fails to signify; it is simply a prime number, indivisible, without factors. Similarly the reader is invited to see Emma (M-A) as a mother figure but cannot really make anything of the equation" (Carl D. Malmgren, "Exhumation: *The Dead Father*," *Narrative Turns and Minor Genres in Postmodernism*, eds. Theo D'haen & Hans Bertens [Amsterdam: Rodopi, 1995] 35).

3.6 "ORPHEUS PUTS DOWN HARP": THOMAS PYNCHON

In the introduction to his 1984 reprinting of his early stories under the title of *Slow Learner* (1984), Thomas Pynchon repudiates his younger self for creating *V.* (1963), *The Crying of Lot 49* (1966), and *Gravity's Rainbow* (1973), all results of his "notion that one's personal life had nothing to do with fiction, when the truth, as everyone knows, is nearly the direct opposite" (*SL*, 23). His early work had ignored what he had already known, that the fiction "that moved and pleased me then as now was precisely that which had been made luminous, undeniably authentic by having been found and taken up, always at a cost, from deeper and more shared levels of the life we all really live" (*SL*, 23). The developments of Burroughs, Barth, even Gaddis and Barthelme, all reached the peak of their linguistic experimentalism sometime between the mid-1960s and mid-1970s, with a turn in the early 1980s toward a more traditionally narrative prose; but nowhere did this turn entail an effective renunciation of the previous endeavour, as in Pynchon's case.

Pynchon is a Joycean writer chiefly through his foregrounding of complexity, his conflation of a multitude of symbolical systems of signification which he imposes upon, and through which he shapes the fictional reality of his narratives. Few other writers after Joyce have been as interested in encoding and decoding, in interpreting, in construing fictional reality by means of structurality—concatenation of ciphers, symbols and signs—as Pynchon. This complexity has also bred an equally complex and sizeable critical material that surrounds Pynchon's fiction: again, few authors after Joyce can boast of quite as many reader's guides or books devoted to mere plot summaries and basic sense-making of their work, as Pynchon. Also, one can note the biographical parallel between Joyce and Pynchon, the latter living the former's dictum of the artist's refinement out of existence.[77]

The more relevant, theme-based affinity between Joyce and Pynchon concerns their encyclopaedism, recognised in one of the first critical responses to *Gravity's Rainbow*. In his 1976 essay in a collection on Pynchon entitled *Mindful Pleasures*, Edward Mendelson included Pynchon's novel in a genre composed of "only a few books in the Western tradition," that of the "encyclopaedic narrative," in which it joined not only *Moby Dick* but also "Dante, Rabelais, Cervantes, Goethe, and Joyce's *Ulysses*."[78] Connected with the first

---

77 "James Joyce's dictum that the artist should be refined out of existence seems to have been taken literally by Pynchon: only one photograph of him exists; his dossier at Cornell has mysteriously vanished; and records of his service in the navy were burned in a fire at the records office in St. Louis" (Robert D. Newman, *Understanding Thomas Pynchon* [Columbia: University of South Carolina Press, 1986] 4).

78 Edward Mendelson, "Gravity's Encyclopaedia," *Mindful Pleasures: Essays on Thomas Pynchon*, eds. George Levine & David Leverenz (Boston: Little, Brown, 1976) 161.

on the list is another trace shared by Pynchon with Joyce, their interest in science and technology vis-à-vis culture and fiction – in his dauntlessness as regards science and technology, Pynchon has been seen by critics as belonging to the "apostolic succession from James Joyce."[79] At the same time, however, the difference in the purpose served by these parallel efforts is as marked and should not be understated. For instance, myth, in Pynchon, is treated encyclopaedically in that mythical referents—in *Gravity's Rainbow* but also elsewhere—are derived not merely from the customary sources (as the *Nibelungenlied*, for example), but also from literature (Dante, Borges, Grass, as well as Joyce), from science and psychopathology (Newton and Einstein, Sacher-Masoch and Pavlov), and from history itself.

As Levitt notes, this diversified, encyclopaedic basis of myth is ultimately used as a refusal of the modernist mythopoesis, in favour of the injunction that "we must invent myths today, often outrageously, precisely because we can no longer experience them, that we have lost our mythological heritage."[80] Clearly, most criticism pitting Pynchon against Joyce on the basis of their treatment of myth and discursive parody reduces Joyce unfavourably to a mythmaker à la the one portrayed in Eliot's 1923 *Ulysses* review. However, Eliot's is a problematic and limiting reading that in no way does justice to Joyce's destabilisation, if not debunking of the Homeric parallels, the fashion in which Homer is brought into contact with the Shakespearean intertext and, last but not least, how the later *Ulysses* chapters take as targets of their satire all sorts of discursive systems, whether that of nationalist propaganda ("Cyclops"), popular women magazines ("Nausicaa"), or science ("Ithaca"). Differences not in degree but in kind are, therefore, to be sought elsewhere. Linked with their shared encyclopaedism is Pynchon's and Joyce's commonly perceived "difficulty" with the reader.

Richard Poirier's meditation on "The Importance of Thomas Pynchon" is instructive[81] in its identification of a dilemma for those fond of Pyn-

---

79   "Pynchon lies in the apostolic succession from James Joyce, who felt compelled to master in lucid prose not only the process by which thermal energy from the sun, stored for millennia as fossilized vegetable matter, eventually came to heat Leopold Bloom's shaving water, but also the process by which the water itself got from Dublin's reservoir to Bloom's tap. Joyce once described his mania for detail by saying that he had the mind of an assistant greengrocer. With a similarly all-embracing mind, Pynchon joins the staff of Joyce's implied word-grocery, with an even more formidable determination not to leave the higher or more remote shelves uninventoried" (David Cowart, *Thomas Pynchon: The Art of Allusion* [Carbondale/Edwardsville: Southern Illinois University Press, 1980] 1).

80   Cowart, *Thomas Pynchon*, 86.

81   "We can't with Pynchon—any more than with Joyce or with the Eliot of the loveably pretentious notes to The Waste Land—possibly claim to be as conversant as he wants us to be with the various forms of contemporary culture. He may be as theatrically enlivening and entertaining as Dickens, but a reader needs to know relatively little to appreciate Dickens. Really to read Pynchon properly you would have to be astonishingly learned not only about literature but about

chon's work: "We don't want to stop the game, we don't want to get out of the rhythm, but what are we to do if we simply don't know enough to play the game, to move with the rhythm?" Poirier links this to Burgess' popularisation efforts vis-à-vis Joyce, of which he is harshly critical.[82] Bypassing the issue of accessibility—always ultimately subjective and hardly useful— critic Sara Soldberg focuses instead on the different uses, in Joyce and in Pynchon, of encyclopaedism, and goes so far as to speak of apples and oranges.[83]

Winning the William Faulkner Foundation award for the best debut novel of the year, Pynchon's first work, entitled *V.* (1963), invites parallels with Joyce's *Ulysses* on a number of levels. It features two parallel narrative strands, taking turn in a chapter-by-chapter alternation—one set in the New York of 1956, the other taking place at various different moments of historical crises—following two protagonists, Benny Profane and Herbert Stencil, respectively.[84] The two eventually meet in the final chapter as Profane joins Stencil on his quest after a mysterious entity known to him only under the initial V.[85] The single letter V gradually takes on a function akin to that of the acrostic structures of the *Wake* – operating as a sign locus for multiple intersecting meanings.[86] Throughout, Pynchon toys with the possibility that

a vast number of other subjects belonging to the disciplines and to popular culture, learned to the point where learning is almost a sensuous pleasure, something to play around with, to feel totally relaxed about, so that you can take in stride every dizzying transition from one allusive mode to another" (Richard Poirier, "The Importance of Thomas Pynchon," *Thomas Pynchon*, ed. Harold Bloom [Philadelphia: Chelsea House Publishers, 2003] 47-8).

82 "We can't, above all, pretend that such a writer is a regular fellow, the way Anthony Burgess does with Joyce. Burgess' *ReJoyce* is both quite a bad book and an amusing object lesson. With totally false casualness, Burgess has to lay before us an immense amount of requisite learning in the effort to prove that Joyce can be read by Everyman. Burgess makes an obvious, glaring but nonetheless persistent error: he confuses Joyce's material (much of which is indeed quite ordinary and common) with what Joyce does to it (which is totally uncommon, unordinary, and elitist). Another way of answering Burgess, or anyone who says that a writer like Joyce or Pynchon is just a "good read," is to say that nobody in Joyce, and very few in Pynchon, could read the novels that have been written about them" (Poirier, "The Importance of Thomas Pynchon," 48).

83 "Of the major modernists, it is probably Joyce whose degree of connection with Pynchon stands most in danger of overstatement. Although *Gravity's Rainbow* accepts the Joycean demand that would-be great, important books be committed to the practice of an omnibus informal erudition, a great deal of sophisticated stylistic experimentation, and an extremely large thematic purview, these are profoundly different kinds of encyclopedists" (Sara M. Solberg, "On Comparing Apples and Oranges: James Joyce and Thomas Pynchon," *Comparative Literature Studies* 26 [March 1979]: 33).

84 Levitt parallels between the protagonist couple and Joyce's Bloom and Stephen, where Benny Profane becomes "a type of Everyman-Pilgrim, echoing ironically both old allegorical quest heroes and new," like Bloom he is "Part-Catholic, part-Jew" and also "cut-off from conventional family ties" (Levitt, *Modernist Survivors*, 77).

85 David Seed, *The Fictional Labyrinths of Thomas Pynchon* (London: Macmillan, 1988) 84-5.

86 As Levitt has noted, the connotations of V include "various women (Vera Meroving, Hedvig Vogelsang and Veronica Manganese, among others) and places (Valletta, Vesuvius, Venezuela, and the perhaps apocryphal Vheissu), forms human and inhuman (a recurring V-shaped stain on a dish, the delta of Venus), concrete objects and abstract concepts (volcanoes, the viola da

the pattern might yield some overriding meaning and signification, Stencil dreaming "perhaps once a week that it had all been a dream, and that now he'd awakened to discover the pursuit of V. was merely a scholarly quest after all, an adventure of the mind, in the tradition of *The Golden Bough* or *The White Goddess*" (*V.*, 50).

There is a repeated intimation that things might "all at once to fall into a pattern" (*V.*, 280), but ultimately, at a later point in the novel, the narrative concedes that "V. by this time was a remarkably scattered concept" (*V.*, 364), and the novel ends up performing the formerly envisaged "retreat to a diametric opposite rather than any reasonable search for a golden mean" (*V.*, 103). One of the patternings V. follows meticulously is the heritage of the pre-war avant-garde art and literature of the subsequent periods.[87] Parallels notwithstanding, differences are equally palpable: not only does the V-trace ultimately yield no insight, but also the meeting between Stencil and Profane toward which the narrative gravitates throughout—a *coincidentia oppositorum* of sorts—fails to offer any reconciliation or affirmation. However busy and active a text peopled with an immense cast of characters and swarming with activity—and in that sense, reminiscent of *Ulysses*—as Adams has noted, "all the hurry and scurry in the novel [...] lead nowhere. For one tale that is tied up in pink ribbon [...], there are dozens that the author leaves hanging in mid-air."[88]

Similar parallelism in method and difference in purpose can be found in Pynchon's undisputed opus magnum, *Gravity's Rainbow*, including the vicissitudes of its reception, the rejections of the novel by the Pulitzer Advisory Board and by other members of the literary establishment, as an affront to good taste. The novel's many plottings are so complex as to warrant a whole library of exegetic critical material: it contains over 400 characters and involves many different threads of narrative which cross-sect and weave around one another. Recurring themes feature the rocket programme of

---

gamba, vision, venality, a sewer rat named Veronica, the Machiavellian virtú" (Levitt, *Modernist Survivors*, 79).

87   "There are parallels, for example, between the scandals of Cubism and the *Sacré* and the scandals of Abstract Expressionism and free jazz. There are anticipations, of absurdist literature in Conrad and Kafka, of the absurdist universe in early Wittgenstein. There are direct links: Henry Miller is the acknowledged forerunner of Kerouac and the Beats, Sartre uses Rilke's *Notebooks* as a model for *La Nausée*; Beckett is Joyce's protégé; the "old Dadaists" reappear as new Dadaists like Oldenburg and Rauschenberg; the Theatre of the Absurd is a development of Surrealism" (John Dugdale, *Thomas Pynchon: Allusive Parables of Power* [London: MacMillan, 1990] 102–3).

88   Unlike Bloom's and Stephen's respective quests for a spiritual son and father, in *V.*, notes Adams, "what is important to the book takes place outside the realm of the characters' actions, and to a large extent outside their comprehension; and it's only indirectly, semi-allegorically connected with Stencil's search for V. That is more in the nature of a private anxiety, since the woman in whom the principle of V was momentarily embodied, insofar as she was an individual at all, was dead well before the action of the novel starts" (Adams, *Afterjoyce*, 171–2).

Nazi Germany, the interplay between theological concepts of human free will versus divine providence and predestination, monstrosity as violation of the natural cycle, behavioural psychology, sexuality and its discontents, paranoia as epistemological paradigm, and the many plottings of history, whether factual, fictional, or (in between) conspiratorial. Here, the Joycean presence goes well beyond the historical reference to Joyce's sojourning in 1916 Dadaist Zurich and frequenting the local Odeon Café, together with Lenin, Trotsky, Einstein, and Tzara (*GR*, 266). Among the most markedly *Ulyssean* techniques employed by Pynchon for the sake of discontinuity is his use of headings separating textual items, e.g., in chapters 69 and 73, a mythical reference introduced by the heading "Orpheus Puts Down Harp," which when translated from journalese reads "Orpheus Theatre Management Denounces the Harmonica" (*GR*, 754) – a strategy reminiscent of the "Aeolus" episode of *Ulysses*.

Pynchon, again, plays with visual typography; the novel is composed of four parts, each consisting of a number of episodes whose divisions are marked not by subheadings or numbers but by means of a graphical depiction of lines of empty squares. As suggested by Richard Poirier in one of the first-ever reviews of the novel, these squares might represent "sprocket holes in a film" that engage with the teeth in a camera or projector," [89] although their origins in the engineer's graph paper, on which the first draft of the novel was written, cannot be disproved. Pynchon also peppers his text with the occasional verbal conglomerate smacking of Joyce's verbal amalgamations, as in his imagist coinage of "Swirlinggrainoftreeslikefrozensmoke" (*GR*, 76). In passages focusing on *Gravity's* protagonist, Tyrone Slothrop, Pynchon employs the narrative techniques of interior monologue and stream of consciousness – and again, the immense narrative panorama can be reduced to two parallel and opposing tendencies: the assembly of the Rocket, and the disassembly of Tyrone Slothrop.

Last but not least, critics have argued for the circularity of *Gravity's Rainbow* as narrative, its incomplete last line—in which supposedly the explosion of the Rocket takes place—harking back to the "cry coming across the sky" from the novel's opening.[90] However, the list of parallels is again as long as the list of differences: mythological parallelism goes only so far. First and foremost, against Joyce's stylistic plurality stands the relative uniformity of Pyn-

89   Richard Poirier, "Rocket Power—*Gravity's Rainbow*," *The Saturday Review* (3 March 1973). Online: https://thomaspynchon.com/rocket-power-gravitys-rainbow-reviewed-by-richard-poirier -1973/#more-1847

90   "The incomplete last line shows the novel resisting its own termination, engaging in yet another struggle of opposites between entropy and energy. [...] In the last line, a rocket is about to explode over "our" heads. The novel's first line describes the sound of a rocket rushing in, *after* the supersonic missile has already exploded. [...] So the novel's conclusion leads us back to its beginning: its ends are joined. The annular structure of *Gravity's Rainbow* refutes the entropic curtailment of its own narrative energy" (Stonehill, *The Self-Conscious Novel*, 154).

chon's style, as evidenced by Newman: "Joyce, a stylistic chameleon, imitates and parodies every stylistic tradition while ultimately subscribing to none. Pynchon uses Laurence Sterne and Joyce as his models for parody, deflating all norms, offering multiplicity and randomness so that patterns may be discovered only in redundancy."[91] As in *V.*, Pynchon's point is pointlessness, and his obsessive problem-solving results in the concluding irresolution.[92] Pynchon's is a parody that exceeds the shadow of its paradigm. So, if Joyce pushed parody to the point of literary self-parody in order to demonstrate how "the available styles and forms of literature were insufficient constraints in which to ossify the flow of life," Pynchon "extends this perception from literature to all systems, whether in science, pop-culture, politics, or history, to show that any attempt at recording life is a form of rigidification and repression."[93]

Vineland (1990), Pynchon's first novel after his professed breakup with his earlier fictional output, features as many parallels as differences vis-à-vis his earlier work. Again, the main plotting of *Vineland* is built around a diagrammatic story of personal and political obsession that has little to do with lives that anyone has ever lived. But as Edward Mendelson has observed, "the relations between parents and children in the book, relations often tangential to the main plot, intermittently make Vineland 'luminous, undeniably authentic,' and give it a warmth that the intellectual exoticism of his earlier work excluded."[94] The main storyline involves yet another quest, but this time one after the secrets of a parent's past, centring on a private sexual obsession, set against the U.S. politics of the twenty-five years between 1965 and the time of the novel's publication.

After this personally rendered detour, Pynchon's production took yet another unforeseen turn in *Mason & Dixon* (1997), an 18th-century historical novel detailing the travels of Charles Mason and Jeremiah Dixon in search of a solution to the border dispute between British colonies, resulting in the eponymous line which would, a hundred years later, divide the anti-slavery North from the pro-slavery South. Their story, in a perfectly 18th-century fashion, is a framed narrative, mediated by a certain Reverend Wicks Cherrycoke as he attempts to divert his large family on a cold December evening. In a yet more perfectly 18th-century fashion, Pynchon tailors his language as mimicry of the novelese of the period. *Mason & Dixon* opens as follows:

---

91   Newman, *Understanding Thomas Pynchon*, 96.
92   "Again, *Ulysses* is a signpost on this twentieth-century track, for the Blooms never resolve their marital problems in the time frame of the novel and, like Slothrop, Stephen Dedalus disappears from the novel, his destiny unknown. However, the meeting of Stephen and Bloom and the favorable shift toward Bloom that occurs in Molly's soliloquy offer the reader an implicit sense of completion and hope. Completion and hope are neither implicit nor explicit in *Gravity's Rainbow*" (Ibid, 96).
93   Ibid, 95.
94   Mendelson, "Levity's Rainbow," *The New Republic* 203.2–3 (July 9–16, 1990): 41.

Snow-Balls have flown their Arcs, starr'd the Sides of Outbuildings, as of Cousins, carried Hats away into the brisk Wind off Delaware,—the Sleds are brought in and their Runners carefully dried and greased, shoes deposited in the back Hall, a stockin-g'd-foot Descent made upon the great Kitchen, in a purposeful Dither since Morning, punctuated by the ringing Lids of various Boilers and Stewing-Pots, fragrant with Pie-Spices, peel'd Fruits, Suet, heated Sugar,—the Children, having all upon the Fly, among rhythmic slaps of Batter and Spoon, coax'd and stolen what they might, proce-ed, as upon each afternoon all this snowy Advent, to a comfortable Room at the rear of the House, years since given over to their carefree Assaults. (*M&D*, 1)

This clamorous opener, dense with the chaotic rush of new sensation, brims with the novel's animating themes – the ascents and descents of lives bene-ath those of the stars. As William Logan's review of the novel shows, the opening sentence belongs to the tradition of well-wrought openers synec-dochally encapsulating and presaging some of the entire novel's concerns.[95] Pynchon's linguistic mimicry chiefly consists of a loosened syntax and spe-lling, particularly through the irritatingly comic capitalisation of nouns for emphasis sake. The effect of Pynchon's technique of concatenating these topi-cal metaphors and images, of moving from detail to design, can be viewed as an ultimately poetic technique.

Pynchon's viewpoint, again, is an encyclopaedic one, involving snippets of lectures and obscure information on themes as abstruse as the Mithraic origins of ley lines, lamination, the switch from the Julian to the Gregorian calendar, the marine chronometer, and Pynchon's vintage conspiracy theory involving Jesuits and their Chinese converts. This layering of designs and schemata has, again, called up the spectre of Joyce – Logan has a point in showing how Pynchon's is "a curious way of disabling the anxiety of influ-ence—by placing his own style so deep in history, he seems Joyce's ancestor, not his descendent."[96] Like Joyce, Pynchon exhibits a penchant for linguistic exuberance, for bad jokes and worse puns, as well as cheap anachronistic references to contemporary phenomena – again, with a notable metaphoric link to science: "Pynchon's invention in language mimics the inventions of

---

95   "Jeremiah Dixon is a journeyman surveyor, Charles Mason an assistant to the Astronomer Royal at Greenwich. The arcs and stars of those hurled snowballs are the heraldic signs of their pro-fessions: in the comedy of their lives, cutting arcs across oceans, sitting stars, these characters make order from the anarchic motions the children in their hurtling suggest. The heated sugar is the earliest intimation of the trade that drove colonial expansion (its sweetness cost the lives of slaves): the lively microcosm (the whole novel might be said to be upon the fly, the characters ever in purposeful dither) serves a macrocosm yet unknown, a universe whose existence, whose author, is adumbrated by fond jokes—of punctuation called up by punctuated, of beginnings (and religious awakenings) summoned by Advent" (William Logan, "Pynchon in the Poetic," *Southwest Review* 83.4 [1998]: 430).

96   Logan, "Pynchon in the Poetic," 437.

science, where one explosion is always fuse of the next."[97] The novel's episodic structure allows for an infinite deferral and postponement of any consummation (including the sexual one), and finally it is as if the sheer fact of narration has become its own sole goal, an aversion to any conflict or resolution.

In *Mason & Dixon*, Pynchon creates an essentially atelic narrative, whose episodes collapse without consequence, whose characters part ways, and ultimately it is as if the author himself has lost interest, no longer bothering to even pare his fingernails – the Joycean aesthetics of detachment consummated to their extreme.

Concluding the first tandem of Anglo-American chapters is one final example of the kind of "transatlantic" dialogue (à la Jolas) in the British reception of American writing, which will illustrate how out-of-step the British reception was with the "progressive" American letters well into the late 1970s, even when meant as positive appraisal and critique of domestic "backwardness."

William Buford's introduction to the first (Spring 1979) issue of *Granta* magazine—co-edited with Pete de Bolla—on "New American Writing," sought to bring the advances in the American fiction of the 1960s and 1970s into dialogue with the British scene of that period. Buford's dissatisfaction with the "neither remarkable nor remarkably interesting" contemporary British novel that "lacks excitement, wants drive, provides comforts not challenges," is juxtaposed with the "literary renaissance" in the States, producing "some of the most challenging, diversified, and adventurous writing today."[98] He criticises the perceived lack of recognition—all through England—of the "new voice," the "new kind of dialogue in fiction" which has developed in the US through the 1960s and 1970s. This lack of recognition is manifest in the UK publishing policies.[99] If Jolas' *transition* strove for a "transatlantic" dialogue, it would appear that in Buford's estimation, no such dialogue took place in the two decades under focus, Burroughs' sojourn in London and the cult following of the Beats notwithstanding.

97   Ibid, 439.
98   William Buford, "Introduction" to *Granta* 1 (Spring 1979): 3.
99   "A new voice has developed, a new kind of dialogue in fiction. But has England even recognized that it exists? Who are the current American writers current in England today? Bellow, Updike, Pynchon, or Mailer? Pop stars like Jong, Robbins, or Brautigan? The less conventional authors, Kurt Vonnegut, Joseph Heller, Philip Roth, John Hawkes, Robert Coover, Grace Paley? Less conventional and less known. Barthelme, probably the most influential American author? A name. [...] John Barth has barely survived the British Press. Stanley Elkin's last novel, already three years old, still does not have a British publisher; and the same applies to the last work of Leonard Michaels or Barry Hannah or Walter Abish, Tillie Olsen, or Ronald Sukenick. William Gass has only one book in print in England; Coover has only two; Gaddis, one; Percy, one; McMurty, one; Purdy, one. [...] American fiction is still not recognized in England; or if recognized, that recognition is not acknowledged" (Buford, "Introduction," 4).

Buford discerns "a paradox central to many American writers, the paradox of being unable to believe in the objective validity of meanings but unable to do without them," and his stress falls on authors whose work represents one kind of writing that presupposes the inadequacies of linear logic, linear relationships, linear reality and projects a kind of art that exists almost as pure possibility, no longer enthralled by an empirical or normative order, or even necessity itself. Buford's exemplars are Barthelme, Pynchon, Gass, Barth, and Coover. However, he points out in the same breath that these writers can represent "*only* one kind and their narrative *only* one kind of rejection of the conventional."[100] Pitted against their work is what Buford terms "non-fiction fiction" (represented by such household names as Norman Mailer, Truman Capote, and Hunter S. Thompson). Although inherently in favour of experimentalism as opposed to the perceived British conservatism, Buford's preference lies not with the "gleeful and gratuitous experimentation as regularly insensitive as the America depicted" of experimental fiction. "Something else is demanded," he insists, "and the demand is obvious as an increasing dissatisfaction elicited by fiction which demonstrates its ultimacies and nothing more; an irritation with the non-linear story that gets nowhere and takes forever not getting there."[101] Thus, despite his conciliatory conclusion, in which American fiction is praised for the "discord" of its "many voices" that is "the source of the literary development, the energy, the achievement," Buford's alliances clearly lie elsewhere than with Pynchon, Gass, or Barth.[102]

Buford's introduction and most of the essays collected in the *Granta* magazine issue attest to how the aesthetic tide in the aftermath of their works was on the turn away from the post-war mutations of the great American novel. But what Buford fails to make explicit is that most of the "newer" writers — i.e., writers of the second post-war generation — championed by him, e.g., Kathy Acker or Ronald Sukenick (see Chapter Six), took up the other pole of 1950s-1960s experimentation and — rather than dealing with conceptual and narrative complexity — preferred to deal with linguistic experimentation and anarchic verbal and discursive practices. In a final anachronism emblematic of so much of the British misperception of the larger processes in American letters, it becomes clear that while from 1980 onward, writers as diverse as Gaddis, Barth, or Pynchon tended toward increasingly conventional, mimetic modes of fiction, the experimental baton was handed over to writers departing from their earlier work of the 1960s – as will be shown in the next "American" chapter.

---

100 Ibid, 7.
101 Ibid, 8.
102 Ibid, 10.

4.
JOYCEAN OULIPO, OULIPIAN JOYCE: 1960–1978, BEFORE AND AFTER

Has Joyce's avant-garde project been co-opted into the canon of the Oulipo group's "anticipatory plagiarists"? If not, what has been the rationale behind this omission? If yes, is this an acknowledged influence? What other influences is it recombined with? The task of this chapter is both to conceptualise a Joycean "Oulipo avant la lettre," and to trace a streak within the Oulipian literary output following both *Ulysses* and *Finnegans Wake*. It tackles this task by tracing Joyce's recognised significance for perhaps the two most canonical Oulipians, Raymond Queneau and Georges Perec, their second-generation successor Jacques Roubaud, and the "strange case" of Harry Mathews, the only American member of the group.

4.1 THE JOYS OF CONSTRAINT AND POTENTIAL

Oulipo was established on 24 November 1960 by François le Lionnais and Raymond Queneau, its founding members including Noël Arnaud, Jacques Bens, Claude Berge, Jacques Duchateau, Latis, Jean Lescure, Jean Queval, and Albert-Marie Schmidt. As such, it is France's longest-lasting literary group, their monthly conventions, the famous "jeudis Oulipo," still taking place at the Bibliothèque National de France to this day, more than sixty years after its inception and long after the deaths of Oulipo's founding fathers, giving proof to Hervé le Tellier's observation, in his study on the group's history and poetics, that Oulipo was "born of a friendship."[1] With Oulipo, it is important to say "group" (or, more precisely, "workshop") while resisting the common appellation of "movement," for as the (unsigned) note of the editor of the first Oulipian compendium made explicit, insofar as a negative definition of Oulipo is simpler than a positive one, it runs as follows:

---

[1] "Oulipo est né d'une amitié. De celle que se portaient Raymond Queneau, écrivain, éditeur, amateur de mathématiques, et François le Lionnais, grand collectionneur de savoirs hétéroclites, mathématiques, échiquéens, littéraires et pataphysiciens, [...] la pierre fondatrice du groupe sera l'exploration du lien entre mathématique et littérature, un lien qui va se décliner [...] autours de notions évolutives et mobiles : structure, contrainte, consigne, axiomatique, manipulation, combinatoire, procédé, procédure, etc." (Hervé le Tellier, *Esthétique de l'Oulipo* [Bordeaux : Le Castor Astral, 2006] 7, 13).

1. Ce n'est pas un mouvement littéraire. (It is not a literary movement.)
2. Ce n'est pas un séminaire scientifique. (It is not a scientific seminar.)
3. Ce n'est pas de la littérature aléatoire.[2] (It is not aleatory literature.)

Neither a literary movement, nor a scientific seminar, and not a practice of aleatory literature either, then – members of Oulipo have been likened by Raymond Queneau to "rats who must build the labyrinth from which they propose to escape."[3]

The acronym stands for *Ouvroir de littérature potentielle*—"A Workshop for Potential Literature"—and the "workshop" in question, significantly, denotes a "sewing circle": not of wealthy elderly females knitting quilts for the benefit of the poverty-stricken, but of mathematicians / writers devising systems of constraints for the use of those suffering from writer's blocks. A workshop, in short: not of textures, but of texts, nonetheless. It is important to keep in mind Point Three of Le Lionnais' negative definition above, particularly in view of the fact that Queneau had been a member of Breton's Surrealist group back in the 1920s, before rather vehemently and tumultuously breaking up with the ensemble in 1929. Taking, as late as 1960, the automatic free-association writing of the Surrealists as a foil, Queneau postulated as the motto for his own group the contention that "il n'y a de littérature que volontaire" ("the only literature is a voluntary one").[4]

This norm of voluntary, "willed," writing had, in Queneau's writings at least, a twofold ramification: texts were devised according to a system, usually, with a sort of formal constraining device at work; and there were also texts presented in a perennially nascent and incomplete state. Here, the precisely calculable potential, according to a rather strict formulation from Le Lionnais, is meant to substitute for the traditionally vague notion of inspiration.[5] Queneau sought to reconcile these two opposites in a milder summary of the main objective of Oulipo's "littérature potentielle": "Proposer aux écrivains de nouvelles 'structures,' de nature mathématique ou bien encore inventer de nouveaux procédés artificiels ou mécaniques, contribuant

---

2   "Note de l'éditeur," *Oulipo – La Littérature potentielle: créations, re-créations, recreations* (Paris: Gallimard, 1973) 11, my translation.
3   Jean Lescure, "A Brief History of the Oulipo," *The New Media Reader*, eds. Noah Wardrip-Fruin & Nick Montfort (Cambridge/London: The MIT Press, 2003) 29.
4   Qtd. in Lescure, "Brief History of the Oulipo," 32.
5   "It is possible to compose texts that have poetic, surrealist, fantastic, or other qualities without having qualities of potential. Now it is these last qualities that are essential for us. They are the only ones that must guide our choice [...] The goal of potential literature is to furnish future writers with new techniques which can dismiss inspiration from their affectivity. Ergo, the necessity of a certain liberty. Nine or ten centuries ago, when a potential writer proposed the sonnet form, he left, through certain mechanical processes, the possibility of a choice" (Ibid, 30).

à l'activité littéraire: Des soutiens de l'inspiration, pour ainsi dire, ou bien encore, en quelque sorte, une aide à la créativité" (*BCL*, 321).

These "aids for creativity" include the famous Oulipian constraints of numerical, alphabetical, graphic, or prosodic nature, always combinable and re-combinable to generate an infinite array of new forms. Among the more popular are lipograms (texts omitting one or more letters of the alphabet), heterograms, pangrams (phrases or sentences in which no letter of the alphabet occurs more than once), anagrams, perverbs, antonymic or homophonic translations, spoonerisms, palindromes, or the famous "S+7" method. In the light of these "conventions," the adjective *new* from Queneau's definition appears particularly dubious: and one need not have recourse to Le Lionnais' avowal in order to see that these procedures were neither "discovered" nor "invented" by any of the Oulipians, but had instead, known variously as "the cento" or "Sortes Virgilanae," served as tools of plagiarist expropriation ever since late Antiquity. As Queneau himself made clear, "the word 'potential' concerns the very nature of literature."[6] The recurrence of the formalist notion of "structure" should not pass unnoticed, harking as far back as Ferdinand de Saussure, according to whose famous metaphor "language is like a machine which keeps going regardless of the damage inflicted on it."[7] Analogously, the procedure theorised and practiced by Queneau's group lays bare the fact that poetic language is like a machine which keeps going, not regardless of, but precisely only thanks to the damage inflicted on it by its author, shape, form, or stylistic gesture—a constraint that brings it into being. There is, in other words, no "unrestricted freedom" into which "a rat" could escape (no "unrestrained freedom" of Surrealist automatic writing), and beyond the wall of its labyrinth lurks yet another wall.

As argued by Jacques Roubaud in his introduction to *Oulipo Compendium*, if the literary impetus behind the Oulipo's origins was a primarily negative one (i.e., against surrealism), the other, mathematical impetus was one of "an homage to" and "an imitation of" the Bourbaki group of mathematicians, who decided, in Roubaud's words, to "perform an Oulipian rewriting of mathematics" in that they drew their inspiration from the axiomatics of David Hilbert and made set theory the basis of their undertaking. This Oulipian bipolarity of mathematics and literature leads to a fourfold classifica-

---

6   Queneau continues: "that is, fundamentally it is less a question of literature strictly speaking than of supplying forms for the good use one can make of literature. We call potential literature the search for new forms and structures that may be used by writers in any way they see fit" (Ibid, 30).

7   Ferdinand de Saussure, *The Third Course of Lectures in General Linguistics (1910–1911)*, trans. & eds. E. Komatsu & R. Harris (Oxford: Pergamon, 1993) 113.

tion of its members.[8] The choice of the "limiting and at the same time crucial role" mathematics played in Oulipian writing made by its founders, Roubaud points out, was one whose rationale dictated that "after the exhaustion of the generative power of traditional constraints, only mathematics could offer a way out between a nostalgic obstinacy with worn-out modes of expression and an intellectually pathetic belief in 'total freedom.'"[9]

In addition to these two aspects—i.e., longevity and mathematical foundations—Roubaud singles out three other essential Oulipian features. So long as its aim is "to invent (or reinvent) restrictions of a formal nature and propose them to enthusiasts interested in composing literature," then *as a group*, Oulipo "does not count the creation of literary works among its primary aims" – for it is equally important to originate the creation of new (even non-Oulipian) works by means of formal restraint.[10] A peculiar notion of authorship arises, with the adjective "Oulipian" acquiring a two-fold adaptability: "Whatever its other merits, a literary work that deserves to be called Oulipian may have been written by a member of the Oulipo, but it may have been written by a non-member of the Oulipian." Hence, the third Oulipian characteristic is the *collaborative* nature of its work, its products (proposed constraints) being "attributed to the group, even if certain constraints are invented by individuals."[11]

The next step for this collaborative attitude towards creation is Oulipian feature number four, its *potential universality*, which renders Oulipian procedures not only applicable to all languages apart from French, but also successive to a vast and old literary tradition, recognised as "anticipatory plagiarism," an expression which "delimits a part of past literature as susceptible of being examined with freshened eyes in the light of the constraint." Roubaud's "masters" of the Oulipo include Lewis Carroll, Raymond Roussel, Alphonse Allais, and Alfred Jarry.[12] Finally, the fifth characteristic, consequent to and subsuming the preceding two, is that Oulipian literature is "neither modern nor postmodern" but what Roubaud calls "a traditional literature true to tradition" – hence its remarkable links (especially as regards poetic texts) with oral poetry.

What, then, are the relationships between constraints, combinative procedures, and potentiality? Chiefly twofold: First, there are works in which

---

8   "(i) the first sort are composers of literature (prose, poetry, criticism) who are not mathematicians; (ii) the second sort are mathematicians who are not composers of literature; the members of type; (iii) are composers of literature and mathematicians; those of type (iv) are mathematicians and composers of literature" (Jacques Roubaud, "Oulipo - Introduction," *Oulipo Compendium*, eds. Harry Mathews & Alastair Brotchie [London: Atlas Press, 1998] 38).

9   Roubaud, "Oulipo - Introduction," 40.

10   Ibid, 38-9.

11   Ibid, 39.

12   Ibid, 40.

Oulipian constraints provide "the rules of a language game (in the Wittgensteinian sense) whose 'innings' (texts composed according to its rules) are virtually unlimited and represent linguistic combinations developed from a small number of necessarily interdependent elements." And second, there are also those works which chart out the particular potentiality that gives rise to them: "Potentiality is here explicitly linked to research in a new *combinatorial art* which, after Llull, proceeds from Bruno to Leibniz and which eventually finds support in the most recent developments in mathematics."[13] Roubaud's examples of both these types are two works by writers both most famous of the entire group and, as will be seen, most Joycean – the most illustrious example of a work of Oulipian potential literature is Raymond Queneau's *Cent mille milliards poèmes* (*A Hundred Thousand Billion Poems*), whereas a case in point of a constraint-ruled Oulipian work is George Perec's *La Disparition* (*A Void*).

4.2 "NOTHING LEFT TO CHANCE": RAYMOND QUENEAU

It is difficult to overstate Raymond Queneau's significance for the Oulipo group, which is due not only to his functioning as the group's founding father, as the dedicatee of some of the crucial works of the other Oulipians, as the inventor of some of its most celebrated constraints and techniques, but also due to his Nestor-like status of a writer whose earlier works precede the founding of the group by more than two decades.

It was Queneau's violent split with Breton's surrealist group in the late twenties that would, thirty years later, shape Oulipo's notions of "voluntary" writing opposed to "inspiration." Queneau's biographers detail how he had met André Breton and become part of the Surrealist milieu, which was then in full effervescence in Paris, contributing a poem and two examples of automatic writing to the journal *La révolution surréaliste*, and signing the Surrealist manifesto *Déclaration du 27 janvier 1925*. However, following a series of personal incidents as well as Queneau's increasing dissatisfaction with the group's political position— i.e., its support of Joseph Stalin after the purging of Leon Trotsky from the Soviet leadership in 1926—alienation between him and Breton escalated. The last straw, for Breton, came in 1930 when Queneau published "Dédé," in *Un cadavre* (*A Corpse*, 1930), a vehemently anti-Breton pamphlet co-written by Jacques Prévert, Georges Bataille, Robert Desnos, Michel Leiris, and others. As Queneau recalled in his *Bâtons, chiffres, lettres*: "That is what happens to those who are excluded or exclude themselves from tightly knit groups. I did not know what to do; I took refuge in the National

---

13   Ibid, 41.

Library, where I began to study literary madmen."[14] Biographer André Leroux also mentions that Queneau "had read the *Dictionnaire Larousse* from A to Z" by the age of fifteen.[15] His obsession with dictionaries might be seen as indicative of his Joycean literary disposition, tending toward the literary encyclopaedia – and Queneau's multifaceted and variegated oeuvre stands as clear testimony to this particular tendency.

Queneau's early essay entitled "Technique du roman" (1937) opens with a "précaution [...] de reconnaître ma dette envers les romanciers anglais et américains qu'il existait une technique du roman, et tout spécialement envers Joyce" (*BCL*, 28).[16] Queneau's 1937 avowal of his "debt" to Anglophone authors and "especially" to Joyce was followed in 1938 by his article entitled "James Joyce, auteur classique" (published in *Volonté*, no. 9, septembre 1938), which reclaims Joyce to the heritage of classicism, for, according to Queneau, the author of *Ulysses* has "une parfaite connaissance de ses buts et de ses moyens" and "rien, dans ces œuvres, n'est laissé au hasard," without which "rien ne manifeste une contrainte." According to Queneau, Joyce's work tends "vers l'universel" and is "une nouveauté continuelle," resting upon "une connaissance de la tradition et des œuvres anciennes."[17] Although a classicist, Joyce, for Queneau, is an author of "continuous novelty" and experimentation— which he seeks to perpetuate in his own oeuvre.[18]

---

14   "C'est ce qui arrive, je crois, à tous ceux qui s'excluent ou sont exclus de groupes fortement constitués. Je ne savais que faire et je me suis réfugié à la Bibliothèque Nationale où je me suis mis à étudier les fous littéraires." Qtd. & trans. in André Leroux, "Raymond Queneau," *Dictionary of Literary Biography, Volume 258: Modern French Poets*, ed. Jean-François Leroux (University of Ottawa: The Gale Group, 2002) 355.

15   Leroux, "Raymond Queneau," 354.

16   In the estimation of the author of the most comprehensive work (well over 500 pages) on the subject of Queneau's Anglo-American influences, this group of writers included "Caroll, Joyce et Faulkner bien sûr, mais aussi Edgar Allan Poe, Joseph Conrad, Henry James, Gertrude Stein, Ernest Hemingway, Henry Miller et Caldwell" (Lise Bergheaud, *Queneau et les formes intranquilles de la modernité* [Paris: Éditions Champion, 2010] 21). On the subject of Joyce, Lise Bergheaud's *Queneau et les formes intranquilles de la modernité* surveys his meticulously kept *Journaux*, detailing Queneau's early acquaintance with *Ulysses* (which he read twice, in 1929 in French translation and, in 1933, in the original, and kept rereading throughout his life, together with relevant criticism) and the care with which he followed the chapter instalments of Joyce's "Work in Progress" in the *transition* magazine. As late as 1971, Queneau reads the 1959 volume of Joyce's *Critical Writings*, showing, according to Bergheaud, that "jusque dans les toutes dernières années de sa vie, il restera fidèle au Joyce à la fois écrivain et théoricien" (Bergheaud, *Queneau et les formes intranquilles de la modernité*, 66).

17   Qtd. in Bergheaud, *Queneau et les formes*, 69.

18   On the whole, Bergheaud's well-informed survey of Queneau's diaries reveals "un regard extrêmement aiguisé sur l'œuvre de l'Irlandais. On y trouve des synopsis de certaines sections de *Ulysses*, des tableaux de correspondances entre différentes éditions de ce texte, de longues citations extraites de l'essai d'Edmund Wilson sur *Work in Progress*, des notes relatives aux personnages de cette même œuvre [...] ou encore le recopiage d'un tableau, élaboré par Joyce lui-même, qui met en relation chaque épisode de *Ulysses* avec un organe, une science, une couleur, un symbole ou une technique littéraire" (Ibid, 70).

As Queneau reveals in "Technique du roman," two of his first three novels had elaborate arithmetical structures. Queneau's first novel *Le Chiendent* (1933; *Bark-Tree*, 1968) is constructed in a fashion which would become typical of Queneau's 1930s novels, and was written after Queneau's trip to Greece (as the concluding postscript, "*Athènes et Cyclades,* juillet–novembre 1932," makes clear [*C* 432]). Translator Barbara Wright's introduction teases out the importance of the trip to Greece for Queneau's reconceptualisation of modern literary French:

> Here he became acutely aware of the difference between classical, written Greek and modern, spoken Greek, and this acted as a catalyst to the ideas he had long been forming about the French language. Written French had become fossilized, spoken French was a totally different language; since he wanted to write in what he considered his maternal language […], he wasn't merely aiming at a transcription of the "language of the ordinary man," but at a transformation of it, something which would become a third language, a new, viable literary language. (*BT*, 1)

As he revealed later in *Bâtons, chiffres, lettres,* Queneau had taken Descartes' *Discourse on Method* with him on his trip, and sought to translate it into spoken French: "With this idea I began to write something which later became a novel called *Le Chiendent*" (qtd. in *BT*, 2). Robbe-Grillet would later on pay *Le Chiendent* homage by calling it "the new novel, twenty years ahead of its time" and giving it an honourable mention in *For a New Novel* (*BT*, 1). The title itself is ambiguous, as revealed in Wright's introduction: "The title, *Le Chiendent,* has many meanings. *Chiendent* is the weed, couch grass. *Voila le chiendent* is Hamlet's: *Ay, there's the rub.* The word is made up of *chien* (dog) and *dent* (tooth). Dogs have always had great significance in Queneau's private mythology... And so on" (*BT*, 1).

Le Chiendent is composed of a mélange of a detective novel set in a proletarian background against bits of Cartesian philosophy, memories of Homer, embedded in technical devices of Joyce and Faulkner. It has been hailed by critics as an epic of the Parisian suburbs in that it features several typified individuals representative of class/social function (e.g., the petit bourgeois, the concierge, the junk-dealer, the bartender, etc.) who emerge little by little from the crowd to rush into a treasure hunt which finally becomes a world war. In *Entretiens avec Georges Charbonnier*, Queneau says à propos of his first novel that the inspiration was Joyce's tables of correspondences for *Ulysses*, and that he drew up similar tables, "as formal as a chess game," for *Le Chiendent*.[19] *Le Chiendent* consists of seven chapters, each containing thirteen sections:

---

19   Raymond Queneau, *Entretiens avec Georges Charbonnier* (Paris: Gallimard, 1962) 49.

every thirteenth (the last in each chapter, consequently) is situated outside of this chapter, in another direction or dimension; they are pauses and their genre can only be monologue, report of a dream, or newspaper clipping. Naturally, the 91st breaks the rule and becomes narrative once more to end the whole. (BCL, 25)

As one of the earliest Queneau critics and author of the first book-length study on the novel, Claude Simonet, has argued, *Le Chiendent* is an accomplishment of the revolution of language in French,[20] by following the Joycean revolution of language in chiefly two ways, conceptual and thematic: by creating imaginatively a "monde autonome et sans autres limites que celles d'une poétique rigoureuse" and by combatting "la tyrannie du temps"[21] in that the first two sentences are also the text's last:

The silhouette of a man appeared in profile; so, simultaneously, did thousands, There really were thousands. He had just opened his eyes, and the teeming streets were seething; seething, too, were the men who worked all day. [...] The silhouette, detached from the wall now, oscillated, jostled by other shapes, not visibly behaving as an individual, pushed and pulled in various directions, less by its own anxieties than by the sum of the anxieties of the thousands of people surrounding it. (BT, 7)

A mask traversed the air, causing people of multiple and complex lives to disappear, and took human form at a café terrace. The silhouette of a man appeared in profile; so, simultaneously, did thousands. There really were thousands. (BT, 280)[22]

Le Chiendent tells the tale of Étienne, who embarks on a metaphysical "cogito ergo sum" journey after the trivial incident of spotting two rubber ducks swimming in a waterproof hat displayed in a shop window. This transcendence in the banal might again recollect the Joycean epiphany, but *Le Chiendent* abounds in more substantial Joycean elements. It would of course be mistaken to regard *Le Chiendent*'s circularity as a token of Que-

---

20   Simonet cites the Jolasian pamphlet, observing that "les auteurs traduisent en préceptes la leçon qu'un jeune écrivain des années 30 pouvait tirer de l'exemple de Joyce et il est curieux de voir qu'ils manifestent une attitude littéraire à laquelle *Le Chiendent*—dans une manière très personnelle—correspond assez exactement" (Claude Simonet, *Queneau déchiffré* [Paris: René Juillard, 1962] 1).

21   Simonet, *Queneau déchiffré*, 2; 10.

22   "La silhouette d'un homme se profila ; simultanément, des milliers. Il y en avait bien des milliers. Il venait d'ouvrir les yeux et les rues accablées s'agitaient, s'agitaient les hommes qui tout le jour travaillèrent. [...] Détachée du mur, la silhouette oscilla bousculée par d'autres formes, sans comportement individuel visible, travaillée en sens divers, moins par ses inquiétudes de ses milliers de voisins" (LC, 9).
"Un masque traversa l'air, escamotant des personnages aux vies multiples et complexes, et prit forme hu-maine à la terrasse d'un café. La silhouette d'un homme se profila ; simultanément, des milliers. Il y en avait bien des milliers" (LC, 432).

neau's *Wakean* inspiration, as in 1933 the circular structure had not been announced or made clear by Joyce. But more importantly, *Le Chiendent* is first of Queneau's so-called "novel-poems," characterised by Simonet in some highly Joycean aspects: "like all Queneau's novels, *Le Chiendent* both has no meaning and at the same time conceals a profusion of meanings [...] a supreme example of the novel whose story cannot be told" (qtd. in *BT*, 4). Wright even speaks of *Le Chiendent* in terms identical to Beckett on the *Wake*.[23] Even more conclusive and explicit Joycean references and allusions begin to appear from Queneau's second and third novels onward. *Gueule de pierre* (1934) is less structurally complex than *Le Chiendent*, mathematically at least consisting of only three parts, as Queneau explains in "Technique du roman," each in a different technique: "monologue of the solitary man in the first, narrative and conversations when he returns to the people of 'La Ville natale,' a poem finally in the third part when he elevates himself." However, as Vivian Mercier points out, each of the three parts also corresponds to one of the domains of nature—animal, vegetable, and mineral—and the third contains all twelve signs of the Zodiac.[24]

Les derniers jours (1936; *Last Days*, 1990) is the first instalment of Queneau's autobiographical quartet, prompted by his psychoanalytic treatment begun in 1933, and comprising *Odile* (1937), *Chêne et chien* (1937), and *A Hard Winter* (1939). *Les derniers jours* was originally planned to have 8 x 6 + 1 = 49 chapters, with every sixth forming a pause; however, the published version has only 38, Queneau having "taken away the scaffolding and syncopated the rhythm" by suppressing certain chapters. The play on the number 7 should be seen as indirectly autobiographical, as both the author's first and second names contain seven letters each. *Les derniers jours* has been called by Simonet "une sorte de 'portrait de l'artiste en jeune homme'" (*LC*, 9), sort of 'a portrait of the artist as a young man,'" as it is Queneau's autobiographical novel of his Parisian student life in the 1920s. His alter ego is called Vincent Tuquedenne and his struggle is less with the nets of nationality and the Catholic church than with the staleness of the university curriculum and the sterility of older-generation academics in "the establishment on the hill" (*LD*, 143), the Sorbonne. Queneau wears his Joycean credentials proudly, and not only on account of an explicit mention of *Ulysses*: "Tuquedenne passed in front of Shakespeare and Company and stopped, coveting the big *Ulysses* in the blue

---

23   "What is Le Chiendent about? Well, it is not about anything, it is something. And that "something" includes a vast amount of what goes to make up human life. [...] How it is—that is what Queneau, in his own way, is always describing. How life is. His own way is not anyone else's— hence something of his quality, and hence, also, the difficulty people do sometimes have in knowing how to read him" (BT, 5).

24   Mercier, "Raymond Queneau: The First New Novelist?" 108.

jacket" [25] (*LD*, 198). Vivian Kogan's introduction to the English edition identifies Laforgue, Kahn, Flaubert, and Gide as "most fully developed" French
intertexts, and of the Anglophone ones, singles out "Melville, Conrad, and
Poe" (*LD*, xii), but Joyce is present not only according to the letter but also
in spirit, in Queneau's highly allusive, punning style. As when early on, one
of his elderly professors named Tolut mentions in passing his nickname
"The Lozenge" / "La Pastille," referring to a cough syrup called Sirop de Tolut, but also playing on the double entendre of *pastille* meaning "anus," and
Tolut rhyming with *trou de cul* (*LD*, 5). Or when one of his characters, before
falling asleep, performs an action described as *se trondela,* where *trondeler* is
not to be found in any French dictionary, as it is—translator Barbara Wright
explains—a portmanteau word, "a combination of the way a dog curls up
en rond, and *tendelet* (an awning) that one rolls up (*enroule*)" (*LD*, 236). Queneau also keeps punning on his own name throughout, as when he writes
"queneau-coutte" for "knock-out" (*LD*, 59).

Queneau's most explicitly Joycean texts came into being in the period
shortly after World War II. *On est toujours trop bon avec les femmes* (1947; *We
Always Treat Women Too Well*, 1981), published as the purported French translation of a novel by fictional Irish woman writer Sally Mara, came out not
with the respectable Gallimard, but with the Éditions du Scorpion, which
specialised in American-style thrillers and had published Boris Vian's *J'irai
cracher sur vos tombes* just the previous year. Accordingly, the novel is set
in Dublin during the 1916 Easter Rising, its storyline concerns the siege of
a small post office by a group of rebels, and its language is peppered with
Celticisms and Anglicisms, i.e., transatlantic slang, the style of choice of the
thriller genre. Classified as a "sado-erotic thriller" by critic Valerie Caton,
perhaps the most jarring effect of *We Always Treat Women Too Well* is the off-
hand, flippant treatment of its brutal violence, a good example of which
comes on page one: "Corny Kelleher had wasted no time in injecting a bullet
into his noggin. The dead doorman vomited his brains through an eighth ori-
fice in his head, and fell flat to the floor" (*WATW*, 1).[26] As commented upon by
Caton, "here the playfulness of the slang and the preciousness of the 'eighth
orifice' jar with the violence of the scene itself and with the forcefulness
of the verb 'vomited'" (*WATW*, x). In this respect, *We Always Treat Women
Too Well* parodies not only the gangster thriller, but also the poeticisation of
violence and the "black humour" cherished by the surrealists, especially in
view of the recent aestheticisation of violence at the hands of the fascists.

---

25 "Tuquedenne passa devant Shakespeare et Cie et s'arrêta convoitant le grand Ulysses à couver-
    ture bleue" (*LDJ*, 213).
26 "Corny Kelleher, pressé, lui avait injecté une balle dans le citron. L'huissier, mort, vomit sa cer-
    velle par un huitième trou de la tête et s'étala, tout plat, sur le plancher" (*OCSM*, 191).

Caton quotes a 3 November 1945 column Queneau wrote for *Front National*, where he remarked:

> Once one has clarified the political nature of fascism, once one has brought out what is specifically Germanic about Hitlerism, there remains nonetheless a certain ideological and practical system which gives to the fascist regime its moral colouring and its philosophical background. Now, this system is not without its links with this or that aspect of the intellectual life of other Western peoples, and notably with the gangster novel and with black humour. (*WATW*, xi)

In order fully to sabotage its novel's "realist" or "high literary" credentials, Queneau creates a mimicry of the city of Dublin based entirely on a pastiche of *Ulysses*. Not only does one of the rebels go by the name of "James Joyce," and not only is the rebels' secret password the exclamation "Finnegans Wake!," but many other rebels' names are lifted from the pages of Joyce's book—there is Corny Kelleher, Larry O'Rourke, Caffrey, and Dillon, with the odd addition of "Gallaher" from "A Little Cloud"—and the chief cause of the narrative merriment is the insurgents' realisation that a female postal clerk, Gertie Girdle (a.k.a. Gerty MacDowell, Bloom's temptress from "Nausicaa") has been stuck in the lavatory long after the elimination of the rest of the post-office staff. In fact, the list of Joycean correspondences is so long that translator Barbara Wright refers the interested reader to Pierre David's long list of "correspondences, similarities, analogies, equipollences, coincidences, etc." to which he keeps adding on a yearly basis (*WATW*, xiii). *We Always Treat Women Too Well* could easily be termed an exercise in postmodern pastiche *par excellence*, parodying and remixing the high and the low, had it not been published some two decades before such pastiche was all the rage.

However, it was in 1948 that Queneau's linguistically most innovative text appeared—his novel *Saint Glinglin* (1948). Although undated, a very plausible avant-text to the novel is a short exercise entitled "Une traduction en joycien" – "A Translation into Joycean." With the motivation to "appliquer la méthode joycienne à un texte quelconque," this little vignette translates the two opening paragraphs of Queneau's second novel *Gueule de Pierre* into Joyce's *Wakese*:

> Drôle de vie, la vie de poisson !... Je n'ai jamais pu comprendre comment on pouvait vivre comme cela. L'existence de la Vie sous cette forme m'inquiète bien au-delà de tout autre sujet d'alarme que peut m'imposer le Monde. Un Aquarium représente pour moi toute une série d'énigmes lancinantes, de tenailles rougies au feu. Cet après-midi, je suis allé voir Celui dont s'enorgueillit le Jardin Zoologique de la Ville Étrangère. J'y restai, bouleversé, jusqu'à ce que les fonctionnaires m'en chassent.

Doradrôle de vie la vie de poisson. Je n'ai jeunet jamais pu unteldigérer qu'on ment on pouvait vivier comme ce la sol dos rêt. Fishtre, ouïes ! Son aiguesistence sucette mort-phe m'astruitte et me cotte, mets ta mortphose dans la raie en carnation, euyet-moi ça, l'alarme dont crevette le monde, ô mort fausse, hue mor ! Quelle hummer ! Quelle hudor ! Où mort ? Où deurt ? Lamproie du rémore, je me limandais où j'allais j'irai. A quoi rhum ? Akvarium. Vite ! Je m'alosais, tourd torturé tourteau tortue matelote d'aiguilles, mais je n'avais pas d'anchois. J'allé je fus à l'énorgueil du gardin-patrie de la ville étrangère, l'acquarius où va-t-Hermann où là oulla verse le couguard. Qu'où gars ? Mais, m'amifère ! Was Herr Mann ? Raie l'action ! Esaüso qui coule o verso d'alpha fo-malo fiché dans les tmimamellisfères bornéo ! Siaux d'os du sciel, piscez jusqu'o ramo ! Bélier ? Wieder ! Videz ! Vide pisces vide ariem. Ariestez-vous ici ! Arrêtes ! Enchristez--vous dans votre shell ! G'y menotais jusquiame que mussel funkchionnaire mé duse : sélassiez ! Ras d'eau ! Merduse ! qu j'grondinais, merlouze ! que j'harenguais. (BCL, 240-1)

The subject, here, is human wonder at the strangeness of the life of fish and water species (incidentally, another hidden "signature" of Queneau's, as Pisces is his zodiacal sign). Accordingly, Queneau "translates" a large portion of dictionary words into portmanteaus that pack together sea- or water-vocabulary: *drôle*, "funny," becomes "*doradrôle*," echoing *dorade*, "sea bream," a Mediterranean fish species; "existence" under the restricted water conditions becomes "*aiguesistence*" – an "acute-sistence" but also echoing compounds like *aigue-marine*, "aquamarine."

Queneau also employs the *Wakese* technique of phonological transliteration – *métamorphose dans la réincarnation* becomes "mets ta mortphose dans la raie en carnation"; "Quelle hummer ! Quelle hudor !" is echoed in "Où mort ? Où deurt ?"; etc. Like Joyce, even though to a more limited degree, Queneau doesn't restrict his wordplay to one language only: thus, "Was Herr Mann?" echoes the German *Wassermann*, "waterman"; "*Wieder!*," German for "again," evokes via homophony the French *Videz!*, the imperative for "Empty!"

Saint Glinglin—a rewriting and augmentation of *Gueule de pierre* and *Les temps mêlés*—is proof that this *Wakean* wordplay was not a solitary enterprise on Queneau's part, but a new tendency and interest of his writing. Its seven parts comprise the three sections of *Gueule de pierre* ("Les poisons," "Le printanier," and "Le grand minéral," here redubbed "Le caillou"), the second and third section of *Les temps mêlés* (nameless, in *Saint Glinglin* entitled "Les ruraux" and "Les touristes") and two "original" sections, "Les étrangers" and "Saint Glinglin." Referring to the fictional French saint, whose celebration day never comes (and thus serves as a convenient point of reference to endless deferral), *Saint Glinglin* retells the primal Freudian myth of the fraternal patricide in a kaleidoscope of styles ranging from soliloquy and interior monologue to quasi-biblical verse or theatre-play dialogue. The mythical, utopian tale of a Ville Natale ("native city") where it never rains, where a bizarre festival is held every Saint Glinglin's Day, is narrated by way of fractured syntax, hidden structures, self-imposed constraints, playful allusions, and puns and neologisms through which Queneau explores the most basic underpinnings of culture. A large portion of Queneau's verbal experimentation in *Saint Glinglin* has as its source the rewriting of his earlier texts.

Though less linguistically daring than his "traduction à joycien," Queneau's *Saint Glinglin* does keep several of his neologisms. Especially the word "existence" is treated in a *tema con variazioni*-like fashion: from "aiguesistence" (*RQ III*, 201–2, 205, 212, 273, 313, 385) to "aigresistence" (*RQ III*, 220, 273, 315, 368), via "eggzistence," "ogresistence," "hainesistence," "alguesistence," or still "âcresistence" (*RQ III*, 203, 05–6, 12, 18). There are, in addition, the occasional monstrous portmanteaux, such as the adverb "méthodethnologiquement" (*RQ III*, 304), meant to mockingly combine method with ethnology in a pseudo-scientific approach to the Ville Natale and its inhabitants. Another neological trait of Queneau's text is its deployment of non-lexical onomatopoeia, its idiosyncratic transliteration of non-linguistic sounds and fragmented speech: "sgâla," "seuksé," "mieucnou," "ptitapti," "sovostrespé," "paskivnait dparler," "Dédicacélemeuh!" and "Imélamin'hocudlastar" (*RQ III*, 236, 7, 324, 364, 383, 320, 7). Such lists, in Bergheaud's estimation, in addition to Queneau's other "véritables innovations linguistiques et littéraires," are indications of "l'inscription, dans le roman, d'une filiation directe entre Joyce et Queneau."[27]

Another exercise in stylistic rewriting, and perhaps the most famous of all Queneau's works, appeared just a year before *Saint Glinglin*. In *Exercices de style* (1947), the Joycean trait is much less conspicuous, even though quite perceptible. Famously, Queneau's text features 99 stylistic exercises in which to narrate a rather banal mini-story featuring two separate events (a minor argument between two voyagers on a busy bus; an overheard bit of conversation regarding a supplementary button to be sewn onto an overcoat) joined by a common protagonist and a narrator. The crucial structural point is the missing 100th element – the presumed "theme" upon which variations are played. Since according to music tradition, the theme must precede its variations, one would naturally look for it at the beginning:

Notation
"In the S bus, in the rush hour. A chap of about 26, felt hat with a cord instead of a ribbon, neck too long, as if someone's been having a tug-of-war with it. People getting off. The chap in question gets annoyed with one of the men standing next to him. He accuses him of jostling him every time anyone goes past. A snivelling tone which is meant to be aggressive. When he sees a vacant seat he throws himself on to it.

---

27   Bergheaud, *Queneau et les formes*, 288.

Two hours later, I meet him in the Cour de Rome, in front of the gare Saint-Lazare. He's with a friend who's saying: "You ought to get an extra button put on your overcoat." He shows him where (at the lapels) and why."
(*EiS*, 19)[28]

The book's first section, written in the "Notations" form, would appear to pose, in critic Teresa Bridgeman's words, as "a linguistically minimal way of recording events," and yet, upon closer inspection, it is not such.[29] Queneau's point, thus, seems to be that there is no "neutral" telling, no "ground zero basis" from which to build one's stylistic edifice, no *fabula* to precede the *sujet* (in Formalist terms), or in music notions, no "theme" upon which to play one's variations – all narrative rendering of reality is always already *stylised*.

English translator Barbara Wright's introduction has identified seven types of Queneau's exercises, and again it is a taxonomy conspicuously incomplete and imperfect:

The first—different types of speech. Next, different types of written prose. These include the style of a publisher's blurb, of an official letter, the "philosophic" style, and so on. Then there are 5 different poetry styles, and 8 exercises which are character sketches through language—reactionary, biased, abusive, etc. Fifthly there is a large group which experiments with different grammatical and rhetorical forms; sixthly, those which come more or less under the heading of jargon, and lastly, all sorts of odds and ends whose classification I'm still arguing about. (*EiS*, 14)

Queneau generates a fabula of sorts not only through the "Notation" exercise, but also through a few others, such as "Analyse logique," which seems to supply answers to the "Hésitations" section (replete with questions), only to subject it to a vast array of further destabilisations and challenges – e.g., "Le côté subjectif," where the events are focalised through the unreliable

---

28   "Notations : Dans l'S, à une heure d'affluence. Un type dans les vingt-six ans, chapeau mou avec cordon remplaçant le ruban, cou trop long comme si on lui avait tiré dessus. Les gens descendent. Le type en question s'irrite contre un voisin. Il lui reproche de le bousculer chaque fois qu'il passe quelqu'un. Ton pleurnichard qui se veut méchant. Comme il voit une place libre, se précipite dessus.
Deux heures plus tard, je le rencontre Cour de Rome, devant la gare Saint-Lazare. Il est avec un camarade qui lui dit: 'Tu devrais faire mettre un bouton supplémentaire à ton pardessus.' Il lui montre où (à l'échancrure) et pourquoi" (*EdS*, 13).

29   Not only does it have "a strong individual style, involving the suppression of certain elements which are usually necessary to a well-formed sentence," but it also "fails to qualify as neutral telling" in that it "not only establishes a series of events, but also includes other elements which we encounter in the texture of narrative, that is, description and evaluation, which cannot be seen as neutral and objective" (Teresa Bridgeman, "Telling Stories," *Raymond Queneau, Exercices de Style* [Glasgow: University of Glasgow, 1995] 13).

first-person narrator, or "Rétrograde," where they are related in reverse. Other exercises position the event sequence in narrative frames, as e.g., "Rêve" provides the oneiric frame, or "Comédie," the theatrical setting, or "Télégraphique," the textual medium of the telegraphic transmission. Still other exercises work not so much on the text's narrative dimension as on its linguistic material: "Anagrammes" begins a comprehensive breakdown of the morphology of the text, shifting the position of letters only within each word, preserving the word as an identifiable unit through spacing and punctuation; the four "Permutations" sections go a step further in altering the linguistic material beyond easy recognition ("Jo un ve ur mi rs su di ap rl te la rm fo rr ea re iè na d'u o but de us li la eS" etc. [ES, 66]. "Aphérèses" and "Apocopes" enhance the typographical dimension of textual presentation, laid out as they are on a double-page spread, allowing the reader to combine them into a single text.

Although present in spirit throughout, the Joycean heritage of multilingual punning and paronomasia is most palpably drawn upon and remembered in two sections of Queneau's *Exercices*, in "Anglicismes" and "Italianismes" (replaced with "Opera English" by Wright):

Anglicismes: Un dai vers midday, je tèque le beusse et je sie un jeugne manne avec une grète nèque et un hatte avec une quainnde de lèsse tressée. Soudainement ce jeugne manne bi-queumze crézé et acuiouse un respectable seur de lui trider sur les toses. Puis il reunna vers un site eunoccupé.

A une lète aoure je le sie égaine; il vouoquait eupe et daoune devant le Ceinte Lazare stécheunne. Un beau lui guivait un advice à propos de bouton. (*EdS*, 74)[30]

Italianismes: Oune giorne en pleiné merigge, ié saille sulla plataforme d'oune otobousse et là quell ouome ié vidis? ié vidis oune djiovanouome au longué col avé de la treccie otour dou cappel. Et lé ditto djiovanouome oltragge oune pouovre ouome à qui il rimproveravait de lui pester les pieds et il ne lui pestarait noullément les pieds, mais qua nil vidit oune sédie vouote, il corrit por sedersilà.

A oune ouore dé là, ié lé révidis qui asoltait les consigles d'oune bellimbouste et zerbinotte a proposto d'oune bouttoné dé pardéssousse. (*EdS*, 82)

These two sections transcribe English and Italian vocabulary into French notation, sometimes blending the two together: "young" and *jeune* combined in "jeugne," "becomes" transcribed as "bi-queumze," "walking up and down"

---

30   "Gallicisms: One zhour about meedee I pree the ohtobyusse and I vee a zhern omm with a daymoorzuray neck and a shappoh with a sorrt of plaited galorng. Suddenly this zhern omm durvya loofock and praytongs that an onnate moossyur is marshing on his pyaises. Then he jetéed himself on to a leebr plahss.
      Two hours tarder I saw lur angcore; he was se balarding de lorngue ang larzhe in front of the gare Saint-Lazare. A dahndy was donning him some cornsayes à propos of a button" (*EiS*, 87).

disguised in "vouoquait eupe et daoune" (the Italian section performing largely similar operations on the Italian lexicon). Thus, both in overall design, in its stylistic obsession, and in some of its particular wordplay, *Exercices de style* can be seen, together with Mercier, as "a serious product" of Queneau's "discipleship to Joyce." Yet, some of its exercises already point to the mathematical approach to language as series of signs, to be re-arranged according to general principles of variation and permutation, a tangent alien to anything in Joyce's poetics.[31]

In other words, *Exercices de style* is Queneau's proto-Oulipian text, after which (and after *Saint-Glinglin*) his novelistic output would gradually be superseded by his poetic works and Oulipian essays and exercises. One of Queneau's most celebrated and lasting innovations is his variation on Jean Lescure's "La Méthode S+7," in which every adjective, noun, and verb is abstracted from a given text and replaced with the seventh adjective, substantive, or verb following it in the dictionary, thereby transforming the original text. One of Queneau's contributions included in the 1973 *Littérature potentielle* anthology was his rewriting of Jean La Fontaine's fable, "La Cigale et la fourmi," central to the *Wake*'s "Ondt and the Gracehoper" story. The title of Queneau's textual transposition is "La Cimaise et la fraction," and although ludic and presented as wordplay, it isn't quite devoid of ramifications regarding the functioning of literary texts, i.e., their intertextuality:

LA CIMAISE ET LA FRACTION
La cimaise ayant chaponné tout l'éternueur
se tuba fort dépurative quand la bixacée fut verdie :
pas un sexué pétrographique morio de moufette ou de verrat.[32]

As critic Warren F. Motte has observed, this method gives rise to a certain spectral doubleness in the perception of the text, especially when read aloud.[33] To be sure, Queneau's S+7 method is decisively un-Joycean and un--*Wakean* in treating words as dictionary-defined, immutable entities, interchangeable on the basis of a numerical procedure. Still, in his pre-Oulipian novels and essays, and in the idiosyncratic, proto-Oulipian *Exercices de style*, Queneau appears as a writer whose taste for verbal experiment and stylistic

31   "Among the weirdest variations are those called 'Permutations': one written in groups of from two to five letters; one in groups of from five to eight; one in groups of from nine to twelve. Here we see again the mind of a mathematician rather than that of a literary artist at work" (Mercier, "Raymond Queneau: The First New Novelist?" 110).

32   Queneau, "Contribution à la pratique de la méthode lescurienne S+7," *Oulipo – La Littérature potentielle*, 152.

33   Warren F. Motte, *The Poetics of Experiment – A Study of the Work of Georges Perec* (Lexington: French Forum Publishers, 1984) 58–9.

innovation would not have formed as it did had it not been for his debt "tout spécialement envers Joyce."

4.3 "A MAN OF LETTERS": GEORGES PEREC

Even today, over forty years after his death, Georges Perec is still a member of the Oulipo group, which—and this dovetails with what has been noted about its relation to tradition—makes no distinction between living or deceased membership.

This membership began in 1967 when his friend Jacques Roubaud introduced Perec to the Oulipo, and a mere two years later Perec published his first novel directly inspired by his relationship with Oulipo, the remarkable *La Disparition*. In the same year, he began assembling and organising material for the masterpiece he would take ten years to complete, *La vie mode d'emploi*. In an appropriately precise mathematical fashion, he declared himself to be "a genuine product of the Oulipo," his existence as a writer being "ninety per cent dependent on my knowing the Oulipo at a pivotal point in my formation, in my literary work."[34] He referred to this formation as one of becoming a "man of letters": "a man whose work revolves around letters, around the alphabet. My work is not done with ideas or sentiments or images."[35] This work with and around letters involves, in an eminently Oulipian fashion, a formal constraint generative of literary inspiration. However, there is also the ten per cent outside of the commonality, which is more interesting to pursue as it is precisely in places where Perec diverges from the Oulipian doctrine that his *raison d'être* as writer and man might be located.[36]

Although a "product" of the Oulipo, Perec is an outstanding Oulipian. His difference from the group is twofold, in degree and in kind. Perec substan-

---

34   "J'ai donc fait connaissance avec l'Oulipo, j'ai été invité à l'Oulipo, pris comme membre, comme associé ou correspondant [...] Je ne me considère pas comme héritier de Queneau, mais je me considère vraiment comme un produit de l'Oulipo. C'est-à-dire que mon existence d'écrivain dépend à quatre-vingt-dix-sept pour cent du fait que j'ai connu l'Oulipo à une époque tout à fait charnière de ma formation, de mon travail d'écriture" (*Georges Perec – Entretiens et conférences, Volume II: 1979–81*, eds. Dominique Bertelli & Mireille Ribière [Paris: Joseph K., 2003] 148–9).

35   Qtd. in Bernard Magné, "Georges Perec, Oulibiographer," trans. Daniel Levin Becker. Online: http://d7.drunkenboat.com/db8/oulipo/feature-oulipo/essays/magne/oulibio.html

36   As critic Paul Schwartz has similarly observed, "the importance of literary experimentation in Perec's development as a writer is clear: through constraint he discovered imagination. But there is another, more significant factor in his development which surfaces in his autobiographical works of 1973–78: his discovery and gradual understanding—with the aid of analysis—of the effect of his parents' death, especially his mother's, upon his creative imagination" (Paul Schwartz, *Georges Perec – Traces of his Passage* [Birmingham, Alabama: Summa Publications, 1988] 3).

tially differs from Queneau and other Oulipians in the degree of control over, and exhaustiveness of, the combinatorial play of formal elements staged in his work. He can be said to push the Oulipian *potentiality* toward *actuality*, never regarding the method itself as sufficient without its extreme realisation. This obsession with exhausting the subject secured him the first place in quite a few of the Oulipian top charts, most notably, for his 1969 *Grand Palindrome*, with 5 566 letters, the longest palindrome in the French language, and his 300–page novel *La Disparition* (also from 1969, translated into English as *A Void*), a book-length lipogram managing to do without the letter *e* throughout, complemented in 1972 by the monovocal text, *Les Revenentes*, where the only vowel used is *e*. Perec invokes this desire for totality, completion, and exhaustive inclusivity in discussing his aspirations as man of letters—"to write all that a modern man can possibly write," "to fill a drawer at the Bibliothèque nationale," "to use every single word in the dictionary"—evident everywhere in his attempts at "description," "inventory," and "exhaustion."[37]

His ambition is to recycle or invent methods, certainly, but above all to push them to their extremes in order to imbue the sphere of their realisation. However, there is also a more substantial difference marking Perec off from others, more substantial because in kind rather than degree: his systematic determination to *motivate* the constraint. This motivation takes place not only in the sense of Jacques Roubaud's principle according to which "a text written according to a given constraint must speak of this constraint,"[38] which assumes the primacy of the constraint over the generated text, but also in the sense of a sort of constraint generated from within the text, a sort of modernist mimetic form imbued by Perec's biography.

Both these Perequian particularities and divergences from the Oulipian doctrine make him closer in spirit to Joyce than any other Oulipian. Still, unlike Queneau, neither his criticism nor his non-fiction writing (e.g., the 1985 posthumous volume *Penser/Classer*) contains much by way of homage to, or address of, Joyce – it is to Perec's interviews and talks, and of course his own fiction, particularly *La vie mode d'emploi*, that one must turn for specific textual evidence. Of the early interviews, one instance specifically stands out: in 1974, Perec acknowledges the destructive aspect of Joyce's heritage and voices the need to surpass it, to "reinvent" the writing destroyed, tying this project to his Oulipo membership.[39] Nonetheless, in his later interviews, most of them to do with *La vie mode d'emploi*, Joyce begins surfacing as an exclusively positive influence: in an interview for *Le Devoir* from June 1979, Joyce's status

---

37 Qtd. in Magné, "Georges Perec, Oulibiographer."
38 Roubaud, "Introduction," 42.
39 "Joyce a montré qu'il est facile de détruire l'écriture; le problème me paraît être maintenant de la réinventer. C'est pour ça que je suis à l'Oulipo. Je le répète, nous sommes des artisans" (*Entretiens et conférences, Volume I: 1965–78*, 188).

is heightened through association with *La vie mode d'emploi*'s key image of puzzle-making and solving; Joyce, together with "Butor, Kafka or Melville," is an author who draws "une sorte de constellation avec au centre (ou sur les bords) une pièce vide qui est celle que je vais venir remplir."[40] Elsewhere, placing Joyce's *Ulysses* firmly into the genealogy of his development as both reader and writer, Perec avows freely that his earliest work, for "reasons which I absolutely couldn't explain to myself," was parody and pastiche of some of his favourite writers.

Again, just as Queneau, Perec emphasises Joyce's influence as part of his own general interest in Anglo-American fiction – as he confided in an answer to Gabriel Simony's question regarding the "shaking off of the weight of all our literary heroes," the "weight" is felt "particularly with Anglo-Saxon litera-ture," much more so than with the native French.[41] Joyce, just as Henry James or Dickens, even serves Perec in the role of an antidote to Flaubert's literary "terrorism" – *Ulysses* is singled out as giving Perec the reader "l'impression d'être dans une ville immense, une métropole, une capitale."[42] Even though Joyce, for Perec, is first and foremost the author of *Ulysses* whereas *Finnegans Wake* is usually associated with "failure," in a late 1981 interview, Perec points out that the risk Joyce was running with his last work is one common to "all writers at any given time."[43] Any writer who "destroys the conventions exist-ing before him" will eventually "find himself facing a wall," without "succes-sors." Still, Perec himself is proof that in France, Joyce's *Ulysses*-project turned out engendering a steady, innovative succession.

The first thing to note about Perec's corpus is that it stands as testimony to its author's intention, voiced in his autobiographical essay "Notes sur ce que je cherche," to "never write two similar books," to never repeat "the same formula" already "elaborated in a previous book."[44] The Perequian corpus—comprising 22 texts from 1965 to 1981 and 15 more volumes of the posthumous editions of his manuscripts, non-fiction, criticism, collected interviews, etc.—is notable not only for its scope and sheer bulk, but also for

40   Ibid, 76.

41   "Moi, ce poids, je le ressens encore plus avec la littérature anglo-saxonne ; avec Joyce, Henry James, Dickens. Mais aussi très forte avec Flaubert. Cela m'a empêché d'écrire. À la fois empêché et tellement donné envie! Effectivement, si on reste terrorisé par Flaubert, c'est vrai que l'on se dit que l'on n'y arrivera jamais, que ce n'est pas possible" (Ibid, 219).

42   Ibid, 224.

43   "C'est un risque que tout écrivain court tout le temps, que tout poète court, à savoir qu'il a im-pression que […] à force de faire un travail qui détruit les conventions qui existaient avant lui, il va se retrouver en face d'un mur et qu'il n'aura pas de successeurs. C'est sûr que pour Joyce… il y a… à la fin de *Finnegans Wake*, il y a quelque chose qui est du domaine de l'échec" (Ibid, 290).

44   "Si je tente à définir ce que j'ai cherché à faire depuis que j'ai commencé à écrire, la première idée qui me vient à l'esprit est que je n'ai jamais écrit deux livres semblables, que je n'ai jamais eu envie de répéter dans un livre une formule, un système ou une manière élaborés dans un livre précédant" (P/C, 9).

its unique variety. As Schwartz has remarked, the differences of style and subject in Perec's first three novels—*Les Choses* (1965), *Quel petit vélo* (1966), and *Un Homme qui dort* (1967)—give the impression of "a man with a need to write, searching for a personal means of expression,"[45] but with Perec, this is no symptom of youthful search and uncertainty, but of a constant writerly disposition. Critic David Gascoigne speaks of Perec's "heterogeneous memory-bank of choice morsels" and their "unexpected juxtapositions" that "nourish his writing."[46] Zooming in on just five years of Perec's career, 1973–78, during which he was most involved with *La vie mode d'emploi*: there are volumes like *La Boutique obscure: 124 rêves* (1973), Perec's dream book where he recounts the dreams dreamt from May 1969 to August 1972, an explicitly oneiric text whose narrative poses questions about the relation of lived experience and writing.

Espèces d'espaces: Journal d'un usager de l'espace (1974) resists generic classification, composed as it is of a series of texts which resemble essays more than anything else, thematically dealing with the ways in which people furnish space – here, Joyce's importance for Perec as a writer of "space," mentioned in several interviews above, directly reflects Perec's own involvement. *W ou le souvenir d'enfance* (1975), again, is formally unique in that its structure is doubly bipartite. First, two separate narratives are juxtaposed throughout the text, an autobiographical narrative and a fictive narrative which Perec had first written at the age of thirteen. Passages of the two are interpolated in *W* in alternating chapters. Second, each of the two narratives is in itself bipartite; their respective caesurae coincide, so that the text as a whole is divided into two parts. *Alphabets* (1976) is a collection of heterogrammatic poetry, i.e., poetry written in successive anagrams of a given series of letters, each anagram constituting a "verse." Finally, *Je me souviens* (1978), perhaps the most immediately accessible Perec text, is an experiment in collective memory, containing 480 short allusions to recent history (political, cultural, and popular), each prefaced by the phrase "je me souviens," "I remember," recuperating the banal element of the past.

Still, Perec himself provided a useful and as exhaustive as possible classification of his works into four categories, to do with his central concerns as writer: first, the "sociological" order, dealing with "how to regard the

---

45 Schwartz, *Georges Perec*, 1.

46 Perec is the most eclectic of writers. Magpie-like, he evidently gleaned from his voracious reading, as well as from his work as a scientific documentalist, a heterogeneous memory-bank of choice morsels—sentences, odd names, incidents real and fictional, technical terminologies— on which he drew in profusion and in unexpected juxtapositions to nourish his writing. In the literary and narrative games which he plays, many of the constituent materials and of the particular techniques can be found to be derived from writers whom he admired and constantly reread" (David Gascoigne, *The Games of Fiction – Georges Perec and Modern French Ludic Narrative* [Oxford: Peter Lang, 2006] 47).

everyday" (exemplary texts: *Les Choses, Espèces d'espaces, Tentative de description de quelques lieux parisiens*); second, the autobiographical order (*W ou le souvenir d'enfance, La Boutique obscure, Je me souviens, Lieux où j'ai dormi*); the ludic order ("all of the works inspired by the Oulipo research: palindromes, lipograms, pangrams, anagrams, isograms, acrostics, crosswords, etc."); and finally, the novelist order, inspired by Perec's "taste for stories" and his hope "to write books that get devoured" by readers "lying on their bellies in bed" – Perec's example is, of course, *La vie mode d'emploi*.[47]

Given the primary focus of this study, attention will be paid to just Perec's two crucial novels, *La Disparition* and *La vie mode d'emploi*. As Warren F. Motte has observed in his excellent study on Perec, *The Poetics of Experiment*, all of his texts partake of the literary tradition of constraint, however, with a particularly Perequian twist, a "constraint voluntarily imposed."[48] *La Disparition* and *Les Revenentes* are the most purely Oulipian of Perec's longer works, not only because of their constraint-observance and self-reference, but also because they are guided, as Motte has put it, by the essentially Oulipian questions of renewal and revitalisation: "Might the modern novel be revitalized through an increase rather than a decrease of formal rigor? Is the means through which this is to be effected a Draconian system of constraint? A castration of the alphabet?"[49]

Although *La Disparition* is the first of Perec's longer texts to adopt the structure of the game overtly, Motte's questions are not merely rhetorical, as both a positive and a negative answer would only tell part of the story. The ten per cent of the non-Oulipian impulse in Perec has to do with his uniquely personal and painful experience. As Perec himself made clear in his "Histoire du lipogramme," the form and the gadget itself are no inventions of his – he duly credits the American Ernest Vincent Wright and his *Gadsby* (1939) as the first novel written entirely without the letter *e*. However, it is in comparison with Wright's text that the truly experimental character of Perec's novel crystallises.

Already the first edition of Wright's book is furnished with an introduction presenting the book's chief constraint and the sundry difficulties ("trouble with pronouns," "the past tense of verbs, -ed," etc.) entailed in its composi-

---

47 Perec, "Notes sur ce que je cherche," 10.
48 "All works of art are composed according to a system of constraint; any human artifact bows to the constraints inherent in the medium within which it is produced. [...] For the literary text, the minimal constraints are those of the language: in Saussurean terms, the *langue* constrains the *parole*. Generic constraints are culturally codified and may be more or less rigorous in various instances, depending upon both the specific genre [...] and the relation of the text thereto, whether it proves itself submissive or antagonistic to the body of literature which precedes it. It is the third case, that of constraints voluntarily imposed, which concerns us here, for it is this that came increasingly to color the work of Georges Perec. [...] It is also characteristic of the literary experimentation of the Oulipo as a whole" (Motte, *The Poetics of Experiment*, 18).
49 Ibid, 31.

tion. Wright also states that "this story was written, not through any attempt to attain literary merit" and that his sole hope is that the reader "may learn to love all the young folks in the story, as deeply as I have, in introducing them to you. Like many a book, it grows more and more interesting as the reader becomes well acquainted with the characters."[50] The narrative of Wright's book relates the rather inane story of a certain John Gadsby whose community activism helps to transform his hometown, Branton Hills, from a stagnant municipality into a prosperous urban space – nowhere in Wright's story is the central constraint substantiated, referred to, conceptualised.

However, if Perec pulled off the feat of doing without the letter *e* for over 300 pages so adroitly that none of *La Disparition*'s first reviewers even noticed, it was not just "for the heck of it" (like Wright), nor in order to draw his overarching narrative scheme (the mysterious disappearance of, and feverish quest after the novel's protagonist, Anton Voyl / *Vowl*) from a recurring metaphorical designation of its constraint. This designation ranges from the overall structure (26 chapters—the number of letters in the French alphabet—with chapter 5 left out, 6 sections—corresponding to the 6 French vowels—with the second section missing) to the minutest narrative details (26 books on the main character's shelf, with the fifth volume mysteriously missing, a pseudo-Oedipal episode with the Sphinx' question after an animal "that has a body as curving as a bow and draws back inwards as straight as an arrow," i.e., the letter *e*, etc.).

It was rather for the sake of turning this familiar undertaking into the central figure of Perec's personal universe marked by loss, absence, and disappearance. The central absence of Perec's life was of course the disappearance of his parents (who were naturalised Polish Jews): his father on the battleground and his mother in the most gruesome concentration camp of World War II. As critics have noted, together with the disappearance of the letter *e*, both "père" and "mère," the author's "famille" must remain absent from the text, as well as its author's name (itself a French transcription of its Polish original). As Robert Bober has argued, *La Disparition* is "a book which in effect demonstrates the following: just as a book can be written without the most indispensable letter of all, the *e*, so Perec has showed what sort of a life could be lived without the most indispensable thing of all, a mother and a father. One *can* live in such circumstances [...] only it's a different sort of life."[51]

In *La Disparition*, the lipogrammatic structure creates all sorts of ancillary wordplay, such as the transformation of the well-known pangram: "Por-

50   Ernest Vincent Wright, *Gatsby* (New York: Ramble House Edition, 1939) i-iii.
51   Qtd. in Gabriel Josipovici, "Georges Perec's Homage to Joyce (and Tradition)," *The Yearbook of English Studies – Anglo-French Literary Relations* (15.1982): 199-200.

tez ce vieux whisky au juge blond qui fume" into the form demanded by the lipogram in *e*: "Portons dix bons whiskys à l'avocat goujat qui fumait au zoo" (*LD*, 51). The same sort of Oulipian exercise is involved in the transformation of six poems, "Brise marine," "Booz endormi," "Recueillement," "Correspondances," Baudelaire's "Les Chats," and Rimbaud's "Voyelles" – a veritable feat in transcription and literary encoding. As Motte has put it, Perec's text becomes a detective novel in which "the relation of the author to the reader [...] is dominated by the ludic element; the text is a game proposed by the author to the reader" and "the hermeneutic task of the reader is analogous to that of the detective, of the exegete, of anyone who attempts to decipher an enigma."[52] Even though traumatically personal, the elision of the letter *e* again forms part of Perec's lifelong mission of a "man of letters," a writer privileging the status of the individual letter – as will be shown, apart from *e* in *La Disparition* and *Les Revenentes*, there is also the famous double example of Perec's interest in *w* – *W ou le souvenir d'enfance* and *La vie mode d'emploi*.

Perec's insistence on the materiality of the letter can, at least partly, be attributed to Joyce's materialist poetics privileging the letter as the smallest semantic/emblematic unit – observes Motte, "in this, Perec recalls other writers [... like] James Joyce, who exalts the *e* in *Finnegans Wake*."[53] However, unlike works "privileging" certain letters, *La Disparition* is marked uniquely in how the *e* dominates the entire text *in absentia*. Since *e* is the most frequently used letter in the French language, its suppression clearly imposes a constraint which radically modifies linguistic normativity. Significantly, the return of the repressed *e* comes in the text entitled *Les Revenents*, meaning "ghosts" or "revenants," literally "those that have returned." The same letter which controls *La Disparition* in its absence dominates *Les Revenentes* by its presence; even though, from another perspective, *Les Revenentes* appears as a lipogram in *a*, *i*, *o*, and *u*. *Ulysses* is featured, in *La Disparition*, in the very final chapter. On their futile search for Vowl, Savorgnan, Ottaviani and Swann had just been faced with a piece of lipogramatic text without *a*, *y*, and neither of course, "has it got a solitary..." (*V*, 272) *e* – which is the void into which the penultimate chapter falls. Then in chapter 26, Ottaviani—who begins to see the point in a quasi-Joycean epiphany—receives the following description:

> Crimson, florid, Ottaviani starts inflating. As imposing and plump as Buck Mulligan standing on top of a spiral stairway whilst intoning an "Introibo," his slowly magnifying body brings to mind a purplish balloon, of a sort that you might buy for your child in Pare Montsouris. And, in a twinkling, just as such a balloon will combust if brought into contact with a sharp point, Ottaviani burst, his body ripping apart, making a din as

---

52   Motte, *The Poetics of Experiment*, 60.
53   Ibid, 83.

loud as an aircraft attaining Mach III and outstripping sound with a mirror-smashing bang. And, in an instant, not a nail, not a button – poor Ottaviani is nothing but a puny, chalky mass as small as a tiny turd of ash from a cigar but so oddly whitish in colour you might think it was talc. (V, 273)

Neither "Joyce" nor his altered ego "Stephen Dedalus," nor the "Ulysses" of his Dublin Odyssey "Leopold" can possibly enter Perec's lipogramatic charade, and so entry is allowed to Buck Mulligan, the buffoon from the famous incipit to Joyce's novel.

Dedicated to the memory of Raymond Queneau is Perec's longest text, *La vie mode d'emploi* (1978), "fictions" (as its subtitle indicates the plural) of some 700 pages, based upon two rigid systems of formal constraint. They preside over, respectively, the sequence of the chapters and the constitutive elements of each chapter. The novel deals with a Parisian apartment building and its inhabitants. The structure of the building is 10 stories high and 10 units wide, suggesting a *10x10* grid, an expanded chessboard. Perec chose this image as the basis for the system of formal constraint which governs the sequence of chapters.[54] Having established a system by which the sequence of chapters is regulated, Perec goes on to regulate the constitutive elements of each chapter, [55] devising 42 categories, each of which contained 10 variables, to be included in each chapter. As he made clear in numerous interviews, the groups of 10 included body positions, activities, colours, numbers of characters per room, events (like America before Christopher Columbus, Asia in ancient times, or the Middle Ages in England), details about the furniture, literary quotations, etc. To take just the first two of these, since each category contains 10 variables—for body position, the variables are: kneeling, sitting, lying on the stomach, lying on the back, an arm up in the air, etc.; for activity: painting, having an interview, consulting a map, performing an erotic act, etc.—each one will be used, in principle, 10 times. The kneeling position will be repeated in 10 chapters, standing in another 10, and so on, thereby filling all the 100 chapters/rooms of the book. Furthermore, each body position is paired with one of 10 activities, and each of these activities will in turn be repeated in 10 different chapters. 10 different positions paired with 10 different

---

54 Motte points out that, for Perec, "it is not chess itself, as distinct from other games, which provides the interest, but the fact that it has historically been seen as a ludic framework within which problems are posed and then solved, very much akin, therefore, to his conception of literature itself" (Ibid, 36).

55 As Perec himself explained, there were "21 fois 2 séries de 10 éléments qui sont ainsi permutées et qui déterminent les éléments constitutifs de chaque chapitre [...] Au terme de ces laborieuses permutations, j'en arrivai ainsi à une sorte de « cahier de charges » dans lequel, pour chaque chapitre, était énumérée une liste de 42 thèmes qui devaient figurer dans le chapitre" (Georges Perec, "Quatre figures pour *La vie mode d'emploi*," *Atlas de littérature potentielle* [Paris: Gallimard, 1981] 387).

activities will, in principle, yield 100 unique position/activity pairs, one for each chapter of the book. This is in principle only, because there are merely 99 chapters in the book; Perec threw a (systematic) monkey's wrench into his system in order to deconstruct or "de-complete" it.

Furnished with 42 elements to feature in each of the 99 chapters, Perec could then proceed with the design of the storyline proper. Set on June 23, 1975, at 11 Rue Simon-Crubellier, the narrative of *La vie mode d'emploi* concerns the recounting—in what amounts to a dazzling total of 179 stories featuring over 200 characters—of the personal histories and present states of the flat's inhabitants. What emerges from within this immense kaleidoscope as possibly the organising leitmotif linking them all together is the story of a whimsical project undertaken by one of the flat's tenants, an English millionaire Perceval Bartlebooth, which involves learning the art of the watercolour. Bartlebooth travels the world painting 500 watercolours of seaports, sending these to Gaspard Winckler, an assistant craftsman who partitions these into a 750–piece puzzles. Then, upon returning from the voyage, Bartlebooth aims to reassemble the puzzles into the paintings again, sending each painting to the location of its creation, with the intent of having it washed with a detergent, leaving only a blank sheet of paper. The nothing that was at the beginning would be the nothing at the end.

However, the project misfires as Winckler, avenging himself on Bartlebooth for the twenty years of pointless labour, produces puzzles of an increasing level of difficulty, and at 8 p.m. on June 23, 1975, the almost-blind Bartlebooth dies as he haphazardly attempts to finish puzzle number 439:

> It is the twenty-third of June nineteen seventy-five, and it is eight o'clock in the evening. Seated at his jigsaw puzzle, Bartlebooth has just died. On the tablecloth, somewhere in the crepuscular sky of the four hundred and thirty-ninth puzzle, the black hole of the sole piece not yet filled in has the almost perfect shape of an X. But the ironical thing, which could have been foreseen long ago, is that the piece the dead man holds between his fingers is shaped like a W. (*LUM*, 497)[56]

The ordering of the book's chapters, then, follows a design of dexterity and complexity taken to their extreme degrees and thereby nullified because no longer perceptible – the 99 chapters follow the famous Knight's tour, a mathematical problem involving a knight moving around chessboard (here, of a 10x10 grid), visiting each square only once.

---

56   "C'est le vingt-trois juin mille neuf cent soixante-quinze et il va être huit heures du soir. Assis devant son puzzle, Bartlebooth vient de mourir. Sur le drap de la table, quelque part dans le ciel crépusculaire du quatre cent trente-neuvièmes puzzles, le trou noir de la seule pièce none encore posée dessine la silhouette presque parfait d'un X. mais la pièce que le mort tient entre ses doigts a la forme, depuis longtemps prévisible dans son ironie même, d'un W" (*LVME*, 600).

Thus, with 10 stories and two flights of stairs for either of the two cellar complexes, there are 12 "On the Stairs" chapters; since his is a 5-room apartment, indeed, there are 5 "Bartlebooth" chapters. The knight's tour performed by Perec's narrative is a closed one, that is to say, the last square of the voyage would be the one from which it was commenced – a leap two squares outside Bartlebooth's apartment and one down would indeed bring us back to the landing "between the third and fourth storey" of the first chapter. Just as Bartlebooth's own absurdly self-cancelling endeavour, the knight would be left at exactly the same spot from which it had set out. Consequently, the opening of the novel is equally random, as the closed knight's tour can be begun at every single one of its steps – and accordingly, the novel opens: "YES, IT COULD begin this way, right here, just like that" (*LUM*, 3), or "Oui, cela pourrait commencer ainsi, ici, comme ça..." (*LVME*, 19).

The opening meditation in *La vie mode d'emploi* on jigsaw puzzles is quite obviously designed to be taken as a metafictional commentary on the book itself, as its main narrative line plus the sundry digressions from which it is inseparable—indeed, indistinguishable—involves riddle- and puzzle-solving and its overall formal setup is meant to evoke, as much as possible in the essentially temporal medium of language, the spatial organisation of a jigsaw puzzle. The entire "Préambule" is repeated, with only minor variations, in chapter 44; this is singularly appropriate, since the chapter recounts the meeting of Percival Bartlebooth and Gaspard Winckler, to become the former's puzzle maker – at the centre of *La Vie* is the distant, but no less fierce combat between Winckler and Bartlebooth, between puzzle-maker and puzzle-solver.[57] Perec starts off by pointing out that the English word "puzzle" signifies an enigma; and like all enigmas, the jigsaw puzzle seems rather trivial when solved.

His ultimate point, however, in the "Préambule" is the insistence on the communicative role of puzzle-making and puzzle-solving:

> Despite appearances, puzzling is not a solitary game: every move the puzzler makes, the puzzler-maker has made before; every piece the puzzler picks up, and picks up again, and studies and strokes, every combination he tries, and tries a second time, every blunder and every insight, each hope and each discouragement have all been designed, calculated, and decided by the other. (*LUM*, 19–20)[58]

---

57 As Motte rightly insists, "Perec's theory of the puzzle is entirely consonant with his theory of literature; he used the image of the puzzle to characterize his writings." Perec the puzzle maker proposed, then, "his work as a ludic and enigmatic whole. His reader, the puzzle solver, enters therein at his own risk and peril; he will undoubtedly come to regard Bartlebooth's obsession with increasing sympathy and comprehension" (Motte, *The Poetics of Experiment*, 66-7).

58 "En dépit des apparences, ce n'est pas un jeu solitaire : chaque geste que fait le poseur de puzzle, le faiseur de puzzles l'a fait avant lui ; chaque pièce qu'il prend et reprend, qu'il examine,

A "user's manual" of sorts to Perec's own text, one might use the "Préambule" to follow the "line laid down" for the reader and deduce from the thorough disquisition on the art of jigsaw puzzles Perec's own theory of reading.

To substantiate this link which might seem haphazard, one only needs to refer back to the numerous etymologies of the word 'to read' (the English word itself having to do with 'solving, interpreting riddles'), as they occur across the various branches of the European linguistic family: the Latin *legere* meaning both 'to read,' 'to cull,' and 'to tie together,' the German *lesen* meaning both 'to read' and 'to collect,' the Czech (and more broadly Slavonic) *číst* having also to do with 'counting,' 'adding.' Most relevantly for Perec, the French *lire* is anagrammatically (if not perhaps etymologically) connected with *lier*, 'to join,' 'to put together'; as the passage itself reminds us, "the pieces," after all, "are readable only when gathered." Moreover, if one keeps in mind the often-cited homophone of "pieces" / *pièces* ("rooms") of a building, these two words also refer to the act of relating spaces or going from one space to another, whether that space is a room in a building, or a chapter in a book – or more precisely, a chapter in a book on the subject of a room in a building. Chapters in prosaic text, as well as stanzas in poetry, both have to do with building textual rooms.

Where does Joyce fit into Perec's textual jigsaw puzzle? The novel comes with a number of appendices: an "Index" (which runs to 40 pages), a "Chronology," an "Alphabetical Checklist" of some of the "Stories Narrated," and a "Postscript," in which it is revealed that:

> (This book contains quotations, some of them slightly adapted, from works by: René Belleto, Hans Bellmer, Jorge Luis Borges, Michel Butor, Italo Calvino, Agatha Christie, Gustave Flaubert, Sigmund Freud, Alfred Jarry, James Joyce, Franz Kafka, Michel Leiris, Malcolm Lowry, Thomas Mann, Gabriel Garcia Marquez, Harry Mathews, Herman Melville, Vladimir Nabokov, Georges Perec, Roger Price, Marcel Proust, Raymond Queneau, François Rabelais, Jacques Roubaud, Raymond Roussel, Stendhal, Lawrence Sterne, Theodore Sturgeon, Jules Verne, Unica Zürn.) (*LUM* 579)[59]

Perec, thus, reveals a novel which had seemed such a highly original, hyper-realistic universe unto itself, as a veritable mosaic, tissue, or jigsaw-puzzle of

---

qu'il caresse, chaque combinaison qu'il essaye encore, chaque tâtonnement, chaque intuition, chaque espoir, chaque découragement, ont été décidés, calculés, étudiés par l'autre" (*LVME*, 18).

59 "Ce livre comprend des citations, parfois légèrement modifiés, de: René Belleto, Hans Bellmer, Jorge Luis Borges, Michel Butor, Italo Calvino, Agatha Christie, Gustave Flaubert, Sigmund Freud, Alfred Jarry, James Joyce, Franz Kafka, Michel Leiris, Malcolm Lowry, Thomas Mann, Gabriel Garcia Marquez, Harry Mathews, Herman Melville, Vladimir Nabokov, Georges Perec, Roger Price, Marcel Proust, Raymond Queneau, François Rabelais, Jacques Roubaud, Raymond Roussel, Stendhal, Lawrence Sterne, Theodore Sturgeon, Jules Verne, Unica Zürn." (*LVME*, 695).

quotations. Notably, Joyce is one of only four English-language authors (the other three being Lowry, Sterne, and Mathews). Perec's "Citations" notebook consists of precise references to quotations carefully garnered from a list of twenty authors. Here is Perec's list for Joyce:

JOYCE

1	ch 23	*Ulysse* p 637
2	ch 32	*Ulysse* 550 (carte postale)
3	ch 36	"Homme Libre
4	ch 43	"p 151 (gomme Héphas)
5	ch 59	"p 608 (instruments)
6	ch 60	"p 471 (le lino) + des mots du diction
7	ch 67	"p 150 CABINET DE CONSULT.
8	ch 93	"p 447
9	ch 46[60]	

To the left is the number of the quotation in Perec's listing, followed by the number of the chapter in *La vie mode d'emploi* in which it is inserted, and then the title of the book from which the quotation is drawn. The words to the right indicate that Perec was working from the French translation produced by Auguste Morel with Stuart Gilbert and Valéry Larbaud in 1929, and the pagination in the previous column refers to the 1948 Gallimard edition, which, as the catalogue of Perec's library confirms, was the one he owned.[61]

Although Perec's quotations from Joyce have certain distinguishing characteristics and generate particular kinds of intertextual meaning—often relating, for instance, to the theme of translation that they both enact and represent—they are not of a markedly different kind from Perec's other adapted quotations. In *La vie mode d'emploi* a deliberate structural flattening or equalisation prevails: the lists, the chess and complex mathematical formulae that govern the trajectory of the narrative within the building and regulate the distribution of elements within each chapter, preclude the possibility of one author being elevated above another. Evenly weighted, these voices form a gigantic intertextual puzzle. To quote in this way, for Perec, is to conjure a personalised literary microcosm within the wider literary macrocosm, a fictional constellation in which the coordinates of specific authorial

---

60 N.B. The list is left purposefully incomplete. Georges Perec, *Cahier des Charges*, eds. Hans Hartje, Bernard Magné, and Jacques Neefs (Paris: CNRS Éditions, 1993) 61. For more on its incompletion, see Scarlett Baron, "Hoaxville: Reading Perec Reading Joyce," *James Joyce Quarterly* 52.2 (Winter 2015): 369–412

61 For a closer and perceptive analysis of these quotations, see Baron, "Reading Perec Reading Joyce."

reference points define a space of writing in which "work on genres, codes and models" takes place.[62]

So Perec, like Joyce, consciously and self-consciously opens up his text to a plethora of other voices. Like Joyce, he makes intertextuality a compositional principle, and in his own eye-popping Oulipian style, finds astonishingly ingenious ways of flooding his text with quotation, even though Perec's intertextuality is of an order different from that of Joyce's.[63] Still, as Jacques Mailhos has argued in "The Art of Memory: Joyce and Perec," there is one *Ulysses* borrowing (the first one, in chapter 23) that stands out and above the others in that it "includes" the entirety of Joyce's *Ulysses*. Discussing how Perec resorts to similar solutions to the similar sorts of compositional problems faced by Joyce while organising his encyclopaedic narrative, Mailhos shows "the extent and importance of Joyce's presence in *Life: A User's Manual*, while concentrating on an analysis of the similar use, by both writers, of the art of memory as a basis for the creation of the fiction."[64]

It is in its functioning as mnemonic system that Perec's intertextuality should be given its proper due without necessarily regarding it as inferior to Joyce's.[65] The notion of "memory places," in Mailhos' essay, gives rise to the idea of the book as textual space, a "house" of sorts, conjuring up Perec's first "altered quotation" from *Ulysses*, his borrowing of the character of "Mr Henry Fleury" (Bloom's pseudonym in "Lotus Eaters") in chapter 23 of *La Vie*, turning him into a room decorator – with reference to a "doll's house" taken from the end of the "Ithaca" chapter, where it forms part of Bloom's fantasy of his "ultimate ambition." Mailhos shows how via this doll's house, *Ulysses* as

---

62   "Mon ambition d'écrivain est donc de balayer, ou en tout cas de baliser, les champs de l'écriture dans tous les domaines où cette écriture m'a permis d'écrire à mon tour. Cela implique un travail sur les genres, sur les codes, et sur les "modèles" dont mon écriture procède : un certain nombre d'auteurs (de Joyce à Hergé, de Kafka à Price, De Scève à Pierre Dac, de Si Shonagon à Gotlib) définissent, circonscrivent le lieu d'où j'écris" (Bernard Pingaud, "Ceci n'est pas un puzzle," *Arc* 76 [1979]: 3).

63   As Scarlett Baron has pointed out, "Authorial omniscience and omnipotence are presented as absolute principles: the picture tauntingly outlined here is one of supreme, invincible intentionality. This is in accord with the impression of complete control produced by Perec's work, in which contingency is reduced to a finely calibrated minimum. [...] Perec replicates the dizzyingly broad incorporative energies of Joyce's own writing. But in his idiosyncratic approach – all at once personal and impersonal, individual and Oulipian, mischievous and algorithmic – Perec adapts, translates, and transposes Joyce's intertextual vision, adding his piece to the expanding puzzle of Joycean, and universal, literature" (Baron, "Reading Perec Reading Joyce," 394–5).

64   Jacques Mailhos, "The Art of Memory: Joyce and Perec," *Transcultural Joyce*, ed. Karen Lawrence (Cambridge: Cambridge University Press, 1998) 151.

65   "It is precisely because *Life: A User's Manual* functions as a mnemonic system that the most insignificant references, the most trivial borrowings (and they are often particularly trivial) are (A) possible (they have found the structure which seals their places in the narration), and (B) import their original context with them" (Ibid, 162).

a whole enters Perec's novel.[66] Moreover, as concerns the Perec/Joyce relation, one need not stop with intertextuality. Gabriel Josipovici's 1982 review of Perec's novel for *The Yearbook of English Studies* went so far as to speak of "Georges Perec's Homage to Joyce."[67] Josipovici's argument is most convincing in its discussion of Perec's hyper-realism: "Is Perec a hyper-realist, only concerned to detail what is to be found in the average Parisian building around 1975? Or does he perhaps wish to tell us something about the characters through the descriptions?" is the question, and Josipovici answers in the negative.[68]

Another feature, one in which Perec surpasses even Joyce, is the extreme non-linearity of his narrative – in the light of which even a text like *Ulysses* appears to grow pale.[69] In Perec's jigsaw puzzle, no affirmation of linearity and archetypical status can be said to take place. Josipovici's intervention makes a compelling case for Perec's *La Vie* as "a homage to tradition, the storehouse of possibilities" and in particular, "a homage to Joyce, the man who above all others made it possible," by which is meant "the book as it stands possible, but also made possible the pleasure which work on the book no doubt gave to Perec."[70] Even though less concerned than Queneau with expressive verbal deformations à la the *Wake*, Perec's *La vie: mode d'emploi* stands as Oulipo's most *Ulysses*-like novel: a novel of grids, schemas, as well as dazzlingly broad and complex intertextuality.

---

66   "Through this doll's house, *Ulysses* as a whole enters *Life: A User's Manual* (in the same way as whole characters and books enter *Finnegans Wake* through assimilations, puns, cryptic references, etc.). This doll's house is a typical memory image which contains Bloom, Bloom's dreams, but also the idea (the possibility) of a different *Ulysses* with a different character [...]. Thus, in a way, Bloom himself was present—*under cover*—in Perec's Parisian building (and book), and Bloom himself, as an interior decorator, set all the elements in one of the apartments. [...] Given the way in which this book functions, Bloom, as an interior decorator, thus becomes something like the author of one of its chapters" (Ibid, 165).

67   Josipovici, "Georges Perec's Homage to James Joyce," 179.

68   "On the contrary. What we realize as we read this book is how very selective the ordinary novelist is and how Perec's method actually destroys the delicate balance of foreground and background on which novels depend for their effect of reality. But then this is in keeping with what new art always does: it does not render the old obsolete but helps to make us see the often hidden parameters and conventions of the old" (Ibid, 183).

69   "Even when a writer as boldly innovatory as Joyce wants us to get away from the anecdotal and the linear he can only do it by trying to present Bloom as Everyman. Joyce, like Freud, was very often confused by his own instincts and interpreted his discoveries in terms of the nineteenth-century patterns of thought which these very discoveries were in the process of subverting. Thus "Cyclops" and "Ithaca" pull in one direction, centrifugally, while "Circe" and "Penelope," for all their flirtation with fragmentation and the dissolution of self, really affirm a rather old-fashioned view of character and archetypes" (Ibid, 189–90).

70   Ibid, 200.

4.4 "A PRE-MODERN, ENCYCLOPEDIC CAST OF MIND": HARRY MATHEWS

Harry Mathews was a writer officially Oulipian, even though he was born in New York, studied music at Harvard University and frequently taught writing in the United States, and only in 1952 relocated to in France. As he confided to John Ashbery,

> in 1952 I ran away from America. Which was not America: it was the milieu in which I'd been raised, and I thought that's what America was, that is to say, an upper-middle-class Eastern WASP environment, which I read as being extremely hostile to the poetic and artistic enthusiasms that I felt were most important at that time.[71]

Already influenced by Raymond Roussel's proceduralism, Mathews gradually came under the influence of the Oulipo group, becoming in 1973 its only American member to date. However, a body of his work predates his accession to Oulipo, significant in its own right so as to set it off as a separate, self--contained period in his overall *oeuvre*. Symptomatic of his Oulipian turn in 1973 is that ever since the mid-1970s publication of *The Sinking of the Odradek Stadium and Other Novels*, Mathews has written only two works of fiction that can be loosely labelled as novels, i.e,. *Cigarettes* (1987) and *The Journalist* (1997), and that neither of these two can be said to follow any strict Oulipian "programme" or "poetic agenda." Mathews himself has provided the following personal view on his pre- and post-Oulipian development:

> How much has the Oulipo mattered to me, and why? It is hard to answer simply, because its influence has been gradual, because I had strong non-Oulipian feelings about three of its members, because my devotion to the group involves much more than its ideas. [...] I had written my first three novels without even hearing of it. [...] I was not yet aware of what the Oulipo was in fact changing: my understanding of the act of writing. (*CPM*, 85)

In the many interviews and public pronouncements made over the course of his life, three instances in particular cast light on the significant, yet limited role played by the modernist heritage in Mathews' understanding of literary history and his own influences. Mathews opens his 1987 interview with John Ashbery for *Review of Contemporary Fiction* with acknowledging his debt to Ronald Firbank, about which he is "delighted," observing that "of course Firbank was the great formal innovator. He invented modernism, more so

---

71   "A Conversation with Harry Mathews by John Ashbery," *Review of Contemporary Fiction* 7.3 (Fall 1987): 46.

than Joyce really," and going on to specify Firbank's stylistic influence on the example of the opening of his first novel, *Conversions*.[72] Two years later, in an interview included in Warren Leamon's book-length study, Mathews specifies the relative importance of Joyce vis-à-vis Firbank more generously.[73] Finally, in a 1994 interview with Lytle Shaw, Mathews is again outspokenly in favour of what he sees in Firbank or Kafka as minimalist subversion to Joyce's medieval monumentality or encyclopaedism.[74] This encyclopaedism of *Ulysses*, admirable though it is, by Mathews' own admission, "isn't pushing me to see what I can do next." For the *Wake*, the praise is similarly limited and qualified: although "fabulous" and "haunting," some passages (e.g., the whole ALP section) are found "sentimental and self-indulgent." Moreover, as the interviewer suggests, there looms the sense of Joyce's texts' pre-programmed and omniscient nature, which renders the reading experience into a passive one.[75]

All three Mathews' pre-Oulipian novels start off as seemingly simple quest narratives that become gradually enmeshed in complex realms of arcane knowledge and abstruse erudition. His most common procedure is to break the linearity of the simple framing quest-narrative by inserting sundry tales within tales, the effect of whose multiplication is to collapse plot into a patchwork of diversions. As quest narratives, each of the first three novels involves the use and reworking of some sort of mythology—with the hindsight of a long-term Oulipian, as Mathews discerned in his own preoccupation with mythology an Oulipianism *avant la lettre*—and it is also one that departs from the modernist mythological project:

---

72 "The sentences are very simple, but there's something slightly out of kilter about them. There's something about their lack of emphasis or the way the emphasis falls in an unexpected place. Firbank did this first of course, and it's almost a source of irritation that there are so many things one can't do without sounding like him" (Ashbery, "A Conversation," 21).

73 "To my mind Firbank's superiority resides in this: Joyce's innovations have affected us mainly in the domain of style and the way his material is presented, whereas Firbank transformed the basic narrative procedure of fiction. This is a hastily concocted remark; I wouldn't find it interesting to get stuck in an argument defending it" (Warren Leamon, *Harry Mathews* [New York: Twayne Publishers, 1993] 16).

74 "The "Night Town" scene above all is an extraordinary work of subversion. What struck me in re-reading Ulysses was [Joyce's] encyclopedic view of "reality": if you find a narrative that is valid, you can load it with any amount of cultural freight, and the more you load, the truer it will become. In spite of syntactical or rhetorical alertness, in a sense he remained pre-modern because of this encyclopedic cast of mind" (Lytle Shaw, "An interview with Harry Mathews," *Chicago Review* 43.2 [Spring 1997]: 36).

75 "It's a passive experience [...]. (In *Ulysses* that's not always the case and that's why I love the "Night Town" scene.) A kind of all-knowingness. I suppose someday I will write a long book and everyone can say it's my magnum opus. But I prefer classical subversion to monumentality. That's why I love Firbank: such explosive froth! There is something about small books – a book is like a time bomb, and a small, demure time bomb seems to me most efficient of all. But someday self-interest may beguile me into Grand Design" (Shaw, "An interview with Harry Mathews," 36).

My first three novels depend on a non-systematic Oulipism, if such a phenomenon exists – a combination of techniques of variation and substitution that often determine the nature of narrative materials as well as their use. In *The Sinking of the Odradek Stadium*, the accumulation of these procedures has become an omnipresent "table of obligations" (Perec's *cahier de charges*): the text is, to put it mildly, overdetermined. From *The Conversions* to *Odradek*, the use of "justifying myths" in the manner of Joyce and Eliot yields to that of "non-certifiable" materials organized in quasi-systematic ways – a tendency pointing eventually to a complete Oulipisation. (*CPM*, 88)

For Mathews, hand in hand with mythology goes the discourse that supplanted it, at least in the European cultural space – as he confided to Lynne Tillman, "the substratum of the first three novels is a religious one."[76]

In *The Conversions* (1962), the quest is one after the answers to the three riddles contained in the last will of a late millionaire, Mr Wayl, whose vast estate is to be left to the person who knows "When was a stone not a king? What was *La Messe de Sire Fadevant*? Who shaved the Old Man's Beard?" (*C*, 46). His quest for these answers takes the narrator on a journey both in space and time, into areas of conceptual and factual obscurity (the secret Cult of Silvius being just the most conspicuous among them). The quest turns out futile as, just as he is on the brink of finally solving all three riddles, the narrator learns that "Mr Wayl's will had been thrown out as a complete hoax" (*C*, 165). The quest, thus, acquires a twist, as it becomes the reader's quest to determine the reasons that motivated the narrator's quest in the first place. Crucial, in this sense, is the opening scene of the novel, the narrator's meeting with Mr Wayl and his introduction to the mystical adze that later on forms part of the inheritance. Of the literary inheritance upon which *Conversions* has drawn, Mathews himself acknowledged his debt to Firbank.[77]

If the first novel was a first step in using the plot as a frame for other stories and games, then in *Tlooth* (1966), Mathews takes this even further. His second novel can be (and has been) described as an elaborate game, a compound of absurd adventures, faked documents, diagrams, and word puzzles, and its very loosely traced storyline is that of travelogue-adventure in which all places are very much the same, whether they be called Russia, Afghanistan, India, Morocco, or Venice. These are the locales featuring in the itinerary of the narrator's quest, which takes the form of a crazy pursuit of a certain Dr. Evelyn Roak, who is believed to have caused the mutilation of the

---

76 Lynne Tillmann, "Harry Mathews," *Bomb* 26 (Winter 1988–9): 35.
77 Leamon concurs: "Like Firbank, Mathews creates a world in which all the parts are 'representational,' but when put together they come to 'represent' something other than what the reader expects. [...] Mathews' style is both limpid and opaque in that there is nothing difficult about the 'stories' that make up the novel but how (or if) those stories go together presents great difficulty" (Leamon, *Harry Mathews*, 33).

narrator's hand. The quest, then, is revenge – and it is a quest from a failed attempt at it to a refusal to take it; again, the quest is incomplete, it rejects to convey any ultimate "message" or "moral."

One of the games played by Mathews in this narrative is obscuring the narrator's gender – an incipit successful wooing of Yana (a woman) establishes the narrator's falsely assumed masculine identity, and only the concluding proposal of marriage to Joan (a man), and his calling the narrator "Mary," restores her feminine gender. One of the chapters, "Spires and Squares" (*T*, 63–71), contains a witty debunking of one of the text's key preoccupations: code deciphering and cracking. There is the mysterious message containing the inscription "r e s," accompanied by the incomplete sentences: 'The Mother cannot ... her Son. The Son ... his Father. The Mother ... their Spirit." This message is exposed to many elaborate exegetic tools, including Biblical and Christian allegorical reading, *res qua res*, etc., only to be found discovered as an incompletely copied text taken from a German grammar textbook. In fact, the fabric of the novel's multiple plotting is interwoven with a plethora of heretic or cultic conceptual frameworks: Fideism, Resurrectionism, Darbyism, or Nestorianism, all having to do with the medieval attempts to solve the problem of the trinity's hypostatic union.

The language of *Tlooth* undergoes distortion in some of its most explicitly erotic passages, where it seems to result from an intensification of experience and sensory perception on the part of the narrator who, in the following scene, is writing (and living) a pornographic screenplay. "Bewildered with desire," the narrator's language goes from fairly minor departures from standard spelling ("She ceemed exsited") to some witty double entendres ("I followed her into the atartment" [*T*, 120]) to full-fledged systematic (and largely phonetic) distortion of the written language:

'Yeu. Kwik and kan yoo raiz yoohr as u lit'l? Uy waunt too prupair dhe waiy.' 'Yoo noh darling Uym priti wet dhair aulredi.' 'U lit'l riming nevur hurt eniwun, and dohnt let goh uv mee—Uy dohnt waunt too loos u hair auf dhar ureksh'n.' 'Noh, ainjul, noh.' [...] 'i held eel while she wifted her shun lit (her pan dlazing her crup bate and so grinly i could hard shoff it) and it was lee, when she farted to hum, who with spast kong mugs of her fips and a clangled hie of 'Flip it, yoo shit!' drew my sweering seef ooss inte the rut famp-hole of her jassness, constreasured by her own savaging reizure of plicter and pain. I uuuuuuuuuuuuucccc lought of Dante's whines at that foment, *L'altra piageva sì, che di pietale, &c.* (*T*, 122–3)

The Sinking of the Odradek Stadium is an epistolary novel developed by means of an exchange of letters between Zachary McCaltex, a librarian living in Miami, and Twang, his Southeast Asian wife sojourning in Italy, and centres around their treasure hunt. Twang's letters are written in an amusingly broken Pidgin English, which improves as the novel progresses – it is here that one can again find some witty language distortion effects reminiscent of Joyce's *Wakean* project.

But the *Wake* is present on two other levels: the novel opens midsentence of a letter ("...confidence in words, Twang" [*O*, 365]) and ends with an incomplete letter with no period at the end of it ("I have telephoned but it will not answer, and shall wire but you will not believe it" [*O*, 554]). Moreover, one of the lesser characters, Lester Greek, is seen at work on a study called *The Confidential Walrus*, which seeks to establishes "the palindromic precedence of 'Eve' over 'Anna' in *Finnegans Wake*" (*O*, 446–8). Letter-writing presents, again, not only the form, but also the content of the novel, since much of its main storyline revolves around and departs from the confusion caused by one letter that goes undelivered – as becomes revealed only in the final letter. Having found out that their correspondence is being opened and read by a third party, Twang sends Zachary a letter secretly apprising him of this fact and informing him that henceforth she will write "fake" letters to which he is to pay no attention, and devises a code by which he is to communicate the date of their next reunion.

This letter, as is revealed in a footnote, is returned to the sender due to insufficient postage applied – thus Zachary takes Twang's nonsense letters seriously, and Twang believes that Zachary's serious letters are nonsense. It is not until Twang's final letter, "written in an English that signifies Twang's conquest of more than language," that the crucial confusions are clarified.[78] However, the mystery of the title—although now revealed to refer to the ship carrying the treasure in question—is not completely explained away (in a text riddled with "mistakes," the transition from the Greek *Stadion* to the Roman *Stadium* is hardly surprising), nor can it ever be established whether this crucial letter does or does not reach its destination. In Leamon's estimation, "one thing is certain: not all questions are answered by the title of the novel any more than solving the final riddle in *The Conversions* answers all the questions in that novel. In fact, the title, *The Sinking of the Odradek Stadium*, is, like everything else in the novel, successful on a number of levels."[79]

The narration of Mathews' fourth novel, *Cigarettes* (1987) is structured by the depiction of fourteen character-relationships, prominent among whom is Elizabeth, around whom (whose portrait) the other thirteen revolve. In his own words, the novel "started as an attempt to solve a specific problem [...]

---

78   "(1) that a letter that never reached its destination has caused great confusion; (2) that the treasure never left Italy; (3) that Twang is the rightful heir to the treasure; (4) that the treasure has been secured and loaded for shipment to Burma on a ship called the *Odradek Stadion*" (Ibid, 72).

79   Ibid, 73.

how to tell a story about a group of people belonging to the New York art and business world in a way that would allow the reader to make it up."[80] The narrative covers two time periods: 1936–8 and 1962–3, with no causal connection established between them, the sole link being the portrait of the character Elizabeth, painted in 1936 and copied, stolen, bought, sold, and seemingly (but not actually) destroyed sometime in the early 60s. However, apart from its flirtation with circular structures and haphazard sequencing of events (left up to the reader to "make up"), *Cigarettes* adds little to Mathews' linguistic experimentation undertaken in *Tlooth* and *Odradek* – as he himself observed, the constrictive structure in *Cigarettes* is not *syntactic*, affecting the "material aspects of language (letters, words, syntax)," but instead *semantic*, affecting "'what language talks about' (subject, content, meaning)" (*CPM*, 136) and so need not be followed in any more detail, here.

The same goes for *The Journalist*, Mathews' latest novel from 1997, presenting a journal of the protagonist's daily activities in which he embarks on an elaborate scheme intended to organise his life, reminiscent of B. S. Johnson's *Christy Malry*. As critic Joseph Conte has observed, the chief constraint, for both Mathews and his protagonist, becomes the system for indexing lived experience "in the presence of an always unclassifiable 'other.'"[81] As each subdivision of his categories makes finer distinctions, each leaves behind an intransigent remainder of "other actions and events," "other matters," "other people," until the realisation dawns on him that "it's not this or that category, it's the overall problem I can't master. The more I put in, the more I leave out" (*J*, 84; 110).

Although parodying and subverting, in his later works of fiction, the modernist obsession with all-inclusiveness, Mathews' early work clearly partakes of and continues in the footsteps of the modernist "revolution of the word," reworking the material aspects of language most outspokenly, in the postmodernist fascination with, and critique of, the sundry systems of meaning, governance, and control that make up contemporary social-political reality.

4.5 "THE BABEL EFFECT": JACQUES ROUBAUD

Of contemporary Oulipians alive and active in the 21st century, it is most clearly Jacques Roubaud whose literary output follows in the footsteps of Queneau's and Perec's novelistic careers. Trained as a mathematician specia-

---

80   Ashbery, "A Conversation," 31.
81   Joseph M. Conte, *Design and Debris: A Chaotics of Postmodern American Fiction* (Tuscaloosa: University of Alabama Press, 2002) 102.

lising in algebra, Roubaud began "composing"—as he refers to the activity—poetry before producing vast prose works. A member of the Oulipo since 1966 (the first new member apart from the founders, making him the longest-serving member in the group's history), his mathematical disposition was revealed already in his first notable poetry collection, published in 1967 and entitled ϵ, the mathematical symbol for "belonging" or "contained within," where mathematical strategies, chiefly from the field of combinatorics, are used for producing multiform sonnets according to the moves in a masters match of the Japanese game of Go.

His poetry collections, *Mono no aware* (1970) and *Trente et un au cube* (1973) reflect his lifelong interest and source of inspiration in Japanese poetry forms, mainly haiku and tanka. But Roubaud's production is proverbially variegated and vast: he has rewritten French medieval texts (especially of the Holy Grail cycle), translated 20th-century American poetry (Charles Reznikoff), identified himself as inheritor to Lewis Carroll, written on the history of the evolution of European verse forms, etc. Before embarking on his "Projet," Roubaud played an Oulipian game in his "Hortense" series,[82] which presents a zany pastiche of the English detective novel – if, as Taylor has rightly remarked, "*pastiche* is a word wild enough to embrace the perpetually disarming 'distancing effects' sustained by the author in this trilogy."[83] The reader is constantly made aware that he is holding "a detective novel" to the extent that the "enigma" becomes less a "plot" than a series of evolving narrative structures.

In his own development as writer, the year 1983 marks a turning point in both Roubaud's life and work, as with the death of his young wife (aged thirty-one), he fell silent for thirty months, and in the years following, commenced an extended meditation on "her death and the intimate inter-relationship among absence, loss and writing,"[84] resulting in two volumes of poetry, *Quelque chose noir* (1986) and *La pluralité des mondes de Lewis* (1991), and the multi-volume work *Le grand incendie de Londres* (1989). The last work, *The Great Fire of London*, is the first volume of the so-called "Projet," a six-part series of large works of prose continued over the course of twenty years. Already the first volume is marked by stylistic variability, even though, as has been pointed out by critic Véronique Montémont, author of a book-length study on Roubaud's work, the possible analogy with Joyce is a faulty one. Since to every "branch" of *The Great Fire of London* corresponds not a distinct

---

82 *La Belle Hortense*, 1985, translated as *Our Beautiful Heroine; L'Enlèvement d'Hortense*, 1987, translated as *Hortense Is Abducted; L'Exil d'Hortense*, 1990, translated as *Hortense in Exile*.

83 John Taylor, "On Reading Jacques Roubaud," *Paths to Contemporary French Literature, Vol. 2*, ed. John Taylor (New Brunswick, New Jersey: Transaction Publishers, 2009) 141.

84 Greg Kinzer, "Possible worlds: trans-world travel, haecceity and grief in Jacques Roubaud's *The Plurality of Worlds of Lewis*," *Journal of Modern Literature* 34.3 (Spring 2011): 162.

style, but a sort of characteristic "cocktail" of styles, Roubaud's project differs from Joyce's.[85]

It is useful to consider the contrastive example of Joyce in the context of another critic's definition of a "Roubaudian poetics."[86] As long as "an attitude of homage and profanation toward literary tradition," one of "revising, recollecting and rewriting tradition" is perfectly Joycean, or more broadly modernist, then approaching "language as a series of numbers," as abstract units recombinable in permutative series, goes beyond the modernism of Joyce. Similarly, what Poucel terms Roubaud's "art of memory" is not without its Joycean conceptual overtones, and yet ultimately different in effectuation, as Roubaud's writing under constraint is more of "a game that directs experimentation with the explicit goals of the invention, recollection, and transformation of tradition" than Joyce's encyclopaedic memory machine.[87] What Roubaud's "art of memory" ultimately amounts to, as Taylor has observed, is a confrontation with Proust and Bergson rather than a filiation with the Joycean "hypermnesis."[88]

Roubaud's difference in degree and kind from the *Wake* is not without its Oulipian predecessors and co-adherents. The only extended mention of Joyce in Le Tellier's *Esthétique de l'Oulipo* comes in the "L'effet-Babel" section, where the question becomes "où situer l'idiome du 'maçon des hommes francs' Tim Finnegan, héros du roman inachevé de James Joyce *Finnegan's wake*?" [sic].

---

85   "Le projet n'est pas sans rappeler l'entreprise joycienne qui opte pour un style nouveau à chaque chapitre d'*Ulysse* [...], mais chez Roubaud, le style n'est pas un facteur parodique, étant donné que la plupart des lecteurs occidentaux ignorent tout de ces distinction, et auraient de toute façon beaucoup de mal à les percevoir s'ils en étaient informés" (Véronique Montémont, *Jacques Roubaud, l'amour du nombre* [Lille : Presses Universitaires du Septentrion, 2004] 213).

86   "Plainly stated, it is a strategy by which a methodical memory of tradition becomes the basis of literary innovation. Two imperatives ground Roubaud's overall poetics. The first, borrowed from Raymond Queneau and François Le Lionnais [...], is the decision to comport oneself toward language as if it could be mathematized. [...]. The second precept underlying his poetics, purportedly borrowed from Octavio Paz, is the imperative to adopt an attitude of homage and profanation toward literary tradition" (Jean-Jacques F. Poucel, *Jacques Roubaud and the Invention of Memory* [Chapel Hill: University of North Carolina Press, 2006] 12).

87   "His art of memory powerfully presents and reconfigures a collective and personal tradition; his work postulates that there is continuity and change in literary and linguistic developments, and that they may be traced along an interconnected and motivated chain of written occurrences. [...] In fact, we might imagine his collected works as a conglomerate sphere of memory, an organic simulacrum of memory whose form is constantly shifting and whose meaning is transient and essential" (Poucel, *Jacques Roubaud and the Invention of Memory*, 14).

88   "It is in this confrontation between emotion and constraining form, between a pre-planned literary-mathematical structure and the painful vicissitudes of personal history, that Roubaud's writings raise so many essential questions. [...] In contrast to Proust's notion of memory as expanding from some small, insignificant detail (like a madeleine cookie, of which the author of *The Great Fire of London* must surely be thinking when he in turn brilliantly describes a fresh croissant), Roubaud conceives recollecting as a sort of «forest» in which branches and twigs of clustered trees overlap and intertwine" (Taylor, "On Reading Jacques Roubaud," 142).

Factual errors proliferate in Le Tellier's brief disquisition, as he goes on to claim that "une bonne part de ces mots provient aussi de langages artificiels : *milito* vient de l'espéranto et signifie 'guerre,' adyo (adieu) du Volapük, etc."[89] These aside, though, Le Tellier's main issue with Joyce's *Wakean* Babel-project is this:

> Le meilleur argument contre les partisans d'une langue universelle reste celui, re-marquable, de Saussure, lequel rappelle l'évolutivité des langues, que nul ne saurait maîtriser, et à laquelle on imagine mal une langue, fût-elle "la chose de tout le monde" échapper : l'homme qui prétendrait composer une langue immuable, que la postérité devrait accepter comme telle, ressemblerait à la poule qui a couvé un œuf de canard : la langue créée par lui serait exportée bon gré mal gré par le courant qui emporte toutes les langues.[90]

Ironically, the only mention of Joyce in another prominent work of Oulipian historiography and poetics, Mathews' co-edited *Oulipo Compendium*, comes in a similarly twisted manner – as "an interesting use of restricted vocabu-lary":

VOCABULARY, RESTRICTED
[...] An interesting use of restricted vocabulary is James Joyce's translation of the last four pages of "Anna Livia Plurabelle" from *Finnegans Wake* into Basic English: a re-duction of the English language (to 850 words) invented by C.K. Ogden in which, he claimed, "everything may be said." The text appeared in *transition*, 21, March 1932.[91]

In Le Tellier's rendition, as in Roubaud's plenary address, Joyce is "a partisan of a universal language," a utopia doomed to fail, as Saussure's lesson teaches all too clearly, whereas for Mathews' *Compendium*, the interest lies in sub-mitting his *Wakean* project to a proto-Oulipian constraint. A similar position has been expressed by another prominent contemporary Oulipian, Jacques Jouet, in an email to the author:

> *Finnegans Wake* ne m'a jamais attiré [...] le poisson ne peut pas inventer une autre eau que l'eau. Un écrivain ne peut pas créer une langue. Il est dans une langue commune. C'est toute la beauté du poème, du roman, du drame : nager dans une langue commune à un groupe, peuple, etc.[92]

---

89   Tellier, *Esthétique de l'Oulipo*, 106.
90   Ibid, 109.
91   *Oulipo Compendium*, eds. Mathews & Brotchie, 234.
92   Jacques Jouet, email to the author, 11 March 2013.

Jacques Roubaud himself went a step further, claiming on the topic of Joyce that although "je l'ai lu avec plaisir," it was with the exception of "*Finnegans wake*, qui est d'un ennui mortel," and that Oulipo as such "n'a rien à voir avec Joyce."[93] So long as Oulipo works by applying mathematical principles onto language by way of *constraint*, it is profoundly non-Joycean in its formal experimentation and reworking of linguistic matter: and it is chiefly in the pre-Oulipian early work of its founding father, Raymond Queneau, and in the personal, non-Oulipian 'ten per cent' in the formation of Georges Perec, that the most conspicuous and meaningful manifestations of Joycean materiality of language can be found.

4.6 THE ANTICIPATORY PLAGIARIST

As long as the crucial defining traits of Oulipian writing are its (negative) opposition to the aleatory and the (positive) pursuit of "systematic" operations performed upon the "voluntary" rule-based writing that is literature, then Joyce's own understanding of his poetics fits the Oulipian bill almost perfectly. To take but one example from Richard Ellmann's biography:

> But of modem writers in general he remarked, "If you took a characteristic obscure passage of one of these people and asked him what it meant, he couldn't tell you; whereas I can justify every line of my book." And another day he remarked, "I have discovered I can do anything with language I want." But it was like him to counter these statements by saying to Beckett with impressive modesty, "I may have over-systematised *Ulysses*." (*JJ*, 702)

Here, Joyce's objection to modern writers, again, is based on their perceived lack of total control and perfect awareness of "every line" of their writing, their lack of an overriding creative method such as Joyce's—which allowed him to "do anything with language" he wanted—and their lack of a literary "system" – in this case, Joyce seems even worried that the systems imposed upon the linguistic and thematic material that comprise *Ulysses* may have been a few too many. Indeed, David Hayman defines Joyce's "real preoccupation" as one with "systems of presentation": "His development was toward the amplification of the verbal, the creation of autonomous forms in motion; toward the vitalized word in *Finnegans Wake*, the 'collideorscape.' To arrive there he was obliged to alter and recombine, but not to destroy, existing expressive codes."[94]

---

93   Jacques Roubaud, email to the author, 9 March 2013.
94   David Hayman, "Introduction," *In the Wake of the* Wake, 13.

To "combine, not to destroy" the extant formal procedures is very much in tune with the chief Oulipian preoccupations. Since Hayman gives no further specification, one must ask further: which "systems of presentation" could be seen to have informed Joyce's writing and how did it "develop"? The schema is a traditional one, repeated, with minor variations, in Joycean criticism ever since its first pioneers (Stuart Gilbert or Harry Levin), revealing him as an author of a profoundly synthetic sensibility. To confine the argument to just Joyce's three long works of prose: firstly, *A Portrait of the Artist as a Young Man* presents the definitive amalgam of the novel of a young man's experience while growing up, depicts the development of the artist in contemporary society with a criticism of the social malaise of the times, and functions as a work simultaneously psychological and sociological.

Ulysses presents a step further in functioning as the complete modern novel, satisfying all of Northrop Frye's "four types of fiction" simultaneously—romance, novel, confession, catalogue—and blending the naturalistic with the psychological, the conscious stream of thought with the unconscious whirlpool, while still thoroughly developing the pattern of surface events. In *Ulysses*, as Bernard Benstock has remarked, "all previous tendencies in the development of the novel since Fielding were successfully amalgamated into a single, unified work, an inimitable book which was nonetheless imitated, becoming the single most important influence in the European and American novel for several decades."[95] Finally, *Finnegans Wake* ventures into a realm of such personal synthesis of techniques that it constitutes a medium which does not pretend to present any sort of "reality" or, rather, which announces its roots in a purely verbal universe – in Hayman's rendering, "the plays on words, words as self-destroying but resilient objects; the texture of clowning which imitates but does not create chaos, suggests but does not enforce order."[96]

"Ordering" is the most natural consequence to Joyce's "systematisation" of literary expressivity, brought, in *Ulysses* and *Finnegans Wake*, to whole new levels. Despite their differences on the level of the signifier, both *Ulysses* and *Finnegans Wake* present several superimposed systems of ordering of experience – and one of the crucial overlapping systems is the most fundamentally Oulipian one: Joyce's concern with numbers as symbolic and abstract means of interrelating disparate elements of reality. The number most prominent in Joyce is the number three: from the third stroke of Father Flynn in "Sisters" via Stephen Dedalus' Thomistic *claritas, consonantia, integritas* and his own creed of "silence, exile, cunning" in *A Portrait*, to all the trinities and triadic structures of *Ulysses* predicated upon the S-M-P, the subject-middle-

---

95   This account follows the survey in Benstock, "On William Gaddis: In Recognition of James Joyce," *Wisconsin Studies in Comparative Literature* (Vol. 6 No. 2: Summer 1965): 178.
96   Hayman, "Introduction," 6.

predicate, the structure of logical statement analysis. Analogously, *Finnegans Wake*, already on the very surface, advertises number four, or, better said, three-plus-one, as its structuring principle and square-turned-into-circle as its shape. The same Beckett to whom Joyce confided his worry regarding the over-systematisation of *Ulysses* also observed of his "Work in Progress" the following:

> Why, Mr Joyce seems to say, should there be four legs to a table, and four to a horse, and four seasons and four gospels and four Provinces in Ireland? Why twelve tables of the Law, and twelve Apostles, and twelve months and twelve Napoleonic marshals and twelve men in Florence called Ottolenghi? Why should the Armistice be celebrated at the eleventh hour of the eleventh day of the eleventh month?[97]

Numbers, in their definiteness, enable disparity and variety to be measured, brought onto one plane of structural correspondence. Insofar as Beckett´s comment is equally relevant to his own method of shaping texts around a limited amount of numeric constants with value variables, his comment can also serve as a springboard for a reading to which *Finnegans Wake* yields itself most readily – as an immensely intricate structure of sundry, if not infinite, variables, however one which is built around principles that are both definite and constant.

Hugh Kenner has tied this numerological preoccupation in Joyce to his "stoic comedy" of the "inventory," springing from Joyce's aesthetic conviction, departing from "two profound intuitions: that the Thomistic analogy with sight could guide the operations of a writer of prose fiction, that the analogy of the epiphany could govern the release of aesthetic clarity."[98] It is precisely lists of finite sets contained within reality, as well as epiphanic parallelisms with other texts, that govern Joyce's numerological ordering of a text like *Ulysses*:

> There are twenty-four hours in a day, and he accounts for all but the ones spent by his characters in sleep. The spectrum has seven colors, and Bloom names them: roy g biv. The *Odyssey* can be dissociated into specific episodes, which Joyce accounts for. Shakespeare wrote some thirty-six plays; I do not know whether Joyce includes in the library scene an allusion to each of them, but it would not be surprising. The embryo lives nine months in the womb, or forty weeks; the body of the "Oxen of the Sun" episode has nine principal parts, in forty paragraphs, linked furthermore to a sequence of geological eras obtained from a list in a textbook.[99]

---

97   Samuel Beckett, "Dante...Bruno. Vico.. Joyce," *Our Exagmination*, 21.
98   Hugh Kenner, *Flaubert, Joyce and Beckett: The Stoic Comedians* (Boston: Beacon Press, 1962) 58.
99   Kenner, *The Stoic Comedians*, 53–4.

In the cyclical structure of the *Wake*, the number eleven plays a very important role all through the text (as part of number 1132, featured ten times) as
a symbol of "beginning anew." However, as Kenner shows elsewhere, the
number eleven is very much present, though less conspicuously, from the
very start of *Ulysses*, a book "[aware] of numbers: how many people in a room,
shillings in a ledger, even words in a sentence."[100] What deserves pointing out
is how numbers operate at once on the realist (i.e., contained in the narrated
reality), the symbolic (11 as the end and the beginning), and the material (i.e.,
contained in the narrating reality of language – 11 sentences, 11 letters, etc.)
levels. Joyce's work with formal constraints is one of amplification, multiplication, and layering of various means of ordering.

Thus, to revert to Roubaud, if Joyce's "language games" (the numerological one above is by far not the only one) can be seen as Oulipian, it must be
as rule- (if not exactly constraint-) bound, and definitely not as works of
"potential" literature – Joyce's comedy of the list, the encyclopaedic ambition
toward (albeit impossible) all-inclusiveness, seeks to exhaust the actual, not
imply the potential. In his practice of "voluntary" writing based on formal
and stylistic "rules" and his accentuating the plurality of literary technique
functioning "as a bridge over which to march my eighteen episodes" (*JJ*, 542),
Joyce is as perfect a proto-Oulipian, as ideal example of an "anticipatory plagiary," as one can find in the Anglophone literary tradition (except perhaps
Lewis Carroll).

However, apart from his un-Oulipian tendency toward the multiplication
and amplification of rules and systems of presentation, there is another, even
more fundamental sense in which the Oulipian exploration of mathematical
models for potential literature goes counter to the development of Joyce's poetics, in fact reverses it. As Kenner has put it, "Joyce's techniques—it is one of
his principal lessons—are without exception derived from his subject, often
excerpted from his subject. They are not means of representing the subject,
and imperfectly; they are the subject's very members laid on the page, in elo-
quent or ludicrous *collage*."[101] Joyce's techniques, his rules and constraints,

---

100 "A recurrent number is 11: the first sentence has 2 x 11 words, the third one (from "He" to "*dei*")
      has 11: as we become skilled navigators, we recognize 11 as a Ulyssean seamark. For in this book
      11, the fresh start after a decade, is the number for the two primary kinds of events, beginnings
      and endings; and while sometimes it is specified, it sometimes lurks behind a count of episodes
      or paragraphs or words. A sampling of elevens: Rudy Bloom died 11 years ago, aged 11 days; Ste-
      phen's age is 2 x 11; "Marion Bloom" has 11 letters and so has "Hugh E. Boylan," and the hour of
      their tryst is set in the 11th episode; 11 paragraphs of entry and 11 of exit precede and follow the
      40 paragraphs of gestation in "Oxen of the Sun"; as late as 1919, when he conceived "Wandering
      Rocks," Joyce had meant the center of the book to consist of 11 episodes. And in Joyce's final book,
      Finnegans Wake, the last sentence-fragment circles toward a new beginning with just 11 words"
      (Hugh Kenner, *A Colder Eye – The Modern Irish Writers* [London: Allen Lane, 1983] 193).
101 Kenner, *The Stoic Comedians*, 50.

are always *motivated* by the subject matter, and inseparable from it; not—as is so often the case in Oulipo—vice versa, where the text is the *result* and an *illustration* of a pre-conceived method at work. It is in this twofold sense—as both their colleague and a writer of profoundly different sensibility and style—that Oulipians have conceived of Joyce as "anticipatory plagiary."

5.
"THE CENTENARIAN STILL SEEMS AVANT-GARDE": EXPERIMENT IN BRITISH FICTION, 1975–2005

"Lost Prophets" is the title of an article from 1975 by art critic and writer John Berger—whose name, it will be remembered, was featured in B. S. Johnson's list of experimentalists—which paints the bleak picture in which "the revolutionary hopes of the 1960s, which culminated in 1968, are now blocked or abandoned."[1] This comment is relatable to the situation in fiction. After the 1973 death of both B. S. Johnson and Ann Quin, British experimentalism— with the literary historians, critics, and the reading public—fell into a black hole of silence akin to that surrounding the *Wake* in 1939. It was with only slight exaggeration that, on the occasion of the thirtieth-anniversary re-edition of Johnson's *The Unfortunates* by Picador (1998), Jonathan Coe's introduction summarised the thirty years of Johnson's "reception" as follows: "To a nation of literary amnesiacs, B. S. Johnson is already a forgotten writer. [...] It's less than thirty years since he died, but his books have been out of print for most of that time, and the tides of literary fashion have ebbed and flowed often enough to wipe his name from collective memory."[2] The exaggeration was there only because in comparison with the oblivion to which Johnson's work had fallen prey, the misconception of Brooke-Rose's work (not to mention the ignorance of Brophy's or Quin's) was still orders of magnitude greater.

Although not (self-)published until 2012 (and only picked up by Dalkey Archive in 2020), Francis Booth writes in the "Preface" to his monumental *Among Those Left: The British Experimental Novel 1940–1980* that when revisiting the subject matter thirty years after the book's completion, he felt little need for updating it: "This book stops around 1980 because that was when it was first written but in fact this does seem to be roughly the date at which experimental novel writing in this country almost dried up, though Nicholas Mosley, Christine Brooke-Rose and Eva Figes soldiered on. It had never in any case really caught on."[3] Chiefly responsible had been the cultural and critical climate in which the 1960s and 70s experimentation had been received. As remarked by Booth, "unlike in France or America, where novelists, academics and reviewers were often the same people, reviewers in Britain were

1   John Berger, "Lost Prophets," *New Society* (6 March 1975): 600.
2   Jonathan Coe, "Preface" to B. S. Johnson's *The Unfortunates*, v.
3   Francis Booth, "Preface," *Among Those Left—The British Experimental Novel 1940–1980* (self-published, 2012) 14.

mostly unsympathetic."[4] Not only that, but also unlike France or USA, the British literary culture failed to provide the logistics and the background for the cultivation and promotion of the avant-garde: "It was not as if British experimental novelists [...] had a support structure among themselves: most of them did not teach in universities, and none in this country [...] or had access to an academic writing/reviewing cycle as the French and Americans did. They even sniped at each other."[5]

Emblematic of the overall critical tenor is the criticism of David Lodge, whose widely influential books, *The Novelist at the Crossroads* (1971) and *Modes of Modern Writing* (1977), set both the scope and the critical apparatus in which the British novel was discussed, while promoting a type of criticism prescriptive of the kind of fiction practised by its author. Particularly in *Novelist at the Crossroads*, Lodge is explicit in doing away with the realist/experimental binary to suggest that, together with pressure coming to bear on the central "compromise" of realism, possible alternative routes have branched off into different directions – both towards the "non-fiction" novel and towards "fabulation." In addition, Lodge posits a fourth choice available for novelists: to "hesitate at the crossroads" and "build their hesitation into the novel itself."[6] This "problematic novel" label turns out to be a convenient tool of accommodating formal deviations within a basically realist tradition, since it mainly consists of self-reflexive meditation or parody of realist and modernist conventions. Realism is "the road on which [the English novelist] stands." It is the main road, and Lodge concludes with "a modest affirmation of faith in the future of realistic fiction," concluding that "if the case for realism has any ideological content it is that of liberalism."[7] The trend, in British criticism and literary history, of blurring if not eradicating the experimental/conventional opposition, has continued till the end of the millennium, and beyond.

In this context, it is useful to counterpoint Lodge's views with those of Christine Brooke-Rose, who emphasises the confusion, within British literary practice and criticism, of self-reflectiveness with experimentation, which in the British fiction of the 1950s and 1960s was dominated by a tendency toward fantasy, perhaps in order to oppose the social-realist fiction. Brooke-Rose's criticism[8]—whose gist is contained in her

---

4   Booth, *Among Those Left*, 14.
5   Ibid, 16.
6   Qtd. Stuart Laing, "Novels and the Novel," *Society and Literature, 1945–1970: The Context of English Literature*, ed. Alan Sinfield (London: Atlantic Books, 1983) 254.
7   David Lodge, "Novelist at the Crossroads," *The Novelist at the Crossroads* (New York: Cornell University Press, 1971) 33.
8   Brooke-Rose's work as critic and theorist attests to her wide-ranging schooling, reaching back into late 1950s, when in 1958 she published *A Grammar of Metaphor*, an informed survey of poetry from Chaucer to Dylan Thomas in which metaphor is treated as form rather than content, followed in 1971 by *A ZBC of Ezra Pound*, a study of *The Cantos* as diachronic poetics, particularly

two monumental essay collections, *A Rhetoric of the Unreal* and *Stories, Theories and Things*—presents her diagnosis of her contemporaneity, out of which spring the ethical and moral imperatives followed in her fiction. Brooke-Rose's diagnosis is one of "a reality crisis" in which "what used to be called empirical reality, or the world, seems to have become more and more unreal, and what has long been regarded as unreal is more and more turned to or studied as the only 'true' or 'another and equally valid' reality" (*RU,* 3–4). This ontological shift is of crucial importance for fiction since it has occurred chiefly as consequence of "the discourse upon discourse that man has always needed since writing began," which "has now expanded to a vast industry of unprecedented proportions" (*RU,* 11). The two works also introduce a loosely conceived canon of fictional investigations into the un-reality of the real, and thus point to acknowledged precursors and fellow-travellers of Brooke-Rose's own explorations. Brooke-Rose's thematically organised canon includes such diverse writers, movements, and genres as Henry James (whose *Turn of the Screw* she analyses in remarkable detail on the basis of its "surface structures"); magic realism; the new science fiction (Kurt Vonnegut and Joseph McElroy); American postmodernists (in particular, William H. Gass); and Brooke-Rose's favourite writers of the *nouveau roman* (Alain Robbe-Grillet, Nathalie Sarraute) and *Tel Quel* (Maurice Roche, Philippe Sollers).

Regarding Bradbury's equivalence between the fantastic and fabulation in British science fiction, Brooke-Rose notes that if understood differently, not as fabulation but as the perpetuation of a radical uncertainty regarding the ontological status of the events described, the question of the relation between the real and the fictional in the British novel of the 1960s has rather a different history. Instead of Lodge's simplistic equivalence of experiment with self-reflexiveness, Brooke-Rose distinguishes between the "anti-novel" in the tradition of Cervantes and Sterne, which is overtly self-reflexive, and the "experimental novel," which seeks to extend the possibilities of fiction through the exploitation of new techniques. In Brooke-Rose's reading, works like Fowles' *French Lieutenant Woman* or Lessing's *The Golden Notebook*—which for Lodge exemplify the experimental British novel *par excellence*—appear at the crossroads, indeed, but one at which any claim of radicalness and innovation intersects with bizarre anachronism and conservatism. Lodge's writers of "problematic" novels in fact do little more than recast the contemporary equivalent of the material of the nineteenth-century novel in the trappings

through a study of Anglo-Saxon alliterative verse. Simultaneously with *Textermination* (1991), Brooke-Rose published a collection of essays entitled *Stories, Theories and Things*, which also included "A metastory, with metacharacters," her exposé of her own fictional practice. Finally, 2002 saw the collection of "last essays" called *Invisible Author*.

of self-conscious frames and other narrative devices that fragment, distort, or comment on it.[9]

Given the many inherent contradictions and surrounding ambiguities, "postmodernism" will be understood here in the broad, yet possibly only meaningful, conceptualisation, close to the one formulated by Christine Brooke-Rose's earliest critic, Sarah Birch: as a concatenation of certain thematic interests and stylistic strategies from the fiction of 1960s onward. Echoing Brooke-Rose's own repeatedly voiced scepticism regarding the usefulness, or indeed tenability, of the term, Birch makes the following point: "At its best, postmodernism is a concept which enables us to reject the view of literature as so many national trees, each with its own main trunk and subsidiary branches, allowing us instead to see it as a network of overlapping groupings corresponding to areas of interest—technical, ideological, thematic, and so on."[10]

Consequently, a writer like Brooke-Rose will be regarded as embodying the notion of so-called postmodernism as abandonment of nationalist-bound categorisation of literature, as conceptual grappling with the resistance to labelling and grouping: "[Brooke-Rose] has returned to the fold [...] of British fiction, but the 'fold' to which she has returned is a composite of styles and approaches, and the term 'English,' or even 'British' is often inadequate to describe many of its members."[11] Birch's "British Postmodernism" vis-à-vis Brooke-Rose is marked by two chief features: inter- and hetero-textuality on the one hand, and a persistent tendency toward the fantastic in its various guises (science-fiction, Gothic, magic realism, and so on), on the other. Still, Birch makes sure to voice the following caveat against too simplistic a labelling: "Technically, British fiction in the last two decades has been reluctant to relinquish the conventions of realism and has been content instead to stretch them."[12]

This point has been echoed in Randall Stevenson's authoritative account in *The Oxford English Literary History*, which distinguishes between the two

---

9   Birch goes so far as to say: "Upon closer examination it becomes obvious that even the 'radical' philosophical concepts behind the novels on the extreme edges of Lodge's schema [...] rely heavily on a tradition of existentialist though associated with realist fiction and a pre-structuralist conception of "reality' as a domain sealed off from the constitutive processes of language" (Birch, *Christine Brooke-Rose*, 200).

10   Birch continues: "We can then talk about the tendency toward ludic manipulation of language in the work of some writers, gender-consciousness in the work of others, the recent trend in science fiction toward the use of metafictional techniques, as well as developments specific to a given culture, as so many "postmodernisms" which together comprise a loose coalition. According to this view of postmodernism, each individual writer could be seen as having a stake in a number of different postmodernist enterprises" (Sarah Birch, *Christine Brooke-Rose and Contemporary Fiction* [Oxford: Clarendon Press, 1994] 217).

11   Birch, *Christine Brooke-Rose and Contemporary Fiction*, 225.

12   Ibid, 218.

options of "innovative techniques" versus "conventions modernism had never wholly displaced."[13] With recourse to Harry Levin's famous observation regarding the decade-by-decade alternation between "progress" and "regression" in literary history, Stevenson goes on to observe that as long as the 1960s were marked by "a renewed readiness for experiment [...], often drawing on the examples of modernism and its successors," the 1970s saw "a return towards conservatism," and the combined heritage of these two periods contributed to the "eclectic" fashion in which "many authors in the 1980s and 1990s" took the liberty of choosing from "stores of literary technique, and to recombine devices they found there, rather than favouring either of the major branches too exclusively."[14] Insofar as to choose from "stores of literary technique" was also to choose whether or not to continue the Joycean revolution of language and wage Johnson's war on the "anachronistic, invalid, irrelevant, and perverse" (*ARY*, 13) realist mode of the nineteenth-century novel, overt alliances with Joyce ceased to have the dissentious charge they had held for the 1960s avant-garde circle around Johnson.

No more pledges of devotion to Joyce à la Johnson or Burgess: the predominance of the realist sensibility from the 1980s onward would be reflected in the dismissal of the relevance of Joyce and the modernist literary innovation across the literary field. Nonetheless, apart from the ongoing career of Christine Brooke-Rose, this chapter will single out six other writers who continued in the avant-gardist project of the 1960s, and departed on their variegated trajectories informed by the Joycean materialist poetics.

5.0 "OF NARRATIVE STYLES, THE DISSOLUTION OF CHARACTER": CHRISTINE BROOKE-ROSE, 1984–2006

The two novel quartets Christine Brooke-Rose produced in the second half of the 1980s and from the mid-1990s to mid-2000s, respectively, offer in themselves a possible framework for the classification and categorisation of the various strands of so-called postmodernist writing. Her two post-1984 tetralogies present a panorama of techniques and styles that develop Brooke-Rose's earlier commitments to aesthetic experimentation (in particular, the

---

13   "For any English writers [...] at least two sets of possibilities were apparent by 1960. Innovative techniques and postmodernist 'prophecy' offered themselves alongside conventions modernism had never wholly displaced—ones often surviving since the nineteenth century, and recently strongly revalued by Movement writing. Twentieth-century literature could even be seen as divided almost decade by decade in terms of allegiance to one or other set of priorities, with the revolutions dominating the 1920s followed by the formally conservative writing of the 1930s and 1950s" (Randall Stevenson, *The Last of England?* [Oxford: Oxford University Press, 2004] 85).

14   Stevenson, *The Last of England?*, 86.

technique of the Oulipian constraint in the case of *Between*), but also depart from it in radically divergent directions. Almost a decade had passed since *Thru* (1975) before Brooke-Rose launched the third tetralogical period of her career. The first volume of her "Intercom Quartet" was published shortly after her retirement from Paris-Vincennes and relocation to the south of France in order to concentrate fully on her fiction, a decade spent teaching and writing works of literary theory and criticism. It is from the conclusions of *A Rhetoric of the Unreal* that her "Intercom Quartet" departs.

The first part of Brooke-Rose's "Intercom Quartet" already bears the marks of a *Wakean* influence well beyond anything discoverable in the preceding tetralogy. *Amalgamemnon* (1984) presents a striking departure from Brooke-Rose's trademark third-person, present-tense narrative mode in favour of a first-person narrative and the utilisation of a new constraint. The entire novel is written in the future and conditional tenses, the subjunctive or imperative moods – i.e., in "non-realising" forms (tense or mood): future, conditional, hypothetical, etc., as opposed to the preterit which, as a distinctive mark of the discourse of official recorded history, is avoided in Brooke-Rose's poetics. The narrative setting and situation centres on the female protagonist lying in bed next to her sleeping/snoring partner/lover, entertaining herself in her insomnia by impersonating several major prophetic voices in the history of Europe.

She is Professor Mira Enketei, who, in view of the impending termination of her academic career in the classics, "mimages" herself as many other characters, reflecting on the possible futures of humanity. Thus, the constraint is in full service of the mimesis and ideological thrust of the text. Brooke-Rose stages a prophecy, a mock-ancient oracle with which she divines the future on the basis of diagnosing the present:

> I shall soon be quite redundant at last despite of all, as redundant as you after queue and as totally predictable, information-content zero. [...] Who will still want to read at night some utterly other discourse that will shimmer out of a minicircus of light upon a page of say Agamemnon returning to his murderous wife the glory-gobbler with his new slave Cassandra princess of fallen Troy who will exclaim alas, o earth, Apollo apocalyptic and so forth, Herodotus, the Phoenicians kidnapping Io and the Greeks plagiarizing the king of Tyre's daughter Europe, but then, shall we ever make Europe? (A, 5)

From the very start, Brooke-Rose engages in her favourite strategy: exposing scientific discourses to the effects of fictional practices, here the discourse of computer science. In the age of 0 and 1, Brooke-Rose's narrator suggests, "I" and "you" become as voided of information content as "u" after "q," or "you after queue." As a classics professor, Mira has much at stake in countering the impending hegemony of computerised technology, whose pre-programming threatens to replace the function of the oracle, ordering both the "foetus" and the "prophetus" into wholly predictable patterns (*A*, 82–3). As a woman and a classicist, her "prophersigh" (*A*, 53) assumes the voice of Cassandra (or, as she appears in the text, Sandra) and aims to counter the "Father of History," Herodotus. In her discussion of *Amalgamemnon* in *Invisible Author*, Brooke-Rose points out that "the word plagiarize [...] originally meant 'kidnap,' and this etymological connection provides 'an invisible pun' in the text" (*IA*, 50).

As Karen Lawrence has observed, by "plagiarising" Herodotus, Brooke-Rose demonstrates "the violence against women in classic history, not only physically, but psychically, with the loss of their voices."[15] This silencing takes place on both the macro-level of the history and mythology of plagiarism/kidnapping, and the micro-level of the narrator's household:

> Soon he will snore, in a stentorian sleep, a foreign body in bed. There will occur the blanket bodily transfer to the livingroom for a night of utterly other discourses that will crackle out of disturbances in the ionosphere into a minicircus of light upon a page of say Herodotus and generate endless stepping-stones into the dark, the Phoenicians kidnapping Io and the Greeks in Colchis carrying off the king's daughter Medea [...]. We'll take that predge when we come to it. [...]
>
> Tomorrow at breakfast Willy will be pleased as punch bring out as the fruit of deep reflection the non-creativity of women look at music painting sculpture in history and I shall put on my postface and mimagree, unless I put on my preface and go through the routine of certain social factors such as disparagement from birth the lack of expectation not to mention facilities a womb of one's own a womb with a view an enormous womb and he won't like the countertone at all, unless his eyes will be sexclaiming still what fun, it'll talk if you wind it up . . . (*A*, 16–7)

The two passages above are characteristic of *Amalgamemnon*'s style, marked by flippancy in tone and anacoluthon in syntax. References to Medeia, the kidnapped Io, and the Woolfian "womb of one's own," as opposed to Willy's "sexclamations" over breakfast, are all part of Brooke-Rose's amalgamation of women's voices throughout the male-dominated history, mythology, and imagination of the West. This amalgamation—present in its "predge" to be taken "when we come to it," i.e., both pledge and bridge—is staged in Brooke-Rose's text already on the level of the signifier. The prophetic protagonist, (Cas)Sandra, imagines herself as a determined counterculture "graphomaniac," who will be imprisoned for her "graffitism" (*A*, 20).

15   Karen R. Lawrence, *Techniques for Living: Fiction and Theory in the Work of Christine Brooke-Rose* (Columbus: The Ohio State University Press, 2010) 103.

Portmanteau amalgamations and subversive etymologies have already been exemplified, but there are more strategies employed – for instance, the numerous *détournements* of clichés, often polyglottic, and often to a satirical effect: "Che sera sera, you shall see what you shall see and may the beast man wane" (*A*, 30) or "On verra ce qu'on verra may the boast man whine" (*A*, 52), where the narrator's reversion of stock phrases about male competitiveness ("may the best man win") undermines the values of the male-dominated society that has designated her as redundant. The narrator's "prophersighs," having traversed areas as diverse and panoramic as Greek mythology, Britain's postcolonial situation, as well as (what amounts to a truly prophetic feature of Brooke-Rose's 1984 vision) Somali famine or the "budding" Arabian terrorism (*A*, 127), ultimately returns to the domestic gender policy and power politics:

> But Wally we'll have to have something in common surely, what shall we talk about when we'll stop talking about love? My love I'll never believe the day will come when we'll have nothing to say, why if we love each other we should never stop talking! Why pin it all on intellectual exchange?
>
> It'll be a very good question, but if there could at least be exchange it might be fun for a while providing he doesn't atomize not only my inquiries, which I'll have to stop, but my own lifelong passions multitudinous, from astronomy to Zeus from Borges to Yggdrasil from choreography to xylophones from Dante to the Wits from ethnology to Vitruvius from fiction to utopias from grammatology to theororism from heresies to sestinas from ideograms to rhetoric from jazz to quattrocento from Kierkegaard to Plotinus from Lear to Oedipus from mimesis to aporia to nihilism, he may dyscognize them all and all the others out of his epistemes.
> (*A*, 130)

As Ellen G. Friedman and Miriam Fuchs have argued, although the stories running "through the madlanes of Sandra's memory" will not help her to find a job, "by inscribing her presence in language, she defies the deadening and ever-growing bureaucracy around her."[16] This inscription takes place by means of multilingual punning and the creation of a neologistic idiolect, i.e., through the deployment of a Joycean strategy *par excellence*, whose importance goes well beyond character parallelism remarked upon by Lawrence.[17]

---

16 Ellen G. Friedman & Miriam Fuchs, "Introduction – Contexts and Continuities: An Introduction to Women's Experimental Fiction in English," *Breaking The Sequence – Women's Experimental Fiction* (Princeton: Princeton University Press, 1989) 31.

17 "Like Joyce's Finnegan, Mira assumes historical, mythic, and astronomical proportions. Her mission, however, remains constant: to awaken those around her to the impending doom she sees on the horizon" (Lawrence, *Techniques for Living*, 101).

Following Brooke-Rose's outspokenly feminist and linguistically innovative *Amalgamemnon* is a relatively straightforward, dialogue-based novel partaking of the sci-fi genre, *Xorandor* (1990). Its two most anomalous aspects, as far as Brooke-Rose's previous output is concerned, are its explicitly English setting (Cornwall) and the dialogical form of the thrust of its narrative, presenting yet another departure from Brooke-Rose's staple narrative sentence. The narrative consists of a transcript of the efforts of fraternal twins Jip and Zab to write the story of their discovery of Xorandor, a nuclear-waste-eating rock that produces similarly abled offspring, as they dictate contrapuntally into a pocket computer the story of their relationship with the ancient silicon life-form. Thus, *Xorandor* revisits the technological anxiety of *Amalgamemnon*, turning computer science from a thematic concern into the very narrative mode: as the two "whiz-kids" talk, the computer transcribes their speech onto their "Poccom 3" computer screen and then replies directly: the twins' "softalk" thus stands in opposition to the "softwary" Mira in *Amalgamemnon* (*X*, 9).

The name of the rock-machine, then, derives from the operand XOR (exclusive OR) and ANDOR (nonexclusive OR). Just how mimetic are Brooke-Rose's narrative device and the consequent style comes to the forefront in *Xorandor*'s very opening:

1 BEGIN
The first time we came across Xorandor we were sitting on him.
Correction, Zab. Sitting True, came across False. We didn't come across Xorandor, he contacted us.
True, Jip. We'd come to our usual haunt by the old carn and we were sitting on this large flat stone.
It was the middle of our summer eprom and we'd taken Poccom 2 out with us to play on.
(*X*, 9)
Correction not accepted. You agreed to introduce the storytellers cos they're also characters. If the storytellers are characters THEN their confusion is part of their characters ENDIF. Inversely IF the characters are the storytellers THEN the confusion is part of the story ENDIF. REMark.
(*X*, 11)

As Brooke-Rose herself admitted, one of the practical reasons for her construction of youth slang out of electronics and physics jargon was that she "had no idea (generation gap + living abroad) how kids talk. The reason was practical, the result, again, a particular style" (*STT*, 10). The more philosophical significance of the dialogic form lies in its foregrounding of the human/machine interface, out of which grows the storyline of the conventional "nuclear disaster averted" story: in nourishing themselves on nuclear material, the computer's progeny promises to solve nuclear crisis.

However, when one of Xorandor's offspring mistakes nuclear waste for nuclear bomb material and neutralises it, upsetting the fine balance of world power, the threat begins to loom of nuclear missiles randomly disarmed by this process. The twins, like all storytellers, have privileged information, but it is so weighty that either revealing or concealing it would influence the course of history, and so, in the end, Jip and Zab decide not to "save" their computer file-story. Again, in anticipation of the 1990s "end of history" debates, Brooke-Rose has the twins reflect on their own status as narrators in a story without a hero, fiction without history:

"Poor Us! We're storytellers without a hero. . . . We're not even autobiographers since we've dropped out of our own story. *Nothing is happening, Zab.*"
"Something is happening to us, Jip, we're growing up. Even story-tellers can change, during the story."
"What on earth do modern historians do, Zab, *when history seems to stop?*"
"They wait."
"Until something happens?"
"*Until they discover that something has been happening all the time, away from their camera-eyes, unbeknown to them.*"
(X, 159, my emphasis)

Thus, although firmly embedded within the science-fiction genre, it is chiefly through *Xorandor*'s combination of form and content, as well as its computerised style, that Brooke-Rose performs her typical experimentation with the discursiveness of science.[18]

Verbivore (1990) represents a novelty in its status as a sequel both to *Amalgamemnon* and *Xorandor*, developing and enhancing their stylistic effects and thematic concerns. *Verbivore* presents their "realisation" of sorts, insofar as *Amalgamemnon* insists on its "unrealised" verbal tense and mode and *Xorandor*'s narrative culminates in self-effacement. However, this realisation is problematised by Brooke-Rose on many levels, primarily because "the real," throughout *Verbivore*, is presented as "simulation." If Xorandor reappears, it is with the hitherto unknown ability to "simulate a reality and decide when a different version was required" (V, 61). *Verbivore* creates a fictional world inhabited by an over-computerised race of beings who have lost control of their words and memories, life having been completely absorbed and distanced by screened writing, floppy disks, and media.

---

18   Lawrence speaks of Brooke-Rose's "radical science fiction": "Eschewing traditional science fiction, which on numerous occasions she refers to as 'unimaginative' and, paradoxically, too reliant on the codes of realism, Brooke-Rose is clearly after some more radical kind of science or scientific fiction that derives its *techne*, rather than merely its content, from computer technology" (Lawrence, *Techniques for Living*, 125).

The driving narrative "incident," which again determines the peculiar style, consists in the reaction of a mysterious megacomputer (very likely Xorandor's offspring) to the overload of information by sudden cuts in the flow, during which words disappear and writing undergoes erasure. Just how different a world *Verbivore* presents can also be seen in how the revenant Mira Enketei is only left to perversely enjoy the classicist etymologies: "In fact the press soon named the whole phenomenon Verbivore. Some journalists tried Logophagoi—which pleased me more, as an ex-Greek scholar, and also re-called the Xorandor affair with its Alphaphagoi" (*V*, 28). The erasure of writing staged in *Verbivore* commences from the very outset:

> On the first day of Verbivore I was wordprocessing a difficult farewell letter to my wife and listening to the radio when it suddenly went phut. But this often happened, so I just waited patiently, erasing and retyping sentences and whole paras. It was only later that.
> When Verbivore began I was watching the last instalment, well, not *the* last I mean but it came to be the last instalment of.
> What was I doing when Logfag began? Why I was calling Jimmy, he's in Zambia you see, and as I got through I realised I had the telly on but then.
> I can't remember the beginning of Verbivore. It seems quite.
> I can't remember, I was coming-to after having me womb out.
> (*V*, 7)

However, as long as her previous two novels raise their admonishing fingers against the predatory computer technologies and discourses, here Brooke--Rose explicitly engages in computerised cannibalism by feeding upon the words, phrases, and motifs of *Amalgamemnon* and *Xorandor*, as well as recasting their characters, cutting the former and reshuffling the latter, before concluding with: "Blank screen, black with millions of white dots, like a universe. Decibel dies" (*V*, 196). Moreover, Brooke-Rose accentuates the narrative obsession with simulation by displacing the narrative as a whole upon the level of simulation – shortly before the concluding blank screen, the whole "Verbivore affair" is revealed as fiction within fiction, part of a novel somebody is writing, maybe Perry Hupsos (original Greek title of *On the Sublime*), maybe a character in a radio-drama written by Perry Hupsos and produced by Mira Enketei. In letting her own characters comment on their own displacement—as fictions—from "the real," while constantly undermining the textual reality as fictional and fictitious, Brooke-Rose is already paving way for the climax of her tetralogy.

Textermination (1991), despite reverting to a trademark Brooke-Rose narrative strategy—i.e., the third-person present-tense narrative sentence—takes intertextuality and fictionality to unprecedented heights. "A sequel to something like the entirety of world literature,"[19] *Textermination* features dozens of characters grafted from the classical texts of fiction of all periods and national literatures, who gather at the San Francisco Hilton to petition the Reader (a divinity whose name is appropriately capitalised) to spare them from the oblivion of no longer being read. This grafting, needless to say, happens not only on the level of the character, but also of each and everyone's own life-world, which results in a collapse of the ontological demarcations among these respective worlds. But Brooke-Rose does not settle for having Humbert Humbert leer at an unsuspecting Maisie, or depicting the surprise of Casaubon from *Middlemarch* upon realising that the conference paper on himself he takes pains to listen to deals in fact with the Casaubon from Umberto Eco's *Foucault's Pendulum*. With evident relish Brooke-Rose also stages the spectral presence of, e.g., Calvino's Nonexistent Knight or the anonymous soldier from Robbe-Grillet's *In the Labyrinth*. Part of this procession is a caricature of Joyce's Leopold Bloom:

> On the excursion upcoast, Lotte looks as ever for Goethe but finds herself with a Dublin Jew called Leopold Bloom, who talks a great deal but of things quite beyond her ken, except when he describes the preparation and eating of fried kidneys. Ugh! [...] Leopold Bloom is watching from a safe corner far away, talking to Ulrich about the Irish troubles while Ulrich listens politely and looks on, thinking of the empire. (*T*, 112–5)

In order further to blur distinctions, thrown into this medley are the characters' professional "interpreters" – both academics with careers based on their exegeses, as well as actors, their cinematic re-embodiments (Lillian Gish as Hester Prynne meets her literary paradigm in what is bound to be an awkward encounter). The point about the cultural dominance of television is brought home when the literary convention is overrun by an overweening crowd of "movie-star" characters from soap operas and TV series.

In Lawrence's apposite remark, Brooke-Rose's exploration of these ontological compounds undertakes "a sociology of cultural oblivion," aiming to address its causes and effects.[20] Indeed, Brooke-Rose does not "merely" experiment for experiment's own intertextual sake. At the time of crisis and

---

19 McHale, "The Postmodernism(s) of Christine Brooke-Rose," 205.
20 Lawrence has usefully categorised these into five groups which cover most of the *Textermination* crowd: literary characters who are upstaged by popular culture icons, both television and film characters and the actors who play them; literary characters who are upstaged by the news, that is, the real has become unreal, sometimes beyond the wildest dreams of fiction; literary characters who have become irrelevant, no longer able to matter to readers; literary characters who are not memorable to readers; literary characters who are threatened by the deadening effect of academic critical practice, particularly, the narrow theoretical and political axes that critics grind (Lawrence, *Techniques for Living*, 144).

downfall of traditions, literary or other, Brooke-Rose incites the reader to recognise both fiction's powers and its limits, particularly in terms of the confusion between fiction and politics. *Textermination* contains the thriller-genre subplot in which Gibreel Farishta of Rushdie's *Satanic Verses* is, just as his real-life author, hounded by terrorists – a metonymy for the danger of literature as such when facing oppressive ideology, religious or political.[21]

Brooke-Rose has a personal stake in the danger of literature becoming obsolescent and irrelevant, which is brought home by the poignant *memento mori* she stages round the middle of the text; her own Mira Enketei, originally Brooke-Rose's fictional surrogate, finds her own name on the list of forgotten characters:

> Idly she lifts the zigzag scroll at an eighth or so of its thickness and her eye falls on a long list of forgotten names in alphabetical order. She can't resist, lifts another thickness, runs her finger down to EL, lifts another small thickness, finds EM, then EN, and moves down to ENK. Yes, she too figures in it: Enketei, Mira. She can't go on. She doesn't exist. (*T*, 105)

In the ultimate metafictional twist, and with a poignant wink to Beckett, Brooke-Rose "herself" takes the stage:

> If she can't go on, I suppose I'll have to. I am not Mira of course, though many readers think I am. For one thing I have little Latin and less Greek. Curious how one can invent knowledgeable people without possessing their knowledge. One cheats, quite simply. [...] Be that as it may, I am the author, take it how you will, and I am still alive and well, if not in Texas, at least here, and for a little while yet. (*T*, 106–7)

For Brooke-Rose, the author's survival ironically manifests itself in her ability to "write off" her character. But the same also applies conversely: after Farishta has been gunned down by his chasers, Brooke-Rose exercises the writer's rare numinous privilege of restoring her creations back to their "lives." Despite ending *Textermination* with an *ekpyrosis*—commensurate with the burning of the Alexandrian library—during which the San Francisco Hilton is burned to the ground, burying all its temporary inhabitants and together with them the whole of literary history, Brooke-Rose was to "go on" – again, in surprisingly innovative and unforeseen directions.

---

21   McHale makes a similar point when observing that for Brooke-Rose, "the character of Farishta has come to stand metonymically for literary fiction itself, which is similarly in mortal threat from ideologies intolerant of its speculativeness, pluralism, and ontological irresponsibility" (McHale, "The Postmodernism(s) of Christine Brooke-Rose," 207–8).

Brooke-Rose's final, third experimental tetralogy comprises *Remake* (1996), *Next* (1998), *Subscript* (1999), and *Life, End Of* (2006). Of these, the first and last present her fictional autobiographies, grappling with "the paradoxical task of looking back in the present tense."[22] However poignant and painfully candid in their depiction of mental and physical senescent deterioration, and apart from their (particularly the latter's) staging wordplay and punning as the aging writer's only diversion, *Remake* and *Life, End Of* are only truly novel in Brooke-Rose's canon by staging their author as their protagonist. On the other hand, with *Next* and *Subscript*, Brooke-Rose was still able to expand upon and depart from her best narrative experiments.

Next is Brooke-Rose's at once most Oulipian as well as English, or, more precisely, London-based, novel. The cover-blurb advertisement touches on most of the Oulipian devices: set amid the London homeless community (and its narrative concerning an investigation of one of the homeless characters' violent death), this well-nigh sociological reportage of an underworld of dispossession painstakingly omits the verb "to have" and reserves the first-person pronouns only for direct speech, for the content is poverty and isolation. The voices representative of the community are legion: 26, to be precise, as many as letters on the keyboard; the initials of the characters living out on the street—thus forming an avant-garde of sorts—spell QWERTYUIOP, i.e., the top rank of keyboard keys. These conceits are combined with an ultra-realist description of the homeless reality – with typographical effects reminiscent of B. S. Johnson, as for instance those opening the text:

> **The Story So Far:** Derica, long married to oil-man Brad, ran his ranch for years and reared the twins Rex and Regina,   but could not ever onceal her   strong   love   for   Trix, born of   an   old   affair with Jesse, business rival to   Brad   and   later married to Tina,   but now pursuing Gina. Doug, a new   riend of Rex, brings Cindy,   who   fasci-   nates Brad, while Gina strongly attracts Doug,   but is herself too po-werfully involved with Rick who now helps Derica ma-nage the estate. After a violent scene with Sal, Derica asks Dan to intervene with Bradley.
>
> (*N*, 1)

---

22   Lawrence, *Techniques for Living*, 175.

The alphabet, termed "alphabête" (i.e., "alphabeast") early on, serves as the acrostic grid for the 20th-century's worst atrocities:

A for Auschwitz. B for Belsen. C for Cambodia.
D for Dresden. For Deportation. E for Ethiopia, for Ethnic Cleansing... F for, what's F?
Famine... Mao's Great Leap into, 1959. Stalin's ditto, Ukraine 1933.
Fundamentalism. There's usually more than one horror for each letter.
(*N*, 3)

These and similar never-ending alphabetical rounds from *A* to *Z* and back are interspersed within the text's ostensibly realist, quasi-documentary mapping of street-level London of the contemporary, millennial moment.[23] Equally remarkable is Brooke-Rose's inventory of the varieties of London Estuary English (termed "Estuarian"), ranging from educated RP and bureaucratese, via variously slanted Standard, down to 'the thing' itself:

Craowded inni, can' even ear the telley. No response above the environmental clatter. No' tha' there's ever anythink on the telly, stiuw, ah lahk ter watch the world ah doow, can' see i' reely in the streey'. Wha' fooar? the sheepskin asks. Putty hair bristles like a Simpson. Ah lahk the ads, thy's ever sao machao. No take-up, no demand for examples. No' tha' thy knaows i', or cares if thy doow.

No feedback. The putty boy says. Ah aonly watch the business neuws. An every tahm i' says NEXT, an wha' bi' of world's camin ap, yer ge's Bu' first wey'll tike a brike.
(*N*, 10–11)

Whether the result of Brooke-Rose's powers of invention or registration, the spoken language as transcribed here allows not only for an entertaining readerly exercise in deciphering, but also enables a re-enactment, whether mental or vocal, of the spoken *as read*, an imaginative and imaginary identification and unification between the reader and the dispossessed voices of *Next*. For the ethics of *Next* is a lesson in pity and sympathy:

(Is there a life before death?)
   under the lullaby of trucks
     as the snow, thickening fast, the now slanting snow,
        greypinkly eiderdowns him over,
     for hours,

---

23   So meticulous is Brooke-Rose's urban mapping that McHale's review hailed *Next* as "a London 'Wandering Rocks' for the nineties," mapping the city as it "track[s] the homeless on their rounds from doorway doss to homeless shelter to job centre and around again, placing Next firmly in the lineage of the great twentieth-century city novels" (Brian McHale, "Review of *Next* by Christine Brooke-Rose," *Review of Contemporary Fiction* 19.2 [Summer 1999]: 127).

as he digests the nan and sausages,
until he is invisible, unpickupable, perhaps,
> into deep sleep
out of time,
> to be debriefed by eternity
> > but with no next.
We'll take a break now. Stay with them.
(*N*, 210)

In *Subscript,* Brooke-Rose once more, and for the last time, revisits the scientific, speakerless present tense, addressing the themes of encryption and legibility on the macro, biological scale of life evolution from the prokaryote cell 4500 million years ago all the way to modern man at the end of the Magdalenian period 11,000 years ago. The title suggests "under-writing," and that which underwrites all biological evolution, of course, is the genetic "code," the record of millions of years of organic adaptation. As Brooke-Rose herself observed, all explicit mentions of "the code" disappear around chapter 9, together with the emergence of humans as conscious beings. The theme, then, is evolution through and in language.

The linguistic evolution, as she herself demonstrated in *Invisible Author* (lest it be lost on future translators), is marked by the (non-)use of pronouns. As revealed in Brooke-Rose's quasi-Joycean "schema," the pronouns, deliberately omitted from the first three chapters, before the appearance of reptiles 300 million years ago, gradually appear in sequences tied to cultural developments. The singular impersonal ("it") appears only in chapter 4 to denote a sentient entity. In the same chapter, the plural impersonal pronoun ("they") surfaces to covey an inchoate sense of group differentiation, etc. The narrative schema, yet again, is keyed to evolutionary stages – hence, the novel opens at its most alienating and neologising, with the style increasingly coming to resemble what appears a "convention":

Zing! zinging out through the glowsalties the pungent ammonia earthfarts in slithery clay and all the rest to make simple sweeties and sharpies and other stuffs. Dust out of vast crashes and currents now calmer as the crust thickens and all cools a bit.
Over many many forevers.
Waiting. Absorbing. Growing. Churning. Splitting.
> Over and Over.
In the thrivering slimy heat. Absorbing and churning acid gas in the hot mud bubbling all around and above and out of the hole in the jutting rock. The acid gas hides inside the cracks around the spouting rock. Delicious.
(*S*, 1)

Linearity is meticulously preserved, and yet its sheer evolutionary macro-
-scale renders it beyond human-scale comprehension – as in the unfathoma-
ble *"Sixty-five million years later"* presiding over chapter 4. *Subscript*'s manifest concern with survival—of her own fiction, of literature as such, of the
humanities, of civilisation and humanity itself—which runs the length of
Brooke-Rose's fiction, finally appears in as universal a proportion as possible, while still providing a backdrop for her favourite exercise – the different
modes of representing the unreal.[24] Typically of Brooke-Rose, her tracing of
life evolution ends on an anticipatory, visionary note; only this time, not of
doom or perdition, but of that which steadfastly resists it:

> The bisons pound across the plain, half men, half pounding animals. No, not half
> men, half women, with floating hair and bison bodies and bison legs. [...] And more
> and more, hordes and hordes of wheat-rearers and animal-tamers invading the huge
> forestless plain, the entire landmass, growing grains and greens and fruits and lambs
> and pigs and horses and having endless offspring and living happily ever after. (*S*, 215)

Poignantly candid in its depiction of mental and physical senescent deterioration, *Life, End Of* is also Brooke-Rose's reflection on post-2001 global politics, literature, and culture. Physical decline—the cardio-vascular troubles
plaguing the nameless narrator—works its way into language as a process
of linguistic punning variation on the name of Vasco da Gama: "Vasco de
Harmer" (*LEO*, 11), "Qualmer" (20), "Charmer" (36), "Harmer" (59), "Balmer"
(88), "Alarmer" (92), "Lamer" (103), "Cardio-vasco-de-gamma-totale" (111),
and finally, "Vasco da Drama" (118). Hand in hand with physical decay goes
the narrator's binarisation of the humans around her into T.F.'s ("True Friends") and O.P.'s ("Other People"): "O.P. also means Old People. Over-sensitive
People. Otiose, Obdurate, Obsolete People. Outrageous, obtuse, obstreprous
[sic], ostracised. All of which bring one Person into line: Oxhead Person, Oxy-
moronic Person" (*LEO*, 43). O.P.'s are desensitised doctors as well as former
True Friends alienated, over time and long-divergent paths: "Omega People
that's what we are. O.P. or not O.P., that is the question. There is rarely any
doubt. Real O.P.s are striking, whatever the efforts to drag the eyelids down
over their insensitivity" (*LEO*, 48).

However, together with the growing awareness of her own self-alienation
comes the realisation that "everyone is someone's O.P. that's hardly news"
(91). Interspersed within these are reflections on contemporary politics and

---

24   Lawrence's conclusion is spot-on: "*Subscript* is the archive of the dead, the extinct, the vestigial
     (forms that continue but have lost their function); the disappeared (forms whose sudden dis-
     appearance is experienced as loss but whose fate is unknown); the monstrous (earlier forms
     preserved in storytelling as horror stories)" (Lawrence, *Techniques for Living*, 170).

state of society and thought, marked by scepticism toward American world supremacy ("The Unilateral States of America? So generous sixty years ago and so polite." [*LEO*, 50]) and suspicion of the current "post-" vogue:

> [T]he correct euphemism now is post-, new and therefore better: post-human for instance, heard the other day. But that will at once be confused with posthumous, as of course it should be, human becoming humus. [...]
> Is that the radio voice?
> But isn't the whole O.P. story the same? Who speaks?
> Ah, the twentieth century question. In fact, since you ask, nobody speaks.
> Don't be silly.
> (*LEO*, 64)

Brooke-Rose's narratological obsession drives her to deliver, from a character to an uninterested author, a last mock-technical lecture on free indirect discourse and the importance of narratorless, present-tense sentence, accepting that experiments in narrative are like pain-killers—actively combating the smarting dullness of convention—and that, like life, they have no ultimate purpose beyond themselves. It is a resignation both saddening and ultimately at odds with Brooke-Rose's lifelong project, in which an experimental technique was always harnessed to broader ethical concerns: the experience of loss.[25] The experienced loss, here, is that of fitness for life, for writing, and ultimately, the impending loss of life and writing itself: "The typing, once touch-typing and swift, slows down to a beginner's speed. And even then produces five typos and three squashed intervals per line, costing each time two whole minutes to correct and creating another non-access: writing" (*LEO*, 111).

The only comic relief—now that there is no physical one—comes through language: the tragedy of losing veiled in the comedy of regaining, of redoing language anew by means of punning. Thus, narrator's polyneuritis requiring treatment on the basis of polyketone polymers becomes "Polly New Writis" and "Polly Kettleon" (88); the haemorrhage of her eyes, the ophthalmological "infarctus" ("How can the eye have a heart-attack? Because it loves, it loves" [117]), gives rise to the chilling farewell note: "Eye eye, bye bye, die die, eye. I? Why?" (*LEO*, 118). Despair is accentuated and poignancy escalated as the text draws to a close and life to its end:

> Those earth-plugged body bits seem less strong, as indeed body bit by body bit is slowly being killed off, except for the brain, and humour, so far an uplift out of that

---

25 As Lawrence has observed, for Brooke-Rose, "new fictional techniques are needed to represent the cultural narratives of the twentieth and twenty-first centuries, narratives that must capture heightened constraint and loss" (Lawrence, *Techniques for Living*, 4).

scrambled ego, because of the wholly captivating groundless ground, the extenua-
ted earth the untrue world the ominous planet the hazy galaxy the lying universe.
(*LEO*, 119)

However, remembering that Descartes deemed the pineal gland to be the seat
of the soul, the "scrambled ego" uplifts itself through humour, adding the
concluding comments: "Dehors before the cart, after all. A cruising mind,
as against the mere word-play fun. Meanwhile: *Les jeux de maux sont faits*"
(*LEO*, 119). A supremely ambiguous coda: Descartes putting "dehors" before
"de cart," Brooke-Rose pitting her "cruising mind" against the "mere world-
-play fun." As it was in the beginning, in the end there will also be the pun:
the evil bets having been placed (cf. the French *les jeux sont faits*), and body bit
by body bit killed off, Brooke-Rose adds her own *consummatum est*, her very
last words, quite emblematically, a French pun: "les jeux de maux" implying
les jeux des mots, wordplays. Up until the very last instance, then, multilingual punning and discursive amalgamation remain Brooke-Rose's means of
inscribing her own presence, her own signature, within language: a signature equally unique and idiosyncratic as it is—and must be—repeatable and
recognisable.

   Christine Brooke-Rose's variegated oeuvre presents a most sustained
and original continuation of a (r)evolution of language, her own experimentation concerning itself with the many levels of fictional narrative
discourse and the aesthetic-political implications of style. As opposed to
her marginalisation within the canon of contemporary fiction, Brooke-
Rose's work has a potentially paradigmatic status in that virtually all of the
chief thematic and stylistic concerns of the fiction of her age—technology,
gender, history, the future, discursivity, subversion, hybridity, linguistic
innovation, playfulness, the various "meta-" morphs—are presented in
her oeuvre as a blend at once indefinable and most intriguing. Brooke-Rose
herself thought it "a good sign" that her fiction resisted critical pigeonholes
and eluded classification. Even though the price to be paid for this resistance was obscurity and near invisibility vis-à-vis the canon, the benefit has
been the power of Brooke-Rose's works to remain challenging, surprising,
and alive. Dealing with Brooke-Rose's signature (her presence as writer in
language), it has largely been the recognisability of some of its features
within certain aesthetic traditions and programmes on which literary
criticism has preferred to focus. The time has come, now that the signer
has passed away and presence has turned into absence, to recognise the
signature's uniqueness.

5.1 "LIFE'S TOO SHORED TO EMBARK ON IT NOW": BRIAN W. ALDISS

When, in his introduction to *Imagination on Trial*, Charles Sugnet surveyed the bleak state of experiment in the traditionalist British literature, he singled out science-fiction as possibly the only lasting British "avant-garde" of the era, in that it led a cultic and partisan existence within the mainstream market and fostered experimentation on the levels of literary form and fiction ideology:

> At its worst, science fiction is as predictable as other pop genres, and a reader can take much for granted, but at its best it provides, in addition to all its other uses, a set of metaphors for alienation, and a perfect technique for expressing alienation. [...] In this way, SF parallels the great project of the "serious" avant-garde, which was founded on its deliberate (but ambivalent) separation from bourgeois society. Certain serious texts by Beckett are both serious avant-garde writing *and* a kind of science fiction creation of the alien universe.[26]

To enlist Beckett as a science-fiction recruit might be stretching the boundaries of the genre beyond meaningful delineation – certainly Burroughs (see Chapter Three) would make for a less problematic example. Still, Sugnet is right that around the time of his writing, science-fiction did enjoy a staunch support of a large partisan cult of followers, as well as reputation for being stylistically daring and innovative, to an extent of which not even Johnson himself could have boasted.

The sci-fi avant-gardism entailed its publication and dissemination via journal platforms and readership subscriptions: most famously, the *New Worlds* magazine, active since 1946 and concentrating the first generation of the classics of British sci-fi (John Wyndham, A. C. Clarke, among others), which—in the 1950s under the editorship of John Carnell and from 1964 onward under the leadership of Michael Moorcock—became the seedbed for the "New Wave" science-fiction. The first issue under Moorcock's editorship included work by Barrington J. Bayley and John Brunner, with a review of a Burroughs novel. Among its frequent contributors and staunchest supporters were also two of the most prolific, influential, and experimental science-fiction writers in Britain: Brian Aldiss and J. G. Ballard. Their careers reached their most experimental heights in the 1960s (Aldiss') and early-to-mid 1970s (Ballard's), during which time they both enjoyed a cult status. 1969 marked the apogee of the influence of *New Worlds* magazine in the form of a major literary conference in Harrogate,

---

26 *The Imagination on Trial*, eds. Alan Burns & Charles Sugnet (Allison and Busby: London/New York, 1981) 11.

organised by publisher John Calder, and focused entirely on science-fiction. In 1970, with the money having run out, Moorcock ended *New Worlds* with is- sue no. 200, marking a steep decline in the production of experimental sci-fi. Aldiss and Ballard were the only two major experimentalists who soldiered on into the 1970s, but by the end of that decade, even they had abandoned the sci-fi genre in favour of a more general mainstream. Consequently, even though it is largely to their credit that science-fiction was reclaimed from the exile in the realm of pop culture as an important element of post-war British fiction, they both ended up enjoying a rather problematic status.[27]

If there ever was a British science-fiction avant-garde, the leader of the pack was Brian Wilson Aldiss, who almost singlehandedly brought about the 1960s vanguard sci-fi rejuvenation. A terrifically prolific author, publishing almost a hundred works only between 1956 and 1970, Aldiss regarded the drug culture and the new sexual freedom as part of the challenge to extend the boundaries of the genre. This extension lay in reflecting contemporary reality, in taking science-fiction "inward," and in renewing its style.[28] Ald- iss' alliance with the Modernists, the Beats and, most outspokenly, with the French *nouveau roman*, can be understood as an effort to link the science- fiction genre with the officially established literary canon. A case in point of Aldiss' ties with the French developments is his project dating from two weeks in January 1962 during which Aldiss wrote 46,000 words defying the orthodoxy of fiction in general and of science-fiction in particular: an anti- novel called "A Garden with Figures." To hear Aldiss tell it, he was

> much persuaded by the French *nouveau roman*, the anti-novel, as practiced by Michel Butor and Alain Robbe-Grillet [...] I admired their scrapping of many literary clichés [...] I was stunned by the Robbe-Grillet-Resnais film, *L'Année Dernière à Marienbad*, with its temporal confusions, mysterious agonies, and alien perspectives. It still embodies for me many of the things I set most store by in science fiction.[29]

---

27   Aldiss' work, according to his critic Tom Henighan, "has been unfairly neglected," largely due to his "versatility" which is "dangerous in an era when writers are marketed by having their names associated with a single literary genre, subgenre, or series" (Tom Henighan, *Brian W. Ald- iss* [New York: Twayne Publishers, 1999] 8). Ballard's ambiguous position "as a novelist writing across high and low, literary and popular paradigms," in Michel Delville's opinion, "has also had the more unfortunate effect of relegating his work to the margins of both the SF canon and the literary establishment" (Michel Delville, *J.G. Ballard* [Plymouth: Northcote House Publishers, 1998] 2).

28   In Henighan's account: "They wanted to get away from technology and even from social extrapo- lation, to explore areas that were previously considered taboo areas. To take this step, however, they would need to extend their stylistics, they believed, in a way that would owe more to Joyce, Virginia Woolf, and William Burroughs, than to H. G. Wells, Heinlein, or Asimov" (Henighan, *Brian W. Aldiss*, 5).

29   *Hell's Cartographers: Sounding Brass Tinkling Cymbal – My Affair with Science Fiction*, eds. Brian W. Aldiss & Harry Harrison (London: Orbit Books, 1976) 198–9.

In an exemplary display of the British resistance against the purportedly imported French experiment, Aldiss' text was rejected by Faber and Faber, excoriated by C. P. Snow, and remained unpublished until 1968 when it appeared as *Report on Probability A*, at a time when the resistance against the anti-novelistic chroniclers of disconnected particularities seemed to wane. *Report on Probability A* plays with conceptions of identity and reality, switching between narratives and viewpoints, and presenting a *mise-en-abime* regress of perspectives: there is the P.O.V. of the "watchers," contrasting with passages in italics of beings watching them, and a group of beings one level higher yet, who are watching the watchers watching. Aldiss' advances in experimental science-fiction continued in a series of stories published in *New Worlds* and its companion magazine, *SF Impulse*, the complete (extensively rewritten) sequence published as *Barefoot in the Head: A European Fantasia* (1969), his linguistically most experimental novel, as documented by Henighan's contextualisation.[30]

Written during the height of the hippie revolution, *Barefoot in the Head* remains Aldiss' boldest statement on the dilemma of the individual in history, articulating the need for social involvement, if one is to transcend the restrictions of solipsism. As Aldiss himself remarked, the novel "took me almost three years to write, and when I'd finished it, I felt I'd written myself out of science fiction."[31] Indeed, despite its near-future setting, the novel is very much an encapsulation of the fights and concerns of its time, i.e., the 1960s. Its protagonist is an atheist believing in the surrogate religion of communism, while at the same time a quasi-New Age follower of the mystics Gurdjieff and Ouspensky. Many of the novel's central topics (psychedelic drugs, sexual liberation, anarchy and social disintegration, urbanisation of landscape, etc.) are quintessentially 1960s, only here taken to some new psychedelic heights. Broaching many popular issues of the time, its narrative follows a displaced Serbian on his travels through a Europe devastated by hallucinogenic bombs (the so-called Acid Head War). Here is a piece of concrete poetry entitled "Acid Head":

---

30   "In this work Aldiss carries the Joyce-derived novel in the direction of postmodern trends such as indeterminacy, selflessness, unrepresentation, and carnivalization [...]. At the level of genre, it can be argued that *Barefoot in the Head* combines dystopia with fantasy, quest narrative with satire: and if this constitutes an unpalatable mixture for the common reader of science fiction, that is exactly what Aldiss expected and strove for" (Tom Henighan, *Brian W. Aldiss*, 72).

31   *Hell's Cartographers*, eds. Aldiss & Harrison, 200.

```
            DACIDAC
          DACIDACID
          ACIDACIDA
   ACID              ACI
          HEAD
   CI      ID      DA
   ID      DA      AC
        ACIDACIDAC
        IDACIDAC
        DACIDACI
          CIDACI
           DACI
           ACID
          (BH, 70)
```

The protagonist takes up the name of Colin Charteris and sets out in the first chapter "Northward," from Italy via France to England, developing a doctrine underway of alternative realities and multiple time streams, encapsulated in the quasi-mediaeval and quite Joycean doctrine that "all other human beings were symbols, nodes in an enormous pattern" (*BH*, 27). Upon his arrival in England, Charteris encounters chaos and paradox reigning supreme, and comes under the spell himself of the mysterious hallucinogenic drug, which gradually transforms his thinking and language, devolving into semi-coherence and opacity. He gets adopted as the rock 'n' roll messiah by a band of young nomads, with whom he sets out back for the continent, leading what he believes to be a crusade of liberation, but his creed promotes nothing but egotism and wreaks havoc, turning him into megalomaniac murderer and schizoid opportunist. Charteris winds up incarcerated in a mental asylum run by a Herr Laundrei, a sadistic exaggeration of the misguided therapist sardonically implied in the writings of the famous sixties "anti-therapist" R. D. Laing. Notes of hope and promises of renewal struck in some of his subsequent speeches get drowned out in the miasma of madness:

> What we have seen is worth all collapse and the old Christianity world so rightly in ruins if you forsake all and live where there is most life in the world I offer. There the laternatives flick flock thickly by [...] a man deminiating the topography related belaying a sparky relationship between this Europlexion and the explexion of conventional time the time by which predecyclic man imposed himself against nature by armed marching cross-wise to conceal body-mind apart hide dissillusion. (*BH*, 224)

Aldiss' paronomasia is interesting here: a war-torn Europe, where "alternatives" to the dominant ideology are so "lateral" as to become "laternatives," is a continent where people become so depleted and "expleted" as to "armed--march crosswise" in the service of hiding their "dissillution" (a double-*S* disillusion that might be "silly"?).

To present the disintegrating systems and ontological ambivalences of his dystopian world, Aldiss develops a complex and compact style that fully exploits his skill at wordplay and lexical innovation. In the best modernist tradition of the expressive form, the language of *Barefoot in the Head* is at one with the tenor of the story, and markedly *Wakean*, as is evident in another passage:

> "Ooh this bloke's body's his mindmap!" All untold the fey atmosfuddle of selforiented libidoting wooze trixfixed the constabulary into poets longhaired boxers instrumentalists vocalists meditationers on a semi-syllable card trick-exponents voyeurs of the world box word-munchering followsphere semi-lovers of course with the greatest pretentions wrackonteurs charmers butchboys frenchmen twokissing mystics like-feathered nestlings vanvogtian auto-biographers laughers chucklers starers strargazers villagers and simple heart-burglars all seeing themselves in their hip-packet mirrors. (BH, 244)

Not only does this bear the clear imprint of the *Wake*'s obsession with lists and their exhaustions, but some of Aldiss' rich neologisms again merit further scrutiny: his rendering of ideology as "word-munchering followsphere" is interesting in foregrounding the necessity of its linguistic transmission and followership—its disastrous consequences are brought home in Aldiss' rendering of "raconteur" as "wrackonteur." That Aldiss' bizarre tale is the diagnosis of a particularly Western modern malaise is brought home through such punning slogans as "Expurience of drugged disorient. / Disorient we want and the nonwestered sun of soma" (BH, 256). Eventually, the prose dissolves into verse, incorporating poems, songs, and word pictures – some 60 pages of the text are comprised of snippets of verse and fragments of song lyrics. The novel does not really end; it gradually peters out, blurring the boundaries between modes of writing as Aldiss consistently overrides differences between the genres of fiction.

Asked about his Joycean inspiration, however, Aldiss was evasive and ironic, if also reverentially punning: "I never set Joyce up as a model, but you know if you write that sort of thing, then Joyce is there, just as Picasso is there if you paint a picture of a goat, or Shakespeare if you write English. I never did finish the *Wake*. And life's too shored to embark on it now."[32] Although flirting, in the first half of the 1970s, with a new form of short fiction—visual,

---

32   Qtd. in *Dictionary of Literary Biography, Volume 14: British Novelists Since 1960*, ed. Jay L. Halio (A Bruccoli Clark Layman Book: Gale Research, 1982) 11.

spatial, and imagistic rather than linear and narrative—called "enigma," often surreal and appearing under poetic titles such as "The Eternal Theme of Exile" and "The Daffodil Returns the Smile," Aldiss was for most of the latter half of the seventies preoccupied with the genre of political dystopia à la Orwell (in, e.g., *Enemies of the System* [1978] or *Life in the West* [1980]). The 1980s were to see his full-blown return to traditional science-fiction civilisation epic à la Wells in the monumental *Helliconia* trilogy. However variegated his subsequent genre-blending and hybridisation, his peak of stylistic innovation had come and gone in the 60s, a period whose immense potential and pitfalls Aldiss captured in his *European Fantasia*.

5.2 "PACKED WITH MEANINGLESS LOCAL REFERENCES": J.G. BALLARD

Aldiss' rather unique, one-off brush with experimentalism in the late 1960s might very well be the reason why in 1981, in Sugnet and Burns' interview collection *Imagination on Trial,* the representative experimental science-fiction writer was J.G. Ballard, rather than Aldiss. Twenty-five years earlier, a brief profile, probably penned by editor Ted Carnell, headed "J. G. Ballard, London" and published on the inside front cover of *New Worlds* magazine no. 54 (December 1956), had introduced the then 25-year-young writer as follows:

After winning the annual short story competition at Cambridge in 1951 he wrote his first novel, a completely unreadable pastiche of *Finnegan's Wake* [sic] and *The Adventures of Engelbrecht*. James Joyce still remains the wordmaster, but it wasn't until he turned to science fiction that he found a medium where he could exploit his imagination, being less concerned with the popular scientific approach than using it as a springboard into the surreal and fantastic.[33]

According to Ballard scholar David Pringle, this youthful pastiche must for all intents and purposes be considered as lost. Ballard's biographer John Baxter seems to concur:

Starting a comic novel in the style of Joyce and Richardson, Jim found, like many before him, that such puns and wordplay demanded steely concentration and the scholarship of an encyclopaedist. He completed about sixty pages of *You and Me and the Continuum,*

---

33   Qtd. in John Baxter, *The Inner Man: The Life of J G Ballard* (London: Weidenfeld & Nicolson, 2011) 122. For more information, see David Pringle, "You and Me and the Continuum: In Search of a Lost JG Ballard Novel" (1993) on the official Ballard website. Online: https://www.jgballard.ca/criticism/jgblostnovel.html

on the theme of Christ's second coming. "I'd been bowled over," he said, [...] "and I think my 'novel' was trying to be an updating of the heroes of religious myth - but it was all totally mad as well as unpublishable, the product of too much scattershot reading."[34]

Thankfully, there is enough in the published and official Ballard corpus to group him together with other post-Joycean British experimentalists.

J. G. Ballard's literary career had begun in the early sixties with *The Wind from Nowhere* (1962), which launched his "catastrophe" quartet, but achieved its radical—and scandalous—reputation only with his fifth book, *The Atrocity Exhibition* (1970). Sugnet's introduction makes considerable effort to draw affinities between Ballard's collection of "condensed novels," exploring a world of "second-hand things," with the modernist practice of intertextuality and textual collage, the pride of place granted to Joyce.[35] More relevant, perhaps, to Ballard's aesthetics than Joyce are Freud (the young Ballard flirted with the option of a vocation in psychiatry before turning to fiction) and Burroughs, as Ballard's chief interest in *The Atrocity Exhibition* lies in subliminal messages, excavated by means of what Ballard calls "analytic techniques." These techniques are a direct analogy to Burroughs' myth of Senders and Receivers in *Naked Lunch* (see Chapter Three) and his collaborative development of the cut-up and fold-in techniques.

In the *Imagination on Trial* interview with Alan Burns, discussing how show-business trivia and celebrity gossip (especially the Kennedys, Marilyn Monroe, and Elizabeth Taylor) are used as the building blocks of his fiction, Ballard does recall Joyce as an example of creative appropriation of the mundane and ephemeral in "great" art: "If one could look at the greatest: Shakespeare's plays are thick with topical allusions. The same is true of *Ulysses* - it's packed with local references which Joyce must have known would be meaningless to anyone who didn't know Dublin as well as he did."[36] *The Atrocity Exhibition*'s fifteen "chapters" are loosely connected with the central figure of a psychiatrist suffering from a nervous breakdown, variously named Travis, Talbot, Traven, Trallis, Trabert, Talbert, and Travers - a portmanteau entity, Ballard alerts the reader, which "appears in a succession of

---

34 Baxter, *The Inner Man*, 45–6.

35 "Joyce, in *Ulysses*, threw away the quotation marks and simply incorporated things (headlines, adverts, soft-core pornography, etc.) into his book without attributing any ownership beyond that which we all have in common. [...] One of the complaints made about Freud is that he was too interested in discovering pathology's origin in the particular stories of middle-class individuals. Joyce's nighttown, Genet's *Balcony* and Burroughs's *Naked Lunch* offer that 'pathology' as norm rather than aberration, and find its origin in the shape of the whole culture, rather than in something exclusively personal. Poldy Bloom as Mayor of Dublin and Poldy Bloom as degraded execution victim map not only the fantasy limits of Poldy's psyche, but also the actual structure of the Irish polity" (Sugnet, "Introduction," *Imagination on Trial*, 7).

36 Burns, "Interview with J.G. Ballard," *Imagination on Trial*, 28.

roles, ranging across a spectrum of possibilities available to each of us in our interior lives" (*AE*, 91).

As critics like Michel Delville have noted, Ballard's experiment lies not so much in the omission or reduction of standard novelistic elements (plot, time and place continuum, or characterisation), but chiefly in that they are "literally organized in the mode of a scientific experiment" – Ballard's is a clinical approach to his subjects "as laboratory data to be analysed in the context of the author's investigation of 'the unique vocabulary and grammar of late 20th century life' (*AE*, 87)."[37] A typical psychopathological space depiction takes place in a two-dimensional, dehumanised mode:

> **Murder.** Tallis stood behind the door of the lounge, shielded from the sunlight on the balcony, and considered the white cube of the room. At intervals Karen Novotny moved across it, carrying out a sequence of apparently random acts. Already she was confusing the perspectives of the room, transforming it into a dislocated clock. She noticed Tallis behind the door and walked towards him. Tallis waited for her to leave. Her figure interrupted the junction between the walls in the corner on his right. After a few seconds her presence became an unbearable intrusion into the time geometry of the room. (*AE*, 43)

However, despite this abstract, geometrical outlook, *The Atrocity Exhibition* is steeped in the contemporary socio-historical examination of subliminal effects of media events (e.g., the Vietnam war and JFK's assassination) triggering unconscious drives essential to its pornographic, fetishist aesthetics, hand in hand with its anarchistic anti-establishmentarianism – episodes such as "The Facelift of Princess Margaret" and "Why I Want to Fuck Ronald Reagan" are emblematic in this respect.

As shown in a paper by Joyce-scholar Richard Brown, the Joycean traces within *Atrocity Exhibition* are conceptual rather than textual, and have to do with Ballard's practice of "apocalyptic intertextuality."[38] Yet, *The Atrocity Exhibition*'s avant-garde credentials can be pinned down to some concrete parodic motifs taken from Dada's grandfather Alfred Jarry. The final section of *The Atrocity Exhibition*, "The Assassination of John Fitzgerald Kennedy Considered as a Downhill Motor Race" fairly explicitly refers to Jarry's outrageous short prose text. As Brown's essay shows, this manoeuvre is to be understood as one of Ballard's "many bizarre attempts to understand the absurdity of the Kennedy assassination"—in order to "kill Kennedy again but in a way

---

37   Delville, *J.G. Ballard*, 23.
38   Richard Brown, "Jarry, Joyce and the Apocalyptic Intertextuality of *The Atrocity Exhibition*," *J.G. Ballard—Landscapes of Tomorrow*, eds. Richard Brown, Christopher Duffy, & Elizabeth Stainforth (Leiden: Brill, 2016) 69–86.

that makes sense" (*AE*, 50)—in this case in "an absurd juxtaposition with the absurdity of accelerated motor-car culture and that of the media circus of the presidential 'race.'"[39]

Ballard's 1973 novel *Crash* is a follow-up on one of the "condensed novels" of the previous book: the eroticised aesthetics of car crashes. A narrator named James Ballard reports on how his own automobile crash—in which a passenger from the other car is fatally injured—brings about in him a cluster of compelling obsessions, all of which are centred on the "perverse eroticism of the car-crash, as painful as the drawing of an exposed organ through the aperture of a surgical wound" (*C*, 17). These obsessions are further enhanced through his acquaintance with the deranged scientist Robert Vaughan, whose sole mission is the self-immolating car-crash union with movie star Elizabeth Taylor, an ultimate sex-death which holds the "keys to a new sexuality born from a perverse technology" (*C*, 13). The crash experience is understood as a breach of immediacy through the consumerist and media mediation of human existence ("The crash was the only real experience I had been through for years. For the first time I was in physical confrontation with my own body, an inexhaustible encyclopedia of pains and discharges" [*C*, 39]). Or, as Delville puts it, the car crash metaphor functions "as a means of investigating the latent and manifest meanings of our technological culture, as well as the relationship between violence and sexual fantasies."[40] Just as in *The Atrocity Exhibition*, violence and perversion seem to have become the only means through which Ballard's characters can "relate to each other or even achieve a sense of transcendence."[41]

Following the 1973 publication of *Crash*, Ballard enjoyed a decade of cult following, hailed as the British Burroughs, the high priest of proto-cyberpunk literature, the most outspoken critic of commodity fetishism and media sensationalism – thereby becoming, of course, a media sensation himself. His cult was cemented by further works of social critique, such as *Concrete Island* (1974), a nightmarish anti-*Robinson Crusoe*, an account of a man in an emergency surrounded by disinterested bystanders, or *High Rise* (1975), an imaginary anti-*Utopia* in which the tenants of one apartment building choose to create their own closed society. As the seventies flowed into eighties, the 1981 *Hello America* presented a return to the more familiar and less controversial genre of speculative fiction, followed by *Empire of the Sun* (1984), a semi-autobiographical account of his childhood experience of Japanese-occupied wartime Shanghai. A great commercial and critical success (a Booker Prize nomination), *Empire of the Sun* also presented the close of Ballard's partisan

---

39   Brown, "Jarry, Joyce and the Apocalyptic Intertextuality, 69.
40   Delville, *J.G. Ballard,* 35.
41   Ibid, 36.

status and his entry into the mainstream. Although productive well into his last years, and occasionally reverting to the mode of scandalous social critique as espoused in his early-seventies output, Ballard's turn to the more familiar realms of the semi-autobiographical novel did secure him a mainstream status at the expense of his erstwhile ability to shock or challenge. Still, as the obituaries produced after his recent death unanimously agreed, Ballard's was a singular vision, critical of the emergence of modern media technology within the domain of the aesthetic and remarkably prescient regarding society in the early twenty-first century.

Francis Booth's concluding chapter on "New-Wave Science Fiction" departs from acknowledging the immense influence of Burroughs' *Naked Lunch* and *Nova Express* on the recuperation of sci-fi as a "serious" literary genre, and a fertile ground for experimentation, in Britain. New Wave Science Fiction, to Booth's mind, is distinguished by several formal traits and themes: "post--apocalyptic setting," that is, travelling not so much in space as in time and concerning itself "not with life on other planets or the far future of the Earth, but the imminent possibility of the destruction of life as we know it"[42]. Connected to this is "politics" in that "the message of post-apocalyptic fiction is highly political: something needs to be done."[43] "Fractured identities", "sex", and "fragmented narratives" – these are traits which enable the historian to classify New Wave sci-fi within the experimental pigeonhole: "like many mainstream experimental novels, the New Wave used fragmented narratives to disorient the reader and question the nature of reality and the omniscient narrator."[44]

Similarly, some other recent accounts have attempted to revisit Sugnet's claims of sci-fi's avant-garde status in the stratification of contemporary literature production. For instance, when reviewing the "resurgence of 'lowly' genres in the 1990s," Roger Luckhurst relates these to the resistance against the "development of a new kind of cultural politics that has been called 'cultural governance.'"[45] According to Luckhurst's account, this resistance has been strengthened by what he perceives as gradual dissolution, throughout the nineties, of the two chief cultural arenas of eighties resistance against the dominant culture – pop music and fine art, "the leading cultural phenomena that were incorporated into the cultural governance operated by New Labour in the late 1990s."[46] Consequently, it has been argued, science-fiction

---

42   Booth, *Amongst Those Left*, 663.
43   Ibid, 664.
44   Ibid, 665–6.
45   Roger Luckhurst, "British science fiction in the 1990s: politics and genre," *British Fiction of the 1990s*, 79.
46   Luckhurst, "British science fiction in the 1990s," 81.

and genre writing in general underwent a revitalisation because they could still find spaces outside the general "de-differentiation" or "mainstreaming" effect sought by the strategy of cultural governance.

For Luckhurst, "the more literary editors dismissed the limitations of genre-writing or *Granta* magazine's stunt to nominate the twenty best young British writers, the more oppositional energy accrued to these genres."[47] However, hardly any of the three authors Luckhurst singles out as presenting this genre resistance in contemporary science fiction—James Lovegrove, Gwyneth Jones, and Ken MacLeod—engage in a writing style that could be termed, however broadly as in the case of Aldiss and Ballard, experimental or revolutionary. In fact, theirs is a realist style and resistance takes place purely on the level of the subject: societal and political critique. Thus, the far less optimistic conclusion of Tom Henighan's study on Aldiss from 1999—vis-à-vis the oblivion to which Aldiss' work had fallen prey ever since the late 1970s—seems more to the point:

> Analysts of social trends suggest that the public has lost interest in the challenge of space and thus in science fiction. Were the Voyageur photographs of bleak planets and barren satellites just too daunting for a public accustomed to little green men and faces on Mars? Does science's beleaguered but still intact "objectivity" condemn it to irrelevance in an age of ideologies and irrational commitments? Has the science fiction genre been swallowed up by postmodernism? Are we ever to acquire a science fiction tradition that is consistent, well-defined, stable, and secure?[48]

5.3 "A POLYGLOT BABBLE LIKE A SYMPHONIC EURO-LANGUAGE": ANGELA CARTER

Angela Carter's direct involvement with Joyce took the form of her participation in the centennial 1982 Dublin Symposium, which resulted in her short but revealing article in homage to the author, "Envoi: Bloomsday." As a British writer, she approaches Joyce primarily as an Irish (post-)colonial writer, terming his "magisterial project" as "that of buggering the English language, the ultimate revenge of the colonialised" (*ED*, 208). Thus, the most momentous ramification of Joyce's position is his linguistic experiment, for "the history of the British Empire came to exercise a curious kind of brake upon our expression in the English language, as it became less and less the instrument of feeling and more and more that of propaganda." More relevantly for Carter in 1982,

---

47   Luckhurst, "British science fiction in the 1990s," 83.
48   Henighan, *Brian W. Aldiss*, 123-4.

> Something even odder has happened since Joyce's day, in these last years, when Eng-
> lish, in the great world, has become synonymous with the language spoken in America,
> which, though it uses the same words, is an entirely other communications system.
> Indeed, Americans threaten to leave us entirely stranded, now, on a linguistic beach
> of history with English turning into a quaint dialect, another Old World survival, like
> Castilian Spanish, stiff outmoded, unapposite. And what shall we do then? Why, we
> shall be thrust back on Joyce, who never took English seriously and so he could conti-
> nue, as we will do. (*ED*, 209)

Carter details how in *Ulysses*, Joyce "sheared away the phoney rhetoric that
had been accreting over the centuries," transforming English "into something
intimate, domestic, demotic, a language fit not for heroes but for husbands,"
then, in *Finnegans Wake*, "stripped it of its linguistic elements," producing
"a polyglot babble that, perhaps, begins to approximate something like a sym-
phonic Euro-language, in which English is no more than a dominant theme."
In a word, Joyce "disestablished English" (*ED*, 209–10). More personally, had
it not been for Joyce, Carter, as a writer in post-imperial Britain "would not
even have had the possibility of a language, for Joyce it was who showed how
one could tell the story of whatever it is that is going to happen next." That
this liberating effect should come for the colonially oppressed is a paradox of
which Carter is well aware, but she cannot but insist on Joyce's far-reaching
importance:

> Nevertheless, he carved out a once-and-future language, restoring both the simplicity
> it had lost and imparting a complexity. The language of the heart and the imagination
> and the daily round and the dream had been systematically deformed by a couple of
> centuries of use as the rhetorical top-dressing of crude power. Joyce Irished, he Euro-
> peanised, he decolonialised English: he tailored it to fit this century, he drove a giant
> wedge between English literature and literature in the English language and, in doing
> so, he made me (forgive this personal note) free. Free not to do as he did, but free to
> treat the Word not as if it were holy but in the knowledge that it is always profane.
> (*ED*, 210)

At the same time, Carter notes that Joyce's profoundly anti-British (in the
sense of the Great Tradition) example remains equally, even four decades
after his death, unfinished and open-ended: "You could also say, he detached
fiction from one particular ideological base, and his work has still not yet
begun to bear its true fruit. The centenarian still seems avant-garde" (*ED*,
210–1).

Of all authors addressed here, Carter is the only one included in B. S. Johnson's 1973 list of writers who "write as though it matters." It has been already
argued that her inclusion was perhaps prophetic on Johnson's part, since very

little of her early (beginning in mid-sixties) output seems to warrant Johnson's championing of Carter. However, from early 1970s onwards, Carter went on to establish herself as one of the most inventive and prolific writers of the next two decades. Before producing, in the opinion of critic Lorna Sage, "two of the most festive and disturbing novels of the last years of the century,"[49] i.e., *Nights at the Circus* (1984) and *Wise Children* (1991), Carter wrote poetry, short fiction, children's books, drama, radio plays, television adaptations, innumerable newspaper articles and reviews, as well as the provocative contribution to feminist theory, *The Sadeian Woman and the Ideology of Pornography* (1978), a feminist reappraisal of the Marquis de Sade, whom she regarded as a "moral pornographer," putting pornography into the service of women.

Carter's first full-blown attack on the questions surrounding gender, a feminist book at odds with the "madwoman in the attic" version of a woman's place in the house of fiction, came in her *The Passion of New Eve* (1977), where woman is born out of a man's body again, as in the Genesis story. This image has been regarded as referring to the "painful process by which the 1970s women's movement had to carve out its own identity from the unisex mould of 1960s radical politics."[50] Set in a dystopian, but palpably contemporary USA, its plot entails a picaresque quest of Evelyn, a male English professor on the run westward, away from his black lover Leilah (and her bloody abortion) and in pursuit of Tristessa, a divine figure of the Hollywood silent-era glamour. His quest takes him to the desert, where he encounters a subterranean female city of Beulah run by technological matriarchy which surgically transforms him into a centrefold Eve (removing his *-lyn*), then to a commune composed of a harem dominated by a certain Zero character, akin to Charles Manson's "family"; and lastly to the glass mausoleum of Tristessa, who turns out not a woman at all but a transvestite – a Tiresias with whom Eve gets pregnant. In the concluding scene on the beach, after a symbolic rebirth as a woman and renouncing Evelyn's male past—Eve launches herself into the ocean on a skiff.

That *The Passion of New Eve* is also a *Bildungsroman* in the tradition established by Joyce's *A Portrait*, becomes clear in Carter's perhaps most evident intertextual nod to Joyce, which ends the novel:

We start from our conclusions. I arrived on that continent by air and I left it by water; earth and fire I leave behind me. And all this strange experience, as I remember it, confounds itself in a fugue. At night, dreaming, I go back again to Tristessa's house,

---

49   Lorna Sage, "Angela Carter," *Dictionary of Literary Biography, Volume 207: British Novelists since 1960*, ed. Merritt Moseley (Farmington Hills: A Bruccoli Clark Layman Book, Gale Group, 1999) 72.
50   Sage, "Angela Carter," 77.

that echoing mansion, that hall of mirrors in which my whole life was lived, the glass mausoleum that had been the world and now is smashed. He himself often comes to me in the night, serene in his marvellous plumage of white hair, with the fatal red hole in his breast; after many, many embraces, he vanishes when I open my eyes. The vengeance of the sex is love.

Ocean, ocean, mother of mysteries, bear me to the place of birth. (*PNE*, 191)

Here, Eve's "arrival by air" echoes Stephen Dedalus' departure by the same element, her dream of Tristessa's "marvellous plumage of white hair, with the fatal red hole in his breast," a gender-reversed image of "the breast of some darkplumaged dove" and the "long fair hair" (*P*, 171) of the "birdgirl" of Stephen's epiphany. Finally, the concluding invocation of Carter's novel inverts the "father, old artificer" from *A Portrait*'s ending into "ocean, ocean, mother of mysteries," replacing the futurity of Stephen's "stand me now and ever in good stead" (*P*, 253) with the circular return to the beginning.

In her last two novels, *Nights at the Circus* and *Wise Children,* Carter faithfully followed the creed formulated in her 1983 essay "On Gender and Writing." Exasperated at being typecast as a feminist "mythologist," Carter counters these claims by insisting that "I'm in the demythologising business. I'm interested in myths [...] just because they are extraordinary lies designed to make people unfree."[51] Both these novels follow along the genre lines already established in Carter's *New Eve*, and neither presents a stylistically innovative work – it is, thus, more appropriate to end this exposé with a brief mention of her short fiction from the late 1970s and early 1980s, collected in *Black Venus* (1985), where a Joycean reworking of myths seems precisely her chief concern. She inserts new episodes into ready-made myths, for example, into Charles Baudelaire's and Edgar Allan Poe's life stories (the former's rewritten from the perspective of Jeanne Duval, his "mistress of mistresses," the latter's from the viewpoint of his obsession with dying or dead women, originating with his mother) or into *Robinson Crusoe* rewritten from the standpoint of Friday. Last but not least, Carter's "Overture and Incidental Music for *A Midsummer Night's Dream*," first published in the science-fiction magazine *Interzone* in 1982, is an irreverent salute to England's national literary hero.

5.4 "REALISM IS ANTI-ART": JEANETTE WINTERSON

Jeanette Winterson is an author steeped in modernist sensibility. Her own project combining gender studies with queer fiction constitutes no break

---

51   Angela Carter, "Notes from the Front Line," *Gender and Writing*, ed. Michelene Wandor (London: Pandora, 1983) 71.

from modernism, but rather a constant redrawing of its lines of influence, as is evident in her 1995 collection of essays forming a kind of her artistic credo, *Art Objects: Essays on Ecstasy and Effrontery*.

With a radical sense of a clear-cut dichotomy between the two, Winterson here aligns herself with the heritage of experimental modernism as opposed to British realism. Her dismissal of the "realist" impulse in British fiction is unrelenting: "Realism is not a Movement or a Revolution, in its original incarnation it was a response to a movement, and as a response it was essentially anti-art" (AO, 30–1). Elsewhere, her critique of realism is paired with her appreciation for modernism:

> Joyce is difficult. Woolf is difficult. Eliot is difficult. A poet's method, because it works towards exactness, is exacting on the reader. The nineteenth-century novel, and I include in there, 95 per cent of English novels written now, in the late twentieth century, is a loose overflowing slack-sided bag. Much can be stuffed into it and much of that without much thought. (AO, 30–1; 41; 82)

As regards Joyce, Winterson makes a few critical remarks, e.g., charging him, alongside Milton, with having developed a "private" language which she pits against "the poet's" language (AO, 81). Dubious boundaries aside, Winterson draws an interesting parallel between two great literary reformists of the English language, and her irony is one perhaps called-for given the grandiosity of their projects. Winterson is also careful to ally her critique of Joyce's with Woolf's (her literary champion) remarks on *Ulysses*:

> Like Woolf, Joyce had a fine ear, and he is entranced by the rhythm of words [...]. He is Irish and he lets the words lead him down to the sea, through the strange green waters, until he is returned, salt-washed to the streets of Dublin. His pocketfuls of words, that abrade and glitter, he scatters them, grinds them, and eventually reforms them into a great whale of words, a thousand pages long, that spouts and dives and terrifies and welcomes little men with picks. (AO, 81–2)

Thus, even though she excludes Joyce from her canon of "those Modernists whose work I think is vital" and which includes "HD, Marianne Moore, Gertrude Stein, Virginia Woolf, Sitwell, Mansfield, Barney, Radclyffe Hall, Eliot, Graves, Pound and Yeats" (AO, 126), Winterson's close alliance with modernist experiment and her endorsement of its continued relevance for the present is unwavering: "To say that the experimental novel is dead is to say that literature is dead. Literature is experimental. Once the novel was *novel*; if we cannot continue to alter it [...] then we can only museum it" (AO, 176). Experimentation must be embraced and kept alive. This, however, not through nostalgia for the grand old days of modernist avant-garde, and much less so by slavish imitation of the modernist forefathers and foremothers, but rather through a commitment "to a fresh development of language and to new forms of writing" (AO, 177).

Marked by their poetic, lyrical focus on word-repetition and set imagery, symbolic structures and one overriding theme—the exploration of love as indeed a many-splendored thing in its various facets and expressions—Winterson's seven novels from her debut, *Oranges Are Not the Only Fruit* (1985), to her *The.Power.Book* (2001), are very much of one piece, a fact which she herself showed as deliberate on her part: "They are only separate books because that's how they had to be written."[52] Crucial for their thematic concerns is Winterson's openly lesbian sexual orientation, and her apostasy from her parents' strict Pentecostal Evangelic faith. Her first, semi-autobiographical novel bears testimony to her upbringing in a repressively religious family from a small-town England. Its fairly straightforward plotline of the *Künstler-roman* subgenre type is enriched by interpolations of fairy-tale and mythical elements, with its eight chapters structured after the first eight books of the Old Testament (Genesis through Ruth). As critic Lynn Pyket has noted, Winterson's first novel is "a portrait of the artist as a young, working class lesbian who flees the nets of religion and community" in order to become "an artist-prophet." Like Joyce's *Portrait*, Winterson's novel is less a form of self-expression than of self-invention.[53]

Winterson's next novel *The Passion* (1987) features a plotline composed of two parallel stories, both centred around two marginal witnesses to the Napoleonic wars: Henri, a French soldier who ends up as a chicken-neck wringer and personal cook to Napoleon, and Villanelle, who works at the casino as a croupier until she is sold by her husband as army prostitute. The wide-ranging intertextuality employed by Winterson, playful echoes of *A Portrait*, are evident throughout.

During his long imprisonment, Henri resorts to diary-writing, in which he writes of his love for (the increasingly subjective and constructed) Villanelle—the genre of course of Stephen Dedalus' first creation (in turn produced by his love for Emma C—). Where Stephen Dedalus' contemplation of a 'bird-girl' inspired him to write his short lyric poem of Italian-French origin, Henri falls in love with Villanelle, an Italian woman who works for the French. Henri, like Joyce's Stephen, builds his own textual labyrinth and

---

52 Margaret Reynolds, "Interview with Jeanette Winterson," *Jeanette Winterson: The Essential Guide*, eds. Margaret Reynolds & Jonathan Noakes (London: Vintage, 2003) 25.

53 "*Oranges* is not simply the story of the making of the artist, and of the artist's journey towards her position as exiled visionary [...], but it is also, in its form, an embodiment of that artist's aesthetic" (Lynn Pyket, "A New Way with Words? Jeanette Winterson's Post-Modernism," *I'm Telling You Stories: Jeanette Winterston and the Politics of Reading*, eds. Helena Grice & Tim Woods [*Postmodern Studies 25*, Amsterdam/Atlanta: Rodopi, 1998] 58).

begets himself (or so he believes) as an artist in the concluding passages of
A Portrait:

> I re-read my notebook today and I found: I say I'm in love with her, what does that
> mean? It means I review my future and my past in the light of this feeling. It is as
> though I wrote in a foreign language that I am suddenly able to read. Wordlessly she
> explains me to myself; like genius she is ignorant of what she does. I go on writing so
> that I will always have something to read. (*P*, 159)

As Susana Onega has noted in her study, references go well beyond these
obvious parallels: "The logical implication of this intertextual relation is
that Villanelle and by extension the fantasy world she represents are only
figments of Henri's imagination, a reading that enhances the psychological
interpretation of Villanelle as a projection of Henri's ideal woman."[54] Winterson's *The Passion*, thus, posits Joyce's *A Portrait* as an intertext that holds the
key to the text's important semantic dimension.

Written on the Body (1992) features, in a nod to Brophy's *In Transit*, a narrator of unidentified gender whose bisexual orientation leaves him/her gen-
derless throughout the text. Winterson's is a highly unreliable narrative voice
who repeatedly insists on the fictionality of his/her account, and also one
with a proclivity for obsessive parody – accordingly, the novel's key intertext
is Dylan Thomas' *A Portrait of the Artist as a Young Dog*, in itself a parody of
Joyce.

Gut Symmetries (1997) combines together the intertwined stories of three
narrator-characters, Alice (Alluvia), Jove, and Stella, its narrative propelled
by the baroque effect of repetition and excess. The plotline is divided up to
eleven chapters entitled after Tarot cards, in imitation of the Celtic Cross
Spread symbol. The novel's symbolism, again drawing heavily from archetypal psychology, features the mirror as a central unifying element. In a late
scene, upon looking at herself, Stella reveals a compound mirror image of
three juxtaposed faces: her own, and those of an older woman and a younger
shadow man. This reflected image of three-persons-in-one is an emblem both
of the complex nature of each individual and of "The Eternal Triangle" from
the climax of the novel, constituted by Alice, Stella, and Jove, whose archetypal model is the Holy Trinity.

Finally, *The.Power.Book* (2001), a text graphically engaging with the aesthetics of electronic computerised writing, features a series of narrative
interpolations which together form a spatial organisation; storytelling, here,
is ruled by the internet principle that "there is always a new beginning, a different end" (*PB*, 4). Consequently, the story of the love-affair between two

---

54 Susana Onega, *Jeanette Winterson* [Manchester: Manchester University Press, 2006] 75.

women referred to as Ali/x and Tulip, is arranged as a web of thematically related stories that can be accessed, interacted upon, abandoned, and reopened at will by narrator and narratee, as if, notes critic Susana Onega, "they were links in a hypertextual network."[55] The novel's intertexts are *A Thousand and One Nights*, and Jorge Luis Borges' short stories dealing with the labyrinthine (e.g., "The Garden of Forking Paths"). The embedded stories are each introduced by a computer command, such as OPEN HARD DRIVE (which presents a reworking of *Orlando*'s androgyny), SEARCH, VIEW AS ICON, or EMPTY TRASH. For all its narrative variegation, the concluding vision insists on the novel's (and, potentially, the entire Winterson canon's) single narrative line: "a single story of love: the true history of the world" (*PB*, 244).

5.5 "GREAT ART SHOULD NOT MOVE": ALASDAIR GRAY

Alasdair Gray's *Lanark: A Life in Four Books* (1981)—a most detailed and imaginative reworking of Joyce's methods and techniques in *A Portrait* and early *Ulysses*—came as a culmination of the development of the 1970s Glasgow Group (authors such as James Kelman, Tom Leonard, and Liz Lochhead). Three years later, *Lanark* was followed by *1982: Janine* (1984). Sharing some highly idiosyncratic poetics, the two novels will be discussed here together. Their Joycean credentials were acknowledged by the author himself on numerous occasions, most outspokenly in a 1986 interview with Kathy Acker. Here is Gray on *Lanark*'s early beginnings:

> At an early age I wanted to write a Great Book, and kept starting, but each time I read what I'd written I saw my words were those of a child. [...] But when I went to Glasgow Art School in 1952 I had read or was reading Joyce's *Portrait of the Artist*, Joyce Cary's *The Horse's Mouth*, also Orwell's *Nineteen Eighty-four*, most of Kafka and Waley's translation of *Monkey*, the comic Chinese Buddhist epic.[56]

Written over a period of almost thirty years, *Lanark* merges a fictional rendering of contemporary Glasgow with a nightmarish account of its decadent future, featuring a prophetic vision of a dystopian society in which the masses are governed by an elite who systematically perpetuates their gradual dehumanisation. *1982: Janine,* was written, according to its author's explicit statement, in a fashion contrary to his aesthetics:

---

55   Onega, *Jeanette Winterson*, 182.
56   Kathy Acker, "Alasdair Gray interviewed," *Edinburgh Review* 74 (1986): 83.

When I began writing it in 1982 [...], the monologue swelled up by taking in matters I had never intended to use in a book, for I agree with James Joyce when he says that great art should not move, that only improper arts (propaganda and pornography) move us, but true art arrests us in the face of eternal beauty, or truth, or something like that. But this particular story started discoursing of improper things: sex fantasies I had meant to die without letting anybody know happen in this head sometimes, and political diatribes.[57]

Lanark's four "books" are chronologically displaced and, in addition, interpolated with a prologue, an interlude, an epilogue, and a "tailpiece." Its narrative landscape is peopled with second-hand characters drawn from "existing literature" – so much so that its "Index of Plagiarisms" runs down the side-margin of a good 15 pages of its epilogue. In fact, a whole new categorisation of "literary theft" is required:

BLOCK PLAGIARISM, where someone else's work is printed as a distinct typographical unit, IMBEDDED PLAGIARISM, where stolen words are concealed within the body of the narrative, and DIFFUSE PLAGIARISM, where scenery, characters, actions or novel ideas have been stolen without the original words describing them. To save space these will be referred to hereafter as Blockplag, Implag, and Difplag. (*L*, 485)

Couched between "Imperial Gazetteer of Scotland" and "Kafka, Franz" is "Joyce, James" whose *A Portrait* is credited with having inspired "crude Difplag" in "Chap. 22, para. 5" (*L*, 490–1). That this device is meant as a timely deflection of criticism, making a virtue of necessity, and not, as some critics would have it, as his self-conscious alignment with "postmodernism," has been pinpointed by Gray himself on more than one occasion, as for instance in conversation with Mark Axelrod:

I have never found a definition of postmodernism that gives me a distinct idea of it. If the main characteristic is an author who describes himself as a character in his work, then Dante, Chaucer, Langland, and Wordsworth are as postmodern as James Joyce, who is merely modern.

In the same breath, Gray pinpoints typography as the cornerstone of his literary experiment.[58] Typography, graphic devices, and illustrations are also

---

57   Acker, "Alasdair Gray interviewed," 84.

58   "I use a variety of typefaces where this makes the story clearer. [...] In *1982 Janine*—an interior monologue novel—the speaker has a nervous breakdown conveyed by three columns of different typefaces on the same pages, each a stream of thought or feelings at war with the rest. I do not know how else I could have done it" (Mark Axelrod, "An Epistolary interview, mostly with Alasdair Gray," *Review of Contemporary Fiction* 15.2 [Summer 1995]: 113).

essential to the meaning-conveyance in *Lanark*, as Glyn White's essay in his study devoted to *Reading the Graphic Surface* has shown. The already mentioned chronological displacement (also largely typographical, advertised by the sumptuously adorned full-page frontispieces preceding each of the books) serves the function of alienation. Having the books appear in the sequence 3, 1, 2, 4 complicates the relationship between the central character(s) — Duncan Thaw and Lanark — who would otherwise seem to develop one into the other in the numerical ordering of the books. The broken chronology, however, also suggests a possibility fully explored in critic Stephen Bernstein's take on *Lanark*, based on the novel's subtitle emphasising "a," i.e., "one" life, thus treating the two lives as one, or as conjoined, a possibility "leading most readers to look for ways in which these two lives might comment upon one another."[59]

The commentary is provided by the Prologue (*L*, 107–117), which occupies the crossover point or hinge between the Lanark and Thaw narratives, containing the auto-narration of the life of the oracle, a financier who fades out of existence to become a disembodied voice and resurface as the narrator of the story of Thaw, comprising the gist of Books One and Two. Further connectivity is established by the typographic consistency of the text, applying equally to the fantastic and realistic narratives.[60] Gray's use of italics as an indicator of handwriting is motivated, as he explains to Axelrod, by his belief that italic "is a type based on hand-writing rather than Roman chiselling."[61] Capitalised text, then, is most often used to suggest a fictional source by appearing to mimic it; or to represent (not reproduce, as B. S. Johnson would) the display typefaces from adverts. Reproduced, and rather faithfully so, are a fictional road sign (e.g., *L*, 385) and the recurrent "EMERGENCY EXIT" sign (*L*, 376, 378, 381). Another typographical convention are the variable running headers; e.g., the Prologue features the headers across each double page spread in sequence, so that they make up a poem. Last but not least, testifying to Gray's primary vocation as a visual artist are illustrations, which cover five full pages: a frontispiece and the title pages to each of the four books.

What is more, *Lanark*'s metatextual interplay applies not only to the larger units of the individual books or characters; it also involves units smaller than the sentence, bringing about what White has called "a situation in which *Lanark* is on occasions haunted by itself."[62] Early on, there are five frag-

---

59 Stephen Bernstein, *Alasdair Gray* (Lewisburg: Bucknell University Press, 1999) 36.
60 Thus, in White's account, "capitals are used, like italics, for emphasis of speech but with the added connotation of superficiality; the bold text is not representationally motivated and the use of this type clearly emphasises the borrowed status of these words; bold type is used in a second way to indicate something about volume" (Glyn White, *Reading the Graphic Surface* [Manchester: Manchester University Press, 2005] 170–1).
61 Axelrod, "An Epistolary Interview," 111.
62 White, *Reading the Graphic Surface*, 192.

ments of "bodiless voices conversing against the clamour" (*L*, 64) recorded by Lanark (inhabiting a corrections institute at the time), all of which are verbatim quotes from passages interspersed throughout the rest of the novel. Additionally, there are further, less obvious linkages: for instance, on page 181, Thaw overhears a phrase which resurfaces two hundred pages later in a dialogue between Rima and Lanark. The point of this cross-referencing, as with typography or intertextuality, is an indication of *Lanark*'s aesthetic concern with achieving simultaneity through spatial distribution of fragments – what White calls "a fracturing of time, showing that moments in the lives of Thaw and Lanark are simultaneous [...], that *the whole book* is in some sense simultaneous."[63] This aesthetic concern is a technique markedly modernist (and essentially Joycean).[64] The experimental use of typography in *Lanark* is one route for its investigation of textual power – this can also hark back to the "Index of Plagiarisms," running along the main body of text of the Epilogue, struggling for its space as much as striving to classify the various kinds of literary "thefts" and predations.[65]

Analogously to *Lanark*, *1982: Janine* also includes an "Epilogue for the discerning critic" which, among a plethora of others, credits "O'Brien's *At Swim-Two-Birds*, Nabokov's *Pale Fire*, and Vonnegut's *Slaughterhouse-Five*" as models of "an elaborate fantasy within a plausible everyday fiction," and "night town scenes in Joyce's *Ulysses*" as contributing to the formation of "the rhythms and voices" (*J*, 333–4) of its eleventh, most estranged chapter. However, the economy of its temporal-spatial situatedness in one mind in one hotel room during one night's drunken phantasmagoria, as well as this mind's obsessive narrative, brimming with qualifications, self-interruptions, and meta-commentary, can be most fully attached to Beckett's trilogy or monological drama. Jock McLeish is unable to keep the details of his own

---

63 White, *Reading the Graphic Surface*, 199.
64 Dominic Head develops this point by stressing the ideology of the plot's redoubling: "The novel's twin settings, Glasgow and the dystopian fantasy City of Unthank, suggest the two poles – realism and fantasy – between which Gray locates the impetus of his writing. The median position thus established represents a simultaneous challenge to the two fictional codes. The received history of the realist code is disrupted in a famous passage in which Glasgow is said to be neglected in artistic representations, and so unavailable for imaginative inhabitation. At the other extreme, the novel's fantastic elements suggest the dangers of the unfettered imagination, where escapism is in the ascendancy" (Head, *Modern British Fiction, 1950-2000*, 149).
65 In Randall Stevenson's acute analysis, *Lanark*'s playfulness ultimately serves a serious, anti-illusionary political message: "The real achievement of Lanark is not in seducing readers with illusion, but in allowing them to escape from it; in forcing them to consider conjuring and to examine and experience imagination as process rather than securely finished product. Since Lanark fails in his attempt to save the city, its redemption, if any, lies out with the text, in the continuing processes of imagination of readers, empowered by Gray's dystopian fantasy to recognise the destructive forces which prey upon the life of modern industrial cities, and on Glasgow's more than most" (Randall Stevenson, "Alasdair Gray and the Postmodern," *The Arts of Alasdair Gray*, eds. Robert Crawford & Thom Nairn [Edinburgh: Edinburgh University Press, 1991] 61).

life safely disjunct from the story he tells and even at moments of highest entrancement by his "Superb" erotic heroine, he must pause to ask himself: "Why does this imaginary stuff seem familiar? IMPORTANT DIFFERENCES BETWEEN SUPERB AND MY FORMER WIFE [...] Superb is imaginary. Helen was real. Why can't I keep them apart? [...] I wanted to keep fantasy and reality firmly separate" (J, 33, 41). As an instance of interior monologue *par excellence*, it is not difficult for a critic like Stevenson, never one to miss an opportunity to engage in historical labelling, to posit a postmodernist departure from *Janine*'s modernist heritage.[66] Labels aside, apart from exploding the modest, almost puritan sexual coyness of *Lanark* into a full-blown pornography with sodomy or cunnilingus galore, *Janine* also positions itself as a far more outspokenly political text. Sometimes, these are combined, as in the dialogues between McLeish and Sontag, one of his imaginary lovers – here, broaching the subject of the police brutality and the sorry fate of Ulrike Meinhof:

> "Are you aware that the Parisian police commissioner has publicly advised raped women not to take their complaint unaccompanied to a police station, since they are in danger of being raped again?" [...] "But you have read of the death by hanging of the Meinhof girl in that strangely insecure German max-security prison. Did you know that the official investigators found dry semen between her thighs? Did the warders fuck her then hang her, or hang her then fuck the corpse?" (J, 50–1)

The protagonist's escapism into (auto-)erotic fantasy and self-gratification—indeed, any kind of escapism from "ordinary life"—is shown by Gray to be of a political nature:

> But if I had told her the truth about my politics she would have spent hours trying to convert me and I was having a hard enough time protecting my fantasies from her. If she succeeded in connecting them to ordinary life she would make me feel responsible for every atrocity from Auschwitz and Nagasaki to Vietnam and the war in Ulster and I REFUSE TO FEEL GUILTY ABOUT EVERYTHING. (J, 56)

---

66 "Modernism's epistemological concerns fretted over fissures between mind and reality, and a concomitant crisis in language was defined and fuelled by Ferdinand de Saussure's linguistics [...] showing signifier and signified, word and world, related only arbitrarily. *Finnegans Wake* illustrates one extension of this thinking, its language, detached from a secure representative function, forming instead an autonomous world of its own. An extension of another sort appears in the growth of the genres of science fiction and fantasy throughout the twentieth century. If reality cannot be wholly known, nor language any longer conceived as tightly connected to it, why should not words be used to create other worlds?" (Stevenson, "Alasdair Gray and the Postmodern," 56–7).

Just as *Lanark* combined dull-realist Thaw/Glasgow with the eerily surreal Lanark/Unthank, *Janine*'s two different fictional accounts of the same "real" demonstrate the entanglement of erotic fantasies with the miserable political reality of colonial Scotland – what Will Self's preface terms Gray's "socialist unrealism" (*J*, xvii). The overall masturbatory obsession of *Janine* can be seen as a metaphorical re-enactment of the proverb (of Gray's own coinage) that ran the length of *Lanark*: "*Man is the pie that bakes and eats himself and the recipe is separation/hate*" (*L* 62, 101, 411, 188). Gray's political agenda consists in rejecting the idea of individual recognition at the expense of others and advocating collaboration among, rather than exploitation between, individuals. In *Janine*, Gray takes a step further in promoting the connection between the political and psycho-sexual.

By foregrounding, in Cairns Craig's political reading, typography as "the symbol of [Scotland's] own culturally repressed condition" in which "to overthrow the rule of type is synonymous with overthrowing the type of rule under which the culture has struggled for self-expression,"[67] Gray's experimental texts have paved the way for a continuing tradition of textual and typographical experiment in recent Scottish writing. *Lanark* and *Janine* have, over the twenty years from their publication, become paradigm-defining texts for writers as different as Irvine Welsh, the layout of whose *Marabou Stork Nightmares* (1995) or *Filth* (1998) sways toward the "purely" ludic and gratuitous, as well as Janice Galloway, whose *The Trick is to Keep Breathing* (1989) uses various typographical devices in a more mimetic service to depiction of trauma. This rich variety provides ample evidence that the revival in Scottish literature inaugurated by Gray at the beginning of the 1980s has spawned its own tradition.

5.6 "GRAFTING, EDITING: QUOTATIONS, CORRESPONDENCES": IAIN SINCLAIR

Iain Sinclair is a Cardiff-born, Trinity College-educated, and London-based contemporary counterpart to James Joyce's Dublin-based (re-)constructions, Sinclair the parallel to Joyce the paragon—"parallel," not "epigone." For just as Joyce famously created his fictional Dublin from the distance of his European exile in the three very different cities of Trieste, Zurich, and Paris, then so does Sinclair—from his own, albeit less distant, exile in the heart of the Albion metropolis—update and upgrade Joyce's methods from a particular angle, tangential, oblique, and transverse. As Julian Wolfreys' monumental,

---

67 Cairns Craig, *The Modern Scottish Novel: Narrative and the National Imagination* (Edinburgh University Press, 1999) 181.

three-volume compendium on *Writing London* shows, at the heart of the Albion metropolis lies a similar doubling, elusiveness, and spectrality: "London is not a place; it cannot be placed," insists Wolfreys, "it is a fluid city, a city of singular, endless flows, unavailable to any generalization, summarization, or finite identification."[68] At the forefront of the group of contemporary fictional psychogeographers of London stands Iain Sinclair, whose writing of the past four decades has been devoted to charting the maps of London City and Environs past and present, real and fantasised, so meticulously as to secure its full reproducibility should some cataclysmic future event wipe the city off the face of the earth.

Sinclair's work also represents—for most criticism as a solitary *flâneur,* in his own view as part of a vanguard group of such fellow travellers as J. H. Prynne, Douglas Oliver, or Peter Ackroyd—a continued line of influence from William Burroughs' eight-year London sojourn between 1966 and 1974. Sinclair has drawn comparisons with Burroughs especially for his early, dark and hallucinatory explorations of urban London, past and present, both in poetry (*Lud Heat*, 1975, and *Suicide Bridge*, 1979) and prose (*White Chappell, Scarlet Tracings*, 1987). His clearest alignment with the Beats took place as much on paper as in real life. He became the amanuensis of the Dialectics of Liberation Congress held at the Roundhouse in Chalk Farm in July 1967, whose participants included Allen Ginsberg, R. D. Laing, Gregory Bateson, Digger Emmet Grogan, Herbert Marcuse, and Lucien Goldmann. The patchwork of Sinclair's own reminiscence and transcriptions from film and tape—transcribed interviews, poetry-readings, lectures, and debate—came to form the gist of his self-published *The Kodak Mantra Diaries: Allen Ginsberg in London* (1971).

In critic Ben Watson's estimation, the importance of Sinclair's ties with the Beat movement cannot be overstated.[69] In his indebtedness to Burroughs, Sinclair seems on a par with Ballard, another distinctly urban writer of the dark London, however, where Ballard's vision remains distinctly fantastic and only loosely based on the city's real geography, Sinclair takes a far more matter-of-fact approach to both the city's sacred and profane sites, its liminal passages, its underbellies and peripheries (in space), as well as its occult

---

68   Julian Wolfreys, *Writing London* (New York/London: Palgrave MacMillan, 2004) 4.

69   "Modernism's epistemological concerns fretted over fissures between mind and reality, and a concomitant crisis in language was defined and fuelled by Ferdinand de Saussure's linguistics [...] showing signifier and signified, word and world, related only arbitrarily. *Finnegans Wake* illustrates one extension of this thinking, its language, detached from a secure representative function, forming instead an autonomous world of its own. An extension of another sort appears in the growth of the genres of science fiction and fantasy throughout the twentieth century. If reality cannot be wholly known, nor language any longer conceived as tightly connected to it, why should not words be used to create other worlds?" (Ben Watson, "*The Kodak Mantra Diaries*: The Politics of Sinclair's Poetics," *The Work of Iain Sinclair*, eds. Robert Bond & Jenny Bavidge [Cambridge Scholars Publishing, 2007] 83).

histories, its phantom pasts and past phantoms (in time). Whereas Ballard is the visionary of London's possible (dystopian) futures, Sinclair is the meticulous cartographer of its spaces excluded from traditional mapping, and the recorder of its past, repressed or excluded from official history. Thus, *White Chappell, Scarlet Tracings* introduces a group of rare book dealers in search for documentation of Jack the Ripper and other Victorian sadists all across London, and *Downriver; or, The Vessels of Wrath* (1991) takes the reader on a twelve-part roller-coaster ride through the depths of London and the dark souls of its denizens. Another story of an unusual Londoner, this time centred on one protagonist, is the 1999 *Rodinsky's Room*, on which Sinclair collaborated with Rachel Lichtenstein. The two authors used alternating chapters and their own voices to present the life of David Rodinsky, a reclusive inhabitant of the London synagogue attic, where he worked as caretaker and from which he mysteriously disappeared.

A general preoccupation with the fantastic recurs throughout Sinclair's oeuvre in a highly individualised fashion, for Sinclair's psychogeographical project is steeped in occultism, if not of his making, then of his choosing and adapting. Already in his 1975 book-length poem *Lud Heat*, Sinclair launches the process of drawing divinatory lines on maps, which partly dictates his approach towards cultural formation and its poetics. The two axes delineating this mapping are Sinclair's experiences as an assistant gardener with the Parks Department of an East London borough, and the "sacred landscape" delineated by the churches of Nicholas Hawksmoor. "The most notable thing that struck me as I walked across this landscape for the first time," Sinclair recalls in conversation with Kevin Jackson, "were these run-down churches, and I suddenly realised, there's this one here and that one there, and maybe there is some connection. And then I did have this very vivid dream of St Anne's, Limehouse..." (*V*, 98).

One is struck, in turn: "a vivid dream"? "Maybe some connection"? More often than not, Sinclair's progression in his cognitive mapping operates on the principle, "That was my hunch: confirmation followed" (*LH*, 28). Adopting this approach, Sinclair positions himself as heir to the ancient Celtic tradition of the poet as soothsayer, of the bard with the power to alter reality through his word. As he confided to Jackson:

By nature and temperament I'm absolutely one of those mad Welsh preachers who believes that... deliver a speech and you'll change someone's life. Or kill them. I really believe all that, but I can't go around spouting that and survive, so I'll adapt equally to the Scottish side of me, which is cynical, rational and cynical, and I believe in that as well. [...] It's Stevenson, the classic Scottish Jekyll and Hyde thing. One is really deranged and manic, the other is looking at it being deranged and manic, and commenting on it. That's the tension. (*V*, 59)

Sinclair's walk around Hawksmoor's London churches in *Lud Heat* reveals a "web printed on the city and disguised with multiple superimpositions," a web "too complex to unravel here, the information too dense: we can only touch on a fraction of the possible relations. [...] It is enough to sketch the possibilities" (*LH*, 16–7). Drawing upon Alfred Watkins' theory of the ley line, according to which the ancient sites in England and Wales are mutually aligned, thus forming a network of straight routes of communication, Sinclair creates willed ley lines across a chosen area (in *Lud Heat*, this produces a "hieratic map" of London), which generate in his texts a wealth of occult materials for Sinclair to carefully counterpoint with local, matter-of--fact accounts.

The ley line as one of Sinclair's signature tropes has been amply demonstrated in the many prose works that followed *Lud Heat* and *Suicide Bridge*. For instance, his 1997 *Lights Out for the Territory*, a collection of nine loosely collected perambulatory pieces, describes lighting out for various London nooks familiar and obscure, forgotten and re-remembered. As Sinclair himself reveals halfway through, the seemingly random extravagations actually serve a specific purpose – his project of map inscription:

> Each essay so far written for this book can be assigned one letter of the alphabet. Obviously, the first two pieces go together, the journey from Abney Park to Chingford Mount: V. The circling of the City: O. The history of Vale Royal, its poet and publisher: an X on the map: VOX. The unheard voice is always present in the darkness. (*LOT*, 156)

Revisiting this theory in the opening of his novel, *Landor's Tower* (2001)— where the story of a historical figure, Walter Savage Landor, is interwoven with Sinclair's frustrated attempts to write a book about him, along with a subplot about booksellers hunting for rare editions—Sinclair encapsulates Watkins' lesson in the following formula: "everything connects and, in making those connections, streams of energy are activated" (*LT*, 2). Later on, Sinclair makes it explicit that his practice of psycho-geographical fiction is steeped in modernist poetics of juxtaposition and collage:

> All of it to be digested, absorbed, fed into the great work. Wasn't that the essence of the modernist contract? Multi-voiced lyric seizures countered by drifts of unadorned fact, naked source material spliced into domesticated trivia, anecdotes, borrowings, found footage. Redundant. As much use as a whale carved from margarine, unless there is intervention by that other; unless some unpredicted element takes control, overrides the pre-planned structure, tells you what you don't know. Willed possession. (*LT*, 31)

Such is Sinclair's rumination on what the modernist heritage for the present might be: empiricism and encyclopaedism ("drifts of unadorned fact, naked source material"), presented as polyphony ("multi-voiced lyric") and design ("pre-planned structure") open to "intervention by that other," an "unpredicted element." Another example of Sinclair's use of pre-existent, commonplace modern ley lines is *London Orbital: A Walk around the M25* (2002), Sinclair's spiritual travelogue of his walk around the M25, a road that forms the boundary of London, which provides a springboard for his free-form reflections on the most sundry subjects.

A most recent, compelling example of factual-fictional accounts of Sinclair's voyages outside of London is his *Edge of the Orison* (2005). Encompassing the genres of memoir, biography, art theory, and literary criticism, it follows the journey undertaken in 1841 by poet John Clare who—after escaping from a lunatic asylum in Epping Forest—walked for three days to his home in Helpston, (then) Northamptonshire, some eighty miles away. Having "imagind that the worlds end was at the edge of the orison & that a day's journey was able to find it," Clare tellingly conflated "orison" (prayer) with "horizon," bespeaking the indivisible closeness of his poetic vision with a sense of place. Sinclair's retracing of these and other "uncertain tracks that are visible only if you insist on them" is beset with the coincidental, those "unpredicted elements that override the preplanned structure" (celebrated in *Landor's Tower*), starting with Clare's grave, whose "weathered tomb-lid" features the Horatian dictum rewritten as "BORN NOT MAD" (*EO*, 24). Indeed, the madness of John Clare, the peasant poet out of his time and place, is revealed as resulting from his exposure to the London literary establishment, which undid him by turning a farm labourer and versifier of the English countryside into a commodity, a "Peasant Poet" soon out of vogue, securely placed in a "cabinet of curiosities" and thereby "destroyed." (*EO*, 98).

Walking in Clare's footsteps gradually reveals a whole series of relationships linking Sinclair (whose name near-contains Clare's: 'Sin-Clare') and his wife Anna (born Hadman, the book's dedicatee) with the peasant poet. The rumoured kinship between Anna's ancestry and Mary, Clare's wife, is doubled with the claim of a blood-tie between Anna's father and Clare himself. Sinclair's travelogue thus merges with a personal memoir and genealogical search for family roots. Following his aesthetics of free association and imagist juxtaposition, Sinclair uses the fact that Clare spent his last years at the Northampton asylum, and the coincidence that his journey to Helpston took place in pursuit of his first love, a certain Mary Joyce, in order to draw a ley line between his central quest and the chronicling of Lucia Joyce's institutionalisation at the same asylum, 110 years later:

What happened to Lucia Joyce in Northampton? Can her silence be set against Clare's painful and garrulous exile? Visitors came to the hospital to pay their respects, to report on the poet's health. Biographers of Lucia cut out, abruptly, after she steps into the car at Ruislip and drives north, never to return. (*EO*, 233)

Lucia's father surfaces in Sinclair's musings at the most unexpected instances. For instance, upon pondering the river Lea, Sinclair's mind makes the sudden imagist switch to:

> Djuna Barnes, profiling James Joyce, zoomed in on his "spoilt and appropriate" teeth. And that is this stretch of the Lea, precisely: spoilt and appropriate. Hissing trains. Occasional apologetic herons (all spindle and no heft) tipping out of dead trees like faultily assembled kites. Nothing spectacular, nothing to stop your advance on Broxbourne. "Writers," Joyce told Barnes, "should never write about the extraordinary, that is for the journalist." But already, she was nodding off. "He drifts from one subject to the other, making no definite division." (*EO*, 141–2)

Following the oneiric and phantasmal poetics of Sinclair's textual ley lines, Joyce first enters Sinclair's text through a dream dreamt at a Northampton Hotel, which is a rendering of Stephen's dream of the wraith of his dead mother:

> In the Northampton ibis, I dreamt; re-remembered. The drowning. Weaving back, no licence required, on my motor scooter: to Sandycove, the flat beside Joyce's Martello tower. Wet night. A tinker woman had been pulled from the canal. Drunk. The smell of her. My first and only attempt at artificial resuscitation, meddling with fate. Met with: green mouth-weed, slime, bile, vomit. [...] Woodfire on wasteground within sight of a busy yellow road. Bring someone back from death and you're landed with them. (*EO*, 234)

Sinclair's Joycean re-remembering is complete with its Martello tower setting, its textual echoes, its linguistic ("woodfire on wasteground") as well as narratological markers. When Sinclair reveals that his first meeting with his wife Anna in 1962 took place in Sandymount, dreaming becomes re-remembering. The "drowning" in which Sinclair is primarily interested here, however, is Lucia's – which brings forth another tangent, another ley line, pointing toward Beckett:

> James Joyce (always) and Beckett (at the beginning) constructed their works by a process of grafting, editing: quotations, submerged whispers. Correspondences. Joyce read other men's books only to discover material useful to his current project. Libraries were oracles accessed by long hours of labour: at the cost of sight. The half-blind Beckett, aged twenty-two, reading to a man in dark glasses (waiting for the next operation). A theatrical image reprised in Beckett's play *Endgame*. (*EO*, 234–5)

Sinclair's ley-line network of correspondences and energies stretches well beyond mere blood kinship. Echoing Stephen's own troubled relationship with his ancestry, both biological and spiritual, is Sinclair's technique of blending Joyce's photographs with reveries and memories of his male ancestors. The memory of "magnifying glass over etymological dictionary: blood-globe, headache. [...] Stub of period moustache, just like my father" segues into memories of footage of his soon-to-die grandfather, and then back to Joyce again: "This man, a doctor, is very tired. He performs a reflex ritual, perhaps for the last time: remembering how to lift an arm. A moment that parallels Gisele Freund's 1938 photograph of Joyce in a deckchair. More dead than alive. Moving image showing to a still: bleaching to nothing" (*EO*, 234–5). Here as elsewhere, Joycean reminiscences serve Sinclair the particular autobiographical purpose of revisiting and coming to terms with his own past. In this re-remembering, Joyce's ghost becomes Sinclair's grandfather and he himself a ghost of his own father. "He himself?" (*U* 1.156).

Still, the setting is Northampton and the focus remains not so much on the "cold, mad, fiery" Father as on the Daughter. "Drowning" is the metaphorical ground for the ensuing flights of Sinclair's metaphorising fancy. Having observed earlier that "one of Lucia's cabal of expensive doctors, Henri Vignes, prescribed injections of sea water, to no evident effect" (*EO*, 235), Sinclair establishes the following line: "In mid-England, mid-journey, flying and drowning become confused. Drowning and writing. Dreaming and walking. *Finnegans Wake*: Lucia searching out words for her father, the book for which she is the inspiration. The problem."[70] The issue becomes one of "inspiration" in *Finnegans Wake* as well as in his own *Edge of the Orison*, where "drowning and writing" become equivalent to "dreaming and walking."

Interestingly enough, Sinclair here bypasses the common anxiety-of-influence Oedipal drama of literary ancestry, undermining Joyce's authority by identifying himself not with Joyce's fictional alter ego Stephen, but with his real-life, silenced and traumatised daughter Lucia, and "the pain of her involvement with *Work in Progress*," corroborated by the Father Himself in a remark recorded by Ellmann: "People talk of my influence on my daughter, but what about her influence on me?" (*JJ*, 684) Again, Sinclair turns to reminiscences (re-inventions, he calls them) of his own family, adding to the already numerously superimposed plains of linkages yet another layer: re-

---

70   Sinclair continues: "Joyce asks Lucia to look at the song 'Dublin Bay', to change it: the young couple must not be drowned. The man will bide his time at the bottom of the sea, then rise to the surface. Joyce, fond father, continued to believe that Lucia, dosed on sea-water, would swim back to him, to health. Hospitals taught her to breathe underwater. [...] She visited Jung. He couldn't help. There was an unresolved argument with the author of *Ulysses*: a book that dared to trespass on his territory. [...] 'If Joyce was diving into a river,' Jung said, 'Lucia was falling.' Voluntary or involuntary immersion: it depends on who is telling the tale" (*EO*, 238).

membering his aunt in Ballsbridge, Sinclair recalls that she had a connection
with Beckett, whose lectures in Trinity she attended. Then, Sinclair pulls the
final chef-d'oeuvre rabbit out of his magician's hat of magical correspondences: "When Beckett arrived in Paris, he carried a letter of introduction to
Joyce, written by Harry Sinclair. His Aunt Cissie (mother's sister) married
William 'Boss' Sinclair" (*EO*, 241). Bloodline, as all other lines of connection,
calls for reflection: "If there is common blood with Beckett, however diluted,
so much the better. I won't investigate it. I salute him as a great walker, out
alone in all weathers, or with his father, tramping the Wicklow Hills."[71]

Joyce's own work as well as life stand Sinclair in good stead, offering a tex-
tual/biographical ley line between two otherwise non-communicating entities: Clare and Lucia, the mad poet and the mad daughter. The author of the
famous poem "I AM" who later in life claimed to be Byron and Shakespeare;
the daughter of the famous father, who later in life claimed her father was
"watching us all the time," from "under the ground" (*JJ*, 743). Toward the end
of the journey, Sinclair pays his respects to Lucia when passing Kingsthorpe
Cemetery. Ever on the lookout for the aleatory epiphany, before making the
turn, "up the slope to where Lucia is buried, I find a nice marker, the grave of
a certain Finnegan" (*EO*, 347).

Analogously to Joyce's fictional psychogeographies, *Edge of the Orison* is
a centrifugal text that flees from London, while never breaking free from the
centre's spell and gravitational pull. Similarly to Joyce's *Finnegans Wake* and
Clare's *Journey out of Essex*, the text of *Edge of the Orison* poses as a letter from
one spouse to another, and conflates travelling in space and time with writing
with and across texts: its punctuated, short-sentenced prose re-enacting the
rhythms of walking; its meandering, freely-associative narrative guided by
the whimsical workings of memory. Sinclair's fictional biography of his wife
Anna combines with a travelogue of their journeys in the footsteps of the
Mad Poet and exploration into the sinuous histories of ancestries both biological and spiritual. *Edge of the Orison* also stands as a memorial to Joyce's silenced daughter, to Sinclair's creative revisitation and advancement of her
father's literary heritage.

These consist in mapping and bearing witness to the singularity of specific urban spaces and their multiple temporal traces, which have no other connection than the fact that particular events or types of events have occurred

71   Sinclair continues: "Elective affinities: I acknowledge Beckett, from the period of *Murphy*, as
a notable London psychogeographer. James Knowlson tells us how the frustrated novelist
trudged for hours through streets and parks, making a narrative of the city. [...] Reading the
Beckett biography, I came to understand how relationships are based on shared topography,
not mere accidents of blood. Beckett had preceded us to the asylums of London's orbital fringe.
Samuel Beckett was ahead of us, every step on the way: his silence, his eagle stare (the poster
portrait, in the alcove outside the bathroom, that terrified my children)" (*EO*, 242–3).

in the same location (Lucia and John Clare) or via ley lines, whether physical, textual, or genealogical. Where Sinclair differs from Joyce is the performative dimension of his tracings, counterpointing the structuralist paragon (Joyce studying from exilic distance directories for addresses, encyclopaedias for hard facts, and dictionaries for words with which to relate back to his home elsewhere) with a poststructuralist parallel, an open transversal across and through the homeless here and now.

A writer concentrating many diverse lines of influence, combining and transgressing genre and form boundaries, Sinclair's lifelong project of charting the maps of London City and Environs present and past, real and surreal, relays a unique literary endeavour that is at once most idiosyncratic and original, while also profoundly and self-consciously experimental in its pursuit of the material of memory as construed from the materiality of language. Sinclair's ultimate shared commonality with Joyce consists in how for both, the materiality of history becomes translated as the materiality of the letter.

5.7 CONCLUSION: JOYCE EVERYWHERE AND NOWHERE

Despite the palpable lapse of literary experiment following the disintegration of B. S. Johnson's literary circle, certain genre-writing (Aldiss, Ballard), feminist fiction (Winterson, Carter), but also a few mavericks devoted to their own idiosyncratic textual/thematic literary enterprises (Brooke-Rose, Gray, and Sinclair) have kept the materialist linguistic poetics of Joyce (as well as that of his contemporaries) alive, if not exactly kicking in Britain. In systematising Joyce's importance for the British fiction of the last two decades of the twentieth century, the present account challenges the blanket dismissal from his Morton Levitt's *Modernist Survivors* (repeated with variations elsewhere), according to which

> with Johnson's death Britain has lost its sole significant novelist who had been influenced by Joyce [...], the one serious novelist of his generation who had been fearless of "experiment" and of being linked with the Modernists, the creator of a developing canon who almost alone in the land had shown promise of further and challenging development. [...] Albert Angelo is dead, and his creator is dead, victims, in a sense, of their hostile surroundings. But the Neo-Victorian novel of Britain, in the third decade now of its dominance, appears to live on, its critics, practitioners and audience still unaware, it would seem, that it was stillborn.[72]

---

72   Morton P. Levitt, *Modernist Survivors* (Columbus: Ohio State University Press, 1987) 72.

Levitt's generalisation that the "stillborn" Neo-Victorian realist mode has presented the most relevant, or indeed the only, path to be taken by the British novel between 1975 and 2000, is a gross oversimplification. For that, the British novel's orientation, ideological agenda, stylistics, typographical innovation, and linguistic poetics are too broad-ranging, its range of returns to—and departures from—the modernist Joycean tradition of treating language as material, too diverse. However, to merely demonstrate Levitt's summary as simplistic and reductive is not enough, because there is a grain of truth to Levitt's argument: British innovative fiction from 1980s onward very seldom—as was Johnson's case—defined itself against the narrative conventions of the nineteenth-century realist novel.

Following the vast literary synthesis and eclectic miscegenation of the stylistic techniques and narrative strategies of the previous decades, Joyce's presence within the British fiction of the 1980s and 1990s has become virtually all-pervasive, yet together with it also neutralised, dispersed, sometimes well-nigh invisible. This topic will be revisited in the Conclusion to this book.

6.
"THE FUNNYMENTAL NOVEL OF OUR ERROR": JOYCE IN AMERICAN FICTION, 1973–1997

The long post-war period of literary production in the U. S. mapped in chapter three was one whose protagonists were solitary creators. It was in the mid--1970s that this picture of the literary landscape was to change dramatically. For both fiction and poetry, this was a time of collective radicalisation and political commitment, in reaction to what had been the United States' most socio-politically turbulent decade in the history, which critic Kenneth Millard has summed up neatly as follows:

> The years of the Nixon administration, 1969–74, was perhaps the crucial period in recent American history, years that saw the culmination of an extraordinary period of social upheaval which had included the assassinations of John F. Kennedy in 1963, Malcolm X in 1965, Martin Luther King in 1968, and Robert Kennedy in 1969, and which also saw the Apollo moon landing of 1969, the Kent State University shootings in 1970, and the unique disgrace of the resignation of President Nixon in 1974.[1]

The protracted and ultimately disastrous war in Vietnam (1965–75), then, was a mere pinnacle of what historian Paul Kennedy has characterised as "the massive transformation in the nation's self-understanding which took place during those same years," Vietnam functioning as its practical and symbolic consummation:

> In so many ways, symbolic as well as practical, it would be difficult to exaggerate the impact of the lengthy campaign in Vietnam upon the national psyche of the American people. [... It] helped to cause the fissuring of consensus in American society about the nation's goals and priorities, was attended by inflation, unprecedented student protests and inner city disturbances, and was followed in turn by the Watergate crisis, which discredited the presidency itself for a time. [... The effects] were interpreted as a crisis in American civilisation.[2]

For many, the turning point in the post-war development of both society and literature had occurred even before the war broke out. As Federman has

---

1   Kenneth Millard, *Contemporary American Fiction* (Oxford: Oxford University Press, 2000) 6.
2   Paul Kennedy, *The Rise and Fall of the Great Powers* (New York: Random House, 1987) 404–5.

argued, if the 1950s writers were known as "the silent generation" due to their "expressed silent agreement with the official political, moral, and social attitudes of the State," then the writers working in the aftermath of November 22, 1963 found themselves in a markedly different social environment:

> This is why the assassination of JFK (public and televised) had such a traumatic impact on the American consciousness. Suddenly things were not as good as they appeared. Suddenly American people were doubting the very reality of the events they were witnessing, especially on television. It took certain blunders of the Johnson administration, and subsequently the manipulations and lies of the Nixon admin, and of course the Vietnam War, and the Watergate debacle to awaken Americans from its mass media state of illusion and optimism. (*SF*, 24–5)

In addition to political precarity, fiction found itself having to cope with its internal tensions, the situation of "The Death of the Death of the Novel,"[3] so-called by critic Jerome Klinkowitz, where in which reactions to John Barth's seminal "Literature of Exhaustion" essay were chiefly twofold. First, the so-called "New Journalist" movement led by Tom Wolfe and including writers like Norman Mailer or Truman Capote; second, the kind of experimental writing pursuing a new aesthetic for fiction, beyond Barth's precepts, including writers like Richard Brautigan, Steven Katz, Robert Coover, Kurt Vonnegut, or Ronald Sukenick. For both, Klinkowitz argues, a disruption in the "tradition of the great American novel" was necessary were they to develop or even survive.[4]

The "disruption in tradition" observed by Klinkowitz did not cease once the 1960s dust had settled, but kept taking place in the course of the 1970s and well into the 1980s. Nor did it fully supplant the metafictional experimentation dominating the U.S. fiction prior to 1968. It follows from Chapter Three that many of the 1960s pioneers of American experimental fiction were actively publishing well into the 1980s and 90s. Unlike in Britain, where the sense of disconnect between the "avant-garde" generation of the 1960s and 70s (i.e., the B. S. Johnson "circle," brought to its end with B. S. Johnson's and Ann Quin's 1973 suicides) and the second-generation experimentalists (such

---

3   Jerome Klinkowitz, *Literary Disruptions: The Making of a Post-Contemporary American Fiction* (2nd edition, Urbana Chicago London: University of Illinois Press, 1980) 1.

4   "Without a radical disruption in its tradition, the novel might have sustained grievous injury in the late 1960s, a universe away from the times in which fiction was first conceived and the rules for it set. Yet despite all the cultural and historical innovations in topic, it was the old-fashioned *form* for its content—in the guise of a mimetic pretense at life—which was the most debilitating thing of all. [...] To John Barth's valid case for the exhaustion of old narrative forms Robert Coover, Steve Katz, and Richard Brautigan added a new aesthetic for the novel: not just the reporting of the world, but the imaginative transformation of it" (Klinkowitz, *Literary Disruptions*, 32).

as Alasdair Gray or Iain Sinclair) is a tangible one, in the U.S. there is no clear sense of generational sequence, and even less so of a gap or disparity. Nonetheless, 1973 saw Raymond Federman's coinage of the term "surfiction," followed next year by the founding of the Fiction Collective (including, among others, Ronald Sukenick), which formed the first American not-for-profit publishing collective run by and for innovative authors, and will present a convenient starting point in the following chronological arrangement.

The Fiction Collective was started in 1974 when Jonathan Baumbach, Peter Spielberg, Mark Mirsky, Steve Katz, B. H. Friedman, and Ronald Sukenick founded a cooperative fiction publishing venture, venting their discouragement at the stern editorial and marketing strictures of commercial publishing, in Spielberg's memorable phrase, at "literature defined by a committee, books designed by cereal packagers, marketed by used-car salesmen [...] and ruled or overruled by accountants."[5] As Baumbach later recalled, the need for the collective sprang from the conviction that "fiction that redefined the rules, innovative and experimental work, was having the most trouble finding a home in what was clearly (though unacknowledged) a publishing establishment increasingly attuned to the bottom line."[6] Having formulated an editorial protocol, according to which six books were to be published annually, three in the spring and three in the autumn, with the editorial board acting both as authors / editors, and printers / distributors, the Fiction Collective found its manifesto in Ronald Sukenick's *New York Times Book Review* column, "Guest Word," in September 1974:

> The Fiction Collective will make serious novels and story collections available in simultaneous hard and quality paper editions [...] and will keep them in print permanently. The Collective is not a publishing house, but a "not-for-profit" cooperative [...] the first of its kind in this country, in which writers make all business decisions and do all editorial and copy work.[7]

From the five founding fathers, the Fiction Collective grew over the next ten years to encompass over forty published writers, its most notable publications including Sukenick's *98.6*, Marianne Hauser's *The Talking Room*, Raymond Federman's *Take It or Leave It*, Steve Katz's *Stolen Stories*, Clarence Major's *My Amputations*, and Fanny Howe's *Holy Smoke*, among others.

However, by the mid-80s, its massively expanded editorial board made collective decision-making difficult, and the Reagan administration's clamp-

5   Qtd. in Ted Pelton, "How, and How Not, to be a Published Novelist" *Federman's Fictions – Innovation, Theory, Holocaust*, ed. Jeffrey R. Di Leo (Albany: SUNY Press, 2011) 41.
6   Qtd. in Pelton, "How, and How Not," 42.
7   Ronald Sukenick, "Guest Word," *New York Times Book Review* (Sept 15, 1974): 55.

down on culture funding curtailed its grant-funding. And so, in late 1989, a slightly altered sexumvirate featuring Curtis White, Ronald Sukenick, Mark Leyner, Jonathan Baumbach, B. H. Friedman, and Peter Spielberg re-organised the press, rewriting the constitution to create Fiction Collective Two (a.k.a. FC2), a non-profit, author-run press with two editorial offices, one at the University of Colorado at Boulder run by Don Laing, and another at Illinois State University in Normal run by White. Soon a new imprint—Black Ice Books—was launched, designed as "a merging of the avant-garde with the popular" (White),[8] thus promoting an "avant-pop" aesthetic, enjoying national review attention and lively sales of its first titles like Mark Amerika's *The Kafka Chronicles* and Samuel Delany's *Hogg*. As FC2, the revised Fiction Collective has been active to the present day, publishing over two hundred titles by more than one hundred authors over the forty-five years of its existence, with all editorial decisions still made by the authors themselves and virtually all Fiction Collective and FC2 titles still in print. In retrospect, Brian McHale characterised the venture as anticipating the network communities in the digital age of the web:

> The Fiction Collective is not now, and never has been, an aesthetic school or movement on the model of the historical avant-gardes of the first half of this century. It was founded, rather, to serve as an alternative network of distribution and promotion, and so has more in common with current online discussion lists and linked Web-pages than it does with more recognizably school-like phenomena such as Language poetry or 1980s Cyberpunk.[9]

The present account will restrict itself to two of FC2's most Joycean writers, Raymond Federman and Ronald Sukenick, but first—an uncharacteristic detour into the field of poetry.

6.0 "'REALISM,' THE OPTICAL ILLUSION OF REALITY IN CAPITALIST THOUGHT": LANGUAGE POETRY

The poetry digression is necessary for the simple reason that the "disruption in tradition" à la Klinkowitz took place as much in prose as in poetry, as evident from perhaps the most lively revival of Jolas' *transition* avant-garde project in the late-1970s/early-1980s American literary production: the

---

8   For more cf. the exhaustive "The Fiction Collective Story" by Jeffrey DeShell, R.M. Berry, Lance Olsen, and Matthew Kirkpatrick. Online on the Fiction Collective 2 website: https://www.fc2.org/about/

9   Brian McHale, "Sukenick in Space, or, the Other Truth of the Page," *Musing the Mosaic: Approaches to Ronald Sukenick*, ed. Matthew Roberson (New York: SUNY Press, 2003) 139.

language poetry movement. The movement was organised around and channelled through L=A=N=G=U=A=G=E magazine, which ran thirteen issues from 1978 to 1981 under the co-editorship of Bruce Andrews and Charles Bernstein, and featured the work of poets as diverse as Ron Silliman and Lydia Davis, Clark Coolidge and Douglas Messerli, Lyn Hejinian and Tom Raworth.

In retrospect, the two chief editors defined the L=A=N=G=U=A=G=E magazine—in terms similar to those of Jolas' transition—as "a forum for writing that places its attention primarily on language and ways of making meaning, that takes for granted neither vocabulary, grammar, process, shape, syntax, program, nor subject matter" (LB, ix). L=A=N=G=U=A=G=E, just as transition, aimed at blending poetic theory and thereby challenging generic conventions and possibly intervening into the socio-political by means of "exploring the numerous ways that meanings and values can be (& are) realized—revealed—produced in writing" (LB, ix). The primary concern, again as with transition, is primarily an aesthetic one: with "repossessing the word," restoring to verbal expression its non-codified and non-fetishised properties. Similar also were the two projects' social goals: the creation of a community as a shared space for articulation, and the control of the means of production. Also alike was the extent to which they were circumscribed by their socio-historical circumstances: Jolas' transition dissolved together with the disintegration of the Parisian inter-bellum literary scene and democracy, and the language group moment(um) receded together with the erasure of the Cold War political configuration in the early 1990s.

However, similarities stretch as far as here, and hence, differences proliferate. Revisiting transition, it was not so much in the footsteps of the Jolasian/Joycean project of "the revolution of language" that the language poets chose to follow, but its near-opposite counterpart: Gertrude Stein's experiments in syntactic variation and verbal minimalism. Ron Silliman's "Disappearance of the Word, Appearance of the World" describes the logic of late-capitalist commodity fetishism when applied to conventional descriptive and narrative forms as one in which "words cease to be valued for what they are themselves but only for their properties as instrumentalities leading us to a world outside or beyond them." Language in this capitalist stage of development undergoes "an anaesthetic transformation of the perceived tangibility of the word," to the benefit of "its descriptive and narrative capacities," regarded as "preconditions for the invention of 'realism,' the optical illusion of reality in capitalist thought." What language poetry seeks to combat is the commodified tie between "reference" and its deformation in "referentiality" (LB, 125), by posing as a "philosophy of practice in language" and "searching out the preconditions of post-referential language within the existing social fact"

(*LB*, 131). Although Stein and Joyce are mentioned in the same breath, it is clear that Stein's undermining of the "assumption that the free evolution of a narrative art, as such, is possible" by means of her "continuous present" is preferred to Joyce's "reintegration of the novel into language," whose usefulness, for Silliman, is questioned by Joyce's arguably "pre-Saussurean linguistics, that of etymologies" (*LB*, 128–9).

In "The New Sentence," Silliman voices his belief that the historical failure of linguistics to consider the sentence is related to the general tendency under late capitalism to ignore the materiality of language and writing. Silliman pushes the analysis further by claiming that the control exercised at the level of the sentence participates in the restrictive organisation of society as a whole. The ideology of the sentence is such that in its "hypotactic and complete" form, the sentence "was and still is an index of class in society" (*IAT*, 569). Silliman's opposition to such control consists in the effort to maintain the sentence as the focus of attention. In place of hypotaxis, he places parataxis. This mode is not new in itself: Silliman cites as precursors the "fragmented" sentences of Stein's *Tender Buttons*. What is newer or at least reaches beyond the oftentimes reductive accusation of "anti-referentiality" is Silliman's "increased sensitivity to syllogistic movement," which enables works of the new sentence "a much greater capacity to incorporate ordinary sentences of the material world, because here form moves from the totality downward, and the disjunction of a quoted sentence from a newspaper puts its referential content (a) into play with its own diction; (b) into play with the preceding and succeeding sentences [...]; and (c) into play with the paragraph as a whole" (*IAT*, 573).

If "language writing" means anything, Silliman concludes, it is "writing which does focus the reader onto the level of the sentence and below, as well as those units above." The new sentence is ultimately designed to oppose what Silliman views as the "deliberate" late capitalist exclusion—from linguistic as well as literary analysis—of "certain elements of signification, such as reference and syntax." This opposition takes place by means of incorporating "all the elements of language, from below the sentence level *and* above" (*IAT*, 575) – a discursive all-inclusiveness not unlike the Jolasian construction of multilingualism within one language. Still, it is precisely its explicit indebtedness to Stein's exploration of repetition and syntactic minimalism that stands at the root of the crucial difference between the two poetic programmes, marking off the language movement most clearly as different from Jolas' revolution of the word. If Jolas' *transition* chose to combat the rise of nationalism and fascism by positing artistic cosmopolitanism and the Joycean multilingual idiom, then the group of poets around the *L=A=N=G=U=A=G=E* magazine resisted the commodity logic of late capitalism—whose chief effect upon language has been described by Ron Silliman as the "Disappearance of the Word"—by revisiting the legacy of Stein's syntactic innovations and positing a "New Sentence."

The question remains, as critic Marjorie Perloff has put it, "whether the calling into question of 'normal' language rules, or received discourses [...] is a meaningful critique of capitalism,"[10] or indeed whether the same goal can be achieved through resistance against the commodification of language by means of "post-referential" writing. Still, there are a number of writers whose work suggests that the avant-garde heritage of James Joyce's *Ulysses* and *Finnegans Wake* did play a pivotal part in the various conceptualisations of the tasks of fiction in the period in question.

6.1 "THAT LEVEL OF ACTIVITY THAT REVEALS LIFE AS FICTION": RAYMOND FEDERMAN

Raymond Federman's work, in language, style, and subject matter, presents the clearest link between 1970s U.S. fiction and developments in French post-war literary avant-garde, especially the *nouveau roman*.[11] Experimental in nature, but ultimately humanist in theme, Federman's fiction deals with the experience of death and survival, and a very concrete one.[12] In his essay "Before Postmodernism," Federman would not only tie his own writing career with a treatment of his Holocaust trauma, but would go so far as to argue that "postmodernism as a literary notion was invented to deal with the Holocaust."[13]

---

10   Marjorie Perloff, "The Word as Such: L=A=N=G=U=A=G=E Poetry in the Eighties," *The Dance of the Intellect: Studies in the Poetry of the Pound Tradition* (Evanston: Northwestern University Press, 1985) 234.

11   Federman's biographer has summed up the roots of his fiction as follows: "Building on the work of (James) Joyce, (Louis-Ferdinand) Celine, (Samuel) Beckett, and other twentieth-century masters, his fictions are fascinating constructs that combine a brilliant style, unorthodox typography, and a masterful new approach to the development of characters and literary structure. [...] Unlike the traditional novel, these works are not intended to be representations of events; they are events in their own right, language events that reflect on their own mode of becoming and that, in effect, critique themselves. [...] Federman questions the very nature of fiction, the fiction writer, and the reality that the writer's language is supposed to represent" (Welch D. Everman, "Raymond Federman," *Dictionary of Literary Biography Yearbook: 1980* [Farmington Hills: Gale Group, 1981] 201).

12   Born in the Parisian suburb of Montrouge of a Jewish ancestry, Federman underwent a traumatic encounter with the Nazi Holocaust when in the summer of 1942, the Gestapo entered his family's apartment, taking his parents and his two sisters to the death camps. The 14-year-old Raymond, whom his mother had hidden in a closet, was the only survivor.

13   Federman continues: "The prewar split between form and content was incapable of dealing with the moral crisis provoked by the Holocaust, and therefore writers like Beckett, Walter Abish, Ronald Sukenick, Primo Levi, Raymond Federman, Jerzy Kosinski, and many others, invented Postmodernism to search among the dead, to dig into the communal grave, in order to reanimate wasted blood and wasted tears [...] or perhaps simply in order to create something more interesting than death" (C, 122).

In 1947, Federman moved to the U.S. – English was a language he only learned as an adult. In America, Federman embarked on an academic career,[14] gradually coupled with his essayist work. His introduction to the seminal collection of essays entitled *Surfiction: Fiction Now and Tomorrow* (1975) can be read as a critical/theoretical programme accompanying Federman's works of fiction. Federman opens by yet another, then-fashionable denunciation of the "death of the novel" proclamation, arguing that, in its traditional form, this type of novel "is very *healthy* today" – and yet his primary interest lies in "that fiction which the leaders of the literary establishment brush aside because it does not conform to *their* notions of what fiction should be; that fiction which supposedly has no value [...] for the common reader" (S, 6–7). Like Johnson in Britain or Robbe-Grillet in France, Federman is adamantly opposed to the notion of "experimental fiction," arguing that the label serves as an umbrella term for "what is difficult, strange, provocative, and even original," and yet it is misleading in that "true experiments (as in science) never reach, or at least should never reach, the printed page." Hence:

> Fiction is called experimental out of despair. Samuel Beckett's novels are not experi-mental—no! it is the only way Beckett can write; Jorge Louis Borges' stories are not experimental; Joyce's fiction is not experimental (even though it was called that for some 30 or 40 years). All these are successful finished works. (S, 7)

For the kind of fiction that "tries to explore the possibilities of fiction," that "challenges the tradition that governs it," that "constantly renews our faith in man's imagination and not in man's distorted vision of reality," Federman instead proposes the name SURFICTION, based on the avant-garde notion of 'sur'-reality: "Just as the Surrealists called that level of man's experience that functions in the subconscious SURREALITY, I call that level of man's activity that reveals life as fiction SURFICTION" (S, 7). Federman's coinage seeks to abolish the mimetic, fiction-as-reality's-mirror duality: fiction is no longer to be regarded "as a pseudorealistic document that informs us about life," but should instead be judged "on the basis of what it is and what it does as an autonomous art form in its own right" (S, 8).

Having proposed a new notion, it now remains for Federman to deter-mine its functioning and applicability, this by means of four propositions, addressing the four related issues of its reception, shape, material, and meaning. Since the "very act of reading a book," to Federman's mind, has

---

14   Federman earned his PhD at U.C.L.A. in 1963, his dissertation published in book-form in 1965 as *Journey into Chaos: Samuel Beckett's Early Fiction*. This dissertation marked only the beginning of Federman's life-long fascination with Beckett, followed by no fewer than four other scholarly works in the course of the next fifteen years.

become "*boring* and *restrictive*," he calls for a questioning, challenging, and ultimate "demolishment" of the traditional method of reading, this in order "to give the reader an element of choice (active choice) in the ordering of the discourse and the discovery of its meaning" (*S*, 9). Hence, what is called for is concrete prose, a text of distinct visual and spatial properties:

> That space, the page (and the book made of pages), must acquire new dimensions, new shapes, new relations in order to accommodate the new writing. And it is within this transformed topography of writing, from this new paginal (rather than grammatical) syntax that the reader will discover his freedom in relation to the process of reading a book, in relation to language and fiction. (*S*, 9–10)

Given that, in surfiction, life and fiction should become indistinguishable, the linear shape of the narrative "is no longer possible," to be supplanted by a "digressive shape of fiction" whose elements will now "occur simultaneously and offer multiple possibilities of rearrangement in the process of reading," and the discourse will "circle around itself, create new and unexpected movements and figures in the unfolding of the narration," projecting itself backward and forward "along the curves of the writing" – and the extra-literary parallel/paradigm here is the cinema of Jean-Luc Godard (*S*, 11).

Following from this is proposition number three: Federman posits "no limits to the material of fiction—no limits beyond the writer's power of imagination and beyond the possibilities of language." Hence, fiction should not be hampered by the necessity of producing "the well-made-personage who carried with him the burden of a name, a social role, a nationality, parental ties, and sometimes an age and a physical appearance," which should be replaced by "a fictitious creature who will function outside any predetermined condition," who "will be, in a sense, present to its own making" (*S*, 13). Last but not least, what becomes clear from the previous three propositions is that the meaning of the new fiction "will not create a semblance of order," but instead "offer itself for order and ordering," involving the active participation of the reader who "will be the one who extracts, invents, creates a meaning and an order for the people in the fiction," rather than "having simply received, passively, a neatly prearranged meaning" (*S*, 14). What is striking about Federman's four propositions for the purportedly new "surfiction" is that all of them could be quite easily and aptly applied to *Finnegans Wake*. Federman chooses not to draw upon any distinct genealogy or ally his project with any individual predecessor; instead, he identifies a broad companionship of his contemporaries, according the pride of place to Beckett.[15] Why Joyce should

---

15   "I am not alone in these wild imaginings. Many contemporary writers, each in his own personal 'mad' way, have already successfully created the kind of fiction I tried to define in the preceding

not have figured in Federman's surfictionist "manifesto" (despite receiving a few honorary mentions elsewhere in the collection) would become clear in his early-90s essay collection entitled *Critifiction: Postmodern Essays*.

In the opening essay, "Fiction Today or the Pursuit of Non-Knowledge," Federman opposes Sartre's notions of literature involved with the crisis of conscience and consciousness by arguing that instead, "the literature of the last 45 years concerned itself with itself, with literature, with the crisis of literature, with the crisis of language and of communication, with the crisis of knowledge, and not with social and political problems" (*C*, 5). This crisis of literature results in literature becoming "the explanation of why the writer cannot write, why he constantly confronts the failure of expression and communication, why he can no longer represent the world faithfully and truthfully," a dilemma encountered by "many writers throughout the first half of the twentieth century, especially those who were considered avant-garde: James Joyce, Franz Kafka, Louis-Ferdinand Céline, André Gide, Thomas Mann, John Dos Passos, William Faulkner, and Jean-Paul Sartre himself" (*C*, 6). To these are opposed Proust and Beckett who share "a feeling that something is wrong with literature, something is wrong with the act of expressing" (*C*, 7). Federman's crisis of literature turns out a crisis of knowledge.[16]

Today's New Fiction, the plot emerges, seeks to "avoid knowledge deliberately, particularly the kind of knowledge that is received, approved, determined by conventions" (*C*, 9). It is here that Federman acknowledges predecessors other than Beckett – in the visual arts the "epistemological crisis" began in painting which "through Impressionism, Cubism, and Constructivism blurred the lines of the real, and eventually reached total abstraction, that is to say the total erasing of reality." In fiction, the process was slower since "realism (the great imposture of illusionism) held fiction captive" – with the important exception of "James Joyce's *Finnegans Wake* which outrageously blurred meaning by dislocating words and syntax to become a gigantic verbal edifice of unreadability" (*C*, 12). This point is repeated and

---

pages: Samuel Beckett, of course, in French and in English, Jorge Louis Borges and Julio Cortazar in Spanish, Italo Calvino in Italian, Robert Pinget, Claude Simon, Philippe Sollers, Jean Ricardou, Jean-Marie Gustave Le Clézio, and many others, in France, and in their own individual manner, a number of American writers such as John Barth, John Hawkes, Ronald Sukenick, William Burroughs, Donald Barthelme, Richard Kostelanetz, Jerzy Kosinski" (*S*, 14).

16   "Since the Greeks, literature has constituted itself as the vehicle of knowledge in the form of apologies, commentaries, amplifications on other texts, decorations or explanations of knowledge. In other words, literature was an affirmation of faith, of certitude in knowledge. [...] Beckett's novels seem to progress in exactly the opposite direction, retracting knowledge, cancelling knowledge, dragging us slowly and painfully toward chaos and meaninglessness. [...] This is also the case with most works of contemporary fiction known as avant-garde or experimental. The more pages we accumulate to the left as we read a novel, let's say by Alain Robbe-Grillet or Walter Abish, the less we seem to know" (*C*, 8–9).

further solidified in the next essay, "Self-Reflexive Fiction and How to Get Rid of It" – where the self-reflexive novel is portrayed as a "troublesome, irritating, exasperating form of narrative" that is now finished, the question being, "What have we learned from it?" (*C*, 17). Federman traces the development of post-war US fiction through the conservative, "silent" 50s through the period of self-reflexivity in the 1960s, and down to the New Fiction of the 1970s. Of the 1960s self-reflexive novel, he notes that although "the syntax remains normative, discursive, and even linear, and the narrative metonymic," still some of "the novels written during that period are audacious in terms of their subject matter," what Federman terms their "*irrealism.*"[17]

However, one writer does stand out as sounding the knell of "the terms that define modernist fiction – that is to say, [...] the formalism (stream of consciousness, interior monologue, psychological depth, syncopated syntax) associated with the inscribing of the subject into a fictional text" (*C*, 21) and that writer is William Burroughs with his cut-up technique. It is in his footsteps that the New Fiction writers emerging after 1968 follow, writing what Federman terms *critifiction*:

> Their fiction may not be as political as his, but nonetheless is subversive, for these writers are less interested in parodying the world or mocking history than transforming the language through which the world and history are represented. [...] Many novels written in the 1970s read more like essays than pure fiction, or what I call *critifiction*: a kind of narrative that contains its own theory and even its own criticism. (*C*, 31)

Prominent among these are Ronald Sukenick, Walter Abish, and Gilbert Sorrentino (of the writers considered here), alongside Steve Katz, George Chambers, or Clarence Major. These writers, Federman suggests, enter into a ludic relationship with their readers, constantly questioning "the very act of using language to write fiction, even at the risk of alienating the reader" (*C*, 32). Again, the spectre of the *Wake* looms high, again to be dismissed:

> The New Novelists abandon the search for stable points of reference in reality and in history, abandon also the purely formalistic temptation that dominated literature before WWII and ultimately led to James Joyce's *Finnegans Wake*, certainly the greatest unreadable linguistic tour de force ever written. [...] Gradually the stable syntax and

---

17   "In the novel of the 1960s, where official history is mixed with the picaresque and burlesque adventures of the individual, where characters have no other substance than their fictitious personalities since they exist only as verbal beings, the author denounces the symbolic strata that shape history and the individual. Most of these novels propose nothing, they only illustrate the fact that reality is but a fraudulent verbal network, for to replace one reality with another is a senseless undertaking, because one merely substitutes one symbolic system for another" (*C*, 26).

the readable irony of the early parody-novels of the 1960s are disintegrated into a form
of deliberate unreadability not unlike that of *Finnegans Wake*, not simply for aesthetic
reason, however, but for subversive reasons. (*C*, 33)

Federman's binary opposition of "aestheticism" versus "subversion" is
highly dubious, as the "revolutionary" Jolasian project alone clearly shows.
Especially since the "subversion" of such texts as Abish's *Alphabetical Africa*,
Reed's *Mumbo Jumbo*, Sorrentino's *Mulligan Stew*, Sukenick's *Long Talking Bad
Condition Blues*, or Federman's own *The Voice in the Closet* lies in "their extreme
self-reflexivity and their typographical 'exuberance,'" which raise "fundamental questions about the role of fiction today" by exposing "the fixation of
desires in language" (*C*, 34).

Federman's first novel, *Double or Nothing* (1971, 1976), is a "typographically
exuberant" text *par excellence*, described variously as a multi-layered, bleakly
comic work whose plot focuses on a young French immigrant who, having
lost his family in the concentration camps, emigrates to America and is
gradually initiated into a strange new world, simultaneously with an inventor's creation of these "events." The narrative is construed as taking place by
means of multiple mediations and removes: the immigrant's story is told by
a would-be author who imbricates his narration with narrative interferences
from his own life, as well as intertwining the narrative with comments on the
writing process itself. At least two additional voices are added to the layering, producing a potentially infinite regression of narrators. There are four
primary ones: "the recorder" (designated by the first-person pronoun), "the
protagonist" (third person), "the inventor" (second person), and "the author"
("that is to say, the *fourth* person"). Curiously enough, the rationale behind
this *dramatis personae* arrangement was only divulged in Federman's next
novel, *Take It or Leave It*:

> This first novel [...] juggles four "voices": first, a rather stubborn and determined mid-
> dle-aged man who decides to record word for word the story of another (second) man,
> rather paranoid and confused, who decides to lock himself up for a year (365 days,
> more or less), subsisting entirely on noodles (that's right), in order to write the story of
> yet another (third) young man, shy and naive, who comes from Europe (perhaps from
> France) to America and who (if the second voice can pull itself together sufficiently
> to write and be recorded by the first voice) will experience various adventures and so
> on but who must for the time being wait until he is charactered – all of which implies
> a fourth voice managing the glorious, sacred, gimmicky confusion craftily jumbled.
> (*TILI*, 361)

As critic Jerzy Kutnik, author of the first book-length study on Federma-
n's and Sukenick's "surfiction," has observed, all these narrative gimmicks

are "eventually reduced to one general problem, which is not so much how to tell this multilayered story convincingly and truthfully, but how to begin telling it at all."[18] The narrative layering becomes gradually so thick that the first person's presence in the "story" becomes undetectable since he exists exclusively through what the second person thinks, says, or does and what he then records "to the best of his ability and as objectively as possible" (*DN*, 00). Federman advertises the fact that within the fictional realm, the protagonist is nothing without his inventor and recorder:

> As for the second person, the one who suffers of paranoia, the gambler, the one who has decided to lock himself in the room for 365 days, his task is much more difficult than that of the first person [...]. The [hero] is nothing in the double setup, the interplay between the first and the second person; as a matter of fact, unless the second person invents him, and the first person records him, he will never become anything. (*DN* 000, 00000)

The theme, as will become Federman's trademark, is the erasure of history and memory, on both mass and individual scales perpetrated through the Holocaust.[19] Typography stages this regression by presenting each page as a complete visual unit. The book is presented as two hundred and two pages of concrete typescript, hence presenting the book as "its own becoming."[20] Federman's solution to the task (of coping with the "unreal reality" of so much of American life) lies in his technique of creating a reality more real: the reality of the book itself. His "real fictitious discourse" (the book's subtitle) is not a sham illusion of some imaginary "real" life beyond the word on the page, but rather just what it says, so many words on so many pages, bound together as a book held in the reader's hands and the unfolding of narration as taking place in the reading process. What critic Marcel Cornis-Pope has termed Federman's "use of the second person as a self-problematizing technique"[21] can be clearly sensed in passages such as the following (and throughout the text):

---

18 Jerzy Kutnik, *The Novel as Performance: The Fiction of Ronald Sukenick and Raymond Federman* (Carbondale/Edwardsville: Southern Illinois University Press, 1986) 182.

19 In Kutnik's words, "the recorder is able to render concretely the unspeakable truth of the past which both memory (the protagonist) and imagination (the inventor) fail to articulate simply by means of typographical symbols: the parenthetical '(XXXX)' which, more powerfully than any words, conveys the reality of the young survivor's erased past" (Kutnik, *The Novel as Performance*, 184–5).

20 Klinkowitz speaks of a "uniquely personal claim to legitimacy" in which "Federman is covered: no shoddy tricks or trumped-up illusion of reality, just so much writing" (Klinkowitz, *Literary Disruptions*, 177).

21 Marcel Cornis-Pope, "From Cultural Provocation to Narrative Cooperation: Innovative Uses of the Second-Person in Raymond Federman's Fiction," *Style* 28.3 (Fall 1994): 414.

you? crazy/or irresponsible Rooms and suitcases that/? fine but a tenor saxophone
that? too/ much Rooms and suitcases it ? living/in one place and traveling someti-
mes/A whole life ? contained between/rooms and suitcases The room ? you ? in one
place The suitcases that you ?/from one place to another That ? the way to ? movement
Movement in/time The time element ? important/too Space and time in other words.
(*DN*, 198)

Klinkowitz notes that Federman's splitting of the authorial, fictional voice up
into thirds runs counter to its "degradation" in the New Novel "back to this
zero point," as well as to its preoccupation with the phenomenology of perception: "Phenomenologists, including Maurice Merleau-Ponty, and many
critics of the French structuralists as well, have regretted that we must deal
with a second-order language, divorced from the thing signified but living
only insomuch as it points back to that thing."[22]

    Take It or Leave It (1976), Federman's second novel in English, is an extended
reworking of his French novel *Amer Eldorado*. A note on the title page calls it
an "exaggerated second-hand tale," whose plot concerns a young French immigrant in the U. S. Army (Frenchy), who has thirty days to travel from Fort
Bragg, North Carolina, to a ship that will take him to Korea, but who must
set out north to upstate New York to retrieve some crucial army papers. The
nameless first-person narrative is constantly interrupted by faceless audience
members and literary critics (the "tellers"), providing the text with Federman's staple meta-critical commentary. The underlying theme, again, is the
Holocaust, and the experience of the exile and the notion of their unrelatabi-
lity; as one of the comments has it, "all fiction is digression" and "a biography is
something one invents afterwards" (*TILI*, 97), particularly in a case like Federman's, where the imperative is to retranslate continually his life story into new
narrative patterns and languages. Both autobiographically and symbolically,
the narrative persona projected by Federman is a "schizotype" that "rides two
languages (-/-) who humps (x/x) two languages at the same time" (*TILI*, 186).
The situation of Federman's exile also underscores the text's preoccupation
with America – here portrayed as land of (largely wasted) opportunity:

No idea what America was about (who does?), geographically speaking (that is), no
idea particularly of the size. Yes! Endless spaces and tremendous colors. Wow! Unbe-
lievable the colors and the spaces [...]. You've got to see that to believe it [...] ENOR-
MOUS distances – between places! Between people too! Between words also And all

---

22   Klinkowitz ties this phenomenological concern on Federman's part to his Beckettian interests:
    "From his studies of Samuel Beckett, Federman knows that literature fails when it claims to
    represent the other, so in his own novel he simply lets it represent itself. As such it is a system,
    an esthetic one, but by claiming to be nothing else it becomes a real entity" (Klinkowitz, *Literary
    Disruptions*, 178).

these people (all these words) all of them Americans who look (what a way to start!) at you, who scare you shitless who scare the hell out of you. (*TILI*, 19)

By means of his "tellers," Federman puts his narrative experiments in dialogue with similar contemporaneous advances in, e.g., the *Tel Quel* group: as he explains, this novel pits "the singled narrator's voice (varied and disguised, to be sure)" against "those of various unnamed but easily identifiable others (the TEL QUEL boys, some odd strangers, plus everyone else Hombre has even known or imagined)" (*TILI*, 361). The traditional triumvirate of narrator-hero-reader is redefined here as main teller, character-teller, listener, to suit the economy of a "recitation," a term borrowed from Beckett that designates a self-conscious, histrionic activity combining memorisation with invention, oral production with the rewriting of pre-existing scripts. Indeed, the most pronounced presence, in Federman's narrative experiments, of Beckett's dramatic monologues is acknowledged in a passage where his own version of narrative purgatory is called (with a word borrowed from *Finnegans Wake*) a "Bethickett," a Beckett-made thicket: "all good story tellers go to BETHICKETT on the way to Heaven and that is why perhaps they are so long in reaching their destination" (*TILI*, 176).

Federman's *The Voice in the Closet* (1979), published in a bilingual English-French (*La voix dans le cabinet*) edition together with "Echoes" by *Tel Quel*'s Maurice Roche, is the most voluble testimony to both Federman's bilingualism and to the biographical and deeply personal basis of his writing. It ranks among Federman's staple book-objects: a visual art-book without pagination, consisting of twenty pages with eighteen lines per page and sixty-eight characters per line. From this constricted form—which parallels the physical constriction of a closet—emerges the voice of a boy hiding in a closet while the Nazis take away his family. The voice speaks to a writer named "federman," who has repeatedly tried and failed to tell the boy's story. *The Voice in the Closet* is Federman's fictional re-living and re-enactment of his personal war trauma – a textual flow, without punctuation or capitalisation, which opens as follows:

here now again selectricstud makes me speak with its balls all balls foutaise sam says in his closet upstairs but this time it's going to be serious no more masturbating on the third floor escaping into the trees no the trees were cut down liar it's winter now delays no more false starts yesterday a rock flew through the windowpane voices and all I see him from the corner of my eye (*VC*, unpaged)

"*Foutaise*" is French for "bullshit" or "garbage"—idle talk, and Federman's childhood memory is saturated with the occasional leaps from English into French as he recalls what he terms his "symbolic rebirth":

> my life began in a closet a symbolic rebirth in retrospect as he shoves me in his stories whines his radical laughter up and down pulverized pages with his balls mad fizzling punctuation question of changing one's perspective view the self from the inside from the point of view of its capacity [...] they pushed me into the closet among empty skins and dusty hats my mother my father the soldiers they cut little boys' hands old wife's tale send him into his life cut me now from your voice (VC)

The existential plight and the static, almost paralysed state of the speaking subject (referring to himself in the third person) resembles Beckett's dramatic monologues ("Sam" is recalled in the very first line), but *The Voice in the Closet*, as a text toying with and problematising its status as recorded speech, is also in the lineage of textual streams of consciousness, in passages such as

> how I crouched like a sphinx falling for his wordshit moinous but where were you tell me dancing when it all started where were you when the door closed on me shouting I ask you when I needed you the most letting me be erased in the dark at random in his words scattered nakedly telling me where to go (VC)

The "wordshit" and "moinous" compounds ("moinous" combining the French *moi* and *nous*, a partly successful synthesis of voices and pronominal persons, but also functioning as an anagram for 'ominous') also bear a Joycean imprint, as does Federman's playful variation on his surname, "featherman." The wordshit image is further strengthened in scatological passages emphasising the parallels between writing and excreting:

> I am not ready for my summation nor do I wish to participate any longer willy nilly in the fiasco of his fabrication failed account of my survival abandoned in the dark with nothing but my own excrement to play with now neatly packaged on the roof to become the symbol of my origin in the wordshit of his fabulation that futile act of creating images of birth into death backward into the cunt of reality regressing toward my expulsion there must be a better way to manifest myself to assert my presence in his exercise-book speak my first words on the margins of verbal authenticity (VC)

As critic Davis Schneiderman has noted, the scatological dimension is a constant in Federman, rendering him part of a tradition including, quite prominently, Joyce.[23] *The Voice in the Closet* is thematically most concerned with the

---

23 Federman's narratives [...] map a postmodern scatology of misdirection, a topos of the excremental. [...] His excreted words, layered like mortar over traditionally communicative prose, become in his works (and certainly in Sterne, Swift, Cervantes, Diderot, as well as the endless host of moderns including Stein and Joyce) a non-apprehensible sludge surrounding and swallowing the communicative literal language of "plot" in order to expose the impossibility of second-degree fidelity" (Davis Schneidermann, Surfiction, Not Sure Fiction: RF's Second-Degree Textual

paradox of narrating the trauma of birth (even though a second and merely "symbolic" one), an experience usually unavailable and inaccessible to the (already speaking and writing) subject. The tone is one of sheer exuberance, a cadenced, repetitive incantation:

> already said already seen foolish pleasures to proliferate in verbal mud to build come back upon retrace already traced lines inscribed a course of action only certitude here in closet alone outside mystery to be found helplessness of an elsewhere beginning veiled fingers of plagiarism who speaks to whom with neutral voice (VC)

There are, to be sure, metafictional passages in which the text comments on itself, its structure and procedure, such as "questions affirmations texture designs negations speculations double or nothing where sun and other stars still burn neither symbols of a beginning nor metaphors microcosm reality gigantic mythocosm edifice of words integrating space figures inside rhetorical perfection," and finally, *Wake*-like, it comes to its own beginning in the concluding passage:

> [his life] begins again closet confirmed as selectricstud resumes movement among empty skins images crumble through distortions spins out lies into a false version leapfrogs infinite stories falling silently into abyss to be replaced retold confusion foretelling subsequent enlightenment
> but to commit transgression for those above those below negates survival time now then to be serious upstairs in his closet foutaise to speak no more my truth to say from fingers federman here now again at last
> (VC)

Not only is "again at last" an echo of the *Wake*'s own ending ("a way a lone a last a loved a long the" [*FW* 628.15–6]), but just as there was no capitalised letter at the beginning, nor is there a full stop at the end, the concluding "again" a mirror image or a direct echo of the opening one.

From Federman's later, typographically and formally less innovative work, one deserves special mention here: *To Whom It May Concern* (1990), his most heavily Beckett-indebted work which uses the "pla(y)giaristic" talent of its protagonist to rewrite personal and collective history.[24] It begins in a familiar dialogic mode with an apostrophe to a narratee who is most prob-

---

Manipulations," *Federman's Fictions – Innovation, Theory, Holocaust*, ed. Jeffrey R. DiLeo (Albany: SUNY Press, 2011) 115.

24   Following Beckett's example, "Federman's fiction has struggled with versions of the 'unnamable,' replacing 'plot' with a conditional 'story' that allows for rupture but also for some development, at least of the circular kind" (Marcel Cornis-Pope, *Narrative Innovation and Cultural Rewriting in the Cold War and After* [New York: Palgrave, 2001] 197–8).

ably a friend and fellow writer: "Listen [...] suppose the story were to begin with Sarah's cousin delayed for a few hours in the middle of his journey [...] stranded in the city where he and Sarah were born" (*WMC*, 9). Against the background of this personal post-Holocaust story of separation and reunion is set also the dramatic history of the last fifty years that has impacted it. However, in a perfectly Beckettian fashion, this narratee appears at times to be little more than a figment of the narrator's imagination, the second person actually indicating a form of self-address, again stimulated by the momentous, or almost impossible, nature of the task for a single narrator – the burden of history must be shared through a spectral splitting of the speaking subject into two, an act of ventriloquism. The narrator's ambition is to create "a stereophonic effect" in the linear discourse of history: "If only one could inscribe simultaneously in the same sentence different moments of the story [...]. That's how it feels right now inside my skull. Voices within voices entangled within their own fleeting garrulousness" (*WMC*, 76–77).

Federman's surfictionist project of creating fiction not as a representation or imitation of a "reality," but as a rhetorical and narratological embrace of its own particular "reality" within the space of the book, creates a new sort of referential link between writing and the world. Even though more clearly informed by Beckett, Federman's project follows in the footsteps of the Joycean "revolution of the word" as proclaimed by Jolas, and parallels the contemporary advances of B. S. Johnson in Britain and Maurice Roche in France.

6.2 "A NOVEL AS A CONCRETE STRUCTURE RATHER THAN AN ALLEGORY": RONALD SUKENICK

As was the case with Federman, Ronald Sukenick's debut as novelist was preceded by his scholarly work—on Wallace Stevens—although unlike Federman, by the mid-1970s and the time of the *Surfiction* essay collection, Sukenick had published no fewer than four works of fiction.

His contribution to the volume, "The New Tradition in Fiction," provides a useful insight into his own practice – and an appreciation for the Joycean materiality of language far deeper than Federman's. Sukenick opens with a reflection on tradition and "progress" in fiction, unmasking both as conceptual inventions rather than empirical entities.[25] Consequently, this

---

25   "Obviously there's no progress in art. Progress toward what? The a-g is a convenient propaganda device, but when it wins the war everything is a-g, which leaves us just about where we were before. [...] Traditions, also, are after the fact. Traditions are inventions—a decision accumulates about which part of the museum is most useful to us in the ongoing present. Now and then a reorganization seems in order. [...] But suppose fiction is something other than

"new tradition of fiction" makes itself felt "as a presence rather than a development" and instead of "a linear sequence of historical influences," it resembles "a network of interconnections revealed to our particular point of view." Still, there is a distinct beginning to it, and a traditional one at that: François Rabelais, from whom it "might go almost anywhere—to encyclopedic multiplicity unified by wordplay in *Finnegans Wake*, or to Sterne via a joke borrowed from Rabelais in *Tristram Shandy*" (S, 37). Part of this new tradition is what Sukenick terms "spatialized writing" – with an appropriate tip of a hat to Hugh Kenner's "technological reality" of the book: "A novel is both a concrete structure and an imaginative structure—pages, print, binding containing a record of the movements of a mind. The form is technological, the content is imaginative. The old novel tends to deny its technological reality" (S, 38).

Instead, a change in consciousness is to take place:

> We have to learn to think about a novel as a concrete structure rather than an allegory, existing in the realm of experience rather than of discursive meaning and available to multiple interpretation or none, depending on how you feel about it. [...] One slogan that might be drawn from Sterne's anti-art technique is that, instead of reproducing the form of previous diction, the form of the novel should seek to approximate the shape of our experience. (S, 40)

There are, however, predecessors far more recent than Sterne, and Sukenick is quick to recognise them, identifying "two important types of fiction that disappeared almost completely during the literary depression of the forties and fifties," both stemming from "the revolution of the word, [...] probably still the critical element in a renewed fiction, and the one least reckoned with by contemporary novelists." The reason it is crucial is that it "deals with the nature of language itself, and any art [...] is fundamentally about its medium," and the two types of this fiction are, indeed, the already identified Joycean and the Steinian ones:

> Both the impossibly overloaded punning in *Finnegans Wake*, and the impossibly opaque wordplay in Stein's *Tender Buttons*, raise the question of whether it is really the pragmatic, discursive, rationally intelligible side of language that best puts us in touch with our experience of the world and of ourselves. [...] John Ashbery wrote recently that there are two ways of going about things: one is to put everything in and the other is to leave everything out. Joyce tends to put everything in and Gertrude Stein tends to leave everything out, and they both arrive at an enigma. (S, 42)

---

what we tend to think it is? I would like to propose the invention of a new tradition for fiction" (S, 35-6).

There are, to be sure, other possible predecessors (e.g., the "sexual" ico-noclasts Henry Miller and Anaïs Nin) and many different lines of develop-ment: there is the "revitalization of narrative in the exuberant inventions of writers like John Barth and Gabriel Garcia Márquez," or the work of "the mythmakers and fairytalers like William Gass and Robert Coover." But the new style derived from "the revolution of the word" and the duality of Joyce and Stein is distinct from these. Sukenick calls it "the Bossa Nova" style and provides the following negative definition: "no plot, no story, no character, no chronological sequence, no verisimilitude, no imitation, no allegory, no sym-bolism, no subject matter, no 'meaning'" (S, 43). It is this style that Sukenick chooses to approximate in his own work.

Joyce makes similarly important appearances in Sukenick's crucial book-length work on the theory of fiction, his *In Form: Digressions on the Act of Fiction* (1985). What can be gleaned from the essay collection as a whole is a theme central to Sukenick as theorist and writer: the immediacy of experi-ence as the greatest value of the genre of the novel, whose uniqueness is in that, like no other genre, the novel "can so well deal with our strongest and often most immediate responses to the large and small facts of our daily lives" (*IF*, 242). This immediacy of experience, something inherently disorganised and inchoate, is reflected in what Sukenick posits as three compositional principles for the novel: the embrace of the arbitrary, improvisation, and collage linkage, which together work to equate the sense-meaning within experience to that of reading.[26]

Another key notion, for Sukenick, is the "truth of the page," which does not refer narrowly to the arrangement of print against blank space but to the acknowledgement of the autonomic nature of the medium of fiction in general, whose meaning is really a matter of the experience of writing and reading the text. This poetics of "fiction-as-composition" is a holistic and pro-cessual theory based on the conception of the imagination as "the means of uniting the self with reality" (*IF*, 26). It is also expressive of the writer's gen-eral aesthetic views, according to which "the successful work of art is a dis-crete energy system that takes its place among the other things of our world" (*IF*, 29). It is as part of these general concerns that Joyce's work receives its due in Sukenick's theory of fiction.

In a digression "against expression," Sukenick moves from the opening maxim, "Art is not imitation; it is example" (*IF*, 25), toward a consideration of how 20th-century fiction moved beyond expression and imitation, and argues

---

26   "As critic Jerzy Kutnik has put it: "Just as the meaning of experience comes, or is perceived, "after the fact," so the meaning of a novel is a product generated in the creative act and not something preexisting it and only reproduced in, or transmitted by, a literary form" (Kutnik, *The Novel as Performance*, 64).

that this move occurred between Joyce and Beckett.[27] Elsewhere, meditating on the notion of the "holy book," relevant in the sense that "narrative fiction, unlike history or journalism, is about what hasn't happened" and "like religion, though in a different way, it deals in faith," Sukenick draws on the example of Joyce's *Wake* as a mode of authenticating narrative fiction:

> The narrative might once more authenticate fiction as having some urgency other than the commercial. This is certainly one of the directions indicated in Joyce, especially in *Finnegans Wake*. But along with the repetitions of tradition in Joyce goes a corresponding iconoclasm, a profanation and dismemberment of tradition through collage. (*IF*, 81)

Sukenick's most sustained reflection on Joyce and the *Wake* comes in his four-page "Finnegan Digression," a typographically complex text combining a series of questions and answers on the subject of *Finnegans Wake* in the right-hand column with a quasi-fictional narrative in the stream-of-consciousness method on the left. The questions surrounding the *Wake*, "the funnymental novel of our error," or 'the fundamental novel of our era,' are six in total and concern the text's genre, meaning, "verysimilitude," treatment of time, "newness," and language. Regarding the *Wake*'s genre, Sukenick proposes the following fusion of myth, dream, vision, and art:

> The content of multiple myth (including the private myth of James Joyce in person). The techniques of dream. The omniscience of vision. The tone of a joke. A sacreligious [sic] joke. *The Bible*, starring James Joyce as God the Father paring his fingers on the chamberpot while he makes. Makes what? His mock-epic of creation in one movement, bowel, macrocosm through Mickrocosm [sic]. A dirty joke? It always is. Is the novel out of ordure? Dream, vision, joke? All of these? None of these? Art is finally art, not secondhand life. A record of creation (and all of creation) is a bible. And a bible is a book. And a book is just a book. An edition to creation. Break down restrictive ideas of fiction: suggest concrete reality of book as artifact. (*IF*, 99)

As for the possibility of explicating the *Wake*, Sukenick considers it "an enigma" given to a "constipated rational mind," a "statement so total it becomes totally ambiguous: Babel-babble" in which the following takes place: "Order becomes ordure – it stinks. Drop it. Play around with it. Play becomes serious – a new order. Life is no joke. You can't win. Winagains Fake. The

---

27 "Watt's cryptic word games that treat language as detached, autonomous, hermetic, and that can be read as a parody of Joyce, indicate a literary difference between the friends. For Beckett, however autonomous language may be, it is finally the last sign of the presence of identity and, if only through the act of composition, of a vestigial, irreducible, and perhaps undesirable connection with experience. In his hermeticism, Joyce is modern; Beckett is the beginning of something else" (*IF*, 26).

best you can do is enigma, puzzle, indeterminacy. That's life. Back to enigma means back to life. Winagainst Fate." (*IF*, 99–100). The question of "verysimilitude" brings forth the question of reality, both of and within the *Wake* – the basic question of "what is it?":

> It's not imitation. It's life in process, thought in process, process in process. But not real life – it's static: the more it changes the more it stays the same. If it moves it's alive, if it stays still it's art. If it does both it's *Finnegans Wake*. It's a fake. But it inCORPorates. A symbol indicates, a pun inCORPorates. Some business. Is this corpse dead? Wake up. Similitude? Very. (*IF*, 100)

After further punning on the subjects of character ("From the cul du sac of life to the sac du cul of the Wake") and compositional principles ("Synthesize, don't anal lies" [*IF*, 100]), Sukenick finally tackles the question of the *Wake*'s language, the question of "what's it made of?":

> Words. Not narrative. Not description. Not observation. Not characterization. Not comment. Not detail. Words. The river rather than its containing banks, the water rather than its course, which is in any case circular. The medium itself, language, words as concrete objects. A cure for schizophrenia: no more division between abstraction and sensation, thinking and feeling. [...] *Wake* language is totally particularized in a given context, totally itself, yet it enlarges reality, discovers reality, maybe creates reality. New language connections = new reality connections. The Word gives us life. (*IF*, 100–1)

Thus, Sukenick's approach is a variation on the Beckettian "whatness"-of--language observation, with the paraphrase of Wittgenstein's "connections of my language and the connections of reality." The coda to Sukenick's meditation on the nature and achievement of the *Wake* is a question without a ready answer, one concerning language as historical/social process versus language as bodily product:

> (How about a Wake language whose frame of reference is not fundamentally historical but open to common experience not committed to the black hole of the dead end of the closed circle of simultaneity but part of the endless unpredictable river of sequence: concretion over abstraction/ contemplation over information / esthetic over utilitarian [...] as immediate as babytalk that expresses not only the reality of the head but that of the whole body its feeling energies needs sensations. Language is speech, speech is voice, voice is of the body. A wake is all about a body)? (*IF*, 100)

Written as parody/homage to Joyce's modernist icon, "The Finnegan Digression" comes to view the *Wake* as what Sukenick claims all literary writing must be: both theory and performance, or what Sukenick later on has called *narralogue*, narrative as "a mode of understanding that uniquely is quick enough, mutable enough, and flexible enough to catch the stream of experience, including our experience of the arts" (*N*, 1). Strategically placed after *In Form*'s discussion of the use of typographic play and the breakdown of genres, "The Finnegan Digression" functions as a pivotal point between Sukenick's theory and practice.[28]

Through spatial play, Sukenick's four-page text takes on the polysemous density of poetry, simultaneously asking: What is *Finnegans Wake*; what is fundamental about the novel?; what is novel about our mistaken ideas of the novel?; what is experimental writing? It implies that *Finnegans Wake* is the fundamental novel of our times, seeing how it "went on trucking," how it spawned a tradition that includes the author of "Finnegan Digression," which is an error, in that this path, especially with the commercialisation of literature and the exhaustion of the avant-garde, leads nowhere but down. Still, in its formal properties partaking of those of Sukenick's fiction, the "Finnegan Digression" solicits the same sort of interactive reader's approach called for in both Sukenick's theory and practice of fiction.[29] The question, eventually, becomes one of "What would you do with it?" The answer: "Play with it. Joyce did" (*IF*, 101). And if that were to be redone, "what would you have then?" The answer: "Funnagain" (*IF*, 102). And fun again with Joyce was, indeed, had – in Sukenick's fiction.

Throughout his prolific output, Sukenick advances what would become a staple aesthetic principle of surfiction, "the truth of the page" as derived from the Burroughs quote in *In Form*: "The writer shouldn't be writing anything except what's in his mind at the moment of writing" (*IF*, 25). There are, as Brian McHale has pointed out, two alternative "truths" of the page. In an earlier manifesto, the "Thirteen Digressions" of 1973, Sukenick speaks of "the two realities behind literature: the reality of the spoken word and the reality of the written word" (*IF*, 30).[30] In this context, Sukenick's "directional" titles—*Up*

---

28   As Steve Tomasula has noted, "immediately we see the resistance to convention that is so central to Sukenick; it is there on a sentence-by-sentence level, embodied by this passage's resistance to be controlled, that is, quoted in the traditional academic style. As in much of Sukenick's work, any quote that doesn't include the white space is a misquote; to quote only the words [...] is to separate the dance from dancer, to paint a still life in the original sense of the word" (Steve Tomasula, "Taking The Line For A Walk: *In Form To Narralogues*, A History *In Medias Res*," *Musing The Mosaic*, 16).

29   "Sukenick's columns and word games and spatial arrangement of type make the readerly performance gymnastic. While reader execute linguistic flips (puns) and sommersaults (assonance) and sssssplits (onomatopoeia), they can't help but become aware of their role as co-author, a role easily submerged in the traditional "readerly" text" (Tomasula, "Taking The Line For A Walk, 18).

30   McHale comments: "The first of these corresponds [...] to the underlying orality of spontaneous prose [...], to the writer 'sitting there writing the page.' The second of these realities, the written word, has different consequences. [...] This other 'truth of the page' is the truth of writing's *materiality*, its existence as a structure of real objects: the white space of the page, the shapes that

(1968), *Out* (1973), *Down and In* (1987)—seem to acquire a different connotation: "they come to sound like directional arrows on a keyboard, allowing us to maneuver around the two-dimensional space of the (virtual) page."[31]

Sukenick's debut novel *Up* was published in 1968, a year in which, as recalled by Charles B. Harris, the conventions "most closely associated with postmodern fiction are defined and, in many respects, exhausted," as there are "few 'pure' examples of metafiction" appearing "after the late 1960s, Gilbert Sorrentino's *Mulligan Stew* (1979) and the 1970s 'surfiction' of Raymond Federman being significant exceptions."[32] Contrasting Sukenick's novel with two of the other great 1968 experimental texts, Gass' *Willie Masters Lonesome Wife* and Barth's *Lost in the Funhouse*, brings home the point of Sukenick's novelty in insisting on "experience beyond language" and using autobiographical elements out of the conviction that "experience begins with the self." [33]

Up presents time as measured by page numbers, time reduced to mere present, for each page records only the presence of a thought at the moment of its writing. The narrative, featuring protagonist Ron Sukenick's various attempts at sexual conquest and his relations with the New York avant-garde scene of the 1960s, has no identifiable story line. A collection of disjointed fragments, its improvisational and discontinuous form renders impossible any unitary or unequivocal centre of narrative mediation or narrative authority, as the narrator himself has no stable, definable identity, and nor do any other characters. The party scene that concludes the novel is a farewell party as well as a celebration. Ron invites all of his characters, from whom he realises he is now free – as Harris has observed, "the novel doesn't conclude, then, so much as it terminates, closing on a strange and evocative image."[34] The only stable elements in the characterisation are the characters' names, but these serve merely as placeholders for completely disparate character features.

This destabilisation takes place on the level of the names themselves; Sukenick's key biographical theme of exile (shared with Federman) allows for

---

typography makes, the concrete 'technological reality' of the book (*IF*, 206)" (McHale, "Sukenick in Space, or, the Other Truth of the Page," *Musing the Mosaic*, 143–4).

31   Ibid, 144.
32   Charles B. Harris, "'At Play in the Fields of Formal Thinking': *Up* and Post-modernist Metafiction," *Musing The Mosaic*, 42.
33   "Sukenick's *Up* signals an altogether different direction. For if late-modernist Gass wishes to demarcate literature from life and early-postmodernist Barth wants to illustrate that life, like literature, is also a text [...], Sukenick insists, both in *Up* and in his essays and interviews [...], that fiction provides us with a way to make contact with what he calls 'experience beyond language.' Thus Sukenick begins to use autobiographical elements in his fiction long before most other postmodernists do, not because he wants to write about himself but, as he explains in an early essay, because "experience begins with the self" (Harris, "*Up* and Post-modernist Metafiction," 43).
34   Ibid, 57–8.

the following ironic self-portrait: son of a Brooklyn immigrant, "Ronnie Suchanitch Sukanitch Subanitch [...] Sukenick" (*Up*, 97) feels at home in his East Side bachelor apartment surrounded by "images of heroic isolation, types of exile and self-exile, Kafka, Joyce, Lawrence, Melville" (*Up*, 265). *Up* records the process whereby the writer tries to get at the truth of his experience by imaginatively recording his thoughts and perceptions occurring during and because of the composition of his novel. As a writer actually sitting at his desk and composing a novel, Sukenick naturally regards the book he is writing as both an imaginative and a coherent structure. He reminds the reader of the materiality of the book on several occasions by using various typographical devices (multiple columns, various font sizes, etc.). The imperative, throughout, is on the truthfulness of the record: "it's all true what I've written, every word of it, I insist on that" (*Up*, 329).

Another theme running through the text is the metaphor of writing as flight, most convincingly rendered in the kite-flying episode, where after two unsuccessful attempts, a group of characters finally launch a kite and manage to keep it up in the air for a while. Kutnik has aptly linked this metaphor with Sukenick's overall poetics, his theory of composition as an autonomous and continuous process.[35] However, this project, just as the kite flying, is ultimately doomed. Kutnik points out that "*Up* does not fully satisfy the requirement of Sukenick's aesthetics of failure because it moves in a (closed) circle: it emerges as an experience and then folds back on itself."[36] Moreover, the narrator's own idea of experiential immediacy is fairly self-serving, reducing the flow of experience to his activities as a writer – to which one of the fictional critics in the book objects: "Fiction isn't confession. You and I may be interested in your tribulations and so on. But the reader. To the reader this sounds like a maudlin exercise in group therapy" (*Up* 55). And although these objections come from a reviewer stuck in a canonical version of modernism, with predilection for "something in the first person, as if Bloom were writing Proust in order to recapture the American myth like Faulkner" (*Up*, 57), this self-criticism remains largely valid.

Out (1973) is a text entirely structured by spacing. It starts with chapter 10 and concludes with chapter 0. There are ten lines in each paragraph in chapter 10, nine in chapter 9, and diminishing by one line in each successive chapter. However, the number of paragraphs per page remains constant (three), although in chapter 1, several pages have only two paragraphs. Chap-

---

35   "As a metaphor for writing, the image expresses Sukenick's theory of composition as an autonomous and continuous flowing which is not so much governed by the writer as initiated by him and then imaginatively participated in. Like kite flying, writing is an activity whose meaning is the actual performance of this activity and not some goal to be reached by means of this performance" (Kutnik, *The Novel as Performance*, 97).

36   Ibid, 98.

ter by chapter, the empty space grows, "allowing the novel to move out from between the book's covers and literally disappear from the page."[37] This form has an obvious impact on the reading process, as the reader ends up turning the pages of the book at an ever increasing rate corresponding to the acceleration of the pace of the "action." The first five chapters present the unfolding of the plot while systematically undercutting its "reality" by studding it with hints about its own fictitiousness; the middle chapter, 5, lays bare the fictitiousness of the story told; and the final five chapters replay the fictions of the novel's first half *as* fictions constructed in front of the reader.

Out's journey of an indefinable character, or perhaps a number of characters, across the US from New York to California would be a classic American theme were it not for the blurred personal identity – as in *Up*, the plot effectively develops by an accumulation of causally discontinuous episodes which form random sequences and do not create a meaningful pattern: as is advertised on page one, "it's all chance" (O, 1). The randomness is brought home in a chapter 9 scene in which the purpose of the character's mission is read from a letter soup, via various permutations on the letters. What critics have termed a "stream of character," already hinted at in *Up*, here becomes one of the central tropes, as the main character transforms from Harrold to Carl to Nick to Rex to RS to Ron to Roland Sycamore to be finally reduced to the minimal R. *Out* features numerous metafictional comments on its own procedures as fiction, e.g. "Data accumulates obscurity persists" (O, 100); "Connection develops meaning falls away" (O, 128); "Meaning disintegrates connection proliferates what does that mean" (O, 164). Kutnik aptly ties the letter-soup episode in with the larger concerns of Sukenick's fiction, its "sensual approach to the world, internalized via the sense."[38] Sukenick's novel demonstrates playfully and self-consciously that the most obvious thing done by any writer when writing is that he *writes*; therefore, it is important to render the experience of writing *as* writing – hence, the end of the text foregrounds the end of writing and the move back "out" into the world:

this way this way this way this way this way this way this
   way out this way
way out
(O, 294)

---

37   Ibid, 99.

38   "The meaning is not *behind* but *in* those events. It is not referential but superficial and, like the alphabet soup, it is not to be interpreted but experienced, not deciphered by the mind but ingested by the body, internalized not via the intellect but via the senses. [...] The full value of a self-contained sensual approach to the world can be appreciated by Sukenick only when he finds out that it is the chief source of man's imaginative power" (Ibid, 104–5).

Long Talking Bad Condition Blues (1979) begins as a solid block of unpunctuated prose, followed by a prose block with "gaping holes" in lieu of punctuation, followed by pages in which blocks of prose and rectangles of white space alternate. At the exact centre of the text, page 57 is entirely blank; then the whole sequence is recapitulated in reverse, akin to a second verse in a blues song. The prose, as in Federman's *Voice in the Closet* (published the same year), is unpunctuated, and Sukenick's juxtaposition of words in a free syntax gives rise to subtle wordplay:

> complaints of clams gesticulation of seaweed torpor of sidewalks hullaballoo of slugs gleam of jet planes smudge of stacks rain drops bridge work tin cans knees streets sighs curves sheets the clarity of persistent ellipsis the logic of lacunae the facile discords of discontinuity thinking at the same time the phrase (*LT*, 9)

In passages like the above, Sukenick's "rhythmic prose" brings about a shift in coherence from conventional syntactic units (sentences, clauses, or paragraphs) to what he calls "prose measure," rendering the quality of the spoken word in his writing. Yet the material quality of the text, again, becomes foregrounded by means of the introduction of "smudges" or gaping holes - elisions in the main character's erratic trains of thought:

> he said good I'm going out for breakfast good she said   he went out for coffee smoked five cigarettes was furious wished he had a cat   but he told himself at least he knew he was at ground zero   where everyone else seemed to be
> (*LT*, 9)

Coupled with these smudges is Sukenick's use of the expressivity of page-space. For example, in a section from page 26 to 41, the nervousness and tension in the narrative are reflected in the typographical layout, as the text is printed in a vertical column occupying only one-half of the page, "pressed" and "oppressed" by the blank surrounding. The narrative, here, is reduced to a minimal set of random episodes, which—as Kutnik points out—furthers Sukenick's project of "free[ing] his writing from the traditional obligation to convey ideas, to tell the 'truth' about reality, and creates instead situations in which he can concentrate completely on the observation and recording of the process by which his own consciousness structures experience."[39]

Sukenick's most linguistically experimental work of prose is his later novel *Mosaic Man* from 1999. It performs a parodic rewriting of the five books of Moses, i.e., the core of the Hebrew Old Testament (here, redubbed as "Genes," "Ex/Ode," "Umbilicus," "Numbers," and "Autonomy"), during which Suken-

---

39   Ibid, 145.

ick's eponymous protagonist searches for his Jewish roots. Again foregrounded is the challenge to the binary between fiction and reality, brought home via the *Wakean* pun of the "reel" versus the "unreal" and presented through a huge repertoire of variegated textual material, interspersed throughout the narrative by means of hand-drawn symbols or lower-case boldface captions beneath those symbols. These symbols generate a personal narrative about discovering the "reel/unreal" nature of narrative itself: David's star referring to "Jewish rules," a circle with a dot in the middle to "reality," a dollar sign to "making it/losing it," two horizontal lines, with two semi-lines opposing each other in between them, to "reel/unreal"; and a check sign meaning "the true story, the word" (*MM*, 20).

These are coupled with the insertion of letters, recipes, road signs, newspaper articles, and even Federman's notes on earlier drafts of the manuscript, together with factual texts, excerpts from a biography of Eisenhower and Chayim Bloch's *The Golem*. Blank spaces, known from Sukenick's earlier texts, here take on the additional function of signalling the absence of key information. Rewriting the titles of the Books of Moses, *Mosaic Man* also rehashes some of the stories of the Old and New Testament (Adam and Eve, the motif of the Golden Calf, the Last Supper) from an iconoclastic perspective that emphasises the progress from "Testimony," "Commandments," and "Numbers" to "Writing," the book's last section, which creates a new sort of "bible" out of the "babble" (*MM*, 148) that is the turn-of-millennium political-cultural milieu. These broader thematic concerns are outlined in the novel's opening:

> In the beginning was the WORD which is unspeakable, unreadable and unintelligible. Beyond human perception. Sublime. Writing not yet language. Dazzle. Pure information. Generative. Algorithmic. Digital, i.e., DNA. Digital Not Analog. Helical. The master code. Original. The first person. Iconoclastic. Always beginning.
> Then the WORD says. It says language. It says analogy. A metaphor. A picture. RNA. Real Not Artificial. You. Mensch. Personal. Genetic. Chronic. Iconic. Scripture. A story. Worth thousands of words. All of them analogous. Guilt. Knowledge. Dream. The world, i.e. A mensch in the world. The WORD in the world. In the book of life. There but hidden. Finding it. In the story. As promised. (*MM*, 9)

Via a series of puns, the text deals with the increasingly empty notion of a Jewish identity, taking stock of a broad spectrum of contemporary political concerns – e.g., the extreme right-wing, xenophobic policy of Jean-Marie Le Pen, according to whose anti-Semitic pronouncements "Jews had better keep their mouths shut. Le Pen is mightier than the word" (*MM*, 12). The Jewish theme, throughout, is treated as a means to an end, to examining humanity at large:

Personally, being Jewish is just an advanced case of being human, and being human may be a terminal disease that's run its course. Personally, maybe we're just beings, forget human, beings among other beings, some hairy, some furry, some feathery, some leathery, and some who possibly will soon arrive from other sectors of the universe. (*MM*, 15)

Coupled with the Jewish theme is a retrospection of Sukenick's own career as an "innovative writer" condemned to "progressive invisibility" (*MM*, 182) by the official culture, and thus morphing into a "comic, a crazy" (*MM*, 201), a Mosaic man punning his "genetic language" against "the Babel of background DNA" (*MM*, 208–09), a desensitised Shylock:

He can't say what he really feels because he's not a real person. He doesn't really feel anything. He's a dummy. A manikin. An android. An alien cyberpod. Slapped together. Mosaic man, the man of parts. Ceramic. Or silicon. Prick him he doesn't bleed. He who? The Jew. Of thee I sing. (*MM*, 205)

Mosaic Man links the fate of the post-war innovative writer to his capacity to turn history into a story of possibilities, "opening doors" in the dead-end past (*MM*, 170). Thus, in Cornis-Pope's estimation, *Mosaic Man* participates in "an important recent trend of analytic-utopian fiction that challenges our complacency about human history at the end of the second millennium."[40]

Taken as a whole, Sukenick's is a monolithic experimental oeuvre whose chief thematic concern is with the "reality of fiction" and "fictionality of reality," with what can be identified as the two "truths of the page," in surfictionist writing.[41] As the progress from *Up* to *Mosaic Man* shows, the direction of Sukenick's writing was from the "process-oriented" toward the "materialist" – the kind of writing identified in his piece on the *Wake* with treating "words as concrete objects."

6.3 "ANOTHER AWARENESS, ANOTHER ALPHABET": WALTER ABISH

In the chapter of his book *Design and Debris: A Chaotics of Postmodern American Fiction*, devoted to what he calls American "proceduralism," Joseph M.

---

40   Marcel Cornis-Pope, "Unwriting/Rewriting the Master Narratives of "Bankrupt" Modernity: Ronald Sukenick's *Mosaic Man*," *Musing the Mosaic*, 209.
41   "Just as there are two 'truths of the page,' the truth of the page-as-process and the truth of the page-as-material, so there are two correlative types of narrative content. Improvisatory, process-oriented writing [...] favors narratives of picaresque adventure, restless circulation, the open road. 'Materialist' writing, by contrast, tends to favor fixed sites, bounded spaces, fictions of *place*" (McHale, "Sukenick in Space," 145–6).

Conte makes a useful distinction between proceduralism and formalism. Whereas the value of the latter—common to all literary writing observant of formal/generic conventions—is largely based on its conformity with the rules of the form/genre, the former consists in "the adoption of a rigorous and efficient design in advance of the composition of a work of literature as proceduralism." Proceduralists, then, "invent forms without knowing the precise manner of text that will be generated" and "welcome a degree of indeterminacy in literary production and do not confuse the value of the text with its conformity."[42] Conte places the American proceduralists—most prominent among whom are Harry Mathews, Gilbert Sorrentino, and John Barth—within the 1970s American avant-garde surfictionists.[43]

The necessary components of a procedural text, in Conte's account, are invention, constraint, generation, and synergy – and it is with reference to Marcel Bénabou's essay on "Rule and Constraint" that the latter is distinguished from the former, analogously to the formalist vs. proceduralist distinction. Whereas "rule" is inherent to all literary production, "constraint" takes its prescriptiveness a step further, achieving a degree of difficulty that is exceptional, forcing the system out of its normal functioning. The paradox, here, is that "what appears to be an unnecessary and deliberate restriction on the writer's practice can actually serve to liberate the writer from conventional means of expression and the tyranny of having to invoke some personal font of inspiration."[44]

Hand in hand with this sense of liberation comes the principle of synergy – opposed by Conte to the notion of "design" which "produces a text with little more than a one-to-one correspondence to the effort expended," the system tending "toward an unpromising steady state." Synergy, on the other hand, arises when "the complex dynamical system initiated by the constraint has the capacity of exceeding authorial control," and when "the unpredictable nature of the language system" results "in a creative autonomy, a generative text that far exceeds the enumeration of its preordained structure."[45]

As shown before the Oulipo group,[46] even though primarily Francophone and France-based, has been an international movement, as its membership

---

42 Joseph M. Conte, *Design and Debris: A Chaotics of Postmodern American Fiction* (Tuscaloosa: University of Alabama Press, 2002) 76.

43 "Proceduralists share a penchant for "blatant artifice" in literature with other practitioners of metafiction. They are allied with the surfictionists, especially in the use of graphical typography and the manipulation of textual space that one finds in Raymond Federman's *Take It or Leave It* or Ronald Sukenick's *Long-Talking Bad Condition Blues*. In this regard proceduralism is always antimimetic, a contrivance that disturbs a reader's willingness to become absorbed in the regime of representation" (Conte, *Design and Debris*, 83).

44 Ibid, 83–4.

45 Ibid, 84.

46 The subject proper of Chapter IV.

features Italo Calvino and Oskar Pastior, an Italian and a German, respectively, while also involving one British (Ian Monk) and one American (Harry Mathews) writer. Despite making a point of basing their lives and literary activities in France, both Monk and Mathews have functioned as translators/propagators of the group's works in the Anglophone world, as mediators between the two linguistic cultural spaces. For, to be sure, there have been—particularly in the US of the 1970s—writers formally unconnected to the group who, however unwittingly, still displayed interest in Oulipian procedures. A case in point is a work on which Mathews' co-edited *Oulipo Compendium* bestows the appellation of one of "the most remarkable Oulipian works by an author not belonging to the group"[47] – the first novel by Walter Abish, *Alphabetical Africa* (1974).

The reason for this special status is the compositional method—and the constraint—governing the text's form and style. Exploring the "idea" of Africa literally from A to Z, this novel's opening and closing chapters consist wholly of words beginning with the letter A, and the intervening forty-nine chapters gradually accumulate (from A to Z) and then repress (from Z to A) words beginning with each of the remaining twenty-five letters of the alphabet. The other rule observed throughout stipulates that every chapter begin with the letter which is being "added" in the first, accumulative half, and then "omitted" in the other, repressive half of the text. For Mathews, this method—of Abish's own devising—is Oulipian "both in its axiomatic simplicity and in the extent to which it determines both the ingenious narrative and its beguiling linguistic texture."[48]

The *determination*, here, is significant, for indeed the restraint determines the narrative—chiefly dealing with two murderous jewel thieves pursuing their perfectly proportioned, promiscuous partner throughout Africa—to an unprecedented degree, the form "creating" the content, the medium "conveying" the message. If in the first chapter, the narrative consists largely of lists—"Africa again: Antelopes, alligators, ants and attractive Alva" who is "apprehend[ed] anatomically, affirmatively and also accurately" (*AA*, 1)—then with B comes temporal distinction—"Before African adjournment, Alex, Allen and Alva arrive at Antibes" (*AA*, 3)—and it isn't until the ninth chapter that interiority can enter into the narrative together with the introduction of the first-person pronoun: "I haven't been here before. I had hoped I could hire a car, but I can't drive. I have been awfully busy finishing a book about Alva" (*AA*, 21). As the first list shows, the combination of alphabetical constraints and the difficulties entailed in representing Africa as conforming to Western orthodoxies give rise to a narrative that often reads like a comical tour-guide

47   *Oulipo Compendium*, eds. Mathews & Brotchie, 45.
48   Ibid, 47–8.

through the "dark" continent: through an Africa of the images, stereotypes, prejudices, and fantasies of Western imagination; one of "antelopes, alligators, ants." However comic in this thoroughly self-referential game of constraint, *Alphabetical Africa* is also a highly difficult, arduous text to read, as the amount of what is unsayable always vastly surpasses and haunts what can be said.

This obsession with the ability of linguistic forms to construct the familiar and to neutralise the uniquely unfamiliar does, in Tony Tanner's words, achieve "some distinctly novel effects, as the text moves from constriction and gradually expands until it seems to have achieved a new kind of freedom."[49] The main relationship is not merely a dual one—author and the alphabet at his disposal—but a triadic one: author, alphabet, and Africa. However Oulipian in its making, it would be a mistake to dismiss it together with Tanner as merely "a one-off book" based on "an interesting experimental idea" which "produced certain unusual effects."[50] For, Abish's treatment of the inherently thorny issue of European (Abish was born in 1930 in Vienna and did not become a US citizen until 1960) representation of a strikingly non-European experiential framework is replete with political import. Claire Fox has drawn powerful analogies between Abish's work and that of his clearest precursor in terms of subject matter, Joseph Conrad, arguing that both "have demonstrated that 'Africa' is an image constructed in language, but they have also demonstrated that writing itself is creation,"[51] while Anthony Schirato has emphasised the twofold nature of language in Abish's understanding, both as "an ontologically empty system of reproduction" and as "discourse full of references to its connections with the world outside."[52]

As Katalin Orbán has perceptively argued, what saves *Alphabetical Africa* "from being merely a *tour de force* by The Incredible Rubber Author" is "the grim relevance of its machinery to its colonial subject," or in other words, "if Abish's language keeps pointing to itself, that 'itself' would be thoroughly different without an 'Africa,' however alphabetical in its appearance in the text."[53] As Orbán shows, it is the colonial subject matter that provides the

---

49   Tony Tanner, "Present Imperfect: a Note on the Work of Walter Abish," *GRANTA 3: New American Writing*, eds. William Buford & Pete de Bolla (Spring 1979): 66.

50   Tanner, "Present Imperfect," 67.

51   Claire Fox, "Writing Africa with Another Alphabet: Conrad and Abish," *Conradiana* 22.2 (1990): 125.

52   "There is in *Alphabetical Africa*, a play between, on the one hand, the notion of textual discourse as nothing more than the product of a system that is capable only of reproducing that system and is, therefore, ontologically empty, and, on the other, a notion of discourse as being full of references to its connections with the world outside language and of its dealings and relationships with politics, colonialism, and exploitation" (Anthony Schirato, "Comic Politics and Politics of the Comic: Walter Abish's Alphabetical Africa," *Critique* 33.2 [Winter 1992]: 136).

53   Katalin Orbán, *Ethical Diversions – The Post-Holocaust Narratives of Pynchon, Abish, DeLillo and Spiegelman* (New York/London: Routledge, 2005) 79.

textual demonstration of the culpability of any systemic apprehending and structuring.[54] Here, it should be noted that the last chapter recounts a long list of alternative options, finally concluding on "another awareness another awakening another awesome age another axis another Alva another Alex another Allen another Alfred another Africa another alphabet" (*AA*, 152). As Orbán points out, it is no accident that "another alphabet" rather than "another Africa" is granted the final position in this list, it is significant in positing "otherness and language in relation: the problem at the core, yet farthest out of reach."[55]

Despite its discursive preoccupation and decidedly experimental character, *Alphabetical Africa*—though certainly qualifying as a *tour de force* in Oulipian constraint writing—might hardly be conceived of an essentially "Joycean" experiment. Neither can Abish's other novel, *How German Is It* (1982), which deals, similarly to *Alphabetical Africa*, with questions of visibility and concealment and the representation of the two – only this time the framework is not postcolonial, but post-Holocaust. Nor do Abish's short stories, particularly *In the Future Perfect* (1977), which are similarly concerned with familiarity, otherness, and constraint (even though, here, one of the narrative viewpoint, reduced to its visual, scopic component) and which oftentimes treat language as both a barrier and an opening (cf. the last short story, "Language Barrier"), quite repeat the same intensity of the language effect developed in his first novel. Abish's 1990 experimental text, *99: New Meaning*, even ceases to be even remotely Oulipian in embracing chance and textual collage as its procedural and compositional method. It consists of ninety-nine segments by as many authors, each line, sentence, or paragraph appropriated from a page bearing that same, says Abish, "mystically significant number 99,"[56] thereby reminiscent of William Burroughs' cut-ups.

Still, the Joycean impulse of structural overlay, and a certain notion of "economy of writing," i.e., the effort to make the fewest words do maximum work, to achieve the most with the least, that are present in Abish's *Alphabetical Africa*, substantiate his inclusion in this genealogy.

---

54   "*Alphabetical Africa* would collapse without Africa just as promptly as it would without the alphabet; nevertheless, by choosing the alphabet as master structure and by focusing on letters and words as the primary analytic elements, Abish's text keeps restating the question of otherness in linguistic, philosophical and ethical terms much broader than African colonial exploitation" (Orbán, *Ethical Diversions*, 80).

55   Orbán, *Ethical Diversions*, 81.

56   Qtd. in *Oulipo Compendium*, eds. Mathews & Brotchie, 45.

6.4 "THE PARODYING PUNNING PRE-JOYCEAN CAKEWALK": ISHMAEL REED

Ishmael Scott Reed is another example of an innovative U.S. writer who refashioned the Joycean revolution of the word in order to "forge," by means of his highly personal idiosyncratic poetics, "the uncreated conscience" of his race: the Afro-American struggle against political and cultural discrimination and search for an "authentic" minoritarian artistic expression. His most experimental and "Joycean" novel *Mumbo Jumbo* (1972) concerns "Jes Grew," a virus of freedom and polytheism and improvised expression spread by black artists, which overthrows a repressive status quo. And indeed, in *The Paris Review*'s estimation,

> His own groundbreaking literary output over six decades, in multiple languages and every form—essays, fiction, poetry, film, even editorial cartoons—has infected a generation of artists. His work as an institution builder, anthologist, and publisher has spread the work of hundreds of writers from outside the literary mainstream—students, black folks, immigrants, working-class writers, avant-garde experimentalists, and every member of his immediate family.[57]

Reed came to write innovative fiction via his early immersion in the poetry of Harlem Renaissance, the Beats, and American surrealism. This is perhaps why his recent interview with Chris Jackson for *The Paris Review* was titled "Ishmael Reed, The Art of Poetry No. 100." In that interview, Reed spoke of his youthful literary idols, pairing up Dante and Joyce: "I read Dante and realized how much power a writer could have. [...]. I loved James Joyce, too, and really studied his work."[58]

Reed was co-founder, with Walter Bowart in 1962, of the underground magazine *East Village Other*, which employed Dada montage and psychedelic layout and came out as biweekly for a full ten years, bringing out work by such prominent artists as Spain Rodriguez, Robert Crumb, and Art Spiegelman. Also in 1962, Reed joined the Umbra Writers Workshop, a collective of young black writers living in New York, alongside David Henderson, Askia Touré, among others. As an editor of over a dozen anthologies (most notably, *POW WOW, Charting the Fault Lines in the American Experience*, from 2009) dedicated to innovative writing, Reed has—in the estimate of his biographical note in *Mumbo Jumbo*—"published more white authors than white literary magazines have published black, Hispanic, Native American, and Asian American authors" (*MJ*, 295).

---

57   Chris Jackson, "Ishmael Reed, The Art of Poetry No. 100," *The Paris Review* 218 (Fall 2016): 36.
58   Chris Jackson, "Ishmael Reed," 39.

A lifelong academic between Berkeley, Harvard, and Yale, an accomplished jazz pianist and author of a dozen novels (his twelfth published as lately as June 2021), Reed has produced an oeuvre also including over ten essay collections ("American Poetry: Is There a Center?" won him a Pushcart Prize in 1979), ten poetry collections, work in theatre, and songs performed by the likes of Mary Wilson of the Supremes and Bobby Womack. The *basso continuo* of his wide-ranging output is the broadly conceived interest in African American life and its wider relationships to American society, deploying parody and biting satire as tools for dissecting the dominant Eurocentric narratives of history and culture, and subverting dogmas of all stripes. Advocating "for a fully inclusive art, and marked by stylistic variety and playfulness," Reed's work sits problematically within the postmodern pigeonhole, as its humor is "married to a passionate candor about history and social issues" (*MJ*, 298).

Writing in a collection of essays on Reed's work vis-à-vis the genre of satire, Christopher Shinn has observed that Reed is a writer and activist always stressing multicultural diversity and the need not to be limited to a monocultural or restricted identity framework, going so far as to as align himself with the Irish cause.[59] Symptomatically set in Harlem in the 1920s, *Mumbo Jumbo* deals with the "Jes Grew" virus, which is carried by certain black artists, described as "Jes Grew Carriers" (a.k.a. "J.G.C.s."), spreading as an "infection" with ragtime, jazz, polytheism, and liberty. The name itself seems to have been spawned by the early phrase, "We knew that something was Jes Grewing just like the 1890s flair-up" (*MJ*, 10) in Chapter 1. Representing African American culture as a complex set of traditions that evolved out of hybrid contacts among various populations of the Atlantic world, the motif of *Mumbo Jumbo*'s "Jew Grew" viral contagion literalises the replicative, uncontrollable identities that have evolved in the US over the last three centuries, described as

a huge magic snake of electric bloodless dots, and potentially deadly or benevolent depending upon how you look at it, clusters from New Orleans to Chicago on a map of the United States. Rashes are reported in Europe as well. Jes Grew begins to become pandemic, leaping across the ocean but generally forming a movement which points from Chicago to the East. (*MJ*, 83)

---

59   "Reed is a member of the Celtic Foundation, and the late John Maher of the Delancy Foundation once introduced him as an Irish American poet. Reed also tells a story of how he mentioned his "Irish American heritage" to a "Professor of Celtic Studies at Dartmouth" who merely "laughed." [...] Reed also remarks that if Alex Haley's Roots: The Saga of an American Family might have followed his Haley's father's bloodline twelve generations back, he would have instead returned to Ireland, not Gambia" (Christopher A. Shinn, "The Art Of War: Ishmael Reed and Frank Chin and The U.S. Black-Asian Alliance of Multicultural Satire," *African American Humor, Irony and Satire: Ishmael Reed, Satirically Speaking*, ed. Dana A. Williams [Newcastle: Cambridge Scholars Publishing, 2007] 70–1).

The history of voodoo becomes a nexus for the meeting of Orient and Occident, and of Antiquity and Modernity, as its missing link with Judeo-Greek--Christianity is found in their shared ancestor in ancient Egypt. Osiris is posited as the first recipient of Jes Grew, and Moses believed to have stolen the Voodoo practices from Goddess Isis. Furthermore, the Greek admixture is added via Dionysus, portrayed as a follower of Osiris, and the modern-Occidental mythical overlay is added through the Faustian motif, where instead of his pact with Mephistopheles, Faust is depicted as mastering his black magic through connections with black Voodoo practitioners. No wonder, then that "Jes Grew" might conjure up a distant memory of the famous Joycean formula, "Jewgreek is greekjew. Extremes meet" (*U* 15.2097–8), popularised in Derrida's 1967 *Writing and Difference*.

The Jes Grew infection spawns a typical postmodern conflict of three conspiracy groups. The first features the elderly Harlem practitioner of Haiti voodoo, PaPa LaBas, and his companion Black Herman ("real-life" African American healer and root doctor, Benjamin Rucker), on a quest after a mysterious book called The Work, which vanished with black militant Abdul Sufi Hamid (a.k.a. Eugene Brown, one of the earliest Black converts to Islam). Papa LaBas runs a voodoo healing practice at the Mumbo Jumbo Kathedral. and "Mumbo Jumbo," as Reed makes clear in the very first chapter quoting *The American Heritage Dictionary*, is a Mandingo word, meaning "magician who makes the troubled spirits of ancestors go away" (*MJ*, 13). The second group is the Wallflower Order, an international conspiracy promoting to monotheism and control, attempting "to meet the psychic plague by installing an anti-Jes Grew President, Warren Harding" who "wins on the platform 'Let's be done with Wiggle and Wobble,' indicating that he will not tolerate this spreading infection" (*MJ*, 20). On a secret mission track down the cause of and contain the virus, The Wallflower Order, in tandem with the Knights Templar Order, aim to put a stop to the dance crazes spreading among black folks.

Finally, the third group in *Mumbo Jumbo* is the Mu'tafikah, the "notorious art-nappers" (*MJ*, 271), a word with Judeo-Christian meaning since, as per Reed's footnote no. 3, the *Mu'tafikah* were, "according to *The Koran*, inhabitants of the Ruined Cities where Lot's people had lived. I call the 'art-nappers' Mu'tafikah because just as the inhabitants of Sodom and Gomorrah were the bohemians of their day, Berbelang and his gang are the bohemians of the 1920s Manhattan" (*MJ*, 17). The Mu'tafikah are a radical anarchist group who steal art collections from Western museums and ship them to "their rightful owners" in Africa, Asia, and South America (*MJ*, 106). As Berbelang, their leader, puts it, "we would send their loot back to where it was stolen from and await the rise of Shango, Shiva, and Quetzacoatl, no longer a label on a cheap bottle of wine but strutting across the sacred cities [...] like a proud cock" (*MJ*, 115). Accordingly, this group is a hybrid, including a young white American, a Native American, a South African, and a Mayan. For all the seriousness of their holy mission, Reed's representation of this group is satirical, as evident from the very name of the group—a pun on the m- curse word—which reveals Reed's own reservations about all the self-appointed justices of this world.

As so often in Pynchon or Coover, fictional constructs rub shoulders with "real-life" historical, social, and political events. The US occupation of Haiti, white-supremacist attempts to suppress jazz music, and the circulating rumours that president Warren Harding had black ancestry, all are commingled with the main storyline of PaPa LaBas' searching after his mysterious book, the Mu'tafikah's scheming to return museum treasures looted from ancient Egypt to Africa, and the Wallflower Order training the perfect "Talking Android," a black man who will "work within the Negro, who seems to be its classical host; to drive it out, categorize it analyze it expell it slay it, blot Jes Grew" (*MJ*, 20). This Talking Android fulfils the function of an ideological interpellation to be manipulated by those wielding the power over the dissemination of cultural identities. That this satire of robotic samboism is, again, employed in parallel with the tradition of the Stage Irishman is brought home in passages like this:

> What we will do is begin a magazine that will attract its followers, featuring the kind of milieu it surrounds itself with. Jazz reviewers, cabarets, pornography, social issues, anti-Prohibition, placed between acres of flappers' tits. Here we will feature the Talking Android who will tell the J.G.C.s that Jes Grew is not ready and owes a large debt to Irish Theatre. (MJ 88)

The format and typography of *Mumbo Jumbo* match its stylistic fireworks, which have been variously compared and likened to *Ulysses*.[60] At its beginning and end the text employs the style of the movie script, with credits, a fade-in, and a freeze-frame followed by the publication and title pages which occur after chapter one. A closing section of *Mumbo Jumbo* mimics a scholarly book on social history or folk magic by citing a lengthy bibliography of 104 titles drawn upon and freely recombined: that is, Reed posits the novel as research.

Mumbo Jumbo's ambivalent attitude to radicalism and nationalism, both of support and critique, echo the clash between anti-English, anti-colonialist

---

60 Cf., e.g., "The style of *Mumbo Jumbo* is hard to follow: like Joyce's *Ulysses* it is a celebration of idiom and an eclectic collection of cultural myth. Reed mixes the styles of detective stories, voodoo, and academic burlesque, providing unexpected visuals, news stories, history, and stream-of-consciousness. Reed's command of different vernaculars is astounding: he switches mid-sentence from one attitude to another, from popular to academic clichés like the sampling in rap music, satirizing everything: Black English Vernacular, White English Vernacular, and academic language" (Carol Siri Johnson, "*Mumbo Jumbo* and the Mummy," *MELUS* 17.4 [Winter 1991–2]: 107).

sentiments and critique of the blinded Irish nationalist agenda in *Ulysses*. As shown in a detailed account written for *Journal for the Study or Radicalism* by Babacar M'Baye, *Mumbo Jumbo* is at best ambivalent about radical liberationist movements.[61] Most interestingly, the radicalism of *Mumbo Jumbo* is played out as much on the level of political commitment as on that of aesthetic engagement, as when Reed's narrator mentions a suggestion by "another author" that "the Nursery Rhyme and the book of Science Fiction might be more revolutionary than any number of tracts, pamphlets, manifestoes of the political realm" (*MJ*, 21), a sentiment very much in line with the *Wake*'s political materiality of the word. As Gloria Steele has observed regarding this passage, both the nursery rhyme and science fiction are "things of fantasy," something "out of the ordinary," and "transcendent."[62] Jes Grew is the uncontainable and ineradicable spirit of the Diaspora, concentrating the energy of all the lost uprooted souls without a spiritual and cultural "home." One such lost soul, poet Nathan Brown, has repressed his heritage through a doomed attempt at compromising his older faiths by fusing them with Christianity and a belief in a "Black Christ." In a crucial scene, this Nathan Brown asks a hoodoo priest, Benoit Battraville, how to catch Jes Grew and is given the following tour-de-force tirade:

> The Americans do not know the names of the long and tedious list of deities and rites as we know them. Shorthand is what they know so well. They know this process for they have synthesized the HooDoo of VooDoo. Its bleeblop essence; they've isolated the unknown factor which gives the loas their rise. Ragtime. Jazz. Blues. The new thang. That talk you drum from your lips. Your style. What you have here is an experimental art for that all of us believe bears watching. So don't ask me how to catch Jes Grew. Ask Louis Armstrong. Bessie Smith, your poets, your painters, your musicians, ask them how to catch it. Ask those people who be shaking their tambourines impervious of the ridicule

---

61   "*Mumbo Jumbo* both celebrates and vituperates black radicalism and nationalism, suggesting the author's ambivalent views about liberation movements. Yet, despite this duality, Reed's novel is consistent since it definitely promotes multiculturalism over the blind adoration of singular traditions or experiences, allowing us to establish a theoretical framework to explain how both the trickster figure and the subversive black Atlantic formation he calls "Jes Grew" advocate difference and equal, plural meaning, preventing a totalized truth" (Babacar M'Baye, "The Trickster in Ishmael Reed's Dualistic Representations of Black Radicalism and Nationalism in *Mumbo Jumbo*," *Journal for the Study of Radicalism* 10.1 [Spring 2016]: 107).

62   "But what is the nursery rhyme, the science fiction? Things of fantasy [...] as something formerly inconceivable, out of the ordinary, transcendent; above or beneath conventional imaginations or communications. It is the odd. The thing that is not "normal" when normality is assumed to be something common or "mainstream." And the revolution of the nursery rhyme or the science fiction lies in its revelation; its revelation lies in its negation and/or refutation of the normal. This negation is silence. Nonsense, fantasy, things that are outside normality—silence. Gibberish? Mumbo Jumbo? All silence" (Gloria Steele, "Signifying and Placing Significance," *Hypothetical Theological Illogical Scholastica* [January 2006]. Online: https://illogicscholastica.blogspot.com/2012/).

they receive from Black and White Atonists, Europe the ghost rattling its chains down the deserted halls of their brains. Ask those little colored urchins who "make up" those new dance steps and the loa of the Black cook who wrote the last lines of the "Ballad of Jesse James." Ask the man who, deprived of an electronic guitar, picked up a washboard and started to play it. The Rhyming Fool who sits in Rĕ'-mōte Mississippi and talks "crazy" for hours. The dazzling parodying punning mischievous pre-Joycean style-play of your Cakewalking your Calinda your Minstrelsy give-and-take of the ultra-absurd. Ask the people who put wax paper over combs and breathe through them. In other words, Nathan, I am saying Open-Up-To-Right-Here and then you will have something coming from your experience that the whole world will admire and need. (*MJ*, 205–6)

In this marvellous passage, Reed suggests that although in seeking its autonomy, black art must perforce exert resistance to the Eurocentrism of the Western poetics and aesthetics, black art forms (especially those promoted by the Harlem Renaissance group in the 20s) have often grown in tandem with, or even anticipated, the most avant-garde experimental Western art, this through their "dazzling parodying punning mischievous pre-Joycean style-play of your Cakewalking your Calinda your Minstrelsy give-and-take of the ultra-absurd." In this resistance, Joyce is cast in a peculiar role of the double-agent: both a member of the enemy camp and an ally. A similar dynamics lies behind the concern with etymology and "nonsense" as subversion of the linguistic *status quo* in both Joyce's Hiberno- and Reed's Black Vernacular English, as pointed out by Robert Elliot Fox's fine semiotic analysis.[63]

What, ultimately, *is* the forgotten message that Jes Grew comes to articulate in *Mumbo Jumbo*? Perhaps it is nothing more than the truth its title insists upon. After PaPa LaBas finishes narrating the history of Jes Grew and the *Book of Thoth*—the sacred text Isis handed over to Moses in the foundational act of an Egyptian-Hebraic transcultural exchange—he is attacked by the Guianese art critic: "In times of social turbulence men like you always abandon reason and fall back upon Mumbo Jumbo" (*MJ* 260). The truth of nonsense—as Patrick McGee notes, "curiously, Freud and Lacan (and even James Joyce with regard to *Finnegans Wake*) have all been accused of the same thing."[64] *Wakean* is also the last paragraph's insistence on time being "a pendulum, not a river":

63 "The different 'readings' in this instance are not racially determined; they are predicated upon consciousness. But from a black point of view, the transition from "nonsense" to a positive interpretation is one in which the slave becomes the master. Although the English language has basically equated the expression "mumbo jumbo" with "gibberish," the etymology which Reed provides derives from a Mandingo term relating to a process which calms the troubled spirits of the ancestors. Ironically, at the same time that the words lost their original meaning, they took on a meaning which troubled the spirits of whites, invoking the fearful, atavistic vision of the "dark continent" that Africa inspired in the West" (Robert Elliot Fox, "Blacking the Zero: Toward a Semiotics of Neo-Hoodoo," *Black American Literature Forum* 18.3 [Autumn, 1984]: 97).
64 Patrick McGee, *Ishmael Reed and the Ends of Race* (New York: St Martin's Press, 1997) 121.

People in the 60s said they couldn't follow him. [...] What are you driving at? they would say in Detroit in the 1950s. In the 40s he haunted the stacks of a ghost library. In the 30s he sought to recover his losses like everybody else. In the 20s they knew. And the 20s were back again. Better. Arna Bontemps was correct in his new introduction to *Black Thunder*. Time is a pendulum. Not a river. More akin to what goes around comes around. (Locomobile rear moving toward neoned Manhattan skyline. Skyscrapers gleam like magic trees. Freeze frame.) (*MJ*, 286)

Just as Joyce's "revolution of the word" sought to invade and deconstruct from within the language of the coloniser, and the sundry discourses of power in its service, so has Reed's "Jes Grew" functioned as a "virus of freedom, polytheism and improvisation" with which to infect and overthrow the political-cultural powers that be of the ingrained Euro-American cultural racism.

6.5 "DOES LANGUAGE CONTROL LIKE MONEY?": KATHY ACKER

Another writer reworking the Joycean legacy to craft her highly idiosyncratic cyberpunk aesthetics is Kathy Acker. "Words belong to everybody, [...] nobody owns words, [...] there's nothing sacred about words, [...] let's break the word habit."[65] Brion Gysin's famous injunction regarding the material for the cut-up method which he invented (and William Burroughs put to use) is as good as any motto to her work. Or, in the words from one of her books, "The code said: GET RID OF MEANING. YOUR MIND IS A NIGHTMARE THAT HAS BEEN EATING YOU: NOW EAT YOUR MIND" (*ES*, 38).

A cult figure of the punk movement, Acker[66] is widely considered one of the most significant proponents of radical feminism in the American post-

---

65   Harold Norse, *The Beat Hotel* (San Diego: Atticus Press, 1983) 62.
66   Born in New York City, Acker was raised by her mother and stepfather. Her biological father, whom she never met, abandoned her mother before she was born. Her mother later committed suicide when Acker was thirty. Acker attended Brandeis University and the University of California, San Diego, where she earned a bachelor's degree in 1968. Twice wed—first to Robert Acker in 1966, then to composer Peter Gordon in 1976—and twice divorced, Acker returned to New York during the 1970s to work as a secretary, stripper, and performer in live sex shows and pornographic films while promoting her fiction in small press publications. She began a combined doctoral program in classics and philosophy at the City University of New York and New York University, but left after two years. An amateur bodybuilder, tattoo enthusiast, and adjunct professor at the San Francisco Art Institute beginning in 1991, Acker also appeared as a visiting instructor at the University of California at Santa Barbara, the University of California, San Diego, and the University of Idaho in 1994. Shortly before her death, she produced *Bodies of Work* (1997), a collection of essays, and *Eurydice in the Underground* (1997), a volume of short fiction. At age forty-eight, Acker succumbed to breast cancer at an alternative cancer treatment centre in Tijuana, Mexico.

war letters. Born Karen Alexander and using such *noms de plume* as "Rip-Off Red" and "The Black Tarantula," Acker established herself in the 1980s as a well-versed literary theorist and sophisticated experimenter, whose provocative fiction posed a challenge to established literary forms, categories of literary authorship, propriety, etc. Early on, Acker became associated with the discordant, irreverent punk rock culture, which gave her, as she told Ellen Friedman, a sense of community: "We were fascinated with Pasolini's and Bataille's work, but there was no way of saying why or how."[67] Her introduction to the work of Deleuze and Guattari "and somewhat Foucault" gave her a language for expressing her group's ideas and values: "For the first time we had a way of talking about what we were doing."[68]

Acker's iconoclastic, plagiarist fiction (an amalgam of extreme profanity, violence, graphic sex, autobiography, fragmented narrative, and recycled texts) drew on an extraordinarily wide range of sources and a very complex methodology of writing which rejected conventional morality and traditional modes of literary expression. Critic Peter Wollen recalls Acker's pronouncement to the effect that none of her readers are expected to read any of her books cover-to-cover, which to his mind suggests the notion of reading as "perpetuation of Acker's creation." As long as her writing was the result of her reading, then so should any individual reading of her work perform its own rewriting.[69] A critical term often used (by Wollen as well) to describe Acker's practice is the situationist *détournement*, or re-functioning by re-contextualising, by making strange.

As Jeanette Winterson observed in her introduction to *Essential Acker*, Acker was "ahead of her time" in two respects: her fiction is "closer to the European literary tradition of Borges and Calvino" than to "the Anglo-American narrative drive of Salinger or Roth or Amis," plus she was "a woman – therefore she was locked out of tradition and time" (*EA*, vii). Acker's strategies of plagiarism can, consequently, be seen as her revenge upon the patriarchal culture of the past and her times, followed by an attempt at re-appropriating, re-inscribing herself within it – a point brought home in Winterson's introduction.[70] One of *Essential Acker*'s editors, Amy Scholder, has also challenged

---

67 Ellen G. Friedman, "A Conversation with Kathy Acker," *The Review of Contemporary Fiction* 9.3 (Fall 1989): 15–6.
68 Friedman, "A Conversation with Kathy Acker," 16.
69 "In other words, you can make your own montage, you could appropriate and re-order, just as Kathy Acker had appropriated and re-ordered the writing of others [...]. Leslie Dick once remarked that Kathy Acker's writing was an extension of her reading, that her plagiarism was a way of reading, or re-reading, appropriating and customizing what she read, writing herself, so to speak, into the fabric of the original text" (Peter Wollen, "Kathy Acker," *Lust for Life: On the Writings of Kathy Acker*, eds. Amy Sholder, Carla Harryman, Avital Ronell [London/New York: Verso, 2006] 1).
70 "Acker saw herself as dispossessed – from her homeland, because of its politics, and from literature, because she was a woman. [...] Acker took revenge on a male literary tradition by raiding

the notion of "plagiarism" as applied to Acker's writing, the two main problems being that

> 1. she's open about it, and 2. she alters those texts (at times they become unrecognizable), or she embeds chunks of another work into a new context, one that's so unfamiliar that the pirated text's meaning is radically distorted. Let's call it appropriation, for lack of a sexier term – the music industry came up with "sampling" years after Acker tried it in literature. (*EA*, xi)

The formal ingredient of Acker's subversion—plagiarism—is coupled with her thematic concern with pornography and sexual explicitness. This for chiefly two reasons: one loosely biographical,[71] the other conceptual: not only does Acker believe that "desire is the only honest part of us" and that "art is authentic desire" (*EA*, ix), but for Acker, writing porn was a stylistic challenge: "using language, pushing limits, turning on" (*EA*, xiii).[72] Acker's staple style is a pastiche combining sensationalised autobiography, political tract, pornography, and appropriated texts to generate visceral prose in which characters—often famous literary or historical personages—easily move through time and space while frequently changing personalities and genders. Deliberately non-chronological and usually evoking a quest theme, her largely plotless narratives progress through disjointed, jump-cut sequences that juxtapose excerpted texts from various sources.

As Friedman has noted,[73] Acker frequently embodies patriarchal domination in sadistic, cowardly father figures (often adopted or step-) and embodies women's relation to patriarchy with self-destructively dependent daughter figures. Fathers in Acker's work literally control with their phalluses, practicing rape and incest and then abandoning their daughters. In these moves, they are identified with the phallogocentrism of the culture. The daughter's weapon of revolt is irrationality and desire, the feminine language that, by writing the female body, defies the law of the father. Her first publication, *Politics* (1972), is a combination of poetry and prose heavily influenced by the work of William Burroughs and his cut-up method, written

---

it mercilessly; her so-called plagiarism is a way of appropriating what is otherwise denied. As a woman, she can't inherit. As a pirate, she can take all the treasure for herself" (*EA*, ix).

71 As Scholder points out, "At a pivotal time in her life Kathy worked in a strip club in NYC's Time Square. The experience of the sex industry and the stories she heard from the other girls would find their way into almost everything she wrote" (*EA*, xii).

72 "Still, sexuality in Acker's work is a site of confusion – and it's within that confusion that her female characters come alive, expressing who they are and what they want. They are victims who crave and get revenge. [...] Desire is a place of not yet having: it's in the becoming, the longing, the imagining, that Acker wants her women to exist" (*EA*, xiii).

73 Ellen G. Friedman, "'Now Eat Your Mind': An Introduction to the Works of Kathy Acker," *Review of Contemporary Fiction* (9.3): Fall 1989, 41.

in one unpunctuated sentence. *The Childlike Life of the Black Tarantula* (1973) contains the following author note: "All the above events are taken from *Helen and Desire* by A. Trocchi, *The Wilder Shores of Love* by L. Blanch, and myself" (*EA*, 41). *I Dreamt I Was a Nymphomaniac* (1974) already features Acker's staple ingredient of openly erotic, pornographic language:

> I absolutely love to fuck. These longings, unexplainable longings deep within me, drive me wild, and I have no way of relieving them. Living them. I'm 27 and I love to fuck. Sometimes with people I want to fuck; sometimes, and I can't tell when but I remember these times, with anybody who'll touch me. These, I call them nymphomaniac, times have nothing to do with (are not caused by) physical pleasure, for my cunt could be sore, I could be sick, and yet I'd feel the same way. (*EA*, 42)

1978 saw the completion of three short novels: *Florida*, a brief satire of the film *Key Largo*; *Kathy Goes to Haiti*, relating the sexual exploits of a girl visiting Haiti; and *The Adult Life of Toulouse Lautrec by Henri Toulouse Lautrec*. During the early 1980s, Acker moved to London where she achieved a degree of fame and maintained a steady output of novels including *Blood and Guts in High School*, *Don Quixote*, and *Empire of the Senseless* (1988), all among her best--known works.

The English version of *Blood and Guts in High School* (1984) includes the novella *My Death My Life by Pier Paolo Pasolini*, later republished as part of *Literal Madness*. Another one of her fictitious autobiographies, *My Death My Life* reconstructs the 1975 murder of the Italian writer and filmmaker through a series of loosely related vignettes, including Shakespearian parodies and an obscene epistolary exchange among the Bronte sisters. Part One, "Sex," juxtaposes these with meditations on language, capitalism, materialism:

> What is language? The discovery of the urban peripheries has so far has been essentially visual – I'm thinking of Marcel Duchamp's rationality or autism and Sheeler's social-realism that is discontinuity that is seeing without psychology. Wittgenstein seems to understand language as function, therefore, without psychology [...] The question is: Does capitalism which must be based on materialism or the absence of values stink? The question is: What is art? Is art worth anything in the practice of art making (of values) or is it craft? (*LM*, 219)

Acker's plagiarism serves to depersonalise her confessional in passages such as: "I keep trying to kill myself to be like my mother who killed herself. I kept working on the 'Large Glass' for eight years, but despite that, I didn't want it to be the expression of an inner life" (*LM*, 222).

Even at this moment of (apparent) full self-disclosure, Acker is speaking through the work of Marcel Duchamp, whose artwork "The Large Glass" was produced through years of interrogating the gaze. In "Sex," Acker's sexualised pastiche of *Hamlet* and *Romeo and Juliet* is also interspersed with ruminations on language: "How available are the (meanings of the) specifics of all that is given? Language is a giveness like all other givenesses. Let the meanings not overpowering (rigid) but rather within the contexts, like Hamlet's father's ghost who tells the first meaning, interpretation of nothing, be here" (*LM*, 200). This is suddenly interposed by a cutback to Zurich and a meditation on Joyce's grave via a *détourned* passage from the "Hades" episode of *Ulysses*: "—Some say he is not in that grave at all. That the coffin was filled with stones. That one day he will come again. Hynes shook his head. —Parnell will never come again, he said. He's there, all that was mortal of him" (*LM*, 200; *U* 6.923-7).

After another plagiarised passage from the "Aeolus" episode (*U* 7.21-7, 142-4), there is another cut and the scene is Paris, with passages from the "Proteus" chapter of *Ulysses* interspersed:

> Comparison: *Paris rawly waking, crude sunlight on her lemon streets. Moist pith of farls of bread, the froggreen wormwood, her matin incense, court the air.* The milk of architectural tits. *Têtes.* Frenchmen can only think. We invited two hookers to sit with us cause Frenchmen are only polite to language and food before you've fucked them. *There Belluomo rises from the bed of his wife's lover's wife, the kerchiefed housewife stirs, a saucer of sunk* gone oh below the cement. I say, pick up skirts. Show cunt. Smelly fish all over the sides of flesh going slowly arising. (*LM*, 202; *U* 3.209-12, my emphasis)

Here, Stephen Dedalus' lyrical description (possibly in itself a pastiche of his readings, or a self-parody of Joyce's own youthful style) is counterpointed by Acker's provocative stereotypisation of French sexual explicitness. Following this passage is the peculiar avowal "*I can no longer speak English*" with a shift into French. Part Two, "Language," features the minimalist "Narrative Breakdown" dedicated to language poet Carla Harryman:

> The people in the world blow up the world. After the end of the world.
> One. One and one. One and one. One and one. One and one. One and one. One and one. One and one. One and one. One and one.
> One and one and one. One and one and one. One and one and one. One and one and one. One and one and one. One and one and
> One and two. One and two and no more. One and two. One and two and no more. One and two. One and two and no more. One and two. One and two and no more. One and two. One and two.
> (*LM*, 243)

In *Don Quixote: Which Was a Dream* (1986) Acker casts Don Quixote into the role of a woman on a quest to defeat the evil enchanters of the modern American life. Her tool is language, the foundational site of power in Western civilisation, portraying a society so blind to its own incarceration by greed and corruption that it requires an outside perspective to determine what is still human (this outsider comes in the character of Godzilla). Signification itself is subject to Acker's examination, and throughout *Don Quixote*, she relates language to the formation of gender identity; in sentences like "since a broom's sweeping hisandorher bald pate, heandorshe is a which," or "he whom I love is my eyes and heart and I'm sick when I'm not with him, but he doesn't love me; he's my I's; I see by my I's; he's my sun. My son lets me see and be. Thus he's my and the @" (DQ 75; 101), Acker is not simply exploiting puns to form sentences with multiple possible meanings,[74] but purposefully disrupts the illusion of narrative coherence or message. The only Joyce cameo in the novel, again, has to do with the notion of authorship and propriety: "Would not the attributing of *The Imitation of Christ* to Louis Ferdinand Céline or James Joyce be a sufficient renovation of its tenuous spiritual counsels?" (*DQ*, 55).

With *Empire of the Senseless* (1988), Acker turns to mythology as the overarching structure of her work, in particular, to the communal myths that pervade the general culture. *Empire of the Senseless* recounts the picaresque adventures of Abhor, a female protagonist of mixed race and human-robot composition, and her male accomplice, Thivai, on their search for meaning and legitimate modes of expression amid war and revolution. The two become terrorists resisting an institution of power disseminated by the media and governed by money, so that "Empire" refers equally to systems of representation and the Western hegemony that governs them. Indeed, Thivai's initial remark, "Money is a kind of citizenship. Americans are world citizens," comes to fruition later in the novel when he makes precisely this link: "What is language[?] ... Does language control like money?" (*ES*, 38; 164).

Chapter titles in *Empire* such as "Let the Algerians take over Paris" and "On Becoming Algerian" convey Acker's ongoing consideration of the possibility of socio-political opposition for marginalised Others. The "real values" on which to base legitimate modes of expression are found in Acker's female bodies, positioned against a larger, collective body of oppression. The opening section is called "Elegy for the World of the Fathers" and features the following graphic scene of incestuous rape:

---

74   Christina Milletti speaks of Acker's "terrorist aesthetics": "In contrast to James Joyce's work, which celebrates an infinite web of language and meanings, Acker tends to exacerbate fictional language, present it as a faulty tool that, because of its figural structure, lacks an essential clarity. Indeed, for her, narratives seem to be designed so poorly for communicative purposes that understanding itself is a fraud, ineffably deadlocked within language itself" ("Violent Acts, Volatile Words: Kathy Acker's Terrorist Aesthetic," *Studies in the Novel* 36.3 [Fall 2004]: 363).

> At the moment my mother was whining, daddy was smelling my cunt. 'I've reached my best moment now!' he explained. Now I was sure what he was referring to. 'This is the moment of truth!!! ... I'm going off off off jacking it off!!! ... my hands're gonna be broken from this one!!! ... I don't even recognize my own body!!! ... and it doesn't matter!!! ... I know you're mine!!! ... I made you!!! ... I'm making you!!! ... I swore I'd live for pleasure!!! ... My tongue is fucking enormous!!! ... feel it!!! ... it's reaching down to my waist!!! ... God almighty!!! ... nothing matters!!! ... you're my God!!! ... my daughter: I worship you!!! ... I beg you to do it, show I can please you!!! ... now look at it it's big, in my corkscrewing hand!!! ... kiss it!!!' [...] I licked up his sperm. (*ES*, 15)

Together with the breach of the human civilisation's basic taboo occurs a disruption in signification and communicative function of language:

> This is what daddy said to me while he was fucking me: 'Tradicional estilo de p... argentino. Q...es e.mas j...de entablar g ... amistades o t... tertulias a ... es m... similar a. estilo t...: se c... la c... con l. palma de la m... y s. apoyan l... cinco d... se s... y s. baja l. mano, l... de e ... manera y . el c ... se h ... hombre. origen e. profundamente r... y s. han h ... interesantes t... en l... jeroglificos e ... y m ... Es e.mas r ... para d ... de l ... comidas p... no c... la de ...' He had become a Puerto Rican. (*ES*, 17)

Apart from dismantling language as communication tool with these and similar deformations, Acker directs her sarcastic barbs against the powers that be and people who happen to wield power: "In agreement with Dr Freud, Dr Schreber defined paranoia as a defence to homosexual love. Dr Schreber was paranoid, schizophrenic, hallucinated, deluded, disassociated, autistic, and ambivalent. In these qualities he resembled the current United States President, Ronald Reagan" (*ES*, 45). Interspersed with these are Acker's staple poetic meditations on loss, absence, and death:

> The absence of me. Not even the existence of nothingness represented me. When I regained consciousness, unlike the old cashew nut, I lifted up the first public phone receiver I could find.
> Somebody answered me, 'Death.'
> 'That's not my name.' Alive I protested.
> 'It's your code.' I knew his voice. The curer of death. 'For the living, winter is death.'
> (*ES*, 52)

In the "Let the Algerians Take Over Paris (Abhor)" section, Acker's terrorist project is connected to the more abstract category of the exile. As her female protagonist Abhor recounts, "I would have run somewhere if there had been anywhere to which to run. But there wasn't. I know, I know there's no home anywhere. Nowhere: Exile was a permanent condition. A permanent community, in terms of relationships and language. In terms of identity. But from what was identity exiled?" (*ES*, 63). Whatever future or power her terrorist characters possess, Acker never tires of pointing out that it lies in and as writing: that any subject's future is determined by marks on the page.[75] And it is through such textual acts of terrorism that Acker hopes, as she writes in the final line of Empire, to reform society at large:

> I stood there, in the sunlight, and thought that I didn't as yet know what I wanted. I now fully knew what I didn't want and what and whom I hated. That was something. And then I thought that, one day, maybe, there'ld be a human society in a world which is beautiful, a society which wasn't just disgust. (*ES*, 227)

To this end, her manifesto appears in *Empire of the Senseless*, explaining her textual practices and taboo exploration as "an attack on the institutions of prison via language":

> That part of our being (mentality, feeling, physicality) which is free of control, let's call it our "unconscious." Since it's free of control, it's our only defense against institutionalized meaning, institutionalized language, control, fixation, judgement, prison. [...] What is the language of the unconscious? [...] Its primary language must be taboo, all that is forbidden. Thus, an attack on the institutions of prison via language would demand the use of a language or languages that aren't acceptable, which are forbidden. Language, on one level, constitutes a set of codes and social and historical agreements. Nonsense doesn't per se break down the codes; speaking precisely that which the codes forbid breaks down the codes. (*ES*, 133–34)

Here, Acker explicitly refers to Gysin's/Burroughs' famous cut-up technique, which her earlier fiction, in its excision of classic texts, perpetuated at least on the conceptual if not practical level. But now that nonsense is found out to "point back to the normalizing institutions," to disobey the laws of language doesn't mean escaping from the prison house in which it holds its speakers, nor does breaking the societal rules imposed by patriarchy entail acting in a truly "liberated" fashion. Closer to (Acker's) home, the binary opposition also imperils avant-garde writing: as long as it is simply the negation of conventional discourse, it is defined by its opposition to the institutional code and cannot possibly aim to eliminate it. So instead of deconstructing or intervening, Acker prefers instead to attack the codes themselves through speech that is not unintelligible but forbidden, to speak, as it were, the unspeakable.

---

75 Speaking of Acker's "terrorist aesthetic," Milletti puts the equation as follows: "For the terrorist, that mark is a bomb. For Acker the writer, that bomb is a fictional language which creates—not simply spurs—subjects to action" (Milletti, "Violent Acts, Volatile Words," 355).

In the third and final part of Empire, "Pirate Night," Acker's renegades go on a quest after a "society that is taboo," that is established on the very ground of transgressive acts. This section begins by plagiarising *Huckleberry Finn*, and so Thivai and his gay friend Mark (Huck and Tom) go to elaborate lengths to liberate the imprisoned Abhor (Jim), who is part black and referred to as a "runaway nigger" throughout. Acker's détournement, here, consists in replacing racism with sexism as the enslaving practice from which her protagonist must liberate herself. Still, *Empire of the Senseless* concludes on a provisional note, with Abhor facing the risk of, in rejecting rationalism, trapping herself in irrationality. Acker thus construes what critic Nicola Pitchford has called an "unreasonable text."[76] The entire book is dedicated to Acker's "tatooist." Its concluding image, as commented on by Conte in great detail, shows a rose pierced by a knife, wrapped by a banner upon which is inscribed "DISCIPLINE AND ANARCHY." And there is certainly something emblematic about this image: the "tension between discipline of life in a dualistic, gendered body and the anarchy enabled by recognizing that body as a construct"[77] is a *basso continuo* of Acker's writing.

After and together with the many other textual subversions and destabilisations, the tattoo can be both an artistic expression and an identification mark. Both an artful design written of the body and poisonous injection inside, both a décor and a mark of the outcast, a point Acker brings home:

> Cruel Romans had used tattoos to mark and identify mercenaries, slaves, criminals, and heretics. For the first time, the sailor felt he had sailed home. Among the early Christians, tattoos, stigmata indicating exile, which at first had been forced on their flesh, finally actually served to enforce their group solidarity. The Christians began voluntarily to acquire these indications of tribal identity. Tattooing continued to have ambiguous social value; today a tattoo is considered both a defamatory brand and a symbol of a tribe or of a dream. (*ES*, 130)

And yet, Acker's sailors welcome their identifying marks of difference and outcast status—again, Acker's détournement consists in turning "the kind of writing which facilitated the control and purging of the undesirable into

---

76 "Abhor begins again the difficult and constant struggle to fight hegemonic rationalism while maintaining a nonessentialist insistence on gender differences. That these differences are textual and contextual is underlined by the drawing of a tattoo that is the book's last image. It is a rose pierced by a knife, wrapped by a banner upon which is written "DISCIPLINE AND ANARCHY" (Nichola Pitchford, *Tactical Readings: Feminist Postmodernism in the Novels of Kathy Acker and Angela Carter* [London: Associated University Press, 2002] 103).

77 "This is, on the metafictional level, also evident the tension between the discipline of any individual, complete and self-contained text and the anarchy of the contextual mutations that Acker makes of them" (Pitchford, *Tactical Readings*, 103).

an expression of group identity."[78] The iconography of the concluding image suggests that the competing principles of discipline and anarchy, in which the sword of pain pierces through the rose of pleasure, binding the cords of discipline and untying the knot that restrains anarchy. As Acker confided to Friedman,

> The most positive thing in the book is the tattoo. It concerns taking over, doing your own sign-making. In England [...] the tattoo is very much a sign of a certain class and certain people, a part of society that sees itself as outcast, and shows it. For me tattooing is very profound. The meeting of body and, well, the spirit—it's a real kind of art, it's on the skin.[79]

Drawing on an extraordinarily wide range of sources and a very complex methodology of writing which rejected conventional morality and traditional modes of literary expression, Acker's iconoclastic was designed as a challenge to established literary forms, categories of literary authorship, propriety, etc. Acker's novels contain some of the most stylistically difficult writing in the entire period. Her narrative voices, as well as her typeface, page layout, language (portions of *Blood and Guts* and *Empire of the Senseless* are in Persian) have a fragmented quality; the characters' histories, sex, and even species change without warning or explanation. This writing methodology and its destabilising effects accounted for the many scandals, censorships, and suppressions surrounding Acker's texts, but they have also brought about her success, her celebrity status, and her inclusion within the canon. Her, for some paradoxical, achievement has been read as a case in point of "the ways in which capitalism informs publishing to the extent that a writer who 'blasphemes' against every conventional value imaginable can be safely incorporated into consumer culture."[80] For all her attempts at the contrary, Acker has gone down in recent literary history as one of its most easily definable and identifiable (read: marketable and profitable) personae.

This, perhaps, is the ultimate terrorist (i.e., aggressively disruptive of the status quo) act of Acker's work: neither its adumbration of the "language of the unconscious," nor its articulation of "the anarchic dictate of the individual heart," but its foregrounding of the processes whereby it will be re-appropriated by the contexts, relations, and institutions it seeks to oppose. Even Acker's own anti-business revolution was ultimately "good for business":

---

78 Joseph Conte, *Design and Debris: A Chaotics of Postmodern American Fiction* (Tuscaloosa: University of Alabama Press, 2002) 65.

79 Friedman, "A Conversation with Kathy Acker," 17–8.

80 Martina Sciolino, "Confessions of a Kleptoparasite," *Review of Contemporary Fiction* 9.3 (Fall 1989): 63–4.

Any revolution, right-wing left-wing nihilist, it doesn't matter a damn, is good for business. Because the success of every business depends on the creation of new markets." He drummed his left finger into the table. "Do you know what human death means? It means disruption." Drum. Drum. "Disruption is good, necessary for business. Especially comic books. (ES, 182)

Capitalism can indeed profit even off that which strives to annihilate it. Acker's desensitising aesthetics is acutely aware of this—and like Joyce's, her "pelagiarist pen" (FW 182.3) not only anticipates, through its many own plagiarisms, the ultimate theft which shall not be its own to inflict upon others. In doing so, it also actively participates in the expropriation to which it will be subjected, once the empire of the senseless decides to strike the all-too--perfect balance with it.

Echoing some of Jolas' revolutionary pronouncements and sharing his conviction of the necessity of treating (and attacking) the language of official discourses as a political entity, the aggressive, confrontational intertextuality of Acker's novels is arresting and disturbing, and presents a strikingly original reworking of the Joycean fictional exploration of the materiality of language.

6.6 "THE JOYOUS HERESY THAT WILL NOT GO AWAY": GILBERT SORRENTINO

The most explicitly *Ulyssean* and *Wakean* work of fiction of the time and place is doubtlessly *Mulligan Stew* (1979) by Gilbert Sorrentino.[81] However, both preceding and following it is an oeuvre whose experimental character results from Sorrentino's highly idiosyncratic blend of influences and his proceduralist approach to fiction. As he confided to Charles Trueheart of *Publishers Weekly*, "form not only determines content, but form invents content."[82]

Sorrentino's output commingles poetry and prose to an almost equal degree: by the time his first novel was published, two books of his poetry had

---

81   Sorrentino was born in Brooklyn and spent most of his life in New York. He married twice and had three children, and served, via conscription, in the Army Medical Corps from 1951 to 1953, after which he began to write fiction. Early in his literary career, Sorrentino cofounded *Neon* magazine and served as its publisher and editor from 1956 to 1960. When Neon folded, he took a book editor position with Kulcher and then with Grove Press, where he witnessed a revolutionary period in avant-garde publishing. By the time he left Grove in 1970, Sorrentino had published several works of poetry and fiction. From that point forward, he continued to publish consistently and worked in various faculty positions for institutions including Columbia University, Sarah Lawrence College, the New School for Social Research, the University of Scranton, and finally Stanford University, where he served as a professor of English from 1982 to 1999 and then professor emeritus.

82   Qtd. in *Merriam Webster's Encyclopedia of Literature* (New York: Merriam Webster, 1995) 1053.

come out, engaged with spatial presentation of language, a preoccupation shared by his fiction. His first two novels—*The Sky Changes* (1966) and *Steelwork* (1970)—prefer spatial arrangement and non-chronological simultaneity to linear narrative progression. In *Imaginative Qualities of Actual Things* (1973), Sorrentino satirises the New York avant-garde art world of the 1950s and 1960s, with which he had been personally involved but later sought to dissociate himself from. This work is the first in which Sorrentino's modernist heritage clearly surfaces: each chapter is devoted to one of the eight principal characters and the novel proceeds by way of digression, anecdote, asides, and itemisations, all filtered through a single narrator.

First of Sorrentino's formally experimental works is *Splendide-Hôtel* (1973), a short text of twenty-six sections, each based on a letter of the alphabet and the images it suggests. As the back-cover blurb[83] makes clear, *Splendide-Hôtel* comes under the influence of the poetry of William Carlos Williams and Arthur Rimbaud—the title is taken from Rimbaud's "Les Illuminations"—and aims to rescue the poetic language from the grasp of commercialism. Dedicated to his old friend Hubert Selby, Sorrentino's *Splendide-Hôtel* is meant as an antidote to what he saw as a general neglect of prose. The motto is Rimbaud's "*Et le Splendide-Hôtel fut bâti dans le chaos de glaces et de nuit du pôle,*" and below is a sample of the opening lines for a few letters:

A: A continuing rejuvenation? Of flies! *Mouches éclatantes.* The poet has it that this primal vowel is black. The great alpha, black A. "Black velvet coat of glittering flies." Black, black. The A, sitting quietly on the page, wings folded back over the shining body. A, a fly. AA, two flies. [...]
B: B-b-b-b. The sound an idiot makes. I remember Jo-Jo, ah, a perfect idiot name. A Mongoloid, shuffling down the street on the arm of his grey and faded Irish mother, punching himself in the face. [...]
F: A poem may sometimes open to you, a flower; or it will close up suddenly, a trap, inside a nervous rat, moving in swift jerks. One sees, not the poem, but the poet's absolute intent. Or, the floor unexpectedly opens, and a black underworld is glimpsed.
(*SH*, 7; 9; 19)

Sorrentino's letter-based texts employ a whole range of techniques by which to bring home the associations. In the above quotation alone, there is the

83 "Arthur Rimbaud's invented *Splendide-Hôtel,* "built in the chaos of ice and of the polar night," provides the occasion for Gilbert Sorrentino's imaginative meditation on letters and language. Each chapter serves as an opportunity for the author to expand on thoughts and images suggested by a letter of the alphabet, as well as to reflect upon the workings of the imagination, particularly in the art of William Carlos Williams and Arthur Rimbaud. Reminiscent of the philosophical treatise/poem *On Being Blue* by William H. Gass, *Splendide-Hôtel* is a Grand Hotel of the mind, splendidly conceived."

visual/material resemblance ("A" resembling a fly), the auditory/conceptual connection ("B" being "the sound an idiot makes"), or alliterative ("F " evoking a "flower," a "floor," etc.). The remaining parts of the book continue in this celebration of language as material and of creativity as synaesthesia.

Still in 1973, Sorrentino published *Flawless Play Restored: The Masque of Fungo*, a satire in the manner of Ben Jonson, which on its title page declared itself "part of a novel-in-progress presented in play form, but not intended for the stage." In 1975 Sorrentino completed the novel—initially titled "Synthetic Ink"—in which the play was the centrepiece. Sections of the book appeared in various magazines beginning in 1973, but the nearly 450–page work was rejected by many publishing houses before being accepted by Grove Press, on the condition that the title be changed to *Mulligan Stew*, with its punning allusion to Buck Mulligan, and the novel was published in May 1979.

Mulligan Stew, a mélange of literary bits and pieces that serves to demonstrate the breadth of its author's technical skills while dismissing and parodying the avant-garde, is widely considered Sorrentino's masterpiece. Sorrentino uses the simplest narrative frame (the plot of the novel concerning an author who attempts to write a story) on which to hang collective knowledge, cultural awareness, and modernist technical expertise. The title's frame of reference is Joyce, but as shown in its first reviews already, the novel's intertext encompasses Rabelais, Sterne, as well as the Flaubert of *Bouvard et Pécuchet* and the Flann O'Brien of *At Swim-Two-Birds*, to whose "virtue *hilaritas*" the novel is dedicated and who is also the source of an epigraph that prepares the reader for a book considered as a "personal musical instrument." The other two mottoes are "Ber*s*erk. Ber*s*erk. Ber*s*erk! Ber*s*erk? Ber*s*erk! Ber*s*erk . . . ?" (attributed to Philip Vogel, in conversation) and "I done me best when I was let [...] And lilting on all the time," from the penultimate page of the *Wake*.

The novel is prefaced by a series of letters and a reader's report detailing the difficulty of seeing such a novel into publication. One of the letters warns that the following wallows "in the mortal sin of bookishness," and the novel is indeed composed ostentatiously of fictional documents—more letters; extracts from journals, scrapbooks, and notebooks; interviews; reviews; poems; as well as *The Masque of Fungo*. Sorrentino told publisher John O'Brien that "every one of my books is an attempt to solve another fictional problem that I set myself," and one the solutions he uses is "inventing another voice or another group of voices."[84] Sorrentino lifts characters from other novels to

---

84   Qtd. in Julian Cowley, "Gilbert Sorrentino," *Dictionary of Literary Biography, Volume 173: American Novelists Since World War II, Fifth Series*, eds. James R. Giles & Wanda H. Giles (The Gale Group: Northern Illinois University, 1996) 252.

populate *Mulligan Stew*, drawing Ned Beaumont from Dashiell Hammett's *The Glass Key* (1931) and Antony Lamont from *At Swim-Two-Birds*.

Martin Halpin finds himself "plucked out of the wry, the amused footnote in which I have resided faceless, for all these years, in the work of that gentlemanly Irishman, Mr. Joyce" (*MS*, 26), and transplanted into a novel being written by Lamont, within the work of Sorrentino:

> I can't understand how Mr. Joyce allowed him to take me away! Surely, it can't have been for money! Or does Mr. Joyce even *know* that I have gone? Maybe he's dead. [...] Mr. Joyce, knowing that I could do nothing at all, merely stated, *stated*, mind you, that I performed "odd jobs." [...] If there is one thing I learned while working for Mr. Joyce, it is that one cannot escape for long from a writer, unless he decides to completely rewrite a whole section. (*MS*, 26–7)

This "plucking out" occurred from *FW* 266.F2, where Martin Halpin makes a brief cameo as the originator of the phrase "to make hobbyhodge happy in his hole," and is presented as "an old gardener from the Glens of Antrim who used to do odd jobs for my godfather, the Rev. B.B. Brophy of Swords."

The character Antony Lamont is writing a novel within Sorrentino's novel, and midway through the book, Lamont's characters try to escape and go their own way. *Mulligan Stew* traces the decline of Lamont into bitterness and paranoia, and the consequent squandering of his creative energies in his struggle to write. Part of this creative dissipation mapped throughout the book is Sorrentino's staple device: the catalogue structure, which oftentimes takes the form of mere lists of words on exhibit. Lists occur at all levels of narration and include a list of books and periodicals found in the fictional cabin (*MS*, 31–35). The list's humour lies in its allusiveness as well as its treatment of characters as authors themselves: thus, alongside "*How to Understand the Deaf* by James Joyce," there are also books such as "*Having That Affair* by B. Boylan," "*Say Yes to Love* by Molly Bloom," "*The Layman's Missal* by Buck Mulligan," or "*James: Preserves and Jellies* by Stuart Gorman" (*MS*, 31–4). As the narrator remarks in an ironic aside, "whatever one may make of such a list I don't know. Certainly Ned has no idea what it means" (*MS*, 35). There are recurring lists of "questions and answers" in the scrapbook; the answers are often lists in themselves. The embedded short story "O'Mara" is nothing but lists of insufferable clichés cataloguing everything the "hero" likes and everything he dislikes (*MS*, 66–75). The "Anonymous Sketch" begins with the phrase "a maker of maddening lists" (*MS*, 259) and accordingly, the whole paragraph then becomes a list, the sketch construed around lists of editorial descriptions.

There are also lists (in the mode of "Ithaca") of merely potential, not actual items, e.g., a two-page list of what Halpin would have preferred to find instead of what he did find (*MS*, 411–13). *Mulligan Stew* even ends with a list from Beaumont's second letter to Halpin (*MS*, 439–45): "a list of gifts given by writers to characters of theirs who have patiently waited for years and years, after working like dogs, in manuscript and long-forgotten and out-of-print books—waited to be seen and known, loved and hated. Tokens of their employers' esteem and gratitude" (*MS*, 439). The problem of finding a suitable audience for a novel like *Mulligan Stew* is in fact directly addressed in its own initial pages, e.g, through the series of rejection letters received by "Gilbert Sorrentino" (rejecting the book we are about to read). "Lookit," writes one "Edgar Naylor," a "Senior Editor," "you are talking to a man who would have turned down 'Aunt Lydia Plurabelle'—and with no regrets" (*MS*, 7).

James Joyce, notoriously, features among the characters of *The Masque of Fungo*. The list of *dramatis personae* lists "James Joyce, *a grocer's assistant*" alongside, e.g., "Fucking Whore" or "Harry the Crab." His contribution is reduced, by and large, to one-line replicas, witticisms, or shibboleths, all culled from the *Wake*, such as "A vagrant need is a flagrant weed" (*MS*, 198; *FW* 294. F3); "He ought to blush for himself" (*MS*, 199; *FW* 47.1); "Respect the uniform" (*MS*, 201; *FW* 579.14); "One must sell it to someone, the sacred name of love" (207; *FW* 268.F1); "Note his sleek hair, so elegant, *tableau vivant*" (*MS*, 209; *FW* 65.7); "I rose up one maypole morning and saw in my glass how nobody loves me but you" (*MS*, 212; *FW* 249.26); "I believe in Dublin and the Sultan of Turkey" (*MS*, 213; *FW* 266.F1). The conclusion of the masque, then, is the following:

> James Joyce: Ere we hit the hay, brothers, let's have that response to prayer. [*FW* 307.F9]
> ALL: No cheating. Unwary.
> James Joyce: Loud, heap miseries upon us yet entwine our arts with laughters low! [*FW* 259.7–8]
> ALL: With laughters low!
> (*MS*, 216, my brackets)

What is remarkable about these *Wakean* borrowings is that, although lifted from across the book, they are without exception instances of plain, common language, devoid of the *Wakean* punning deformations or portmanteau complexification. In a sense, Sorrentino's *masque* unmasks the myth of the *Wake* as a difficult book, and dismantles its fetishised status of *the* avant--garde text, by showing how so much of it is not "avant-garde" or "experimental" at all.

Sorrentino's metafictional or self-reflexive treatment of characters, their employment at his hands as little more than value functions within the exchange processes at the literary market, as well as the nature of his *Wakean* borrowings, underlie his critique of the mythologies—popular and elitist—

of the *Wake*'s culture. As Werner has noted, this treatment of character as commodity has to do with Sorrentino's suggested antidote to his pessimist diagnosis of the state of American cultural life.[85] Always reduced to being a function of the society, a writer—however subversive, avant-garde, or non-mainstream—writes *of* that society, *within* the society. Nowhere is this clearer than through the foil of Lamont's novel whose ample excerpts are scattered throughout *Mulligan Stew*.

For instance, chapter 10, "Nameless Shamelessness," describes an encounter between Halpin, Beaumont, the woman of their dreams Daisy Buchanan, and Mesdames Corrie Corriendo and Berthe Delamode, a pair of pornographers—prostitutes with whom they have become entangled—literally, as in the following:

> I saw Madame Corriendo lie back on the couch, entreating Daisy to forbidden pleasures with a look so flamy that I quaked with lust. And Daisy, who still talked haltingly on of our moral obligations toward dear Ned Beaumont, suddenly ceased, and gently lowered herself to the floor; on hands and knees, cooing softly and deeply in her ivory throat, she crawled toward the lush rose that Madame Corriendo, panting, proffered her, while I helplessly began to undo my curiously constricting trousers. (*MS*, 324)

Lamont's supposedly "stylish" take on writing is here undermined penchant for the trite phrase ("forbidden pleasures," "quaked with lust," "ivory throat") and the gauche euphemism ("lush rose"); he could be no more successful as pornographer as he is as an avant-gardist (a failure). Stylistic lushness, then, is arguably even less effective in a genre that requires a minimum of obfuscation.

A chapter of Lamont's novel entitled "Making It Up As We Goes Along" (*FW* 268.F2) is not only another allusion to a footnote in the same section of the *Wake* which introduces Martin Halpin to the literary world, but also underscores Sorrentino's point that, indeed, a writer does make up his fiction as he goes along, from the linguistic material conditions of his culture, the inevitable result being that the fiction inevitably reflects the culture. Notes Werner, "just as Joyce filled the *Wake* with references to cricket stars, Sorrentino fills *Mulligan Stew* with allusions to baseball players." Similarly, the literary myth of Joyce's Leopold Bloom is no more important to *Mulligan Stew*

---

85 "He demonstrates that the 'character' Halpin is as much a function of the disintegrating world of the 'experimental' writer Lamont as he was of the 'quiet world' of the 'gentlemanly' Joyce. Sorrentino makes the point that one's view of the universe depends in large part on one's position in that universe; few of the characters in *Finnegans Wake* lead such a sedate life as Halpin. But Sorrentino extends his discussion to indicate that Lamont (and by extension Sorrentino, also an 'experimental' novelist) is himself a function of the culture in which he lives" (Werner, *Paradoxical Resolutions*, 198–9).

than, e.g., the myth of Fitzgerald's Daisy Buchanan. As Werner correctly observes, "Sorrentino, like Joyce, accepts and employs everything which falls within his experience without aesthetic preconceptions either realistic or romantic," insisting only that "we work with the full range of the experience at our disposal."[86]

Echoing Joyce's "first riddle of the universe" (*FW* 170.4), Sorrentino asks, "When is a man not a man?" and while Joyce's answer in the *Wake* was "Shem," Sorrentino's answer, "When he is a sham" (*MS*, 42), is even more explicitly damning. In a culture of sham, men become shams/characters as characters/shams become men, as does the Joyce whom Sorrentino salutes in the closing "credits" to *Mulligan Stew* as "Joky Joyce who lost her undies" (*MS*, 440), as "Joyce the Jewel of the merchant fleet" (*MS*, 444), and as "Jimmy the Joy of Dublin" (*MS*, 445) – a single man of many shams. As critic Daniel Green has noted, the 1979 publication of *Mulligan Stew* marked the climax of the self-reflexive novel in the US letters, appearing alongside such works as Gaddis' *J R*, Robert Coover's *The Public Burning*, and Barth's *LETTERS*. However, Sorrentino's book "appeared at a time when critical attention was beginning to shift toward the various forms of minimalist neorealism that would dominate the 1980s and 1990s," and so "the *Stew* was too easily dismissed as a vestige of a waning era, a wildly excessive book that seemed increasingly out of step with the sour and sober fiction of the minimalists."[87] Sorrentino's style changed, too, and never again did he repeat the stylistic exuberance of the *Stew*; however, he still went on writing experimental works, each of which developed its own unique form.

Indicative of his overall approach is his 1981 review of *Exercises in Style*, Barbara Wright's translation of Raymond Queneau's stunning set of variations on a banal theme (for more see Chapter Four). His conclusion neatly sums up the position from which Sorrentino has written all his fiction, but which appears most immediately pertinent to the works beginning with *Blue Pastoral* and climaxing in the trilogy: "What it posits, in a great bravura performance, is the joyous heresy that will not go away, despite the recrudescence of such aesthetic nonsense as Moral Responsibility, Great Themes, and Vast Issues as the business of fiction, and that heresy simply states: form determines content."[88] In his next novel, *Aberration of Starlight* (1980), Sorrentino turns to a more conventional form, writing a story set on the New Jersey coast towards the end of the Great Depression and concerning four characters, each of whom narrates the events of thirty-six hours at a local

---

86   Werner, *Paradoxical Resolutions*, 199.
87   Daniel Green, "'Terribly Bookish': Mulligan Stew and the Comedy of Self-Reflexivity," *Critique* 41.3 (Spring 2000): 243.
88   Qtd. in Cowley, "Gilbert Sorrentino," 253.

boarding house. *Crystal Vision* (1981) marks a return to intertextuality based on the Tarot deck and featuring a series of seventy-eight unconnected stories.

It is in *Odd Number* (1985), *Rose Theater* (1987), and *Misterioso* (1989), all three of which were published in 1989 under the title *Pack of Lies*, that Sorrentino blends the perspectivism of *Aberration of Starlight* with the design/procedure of *Crystal Vision*. *Pack of Lies* presents the three novels as trilogy, however, on a few noteworthy counts this conventional appellation fails to apply, not least of which is the undermining of narrative linearity and character identity.[89] The basic constraint suggested by the title of *Odd Number* is a division of the text into three sections comprised of thirty-three questions – an interrogation for which no reason is ever provided. In accordance with Sorrentino's creed, the form induces the content: the questioning serves to direct the novel toward a particular discourse, that of the detective or mystery story. The questions are posed by an unidentified interrogator, the answers provided by an unidentified informant:

> Was it still twilight, or had it already grown dark?
> If you'll again permit me to get my notes in order, I'll according to my data, what there is of it, it was not yet quite dark, yet it was just past what is usually called twilight certainly it was not yet dark enough not to be able to see, since it is clear that the three of them were seen in the street, beneath a plane tree it was a soft evening late spring
> (*PL*, 9)

The responses, as can be seen, are presented replete with lacunae, elisions, and deletions, implying a third-agent mediation, and interfering with, the transcript of the interrogation. The fact that the questions of part one are repeated in reverse order in the second part of the novel, suggests that the interrogator has turned to a different informant, one who is, in contrast with the taciturnity of his predecessor, now loquacious, adorning his responses with irrelevant digressions and personal associations. Then, a brief final section follows where the same interrogator (presumably) questions a third informant who presents evidence contradicting the previous two testimonies.

This cyclicality is, then, enhanced in *Odd Number*'s conclusion: a continuous loop of text that would seem to describe the novel before us: "On his desk there is a manuscript, a typescript, to be precise, of a little more than a hundred and fifty pages . . . Next to the manuscript is a single sheet of white paper on which there is typed a paragraph that reads:" (*PL*, 146), with

---

89 As Conte has noted, "the names of characters reprise in each of the novels, but in violation of literary convention, the characters are assigned different attributes. Each is a shifting signifier in a complex lang game. One will have to find some other rationale than linear (narrative) sequence for grouping these three novels together, in the order in which they appear" (Conte, *Design and Debris*, 88).

the text repeating itself up to the colon, implying repetition *ad infinitum*. The absence of a framing narrative that would explain the reasons behind the interrogation ultimately undercuts the teleology of the narrative, as critic Louis Mackey has observed, "What you get in *Odd Number* is lots of language, indeterminately representational, but no determinate representation: narration without a narrative."[90]

Rose Theater contrasts the austerity of *Odd Number* with punning verbal exuberance. In the first section, entitled "Littel alter" (a paronomasia for "little later"), the *Wake* is acknowledged as a source to some of the text's experimentation:

> Do Not Disterb. It was the McCoy, a honeymoon suite from which the ocean could be glimpsed. In the dark, in Asbury Park, for a lark. Quark quark. *Finnegans Wake* that's from. Art which rescued him from the provincial. Right. Quark you. Oh Dick, the thteak is wuined. Just like in the movies. With ascot all undone and in a generally unbuttoned state, the young woman but partically dressed, he ascendeth to the Seventh Heaven. A far cry from Mechanicville. A girdle! That was in a nother country, you can bet the rent on that. He preferred *Dubliners*, yes, I prefer *Dubliners*, to tell the truth. Self-denigrating smile. To tell the what? Father Graham turned to face them, his best vatic smile beaming. It's a sin to laugh in church. (*PL*, 158)

Rose Theater introduces the inner lives and outer circumstances of the principal female characters (ten in total) in *Odd Number*. It is constructed according to the principle of the catalogue, the fiction continuously referring to itself as a "found object," a catalogue of ultimately arbitrary, theatrical properties representing nothing more than the artifice of fiction, its fifteen chapters named for an inventory of props found in London's Rose Theatre in 1598. As Sorrentino states in *Rose Theatre*'s dust jacket, it sets out to correct the errors of its predecessor, but "in its desire to stabilize and clarify, adds new and unsettling material to that which we already possess."

Finally, *Misterioso* takes its title from a song by jazz pianist and composer Thelonious Monk. In 1983, four years before he started writing it, Sorrentino wrote to publisher O'Brien that he envisaged "a book that is a series of lists and catalogues—no narrative, no characters, no author, and no place or time or action, no nothing but those words that 'tend towards maximum entropy.'"[91] Although not quite as chaotic as Sorrentino had anticipated, *Misterioso* is still a singularly opaque recapitulation of figures and events from the first two books of the trilogy. Its structure is based on the alphabet,

---

90   Louis Mackey, *Fact, Fiction, and Representation in Four Novels by Gilbert Sorrentino* (Columbia: Camden House, 1997) 30–1.

91   Qtd. in Cowley, "Gilbert Sorrentino," 254.

and the order into which the names of characters and places, titles, some substantive nouns, and other attributes appear to fall surfaces within the first few pages.

Where Abish's *Alphabetical Africa* unleashes a strict, chapter-by-chapter process of addition and subsequent reduction, *Misterioso* has no chapter or section divisions, only blank slugs that separate text whose scope ranges from a single sentence to several paragraphs in length. If *Rose Theater* concludes on the inconclusive note "Now, what" (PL, 283), then *Misterioso* opens on a hopeful note:

> Perhaps a question will open the way to resolution, for instance: Why does this old A&P supermarket, with its wooden floors, narrow aisles, and overabundance, or so some think, of house-brand canned goods and bakery products, display, as if carelessly forgotten atop a binful of Granny Smith apples, a seemingly well-read paperback copy of *Absalom! Absalom!*? (PL, 289)

The alphabetical constraint is responsible for the orderly disorder of the text. The reader experiences the alphabetised material of the text as blatant artifice, the imposition of an implausible ordering of persons, places, and things. As Joseph Conte has shown, "these materials are brought into proximity by lexicographical accident, selected according to a principle that is foreign to the development of character, scene, or plot."[92] The number of sections, each one featuring names beginning with the appropriate letter of the alphabet, is not twenty-six, but twenty-five: The missing section—crossed out—should be devoted to X; instead, X is found in the penultimate paragraph of the novel, mysteriously lurking among the Z's. With reference to Sorrentino's own pronouncements, Conte has contextualised this anomaly via the Oulipian theory of the *clinamen*.[93]

Sorrentino's next book, *Under the Shadow* (1991), is a genre-defying assemblage of fifty-nine mysterious fragments. Each vignette has a simple noun for its title, so the contents page reads like a heterogeneous list, starting with "Memorial" and concluding with "Things." Its (in)coherence is that of a collage rather than of a narrative, and intertextual: each of the chapters is based on one of the 59 drawings that Raymond Roussel had Henri-Achille Zo produce by way of illustrations for his *Impressions d'Afrique*. With *Red the*

---

92 Conte, *Design and Debris*, 96.

93 "The deliberate anomalies in the alphabetical order of the text are examples of the Oulipian theory of the *clinamen*, or swerve. Georges Perec contends that a system too rigorously ordered will fail to be generative of any new order, remaining perpetually in an undifferentiated state. [...] *Misterioso* enfolds the previous two works within its alphabetical ordering; but as in the folds of a strange attractor, no detail recurs in precisely the same place or with the same attributes" (Conte, *Design and Debris*, 97).

Fiend (1995) Sorrentino returned to the quasi-naturalistic mode of his early output, and none of his subsequent works achieved the kind of complexity and stylistic variety of *Mulligan Stew* or the trilogy. Commenting on Sorrentino's career, *Newsweek* writer Ray Sawhill declared that

> Sorrentino has the mind of an avant-garde experimentalist and the instincts of a profane showman. His novels overflow with elaborate literary contrivances and games, and the titles he gives them [...] lead you to expect one hall of mirrors after another. But there's nothing dry or ingrown about his writing. His novels have the kind of physical charge and excitement more often associated with jazz and improvisational comedy than with literature.[94]

Even though, as Sorrentino himself confided to Dennis Barone, ours is a "Pound era" (in Kenner's coinage), not a "Joyce" or "Eliot era,"[95] his avant-gardism was deeply informed by his reworking of Joyce's *Ulysses* and the *Wake* – a reworking that is at once parodic and (ir)reverential, in service of creating a highly individual and idiosyncratic poetics.

Just how idiosyncratic the programme of Sorrentino's fiction was is teased out in Jeremy Davies' 2010 essay, "Well, You Needn't, Motherfucker: Sorrentino Underground," where criticism is levied against the "establishment," be it academia or the "ever-shrinking world of popular literary fiction," which has "ignored Sorrentino, and continues now to ignore him."[96] Davies' reading of passages from Sorrentino's novels as well as his essays, reviews, or interviews unveils as his key topic a "conflict between a love of elaborate falsification and a disgust for the false fought to a draw over and over again," which, for the reader, is "deeply unsettling," and for the literary establishment "deeply unfashionable, as it must needs be."[97] But Davies goes further, examining and challenging the very claim of Sorrentino's influence in terms of literary tradition: "It may be, then, that Sorrentino does not open ways for writing, but closes them," in that "his work may not be generative, as his own idols/

---

94   Ray Sawhill, *"Blue Pastoral* – A Review," *Newsweek* (July 4, 1983).

95   "Pound. There is no way to gauge his importance. He is by far the most important literary figure of the twentieth century. His energy, his dedication, his brilliance, his critical faculties, his ability to find things out, to locate things, to attack what was rotten and to plug what was good. His casual remarks in letters and his short essays are, by themselves, enough to make most critics seem fatuous. Edmund Wilson is a kind of Tom Swift of letters compared to Pound. Just his services on behalf of Joyce are enough to make him great, and there's his own work. I don›t think it's a mistake that Hugh Kenner called his book *The Pound Era*, which shocked a lot of people. They thought he should have called it *The Joyce Era* or *The Eliot Era*, but it's not. He's right, it's Pound" (Gilbert Sorrentino and Dennis Barone, "An Interview with Gilbert Sorrentino." *Partisan Review* 48, no. 2 (1981): 246).

96   Jeremy M. Davies, "Well You Needn't, Motherfucker: Sorrentino Underground," *Hidden Agendas*, ed. Louis Armand (Prague: Litteraria Pragensia Books, 2010) 96.

97   Davies, "Sorrentino Underground," 100.

models / favourites' were." Still, influence can be measured retroactively as well, as it were: "Joyce, Flann O'Brien, Williams – they are beginnings, and we know this if for no other reason than that Sorrentino built upon what they began."[98] And, perhaps most to the point, Davies concludes by putting his finger on what seems to be the most unsettling, unfashionable, and thus marginalising aspect at stake – the purposeful un- or anti-literariness of Sorrentino's poetics: his fiction is bleak and unpopular perhaps because it is "high" literature with "no interest in romanticizing the literary." For all its intellectual comedy and linguistic sensuality, Sorrentino's writing is "literature that loves literature, but is not broadly in favour of literature." Davies' conclusion is spot-on:

> The sentences we write have already been written. Fiction has its origins in the cliché, so is implicated in the death of sense and feeling. In the end, the hip and the square, the con and the mark, turn out to be in cahoots—they all conspire to break, however temporarily, the embargo of the ersatz. How often do they succeed? More to the point: How often do they like to be reminded of their failure?[99]

---

98   Ibid, 112.
99   Ibid, 112–3.

7.
JOYCE AS SUCH / *TEL QUEL* JOYCE: 1960–1982, AND BEYOND

In the mode of Jolas' *transition*, *Tel Quel*—co-founded by Jean-Edern Hallier and Philippe Sollers and run by the latter (chiefly in co-editorship with Jean--Louis Baudry and Marcelin Pleynet) in the period 1960–1982—is the single most important and most explicitly avant-gardist collective undertaking that consciously and pronouncedly placed itself in the tradition of the Joycean "revolution of the word." As Jean-Michel Rabaté has observed, "*Tel Quel* helped place Joyce into French avant-garde thinking in the 1960s and 70s just as Larbaud and *transition* had done in the 1920s and 30s."[1]

Promoting a broadly international avant-garde, *Tel Quel*'s use of shock tactics, political denunciations, and ideological reversals were all undertaken in order to directly connect literary production with socio-political practice. Another trait shared by *Tel Quel* with *transition* was its penchant for tying literary practice, criticism, and theory with an overriding programme or scheme, which it undertook as an explicitly group project. As Patrick Ffrench has pointed out in his magisterial study, *The Time of Theory*, "*Tel Quel* was unlike most periodicals in committing every article and its author to the programme or project of the group. In this sense it is not just a review, but also a movement in literature and theory."[2]

As journal, it was published in Paris between 1960 and 1982, appearing four times a year and amassing a total of ninety-four issues. However, *Tel Quel* was more than a periodical, and has taken on the different modalities of a group, movement, and ideology, modalities which are far less circumscribed and less institutional than that of a literary journal. As Ffrench argued elsewhere, "if regular involvement in the numerous conferences, seminars and interventions that bear the name *Tel Quel* are signs of belonging, then the group certainly includes Roland Barthes, Guy Scarpetta, Jean-Joseph Goux, and novelists Pierre Guyotat, Maurice Roche, Severo Sarduy."[3] As a move-

1   Sam Slote, "'Après mot, le déluge' 2: Literary and Theoretical Reception to Joyce in France," *The Reception of James Joyce in Europe*, eds. Wim Van Mierlo & Geert Lernout (2 Vols., London: Continuum, 2004) 394.
2   Patrick Ffrench, *The Time of Theory: A History of Tel Quel (1960–1983)* (Oxford: Clarendon Press, 1995) 3.
3   *The Tel Quel Reader*, eds. Patrick Ffrench & Roland-François Lack (London/New York: Routledge, 1998) 1.

ment or ideology, *Tel Quel* is even harder to identify and pin down, since over its twenty-two year history, *Tel Quel* often defined itself punctually in relation to the context of any particular moment.

As a whole, however, *Tel Quel* contributed to the crystallisation of a new style and to the creation of new discourses and disciplines (such as semiology and semiotics) in the intellectual and ensuing institutional revolution, participating—as one of its historians Niiko Kauppi has observed—"in the transition from Sartre's hegemony to that of the human sciences (*sciences humaines*)."⁴ This transition was part of a larger transformation in

> the dynamics of the French intellectual field [...] in the intermediate sector: the sector between scientific culture and literary culture (the poles of the professor and the creator) as well as the sector where the internal legitimation circuits (peers) and external legitimation circuits (the layman public) merged. [...] In this context, *Tel Quel* could present and diffuse avant-garde symbolic goods—paradoxically, those destined for a restricted public—to a relatively large public at a relatively low price.⁵

As Philippe Forest's monumental study, *Histoire de Tel Quel 1960–1982*,⁶ has shown, the magazine's aesthetic-political beliefs shifted from an early identification with the *nouveau roman* to a radical break with it (in the mid-1960s), from an early involvement with phenomenology and structuralism toward a full-fledged "révolution culturelle" (spurred by the student revolution of May 1968), from a Freudian reinterpretation of Marxism via an early-1970s fascination with Maoist communism to Sollers' (and the magazine's) early-1980s conversion to Catholicism.

Hand in hand with this volatility and plurality goes *Tel Quel's* variegated literary programme – even though Ffrench's perceptive account does manage to tease out the crucial trait that remained a *Tel Quel* constant: its occupation with the scientificity of literature and literary criticism/theory.⁷ This scientific outlook, then, pervaded *Tel Quel's* theory as much as its practice of literature.⁸ *Tel Quel's* literary canon was also a "work in progress" of sorts: if Joyce

---

4   Niiko Kauppi, *The Making of an Avant-Garde: Tel Quel* (Berlin/New York: Mouton de Gruyter, 1994) xv.
5   Kauppi, *The Making of an Avant-Garde*, xvii.
6   Philippe Forest, *Histoire de Tel Quel, 1960–1982* (Paris: Seuil, 1995).
7   "When science becomes [...] rhetorical, it shares the ground of literature. The literature that provides science with analogies can itself be construed as scientific (the systematicity of Joyce; Lautréamont's advocacy of a *science nouvelle*) but the significant affect is in the other direction: science becomes undermined by its object. This is happening when, in the theoretical discourse of *Tel Quel*, the twin dimensions of the subjective and the political come increasingly into play" (*The Tel Quel Reader*, eds. Ffrench & Lack, 4–5).
8   "From *Nombres* to *Lois* to *H*, the textual space of Sollers' writing becomes organized as much by Chinese ideograms and exclamation marks as by number and sequence, before finally attaining unpunctuated seamlessness; [...] in Maurice Roche's explosively visual textualizations, from

and Céline are signalled as primary objects of analysis and celebration from early on, then a colloquium in 1972 highlights Artaud and Bataille as "subjects of excess," and Julia Kristeva's *Revolution in Poetic Language* (1974) consecrates Lautréamont and Mallarmé as "proponents of a radical shift in knowledge." Ffrench's account also encapsulates the triple reasons for the importance of literature to *Tel Quel*'s socio-political revolutionary practice.[9]

The 1960 foundation of *Tel Quel* was aimed against another anti-tradition-alism within French writing, the *nouveau roman*. In a 1963 issue of *Tel Quel*, Sollers claims that "a livelier lucidity can in effect, in making *language* the principal subject of all writing, open new perspectives" (*TQ* 17, back cover). As Chapter One strove to show, any notion of an "ideology" of the *nouveau roman*, which *Tel Quel* set out to confront, is itself illusory since the creative practice of each of the New Novelists was unique and different. That said, the New Novel group found their common characteristics in the formalist experimentation with narrative and the reduction of the traditional ele-ments of character and psychology, and it was these common characteris-tics that *Tel Quel* decided to confront in order to establish its own practice as distinct. Vastly different are the two avant-garde's literary and philosophical traditions within which they place themselves – and so, by extension, is their treatment of Joyce's legacy of the materiality of language. As long as in Robbe-Grillet's *Pour un nouveau roman*, Joyce is merely one name alongside Flaubert, Roussel, Proust, Kafka, or Faulkner, in Sollers' tradition of the *œuvre limite*, Joyce occupies a central position.

7.1 *TEL QUEL'S* "ENIGMATIC RESERVE"

In the last issue of the magazine, one of *Tel Quel*'s foremost chroniclers and theorists, Jean-Louis Houdebine, observed that as long as in Robbe-Gril-let's writings, "one would be at pain to find a single remark testifying to 'a real' knowledge of Joyce's work," for *Tel Quel*, from the very start, "the name of Joyce held an important symbolic value."[10] In another context, Houdebine

---

Compact through *Circus* to *Codex*, the space of the scientific equation or diagram is invaded by figures and drawings, turning these "scientific" forms into different, figural space" (Ibid, 5).

9 "The answer to the question "Why literature?" changes according to the different versions of canonicity promoted by or ascribable to *Tel Quel*: firstly, because it is the vehicle of an epistemo-logical radicality reflected in social and philosophical change, and of a rhetorical analysis of it which engages the participation of the reader; secondly, because it is the vehicle of a subjective excess which incarnates political and cultural revolution; and thirdly, because it is dissident with regard to any system, exceptional with regard to any rule" (*The Tel Quel Reader*, eds. Ffrench & Lack, 6).

10 "On serait bien en peine de trouver dans les interventions de Robbe-Grillet, réunies en 1963 sous le titre générique *Pour un nouveau roman*, la moindre remarque qui témoignerait d'une connais-

identified the second half of the 1970s and the beginning of the 1980s as two periods of flurry in *Tel Quel*'s Joycean forays, according Joyce's legacy the status of "an enigmatic reserve."[11] Joyce's prominent position was further cemented in Julia Kristeva's account, which placed Joyce within the group's "cult of the Great Man."[12]

Gradually, however, Joyce's became an influence far more palpable and useful than any "symbolic value" (Houdebine) or "cult [of] a great man" (Kristeva) might have accorded him at the start. Even though Joyce came to prominence only together with the appearance of Jacques Derrida's essays in the mid- to late 1960s (later collected in *Dissemination*), it was thanks to *Tel Quel*'s interdisciplinary bent that discussions of Joyce were not limited to literary critics.

Rabaté has noted how Derrida's interest in Sollers was in fact emblematic of *Tel Quel*'s interest in Joyce, both aimed at the examination of the functioning of language.[13] For *Tel Quel* (and particularly for Sollers), Joyce was part of the lineage from Sade, Lautréamont, Mallarmé, all the way to Artaud and Bataille, which was exemplary of a certain canon of modernist literature subversive of classical codes. As Houdebine would recall much later, the *Tel Quel* "programme" was formulated in autumn 1967, in Sollers' "De Dante à Sade," a text whose historical scope necessarily leaves out Joyce, but whose

---

sance réelle de l'œuvre de Joyce" whereas for *Tel Quel*, "même sous cette forme pour le moins sommaire, l'inscription du nom de Joyce, dans des débats auxquels participent les animateurs de *Tel Quel* dès les premières livraisons de la revue, garde une valeur symbolique importante" (*TQ* 94: 35).

11 Jean-Louis Houdebine, "Histoires de ruptures," *De Tel Quel à L'infini: L'Avant-garde et après? (Colloques de Londres et de Paris – Mars 1995)* (Nantes : Éditions Pleins Feux, 1999) 61. Houdebine has this to say: "la lecture de Joyce, le travail analytique mis en jeu par cette lecture, a été d'une grande importance, à mon avis exemplaire. C'est une longue histoire que celle-là, qui s'inscrit dans *Tel Quel* pratiquement dès les débuts de la revue, dans les années 1960, et qui prend un nouveau rythme, particulièrement actif, productif, dans toute la seconde partie des années 1970 et le début des années 1980, jusque dans le dernier numéro de la revue (le n° 94, en 1982)."

12 "L'originalité de *Tel Quel* consiste à reconnaître le besoin de culte du Grand Homme, au cœur même du langage et au sein d'une société laïque. Et à accompagner ce besoin d'une stratégie qui propose une relecture du christianisme, à la fois pince-sans-rire et sérieusement scandaleuse, dont l'exemple le plus net est le rôle majeur que *Tel Quel* a accordé à Joyce – Joyce le polyphonique –, ainsi que la continuation de cette veine par Sollers. En ces temps de dénigrement des valeurs, la chasse ouverte contre Joyce est un des symptômes du populisme. Et on voit qu'elle se produit non pas pour désacraliser le besoin du Grand Homme, mais pour lui opposer justement d'autres grands écrivains de *best-sellers* ou de bouillons de culture" (Julia Kristeva, "Les Samouraïs tels quels," *De Tel Quel à L'infini*, 23).

13 "Derrida identified in Sollers' novel Nombres the utopia of a purely textual novel soon to become the hallmark of Tel Quel: resolutely 'experimental' texts halfway between poetry and prose. Like Finnegans Wake, they did not represent anything but just exhibited the functioning of language. By showing the codes, cogs, and wheels of literary language, the production of a new poetic and political truth would hopefully shatter the dominant repressive ideology" (Jean-Michel Rabaté, "The Joyce of French Theory," *A Companion to James Joyce*, ed. Richard Brown [Oxford: Blackwell, 2008] 259).

call for a multiplication of styles of writing by means of the "destruction of language" does relate to him, in concept if not name, since Joyce is regarded to have given this process "une ampleur, une profondeur historique [...] littéralement sidérante."[14] But the Joycean presence in *Tel Quel* was far from merely conceptual or "spectral," as even a cursory overview of its most conspicuous manifestations clearly shows.[15] The bulk of *Tel Quel*'s essays on Joyce appeared after 1968, when rather than attempting to change the novel, *Tel Quel* aimed at a full-fledged cultural revolution.

The 1972 issues 50–51 brought Stephen Heath's highly influential essay, "Ambiviolences," one of the earliest attempts at a philosophically rigorous articulation of the operations of the *Wake*'s semantic ambiguity and linguistic materiality, for which it gained so much currency among the *Tel Quel* practitioners, with reference to, among others, Vico, Jousse, Saussure, Kristeva, or Derrida. In the first part of the essay, regarding the *Wake*'s strategies of production of ambivalence, Heath identifies its contrarian attitude to continuity ("le texte n'est pas homogène mais sans cesse discontinue, une fragmentation du sens dans un perpétuel 'plus tard'" [*TQ* 50: 23–4]); its "strategies of hesitation" perceived across the entire Joyce oeuvre ("l'écriture de Joyce se trouve contrainte de poursuivre une activité constant de refus du sens, un constant dégagement de cette nappe continue des significations, explications, orders du discours" [*TQ* 50: 26]); its preference of "intertext" over "context" ("les textes de Joyce, dans leur déstabilisation, renvoient non à un context—et donc non à quelque 'Réalité'—mais à un intertexte" [*TQ* 50: 30]); its staging of the "matérialité des effects d'écriture," and its employment of the rhetorical strategies of "parodie – pastiche – plagiat – contrefaçon" (*TQ* 50: 32). The second half is devoted to the *Wake*'s elaboration of "incomprehensibility" rising from its "narration du langage" (*TQ* 51: 65), its "sillage de l'écriture, interminable remise en place du sens dans la forme, du signifié dans le signifiant" (*TQ* 51: 66); the "scribenery" through which the

---

14   Houdebine, "Histoires de ruptures," *De Tel Quel à L'infini*, 62.

15   Umberto Eco wrote a two-part article on Joyce for *Tel Quel* ("Le Moyen Age de James Joyce," *TQ* 11–12 [Fall 1962–Winter 1963]). *Tel Quel* no. 22 (Summer 1965) featured Hélène Berger (to become Cixous)'s "L'Avant-Portrait Avant-portrait ou la bifurcation d'une vocation," a study of Joyce's *A Portrait* as exercise in literary auto-biography. *Tel Quel* no. 30 (Summer 1967) brought Philippe Lavergne's French translation of the *Wake*'s "Shem" (I.7) chapter, accompanied by Jean-Pierre Faye's "Post-scriptum: Shem trouvé" and Jean Paris' study "Finnegan, Wake!" in which three words from the *Wake* ("venissoon," "cweamy," and "notshall") are subjected to an exhaustive etymological and comparative linguistic examination which yields lists of possible analogues and echoes from several dozen languages. Joyce's work is regarded by Paris as the consummation of Shklovsky's ultimate goal in art: "cette singularisation, cet obscurcissement de la forme qui, en retardant, en déroutant la perception, nous rend au sentiment que 'la pierre est de pierre'" (*TQ* 30: 59). Lavergne's "Avant-Propos" to his translation, then, approaches the *Wake* from the more conservative viewpoint of a text "suivant les lois d'association-dissociation du rêve" (*TQ* 30: 67).

Wake becomes a "theatralisation of language" on whose stage "le langage est retiré du monde de la communication et interrogé dans ses fictions" (*TQ* 51: 71); and finally, the *Wake*'s refusal of origin: "L'horizon de *Finnegans Wake* n'est pas une 'origine' mais le monde s'écrivant [...], non pas la parole vivante mais l'insistance du significant, non pas la Lettre mais le jeu des lettres" (*TQ* 51: 75). Heath's ground-breaking article, in this context, is significant not only in terms of *Wake* scholarship, but also as a blueprint for *Tel Quel*'s own practice of fiction, a guideline for so much of *Tel Quel*'s literary production, often based on the treatment of language as discourse, as material, its "narrative" drive subdued in its sustained exploration of the functioning of language.

Issue 55 (Autumn 1973) featured an excerpt from Joyce's own Italian translation of "Anna Livia Plurabella," accompanied by Jacqueline Risset's study, "Joyce traduit par Joyce." Issue 64 (Winter 1975) brought a print version of Sollers' "Joyce et Cie," his plenary lecture at the Paris Joyce Symposium from earlier that year, in many respects the crucial *Tel Quel* text on Joyce as originator of the *Telquelian* fiction practice. In 1979, issue 81 featured Houdebine's essays "Joyce's signature" and "Jung and Joyce" (dealt with below), and *Tel Quel* issue no. 83 (Spring 1980) was a special Joyce issue entirely dedicated to *Ulysses*, the *Wake*, and the questions of Joyce's Catholicism – what stands out are Houdebine's interview with Sollers ("La Trinité de Joyce"), David Hayman's study "Stephen on the rocks," and Sollers' article "James Joyce, obscénité et théologie."

Here, Sollers analyses the beginning of *Ulysses* as a conflict between Greek paganism and Jesuit Catholicism. Stephen Dedalus' refusal to kneel in front of his mother's deathbed is a symptom, for Sollers, of Stephen's will to attain a distance from matriarchy. Joyce's Catholicism, then, is a refusal of the worship of a pagan, maternal substance, which Sollers' *Paradis* suggests is the condition of society. For Sollers, this refusal on Joyce's part is tied to his conception of writing which offers access to the invisible, to something outside of the order of the phenomenal. Joyce's religious mindset (founded upon trinitarianism) allows him to pass in language through the screen of the phenomenal.

This, as Ffrench has shown, is consistent "with the constant critique in *Tel Quel* of the visual and representational, the spectacle, in favour of language and writing," and also has consequences for the relation of language to the body.[16] Adorning the cover of issue no. 92 [Summer 1982] is a photograph of

---

16 "Again, the body is left behind, as *déchet*, in this passage across and beyond the phenomenal. [...] The voice or le soufflé intervenes in the body to transform it into an incarnation of the divine possibilities of language. The stress on the voice at the expense of the image reveals that the critique of the visual in Tel Quel is the negative side of an affirmation of language [...] The materialism of Tel Quel is not a fetishization of writing but an affirmation of the irrepressible role of the voice in human relations" (Patrick Ffrench, *The Time of Theory: A History of Tel Quel (1960–1983)* [Oxford: Clarendon Press, 1995] 253).

Joyce's death mask, and part of its content is Beryl Schlossman's article "Joyce et le don des langues" ("Joyce and the Gift of Languages"). As Houdebine has noted, what is important about this surge in late *Tel Quel*'s interest in Joyce is that *Tel Quel*'s work on Joyce coincided with "la rédaction par Sollers de ces deux grands textes romanesques qui sont comme la signature du passage de *Tel Quel* à *L'Infini* – *Paradis* (1) et *Femmes*."[17]

Tel Quel's forays into Joyce culminated with Sollers' address delivered at the 1975 Paris Joyce Symposium, entitled "Joyce & Cie," later reprinted in Hayman's collection, *In the Wake of the Wake*. The address opens with the provocative statement that "since *Finnegans Wake* was written English no longer exists […] as self-sufficient language," since "Joyce introduces a permanent carrying over of sense from language to languages, statement to statements, punctuality of enunciation subject to series," (*TQ* 64: 3). Sollers' revisitation of the radically cosmopolitan, multilingual, avant-garde Joyce of *transition* sketches out Joyce's politics of refusal:

> Joyce's refusal to indulge in the slightest dead pronouncement is exactly *itself* the political act, an act which explodes at the heart of the rhetorical *polis*, at the heart of the narcissistic recognition of the human group: the end of nationalisms decided by Joyce at the time when national crises are at their most virulent (fascism in Europe). Nationalism can be characterized as a twofold obstruction—to the unconscious and to the area of the international. Hence […] it is always basically regressive, opening onto all the racist exclusions. (*TQ* 64: 3–4)

Joyce's most important political gesture, however (and here Sollers recalls some of the exagminers) is his "persistent determination to probe the religious phenomenon": for Sollers, Joyce "represents the same ambition as Freud: to analyze two thousand years of manwomankind, and not ten or a hundred years of politics." This enables Sollers to argue his case for the *Wake* being "the most forceful act ever accomplished against political paranoia […], the most formidably anti-fascist book produced between the two wars" (*TQ* 64: 4). Hand in hand with his politics is Joyce's aesthetics – again, as in Jolas' estimation, founded upon the word:

> My hypothesis, precisely, is that *Finnegans Wake* is a word, one immense word but in a state of skidding, of lapsus; a word jam-packed with words, in fact a name full of names, but "open," spiraling. This play on words seems to me to function on a simple nucleus where to give *one* word (or rather an "effect of word") there is a coming together of at least three words, plus a coefficient of annulation. (*TQ* 64: 7)

---

17   Houdebine, "Histoires de ruptures," *De Tel Quel à L'infini*, 62–3.

Examples of such "effects of words" are instructive: "Joyce writes SINSE, reading *since, sense,* and *sin.* The 'syllogistic' development of this condensation is as follows: ever since sense, there is sin; ever since sin, there is sense; ever since since (time), there is sin and sense [...] In one word, as in a thousand, you have a thesis on language and man's fall from paradise; and, simultaneously, it is funny" (TQ 64: 7). This "syllogistic" poetics has also ramification for Joyce's mytho-religious outlook: "[I]n the beginning were neither heroes nor gods, nor even men, but collisions, aggregates of sounds, of syllables," a state which Sollers reads as "laughter towards the one" via a Francophone reading of the *Wake*'s opening word "riverrun" as "*rire-vers-l'un*" (TQ 64: 8).

Such Frenchified re-readings and re-writings of the *Wake* tie in with Sollers' opening statement, later on rephrased in terms highly reminiscent of Jolas: "English for Joyce is an angle and this angle, this filter, must open on the one side onto all languages, on the other onto what 'strictly speaking' has no language, the unconscious" (TQ 64: 10). Sollers agrees with Beckett's insistence that "we are too decadent to read Joyce, too decadent perhaps to read any writing which moves in that direction. Dante, Bruno, Vico, Joyce – challenges to linear meaning, squarings of circles" (TQ 64: 10). Sollers concludes by linking his linguistic exploration of the *Wake*'s mytho-religious conceptual framework to a third crucial Joycean topic, his treatment of sexuality in which "the language is transformed into the joyance of languages" where the last word—both in *Ulysses* and *Finnegans Wake*—is entrusted to a woman.[18]

Sollers' Joyce is a man of revolutionary politics (which he seems to have been only with a considerable stretch of imagination), but he is also a writer of striking linguistic innovation and lasting importance for Sollers' own experimental time and milieu. As argued by Rabaté, for Sollers "radical literary experimentations like those of Joyce were instances of subversion of middle-class complacency and resistance to totalitarianism."[19] Besides that, and even more importantly, they formed the basis on which *Tel Quel*'s three crucial novelists (Sollers, Roche, and Cixous) founded their linguistically materialist poetics, and its chief literary theorist (Houdebine) formed his numerous forays into discursiveness and the politics of language.

---

18   "It is this saturation of the polymorphic, polyphonic, polygraphic, polyglottic, varieties of sexuality, this unsetting of sexuality, this devastating ironicalisation of your most visceral, repeated, desires which leaves you—admit it—troubled when faced with Joyce. Freud, Joyce: another era for manwomankind" (TQ 64: 13).
19   Rabaté, "The Joyce of French Theory," 257.

7.2 "A CERTAIN TYPE OF EXCESS": JEAN-LOUIS HOUDEBINE

Houdebine's essays on (not only) Joyce from the period between 1974 and 1983 have been collected in his magisterial study *Excès de langages*, which deals with linguistic transgression (via excess) of all types of imposed normativity. This is performed across genres (both literature and philosophy / theology), across languages (the German of Hölderlin, Hegel, Marx, and Freud; the Latin of Duns Scot; the English of Hopkins and Joyce; the French of Sollers), and across discourses and traditions (Duns Scot's medievalism, Hegel's phenomenology, Cantor's set theory, Freud's psychoanalysis, Joyce's and Sollers' literary avant-gardism). In a short text on "La question *langage* face aux révolutions totalitaires," Houdebine echoes Jolas' notion of the "Revolution of the Word" while also placing the Joycean project within the philosophical-theological context by claiming that "art is not a matter of concept, and even less of ideology, but a matter of the *word*."[20] The "Dossier Joyce" comprises a substantial part of the book (some 150 pages), beginning with the "Dossier politique" that discusses three types of refusal of Joyce's fiction: the Soviet reaction against his poetics (on the occasion of the 1934 Moscow Congress of Soviet Writers and the famous critique levelled against Joyce by Karl Radek); Carl Gustav Jung's 1932 article attesting to his "fascinated horror" in the face of *Ulysses*; and finally the "silence," occasionally interrupted by "annoyed remarks," from the Surrealist camp, particularly from André Breton and Louis Aragon.

The last of these refusals is worth dwelling on. In Houdebine's opinion, the surrealist hostility toward Joyce was based on the perceived "enormity" and "dangerous proximity" of his project.[21] An even finer difference comes into play when the work of a linguistically more innovative surrealist like Michel Leiris comes to bear resemblance to Joyce's *Wake*, as for instance in his *"Glossaire: j'y serre mes gloses"* (published serially in *La Révolution surréaliste*, nos. 3–6). The difference is the much larger degree to which Joyce's work with language is "subversive" of the cultural-linguistic material operated upon by means of parody, so sorely lacking in the surrealist "automatic

---

20   "Au commencement de l'Art est une expérience du Verbe; d'un Verbe infini se liant à du Nom comme s aspiration même. De cette Trinité, Joyce ne cesse parler, dans *Ulysse* et dans *Finnegans Wake*; et Sollers aujourd'hui, dans *Paradis*. Chacun à sa manière propre, dans l'époque où il leur a fallu naitre, des écrivains en dissent donc l'opération absolument singulière, dont se constitue paradoxalement son universalité absolue" (*EL*, 112).

21   "A nouveau, comme s'il y avait là, dans *Ulysses*, puis dans *Finnegans Wake*, quelque chose d'énorme, de trop énorme, de trop dangereux pour la doctrine et l'écriture surréaliste, et que celles-ci s'avèrent incapables de penser ; quelque chose, pour ainsi dire, de trop dangereusement proche et pourtant de totalement différent, et qui relègue immédiatement au rang de babioles mondaines les poèmes de ces Messieurs" (*EL*, 163).

writing."[22] Breton's 1953 critique of Joyce, ascribing to his fiction an "imitative" status, is countered with Beckett's insistence on the "thingness" of Joyce's words and Jolas' concept of linguistic autonomy.

In Houdebine's "Joyce Tel Quel," Joyce appears as the writer who epitomises *Tel Quel*'s view of fiction during the 1970s via the paradigm of the writer as exception, against such historically totalising movements as fascism and Stalinism. The textual effects commented upon by Heath or Hayman in the pages of *Tel Quel* and followed by practitioners like Sollers, Roche, or Cixous, have a real political importance in that Joyce represents the historical unconscious, a return of the repressed. *Tel Quel* champions the exceptional values of Joyce's texts—mostly *Finnegans Wake*—against nationalism, through the concept of the plurality of languages, a.k.a. *l'élangues*, as Sollers neologises in opposition to Lacan's *lalangue*.[23] Joyce becomes the touchstone of fiction's ability to undermine politically totalising systems, hence the review's stress on Joyce as a political choice, with effects for the review's interaction with the context. Joyce appears implicitly as the exception that returns on the rule to subvert and transform its system.

In Houdebine's two crucial Joyce-focused essays, "Littérature et expérience catholique" and "La signature de Joyce," the emphasis falls on the intertextual, exegetic side of *Tel Quel*'s staple Joyce criticism (rather than its political counterpart). Joyce's Catholic experience is regarded as "fundamentally soliciting" his mode of writing – reference is made to Robert Boyle's *James Joyce's Pauline Vision* and its central analogy between the mystery of religion and the mystery of literature. Houdebine returns to some points raised in his interview with Sollers on the subject of Joyce, which emphasises the theological treatment of *obscenity* as an exceptional dimension through which the status of the sexual and of the symbolic are treated as equivalent in a speaking subject.

Concentrating on the relation between "Ithaca" and "Penelope," which to his mind stages "la possibilité d'un passage à l'écriture de *Finnegans Wake*" (*EL*, 230), Houdebine reiterates the dynamics of the phenomenal and the transcendent, where the transcendent *Summa Theologica* of Aquinas (under-

---

22 "Les petits jeux de mots de Leiris n'ont en fait à voir avec la subversion du langage et des langues que Joyce est alors en train de réaliser : subversion qui met en jeu un matériau culturel et langagier énorme, traité dans une incessante parodisation, dont la démesure est exactement proportionnée à la lucidité maitrisant qu'elle implique et contient pour aussitôt la détruire et l'excéder dans son rire. C'est précisément en ce point que la divergence est effectivement totale, absolue, entre l'écriture joycienne et l' « écriture automatique » des surréalistes, avec ses effets de pacotille et banalité précieuse, dont participe entièrement le *Glossaire* de Leiris" (*EL*, 165).

23 "La différence entre l'économie du sujet de l'inconscient et celle du sujet de l'écriture réside essentiellement dans le fait que la première est réglée par l'assujettissement du sujet à *lalangue* (en un seul mot), tandis que la seconde suppose la traversée de la première pour qu'y advienne le sujet, non plus d'une *lalangue*, mais de ce que Sollers a appelé pour Joyce: *l'élangues*" (*TQ* 94: 39).

lying the catechism of "Ithaca") contrasts with the "*lapsus*" into the phenomenal world of sexuality (in "Penelope"). *Tel Quel*'s feminist slant is evident in
Houdebine's concentration on the central paradox of the episode, that it is
"a man writing a woman's enunciation" ("que c'est un homme qui a écrit cette
énonciation de femme, et que cette opération concerne directement le passage à *Finnegans Wake*" [*EL*, 236]). Joyce's letter to Frank Budgen, identifying
the four "cardinal points" of the female body and equating them with their
verbal representations is meant to convey "the way a body can understand,"
a project viewed by Houdebine as a process of a textual "incarnation" of the
female body, what he also terms the "Incarnation of the Word."[24]

Turning to the *Wake*, Houdebine notes how the Freudian definition of the
"dream" has only partial applicability – Joyce's multilingualism generates not
so much a "language of the dream" at work as a "language of the people."[25]
Returning to the topic of *obscenity*, Houdebine insists that it should be viewed
as "a gesture of language," whether verbal or non-verbal – the status of the
obscene, in Joyce, is always of the semiological order. This inscription of the
obscene has, then, the function of providing access to the sexual prohibitions
and taboos.[26]

"La signature de Joyce" focuses entirely on the *Wake*, viewed as "une multiplication du récit," which is a function of a certain type of excess, defined
as a "multiplication / division of narrative paradigms," "qui correspondraient
assez bien à ce qu'on a pu appeler « mythèmes par filtrage et agglutination »
de langues" (*EL*, 199). This multiplication is of a twofold order: "polynomina-
tion" and "polyglossie." The former takes place "au niveau de la trame narrative qui en est intérieurement et constamment secouée, inquiétée, ironisée,
aux enquêtes toujours reprises, interrogatoires, tentatives d'analyse d'un
document retrouvé par hasard," i.e., on the level of the narrative thread, constantly shaken, disquieted, and ironised (*EL*, 200). The latter echoes Sollers'
observation about Joyce using English as a filter through which to process
dozens of other languages in a syntax which is "ni la syntaxe anglaise propre-

---

24   "Elle nous introduit au contraire à l'ordre de ce que j'ai appelé une Incarnation du Verbe, de Joyce
      devenant Verbe dans l'écriture même d'une énonciation féminine, c'est-à-dire maternelle, dans
      la traversée incestueuse d'une chair enfin parlante, au sein de laquelle il accède à l'infinité « post-
      humaine » du langage. Ce qui signifie qu'il se donne à lui-même, et par un geste de *paternité*
      logique finalement très clair à mes yeux, la possibilité d'écrire *Finnegans Wake*" (*EL,* 239).

25   "Manifestement, ce n'est pas à ce niveau que se situe l'écriture de *Finnegans Wake*, ou du moins
      pas seulement : le recours à un plus-de-langues possible, qui a été soutenu systématiquement
      par Joyce, laisse à penser au contraire que loin d'écrire (dans) une « langue de rêve ," il poursuit
      un projet beaucoup plus ambitieux, qui ne peut se définir qu'en termes de *linguae gentium*, cha-
      cune d'entre elles fût-elle affectée de sa propre déformation onirique." (*EL*, 242).

26   "Dans une écriture comme celle de Joyce, dont je rappelle que ce n'est pas un hasard si elle s'est
      chargée, *du même geste*, des spéculations théologiques les plus sublimantes, l'obscène constitue
      un moyen d'accès privilégié à la symbolicité, et au lieu même de son intensité maximale : celle
      de l'inscription des interdits sexuels" (*EL*, 244).

ment dite, ni même la syntaxe de quelque langue naturelle que ce soit" (*EL*, 206).

Here, Houdebine's conception of Joyce's signature crystallises as precisely the operation of "filtrage" through which some "one" becomes a plurality of voices, "'quelque un' est en train de passer, en pluralité de voix," a parodic plurality of multiplied signatures.[27] Joyce's *Wake* is portrayed as the idea of the post-universal singularity that exists in a temporality of the *pressant*, the infinity of texts pressing behind the moment of writing, a temporality of the *dépense* of the anterior texts. The singularity of the exception, for Houdebine, is a post-intertextual singularity, what is described by a word from the *Wake* as "meandertale": "Énigme, car cela revient à (se) demander : « qui suis-je ? ». « Joyce, » bien sûr, « James Joyce ». Mais « qui suis-je-Joyce » quand « j' » écris ? Qui *joys* quand ça s'écrit, quand ça s'écrit « James Joyce » ? [...] On pourrait appeler cela : écrire son nom comme un *meandertale*" (*EL*, 208-9). In this context, Patrick Ffrench writes about Joyce's traversal of language, which takes place both within one single language or across a linguistic multiplicity:

> This traversal is neither metaphoric nor real. It is not a question of a discourse that is consciously aware of copying all other languages—the *traversée*, moreover, exists within one language, although there are exceptions, of which Joyce is the obvious one—but of a writing that has no consciousness of itself as pure origin and does not close itself off from other texts, or any writing that can be read in these terms. It reveals itself as within the same general corpus (language) as the infinite texture of human interaction.[28]

Houdebine's treatment of Joyce's signature as an intertextual and polyglottal multiplication of the many individual signatures preceding him resonates with some of the crucial concerns of *Tel Quel*'s chief practitioners of fiction.

7.3 "DIS: YES – I.R.A.": MAURICE ROCHE

Maurice Roche (1925–1997) was a writer (and musical composer) of prolific output, a "*bricoleur* with words, letters, drawings, signs, and symbols."[29]

---

27 "Si l'on peut caractériser *Finnegans Wake* comme un ensemble infini (mais théoriquement dénombrable) de séries de signatures, le texte, quant à lui, ne se borne nullement à les amonceler, à les juxtaposer : il les *re-signe*, au contraire, de la même façon que chaque nom s'y trouve *renommé*" (*EL*, 207-8).

28 Ffrench, *The Time of Theory*, 247.

29 Dina Sherzer, *Representation in Contemporary French Fiction* (Lincoln and London: University of Nebraska Press, 1986) 50.

Apart from his experimental novel-triptych, published between 1966 and 1974, his works include *Opéra bouffe* (1975), *Mémoire* (1976), *Macabré* (1979), *Testament* (1979), *Maladie mélodie* (1980), and *Camar(a)de* (1982), all of which are intended to form a single work made up of interdependent panels. *Compact*, *Circus*, and *Codex*, Roche's first three experimental texts explicitly tied with *Tel Quel*, use "deconstructed narratives, typographical music, extended puns, and systematic disfigurations of the white page"[30] along with Joycean verbal neologisms to communicate the "dance of death" of our civilisation—an apocalyptic dimension also present in the *Wake*, published on the eve of World War II.

In *Compact* (1966), Roche draws on his background as a musical composer to structure the novel with alternative narratives, each provided with a specific voice, tense, and typeface. The thin storyline revolves around a blind, dying man whose recourse to imagination enables him to create erotic sensations as he deals with a Japanese tattoo collector who seeks his tattooed skin. The collage of fragments that forms the texture of *Compact* is reminiscent of Burroughs' technique of the cut-up – referred to via allusion to the Beat Hotel: "Sans arriver à oublier complètement que j'occupe, couché sur un grabat, une mansard d'hôtel (rue Gît-le-Coeur, au centre de Paris), je m'imagine gisant de marbre au fond d'une crypte obscure" (*Co*, 27). Paronomasia is redeployed by Roche as "calembours": e.g., *douleur*, "pain," becomes variously transcribed as "doux leurre" or "d'où l'heure?" (*Co*, 31). Portmanteaux appear not as "packed together," but as simultaneously presented alternatives: e.g., "A peine per $\frac{due}{cue}$" (*Co*, 102) or "Percer le cont $\frac{i}{e}$ nu de la vie," and very often the text branches into neighbouring columns.

Where Joyce packs meaning into the word and includes a vast number of oblique and direct allusions to "molecular" details, Roche depends more on the technical shaping, the sentence as polyseme, the text as variable image or gesture. As in Acker, the motif of the tattoo collector allows Roche to meditate on how the surface on which writing is inscribed becomes none other than the body, human skin and flesh – a "bodily" language of yet another order is presented on page 55, with a whole passage transcribed in Braille. Punning, however, is also ample, and quite palpably Joycean: "ET VÉNUS EST VENUE ÈVE NUE AI VEINE EUE" (*Co*, 87), as is mythological parody: "ARIANE EN SOLDE, ISOLDE AU RABAIS, BÉATRICE À CRÉDIT, DIDON BON MARCHÉ, SCHÉHÉRAZADE – RAMENTEUSE DE DORMEUR ÉVEILLÉ" (*Co*, 48).

---

30   Hayman, "Introduction," *In the Wake of the Wake* (Madison: University of Wisconsin Press, 1978) 28.

The concluding macaronic melange, combining the French base with Italian and German admixture (the discourse and catchphrases of Nazi rallies), ties in with *Tel Quel*'s belief in the *Wakean* multilingualism as an anti-fascist strategy:

> EVVIVA ! – « Noi, ci sentiamo forti – W ! – Questa mattina, siamo comunicati – W ! – Quando buffiamo del buon dio possiamo inghiottire qualsiasi cosa – EVVIVA !
>
> ... (hou ! hou ! hou !
>
> hou ! ouououououououn goth et magoth mit uns ! – HEIL ! – Wir versprechen tausendundeine Nachtjahre in der Wüsten ! – HEIL ! – jezt und immerdar ! – HEIL ! – und von Ewigkeit zu Ewigkeit ! – AMEN –...
>
> (*Co*, 158)

"Goth et magoth mit uns" is self-explanatory, and the promise of "a thousand-and-one nightyears in the desert" an interesting portmanteau of the Arabian Nights, the Biblical thirty years of wandering the desert, and Hitler's thousand-year Reich. As observed in a study by Michel Pierssens, by employing such typographical compression and linguistic innovation, *Compact* is thus a novel "of a descent into Hell condensed to the extreme," thus in a line of descent stretching from Homer's *Odyssey* and Virgil's *Aeneid* to Joyce. Except that, unlike Joyce's hell, Roche's is inhabited not by the mother, but the father: "Vous seriez, vous, le fils qui vous regarderait — Vous le père que vous regarderiez allongé sur un chariot dans la chambre frigorifique de l'hôpital..." (*Co*, 114).[31]

Circus (1972) further reduces the narrative drive by zooming in on the labyrinth of the brain filled with noxious and voided commonplaces, a novel made up of the detritus of novels. Its visual presentation looks like the manuscript of a book proofread and corrected, ready to be typeset, with mistakes and their corrections appearing together on the pages and yielding two meanings. As critic Dina Sherzer notes, Roche calls these *coquilles creatives*, drawing attention to the double meaning of *coquille* as a typographical error and as a protective shield for male genital organs. Regarding *Circus*' avant-garde affiliations, Sherzer traces them back to Joyce's Dada Zurich.[32]

---

31   "*Compact* est ainsi le roman condensé à l'extrême d'une descente aux Enfers, comme on en trouve dans tous les grands récits deformation. [...] Là aussi où, chez lesclassiques, l'Enfer est un lieu peuplé, voire surpeuplé, il n'est habité dans Compact que par un seul fantôme — non celui de la mère, comme chez Homère ou chez Joyce — mais celui du père" (Michel Pierssens, *Maurice Roche* [Amsterdam- Atlanta: Rodopi, 1989] 12).

32   As regards the content, Sherzer has wittily suggested that "one way to prepare oneself to enter *Circus* is to think of the memorable Dada evenings of the Zurich Cabaret Voltaire. The readings of prose and poetry in several languages; the shaking of bells and the beating of drums; the use of puppets, masks, and costumes; the interest in nonsense [...], all these created a multimedia, heterogeneous atmosphere" (Sherzer, *Representation in Contemporary French Fiction*, 50).

Circus mingles fragments of discourse (advertisement, history textbooks, lewd songs) in different languages (again, English, Italian, and German are prominent), as well as different registers and styles of French. However, *Circus* goes beyond *Compact* in featuring languages both ancient and modern in their original script: Arabic, Chinese, German, Gothic, Aztec glyphs, Egyptian hieroglyphs. Moreover, there are also some artificial indexical and symbolic languages in their graphic representation: road signs, chemical compounds, mathematical and physical symbols and formulas, shorthand, labels of products, pieces of music, symbols from the Michelin guide, and signs of the zodiac. The typography is also a kind of textual carnival: there are italics, boldface, large and small lowercase and uppercase letters; horizontal, vertical, and sideways writing; passages in parentheses, brackets, braces, and boxes; underlining, arrows, and oscillograms. Examples of Joycean wordplay again abound: "$\overset{r}{\underline{\mathit{ÉcouXterleLaïus}}}$" (*Ci*, 25). Écouter, notes Sherzer, means "to listen to," whereas écourter is "to shorten"; the capital L of Laïus makes it a proper name, the father of Oedipus, but juxtaposed with écouter or écourter it takes on the meaning of *laius*, slang for a long-winded speech.

Roche's typographical emblem (his surname signature arranged so as to form a picture of a skull) is here present on the textual level in passages like "Grossièrement fait ? De cinq lettres (C$\overset{r}{\underset{â}{}}$n E) dont une canine, celle de l'œil. $\frac{\mathit{Démontable}}{\mathit{Incassable}}$!" (*Ci*, 22). Or, more complexly, in such bilingual passages as follows:

qu'eSt-ce QUE LETTrE

entre

le !   objet   sujet   le ?

« l'intérieur est à l'ex-

térieur et l'extérieur

n'existe pas... »

Schrift**K**örp**Er****LETT**ern

zwischen

dem !   dem ?

Objekt

Subjekt

« Das Innere ist außen

und das Außen

existiert nicht. »

(*Ci*, 32)

Here, not only does the inscription form a calligram reminiscent of a skull, but the clever capitalisation of selected letters spells out SQUELETTE and SKELET. There is also the Joycean blasphemous parody, when Roche détourns, e.g., the first line of the Lord's Prayer, "Notre père qui êtes aux cieux," which underlies "Notre Père qui êtes aux yeux du monde sans effet" (*Ci*, 34). In her detailed analysis of the text, Sherzer speaks of *Circus* as constituting "a semiographic space, a constant visual spectacle, in which a compendium of signs and symbols create a polysemiotic environment, a kind of *intersignalité*, comparable to the one that readers are exposed to every day in their lives,"[33] i.e., ,paperspace of the materiality of signs à la Joyce.[34] So long as sexual references and innuendos are present on almost every page of the text, the Eros of the language is closely accompanied by Thanatos or Death. The last page features an image of skull preceded by an inscription and Roche's emblematic signature:

> **Toucher à ce terme emblématique – à l'idéogramme, hiéroglyphe d'un (dernier) soupir, d'un souffle (contenant tous les sens – y compris celui de l'histoire, de toutes les histoires possibles et maginaes).** (*Ci*, 72)

Codex (1974) embarks on charting a schematic apocalypse in which a dying man meditates upon the last things of a civilisation, which he gradually comes to represent. Here, the language frequently becomes one of chemical equations and compound symbols. Again, the focus is the inside of the skull, the workings of the imagination, the structuring of language. This comes across in the following pun regarding the "infinite proportions between *nothing* and *deny*," words which form an anagram in French: "Entre *rien* et *nier* les proportions étant tellement infinies, la cervelle la plus aiguë n'y pouvant pénétrer, devoir—pour échapper à ce labyrinthe inexplicable—admettre une manière" (*Cx*, 48).

The apocalyptic dimension of the text is brought home in the long "Cantate funèbre," which is structured by means of a punning transcription of the sections of the Requiem Mass. Thus, "Requiem aeternam" becomes "Recuit, aimer terne âme":

> **Relax(e) quand tout est terminé bien**
> **Fini car il faut bien que cela**

---

33 Sherzer, *Representation in Contemporary French Fiction*, 56.
34 "Its constant play with signs, letters, and space, and the facile and irritating play with and on words that creates endless polysemies. It is undeniable that the writing appears overtly as techno-narcissism, exhibitionism, mannerism, contrived exaggeration, and constant fireworks. It is also the production of someone who enjoys mixing, cutting, splicing and "joycing" (in the sense of James Joyce) words, languages, sings and symbols" (Sherzer, *Representation in Contemporary French Fiction*, 59).

> **Finisse le dernier terme apportant**
> **La grande lueur d'espoir au napalm**
> **Ou à l'hydrogène.**
> (*Cx*, 105)

"Kyrie eleison" becomes "**Qui riez (patron), réveillez – il sonne ! –;**" "Dies irae," "**DIS, EST-CE IRÉnique, la rogne,**" "Tuba mirum;" "**TUBE, AMI, RHUM – per sepulchra Regionum –;**" etc. (*Cx* 105–6). This "Cantate" also includes a most direct allusion to Joyce in that it buries the concluding line of *Ulysses* within the sado-religious context of the bitterly comic funeral: "LA CRIME Ô SAD – DIS: YES – I.R.A" (*Cx*, 111) transcribes the Latin "Lacrimas a Dies Irae" as a calembour of Joycean and Irish themes. As Hayman has noted, unlike the *Wake*, however, which builds toward a reawakening from the thunderous fall, "Roche's texts build toward a spine-chilling conclusion full of political overtones."[35] The conclusion of *Codex* is Roche's staple image of the grinning skull, the clown's totem, which is visually turned into an emblem for Roche's own name. In the final double hieroglyph of *Codex*, a radar screen (posing as a TV screen) alongside which is written VIDE PARTOUT! is followed on the next page by a skull made of words for peace in many languages, punctuated by bomb-shaped exclamation points.

Roche's is a broadly experimental, multimedial, and visually innovative poetics whose concrete typography, however playful and funny, serves its serious political message: a warning against civilisation's drive toward self-destruction, and an elegy for all it has already destroyed. Where Joyce packs meaning into the word and includes a vast number of oblique and direct allusions to "molecular" details, Roche depends more on the technical shaping, the sentence as polyseme, the text as variable image or gesture.

7.4 "AS CLOSE AS POSSIBLE TO THAT UNHEARD-OF PLACE": HÉLÈNE CIXOUS

Hélène Cixous is an author of an astonishing variety of works of multiple (even hybrid) genres, with fiction, theory, drama, and opera libretti most prominent among them. The range and complexity of Cixous' corpus presents several difficult challenges for any critical summary. First comes the fact of the sheer volume: she has written more than forty book-length works, more than a dozen major plays, and vast numbers of articles and reviews, and still counting. Second, her works blur typical demarcations between critical and

---

35   Hayman, "Introduction," *In the Wake of the Wake*, 34.

creative endeavour. Despite the French habit of drawing neat demarcation lines separating fiction from theory and criticism, Cixous has never respected such taxonomic categories.[36]

If one were to pinpoint just one theme uniting her critical/theoretical writing with her fiction, one would single out her cause of écriture féminine, a feminist concept elaborated in the early-to-mid-1970s in works like *Le Rire de la Méduse* (1975) and *La Jeune Née* (1975). In close, oftentimes personal, association with the work of other French philosophers and post-structuralist theorists—in particular, Derrida, Deleuze, Lyotard, and Lacan—and in a constant dialogue with her predecessors—most prominently, Freud, Heidegger, Nietzsche, and Marx—Cixous' writing is similarly informed by the desire to dismantle philosophical, social, and cultural orthodoxies in an attempt to develop theoretical systems capable of taking stock of the complexities of cultural signification.

Unlike both her predecessors and contemporaries, however, Cixous has a ubiquitous interest and investment in feminist issues, usually explicit, and powerfully expressed in her writing. The structures she seeks to deconstruct are those culpable in the oppression of women and marginalised social groups, and her deconstruction, first and foremost, is designed to unmask and challenge sociocultural, patriarchal operations. For her cause of écriture féminine, Cixous is not content with enlisting female writers only (most prominent among whom would be Brazilian experimentalist Clarice Lispector), but also a whole genealogy of male writers whose linguistically innovative work underscores, attacks, and ridicules the many various discourses of Western phallogocentrism – most prominent among whom would be James Joyce. Morag Shiach has aptly outlined the crucial interdependence between Cixous' fiction and theory as a joint exploration of "the transgressive potential of language."[37] Like Derrida and Camus, Cixous was born in French Algeria, and only moved to France at the age of eighteen (already married to Guy Berger) – her childhood and youth spent in the colonised North Africa is

---

36 As Ian Munro has observed in a biographical entry on Cixous, in her work, "fiction blends into literary criticism, into cultural theory, into feminist manifesto, into political analysis, and into personal history, with no clear boundaries separating the different genres of writing," and so, in the broadest terms, "Cixous could be perhaps most accurately described as a cultural philosopher, as long as that label is not thought to depend on a narrow, discrete, or even cohesive theory of culture" (Ian Munro, "Hélène Cixous," *Dictionary of Literary Biography, Volume 242: Twentieth-Century European Cultural Theorists*, ed. Paul Hansom [University of Southern California: The Gale Group, 2001] 83).

37 "Cixous' explorations of the transgressive, and the transformative, potential of language, take place in the context of a sustained engagement with other fictional and theoretical writers. Her readings of Kleist, or Joyce, or Lispector, are always linked to her desire to theorize the power of language to evade the habitual, to move beyond the hierarchies of dual opposition, and to challenge the deathly economy of intersubjectivity" (Morag Shiach, *Hélène Cixous – The Politics Of Writing* [Routledge: London and New York, 1991] 40).

a constant reference throughout her work, as it is, according to critic Verena Conley, the cause of her threefold stigmatisation.[38]

In 1959, at the tender age of twenty-two, Cixous became the youngest-ever *agrégée de lettres* (holder of the *agrégation* in literature) in France, a distinction she repeated in 1968 when she completed her doctoral thesis on James Joyce (under the supervision of Jean-Jacques Mayoux) and became the youngest-ever *docteur-ès-lettres*. Her thesis, published in 1968 as *L'Exil de James Joyce ou l'art du remplacement*, proceeds by examining selected themes from the Joyce oeuvre using a method purportedly borrowed from the author himself. If Joyce, in *Ulysses*, has his alter ego Stephen deploy a "biographical method" in order to analyse Shakespeare's life by using his writings, then for Cixous, the life and work of Joyce himself are consubstantial, his work functioning as a copy of his life and his life a repetition of his writing. As noted by Geert Lernout in the Cixous section of his overview of *The French Joyce*, "although it is based on extensive research," Cixous' thesis "tends to be more a reflection of the author's preoccupations than of those of his subject."[39]

L'Exil de James Joyce is basically a study of the relations between Joyce's writing and his life, where Cixous reads Joyce's fictional texts in the context of the letters and diaries written by himself and by his brother Stanislaus. Cixous divides her material into four sections: first, the nexus out of which the individual is to develop: the family; next, the individual in three stages of development: the heroic, the heretical (or rebellious), and the exilic. Finally, Cixous concludes with the "poetics" of this development. The "family cell" becomes subject to a consideration of the artist's formative years as history and a discussion of his first poem; the concepts of private and public heroism include Joyce's "choice of heresy" and the creed of *non serviam*; the concept of exile as recovery is understood as flight, as a position of critical realism, and ultimately as the exile of the soul which provides the energy and the structures of Joyce's writing; and the poetics of this development concerns the concept of reality in Joyce, his transcendence of sociohistorical reality by means of the reality of language and linguistic symbolism. Cixous ties the Joycean position of *non serviam*, his refusal of all orthodoxies, and commitment to doubt as the only attitude consonant with reason, with his engagement with the Augustinian concept of *"felix culpa,"* a positive outlook on sin as necessarily linked to the possibility of redemption, or, in Joyce's case, to

---

38   "Her radicalism spills over the boundaries of a narrowly defined feminism. As an Algerian, Jew, and woman, she finds herself thrice culturally and historically marked and vows to fight on all fronts against any form of oppression. [...] Though there is a shift in her work from a covert to an overt "feminism," Cixous has always been interested in the inscription of the feminine in text and society" (Verena Andermatt Conley, *Hélène Cixous: Writing the Feminine* [Lincoln/London: University of Nebraska Press, 1984] 4).

39   Geert Lernout, *The French Joyce* (Ann Arbor: University of Michigan Press, 1990) 42.

spiritual growth and finally to an exploration of the constitutive nature of language in relation to reality.

Joyce's exilic mode of life, in Cixous' biographic approach, makes of Joyce's play, *Exiles*, a crucial text, both in relation to Joyce's biography and in terms of its representation of subjectivity. Shiach has identified one of the important pitfalls of Cixous' biographical/textual method as conflation between fact and fiction, and the consequent collapse of her critical distance.[40] The difficulty lies also in the teleological structure of developing creativity that Cixous reads into Joyce's life, all of whose tensions, conflicts, and contradictions, no matter how random and aleatory, are subsumed into the grand narrative of the development of Joyce the artist. Departing from Lernout's observation, Lynn Perod makes the following claim about Cixous' use of Joyce as backdrop for the articulation of her own creative practice: "While it is not necessarily true that what Cixous has said about Joyce can be used to describe her own fictional world, the affiliation is clearly there."[41]

Just as Cixous' Joyce devoted an entire writing career to making a connection between life and art, so do the works of Cixous herself, even though in a quite different set of cultural constructs, reach toward this same goal. Also, Cixous' concluding consideration of Joyce's innovative approach to representing the relation between language and subjectivity, including his foregrounding—throughout *Dubliners*—of the physical power of words, his dissociation of signifier and signified through unconscious association or pun, and last but not least, his challenge to language as a net, limiting rather than reflecting experience of the real—all form the basis of Cixous' subsequent dealing with Joyce in both her theory and fiction.

The next step in Cixous' theoretical treatment of Joyce came in her *Prénoms de personne* (1974), a collection of critical essays containing twelve major texts, grouped into three divisions, where "Prediction," the opening piece, encapsulates Cixous' creed as writer and thinker: "I ask of writing what I ask of desire: that it have no relation to the logic which puts desire on the side of possession, of acquisition, or even of that consumption-consummation

---

40 "Cixous' conviction that Joyce wrote his life, rather than living it, leads her to read biography and literary text together, using in particular the figures of Stephen Hero and Stephen Dedalus as a means to open out Joyce's aesthetic and ethical commitments. The drawback of this procedure is that it leads to a dissipation of Cixous' own critical voice, which often seems to be swamped by the plethora of texts with which she is engaging. This dilution seems particularly disabling when Cixous seeks to analyse the sexual politics implicit in Joyce's aesthetic practice" (Shiach, *The Politics Of Writing*, 41).

41 Penrod continues: "Both Joyce and Cixous express in their writing the sense of exile or marginalization – Joyce for a set of motives admittedly quite different from those expressed by Cixous. Both Cixous and Joyce are deeply involved in the creation of a fictional "reality" through the most radical and experimental use of language itself" (Lynn Kettler Penrod, *Hélène Cixous* [New York: Twayne Publishers, 1996] 21).

which, when pushed to its limits with such exultation, links (false) consciousness with death" (HCR, 27).[42] Cixous continues detailing her personal tradition informed by such romantics as E. T. A Hoffmann and E. A. Poe, and modernists like Joyce: "Of Joyce, I say that he keeps as close as possible to that unheard-of place until suddenly the marvellous openings appear, in *Ulysses*, from which *Finnegans Wake* is catapulted forth; this is the text of texts, the readable-untranslatable. Here an extremity is invented."[43]

The "ensemble Joyce" features the four texts, "Texte du hors," "Les hérésistances du sujet," "La crucifiction," and "Trait-portrait de l'artiste en son autre j'aimot." The first essay, "Texte du hors," praises Joyce's originality and his work's resistance to interpretation or translation. The second essay, "Les Hérésistances du sujet," is a detailed analysis of the concept of "subjectivity" in Joyce's *Dubliners* and *Ulysses*. A third essay, "La Crucifixion," is a discussion of Joyce's "comedy of castration," which questions the very idea of logocentric mastery and phallocentric concepts of "possession" or property, and economic exchange. The final essay of the volume, "Trait—Portrait de l'artiste," is a reading of a small fragment from *Finnegans Wake* (FW 164, the "Casseous/ Burrus" passage). Cixous uses this section as the basis for an exploration of the disturbance caused to patriarchal thought by the representation of female subjectivity.

Cixous here begins to explore Joyce's writing in a deconstructive manner, stressing the ways in which it challenges readability, resists the reduction to narrative, and interrogates the processes of naming. As Shiach perceptively notes, this deconstructive turn is also one away from "Joyce the Artist" and toward "Joyce the writer" in that "his texts are valued as the point of intersection between fiction and theory, between art and revolution."[44] Joyce's writing practice is described as a form of "permanent revolution" in its resistance to codification, to imperialism, to familialism, and to all forms of propriety (PP, 233–4). Cixous analyses the ways in which the narrative point of view is multiplied, unsettled, undermined, particularly in the "Circe" chapter of *Ulysses*, where Joyce dramatises the collision of all of the subjectivities represented in the text, both living and dead, in a scene that couples erotic fantasy with sex change. Her holistic approach to the entire Joyce oeuvre reveals an evolution in degree rather than kind, without however downplaying the departures

---

42   "Je demande à l'écriture ce que je demande au désir: qu'il n'ait aucun rapport avec la logique qui met le désir du côté de la possession, de l'acquisition, ou meme de cette consummation—consumation qui, si glorieusement poussée à bout, lie (mé)connaissance avec la mort" (PP, 5).

43   Cixous concludes: "This non-place which undoes and reconstructs itself is given to behold to the mass of singularities, the multiple mutating figures which constitute Stephen Bloom, in one of the most funnily, and pitilessly, deconstructive parts of Ulysses: the place called "Ithaca," point of no-return home, so that those returning there are carried off by the text which traverses them, and with which their bodies form a dazzling diaspora" (HCR, 30).

44   Shiach, *The Politics Of Writing*, 45.

undertaken in the *Wake*. Cixous critiques Joyce's early negative theology, his need to ruse with words in a double gesture, both *capable* and *coupable*, capable and guilty. In the resulting "machine of cruci-fiction," Cixous finds a disquieting eroticism predicated on phallogocentrism and castration, which gradually gives way, from *Exiles* to *Finnegans Wake*, to the writing of a new affective economy.

In the *Wake*, where there is no subject/object division anymore and where desire based on respecting otherness outweighs the desire for recognition, Cixous reads a possibility for a change "on the invisible line separating light from shadow [...] where the limitless 'begins' multiply [in] neither gift nor loss, but a sort of errant grace; and it is only there, but hardly begun in the mixture of singularities, that finally phallogocentrism unhooks and blows off course from one to the other border."[45] As long as, in *A Portrait*, Joyce had explored the relation between naming and fixity as an unstable process devolving upon convention, then for Cixous, Joyce's *Finnegans Wake* dramatises the refusal of such naming, the journey of "Personne" (PP, 262).

A fitting, albeit belated, illustration (in English) of Cixous' deconstructive practice vis-à-vis her selected literary canon, came in the form of *Readings: The Poetics of Blanchot, Joyce, Kafka, Kleist, Lispector, and Tsvetaeva*, a collection of her 1980–86 lectures delivered at Sorbonne VIII. Cixous starts off her piece on Joyce, "Joyce's *Portrait*: Silence, Exile, and Cunning," by approaching the *Portrait*'s opening scene through "a kind of multiple reading," which portrays it "as a kind of embryonic scene" in that "the entire book is contained in the first pages, which constitute a nuclear passage" (R, 3). Cixous' psychoanalytic approach is founded on the conviction that despite defying it, Joyce was "impregnated" by psychoanalysis and "in a kind of intellectual echo" with Freud. Cixous pays acute critical attention to even the minutest detail:

> The text begins with an enormous O that recurs in the first pages. It can be taken as a feminine, masculine, or neuter sign, as zero. The o is everywhere. One can work on the o-a, on the *fort-da*. I insist on the graphic and phonic o's because the text tells me to do so. With all its italics and its typography, the text asks the reader to listen. (R, 4)

Cixous' close familiarity with both the Joyce canon and his biography enables her to make perceptive general observations and intriguing comparisons.[46]

---

45 Qtd. in Conley, *Writing the Feminine*, 24.

46 "'Apologise' is the last word of this short introduction and the first word with which Joyce played, which he rolled on his tongue. [...] Joyce, as a Catholic, is never done with the law. His unconscious is completely taken into the Christian space of the fault. [...] Instead of giving up the law [like Kafka], Joyce puts in place an enormous system of transgression. And there can be no transgression without law. It all remains very masculine. At the end, in *Finnegans Wake*, Joyce even managed to make of transgression his law" (R, 7).

Houdebine's and Sollers' insistence on Joyce's Catholicism are echoed in Cixous' observations regarding how Joyce "puts the artist into rivalry with God since both are creators" (R, 8). Joyce, first and foremost, is a creator of words, and the lesson Cixous draws from *A Portrait* is that

> if one reflects on words, if one warms them like a hen, one ends up understanding them. The little boy is constantly before a secret constituted by signifiers or by words. Over hundreds of pages, for Stephen Dedalus it is but a question of enigmas. Where there is a primal scene, there are also primal words, since the two are equivalent. The words hold back, they bind the future artist as young man. (R, 9)

How does Cixous' engagement with Joyce relate to her own practice of writing?

In her preface to *The Hélène Cixous Reader*, Cixous connects her doubled Joycean interrogations with her own practice as writer: "Like all those whose vital substance is cut from the same fabric as writing, I am constantly impelled to ask myself the questions engendered by this structure which is at once single and double" (HCR, xv). Questioning herself, Cixous makes a point of asking, not "who am I?," but "who are I?," and again credits Joyce with giving a literary expression to this trans-individual multiplicity, to this "chaosmos" of us all:

> In French the phrase "who are I?" (qui sont-je?) also plays the music of the difference writing/voice; for our French ear hears, when I pronounce my question, the phrase "who muses?" i.e., who dreams. Who are I when I muse? When I dream who dreams? In dreams am I not all the characters of my dreams? We are all this numerous and coalescent personality, who inspired Joyce's motley heroes, whether Bloom-Ulysses- -Shakespeare Booloohoom or Here Comes Everybody. To rise above the interior chaosmos each one of us gives ourselves a spokesperson I, the social I who votes, who represents me. (HCR, xviii)

Dedans (1969; *Inside*, 1986), Cixous' first novelistic text, appeared in the aftermath of May 1968, participating in the spirit of rethinking and revolution that was then happening across the entire French society and culture. Just as Cixous' Joyce, the novel is profoundly autobiographical in complex and indirect ways, charting the female narrator's strong feelings about the passing of her father. The title tells it all: throughout the text the reader is locked inside the mind and memory, dream-life and fantasy of the narrator as she mourns the untimely death of her venerated father. *Dedans* is an experimental text; just as in the case of all Cixous' other writing, the label "novel" seems inadequate to its rewriting of literary genre. The connection between revolutionary literary style—countering and undoing the realism of the still-dominant *nouveau roman*—and revolutionary politics is clear for Cixous, and her narrative is composed of fragmented blocks of text, coherent within themselves but often inconsistent or random in their relationship to each other.

What is sketched, precariously, through these juxtapositions is a provisional and improvisational account of an emotional experience and a psychic journey dealing with loss and aiming for recuperation. The narrative line is bifurcated, revolving around two periods in the narrator's life separated by twenty years, the second section functioning as a return, a rewriting of the first and the past that reinforces the novel's structuring by means of repetition and remembering. Splitting, fracturing, and dividing are significant dynamics in the book, but so are themes of enfolding and hybridising. As Ian Munro has observed, the title, meaning "Inside," has some wide-ranging ambiguous implications.[47] *Dedans* is also a text invested in the theme of writing, about coming to writing and about the precarious power of words to create, to explain, and to speak. Writing appears as the only possible solution; writing is produced by the pain the narrator feels, and writing is the ability that is celebrated at the very end of Cixous' text: "I hate beauty, dust, patience, passion, the stubborn wish for death, silence, the nobility of the soul, the deprivation of the body, and I rejoice in my power to speak, in the fact that I am ten years old, thirty years old or sixty, and that I can say kiss of kiss off to death" (*I*, 135). Writing allows one to say, as Cixous puts it, "merde merde merde à la mort" (*D*, 208). Munro shows in his detailed overview that the issues and concerns central to *Dedans* animated Cixous' writing through the next decade, with her literary strategies becoming more explicitly theoretical and her style more radically innovative. *Le Troisième Corps* and *Les Commencements*, both published in 1970, blur the boundaries between fiction and theory and extend Cixous' interrogation of writing, selfhood, and the place of the feminine.

It is only in *Souffles* (1975) that Cixous' fiction starts taking aboard further levels of signification and structuration, as well as some explicitly Joyce-inflected linguistic experimentation.[48] *Souffles* deals with the mental and physical experiences of an anonymous, undescribed female narrator who—at times in the first and sometimes in the third person—recounts both her pre-

---

47   "This text is one of transformation and initiation, of passing through thresholds and becoming new. The title could be interpreted as indicating some sort of interiority, a place for the self, but it is also a confining within, a prison, and so on. The self is always necessarily in motion; on one level, engaged in a process of evolution and initiation, but also an unstable, rickety place of construction and deconstruction, forced to keep moving in order to survive" (Ian Munro, "Hélène Cixous," *Dictionary of Literary Biography*, 87).

48   What Sherzer identifies as "play and manipulation with words, which produce excess and multiplicity of meaning" (Sherzer, *Representation in Contemporary French Fiction*, 158).

sent and past. Cixous' style has been described as "poetical, harmonious, and lyrical, shifting abruptly into vulgarity and obscenity and becoming violent and disjointed,"[49] with the important admixture of wordplay and allusiveness to various frames of reference (philosophical, psychoanalytic, literary, etc.). The opening is an ironic echo of the gender stereotype in which the passive female is awoken by an outside voice: "Là! c'est la voix qui m'ouvre les yeux, sa lumière m'ouvre la bouche, me fait crier. Et j'en nais" (S, 9). The narrator inscribes images, visions, and scenes as they arise, without motivating or explaining their appearance. Following Cixous' creed of "passons-nous de causes" (S, 114), *Souffles* is a text in which the unexpected becomes a structuring device, in which cohesion is achieved by the fact that all the experiences described share the ecstatic feature of transporting the speaker into intense and exhilarating states.

Punctuating the narrator's ruminations are adaptations of well-known utterances to her own texts and philosophical context: "Encore un effort mon corps allons, porte-moi" (S, 217) recalls Marx's famous exhortation to the working class; "Écrire, ne pas écrire. Angoisse" (S, 217) is modelled on the beginning of Hamlet's soliloquy. One of the neologisms running the length of the text is "origyne," rewriting *origine* as female (*gyne*) "ori-fice." Eroticism and sexuality are presented by Cixous as ecstatic experiences disrupting the functioning of the symbolic order, experiences of wholeness which affect the entire body and imply activity, equality, and reciprocity in both partners. Cixous writes about bliss, about sexual activity and satisfaction, in a fashion unsettling of the norms of appropriateness in Western society, letting her narrator repeatedly point out what major satisfaction she achieves by using vulgar language. These and other examples corroborate Sherzer's evaluation of *Souffles* as a complex intertextual web[50] that reweaves the threads of Joyce's *Wake* and its lesson of desire based on a respect for otherness. *Souffles* neither rejects masculinity, nor does it privilege femininity, valorising reciprocity instead.

In her 1977 novel, *Angst*, Cixous deals with the breakdown of a love relationship, whose pain and anguish are not expressed in existential, representational terms, but in a metaphoric exchange of letters; her own *écriture féminine* again engages critically with Freudian psychoanalysis. The narrator explores her responses to the loss of her father and her separation from her mother. As noted by Munro, what makes this work into an example of écriture féminine is Cixous' treatment of the psycho-dynamics of the nar-

---

49 "A web of allusions, references, and modified quotations that index a host of meanings. In addition, the narrator's verbal texture mingles flowing passages of sensuous lyricism, didactic essays, pornographic slang, and prose poems with dislocated syntax – with the consequence that rhythms, tones, syntax, registers, and styles constantly shift" (Ibid, 147).
50 Ibid, 153–4.

rator's pursuit. But *Angst* is also adventurous stylistically, thereby works to further its écriture féminine. Much of the novel occurs in dream states and recollected images whose effect is similar to Joyce's use of stream-of-consciousness narration. This technique effectively serves the role of psychoanalysis in the narrative. The narrator achieves finally a kind of rebirth and subjecthood only after she works through her neuroses and anxiety in psychoanalytic terms. In constructing the narrative in such a way, Cixous both accepts and appropriates Freud by showing how the tools of psychoanalysis can be made to deconstruct rather than promote the masculine forces that oppress the narrator and women in general. In a passage included in the *Hélène Cixous Reader*, language, as the representative of this order, is depicted as a "web of metaphors" spun by the masculine *il* ("he") to entrap "her":

> The black words were avoiding something that must have been foul. He didn't "say" them. He "put them forward." They didn't wind their way towards me. They hedged. "You came at the right time for another!" Their power, craftiness—I was stung. Taken in. Their spidery legs. Their web of metaphors, smothered innuendos. (*HCR*, 76)

"He" talks "without hesitation in his own language," spinning "fictions" that annihilate "her" reality. The quote shows the masculine desire to subjugate the other as ultimately self-trapping: "he" too is a fly struggling in the web of his making.

The text of *Angst*, as always one of transformation, led Cixous to another phase in her consideration of women's issues. For the next few years Cixous espoused the cause of women in a more militant language, which also entailed a gradual shift in medium – and Cixous' output from the early-1980s onward is predominantly theatrical and aimed at collaboration with directors (such as Ariane Mnouchkine or Simone Benmussa) rather than literary and based on critical engagement with writers. Still, however, Cixous' theatre work is one which challenges gender roles and subverts patriarchal rule, continuing in her life-long project,[51] one which was crucially informed by her early exposure to, and extended engagement with, Joyce's literary experiment.

---

51 In this project, according to Conley, "writing attempts to break away from cultural stereotypes, essentializing concepts and their attributes such as man/woman, masculine/feminine, active/passive. She tries to displace the conceptual opposition in the couple man/woman through the very notion of writing and bring about a new inscription of the feminine" (Conley, *Writing the Feminine*, 6).

7.5 "A SUBJECT ILLIMITABLE, NUMBERLESS": PHILIPPE SOLLERS

It is difficult to overstate the late Philippe Sollers' importance for *Tel Quel*, the journal he co-founded, edited, and used as his mouthpiece for the entirety of its existence (1960–82), not only as a tool for disseminating his fiction and literary criticism and theory, but also as a platform for propagating his political beliefs. These were far from unified and consistent, and so accordingly, *Tel Quel*'s political/poetic tenor underwent a multiple-stage (r)evolution. In Roland Champagne's account—the first book-length study on Sollers in English—just as Barthes, Sollers too began his literary career by opposing his chief concerns to those of Jean-Paul Sartre's purported Marxism.[52] Sollers' early *nouveau-roman* stage was short-lived, and so was his affiliation with the PCF. The events of May 1968 in France, in which Paris university students and workers cooperated in social revolt without the leadership of the PCF, were pulls in the direction of revolutionary history and the Maoism advocated by Sollers for *Tel Quel* during most of the 1970s, seeking new directions for French Communism in China where Mao was leading what he called his Cultural Revolution. Sollers' vehemence and despotism in his advocating of Mao were what ultimately brought about, in the consensus of many critics, *Tel Quel*'s demise – in Champagne's account, "by 1980, Sollers became aware that he was himself guilty of what he had earlier attributed to a bourgeois mentality."[53]

For Sollers, Joyce is not only a source of creative inspiration, but an object of critical and theoretical investigation—primarily in respect to *Finnegans Wake*. As he confided to Hayman, there are chiefly three aspects in which the *Wake* concerns Sollers the critic and writer: "its tendency to dissolve linguistic barriers through multilingual puns, the rhythmic qualities through which subjectivity is projected, and the manner in which it telescopes history to create the effect of a unified historical (or 'epic') dimension."[54] It is essential to add to these interests the biographical connection between the two: Catholicism, which Sollers believed he shared with Joyce.[55]

---

52 "Instead, Sollers proposed a type of Communism that would clearly be an alternative to either Fascism or colonialism and would be dedicated through *Tel Quel* to inspiring the French Communist Party. In 1960, he began that journal by aligning it with the poet Francis Ponge and his ahistorical literary poetics which soon led Sollers and his colleagues toward the *nouveau roman*, structuralism, Derrida's deconstructive poetics as an affirmation of the text's integrity, and other intellectual positions that diverted the *Tel Quel* group away from history and into formalist exercises subverting the ideologies of bourgeois and capitalist ways of thinking" (Roland A. Champagne, *Philippe Sollers* [Amsterdam/Atlanta: Rodopi, 1996] 21–2).

53 Champagne, *Philippe Sollers*, 22.

54 Qtd. in Hayman, "Introduction," *In the Wake of the Wake*, 25.

55 "Both educated by Jesuits, Joyce and Sollers have strong ties to Catholicism. As Sollers indicates in *Paradis*, Joycean Christianity, like Sollers' Catholicism, participates in the comic and the pathetic. Christian ritual, symbolism, and especially theology play a large part in Joyce's narrative

The inception of Sollers' literary career predates the founding of *Tel Quel* by two years: in 1958, with the psychological novel *Une curieuse solitude*, applauded by such Nestors of the French letters as Mauriac and Aragon, whose praise launched his literary career. At the time of its publication, the name "Sollers" was a *nom de plume*, a mask behind which to hide the real name Philippe Joyaux. *Une curieuse solitude* addresses the issues of masculinity and secrecy surrounding erotism—combined with the fascination for pornography as a means of desacralising sexuality—that were to inform Sollers' writing throughout his entire oeuvre. Here, Sollers' examination is centred on language and eroticism, exploring the issue of moral agenda underlying the narrative explicitness or circumspection vis-à-vis the use of certain words, either too sacred or too sinful. After two texts further exploring—in a *nouveau romanesque* fashion—the nature of subjectivity and linguistic representation of space (*Le Parc* and *Drame*), came a striking new departure in Sollers' writing and its experimental peak between 1968 and 1973, with the three hybrid, visually and conceptually innovative texts: *Nombres, Lois,* and *H.*

The most striking visual aspect of the text of *Nombres* (1968) are the Chinese ideograms punctuating it throughout. The noteworthy function of these is that they usually repeat what has just been mentioned in French, operating as a provocation to the reader in a stance of unreadability.[56] The title suggests the mathematical realm from which *théorie d'ensemble* (set theory) is also derived, the word "numbers" referring to "digits," while *Nombres* is also the French title of the Biblical book of *Numeri*, the census of the Hebrew nation and thus an accounting of the constituent tribes. The text is constructed in the sequential alternations of four voices, identified by the numerals one through four, in twenty-five repetitions, with the first three voices speaking in the imperfect tense while the fourth voice is in the present tense. Malcolm Pollard's chapter on *Nombres* details how the narrative's non-figurative and geometric counter-images provide the lines along which "pronominal identities" develop in an abstract framework" and how these identities come to be undermined by "the themes of violence, destruction, and silence."[57]

The plural voices of *Nombres* are part of the *Tel Quel* project to undermine the "novel" as merely the perpetuation of such bourgeois values as a unified subject in control of its desires, goals, and speaking voice, values which Sollers perceived as propagated by the structuralism so rampant in the mid-1960s in France, which assumed a cohesive self and language its expression.

stances. Sollers especially appreciates the comic subversion of Catholic seriousness" (Champagne, *Philippe Sollers*, 16).

56 As Champagne puts it: "the reader cannot choose how to read this text, the text itself is deciding what is readable and unreadable" (Champagne, *Philippe Sollers*, 43).

57 Malcolm C. Pollard, *The Novels of Philippe Sollers: Narrative and the Visual* (Amsterdam/Atlanta: Rodopi, 1994) 102.

This destabilisation is furthered by the text's radically intertextual nature –
Nombres is a patchwork of quotations from an array of texts from the most
variegated sources and of a multitude of discourses. Thereby, *Nombres* inau-
gurates a process crucial to what Champagne identifies as "the second spire"
of Sollers' writing, devoted to "separating self from language,"[58] setting the
stage for Sollers' crucially Joycean texts. As Sollers' biographer Philippe Forest corroborates in his magisterial study of the author, *Nombres* participates
in a "mouvement par lequel l'écriture se prenait elle-même comme objet,
pour, dans la proximité essentielle avec le Joyce de *Finnegans Wake*, s'engager
dans l'aventure d'une épopée moderne."[59]

   Lois (1972) was written during a personally trying period for Sollers, in
the aftermath of the death of his father in 1969, after which he rewrote the
whole text. *Lois* can be seen today as a cry for action aimed at the young revo-
lutionaries in Paris, a repudiation of "laws" in favour of unhindered action,
textual as well as political. *Lois* continues the fragmentation of *Nombres* while
adding the important aural dimension, introducing the exclamation mark as
the instance of a percussive rhythm. In *Lois*, Sollers presents a text working
as much on the level of sound/rhythm as on a conceptual level.[60] Champagne
has issued the useful reminder that this oral/aural dimension of *Lois* has to
do with Sollers' overall concern with challenging the literary traditions of the
French letters.[61] Sollers devises an interesting mode of structuration similar
to Joyce's "Sirens" episode in *Ulysses* by using the opening sentence "NE FACE
A FACE NIANT LA MEMBRANE L'ENTRÉE" as a sort of verbal acrostic whose
individual words stand at the beginning of each of the six "books" that form
Lois.[62]

   As explained in Sollers' own pedantic back-cover blurb, "on reconnaît le
commencement d'un 'livre' à un mot écrit en capitales reproduisant l'un des

58   Champagne, *Philippe Sollers*, 36,
59   Philippe Forest, *Philippe Sollers* (Paris: Seuil, 1992) 167.
60   As Ffrench has noted, "written mostly in decasyllabic phrases, the text of *Lois* is humorously
     scanned by a repetition of sounds, principally the past participle ending in é, *alliteration, and
     rhyme*" (Ffrench, *The Time of Theory*, 196).
61   "One of the techniques introduced in *Lois* that Sollers would develop in his later work is a writ-
     ing that is sensitive to the ear, that is, a poetic writing that records how people speak French
     rather than how it has been traditionally written. Effectively, oral language, like that of the me-
     dieval troubadours of whom Sollers would like to be recognized as the modern equivalent, is
     the basis for what Sollers claims in this text as 'une sort d'explosion de comédie, de parodie'"
     (Champagne, *Philippe Sollers*, 47).
62   NE (L I.1 5) / FACE dévidée frappée de plein fouet catapulte sèche en gazeux mouillé (L II.1, 25) /
     A FACE de face et b à l'envers et c en surface pour couper l'endroit (L III.1, 41) / NIANT cervelle
     os en tout temps cosmos, frappe de plein fouet son éther de vent (L IV.1, 61) / LA MEMBRANE
     autour juste avant après (L V.1, 89) / L'ENTRÉE nous apprend d'abord que ce n'est pas la nature
     en soi mais les transformations réalisées par l'homme qui sont les fondements de la pensée.
     (L VI.1, 116).

mots de la première phrase du texte." Book I, Sollers informs, is dominated by "cosmo-theogony" (Hesiodic prehistory), while Book II evolves from the floorplan of Greek Antiquity and Christianity. Books III-VI deal with the epoch of modern capitalism, marked by the "accentuation transversale de la réalité révolutionnaire (Chine)," i.e., a transversal accentuation of revolutionary reality, as per China. Then, after quotes from Marx and Engels, comes the avowal that "rappels techniques" are derived from "Rabelais, Joyce," these mnemotechnic aids including the decasyllabic verse, from "chanson de geste, chanson de Roland, vers shakespearien" as well as "actualisation du lexique (depuis mai 68)." This explicit statement has led Philippe Forest to believe that it is in *Lois* that Joyce's presence "is inscribed most profoundly."[63]

The history that forms the subject of *Lois* is far removed from that of schoolbooks. The focal point of Sollers' examination of the various discursive strata whose superposition comes to form the official historical accounts is the taboo of incest, its "prohibition or rather subtilized recommendation" regarded as the inaugural moment of civilisation and its organising principle:

> Soit : la prohibition ou plutôt la recommandation subtilisée de l'inceste, à savoir les rapports cochons et cachés mère-fils-père-fille ou plutôt mère-fille-père-fils, racontent la signature du contrat fondu dérivé, l'autre parent n'étant apparemment posé comme désiré qu'afin de produire le masque de son répété... (L I.1, 6)

The taboo of incest, then, is "the key by which intelligibility is conferred upon social network," the mechanism by which "the infant is inscribed into an Oedipal triangle," out of which there is no escaping, which is merely perpetuated through the generations (L I.3, 11).

Thus, while addressing the larger issues of the relationship of literature and propaganda after May 1968, *Lois* reflects a lust for sexual innuendo and scatological detail. Sexuality is part of all this because both men and women, in their multiform quests for each other, repeat the traditional roles passed on by their society, as the text's voice observes: "En réalité, elles vont chercher plus loin leurs effets, elles n'oublient jamais l'antiquité réglée" (L I.3, 12). So in *Lois* the text stages its own search for a form appropriate to the struggle for social renewal, as incomplete and transitory as so many of *Lois'* contestations of the laws of conventional literary discourse. From *Nombres*, *Lois* takes over the idea that the writing of any text takes place with/through other texts – hence the constant presence of quotations, rehashed,

---

63   "Des toutes livres de Sollers, *Lois* est celui où la référence à Joyce est la plus profondément inscrite. Comme dans *Finnegans Wake*—et souvent selon des procédés similaires—la langue éclate pour se reconstruire et se faire entendre en une musicalité étrange et violente. Une épopée inédite s'invente à la mesure de l'histoire et de ses rêves" (Forest, *De Tel Quel à l'Infini*, 548).

reshuffled, rewritten in what Forrest terms "la réécriture parodique,"[64] i.e.,
a parodic rewriting.

How, then, does *Lois* rewrite *Finnegans Wake*? There are chiefly two strategies. One is an homage-cum-translation of selected sections of the *Wake* (the
opening of *FW* I.1 and IV.1). It is no coincidence that the 1972 publication of
Lois was simultaneous with the propagation of Joyce's *Wake* through Stephen
Heath's influential study "Ambiviolences" on the pages of *Tel Quel*. It was with
Heath that Sollers undertook (and published the next year) a translation of
excerpts from the last section of the *Wake*. One finds fugitive allusions to and
borrowings from the *Wake* in many different places ("Gulls. Gulls. And gulls"
[*L* V.1, 89]), but most explicitly at the beginning of Book III, where the begin-
ning of *FW* I.1 and *FW* IV.1 are conjoined in translation-cum-pastiche:

> en rune et rivière pour roulant courant, ravage battant dans le rebaignant, *passée la
> douadouane du vieux de la vielle*, de mèrève-adam se repomnifiant, recyclons d'abord,
> foutrement commode, circulés viciés *ou gesticulant*, le château-comment sous périphé-
> rant, *là où ça méthode, où ça joue croulant... Il y va-repique au volant...* Sandhyas! Sandyas!
> Sandyas! dourmourant le bas, appellant l'eau bas, résuractionné l'airveilleur du bas,
> ô rallie-rallie, ô rellie-ravis, ô reluis pleinphix tout brillant luilui, soit l'oiseau en vie,
> notre râle écrit, nos sémématières sur l'ossiéanie... (*L* III.1, 41, my emphasis)[65]

This passage runs for three pages total (and includes parts of the *Wake* other
than the two crucial ones, e.g., "Sacer esto? Semus sumus" from the end of
FW I.6 [*L* III.1, 51]), but the above excerpt will suffice. The emphasised parts
in the Sollers text mark passages that creatively elaborate upon Joyce's original rather than attempting translation. Sollers' strategies of pastiche
concern rhythmical/ associative properties of language (reduplication in
"douadouane"; alliteration in "vieux de la vielle"; rhyme in "croulant/volant,"
etc.). There is also a tendency toward expansion, "unpacking" of the Joycean
portmanteau into its multiple components ("recyclons d'abord, foutrement
commode, circulés viciés ou gesticulant" for "commodious vicus of recircula-
tion"). Several of Sollers' punning neologisms have a poetic potential equal to
that of their Joycean counterparts ("résuractionné" for "Array! Surrection!"
and "l'airveilleur" for "Eireweeker" are particularly apt).

Apart from translating and incorporating fragments of the *Wake* into its
own textual body, *Lois* "countersigns" Joyce's *Wakean* signature in a far more

---

64   Forest, *Philippe Sollers*, 180.

65   "riverrun, past Eve and Adam's, from swerve of shore to bend of bay, brings us by a commodius
     vicus of recirculation back to Howth Castle and Environs." [...] "Sandhyas ! Sandhyas ! Sandhyas
     ! Calling all downs. Calling all downs to dayne. Array! Surrection! Eireweeker to the wohld blu-
     dyn world. O rally, O rally, O rally! Phlenxty, O rally! To what lifelike thyne of the bird can be.
     Seek you somany matters. Haze sea east to Osseania" (*FW* 3.1–3; 593.1–5).

relevant manner: by borrowing and re-using its compositional strategies, its project of writing by which the text is constructed and reproduced. Like the *Wake*, *Lois* relies on a series of mythical narratives and allusions that provide the narrative framework, engaging in a similar kind of parodic appropriation of their styles and discourses via a similar deformation on the level of the signifier. This deformation brings them into mutual interaction, so much so that the critical element entailed in parody gives way to the undifferentiated blend of the pastiche. The minimal reference, the elementary particle out of which *Lois* is construed, and the most common target of its playful variations, is the proper name: "Buongorno giordano ! Guten tag friedrich ! A nous la transmute, l'éternieretour par le sous détour. C'est pas tous les jours. Au permier qui mute. Farewell ezra ! welcome jimmie ! C'est l'aurore monsieur isidore..." (*L* IV.12, 87) Giordano Bruno, Friedrich Nietzsche, Ezra Pound, Joyce, and Lautréamont – there are many more passages in which Sollers expresses his admiration for and alliance with these writers / thinkers. Added to these is Hesiod, whose *Theogony* forms the intertextual scaffolding of *Lois* – disguised in passage such as "lui dont le cadavre *hési*tant sentant l'*iode* a été porté par les dauphins dans un cortège marin" (*L* I.2, 8, my italics). This paragrammatic dispersion of an author's name is a common strategy in *Lois* (another Lautréamont example: "Il s'y dore. Conte, chante ça, horreur, mâle, dehors! L'autre est en amont si je suis en aval" (*L* V.2, 92), proof of Sollers' familiarity with Saussure's *Anagrammes*.

A second-type reference is formed by Sollers' rewritings of famous quotations, oftentimes with a parodic oppositional twist, functioning as both homage and ridicule; cf. "My little sleep is rounded by a life" (*L* VI.6, 130) or "Le reste n'est jamais silence" (*L* VI.8. 81), in terms of Shakespearean parody, or Sollers' version of Lacan, "le docteur flacon," and his rewriting of Lacan's famous prosopopoeia in "La Chose freudienne" ("Moi la vérité, je parle") as "moi l'aspérité, je parle, je parle, mais ça vient d'ailleurs, de tout autrefois, de futur en courbe et retourne-moi" (*L* III.9, 58). A third-type reference is Sollers' punning, whether via paronomasia or the portmanteau. To take but a few examples:

> Jasons, jasons, il en restera pour nos argonotes. (*L* VI.9, 136)
> Progressant dans sa conne essence! (*L* II.2, 27)
> Tandis qu'argostronautes pansementés piochent lune ombilic limbé, terriens regardant performance bébé déjà face drapeau enfliqué. (*L* II.11, 38)
> Mordre! Femmille! Patrie! (*L* III.9, 54)

Then there are many passages in which the textual flow breaks up into isolated exclamations, as in the following passage from the age of the dinosaurs to the Neolithic age: "Débuts rageurs cavernés caveurs. Chimie-tic! Anthropo!

Dinobronches! Iganonde! Ptérodoctes! Azor! Popo! Pipi! Tec! Tec! Paleo! Neo! Et au lit! Tic-Toc!" (*L* I.5, 15–6).

Or, finally, passages in which articulated language breaks down altogether (as per the famous *Wakean* "thunderwords"), what Forrest terms Sollers' "glossolalia"[66]:

> broum schnourf scrontch clong pof pif clonck alala toc toc toc cling skock bing glup burp snif pout pout paf crac pot clic crac tchhhh hé hé guili sluuiirp aaa mhouh mmouhou mouh plouts gnouf snoups tchi tchit chiiiiii ê ê ê ê slam ga hou gnin hop drelin drelin braang fochloour badabang ! (*L* V.10, 107)

Lois, like the *Wake*, becomes an assemblage of deformed quotations, fragments of displaced discourse – a product of aesthetics of appropriation and détournement, in that it occupies what the *Wake* calls the "trancitive spaces" (*FW* 594.3), those textual spaces based on silent quotation and pastiche, through the reworking of mythical narratives and the material deformation of the signifier. What to make of Sollers' subversive strategies in *Lois*? Pure destruction, notes Forrest, of habitual forms of language has—in the overriding ideology of the *Tel Quel* magazine and of Sollers of the period—a value in itself. The value consists in resisting the alienation entailed in any passive acceptance of a code which determines us from the outside as speaking subject. Still, *Lois* is no more than a limit—never did Sollers repeat or go beyond the radical degree of its linguistic deformation—and a stage in Sollers' development, whose direction was in fact away from the Joycean multi-layering of the written signifying matter toward forms that would allow a complex voicing to the spoken word.

H (1973) is a text whose most striking visual aspect is its lack of punctuation, capitalisation, or paragraph division, maintained for the entire bulk of 185 pages. All external punctuation is abandoned, Sollers explains, in order for *H* to become injected with the gestural rhythm of writing, its melodic effects, and for it to perform its non-linear movement across themes, allusions, scenes from the present and the past. This foregrounding of the oral and aural aspects of discourse is the result of Sollers' conscious effort to create "the equivalent of a musical act."[67] From the narrative viewpoint, *H* is the pro-

---

66   Forest, *Philippe Sollers*, 193.

67   "It is the equivalent of a musical act, an act that I perform after having listened to music: Haydn, Monteverdi, Schoenberg, Stockhausen [...] My dream would be to succeed in creating a sort of opera of language [...] Thus since *Lois* as I draft I use a tape recorder in order to rework different passages according to their sound effects. It was somewhat like the technique developed by Joyce for *Finnegans Wake*" (Jean-Louis de Rambures, "Interview with Philippe Sollers," *Le Monde* [November 29, 1974]: 24).

duction of an anonymous narrator defined as "the upsurge of the subject."[68] The form *H* adopts, Sollers says in the text, is not the "monologue intérieur" much used by early modernists—which often tended to reflect a notion of subjectivity prior to language—but rather what Sollers calls the "polylogue extérieur" (*H*, 42). As *H* itself theorises this,

> i oppose the interior monologue by means of the external polylogue [...] that's rebellion can we say it's still about logos i'd be surprised if i judged by reality checks i knew the trail to treasure island i carry out a new experience for mankind no-one ever went this way what water what crystal what sand what coral and believe me only then do we become humble in twenty thousand leagues under the sea your frowns are dissolved in the whirlwind of seaweed (*HE*, 53)

H's "illimitable subject" develops a highly mobile and differentiated idiom which touches upon a wide range of issues: literary, political, sexual, and historical. "Polylogue extérieur" grows out of Sollers' understanding of the *Wake*'s political achievement in misappropriating language, of freeing language from what Sollers views as its subjective underpinnings, even though "la question reste posée comment dire ça dans quel rythme comment transformer la langue écrite et parlée dans le sens d'une respiration" (*H*, 83).

The process by which Sollers' self is suppressed, or rather externalised so as to become the object of the narrative, is foregrounded within the first couple of pages:

> i have this phi floating on the lips as any other infans with vultures' tails and if the eight returns without an end [...] my father's latin no you won't find i write it octave yes exactly like octavo which gave him to sign that o turning above itself followed by a tiny dot right before the j elaborate embroidered genus gladiolus bell tower g-clef carrying oyous in music o.joyous with underside the animated signature doubled restarted short diamond topped liquid octave is as well a specialized term with jewellers [...] clearly the name itself was sufficient to excite them why because one hears jacks joy jewish jouissance at a time for example these joyous sirs these joyous what would you like [...] tell me but it's not bright a performance and so forth in calf soft polished style so my name in plural is philip joyous [...] sollers echo of the surname of ulysses of sollus whole intact ars ingenious terrain worker fertile lyrae sollers science of the lyre (*HE*, 12–3)

---

68   "It is the upsurge of the subject; or of what I have been calling the subject; the possibility of saying 'I' within, at the heart of language. Language is not neutral, but it needs to be taken over by a subject, a subject I would call illimitable, numberless, rather like in *Finnegans Wage*. This is not a biographical subject, it is not a 'me'" (David Hayman, "Interview with Philippe Sollers," *Iowa Review* [Vol. 5 no. 4, 1974]: 101).

410 7. JOYCE AS SUCH / TEL QUEL JOYCE

"The eight"—again, a reference to "H" as the eighth letter of the alphabet—
brings forth the association with a musical octave, which in turn produces
"Octave," the name of Sollers' late father, whose surname—just as his son's—
was "Joyaux," the son distancing himself from his father by means of a nom
de plume. The author's "real" surname Joyaux serves him only insofar as
its punning potential can be used, covering the whole gamut from "jewel"
to "joyous" to "Jewish." The historical excursus on the names "Philippe" and
"Octave"—a rhythmic texture of associations combining ancient Greece /
Macedonia with the contemporary—followed by a provocative reworking
of the name "Sollers," aims to turn the writer's own name and identity into
a wholly written / writing persona, open to the many material coincidences
and contiguities of history.

This freeing of language is a political undertaking – *H*'s narrative, blending the plethora of voices reportedly overheard by Sollers in the streets of
Paris in May 1968, brims with references and allusions to Mao Zedong, Marx
and Engels, whilst its literary pantheon contains figures such as Artaud,
Montaigne, Nerval, Pascal, and of course Joyce. The freeing of language also
takes place on a personal level. As Champagne and others have noted, Sollers
experimented with drugs for a period of time in early 1970s, the title "H"
thus possibly referring to hashish or heroin, for "sometimes the text makes
such widely disparate references that one is even reminded of the visions
produced by LSD."[69] *H* continues Sollers' acknowledgement of the rebellious
figure of Giordano Bruno, whose 1588 *Figura* adorns the cover, its intersecting circles representing the intellect, which sees and distributes everything,
corresponding to the structure of *H*.[70] "H" can thus also stand for "heresy,"
as per Bruno, but also for the "hybridity" of thinking. It can also take on the
meaning of "hydrogen," mentioned on the last page, in the penultimate line
of its text, which does not end with a full-stop, thereby connecting back-
wards/forwards with the "bomb" mentioned on the first page. "H," then, for
"H-bomb."

The crucial Joycean feature of *H* is not so much its unpunctuated form—
even though *Ulysses* is recalled verbatim and in the original, e.g., "limit of
the diaphane why in diaphane adiaphane if you can put your five fingers
through if it is a gate if not a door shut your eyes and see" (*H*, 29)—as its
various types of play with sound which foreground the text's aurality. There
are units in which sounds are juggled: "faudrait pas confondre les *populations laborieuses* du *cap* avec les *copulations laborieuses* du *pape*" (*H*, 111);

---

69 Champagne, *Philippe Sollers*, 47.
70 As Sherzer points out, "there is no main or single organizing principle at the center; rather,
    many satellites with their own centers are copresent, forming a polygon. *H*'s structure is pre-
    cisely that" (Sherzer, *Representation in Contemporary French Fiction*, 67).

the repetition of one affix or letter: "nag*eur* travaill*eur*, gland*eur* rêv*eur* et touch*eur* ment*eur* et cherch*eur*" (*H*, 120); verbal skiddings involving the recurrence of one word in a series of words: "la période où nous vivons a un nom *bouleversement* sans precedent sur la *boule* qui se met en *boule* d'où *boulon bouloner boulotter* cham*bouler* sa*bouler* le camp impérialiste" (*H*, 121, my italics), etc. Exploiting and foregrounding the various properties and possibilities of language in general, *H* mimics the phases of linguistic awareness and performance experienced by individuals in their consciousness and unconsciousness.

Sollers enjoys puns that play on culture and how culture forms the self, daring to make his texts unreadable, that is, so representative of contemporary life as to be reflective on the nature of the self as it is produced and directed by mores and language. As Sherzer argues, successions of sounds like "flouc floc" and "noum toum atoum" are like the babble of an infant; successions of words like "oui melissa dorée le miel des abeilles la paillettes ruche cueillie dans les fleurs abeille abeille" (*H*, 105) are similar to the ludic glossolalia of children. Further, *H*'s play with sounds, free associations, constant disjunctions, puns, and anagrams are "characteristic of dreams and hallucinatory states; they are, as Freud and Lacan taught us, manifestations of the unconscious surfacing in signifiers."[71] However, Champagne is correct in tying Sollers' project in *H* together with Deleuze and Guattari's *Anti-Oedipus* (published in 1972) and reading *H*'s opening, "qui dit salut la machine," as reference to their concept of "desiring machine" functioning through the intersection of capitalism and schizophrenia induced by the need to conform to some model of the ideal family.[72]

Typographically *H* is a thick, dense, continuous flow of words, perceptively likened by none other than Roland Barthes to "stains of language in the sense that this word could have in the calligraphy of a Jackson Pollock."[73] Rather than a long sentence, it is more appropriate to call it a long clause without interruption. In addition to the lack of punctuation and paragraph structure, there are never any quotation marks to identify someone else's spoken or written words. The book is a large intertext in which the surfaces are ingeniously tied together to create an ironic commentary on the madness of modern culture – a madness without beginning or end, a point brought home by the fact that the text does not open with a capital letter, nor does it end with a full stop. The text finishes with the questions "que crierai-je" (*H*, 185), a question answered by an intimate who says: "crie-lui toute chair est comme l'herbe l'ombre la rosée du

---

71   Sherzer, *Representation in Contemporary French Fiction*, 69.
72   Champagne, *Philippe Sollers*, 49
73   Roland Barthes, "Over Your Shoulder," *Writer Sollers*, trans. Philip Thody (Minneapolis: University of Minnesota Press, 1987) 80.

temps dans les voix" (*H*, 185). These voices remain to haunt and to defy the text, which, in a sense, can never end.

Joyce's ear for homonyms that go beyond individual written words appeals to Sollers who admires Joyce's discovery of "cette espèce de surface qui doit se voir mais qui doit en même temps s'entendre comme si l'oeil et l'oreille étaient en train de déraper sur quelque chose..." (*TQ* 79: 44). This surface slippage ("déraper") of meaning is one of the strengths of Joyce that Sollers continually seeks to follow. David Hayman was correct when guessing—back in 1978—that "*H* is not a passing phase in Sollers' development" since "his current work-in-progress, *Paradis*, points toward more radical departures in post-*Wake* fiction," that is, toward important modifications in the method of his novels. Significantly, Hayman also suggested that the movement generated by *Tel Quel*, and now called the "new-new novel," should be called the "Wake" in a punning allusion to the book of puns.[74]

Paradis can be regarded as consummation of the *Tel Quel* era of Sollers' writing as well as the beginning of a new one, bound with *L'Infini* magazine. Marking the inception of Sollers' post-*Tel Quel* phase, *Paradis* is also a turning point in the direction away from Joyce's materialist textuality toward further exploration of orality and aurality of the spoken word. Houdebine has expressed the gist of this difference rather neatly.[75]

7.6 "AN AVATAR OF CATHOLICITY": BEYOND *TEL QUEL*

Two events following the experimentalist/political peak in his fiction (*Lois* and *H*) in the course of the 1970s alienated Sollers from his *Tel Quel* enterprise: the 1974 visit (together with Kristeva, Barthes, Marcelin Pleynet, and François Wahl) of Beijing to see for himself the results of Mao's revolution. Although fascinated by the exposure to such a radically different language and culture, the social problems of the workers and the women as well as the Maoist hegemonic political purges brought a certain sober tone from the returning group to the *Tel Quel* agenda, attenuating the harsh cries for Maoist revolution.

---

74   Hayman, "Some Writers in the Wake of the *Wake*," 25.
75   "Sollers: là encore, stratégie très différente; pour m'en tenir à ce seul aspect de la question: non pas tant des récits, que leurs thèmes, ou séquences, repris essentiellement au niveau de leurs charges discursives, et donc articulés – notamment par le rythme (cf. le rôle de la syllabe comme lieu nodal des scansions) qui est en l'occurrence l'opérateur de différenciation-intégration privilégié – sur d'autres discours, à statut scientifique ou philosophique, par exemple, lesquels impliquent le jugement rationnel comme « moment » obligé de la lecture aussi bien que de l'écriture ; ce qui n'est pas vraiment le cas chez Joyce, me semble-t-il ; on pourrait presque dire que celui-ci est encore chronologiquement trop contemporain de Freud, et donc pas assez" (Houdebine, *L'excès de langage*, 199).

Then in 1979, Sollers converted to Catholicism, and started working on his Dantesque / Joycean Christian epic, *Paradis*. And precisely the instalments of *Paradis I* and *Paradis II* in the last *Tel Quel* issues and the negative feedback from his editors at the Seuil brought Sollers, in October 1982, to discontinue *Tel Quel*'s publication. Sollers realised that there was another platform through which to attain his goal of social reform, and the opportunity for exploring another venue was provided by the journal *L'Infini*. Sollers directed sixteen issues of the new journal for Denoël, until Autumn 1986 when he moved the journal to the prestigious if mainstream publisher Gallimard, where it has continued its activities until this day.[76] *L'Infini* offers the possibility for an open forum of selected writers who share a vision for an infinity of affirmation, even if it is to involve contestation, and Sollers appears to be less involved in ideological control with *L'Infini* than he was with *Tel Quel*, concerned instead with a tolerant humanism in the spirit of the pamphleteer Voltaire and the Montesquieu of *Lettres persanes*. *L'Infini* has continued the work of *Tel Quel* in publishing texts by incisive young writers (e.g., the work of Bernard-Henri Lévy and his group of "new philosophers"), encouraging the blending of philosophy, history, and politics: a vision endorsed by Sollers from the beginning of *Tel Quel* without, however, continuing its political and literary radicalism.

The two interviews with Jean-Louis Houdebine from 1980 and published as "La Trinité de Joyce" (*TQ* 83-84 [Spring-Summer 1980]) offer valuable insight into Joyce's gradually transformed importance for Sollers. The chief focus is "l'élément catholique" in Joyce's work and Sollers voices the conviction that "un tel débordement, un tel excès et, surtout par rapport aux dames, une telle aptitude à se balader dans la cochonnerie, ne peut venir que d'une éducation catholique, et par conséquent est prise comme un avatar de la catholicité" (*TQ* 83: 37). The focus, in the first interview, is primarily *Ulysses* and the point of departure the conviction that "bien entendu tout ce livre, beaucoup plus qu'à Homère, est dédié à Shakespeare" (*TQ* 83: 39). Analysis of the opening pages of *Ulysses* and the strained exchange between Dedalus and Mulligan show, for Sollers, how

> le catholicisme de Joyce [...] c'est bel et bien le refus de tout ce qui se ramène au paganisme dans le catholicisme. L'intégration du substantialisme maternel païen par le catholicisme est une de ces ruses par où il s'est donné le temps de révéler en quoi il est porteur d'une vérité insoutenable. (*TQ* 83: 41)

Joyce's project in *Ulysses* is ultimately to "faire changer d'époque à l'inconscient. Il s'agit d'attraper ledit inconscient en formation nouvelle par le biais indirect de la parodie, qui consiste à lui dire ce qu'il ne pourra en aucune

---

76   See more in Ffrench, *Time of Theory*, 22–3.

façon entendre" (*TQ* 83: 42–3). Sollers reviews in detail all the various heresies broached in Stephen's early musing, as well as his rethinking of the doctrines of (re-)incarnation and trans-substantiation, which all point to "une disjunction entre les fonctions du Fils, du Père, et de ce qui éventuellement ferait Verbe dans cette affaire" (*TQ* 83: 47).

In the second interview, the attention turns to Joyce's scatological letters to Nora, which to Sollers' mind are proof that "l'entreprise de Joyce quant au langage retrouve quelque chose qui aurait été perdu […] dans les siècles précédents" this being "l'affaire du sexe" (*TQ* 84: 64). Joyce's obsession with the language of transgression attests to how "dans le cas de Joyce […], ce qui revient sous une forme particulièrement bizarre, ça n'est ni plus ni moins que le bric-à-brac théologique" (*TQ* 84: 66). Moving on to the *Wake*, Sollers identifies its main theological problem in the concept of *felix culpa*: how does *guilt* become a *happy* one? Joyce's method of solving this problem in the *Wake*—unlike in *Ulysses*, where the juxtaposition and recombination of the various heresies and orthodoxies is an external one—is to treat this affair from *within*: "il est complètement dedans, il ne la présente pas comme une représentation, il la représente comme un événement de la voix en elle-même" (*TQ* 84: 73). In Sollers' understanding, the voice—in the Catholic dogma as well as for Joyce—is that by which the paternal body manifests itself in the son.

After his conversion to Catholicism in 1979, Sollers wrote what he considered to be his best novel, *Paradis* (1981). He emulated Joyce and Dante for their impassioned inclusion of Catholicism in their epic visions. The title *Paradis* is derived from Dante's *Paradiso*, but Sollers' work purports to be a parody of the modern conception of heaven. A continuation with *H* is established by the repeated suspension of visual punctuation, so that each page of *Paradis* is an unpunctuated block of words, whose visual density is further emphasised by the use of bold, italicised typescript. This suspension of "visible punctuation" is, according to Sollers' back-cover blurb, in the service of a "readable eloquence."[77] Its textual material is composed of a series of catalogues about life in Florence and in Paris, based on Sollers' extensive research—undertaken while travelling between the two cities for an extended period of time—about the nature of "culture" in these two capitals of Western civilisation. The work reads like a computerised database of details, from the most banal to the most sophisticated. *Paradis* is an encyclopaedic parody of Christianity in Joyce's mode, which is counterpointed with Dante's work, on whose command of language and erudition Sollers bases his portrayal of the pathos of modern Christianity.

---

77 "Pourquoi pas de ponctuation *visible*? Parce qu'elle vit profondément à l'intérieur des phrases, plus précise, souple, efficace ; plus légère que la grosse machinerie marchande des points, des virgules, des parenthèses, des guillemets, des tirets. Ici, on ponctue autrement et plus que jamais, à la voix, au souffle, au chiffre, à l'oreille ; on étend le volume de l'éloquence lisible!" (*P1*, back cover).

The text is an "artificial paradise" of messages embedded in sequences of ideas gleaned from throughout literary and philosophical history, one with a particular flavour because the narrator is similar to a troubadour singing the story of modern times.[78] Sollers' deployment of such neologistic variations on écrire as "écrimeur," "écriveur," and "écriteur" does not detract from the overall tendency of his gradual abandonment of the Joycean model, which is furthered in *Paradis*. As Sollers himself corroborated in an interview with Hayman, where he specifically contrasted his text with the *Wake*: "To read my texts you should be in a state of something like a drug high. You're in no condition to decipher, to perform hermeneutic operations [...] The language of the text is a base over which something slides. That's why you don't have polysemic concretions."[79]

Thus, if in the *Wake* one encounters polysemy, the existence of many meanings in a single word, whether pun or portmanteau, and this practice of polysemy multiplies interpretations, then in *Paradis*, on the other hand, one can speak—together with Hilary Clark, author of a comparative Joyce/Sollers study—of a "polysensibilité," a polysensitivity to literary texture, to the overlapping of phrases, which stymies interpretation by a seemingly endless sameness, an impenetrable verbal surface.[80] A standard *Paradis* passage reads as follows:

> *que la cause trébuche d'effet en effet toboggan lapsus décalé et plue elle se prend pour l'effet et plus elle s'y fait et plus elle y tient et s'y entretient et plus qu'elle y colle et y caracole felix culpa péristole péristoire chlorant l'oxydé tourbillon d'éveurs d'adamnées parmi lesquels j'ai aussi mon compte gobé mouche arachné toile or donc au commencement il était une fois un commencement hors-commencement vol essaim chanté sans rien voir forêt d'ondes nuée grimémoire comme c'est vrai le vrai du ça veut dire vrai vérité du vrai dérivé comme c'est dur d'y entrer béni d'arriver au vrai ça m'a dit lequel vous prend largo des pieds à la tête in illo tempore périplum et péripétie...* (P, 146)

Self-reflexively, the above passage comments on the formal consequences of freeing the text from punctuation, calling it a "toboggan effect." To add to

---

78 "*il faut être non seulement chanteur mais aussi d'abord écrimeur où vois entendez crime rime escrime mais aussi crème et crieur écriveur rivé au rêveur écriteur critère du tireur en tout cas plutôt écririen écrimien plutôt écrisseur crispeur que scribeur plutôt cricin que critien*" (P, 102).

79 David Hayman, "An Interview with Philippe Sollers," *TriQuarterly* 38 (Winter 1977): 129–30.

80 Clark comments further: "*Paradis* thus presents two very different faces to the reader: the eye perceives the cryptic, crabbed surface of the page, whose unpunctuated mass recalls the Hebrew of the Old Testament, and with difficulty penetrates it and divides it into units of significance; on the other hand, the ear picks up the rhythms and intonations of speech, familiar patterns against which the verbal flow is perceived, measured, and invested with sense" (Hilary Clark, *The Fictional Encyclopaedia – Joyce, Pound, Sollers* [New York/London: Garland Publishing, 1990] 129–30).

this effect, several words undergo reduplication and repetition: "au commencement il était une fois un commencement" or "comme c'est vrai le vrai du ça veut dire vrai vérité du vrai dérivé comme c'est dur," where the phonic properties override semantic content.

This effect is not without its philosophical implications. As Clark points out, in an unpunctuated text, where units of sense are not clearly demarcated, where they often overflow or interpenetrate, the notion of cause and effect can become blurred. And once the notion of truth ("la vérité") has been caught up in the verbal play and ambiguity of the text, the term loses its privileged status and becomes reduced to being one word among others, susceptible to transformations and manipulations.[81] Very early on in *Paradis*, punctuation is linked to the repression of unconscious desires, and the practiced lack thereof is portrayed as a form of "jouissance." The text brims with erotic situations, oftentimes juxtaposed with evocations of paradise, the two often being indistinguishable. The text speaks of a "relation between punctuation and procreation":

> *j'avais immédiatement deviné qu'il y avait une liaison entre ponctuation et procreation d'où leurs resistances... à savoir qu'ils n'enregistrent que les points de rencontre avec leur image virgule tiret point virgule conclusion... ce truc donnait directement sur leur hantise à grossesse genre sésame bloqué en deçà de telle sorte que l'inconscient est bien le non-né hors-né jamais né...* (P, 8)

There is, also, a strong impulse in *Paradis* toward encyclopaedic enumeration, as when the phrase "the fruit of thy womb" evokes a digression into a catalogue of types of "fruit": "jésus le fruit de vos entrailles pastèque melon pêche melba grenade est béni" (P, 35). Although muted in comparison with *Lois* or *H*, wordplay and punning are also present, as in the portmanteaux "la rembabelle" (P, 176), a composite of *remballer* ("to pack up") and "Babel," "sécréateur" uniting *sécateur* ("pruner") and *créateur* (P, 93), or "cranaval" combining *crâne* ("skull") with *carnaval* (P, 97).

Neither is *Paradis* devoid of its own parodic rewriting and détournement of famous quotations, particularly Biblical passages: for instance, "au principe de tout et surtout de l'humanitout était la parole et la parole était chez je suis et la parole était je suis elle était au principe en je suis profondément dedans fiche en lui" (P, 46) is a rewording of John 1:1–3, without however the humorous effects of neologisms or sexual innuendo of similar détournerment in

---

81   "Thus hesitations and play subvert the process of defining a word. When this word is "la vérité," a powerful concept—traditionally at the base of philosophical systems and of texts—is put into question. [...] A questioning of such monolithic concepts as truth, cause and effect, thought itself is thus facilitated by the practice of non-punctuation" (Clark, *The Fictional Encyclopaedia*, 131).

Lois.[82] As Clark emphasises, the Word is God, the divine "je suis," and divine speech or action is linked ("profondément dedans fichée") with identity, "I am"-ness, whereas in contrast, writing is the site of the subject's traversal by all the other subjects who have ever written, a practice of self-alienation: no longer the *Wakean* striving for "verbal signature," Sollers' exploration of individuality is that of the voice. Ultimately, the most Joycean trait of *Paradis* lies, as Forest has aptly pointed out, in Sollers' treatment of Catholicism *as a myth*, akin to Joyce's "mythical method."[83]

Paradis II (1986) picks up the last word of *Paradis I* and incorporates it into a Baudelairian series of images repeated throughout this second text: "soleil voix lumière écho des lumières soleil coeur lumière rouleau des lumières" (*P II*, 7), words which are part of an ecstatic poetic vision recurrent six times at various parts of the text. This time, there are no italics to distinguish this text, as there were in *Paradis*, the text entirely set in Roman type, as if to say that these are not specially identified words, as the italics suggest. A key intertextual reference here is an "enfin navigable courageus Debussy" (*P II*, 66), the composer of "La Mer," admired by the narrator who also engulfs the reader in a bizarre dialogue that entices with the invitation "entre ici dans mon paradis" (*P II*, 113) while suspending satisfaction even with the last words, which are not final, referring to "mon échelle bien légère et triste et bien ferme très joyeuse et vive et bien ferme veni sancte spiritus tempus perfectum tactus ciel et terre pleine de l'énergie joie d'autrefois" (*P II*, 115). And even though the repetition of "joyeuse" and "joie" may refer to Sollers' real name "Joyaux" as well as Joyce, this ocean of words is Sollers' verbal "orchestration" of Debussy's works rather than a *Wakean* exercise in polysemy.

Champagne speaks of the two volumes of *Paradis* as constituting a verbal hologram of epic proportions,[84] and what little remains of the Joycean avant-

---

82 As Champagne has pointed out, the humour of *Paradis* lies elsewhere: "The humor of *Paradis* is found in its game of messages embedded in apparently unrelated sequences of spoken text. The messages are inserted by the omniscient voice of the poet/writer for the reader to decipher. These are encoded signals that the poet/writer offers as guides through the text. The poet/writer is basically saying that he is the only one who can find the way through this maze of contemporary culture's language" (Champagne, *Philippe Sollers*, 51).

83 "C'est que la foi catholique, telle qu'elle a été révélée par le texte biblique et théorisée par le discours théologique, joue dans *Paradis* le rôle de ce que l'on nommera du terme largement impropre de « mythologie ». dans un texte célèbre faisant suite à la publication de l'*Ulysse* de Joyce, T.S. Eliot affirmait que la littérature moderne naîtrait de l'adoption d'une « méthode mythique ," qui consisterait pour l'écrivain à emprunter la structure de son œuvre aux mythologies anciennes. [...] A condition toutefois d'ajouter immédiatement que *Paradis* ne vise qu'à dissiper toutes les mythologies, en prenant appui—essentiellement sinon exclusivement—sur l'une d'entre elles : la « mythologie » catholique" (Forest, *Philippe Sollers*, 241).

84 "The multiple volumes of *Paradis* indeed constitute an epic. Their epic vision is a humorous one, however, because of their positing of a heroic model in the voices of humanity and in the heroic manner in which S continues to insist on publishing subsequent volumes. Sollers presents himself as the hero, as the poet who is recording this testament of his times. [...] The stream of

garde heritage in Sollers' output post-*Tel Quel* lies in its epic scaffolding, the formatting device of the catalogue, and the employment of recursive structures. Here, the epic catalogue seems to reiterate phrases so as to stimulate the recognition of repetition and involvement of memory on the part of the reading subject who thereby participates in Sollers' project of writing the chronicle of the culture of his times. Repetition and recursion, as in the *Wake*, becomes the bond between writer and reader in their link to a common past.

In the 1980s Sollers' novels changed even more considerably than in the mid-70s. Since *Femmes* (1983), they contain language which is transparent, engages definable narrative voices, and involves character development, intrigue, and a more traditional format with regard to sentence and paragraph structure. In 1984 he published *Portrait du joueur*, and in 1987 *Le Coeur absolu*, both of which sold well.[85] The subject of *Femmes* is a serious one, even though the tone of Will the narrator—an American journalist in dialogue with S., an avant-garde novelist living in Paris—is sceptical regarding the protean nature of styles that create the various popularised roles accessible to women. The combat is fought between feminism and chauvinism – both essentially marketable topics. *Portrait du joueur* is Sollers' humorous take on the difficulties entailed in autobiographic writing à la *Tristram Shandy*, which Sollers respects because of the shifting narrative strategies of the writer as a gambler and player of games. Sollers' narrator, Philippe Diamant, is an autobiographical voice which could be that of Sollers: not only is he French, having been born in Bordeaux and endowed with many of Sollers' own predilections, but in the following passage Sollers ties the name to his original surname Joyaux: "Remarquez, j'aurais pu aussi bien m'appeler *joyaux*. Au pluriel. C'est le même mot que *jouer*. Ancien français *joel*. Racine latine *jocus*. *Jocalis, jocalia*. *Joyaux, Diamant*, tout ça c'est du pareil au meme" (*PJ*, 224). Thus, in a sequence similar to the one seen in *H*, Sollers arrives at his family name via a play on words which associates *Joyaux* with *juif* (Jew), then *joyau* (jewel), and finally *diamant* (diamond).

As long as the *Paradis* series employed comic intervention through the juxtaposition of textual fragments within its parody of contemporary culture, then in *Femmes* and *Portrait du Joueur*, "the apparently serious return to a more classical style of narration is undercut by the self-deprecating tone

---

words in *Paradis* becomes a hologram that ironically erases visual clues if they are read aloud. The reader must go beyond the materialism of the visual assault of these words strung together with no apparent structure just as Sollers himself goes beyond the materialism of his Maoist cultural position in 1974" (Champagne, *Philippe Sollers*, 59; 60–1).

85   As Champagne observes with irony, Sollers is "certainly proud to be finally the writer of bestsellers. However [...] he is also careful about what this 'popularity' means because he does want to be read" (Ibid, 53).

of the narrative voice."[86] In *Le Coeur absolu* Sollers is the name of one of the characters as well as of the narrator, an aging man beset by the fear of his loss of attractiveness to women and his appeal as a writer to prospective readers. Sollers, his reputation, and his talents, are the subject of frequent discussion amongst characters. In this respect, the less Joycean later Sollers becomes the more Kundera-like he begins to sound. The title, "Absolute Heart," suggests an idealism and a personal pathos far removed from the dialectical material-ism of the politically involved Sollers of the early 1970s – nor does the conven-tional narrative style bear any resemblance to his daring formal experiments, which the *Paradis* series of the early-to-mid-1980s brought to a close. After *Le Coeur absolu* followed four more novels in which Sollers continued his return to formal neo-classicism, elaborating on his examinations of Catholicism (e.g., challenging the Christian repression of sexuality), whose conservative style has the primary realist function of getting the message across.

Still, critics like Forest argue for a holistic approach to the Sollers oeuvre, relating as it does one and the same experience throughout: "the mysteri-ous plunge of the subject into the interior of his/her own speech."[87] The fact remains that never before or after the *Nombres-Lois-H* trilogy was the expe-rience conveyed by Sollers' writing quite as Joyce-inflected. Still, in Cham-pagne's opinion, "the spires of Sollers' creative writing have constituted a moving spiral of his modes of iconoclasm, transgression, and religiosity. [...] And Sollers is intent upon continuing that program of making the world less stupid by implementing a type of generosity that is tolerant of differ-ences and allows others to be other."[88] As long as Champagne's retrospective view is correct, it is quite indisputable that all three of these three modes (iconoclasm, transgression, and religiosity) have been dependent if not based on Sollers' engagement with Joyce's work. Sollers is an author who, most out-spokenly and steadfastly of all post-war French avant-gardists, grounded his theory and practice of fiction on the legacy of the Joycean revolution of the word.

---

86   Ibid, 55.
87   "Cette plongée mystique du sujet vers l'intérieur même de sa propre parole, qui, lui permettant de se soustraire à la mécanique sociale qui le nie—langage pétrifié, ronde sexuelle—lui ouvre la voie vers une forme de vérité qui est aussi jouissance" (Forest, *Philippe Sollers*, 332).
88   Champagne, *Philippe Sollers*, 101.

8.
POST-2000 CODA:
CONCEPTUAL JOYCE

The crucial lines of the post-Joycean development traced in this book have centred around three programmatically avant-garde writers revolting against the contemporary literary mainstream of the early 1960s: B. S. Johnson in Britain, William Burroughs in the U.S., Philippe Sollers in France. Each departed from one of the central modalities of the Joycean materiality of language as manifest in *Ulysses* and *Finnegans Wake*. Johnson, from Joyce's concrete writing, his typographical foregrounding of letters and words as distinct objects; Burroughs, from Joyce's conception of the forgery of fiction, of literature as creative plagiarism; and Sollers, from Joyce's neologising of the logos, his destabilisation of the signifier by means of multilingual punning and the technique of the portmanteau.

Their output reached its experimental peak round the turn of the decades, with Johnson's *The Unfortunates* (1968) and *See the Old Lady Decently* (written 1973), Burroughs' *Nova Trilogy* (1966–8), and Sollers' experimental triptych *Nombres, Lois,* and *H* (1968–73). However, with Johnson deceased in 1973, Sollers' *Tel Quel* discontinued in 1982, and Burroughs abandoning his cut-up and fold-in – none of the three can be said to have continued publishing important experimental work beyond the 1970s. In fact, one can point to the year 1982 as a coincidental marker of an end to the experimental periods for all three of the French avant-garde groupings under focus here. The 1982 New York Colloquium of the *nouveau roman* saw Alain Robbe-Grillet, Robert Pinget, Nathalie Sarraute, and Claude Simon celebrating Jean Ricardou's absence and placing a renewed emphasis on the novelist's expression of their personality. The 1982 death of Georges Perec was the passing of one of Oulipo's most formally inventive and linguistically oriented members, who was also most programmatically Joycean of the entire group. The 1982 discontinuation of *Tel Quel* and the inception of *L'Infini* marked the end of Philippe Sollers' politically committed radical poetics departing from his early-1970s exposure, as critic as well as translator, to Joyce's *Wake*. Last but not least, there is yet another sense in which 1982 marked an end of an era, however symbolically: Joyce's work began to be published in the French *Pléiade* series, and Sollers and *Tel Quel* had been certainly instrumental in this acceptance by sensitising the reading public to the links between the avant-garde and its marginalised historical predecessors. At the same time, the effective acknowledgment of Joyce's acceptance within French intellectual circles and the official "canon" neutralised his radicalness and lessened his importance: never again after 1982 would the Joycean presence within the French letters and thought be nearly as palpable as in the *Tel Quel* years.

Of course, post-Joycean experimentation did not stop in 1982, although the latter was certainly on the wane by the time the decade had been through. The present account has traced the careers of almost all the principal figures well till the end of the 20th century, with some post-2000 enjambments: in the UK, there was the exceptional figure of Christine Brooke-Rose, and, appearing from the late 1970s onwards, the maverick figures of Alasdair Gray and Iain Sinclair; in the USA, there was/is the Fiction Collective and FC2 with Ronald Sukenick and Raymond Federman at the helm, the Cyberpunk aesthetics of Kathy Acker in the 80s–90s, as well as the idiosyncratic Joycean experiment of Gilbert Sorrentino; in France, the Oulipo and some re-incarnation of the "New" New Novel have remained active and evolving to this day, however without much of the innovative and radical impulses that informed these movements in the 60s and 70s.

Before looking back on the long road travelled, eking out the lines of commonalities and differences, of creative synergies and entropies, and before construing—on the basis of the genealogy mapped—a Joycean postmodernity, a final detour is thus in order. A brief overview of the work of a dozen writers active post-2000, designed as a report on the state of the literary experiment and avant-garde fiction in contemporary France, the UK, and the USA.

8.1. "MISINTERPRETING THE AVANT-GARDE": RACZYMOW, HADENGUE, LEVÉ

In his study on contemporary French fiction, *Qu'est-il arrive aux écrivains français?*, Jean Bessière devotes an entire section to "La littérature contemporaine et sa mésinterprétation des avant-gardes." This misinterpretation, for Bessière, is due to how contemporary claims to a literary avant-garde are necessarily tied with the heritage of the "avant-gardes of the 50s, 60s, 70s, and as consequence, of modernism," and this heritage is only possible "at the price of distortion and reification."[1] Bessière traces the constant recurrence of Blanchot's concept of literature as "the book to come" and shows how in generalising this thesis, writers and critics have embraced both the minima-

---

1   "Les écrivains et les critiques s'autorisent à se dire modernes et à proposer une telle pensée de la littérature parce qu'ils se reconnaissent comme les explicites héritiers des avantgardes des années 1950, 1960, 1970, et, en conséquence, du modernisme. Cet aveu n'est possible qu'au prix d'une distorsion et d'une réification de cet héritage" (Jean Bessière, *Qu'est-il arrive aux écrivains français ? D'Alain Robbe-Grillet à Jonathan Littell* [Loveral: Éditions Labor, 2006] 41).

lism and sparseness of the *nouveau roman* and the existentialist imperative of a socio-political engagement, thereby losing sight of the pertinence of the avant-garde project.[2]

That which was constructed as innovative and provocative by the historical avant-gardist project, now finds itself "a constant." Contemporary French fiction is thus marked by an "infidelity to what has been called the tradition of the new," and Bessière furthers the thesis that under these circumstances, neither modernist literature, nor the neo-avant-garde of the 1960s and 1970s, can be the guarantor of contemporary literature. That part of contemporary literature which returns to the playful representation of 1960s and 1970s fiction in search of exemplars remains trapped in contradiction.[3]

Such is also the picture painted by Anglophone critics like Simon Kemp, whose *French Fiction into the Twenty-First Century* (2010) redeploys a 1991 article by Jean-Michel Maulpoix, "Le Retour au Récit," to speak of a "return to story" in its subtitle.[4] While the "story" itself that "returns" is a concept ridden by ambiguity, and where it returns "to" is open to conjecture, there seems to be a broad consensus regarding what it returns "from." Critic Pierre Brunel describes the 1980s and 1990s as "the period in which we generally see an ebbing away of the avant-garde thrust of the three previous decades, and in particular of that extreme and extremist avant-garde of the 1970s."[5] And so the pendulum swings back once again and, to reverse Ricardou's famous statement, instead of the adventure of writing comes the writing of adventures. The only extended mention of Joycean experimentalism in Kemp's book comes in his chapter on Marie Darrieussecq's *Bref séjour chez les vivants* (2001), employing

---

2 "On perd cependant ce qui faisait leur pertinence : la littérature était, en elle-même, un projet et, par-là, un contre-projet social. Cette constitution d'un canon et cette perte de la pertinence expliquent que les écrivains et les critiques réifient de manière paradoxale ce dont ils se tiennent pour les héritiers" (Bessière, *Qu'est-il arrive aux écrivains français?*, 42).

3 "Ni la littérature moderniste, ni celle des années 1950, 1960, 1970, ne peuvent donc être des cautions de la littérature contemporaine. [...] La part de littérature contemporaine, qui sait, de manière exemplaire, le retournement des jeux de la représentation hérités des années 1960 et 1970, reste prise dans ces contradictions" (Bessière, *Qu'est-il arrive aux écrivains français ?* 43-4).

4 "The return to the story is now a commonplace in the analysis of contemporary French literature, so much so that it approaches the status of a received idea, propagated from critical text to critical text, often without being interrogated as to its precise meaning or its possible hidden assumptions[...] What exactly is this récit that we are returning to? Where are we returning from? How might we go about judging comparative degrees of 'story' in different texts?" (Simon Kemp, *French Fiction into the Twenty-first Century: The Return to the Story* [Cardiff: University of Wales Press, 2010] 2).

5 Brunel continues: "The Sollers of *Nombres*, *H*, or *Lois* becomes more relaxed and better behaved in *Femmes* or *Portrait d'un joueur*. Robbe-Grillet becomes an autobiographer while continuing to work through fiction. A new generation of writers receives the legacy of the recent experiments in the novel, while at the same time seeking to differentiate themselves" (Pierre Brunel, *Glissements du roman français au xxe siècle* [Paris: Klincksieck, 2001] 31. Qtd. and trans. in Kemp, *French Fiction*, 2–3).

as stately and stalely a modernist technique as the well-worn stream of consciousness (which ironically even Joyce himself claimed to have appropriated
from a French writer, Édouard Dujardin). And even in as basic a comparison
as with Molly Bloom, Darrieusecq pales in comparison, as her stream of consciousness "makes more concessions to intelligibility"[6] than does Joyce, even
keeping the usual typographical breaks and punctuation intact.

Accordingly, the 1990s in French fiction saw little beyond bizarre Joycean
cameos, quotations and pastiche. An essay by Henri Raczymow entitled *La
Mort du grand écrivain* (1994) can be read in precisely these terms proposed
by Bessière: as nostalgia for the supposed "disappearance" of literature in
which there is no French writer of a status comparable to that of Sartre,
Robbe-Grillet, or Queneau. The choice of framing the debate in these terms
is symptomatic of what Bessière terms "the pathology of belonging to literature" – a belonging that can only take place as an anachronism, and from
a position of inferiority. A similarly contradictory "belonging" finds its fictional counterpart in Henri Raczymow's novel *Bloom et Bloch* (1993) in which
Joyce's Bloom meets Bloch, a boyhood friend of Proust's "Marcel." Through
this reunion, Raczymow expresses his belief that Bloom and Bloch are "brothers" in that they are "personnages devenus des personnes," and entertains
the idea of writing a novel—to be narrated by him—in which they will be
the protagonists. For Raczymow, this is meant to provide an opportunity to
discuss the work of Proust and Joyce, to compare "ses deux heros," in terms
of the topics of their shared Jewishness, Hebrew history and language, love,
the philosophy of art, etc. But *Bloom and Bloch* remains, at best, a symptom of
the pathology of "belonging to literature," with Joyce and Proust "alive" only
as undead zombies.

Similar to Raczymow's is the pastiche of some Joycean motifs in Philippe
Hadengue's first work of fiction, *Petite Chronique des gens de la nuit dans un
port de l'Atlantique Nord* (1988), a "long prose poem," written in extremely
long, meandering sentences, that tells an oblique story in a painfully halt-
ing, sometimes oddly punctuated, sometimes oddly skewed syntax, meant
to represent the narrator's manifest suffering. There is the character of an
adolescent would-be artist called Dedalus, again, and at one point, a ship is
christened the Annalivia Plurabelle – but again this a mere lame borrowing
from the repertoire of Joycean motifs which does nothing to rework or expand his heritage. The appearance of two additional novels in 1999, *L'Exode*
and *Quelqu'un est mort dans la maison d'en face*, brought little if anything by
way of fresh departure,[7] and so Bessière's scepticism regarding the signifi-

---

6   Kemp, *French Fiction*, 89.
7   John Taylor, *Paths to Contemporary French Literature*, Vol. 1 (New Brunswick, New Jersey: Trans-
     action Publishers, 2004) 201.

cance of the post-war literary experimentalism for contemporary French fiction would seem fully justified.

Thus, the only figure in contemporary French writing whose avant-garde "misinterpretation" takes on a critical value and a parodic tenor informed by the Joycean détournement of literary discourse is Édouard Levé.[8] Before his untimely death in 2007, Levé produced four conceptual texts—Œuvres (2002; English in 2014); *Journal* (2004; *Newspaper*, 2015); *Autoportrait* (2005; English in 2012); *Suicide* (2008; English in 2011)—blending extensive references to the world and individuals (in his détournement of the public discourse of *Newspaper*) with highly personal and subjective mentions (in *Autoportrait*) and evocations of a friend's suicide (*Suicide*). All of the four take up an "exhaustive" attitude to their conceptual subjects, and so Levé has been classified as a follower of Perec and the Oulipo.[9]

Oeuvres/Works is at once the librarian's dream and the writer's nightmare, for all narrative art aspires to the condition of the 'non-paraphrasable' and 'not-to-be-summarised.' Works shortly describes 533 possible works, or "projects" as Levé calls them—paintings, photographs, films, architecture, writings, and readings—and gives their "prescriptions," i.e., indicates the materials, ideas, procedures, and actions needed for their production. These "projects" are conceptions of works unrealised, merely imagined, but brought under the rubric of a kind of numbering system, the many instances exemplifying the human power to create. As so many Joycean parodic and impossible lists, Levé kicks off his endless list with the one item it cannot possibly include (i.e., itself): "1. A book describes works that the author has conceived but not brought into being" (*W*, 1).

In *Newspaper*, Levé copies, rewrites, and shortens daily news from various newspapers, turning them into semi-abstractions by deleting all specific identifications of information sources, persons, places, and dates. Its thematic arrangement dabbles in the aesthetics of the collage, while its elision of all proper names performs a typically peculiar alienating effect of a situationist *détournement*: cf. some of the "stories" in the first two sections, "INTERNATIONAL" and "SOCIETY":

APPROXIMATELY TWENTY PEOPLE have died in a suicide bombing at a seaside resort hotel. [...]

TWO CANDIDATES in the presidential election have each claimed victory. They are both "governing" with their respective cabinets. [...]

---

8   For more, see the recent detailed article by David Vichnar & Jean Bessière, "'" *Litteraria Pragensia* 30.60 (December 2020): 76–99.

9   "If there is one recent French author who most exemplifies Georges Perec's philosophy of exhausting a subject, he might be Édouard Levé." Scott Esposito & Lauren Elkin, *The End of Oulipo? An Attempt to Exhaust a Movement* (Winchester / Washington: Zero Books, 2013) 107.

> FOLLOWING THE PUBLICATION of incorrect data, the president has just learned that
> his country is in economic trouble. [...]
> A MAYOR OF A MAJOR CITY HAS WRITTEN A DECREE aimed at expelling all homeless
> people from his city. [...]
> "WE HAVE A LITERARY TRADITION that's damaging our country, and then we have
> a tradition that is beneficial to our nation and ought to be promoted by the govern-
> ment," announced a youth organization linked to a far-right leader.
> (*N*, 5–36)

And so on, and so drearily forth: whether banal or vaguely amusing, these
are skin-and-bones messages stripped of their content-value, boiled down
to their generic structures because lacking in specificity. They also ponder
the status of the proper name ("Which" president? "What" mayor of "which"
city?) in the context of the "information value" of any message.

The writing procedures of *Newspaper* are applied to Levé's self-portrai-
ture in *Autoportrait*, which refuses explicit self-expression, as if immersed
in his own personal information flux. Levé turns his biographical data, actions, memories, and feelings into a flow of information and objectifies them
by sticking to the use of the first-person pronoun as the whole ensemble of
information is *his own*. The published edition of *Autoportrait* offers a typographical figuration of this flow: it comprises 1400 sentences based on first-
person verbal phrases, without any paragraph, subparagraph, without any
particular identification of any single line or word:

> When I was young, I thought *Life A User's Manual* would teach me how to live and *Suicide
> A User's Manual* how to die. I have spent three years and three months abroad. I prefer
> to look to my left. I have a friend who gets off on betrayal. The end of a trip leaves me
> with a sad aftertaste, the same as the end of a novel. I forget things I don't like. I may
> have spoken, without knowing it, to someone who killed someone. [...] I don't know
> why I write. I prefer a ruin to a monument. I am calm during reunions. [...]. I do not ask
> "do you love me." Only once can I say "I'm dying" with-out telling a lie. The best day of
> my life may already be behind me. (*AE*, 5, 104)

Finally, submitted to the publisher ten days before he committed his own,
Levé's *Suicide* deals with a friend's suicide, that is, a manifest, definable, and
singular act and a mystery. *Suicide* returns to the questioning of the power of
words and abstractions, which aim to restore both the information overload
and the flow of accumulated time, the time of a whole life and its broadest
extensions: how to release this flow and make time happen? A long poem,
a self-portrait, presented as written by the unnamed man who killed himself, closes *Suicide*. As a sample quotation shows, "To please pleases me / To
displease displeases me / To be indifferent is indifferent to me" (*SE*, 103),

each line is a quasi-abstraction and a concrete self-characterisation, going against expression. *Suicide* tries to build the time of a whole life, that is, to make Levé's thoughts and abstractions about his friend concomitant with the series of his own life's moments.

The implied post-conceptual poetics of Levé's *Works* finds its development in *Newspaper* and the application of one of its basic principles, "against expression," in two works, *Autoportrait* and *Suicide*, which focus on subjectivities. Levé is a Joycean writer, if not so much to the letter, then in spirit. He détourns the official discourses of the "culture" of late capitalism and subjects them to a critique through emptying akin to what Joyce does to discourses of religious and nationalist power throughout *Ulysses*. Levé also maintains a Joycean attitude to the congruence between the particular and universal: one's subjectivity is made manifest without recourse to personal expression—or "impersonating"—but through the manipulation of the general and circumstantial.

8.2 BREAKING "THE RECURSIVE LOOPS OF REALISM": MITCHELL, HALL, HOME, MOORE

The early 2000s marked a change for the better in the publication and reception of the writers loosely associated with Johnson's avant-gardist circle who finally began receiving their long-overdue critical attention in the ensuing decade. 2001 saw the first book-length critical study on Johnson's work, *A Critical Reading* by Philip Tew, followed, in 2004, by Coe's own monumental biography and by Picador's reprint of *Albert Angelo, Trawl*, and *House Mother Normal* as the *B. S. Johnson Omnibus*. Also in 2004, the first conference devoted solely to Johnson took place, producing the proceedings as a book publication in 2007 under the title *Re-reading B. S. Johnson* (eds. Tew and White). A complete reprint of all four Quin novels was undertaken by the Dalkey Archive Press between 2001 and 2004, followed in 2013 by the first book-length study of her work, Robert Buckeye's *Re:Quin*, and in 2018, by *The Unmapped Country: Stories and Fragments*, an edition of her fifth unfinished novel plus shorter fiction (for a creative revisitation of Quin, see Stewart Home below). In 2004, Dalkey Archive also reprinted Brophy's *In Transit*, with an introduction by none other than Brooke-Rose. Two years later, Carcanet re-issued a twentieth-anniversary *Brooke-Rose Omnibus*. 2010 saw the publication of the excellent book-length study of the Brooke-Rose canon, penned by Karen Lawrence. In 2007, the first book-length study on Rayner Heppenstall, written by G. J. Buckell, was published, again by Dalkey Archive.

While all this was happening on the fringes, the mainstream was busy appropriating the idea of "experimentalism" to suit its purposes. The two UK-focused chapters in this book have shown that the "great tradition" of the novel in Britain—i.e., middle-class realism—is one that dies hard, surviving the disturbances of avant-garde modernism almost unscathed. If any further proof was needed, it came in 2008, when Zadie Smith, another literary practitioner-turned-critic, attempted to tell the story "about the future of the Anglophone novel." In an uncanny echo of David Lodge's 1970s prescriptive pronouncements, she titled her essay "Two Paths for the Novel,"[10] and just as for Lodge thirty years prior, for Smith, these two "paths" are two ways of riding the same merry-go-round, two recipes for making the one and only "realist" pudding. Against Joseph O'Neill's *Netherland*—and its "breed of lyrical realism"—Smith pits Tom McCarthy's *Remainder* (2001), whose rejection of the tenor of O'Neill's book is described by Smith as "a function of our ailing literary culture." The irony is that it is precisely such critical narrowing-down of the spectrum of experimentalism to two kinds of "realism," as engaged in by Smith, that is the prevailing disease.

As Louis Armand's critique of Smith's position entitled "Realism's Last Word" persuasively shows, McCarthy's novel is not all that remote from O'Neill's in that it still simulates all the core tropes of realism – it presents no barrier to comprehensibility for the otherwise dispirited reader. Its only anti-realist motif is to present a trauma-survivor protagonist suffering from amnesia, a gadget whereby his past sense of "self" is erased. But other than this, *Remainder*'s linear, objectively narrated, and only ever so slightly absurdist storyline provides the reader with the comforting impression of returning their thoughts to them, "freshly re-minted."[11] And so, however much Smith's article may try to paint the picture of *Remainder* as "experimental," Armand's exposé shows that this cannot be, "only because of its continuing subscription to key tenets of realist fiction" – even though possibly "materialist" in its "thematic concerns," these are nonetheless related in "a straight-forward, one might say conventional, prose style."[12] Armand's argument—which pits Smith and McCarthy against the formal and linguistically experimental work of, e.g., Philippe Sollers—concludes by metaphorically applying the concluding image from McCarthy's novel to Smith's article:

> The final image of *Remainder* is perhaps appropriate here – a plane flying in an endless figure-eight, a recursive loop which will last exactly as long as the fuel in the plane's tank. It's as if McCarthy is adverting here to precisely the trap that Realism in Smith's "Two Paths" represents, in which deviation always feeds back into normalis-

10 Zadie Smith, "Two Paths for the Novel," *New York Review of Books*, 20 November 2008. Online: https://www.nybooks.com/articles/2008/11/20/two-paths-for-the-novel/

11 Louis Armand, "Realism's Last Word," *The Organ Grinder's Monkey: Culture after the Avant-Garde* (Prague: Litteraria Pragensia Books, 2013) 116.

12 Armand, "Realism's Last Word," 118.

ation: the perverse logic at work in McCarthy's radical materialism remains a *depicted* logic in which the novel's language never itself partakes.[13]

There are not many contemporary British authors that could be plausibly pitted against the kind of "normalised" experiment descried in McCarthy's novel, and neither is there a real sense of the 2000s effecting any major "break" with the past or advancement forward. The difficulties tackled by Patrick O'Donnell's introduction to a special issue of *Modern Fiction Studies* devoted to "New British Fiction" (sub specie 2012)—including the work of Smith, McCarthy, and David Mitchell, among others—in trying to define this "new" fiction in terms of generation or a shared programme are almost tangible. He depicts the "millennial" British writers in the broadest possible terms of a generation that "follows that of Salman Rushdie, Angela Carter, Ian McEwan, Martin Amis, and A. S. Byatt," and if that is not vague enough, goes on to speak of an "evaporation" of any sense of "self-definition":

> The tendency for many of the writers mentioned or closely examined in this issue is to regard postmodern experimentation as something of a toolbox; [...]. This may appear to be claiming that they, or we, have "gotten over" postmodernism, which is of course as silly as saying that they, or we, have "gotten over" modernism. But the point is that for many of the writers considered here, the need to define themselves as part of a movement or labeled departure from what came epochally before has evaporated.[14]

Let us take David Mitchell, whose "cosmopolitan, futuristic multinovels" receive honorary mention in O'Donnell's account. Mitchell's first three novels, *Ghostwritten* (1999), *Number9Dream* (2001), and *Cloud Atlas* (2004), are all "system-novels" in that they deal with the implications of daily global interactions between people (facilitated by modern communications technology), and the resultant co-dependence of actors within this system. In a 2015 interview, Mitchell spoke of the "novel" as "a model of a universe,"[15] and that universe has been variously called "cosmopolitan"[16] and/or "globalised."[17]

---

13   Ibid, 128.

14   Patrick O'Donnell, "New British Fiction," *Modern Fiction Studies* 58.3 (Fall 2012): 431.

15   Paul A. Harris, "David Mitchell in the Laboratory of Time," *SubStance* 44.1 (2015): 9.

16   Cf., e.g., Berthold Schoene, "Tour du Monde: David Mitchell's *Ghostwritten* and the Cosmopolitan Imagination," *College Literature* 37.4 (Fall 2010): 42–60. Schoene speaks of the "cosmopolitan novel" as abandoning "the vertebrate structures of the traditional novel's *tour d'horizon*" and instead experimenting with "what are more cellular modes of representation" (48).

17   Cf., e.g., Jason Howard Mezey, "A Multitude of Drops: Recursion and Globalization in David Mitchtell's *Cloud Atlas*," *Modern Language Studies* 40.2 (Winter 2011): 10–37. Mezey notes that the most "spellbinding and problematic" qualities about *Cloud Atlas* are due to how its form "consists of six interlocking stories with a different, fully realized narrator in each one, and featuring

The nine loosely connected stories that make up *Ghostwritten* (1999) follow certain repeated patterns and motifs and build up a structure of complex interconnections with the circular repeat of the opening/concluding question, "Who was blowing on the nape of my neck?" (*G* 3). But apart from its "global" scope—one of the stories' protagonists is a disembodied Mongolian spirit in search of its origins who inhabits the bodies of people from across the globe—and the subtlety with which the chapters of *Ghostwritten* are interwoven (a shared train compartment, a wrongly dialled telephone number, a chance encounter on the street), little effort is made to diverge from Smith's two well-trodden "paths" of realism. *Number9Dream* (2001), is a coming-of-age tale of an archetypal search after a missing father, structurally broken down into eight full-length chapters, as well as a final chapter "nine" that is untitled and unwritten (empty). By contrast with *Ghostwritten*, it features only one narrator, a Japanese teenager on a surreal trip through the Tokyo underworld, juxtaposed with sequences of dreams, fantasy, and memory, including a found WW2 diary and a reading of a collection of children's short stories. Generically hybrid (combining thriller, tragedy, fantasy, and videogames), this broadly conceived novel also includes some numerical patterning and musical intertext (the "#9" of the famous Lennon song, also riffing off Haruki Murakami's *Norwegian Wood*). *Cloud Atlas* (2004), in structure, is similar to *Ghostwritten*, consisting of six interconnected stories with separate narrators, but even more ambitious in scope of its time-frame: it stretches back to the South Seas of the nineteenth century, moves forward into contemporary London, Tokyo, and California, and then an apocalyptic future, before returning to its starting point. All six of the stories in *Cloud Atlas* are representative of Mitchell's penchant for complex transhistorical and ubiquitous narrative plotting, close in spirit to Joyce's metempsychosis as staged in *Ulysses* on the narrative—and in *Finnegans Wake*, on the linguistic—levels. The theme of reincarnation is developed in some far-flung ways, ranging from a nineteenth-century island near New Zealand, where local tribes viciously subdue the Maoris, to 1970s Buenos Yerba, California, the site of a potentially deadly nuclear reactor.

Similarly to Joyce, Mitchell structures his series of interlocking narratives around a few archetypical motifs or situations which permeate all and provide their conceptual unity.[18] However, although frequently praised for his

---

a time scheme that moves forward across millennia and then doubles back on itself," and how its focus lies "less upon conflicts among humans and their circumstances and much more on the act of storytelling itself" (11).

18   To take but one example, the *Wakean* binary of the fall and ascension: Adam Ewing loses his footing and tumbles down into a hollow whilst ascending the volcano on the Chatham Island (*CA*, 19); Robert Frobisher has to jump from the first floor of a hotel to avoid paying his bill (*CA*, 43); the car of Luisa Rey is pushed off the edge of a bridge, falling into the water (*CA*, 144); the

versatile style, what critics have called "ventriloquism" accounts for Mitchell's ability to speak from many different viewpoints, not for stylistic variance and even less so for linguistic innovation. Mitchell's is a talent for multicultural pastiche, not for innovative recombination. Critics like Sam Munson observed that Mitchell's "lexical flourishes and structural baroquerie" are a poor substitute for insight into human character, and Thomas Jones complained that "all the postmodern trickery in the world can't disguise the fact that *Cloud Atlas* is, like a matryoshka, hollow at its core."[19] Thus, parallels with Joyce are ultimately to Mitchell's detriment, as the conceptual complexity of his narrative is very seldom matched on the linguistic level: to measure Mitchell by a Joycean yardstick would entail denouncing his novels as imitative simulation, along the lines of Armand's critique of McCarthy. Moreover, *Ghostwritten*'s and *Cloud Atlas*' form of loosely interconnected stories from across time and space had the important and largely unacknowledged predecessor in Alan Moore's *Voice of the Fire* (1996), more on which below.

The title of Steven Hall's first novel, *Raw Shark Texts* (2007), refers—via a pun on the Rorschach Test—to the idea of a "conceptual shark" (after Damien Hirst's famous conceptual installation), transforming it into a book which constantly meditates on its own status of a printed text and its "role within an increasingly variegated media ecology."[20] Hall's novel includes over forty pages of visual material, including film stills, photographs, scanned newspaper clippings, as well as experimental typography representing the titular shark (most famously, a 45-page flipbook in which the ever-increasing calligram of the shark seems to be swimming at the reader). As N. Katherine Hayles has noted, "*RST* incorporates other media platforms into its project, including fragments on the Internet, inserted pages in translations of the novel, and other sites, including physical locations. The complete work thus exists as the distributed literary system."[21]

After a motto from Borges ("*Some limited and waning memory of Herbert Ashe, an engineer of the southern railways, persists in the hotel at Adrogue, amongst*

---

author published by Timothy Cavendish throws a literary critic off the 12th floor of a hotel (*CA*, 151); the clone, or fabricant, called Sonmi-451 ascends from the underground shopping mall in which she works (*CA*, 208), and her growing self-consciousness is also explicitly described as an "ascension." Finally, Zachry Bailey and Meronym climb and then descend the Hawaiian mountain of Mauna Kea, Zachry confronting the temptations of the devil (named Ol' Georgie in the book) (*CA*, 282). For more cf. online: https://metacloudatlas.tumblr.com

19   Sam Munson, "Mitchell's Lama," *Commentary* 130.4 (November 2010): 63; Thomas Jones, "Outfoxing Hangman," *London Review of Books* 28. 9 (11 May 2006): 35.

20   Julia Panko, "Memory Pressed Flat into Text": The Importance of Print in Steven Hall's *The Raw Shark Texts*," *Contemporary Literature* 52.2 (Summer 2011): 264–297.

21   N. Katherine Hayles, *How We Think: Digital Media and Contemporary Technogenesis* (Chicago/London: University of Chicago Press, 2012) 172.

the effusive honeysuckles and in the illusory depths of the mirrors") comes a first-person opening in which a "second life" begins: "My eyes slammed themselves capital O open and my neck and shoulders arched back in a huge inward heave, a single world-swallowing lung gulp of air." (*RST*, 3) Throughout *The Raw Shark Texts*—as here in its opening—persists a certain naive insistence on repudiating style in favour of orthographic explorations, as in "My eyes slammed themselves capital O open," where the deviation is commented upon, and thus neutralised. We learn that the first-person narrator is an Eric Sanderson, amnesiac in consequence of having been attacked by a conceptual data-shark feeding on human personalities and leaving them devoid of memories. Gradually he starts to receive letters from his former self, "The First Eric Sanderson," that contain tips and clues to re-educate his amnesiac future self in the lore of the Ludovician, and send him on a quest to defeat it. On this quest, the text explores the possibilities of transporting a human subjectivity into a database (thus transcending it), at the same time that it "enacts the performative power of imaginative fiction conveyed through written language."[22]

By means of the opening heave occurs the single, world-swallowing plunge into the fictional world of the book where human communication is a vast network of streams, rivers, and oceans, and where numerous species of "thought-fish" lurk, the most fearsome of which is the "Ludovician," whose victims are (mis)treated and (mis)diagnosed by psychiatrists: hence the title's punning allusion to the Rorschach ink-blot tests. The other main antagonist to Sanderson's quest is Mycroft Ward, who launches his "the Ward-thing," a huge online database, appropriating and acting through "node bodies" after evacuating and absorbing the personality of the original occupant: ""He wasn't really a human being anymore, just the idea of one. A concept wrapped in skin and chemicals" (*RST*, 178). Hayles speaks of a development of "posthuman subjectivity" in Hall's novel.[23]

During its progression, *The Raw Shark Texts* becomes increasingly a gleeful mash-up of cinematic tropes – as wittily remarked in the *New Statesman* review, "You can imagine it being pitched, with deadly accuracy, as 'Jaws meets The Matrix.'"[24] This becomes evident in the novel's concluding emblem: it ends not with words, but with an old film still (from *Casablanca*), exploiting borrowed emotion. Hall's pastiche of the clichéd noir-genre becomes more foregrounded as the text progresses, and the saving grace is Hall's occasional employment of the affectless descriptive style of an early text-adventure game, to some eerie effects:

---

22   Hayles, *How We Think*, 200.
23   Ibid, 172.
24   Steven Poole, "Jumping the Shark," 5 March 2007. Online: http://stevenpoole.net/articles/jumping -the-shark/

muddy spray of split-second impressions—rainy-day football matches, yellow stamping Wellingtons, skidding trainers—a million tiny moment fragments were being blown free from the wet grass in a fast stripe of pressure moving down the lawn from the hospital towards us. A large conceptual thing just below the soil. (*RST*, 160)

The conceptual shark "itself," again, remains outside Hall's scope of description or presentation, only referred to as "a large conceptual thing." Then, on page 327, the text is brought to a sudden halt after the sentence, "The surface receding in hiss and bubbles below my feet," following which are seven blank pages, after which the conceptual shark begins to emerge, composed of bits of text and inky shapes arranged into a picture of the fish getting bigger as it draws near, the book becoming a flipbook. Then, gradually, the incomplete sentence "Fingers clamped my wrist and forearm and dragged me back up towards the surface with a" emerges in the shark's background, dragging both the protagonist and the text "towards the surface"—after its completion, "with a tug-of-war heave" on page 380, the text resumes its typographical layout. This is the highpoint of Hall's cinematic writing, abandoning words as referential signs and using them as ink-material out of which to compose an indexical image.

Hall's experimentation remains largely conceptual, and little outside of the shark's attack is performed on the materiality of language itself—apart from the momentary shift from the lexical to the ideogrammatic—in addition to its variety of printed media. There is, however, the character of Fidorous, Sanderson's helper and a language virologist, whose passages produce some metacommentary on the possibilities and pitfalls of language in the age of digital media, e.g., its proclivity to "viruses" and its "viral" modes of existence, a state in which it is in constant peril of fossilisation:

"All this machinery reroutes emails, websites, voicemail messages, radio programmes even. I feed my viruses into them and send them back so I can monitor the effects. '*At the end of the day.*' That's one of mine which is particularly virulent in the UK at the moment." "You mean, you invent phrases?" "Phrases, words, alternative spellings, abbreviations, corruptions. And not just invent; manage. [...] I construct language viruses so I might better understand real, naturally occurring ones. My work helps me to recognise the early warning signs and protect against future dangerous epidemics." (*RST*, 244)

The conceptual character of *Raw Shark Texts* also consists in its multimedia presentations: each of its thirty-six core chapters, bound into the novel itself, has an analogical "lost" section, known as "negative" or "un-chapter" which exists outside of the main printed text. These extra "un-chapters" (also of Hall's creation) have been found periodically since the book's initial release, hidden either online or in the real world. The text, thus, exists also as hypertext or as textual "found" object. As Steven Hall observed regarding *The Raw Shark Texts* negatives online: "For each chapter in The Raw Shark Texts there is, or will be, an un-chapter, a negative. If you look carefully at the novel you might be able to figure out why these un--chapters are called negatives. [...] there's also sticky negative discussion thread for folks to chat and post their findings. Happy hunting. Steven H."[25] Thus, despite its rather conservative, realist style and language, *The Raw Shark Texts* embraces the avant-garde idea of a work-in-progress, of an artwork exceeding its single-medium modes of existence or presentation.

Stewart Home, according to Iain Sinclair, is "a dynamo of invention, recycling Dadaist provocation into fugues of inspired counter-terror."[26] Ever since the early 1980s, Home had more or less systematically set about to position himself within the dissenting tradition that runs "from the Free Spirit through the writings of Winstanley, Coppe, Sade, Fourier, Lautréamont, William Morris, Alfred Jarry, and on into Futurism and Dada – then via Surrealism into Lettrism, the various Situationist movements, Fluxus, 'Mail Art,' Punk Rock, Neoism and contemporary anarchist cults" (*AS*, 4). A tradition, critic Richard Marshall adds, of "piss-takers, pranksters and jokers who used their slapstick rhetoric and parodic works to entertain, incite, educate and instruct a huge radicalised readership."[27]

Here is not the place to rehash Home's multicoloured career of spoofs, interventions, adopted public personae, and mock-occult society memberships. In this context, it is perhaps worth mentioning two of his activities occupying him around 2000, at the time he was working on his *69 Things to Do with a Dead Princess*. This was the Neoist Alliance—an occult order with himself as the magus and only member dealing with psychogeographic activities—whose manifesto called for "debasement in the arts" and in a parodic manner plagiarised a 1930s British fascist pamphlet on cultural politics. Symptomatically, this activity was followed by Internet ventriloquism using two MySpace profiles, as Mister Trippy and a ventriloquist doll called Tessie. Home's novels in this period switched from incorporating subcultural elements to focusing on issues of form and aesthetics.

Opening with the epigraphs from Samuel Taylor Coleridge on "truth as divine ventriloquism" and Karl Marx likening himself to a "machine devour-

---

25   Cf. online: http://forums.steven-hall.org/yaf_postst52_What-are--Raw-Shark-Texts-Negatives .aspx

26   Iain Sinclair, "Who is Stewart Home?" *London Review of Books* 16.12 (June 1994): 21–2.

27   Richard Marshall, "The Defiant Pose of Stewart Home," *3AM Magazine* (April 2001) Online: http://www.3ammagazine.com/politica/apr2001_stuart_home.html.

ing books," *69 Things to Do with a Dead Princess* tells the tale of Anna Noon, a twenty-year-old student with a taste for perverse sex, involved with a ventriloquist's dummy and an enigmatic older man alternatively called Callum or Alan. Anna lives in Aberdeen and her sex life revolves around the ancient stone circles in this region, whose sublime grandeur provides a backdrop against which Anna is able to act out her provocative psychodramas. Callum or Alan is planning to kill himself the moment he has read the last of his large collection of books, including the fictional *69 Things to Do with a Dead Princess* by the fictional "cult writer" K. L. Callan. This fictional document brings forth a conspiracy theory about the death of Diana, Princess of Wales, claiming that Diana was murdered, then her corpse was dragged around Scottish stone circles, until it fell apart, and Callum/Alan decides to test this with his ventriloquist dummy.

The novel's textual material falls into three roughly equal categories: one third of the novel is made up of psychogeographic descriptions of Aberdeen and the nearby stone circles; a second third is formed by mock-academic reviews of fiction and philosophy, both real and fictitious; and the last third of the novel is taken up by pornographic sex scenes. As Home's own description for *69 Things* states, "this is a book about the body in which the carnal is a manifestation of consciousness: a book in which it is impossible to distinguish the ancient from the post-modern," and which illustrates that "schizophrenia may well be the only sane response to capitalism,"[28] i.e., detouring toward Deleuze and Guattari's *Anti-Oedipus*.

Home's *69 Things* revisits and updates Ann Quin's *Berg* (cf. Chapter Two). It opens with a sentence unmistakably *Bergian*: "A man who no longer called himself Callum came to Aberdeen intent on ending his life" (69T, 1). In a flattering first footnote to the text, Home posits his intention of "avoiding" such modernist figures as Hemingway, Stein, Beckett, even B. S. Johnson, and suggesting that "our attention could be more usefully directed towards Ann Quin" (69T, 169). But Home refers to Quin in many other ways: not only does *69 Things* directly reverse her evasion of geography in *Berg*'s "seaside town" with its obsessively meticulous psychogeography of Aberdeenshire, it also replaces her reversals of parricidal intention with a suicidal one and upgrades her latent eroticisation of the physical world with full-fledged pornographic provocation. But most importantly, Home's *69 Things* is *Berg*ian by virtue of its style, whose primary gesture is that of merging of discourses, the unscrambling of social codes.

The three social codes, or "text-types," deployed in Home's textual production, have been identified as the academic, the psychogeographic, and the

28   Online: https://www.stewarthomesociety.org/books.htm.

pornographic.[29] The so-called academic type of discourse is marked by a monotonous structure that foregrounds the (bad-)writing process, and thereby prevents the reader from engaging with the text. It also conveys the mechanisation of the syntactical structures of language as a repetitive and recursive code. In the porn text-type, as in sex, the two complementary compositional techniques on full show, so to speak, are those of variation and repetition. As when variation of sex-organ terminology yields such increasingly hilarious results as 'erect tool' (69T, 9), 'phallus' (69T, 10), 'beef curtains' (69T, 10), 'molten genetics' (69T, 69), and 'chief implement for the propagation of our species' (69T, 117). Any literary aspirations of Home's style are systematically subverted by the obvious mechanistic, inelegant, tedious repetition, whose preposterously heightened display bordering on caricature makes the text-type itself into preposterous caricature. Finally, Home's "psychogeographic" text-type presents the strongest commitment to a creative rendering of reality, but also its questioning and erasure – an opposition to the documentary style. As the main narrative action consists of the couple's trips across Aberdeenshire, the novel too traverses tedious sections which describe the landscape and stone circles, in deadpan enumerative style full of lists of measurements.

Home's triad of discourses of pornography, psychogeography, and academia is composed of text-types that do not communicate with one another – a point brought home by perhaps the most problematic part of Home's style in 69 Things: his representation of speech as always reported and indirect. Although narrated by Anna in the third person, and in one third made up of her partner's endless diatribes on books existent or not-so-much so, not once does the novel present direct speech. This creates problems of attributing speech to characters, exacerbated in the use of academic text-types, subverting such concepts as originality and source-attribution, both key for academia.

Most Bergian of all the features of 69 Things is the schizophrenic motif that destabilises Home's narrative, destroying old codes, freeing desires beneath socially constructed identity. The novel's "nervous breakdown" gives birth to multiple voices in constant interplay, where none is allowed to dominate. Coherence lost in schizophrenic bedlam. The form of the novel destroyed, it ends with the parallel between the disappearance of Alan and his suicide within Anna's consciousness, the narrative turning to the beginning only in order to note that "there was no beginning":

---

29   Cf. the maddeningly detailed critical piece, "Does Aberdeen Exist? An Essay Review of Stewart Home's 69 Things," by Kevin O'Neill, most likely a Stewart Home ventriloquised avatar. Online: https://www.stewarthomesociety.org/sex/dead.htm.

> The mystery was revolved with the stroke of a pen. We'd stopped living. The beginning did not, could not, exist prior to the end. A man no longer called Alan came to Aberdeen. He told me his name was Callum. I believed him. Interpretation spelt out the elements of a dream. Hallucinations within the hallucination that was already speech. The body of a dead princess as a metaphor for literature. Works of condensation and displacement. (69T, 168)

The breakdown of identity here is coupled with identification of "speech" with "hallucination." Astonishingly, in a book so loud with apparent talk, nothing is ever explicitly said or surely heard or directly related, and so all remains indefinable, unattributable, ventriloquised. Home problematises the speech situation in order to deconstruct hierarchy and subvert certitude—his narrative contains, to paraphrase Stevick, nothing but "voices in the reader's head."

   The concluding "consummation by the turning of a page" is textually brought home by the final footnote (twelve is the number of chapters and of footnotes) that follows after the concluding aposiopesis—literally inviting the reader to "consume" the book by turning towards the final page. There, *69 Things* takes a step further than even Berg in the self-deconstruction of the text, treating us to an endless loop of self-contradicting statements, a textual *perpetuum mobile* that apparently goes ad infinitum:

> A man no longer called Alan came to Aberdeen. Alan and Callum came to Aberdeen. He told me his name was Callum. Alan left Aberdeen. Somewhere along the line he slipped out of my life. A man called Alan came to Aberdeen with me. The life slipped out of Callum. The life slipped out of him. [...] My life. Slipped. He slipped out. Slipped out. Life slipped out. Along the line. A man called Callum. If I could slip out. Reach out and touch. [...] Alan slipped out of his life. A man called Callum changed his name to Alan and I am no longer sure whether or not I killed him. (69T, 182)

Stewart Home's *69 Things* "detours towards" Quin not just by its parodic recuperation of an obscured precursor, nor is it merely a pastiche of the stock techniques of literary experimentalism. Its first footnote, positing the narrator's dislike for figures like Hemingway, Stein, even the "rumoured B. S. Johnson revival" (69T, 169), makes the provocative suggestion that once a certain "type" of experimentalism has received the official stamp of the establishment, it runs the risk of being fetishised as a paragon of the experiment, its erstwhile radicality neutralised and outsideness integrated, its positions of potential opposition expropriated. Both Quin's and Home's styles attempt to eschew this fate by treating text types with double-coding, pastiche, internal parody, and stylistic parallax in order to challenge any neat critical classification and pigeonholing.

Thus, directing his attention to Quin entails for Home a recuperation of a long-lost unique literary voice, and a redefinition of the category of literary experimentation as such. By Home's own avowal, writing—in the genre-bound sense of the commercial publishing industry and its various academic fronts—has never been a justifiable end in itself, but one of an integrated set of means of pursuing an "abolitionist" programme to undermine "social separation" by "simultaneously confronting 'politics' and 'culture'" (AS, 4).

The legendary figure of the 1980s and 1990s comic book—author of *Watchmen, V for Vendetta* and other cult classics of the subgenre—Alan Moore has also published two works of "literary" fiction. *Voice of the Fire* (1996), the sprawling dozen interrelated stories spanning the 6,000 years in the history of the epicentre of his life and work, Northampton in East Midlands. Starting in 4,000 BC with the story "Hob's Hog," Moore hopscotches via an episode featuring roaming tribes set in 2,500 BC, another in AD 43, another tale featuring a Roman-occupied Britannia in AD 290, a Norman story taking place in 1064, a horror story set in 1618 and written in the late-Elizabethan style, all the way to 1995, concluding the diachronic parade with a story featuring his authorial figure "in the voice of Alan Moore," completing the manuscript of the novel we hold in our hands. Moore's diachronic history of one place ultimately translates into a poetic vision of synchronicity in which history happens at once.

As mentioned in Neil Gaiman's introduction, Moore's own mystical descriptor for the book was the formula, "One measures a circle starting anywhere," to which Gaiman adds that "the circle here is temporal, and the circle is geographical. It is a circle made of black dogs and November fires, of dead feet and severed heads, of longing and loss and lust. It is a circle that will take you several miles and six thousand years" (VF, 10). The tour-de-force of the book's twelve vastly varying styles is the opening chapter, with the opening, "A-hind of hill, ways off to sun-set-down, is sky come like as fire, and walk I up in way of this, all hard of breath, where is grass colding on I's feet and wetting they. There is not grass on high of hill. There is but dirt, all in a round, that hill is as like to a no-hair man, he's head" (VF, 13), reminiscent of the description of "riverrunning" around "Howth Castle and Environs" that opens Joyce's *Wake*. Not least because the 50–page opener is a stylistic *tour de force* written in an invented dialect, full of syntactic deviations, solecisms (cf. the "I's" instead of "my" and "he's" for "his"), and paronomasia, suggestive of the ancient setting and also the "simplistic" mindset of the first-person narrator. This is not so much in service of a mimetic illusionism of a "neolithic" language (which of course is utterly unreconstructible), but an invitation to ponder the ontological effects of language on thought, perception, and consciousness, how we are what we think what we speak. And so when at the opening of the final chapter, Moore writes,

> They're buying it. The last words of the previous chapter, written in grey light, stand there upon the monitor's dark stage, beneath the Help menu that's lettered up on the proscenium arch. The cursor winks, a visible slow handclap in the black, deserted auditorium. The final act: no more impersonations. (*VF*, 281)

Moore's note of "no more impersonations" is not a gesture à la a B. S. Johnson novel renouncing the "lies" of stylised fiction in favour of some autobiographic "truth," but the embrace of his own alter ego as a fiction, a narrative-discursive construct. As is evident in the lyrical style of the chapter throughout, as well as its finale, the "revelation of syllables" that make up "our world": "These are the times we dread and hunger for. The mutter of our furnace past grows louder at our backs, with cadence more distinct. Almost intelligible now, its syllables reveal themselves. Our world ignites. The song wells up, from a consuming light" (*VF*, 306).

When towards the end of *Edge of the Orison*, Iain Sinclair makes it—in the footsteps of John Clare—to Lucia Joyce's grave, his guide around Northampton cemetery and environs is Alan Moore, who in conversation with Sinclair

> broaches a relativist's General Theory of Northampton, loosely based on some late pronouncement by Stephen Hawking. The town, it seems, is a black hole from which only 'mangled information' can escape. And that, Alan acknowledges, is his lifelong task: to de-mangle (and interpret) Northampton's cuneiform script. Its codex of madness and possession. Old magick is the new physics. (*EO*, 334)

Ten years later after *Edge of the Orison*, Moore's "General Theory of Northampton" materialised in the behemoth (1175 pages) "novel" called *Jerusalem*, an encyclopaedic and fantastically stylised "semiotic ocean of a book which makes *Ulysses* look like a primer [...] what we've been waiting for—the great British novel" (Michael Moorcock on the back cover). Unlike Sinclair's kinetic travelogue, the emplacement of Moore's narrative is static, centring on just half a square mile of the town, the ill-reputed Boroughs, a working-class area with a "multitude of pubs — what was it, eighty-something?" (*J*, 34) and more than its fair share of prostitutes, tramps, and ASBOs (youths hit with "anti-social behaviour orders" [*J*, 73]). Squalor is rampant all around in the Boroughs present and past, but Moore reminds us that Northampton, sitting almost in the centre of England, has seen the likes of Thomas Becket, Samuel Beckett, Oliver Cromwell, John Clare, Malcolm Arnold, as well as some decisive battles in the English Civil War and the War of the Roses. One of Moore's characters "couldn't help but think if England was America, and if you had a place where both the War of Independence and the Civil War had finished up, then there'd have been a bigger thing made out of it" (K, 208).

Divided into three Books ("The Boroughs," "Mansoul," and "Vernall's Inquest"), the multiple storylines develop over centuries, set in the Boroughs, Northampton's most ancient if also decrepit neighbourhood. The colophon insists that the fiction is "based on a 'true story,'" in quotation marks. Featuring a large collection of characters—mythical, fictional, fictionalised historical, and historicised fictional, *Jerusalem*'s encyclopaedic scope, ten years in construction, includes Moore's family's oral traditions, life experience, and ideas such as "eternalism" explored in other writings. A key plotline culminates in 2006 with an exhibit of paintings—the first of which, just as chapter 1, is called "Work in Progress"—by one of the protagonists, Alma Warren, Moore's foil and authorial stand-in. In multiple instances, episodes are told and retold with different character focalisation, and different writing styles adapted to their inner voices.

Excavating the plethora of half-forgotten riches of Northampton's "working-class mythology"[30] on the twelve hundred pages of this novel, Moore saves the best for last. As *Jerusalem*'s final chapter reveals, Northampton had also been the backdrop for Adam Smith's "half-baked idea about a hidden hand that works the cotton looms" – the site of the first "dark, Satanic mills" of Blake's eponymous poem, harbingers of modern-day free-market capitalism:

> That's the monetarist mystic idol-shit, the voodoo economics Ronald Regan put his faith in, and that middle-class dunce Margaret Thatcher when they cheerily deregulated most of the financial institutions. And that's why the Boroughs exists, Adam Smith's idea. That's why the last fuck knows how many generations of this family are a toilet queue without a pot to piss in, and that's why everyone we know is broke. It's all there in the current underneath that bridge down Tanner Street. That was the first one, the first dark, satanic mill. (J, 1173)

In Moore's, as in Sinclair's, fictional psychogeography, the materiality of history becomes translated as the materiality of the letter. Through this transformation, both Sinclair's and Moore's texts perform an ideological intervention in the political and historical stakes of literary representation, interrogating who lays claim to it and why. Just as Sinclair's, so does Moore's psychogeographical rewriting of Northampton history hinge around the figure of Joyce's daughter, who again interconnects creativity and madness, and becomes the embodied target of the politics behind both. Lucia makes

---

30   Ben Graham, "A Working Class Mythology: *Jerusalem* Reviewed," *The Quietus* (30 Oct 2016). Online: https://thequietus.com/articles/21230-alan-moore-jerusalem-novel-review-working -class-mythology.

her first cameo in the more "objective" style of the opening chapter of Book Three, "Clouds Unfold":

> Lucia Joyce is dancing on the madhouse lawn. Her twirling body is a fragile coracle, becalmed there on the still green sea of grass. She circles beautifully without effect, one of her inner oars misplaced. [...] Her Da, while living, sees her as a work in progre-ss and perpetually unfinished, an abandoned masterpiece. Perhaps one day he'll have another go at her, fiddle with her a bit and try to sort out the stalled plotlines, all the uncompleted sentences, but then he dies and leaves her stranded there in the excluded information, the ellipses... Lucia's family have edited her out, reduced her to a footnote in the yarn, all but excised her from the manuscript. (J, 768)

But more importantly and notoriously, *Jerusalem* includes a chapter entitled "Around the Bend" composed in *Wakese*. The "unreadable chapter" in Alan Moore's *Jerusalem* opens as follows:

> Awake, Lucia gets up wi' the wry sing of de light. She is a puzzle, shore enearth, as all the Nurzis and the D'actors would afform, but nibber a cross word these days, deep-indig on her mendication and on every workin' grimpill's progress. Her arouse from drowse is like a Spring, a babboling book that gorgles up amist the soils o' sleep, flishing and glattering, to mate the mournin' son. Canfind in this loquation now she gushes and runs chinkling from her silt and softy bed, pooring her harp out down an illside and aweigh cross the old manscape to a modhouse brookfast. Ah, what a performance, practised and applausible. (J, 829)

A relatively straightforward opening, aimed to ease into the increasingly dense Joycean style, in which many words primarily mean what they say. Still, some of Moore's neologising style does bring about some unsettling semantic ambivalence: "rising of the sun" in the first sentence becomes "wry sing," suggesting Lucia's mood of wryness and artistic disposition. She is a "puzzle, sure enough," but "shore enearth" suggests her secret—which the "Nazi nurses" and "death actors" / doctors try to extract from her, is dug in deep (with her father?), or "deepindig." In "workin' grimpill's progress," Joyce's "Work in Progress" is blended with Bunyan's *Pilgrim's Progress*, one of *Jerusalem*'s crucial intertexts (Bunyan himself is a character in the chapter "The Steps of All Saints"), to also comment on Lucia's "grim pill" unsatisfac-tory treatment. "Babboling book that gorgles" might quite obviously a refe-rence to the gurgling of the local Dallington Brook, but more interestingly, to Lucia's father's "babbling book," i.e., the *Wake* again—where "babbo" is Italian (Lucia's native tongue) for "daddy"—and to her brother Giorgio, who are brought to mind as Lucia readies herself to "meet the morning sun," but more disturbingly, "to mate the mourning son," suggesting a brother/sister incest, one of the refrains of this chapter. And so on and so ingeniously forth for another 40-odd pages.[31]

Lucia's chapter is a microcosmic sampling of a macrocosm—a normal day in her very unnormal life at the St Andrews Infirmary. She wanders the grounds of her institution, recalling her childhood relationships with the family members, her numerous commitments to various asylums, the Charlie Chaplin films she liked to watch in her Paris youth, and meets the various institutionalised inmates—both past and present—such as John Clare (who mistakes her for Mary Joyce, his "first wife") and Dusty Springfield (famously rumoured to be lesbian), with both of whom she has passionate sex. She also contemplates the Parisian avant-garde of the 1930s and British surrealism of the 1960s, she ponders the future of English as a "language of visions." She also runs into 1930s comic-book artist Ogden Whitney and 1960s composer Malcolm Arnold. She also encounters the threatening figure of poet J.K. Stephen, one of the Jack Ripper suspects, and has a sympathetic conversation with Audrey Vernall, one of Moore's fictional creations (cousin to Alma Warren).

After the lengthy trip down memory lane, Lucia re-emerges in the present, returns to the institution, and a summary of her adventures in the form of six variations on her theme ends the chapter such as, "John signs clearly on the water, / Says the Queen's his daughter, / Longs for young Miss Joyce, the wife he barely even knew, / And no more how's-your-father now. / He's a product of his class / Who eats the grass / Along the path he's made" (J, 870), and "Dusty's cunningly linguistic, / Jem's misogynistic, / But they dance the night away. / Manac es cem, J.K, / And no more how's-your-father now. / Grinding signal into noise / The crowd enjoys / This final white parade" (J, 871). A final repeated invocation—"An embress of textistence and embiddyment aflight, Lucia dawnsees on the meadhows grase floriver" (J, 871)— ends the chapter, with Moore's concluding "floriver"—meaning both "flow, river" and "forever"—paralleling Joyce's "riverrun."

Jerusalem is a monumental work, Moore's "endgame of epic modernism" (as described by Sinclair on the back cover), whose "end" is nowhere in sight so long as the "game" continues. And, in Moore's epochal work, it does.

31 For more see the excellent online "Annotations for *Jerusalem* by Alan Moore, a collective anonymous work of scholarship. Online: https://alanmoorejerusalem.wordpress.com/alan-moore-annotations-index/j3-03-round-the-bend/.

8.3 "CRUCIAL TO THE HEALTH OF THE ECOSYSTEM": AMERIKA, FOSTER WALLACE, GOLDSMITH, DANIELEWSKI, COHEN

Joyce's seminal importance for the theorisation and practice of artistic hyper-text and hypermedia has been well-documented.[32] Here, it will suffice to rehash it just by way of sketching out parallel genealogies. The theoretical one began with Ted Nelson and Marshall McLuhan in the mid-60s and culminated with Jay D. Bolter, Stuart Moulthrop, and George P. Landow in the mid-90s, with Donald Theall, Darren Tofts, and Louis Armand acting as "transmitters" of hypertext theory into Joyce studies. The practical/artistic one, starting with Borges' textual labyrinths, Queneau's *Hundred Thousand Billion Poems*, and Nabokov's *Pale Fire*, and via the surfiction of Federman and Sukenick and the punk aesthetics of Burroughs and Acker, reached the present moment and the numerous American writers and artists working with/in the medium.

Mark Amerika, an American artist, theorist, novelist, publisher of the Alt-X Online Network—a website of online art, literature, and new media theory—was among the first members of the redefined Fiction Collective 2, where he debuted as novelist with *The Kafka Chronicles* and *Sexual Blood* in the mid-90s. Here, Mark Amerika's 1997 project *GRAMMATRON* will serve as a good example of pioneering conceptual cyber-work in the digital hyper-textual age marked by the "playgiarist" impulses of Joyce's poetics. Described by *The New York Times* as "a colossal hypertext hydrogen bomb dropped on the literary landscape [...], grappling with the idea of spirituality in the elec-tronic age,"[33] Amerika's GRAMMATRON net-art project, launched in 1997 and garnering over 500,000 visitors upon its release, became in 2000 the first online artwork ever to be exhibited at the Whitney Biennial of American Art. Its motto, "I link therefore I am," is as much the creed of any hypertextual writer as a formula known to all Joycean avant-gardists.

A self-described "addict of Degenerative Prose [...] that re-synthesises hy-bridized forms of prose including fiction, faction, friction and non-diction,"[34] Amerika created *GRAMMATRON* out of eleven hundred (partly randomised) text elements and 2000 links, 40+ minutes of original soundtrack delivered via Real Audio 3.0, hyperlink structures as specially-coded Javascripts, a vir-tual gallery featuring scores of animated and still-life images, and more "sto-ryworld de-velopment" than any other narrative hitherto created exclusively for the Web. The work consists of different text-layers from which the user is

---

32   Cf., e.g., Donald Theall, *James Joyce's Technopoetics* (Toronto: Toronto University Press, 1997) and Louis Armand, *Techné: James Joyce, Hypertext & Technology* (Prague: Karolinum, 2003).

33   Online: http://www.grammatron.com/about.html

34   "A Virtual Intro," *Degenerative Prose*, eds. Mark Amerika & Ron Sukenick (CF2, Illinois University Press: 1995) 1.

free to choose, including a theoretical essay titled "Hypertextual Conscious-ness," the animated text "Interfacing," and the main hypertext "Abe Golam." Narrated from various authorial perspectives, the story keeps searching for its protagonist Abe Golam, a pioneering Net artist who creates *Grammatron*, a writing machine. Endowed not with the Word (as in the original myth) but with forbidden data—a specially coded Nanoscript—the creature becomes a digital being that "contains all of the combinatory potential of all the writ-ings." Clicking on the hyperlinks in a similar fashion to how today—more than twenty years later—one would Wikipedia, the reader follows Abe Golam's search for his "second-half," a programmer named Cynthia Kitchen, whose playful codes of interactivity lead both Golam and readers through a multi-linear textscape with eerie-sounding remixes of rock n' roll tunes and perhaps the grainiest gifs of this side of cyberspace.

What is *GRAMMATRON*? According to Amerika, "many things at once," but the things he does specify include "experimental narrative riffs from the likes of James Joyce, Arno Schmidt, and Jean-Luc Godard" (*MD*, 167–8). Indeed, *GRAMMATRON* is most explicitly indebted to Derrida's "grammatology" as the study of signification within systems of inscription, to which it alludes not only by its title, and to Wittgenstein's *koan* that "the self is grammatical." But as a story of Golem/writing machine in the age of electronic textuality, it is also steeped in the ritualism of naming, the practice of encoding and de-coding the sacred name, and the self-emptying and replenishment involved in any recreative, playgiarist activity – practices and motifs borrowed from the cabalistic tradition, but also remixed from Joyce's oeuvre. In his recent work *Remixthebook*, Amerika posits that the general idea behind his version of applied aesthetics/remix(grammat)ology is, "don't do as I say or do as I do but remix your own creative potential as a singular fringe-flow sensation," since (and this is a *Wakean* lesson), "the One is not one" (*RB*, 53) but, one might add, three-plus-one. Just as the *Wake*, *GRAMMATRON* brims with abstract thought, self-reflexion, self-redefinitions, and descriptions of the indescribable. It pul-sates with an acute fear of the Internet and an urgent desire to harness it.

It is the *Wake's* cabalistic obsession with textual recombination and inter-linkage, with the deciphering of codes and pluralising of readings, that Mark Amerika chooses to revisit in his own recreation of the Golem myth for the digital age. Just as the *Wake*, *GRAMMATRON* is a paradoxical, looping narra-tive that chooses confusion over coherence and in which individuals manifest inside the electro-sphere as both fleshy and digital versions of themselves simultaneously, their existence "written" by the machine as they experience it. But parallels go further than that. In his book of essays titled *ME-TA/DATA: Digital Poetics*, Amerika expounds on his practice of "playgiarism," associat-ing it with "an entire heritage or rival tradition of literature" (which apart from Joyce includes Burroughs, Federman, and Acker), whose authors readily write cyberspace as a kind of playgiaristic practice, the supplemental *y* signifying play and performance in the "self-organizing world of the artificial intelligentsia" (*MD*, 43–4).

Similarly, the futurist and dystopian aspects of Amerika's *GRAMMA-TRON* could have only been born in the early chaotic days of 1990s cyberculture, when the Internet's utility still lurked in-between its gears. *GRAMMATRON* is the raw expression of early Internet adoption, and an allegory for the tug-of-war between the artists and scientists who flocked to create, and the corporate entities that sought to turn cyberpace into a corpocracy. Amerika depicts the digital world as a living, breathing warzone – a land too vast to be tamed. Just as the *Wake* is very much the product of the avant-garde context of the then-new technologies it thematises, Amerika's 1997 project in turn reminds us of a time when we were not so sure of our place in the digital world, which had not yet been partitioned by corporations and auctioned off to the highest bidder. By existing as moving images on the alternately full/empty screen of fleeting textual formations, *GRAMMA-TRON* rethinks representation by "moving beyond the knowing and entering a world of immersive topographies that open up unknown narrative worlds composed of unstable identities, ambiguously located intentions, and surrogate lovers."[35]

The death of Kathy Acker in 1997 overlapped with the publication of David Foster Wallace's *Infinite Jest*, a monumental thousand-plus-page novel in the great American tradition, with a complexity of themes and styles well beyond the scope of the present résumé, yet a work ushering in a new sensibility characteristic of much of contemporary U.S. fiction.

Wallace's clearest, most programmatic explanation of his theory and practice of writing came in his 1993 essay, "E Unibus Pluram: Television and U.S. Fiction," one of the most important pieces in Wallace's corpus of nonfiction, which preceded the publication of *Infinite Jest* and in many ways prepared the way for that career-making book, as a response to John Barth's "Literature of Exhaustion." For Wallace, the self-reflexive quality of Barth's work, the way it challenges the belief in literature's ability to address directly the world outside itself, serves as a necessary and even useful response to the modernist project. In "E Unibus Pluram," Wallace accuses television as being the primary cause of this shift from a liberating to an isolating anxiety driving the postmodern project. The salient points about TV are its emphasis on surface, and its adoption of self-referring postmodern irony as a form of self-defence.

---

35 "'Amerika Online'—a column by Mark Amerika" (1995). Online: http://www.altx.com/amerika.online/amerika.online.2.1.html

The essay primarily seeks to demonstrate how current trends in television have succeeded in dissolving the subversive power of postmodernist metafiction. Wallace distinguishes among three evolutionary stages in the responses of American fiction to this medium since the 1960s: first, the early work of Gaddis, Barth, and Pynchon, which engaged with pop culture; then, in the 1970s and 80s, with the medium's increasing importance, irony became fiction's ground-clearing tool, utilised with the idealist belief that "etiology and diagnosis pointed toward cure"; in the third wave, with which Wallace associates himself, fiction does not simply use televisual culture, but attempts to restore the television-flattened world "to three-whole dimension."[36] Thus, Wallace's own method emerges, one that attempts to join "cynicism and naïveté," as Wallace puts it, or "to turn irony back on itself, to make his fiction relentlessly conscious of its own self-consciousness, and thus to produce work that will be at once unassailably sophisticated and doggedly down to earth."[37] In this respect, *Infinite Jest* stages Wallace's attempt to prove that cynicism and naïveté are mutually compatible by fictional means, ironising hip irony in such a way that the *opposite* of hip irony, that is, "gooey sentiment," can emerge as the work's indirectly intended mode, in the service of fiction's primary task of articulating "what it is to be a fucking *human being*."[38] The influence of Wallace's allusive style in service of conveying his very basic message has been remarkable.[39]

Set sometime in the early 2000s in the slightly dystopian world of ONAN (Organization of North American Nations), the first storyline centres around Hal Incandenza, a richly talented student at the Enfield Tennis Academy (E.T.A.) in Massachusetts, the son of the extravagantly gifted optics expert and filmmaker James Orin Incandenza (a.k.a. JOI), from whom he has inherited an addictive personality. After his father's eerily bizarre suicide—caused by his alcohol addiction and the suspected infidelities of his wife Avril Mondragon (a.k.a. "the Moms")—Hal, his widowed mother, and his two elder brothers, Mario and Orin, have to come to terms with the downfall of the family business accompanied by the disintegration of the family as such. In one of *Infinite Jest*'s numerous gloomy symmetries, Hal's decline and

---

36 Qtd. in Stephen Burn, *David Foster Wallace's Infinite Jest – A Reader's Guide* (London/New York: Continuum, 2003) 16.

37 A. O. Scott, "The Panic of Influence," *New York Review of Books*, 47.2 (Feb 10, 2000): 40.

38 Larry McCaffery, "An Interview with David Foster Wallace, *Review of Contemporary Fiction* 13.2 (Summer 1993): 131.

39 As Boswell has argued, "since *Infinite Jest*, a whole new group of emerging young writers has copied the elusive Wallace 'tone,' that paradoxical blending of cynicism and naïveté, as well as Wallace's use of self-reflexivity for the purposes of moving beyond irony and parody" and his examples include Dave Eggers' *A Heartbreaking Work of Staggering Genius* and Jonathan Franzen's *The Corrections* as "the most prestigious confirmation of Wallace's revolution in literary sensibility" (Boswell, *Understanding David Foster Wallace*, 19–20).

withdrawal is inverted in the second storyline, which traces the recovery of former burglar Don Gately from his addiction to painkillers, undertaken at Ennet House, an A.A. centre and a halfway house that is literally and metaphorically down the hill from E.T.A. This storyline is a loose series of episodes from the many inmates' lives, detailing the many reasons for their fall into addictions. Finally, entangled in these two narratives is the larger political plot concentrating on a fringe group of Quebecois radicals, the A.F.R. group, plotting a violent political coup using as weapon the last work of Hal's father, the eponymous short *Infinite Jest*, a film so compelling as to render its spectator incapable of not watching and rewatching it *ad infinitum*, thereby entertaining themselves to death. The third plotline details the race between Quebecois separatists and American agents to gain a master copy of this film.

The one key theme uniting these three plotlines is addiction: to alcohol, drugs, sex, and "spectation," the human obsession with watching and being watched, Wallace's central metaphor for the desperation and isolation of modern American life; after all, when towards the end of the opening chapter, Hal is about to pass out, his encyclopaedic mind thinks of "nineteen nonarchaic synonyms for *unresponsive*" (*IJ*, 17). The crucial three narratives' interconnection is then designed as an antidote to said unresponsiveness, illustrating how microcosmic individual actions affect, and are in turn shaped by, the macrocosms of larger communities we inhabit, and should inhabit more fully.

Very much in the spirit of *Ulysses*, the 1100 pages of *Infinite Jest* are chiefly invested in letting these three storylines parallel and intersect with each other. The title of course is a reference to *Hamlet*'s Yorick, the "man of infinite jest," and the chief "mystery" has to do with the quest after the missing skull of the dead father. How come that, during his nervous breakdown in chapter one, Hal may hallucinate that "Donald Gately and I dig up my father's head" and 900 pages later, the unconscious ICU-ridden Gately may dream that "he's with a very sad kid and they're in a graveyard digging some dead guy's head up and it's really important" (*IJ*, 18, 934)—especially given that never the twain have met or shall meet, in the "real world" of the novel— Foster Wallace leaves perfectly ambiguous.[40] To hammer home the point of Joyce's haunting of *Infinite Jest*, the first case of this spectral revisitation of Himself's spectre at Gately's ICU some hundred pages earlier is couched in explicitly Joycean terms: when "the ghostish figure that's been flickering

---

40   "*Infinite Jest* takes hold of Joyce's masterwork and systematically refashions it, appropriating not only the structure of the two wandering protagonists who eventually converge but also the radical experiments with language and point of view, the crucial engagement with Shakespeare, and the figure of the amiable Everyman" (Jeff Staiger, "David Foster Wallace's Contest with Himself," *New England Review* 36.2 [2015]: 94).

in and out of sight around the room finally stays in one spot long enough" (*IJ*, 829), Gately concludes that the wraith's appearance "could be a sort of epiphanyish visitation" (*IJ*, 833).

The encyclopaedic form of *Infinite Jest* most clearly recalls the tradition of massive fictions written by first-generation post-war American writers, beginning with Gaddis' *The Recognitions*, and later including works like Pynchon's *Gravity's Rainbow* or John Barth's *Letters*. But lurking behind them is of course Joyce's encyclopaedic project undertaken in and between *Ulysses* and the *Wake*, with which Wallace's *Infinite Jest*, based on detailed "data-retrieval" (*IJ*, 332), overlaps. Joyce's presence in *Infinite Jest* is not only conceptual, but literal, acknowledged, e.g., in Wallace's repetition of Buck Mulligan's adjective "scrotum-tightening" (*IJ*, 112; 605) and his shared *Ulyssean* interest in "telemachy" (*IJ*, 249). By the same token, however, Wallace is keen on foregrounding the limitations of the encyclopaedic impulse. Part of Wallace's aim seems to be to break with self-reflexivity and direct the reader outside of the book, to find what has escaped the encyclopaedia and the self-reflexive, autonomous world of fiction.

Were the Joycean presence in *Infinite Jest* restricted to a few memorable coinages, it would hardly substantiate its inclusion in this genealogy. Joyce's *Ulyssean* concepts underwrite not only the aesthetics, but also the ethics of Wallace's project, its polyphony of narrative voices. As Dowling and Bell emphasise on this note, *Infinite Jest* takes "polyphony to glorious extremes; nearly everybody has a story and gets to tell it," and so within the first 100 pages, "the narrative hones in upon thirteen distinct characters."[41] Thus, borrowing a term from astronomy but popularised in fiction by Joyce's *Ulysses*, Wallace speaks of "parallaxing" (*IJ*, 556) his story-telling technique, with an emphasis on the many dependencies of what one sees upon where one stands. James Orin Incandenza, the *Hamletian* dead father whose ghost keeps haunting the world of his son Hal, is after all referred to via the acrostic JOI, which suggests a "JOIcean" homage to the spectre of the great precursor, paired with the Shakespearean situation of "Prince Hal" despairing the passing of his cuckolded father.[42]

In fact, Wallace's investment in *Ulysses* is part of his programmatic break with postmodernist self-defeating irony and escapist pastiche, back to modernist critique of the world and engagement with it. Of the many meta-comments *Infinite Jest* provides regarding its literary politics, the following is perhaps the most illustrative: JOI and Avril Mondragon, the King

---

41   William Dowling & Robert Bell, *A Reader's Companion to Infinite Jest* (New York: Xlibris, 2005) 211.

42   "Figuratively, *Infinite Jest* conjures the spirits of Wallace's literary masters hovering over his project. He has many 'fathers' - Joyce and Nabokov, Pynchon and Barth – in the tradition of the novel. Himself, JOI, may represent James JOIce, whose *Ulysses* is a book of "many happy returns" for all manner of dead authors and departed souls" (Dowling & Bell, *A Reader's Companion*, 217).

and Queen of Wallace's American tragedy, met at an an academic conference on "Reflective vs. Reflexive Systems." "Reflective" refers to the classic conception of art and of language as mimetic systems, holding their mirrors up to nature, and *Infinite Jest*'s allegiance to reflective art is evident in its meticulous elaboration of its fictional "real" (the *genius loci* of its settings, the real historical events of its present and "future," etc.). Hand in hand, and sometimes face to face, with this tendency is "reflexivity," breaking through the mimetic illusionism and revealing/reveling in its own artificiality. While his postmodern fathers have stressed the latter tendency in literary discourse, Wallace aims at least to restore balance between them, reverting to the pre-postmodernist aesthetics of reflectivity. This is tied with *Infinite Jest*'s central Artifex JOI's repudiation of "anticonfluentialism." JOI's early films celebrate radical and disorienting tonal shifts, grotesque shock value, and hyperbolic excess of disjunctive leaps—and so much of *Infinite Jest* is just that, but this aesthetics is repudiated, since

> in his last several projects he'd been so desperate to make something that ordinary U.S. audiences might find entertaining and diverting and conducive to self-forgetting that he had had professionals and amateurs alike emoting wildly all over the place. Getting emotion out of either actors or audiences had never struck me as one of Himself's strengths. (*IJ*, 944)

And so, just like Himself's cinema after his rejection of postmodernist pastiche, *Infinite Jest* strives for a "technical feck and for a pathos that was somehow both surreally abstract and CNS-rendingly melodramatic at the same time" (*IJ*, 64). This is what critic Jeff Staiger's essay has called Wallace's "Contest with Himself,"[43] the contest of writing modernist fiction in a (post-)postmodernist world, one informed by Wallace's creative revisitation of Joyce's *Ulysses*.

In the editorial preface to the monumental 2011 *Against Expression: An Anthology of Conceptual Writing*, Kenneth Goldsmith makes the claim that "with the rise of the Web, writing has met its photography," meaning that in "a situation similar to that of painting upon the invention of photography," after which "the field had to alter its course radically," writing too "needs to redefine

---

43   "In a textual environment so thick with allusions to other texts, it becomes nearly impossible to say just what the chief influence is: is it the Shakespeare of Hamlet and/or the Hal plays? Is it Joyce, whose *Ulysses* provides the basic structure of the two protagonists parallel course? Is it Pynchon's *Gravity's Rainbow*, the chief precedent for any zany, sprawling romp through a dehumanized postmodern technocratic world? I believe that it is ultimately Joyce" (Staiger, "David Foster Wallace's Contest with Himself," 99–100).

itself to adapt to the new environment of textual abundance."[44] Goldsmith is a poet, a visual artist, and the founding editor of UbuWeb (1996)—a large web-based educational resource for avant-garde material available on the Internet—whose practice of "uncreative writing" over the past two decades has engaged with textual practices steeped in the plagiarist heritage of Joyce's materialist poetics.

Set on 16 June, 1997 Goldsmith's 2000 text *Fidget* is divided into eleven sections, corresponding to Goldsmith's eleven hours awake that day, in clear homage to the hour-by-hour chapters of Joyce's *Ulysses*, the epic of the body. And as in *Ulysses*, different actions dominate different hours. Goldsmith's performative Bloomsday experiment has a number of interesting consequences. *Fidget*'s breakdown of bodily functions into their smallest components has a strong effect of defamiliarisation, a synecdochal decentring of human subjectivity, which also marks so many of *Ulysses*' descriptions of bodily movements or actions. Goldsmith's transcription of the first chapter in reverse order also achieves some highly poetic effects, words breaching new, unexpected meanings: a key word is "morf" (from), a word highly applicable in the context along with "woble" (elbow), or "pil" (lip). There is much "dna" (and) about. When finally the language game has occluded the multiform activities of the moving body, "Eyelids close."

Having recorded every move his body had made in a day (*Fidget*), or every word he uttered over the course of a week (*Soliloquy*, 2001), Goldsmith followed with perhaps the most famous of his "uncreative projects": *Day* (2003), where he turns his attention to quotidian documents. What Goldsmith has termed "uncreative writing," here becomes a constraint-based-process, a creative practice. As Goldsmith claims on the back cover of *Day*, "It's one of the hardest constraints a writer can muster, particularly on a project of this scale; with every keystroke comes the temptation to fudge, cut-and-paste, and skew the mundane language. But to do so would be to foil the exercise." Typing page upon page, levelling the difference between article, editorial, and advertisement, disregarding all typographic and graphical treatments of the word, Goldsmith reduces the newspaper to mere text, producing an 840-page book-object. In so doing, Goldsmith again out-Joyces Joyce in the ambition of an all-inclusive single-day record of the ephemeral, news transmitted by paper: "a fleeting moment concretized, captured, then reframed into the discourse of literature" (*Day*, back cover). In 2002, Goldsmith created a slightly different "uncreative project." In *Head Citations*, he presents 800 variations, paronomasiac and malaprop-

---

44 Goldsmith, "Why Conceptual Writing?" *Against Expression: An Anthology of Conceptual Writing*, eds. Kenneth Goldsmith & Craig Dworkin (Evanston, IL: Northwestern University Press, 2011) xvii.

istic, on famous pop song lyrics. Christian Bök's back-cover blurb describes Goldsmith as "the Napster of the malapropism" who "downloads the poetic genius of the masses as they croon to themselves in their showers." Craig Dworkin's back cover blurb for the book even quotes *Finnegans Wake*: "'Our cubehouse still rocks as earwitness' to this book of earrors and close listing, as Joyce would put it. So prick up your arse and glisten well. Besides, 'e'erawhere in this whorl would ye hear sich a din again?'" To be sure, the parody of the mythology of the popular song is performed with a similar ear for possible eroticised *détournement*, and to similarly amusing effect, as in the *Wake*. *Head Citations* (the title coming from "11. She's giving me head citations" [Goldsmith 2002, 7]) moves from "1. This is the dawning of the age of malaria. 2. Another one fights the dust. 3. Eyeing little girls with padded pants. 4. Teenage spacemen we're all teenage spacemen" (Goldsmith 2002: 7) all the way to "800. Sleep in heavenly peas" (Goldsmith 2002, 87), and throughout, its punning humour brings about destabilising effects, as for instance in this passage:

> 673. Are you going to Harvard or Yale. / 673.1. Are you going to Scarlet O'Hare. / 673.2. Parsley, sage, rosemary and Todd. / 673.3. Parsley's age grows merry in time. / 673.4. Parsley's angels, Mary and Tom. / 673.5. Partly saved, Rosemary and Tom. / 673.6. People say it was Mary and Tom. / 673.7. Parsnips say Rosemary is blind. (*HC*, 72)

To simply equate or parallel *Head Citations* with *Finnegans Wake* as Dworkin does is absurd, of course, as Joyce's *Wakean* variations endow the ancient clichés with a variety of new meanings garnered from contexts ranging from the historical to the socio-pedagogical to the political, a contextual depth that Goldsmith's mechanical, context-less permutations almost purposefully avoid. Still, Goldsmith's parody of the mythology of popular song is performed with a similar ear for possible eroticised *détournement*, and to similarly amusing effect.

Most recently, Goldsmith's *Uncreative Writing: Managing Language in the Digital Age* (2011) opens with the premise that today, "digital media has set the stage for a literary revolution. In 1974 Peter Bürger was still able to make the claim that 'in literature, there is no technical innovation that could have produced an effect comparable to photography in the fine arts.' Now there is." If painting, a hundred years ago, reacted to photography by abstraction, then, Goldsmith observes, the reaction of writing could be the opposite: "It appears that writing's response—taking its cues more from photography than painting—could be mimetic and replicative, primarily involving methods of distribution, while proposing new platforms of receivership and readership" (*UW*, 15).

One of the pioneers of writing's response to the advent of new recording media, Joyce "presages uncreative writing by the act of sorting words, weighing which are 'signal' and which are 'noise,' what's worth keeping and what's worth leaving. Identifying—weighing—language in its various states of 'data' and 'information' is crucial to the health of the ecosystem" (*UW*, 28). The most literal literary analogue to such filtering of signal and noise is Joyce's meditation on the universal properties of water in the "Ithaca" episode, the musings of Bloom "the waterlover, drawer of water, watercarrier" (*U* 17.183), inspiring Goldsmith's rumination on digital language:

> When Joyce writes about the different forms that water can take it reminds me of different forms that digital language can take. Speaking of the way water puddles and collects in "its variety of forms in loughs and bays and gulfs," I am reminded of the process whereby data rains down from the network in small pieces when I use a Bit-Torrent client, pooling in my download folder. [...] When Joyce speaks of water's mutability from its liquid state into "vapour, mist, cloud, rain, sleet, snow, hail," I am reminded of what happens when I join a network of torrents and I begin "seeding" and uploading to the data cloud. (*UW*, 27)

Thus, in Goldsmith's many "uncreative" appropriations of motifs and techniques from both *Ulysses* and the *Wake*, Joyce's plagiarist poetics is to be found among the cornerstones of contemporary conceptualism.

Mark Danielewski's two best-known works to date, *House of Leaves* (2000) and *Only Revolutions* (2006) face dilemmas and challenges of the digital age similar to those identified by Amerika and Goldsmith, even though their reactions and proposed solutions are markedly different.

A counterpart to Amerika's hypertextual exploration and Goldsmith's verbally conceptual experimentation, Danielewski's momentous 700–page novel *House of Leaves* (2000) is, most simply, "a story about a story about a story about a film about a house with a black hole in it,"[45] a summary that immediately reveals it as one of multiple remove and framing. Hence also the notion of *House of Leaves* as textual labyrinth, pervasive throughout its literary criticism, which always, in one way or another, seeks to provide precursors, labyrinthine authors anticipatory of Danielewski's project.[46]

---

45   Robert Kelly, "Home Sweet Hole – A Review of *House of Leaves*," *New York Times* (26 March 2000). Online: https://archive.nytimes.com/www.nytimes.com/books/00/03/26/reviews/000326.26 kellyt.html

46   Two examples: "Mark Danielewski's debut novel, *House of Leaves*, is a work of experimental fiction [... whose] roots can be traced back to familiar themes and important literary predecessors, most notably Jorge Luis Borges. Danielewski's use of the labyrinth as a theme, symbol, and form, and the mise-en-abyme structure of the text within a text within a text, as well as more direct allusions, underscore his debt to the work of Borges" (Natalie Hamilton, "The A-mazing House: The Labyrinth as Theme and Form in Mark Z. Danielewski's *House of Leaves*," *Studies in Contemporary Fiction* 50.1 [Fall 2008]: 3). "While these narrative games are all good fun, *House of Leaves*

House of Leaves is simultaneously revolutionary and representative of the state of the contemporary novel in its conscious relationship to and incorporation of emergent forms by enacting the process on the level of the medium itself: presenting the book of the 21st century as printed medium open to, and evolving into, its digital and electronic contexts. A possible synopsis outline for *House of Leaves* would run as follows. The novel is comprised of an extensive narration by a blind man, Zampanò, who dictates his critical commentary about the documentary film "The Navidson Record" shot by photographer Will Navidson. The film details Navidson and his family's terrifying ordeal living in a house whose insides gradually grow larger than its frame; the house's hallway mutates into a labyrinthine black hole that devours sound, light, and eventually human beings. Zampanò's ekphrasis of the film is a scholarly one, incorporating analyses and judgments from literary critics and scientists, both real and imagined.

After Zampanò's mysterious death, his scholarly manuscript, The Navidson Record, is discovered by one Johnny Truant, a psychologically damaged but highly literary maverick who, in one of the book's many self-descriptive passages, encounters Zampanò's text as a collection of multimedia scraps: "Endless snarls of words [...] on old napkins, the tattered edges of an envelope [...] legible, illegible; impenetrable, lucid; torn, stained, scotch-taped" (*HL*, xvii). Piecing together these disparate fragments, Truant weaves them in his own narrative layer through a set of footnotes that describe his hyperactive sex life, traumatic childhood dominated by a deranged mother Pelafina, and devastating experience with the editing of Zampanò's text. Truant's version of Zampanò's critique of "The Navidson Record" is then edited by the corporate entity, "The Editors," whose presence is noted by the monosyllabic "-Ed." Proceeding in an objective tone that contrasts with Truant's highly emotive commentary, the Ed. produce an additional set of editorial commentary, footnotes demarcating emendations to the text or acknowledging missing information.

At the same time, *House of Leaves* is a text structured explicitly as hypertext, and this for reasons and with consequences deeper and further-reaching than the use of multiple footnoting and framing superimposition. The technology of hypertextual writing is present on the micro, textual level. Every appearance of the word "house" is blue, the colour of an active hyperlink on the Internet, inscribing the Internet's interface into the book's print pages. Besides imitating the interface and navigation structure of the Web, *House of Leaves* positions itself as a node on the information network before

adds up to more than playfulness. As it should be in such a nightmarish fantasy, what appears to be a barrier is actually a gateway. Like Joyce [...], Danielewski isn't rejecting narration as much as customizing and turbo-charging it" (Michael Sims, "Interview with Mark Z. Danielewski," *Bookpage* [Sept 2, 2007]. Online: http:// www.bookpage.com/).

its narrative even begins. Beneath the copyright and publisher's information is the web address for the official *House of Leaves* website: www.houseofleaves.com. Sharing the title of the novel and its publication date, the website is its fraternal twin – the point being, as critic Jessica Pressman puts it, that "the Internet is a constitutive part of not only the novel's narrative and aesthetic but also its production history," in that "the digital network that housed the first edition of the novel is shown to be an inherent part of the print novel that emerged from it."[47] Critic Mark B. N. Hansen has identified the novelty of *House of Leaves* in its enactment of the horror produced by a very real shift in ontological reference due to the influence of digital technologies, as "the novel is about an impossible object, a referent that is absent not simply in the sense of being lost," which makes it "a realist novel about an object that, for precise technical reasons, cannot belong to the 'reality' we inhabit."[48]

In his introduction, Johnny Truant warns the reader that "old shelters— television, magazines, movies—won't protect you anymore. You might try scribbling in a journal, on a napkin, maybe even in the margins of this book. That's when you'll discover you no longer trust the very walls you always took for granted" (*HL*, xxiii). It is not just the man-eating house that haunts *House of Leaves*; it is the mutation of "old shelters" (e.g., books), induced by digital technology. Zampanò identifies the digital as the ghost haunting the film "The Navidson Record": "even though the spectre of digital manipulation has been raised in *The Navidson Record*, to this day no adequate explanation has managed to resolve the curious enigma" (*HL*, 335). The real ghost in the film, and the novel that subsumes it, is the "spectre of digital manipulation" – the presence of an invisible network of technologies that infiltrate our existence, our access to information, and our ability to read our world and its narratives.

The "horror" effect of Danielewski's text is achieved through the well-known identification technique – by conflating the House with the book, he casts the novel's reader in the position of a reader *within* the text. This is evident in the pivotal scene when Will Navidson's brother, Tom, struggles to save Will's daughter Daisy from certain death. The house swallows him into its dark abyss, and in this moment of horror and ontological impossibility, the house is described as a text:

The whole place keeps shuddering and shaking, walls cracking only to melt back together again, floors fragmenting and buckling, the ceiling suddenly rent by invisible

---

47   Jessica Pressman, "*House of Leaves*: Reading the Networked Novel," *Studies in American Fiction* 34.1 (Spring 2006): 108.

48   Mark B. N. Hansen, "The Digital Topography of Mark Z. Danielewski's *House of Leaves*," *Contemporary Literature* 45.4 (2004): 607.

claws, causing moldings to splinter, water pipes to rupture, electrical wires to spit and short out. Worse, the black ash of below, spreads like printer's ink over everything, transforming each corner, closet, and corridor into that awful dark. (HL, 345)

The "black ash" of the house's internal abyss is compared to "printer's ink" whose "transforming" power rewrites every space with which it comes into contact. The house is like a book: made of ink, it becomes a thing to be read and analysed, navigated, and referenced. Thus, rather than vie-wing the central symbol of the text, the eponymous House, as an updated gothic/horror version of a (Borgesian) textual labyrinth, there is evidence enough to suggest that more appropriate is to treat Danielewski's *House of Leaves* as fictional conceptualisation of the situation of the book in a digi-tal age.

Danielewski's second novel *Only Revolutions* (2006) is another book-object of the "metatextual," concrete sort, undermining several of the basic conven-tions underlying the very process of reading. *Only Revolutions* is printed with both the front and the back covers appearing to be the "main" front of the book, the two sides corresponding to the central duo of characters: the side with the green cover introduces the story told by Sam, the side with the gold cover the story told by Hailey. Every page thus contains upside-down text in the bottom margin, which actually later on turns into pages of the opposite volume: thus, the first page of Hailey's story contains the last several lines of Sam's story, and vice versa. These double-block texts create a parallelism, as the plotline and the book as object falls into two equal 180–page halves mir-roring one another. To reconstruct the parallelism, one must leaf back and forth between the two-page layouts, flipping and "revolving" the book in the process. The book is designed to be read in both directions: beginning at the title page, one reads the top parts of every page; then, rotating the book 180 degrees and flipping it over, one *rebegins* at a *new* title page, again reading only the top portions of every page.

The two narratives converge in the middle, so that on pages 180–1, the same events are narrated in unison by the two characters, though in passages of op-posite orientation; after which they diverge again.[49] The episodic story of *Only Revolutions* is told twice, once in Sam's voice, the other in Hailey's, and the two versions are often at odds: *Only Revolutions* is a classic exercise in modernist

---

49   As critic Brian McHale notes, "parallelism here is *four-fold*. Each passage has an equivalent in the *other* narrative, but it also parallels (with conspicuous variations) another passage in the *same* narrative. The effect is one of *double mirroring*, as it were: mirroring above and below the horizontal line that divides the two narratives, but also mirroring *across* each narrative, on the same plane" (Brian McHale, "Only Revolutions, or, the Most Typical Poem in World Literature," *Mark Z. Danielewski*, eds. Joe Bray & Alison Gibbons [Manchester/New York: Manchester Uni-versity Press, 2011] 153).

narrative perspectivism, however, transposed from the conceptual / narrative level to that of the text / book itself. Since it is impossible to read both passages together at once, in McHale's words, "to integrate them at all requires a dimensional shift from the 2-D space of the page to the 3–D space of the book," a move "beyond the space of the page to the space of the *whole book.*"[50]

Only Revolutions reworks the road-movie genre as its plotline traces the journey of the teenage couple moving through various places and moments in time as they try to outrace history. If *House of Leaves* invoked as its media-intertext the Internet, then *Only Revolutions'* circularity and the changes evoked in its reading process recall the medium of cinema, as is evident in Danielewski's insertion of "periods" in the upper right corner of every 20 pages, referring to the cinematic technique of movie projection, resembling the changeover cues marking the end of a reel in movie projection. The conceptual tie of this book's circularity to that of the *Wake* is evident, but as the Joyce critic Dirk Van Hulle has shown, *Only Revolutions* employs also various specifically textual references. For instance, its very opening, "Bend by bend I leave every curve / blossomingly," in the upper text (OR, H4), counterpointed on the same page (upside down) with Sam's text (OR, S357) mentioning "swerves of Peace," echoes the *Wake's* own opening sentence and its "from swerve of shore to bend of bay" (FW 3.4).

Toward the very end, on page 355, with a dot in the upper right corner announcing the changeover cue, the text alludes to the *Wake's* "bend of bay" again, announcing the imminent "pause" button (359), the final change-over cue: "What bending she allways resolves. / What evolving she allways ends." (S355); "What resolving he allways bends. / What ending he allways evolves." (H355). Another example of a *Wakean* echo would be a scene of bee-stinging: "But O what a sting! Now? Me? Over with?" (S322), ends the page abruptly, and the next page starts with the word "Wake?" (S323). The corresponding page in Hailey's part (after her fall, H321) opens with "Hit? / But softly," recalling Anna Livia Plurabelle's moving end on the *Wake's* last page: "Finn again! Take. Bussoftlhee, mememormmee!" (FW 628.14). These and other playful redeployments and "literalisations" of the Joyce's materialist poetics make *Only Revolutions*, in Van Hulle's witty commentary, into a markedly modernist text in that its "chiastic structure has the effect of marking a centre of indifference in the middle of the whirlpool of revolutions."[51]

---

50 McHale, "The Most Typical Poem in World Literature," 148.
51 Van Hulle continues: "Joyce seems to have employed this marker as a kind of stylistic equivalent of the penciled *x* with which one marks an interesting passage in a boo, thus drawing attention to epiphanic moments, comparable to Marcel Proust's *mémoires involontaires* or Virginia Woolf's 'moments of being.' But *Only Revolutions* does not seem to imply the same modernist suggestion that a special meaning could be attached to such moments of 'beeing'" (Dirk Van Hulle, "Joyce's and Danielewski's Works in Progress," *Mark Z. Danielewski*, 136).

Taken together, Danielewski's *House of Leaves* and *Only Revolutions* present a highly imaginative reconceptualisation of the role and function of the book in the digital age, as well as an innovative project of creating a language capable of responding to its many challenges.

His novel *Witz* having just been published, to mark Bloomsday 2010, Joshua Cohen wrote a column for *Daily Beast* detailing the "12 novels that have been described, whether by critics or the authors themselves, as the *Ulyssi* of their respective cultures," from Turkey to Argentina, from Brazil to Israel. Of his own novel, Cohen observed:

> So I wrote a book called *Witz*. It's capacious (800 pages). It's complex (puns in a dozen languages: fun in a daze of longuages). And it's about a Wandering Jew—the Last Jew in the world. A friend of my father called after having tried a page to say, "It's like the Jewish *Ulysses*." That wasn't a compliment. Problem is, James Joyce's *Ulysses* is already the Jewish *Ulysses*. [...] That's what I said to my father's friend. "Yes," I said, "yes." That wasn't a compliment either: I knew he wouldn't get the reference.[52]

As long as for Cohen, *Ulysses* is "the summa of a culture," the culture of the European Jewish diaspora at the turn of the 19th/ 20th century, then *Witz* is Cohen's upgrade and update of that vis-à-vis the American Jewish culture a hundred years on.

In the perfect Hebraic tradition, *Witz* opens with an allegorical parable and self-reflexive story taken from "one of our many pious books," followed by an empty "motto," "deadication," and an explanatory, etymological note on its titles:

> One should not stack books of a lesser holiness atop books of a greater holiness. Tellingly, in another one of our pious books this dictum is turned on its head—in a story: A rabbi stacked a book of the Talmud atop a book of the Torah. Another asked him, Why are you doing that? And the rabbi answered him, In order to preserve the book of the Torah, because by covering it with this I will save it from the dust and the ashes that might fall upon it. Regardless of which one follows, the book you are holding now should, when stacked, always be placed in the middle. This book you are about to read contains no holy words or letters, neither words nor letters in the Holy Tongue, and nowhere within it are mentioned any of the many names of God. Therefore, this book may be ripped or torn, burnt, otherwise destroyed, and whatever remains require(s) no burial.
> " "
>
> —God

---

52   "A Bloomsday Celebration by Joshua Cohen, author of *Witz*," *Daily Beast* (15 Jun 2010). Online: https://www.thedailybeast.com/a-bloomsday-celebration-by-joshua-cohen-author-of-witz

DEADICATED to mine enemies, without whom none of this would have been possible
And Thy write hand shall save me...
Witz: being, in Yiddish, *a joke;* and, as the ending of certain names, also meaning *son of:*
e.g., *Abramowitz, meaning son-of-Abram*
(also found as –wic, –wich, –wics, –wicz, –witch, –wits, –wyc, – wych, –wycz, –vic, –
vich, –vics, –vicz, –vitch, –vits, –vitz, –vyc, –vych, and –vycz).
(*W*, 3–5)

From the very start, *Witz: A Novel* is concerned with the impossibility of summary and the issues of naming, categorising, and belonging—both in the "genre" of the novel, and the "genre" of the "Jew," a word which—as many *Witz* reviews would start off by pointing—does not appear once in the entire 800–plus pages, Cohen replacing the "J-word" with the term "Affiliated."[53] As is made evident in the publisher's back-cover blurb,[54] *Witz* is a hilariously outrageous ("*Witz*" of course is "joke" not just in Yiddish but also in German) meditation on the commodification of the Jewish identity, including but not limited to the museification of the Holocaust—one of the "witzes" so conspicuously missing from the opening etymological excursion being Auschwitz—and the additional problems of bearing-witness, and "living on" surviving. As noted by critic Jonathan Liu, "at its most polemical and problematic, Joshua Cohen's *Witz* is a [...] vaguely novelistic exegesis on the moral and epistemological impossibility of future Jewish novels. At *Witz'* most compelling [...] it's a primal plea for the return of a tradition to its messy, marginal, but living roots from an ossified privilege in the lucrative, self-satisfied center of mass culture."[55]

Opening with "IN THE BEGINNING THEY ARE LATE" (*W*, 13), *Witz* is a book of the "end times," which again is a trace that is unique to it and one of

---

53   Cf. Louis Armand's account of *Witz'*s deployment of generic supplements and reductions in his essay on *Witz,* "Laughlines from the Shoahshowbusiness": "Is it Cohen's intention that we confront these two circumstances, equally founded upon an act of reduction, in terms of a problem of genre: the genre of the novel and the genre of the Jew? The one named, the other unnamed but everywhere evoked, characterised, taxonomised and genealogised" (*Terrain—Essays on the New Poetics*, eds. David Vichnar & Olga Pek [Prague: Litteraria Pragensia Books, 2014] 174-5).

54   "On Christmas Eve 1999, all the Jews in the world die in a strange, millennial plague, with the exception of the firstborn males, who are soon adopted by a cabal of powerful people in the American government. By the following Passover, however, only one is still alive: Benjamin Israelien, a kindly, innocent, ignorant man-child. As he finds himself transformed into an international superstar, Jewishness becomes all the rage: matzo-ball soup is in every bowl, sidelocks are hip; and the only truly Jewish Jew left is increasingly stigmatised for not being religious. Since his very existence exposes the illegitimacy of the newly converted, Israelien becomes the object of a worldwide hunt... Meanwhile, in the not-too-distant future of our own, "real" world, another last Jew – the last living Holocaust survivor – sits alone in a snow-bound Manhattan, providing a final melancholy witness to his experiences in the form of the punchlines to half-remembered jokes."

55   Jonathan Liu, "*Witz* by Joshua Cohen," *Barnes and Noble* (3 Jun 2010). Online: https://www .barnesandnoble.com/review/witz

its most universal aspects that it shares with all the other "summative" works of encyclopaedic fiction. A crucial passage from the book's midpoint speaks of "massing losses" in a "time to end all times and Time":

> we all must stand ourselves, alive, aware, out on the far ice to reflect above the tide. Namely, that it's the destiny of every individual, of even the symbol, even the ultimate, to think their time the end, to think their world the last – and this especially today, especially fastdeadly, with everything In the beginning again at the already begun, history eternally returning as always, as eternally as ever but rather quickly, evermore and more quickly now, with a precipitate urgency, an Apocalyptic insistence. Now the time in which you live the time to end all times and Time; now the Never again. In mourning, standing atop the furthest spur of frost above the deep, they mourn themselves, a little soon: their failure, their ill luck, the ruinous stars above with their frustrated mazel. It's understood, which means it's itself mourned, our knowing hope, our dreaming: how we can't all be prophets, we can't all be priests, we can't all be kinds; that despite what the scholars once believed, there's only one Moses; that despite what the sages once bowed down to, there's only our God; thinking, too, if everyone's their own Messiah, what's that worth, what's in it for me. Better to unify, best to hold One indivisible. (W, 302)

The torrential quality of overflowing, sprawling sentences and the musical ear for the euphony of language, on display in the passage above as well, makes itself felt almost tangibly throughout *Witz*, brimming with sentences like "A scattering of vases with even their cracks chipped, their fill a handling of left umbrellas, corrupt caducei" (W, 263), where a sentence on "cracks" itself brims with the sharp cracking sounds of [k]'s and [tʃ]'s. Another Joycean technique employed in *Witz* is the acrostic distribution of B's and I's (for Benjamin Israelien), as in "B spits on a finger to erase, a clean slate, saliva daubed with blood. A thumbprint's trace. Upside-down, it doesn't matter . . . I will write myself" (W, 564). Replete with neologisms, *Witz* teems with "Joysey" for "Jersey," "Los Siegeles" for "Las Vegas," "Polandland" for "Poland," "Palestein" for "Palestine," "Yo Semite" for "Yosemite," and "Whateverwitz" for you-know-what. "Rhinoplastics" is all the rage, the most popular beer-brand is "He-Brew." The style is a peculiar blend of distinctly oral rhythm and colloquialisms moulded by a literate and literary diction.

Toward the end of *Witz*, a grave is visited—not of Joyce but of his strange, modernist attractor from afar, Kafka:

> Kaye graves his hands into his pockets, kicks a heel into the mud, turns from the gate only after his trainload's dispersed: only after many have lifted themselves up on their tiptoes to peer over the low falling fence, a few attempting to decipher the inscriptions in an alphabet foreign, in a few alphabets equally foreign, abbreviated then acronymed

to unintelligibility, dazzled into diacritics forgotten: acutes, graves, breves, carons, hooks and horns, dots and diaereses . . . it's not that they'll never understand, rather it's that these invocations will always only make sense to the dead: a readership as obsolete as the language in which they're left reading themselves – they'll be literate in no time, give them a night. (*W*, 676)

This futile attempt to visit Kafka's grave (a Jew famously disappeared behind his minority German in a Czech environment) takes place in a literal linguistic graveyard—in Cohen's elegy for the great novel and readership of the past, even the global functioning of English as *lingua franca* takes place at the cost of an elision, which is always a type of death. As the reviewer for *With Hidden Noise* has noted, "*Witz* is a book about the disappearance of a certain sort of culture: Jewishness, here, is only really appreciated after it's gone, which is a misguided project [...] this is a book about loss, mourning a literate world."⁵⁶ In another critical appreciation, Cohen's *Witz* might be "the last High Modernist, or the first New High Modernist" work, which also speaks of its demands on the reader.⁵⁷

Witz ends, *Ulysses*-like, with 30 pages of unpunctuated musings by the last Holocaust survivor as he dies aged 108—and so *Witz*'s finale treats us to 108 punchlines to 108 Jewish jokes. The concluding monologue links assimilation to fire, suggesting a kind of attenuation of tradition to almost nothing: "assimilationist tendencies from ash into air into academics and stories inventions the deconstructivist dated that's what we do we redact each and every storied second season bedded down in the ground in the air in the pole of the Himmelhow sky theres nowhere else to die nohow to sleep and yet why" (*W*, 801). A lipogram of sorts, the ultimate "Jewish novel" for the 21ˢᵗ century without the word "Jew," *Witz*' stylistic tour de force that shows the extreme and grotesque events at the centre of its plot—the catastrophic extinction of the Jewish race and the abrupt affiliation of the entire US population—to be logical, if extreme, extrapolations of some clearly-present realities for 20ᵗʰ-century American Judaism.

As if to make up for the conspicuous absence of the Internet in *Witz*, Cohen's *Book of Numbers* (2015) opens as follows: "If you're reading this on a screen, fuck off. I'll only talk if I'm gripped with both hands. Paper of pulp,

56 DBV, "Joshua Cohen's *Witz*," *With Hidden Noise* (4 Nov 2010). Online: https://withhiddennoise.net/2010/11/joshua-cohen-witz/

57 "Cohen's readers not only need the same working familiarity with Jewishness that a reader of *Ulysses* needs with Irishness, they also need the same patience in tracking syntax through a labyrinth of subordinate clauses that a reader of *Swann's Way* needs. They need to follow the smoky plumes of consciousness the way a reader of *To the Lighthouse* does, and to recall ephemeral detail from many pages back the way a reader of *Ada* does" (Paul Scott Stanfield, "The Promised Land and Its Discontents: The Fiction of Joshua Cohen," *Ploughshares* 42.1 [Spring 2016] 184).

covers of board and cloth, the thread from threadstuff or—what are bindings made of? hair and plant fibers, glue from boiled horsehooves? [...] I'm writing a memoir, of course—half bio, half autobio, it feels—I'm writing the memoir of a man not me" (*BN*, 1.5). Highly inclusive of all sorts of textual material—photos, graphs, diagrams, text messages, emails, notes, drafts, footnotes, crossed-out *disjecta*—*Book of Numbers* details the interactions between one Joshua Cohen, a novelist (but with a "bio" entirely different from the Cohen on the cover page), with another Joshua Cohen, the genius founder of search engine Tetration and internet tech billionaire, who hires the first JC as the ghost-writer of his biography. Like the word "Jew" absent from *Witz*, and supplanted by "Affiliated," the word "Google" never appears in *Book of Numbers*, with Tetration its substitution.

Another story, then, which like *Witz* hinges on the coincidences of naming and arbitrary relations of words. Unlike *Witz'* picaresque merriment, *Book of Numbers* develops a spy-thriller-type plot. Gradually—digression after distraction after yet another inconsequential email or trivial text message—it dawns on Josh-the-failed-writer that the sinister motives behind Tetration-Josh's autobiography project might have world-altering consequences: the thinly veiled Julian Assange and Edward Snowden characters, persecuted by the global info-tech and political elites, are just the beginning. Realising the dark secrets at the heart of the tycoon's dictations, the writer goes on the run and offline, travelling much of East Europe again, and then off to the deserts surrounding Dubai.

Divided into three sections bizarrely titled, "1.1," "0.161," and "1.419," *Book of Numbers* is another polymathic work of fiction, this time on the subjects of computing, comparative religion, art history, and the role of the book in the digital age of hypertext and hypermedia—brought home by its quasi-catastrophic climax set at the Frankfurt Book Fair. Paul Stanfield has demonstrated the rationale behind Cohen's employment of the eponymous Biblical intertext: "In the *Torah*, the Book of Numbers tells of what became of the Israelites between Sinai and entering Canaan; its namesake novel gives us a Joshua Cohen who has entered the Promised Land and a Joshua Cohen who is dying in the wilderness. [...] Cohen's novel makes us ask, what Promised Land is this, what wilderness?"[58] Coding and encryption are again in the forefront of Cohen's interest, as in the following passage where:

> This is exactly where a code's required, extra shorthand, an abbrev: like how red ink indicated lies in memoranda sent to and from the gulag, like "an inlaw" meant "an SS officer" in the partisan encryption of the Warsaw Ghetto, while the Nazis themselves used "solution" to mean "mass extermination. "There are two great innovations to

58   Stanfield, "The Promised Land and Its Discontents," 184.

recall: (1) all relationships between two or more quantities can be expressed as equations [...], and (2) all numbers, no matter how large, can be expressed by the sequential combination of the smallest numbers: zeroes and ones. (*BN*, 98)

This notion of all-pervasive figurations of numbers in the contemporary ubiquity of binary code is again both 2015 and ancient: the numbers of Book no. 4 of the Pentateuch have to do with the counting of Israelite tribes, with the maintenance of the polis, with raising the requisite revenue, and thus economy. But 2015 is computer-world, and so issues of naming, belonging, and collectivity that formed the backbone of *Witz* resurface here again, except holiness here in the age of computerised simulation is the technological sublime, not the "letters themselves" but "merely a representation":

"The Israeli chief rabbinate has ruled that it is permissible to delete the Tetragrammaton—the four letter Name of God—from both computer screen and file, AND from a server (meaning from anywhere online). As the responsum explains, a computer cannot inscribe or be inscribed by anything, and the proscription against destroying the Name pertains exclusively to physical scripture, to writing by hand (though as dot matrix printer ink impregnates the paper, printed copies must still be "interred). In a computer file, the Name of God, like any other word, exists only as a binary series of numbers, as 1s and 0s signifying the sequence of the letters—they are NOT the letters themselves! [...]
—askandtherabbianswers.com"
(*BN*, 421-2)

Thus, counting again has ultimately to do with survival, matters of life and death, and *Book of Numbers* covers that aplenty. In the estimation of Jerome A. Chanes, "*Book of Numbers* is about being a human in the age of the computer. [...] With his fourth novel, Joshua Cohen has emerged not only as a significant American writer but perhaps as a major literary voice. His new novel will stand as one of the impressive novels of the decade."[59] Just as *Witz* is an elegy for the big and serious encyclopedic novel, *Book of Numbers* is an "elegy for the written word" (Joshua Ferris on the back cover), which in the age of online communication, computer programming, data streaming, cloud uploading, and other operations of virtuality, might be as obsolescent as the notion of burying books containing the Holy Name.

From pastiche and simulation to "uncreation" and re-creation: such is the movement of this concluding overview of some of the trends of contemporary

---

59   Jerome A. Chanes, "Joshua Cohen's Circuit Overload," *Jewish Week* (30 Jun 2015).
     Online: https://jewishweek.timesofisrael.com/joshua-cohens-circuit-overload-2/

fiction in France, Britain, and the U.S. vis-à-vis the avant-garde heritage as exemplified by the refracted field of Joyce's materialist poetics. This refraction covers a whole spectrum of responses: from the passive nostalgia and fetishisation (Raczymow, Hadengue), and simplifying realist levelling (Mitchell) to more productive hypertextual and medial updates (Amerika, Danielewski), creative repurposing (Foster Wallace, Cohen), and more than less successful pastiche (Moore). It is in the strand of conceptual writing (Levé, Hall, Home, Goldsmith) that the five key tropes of the Joycean avant-garde are reworked to some highly (un)original ends. The hypertextual and medial proclivities of some post-2000 fiction revisits the chief concerns of Joyce's "technopoetics" and linguistic materialism. Amerika's attempt at rethinking of literary representation within electrosphere, Goldsmith's conceptual experimentation with linguistic innovation, and Danielewski's textual and typographical exploration of the book-object—all these attest to the fact that Joyce's heritage for the contemporary literary experiment springs chiefly from his avant-garde techno-poetics and intermedial writing in *Ulysses* and *Finnegans Wake*. Each of the twelve authors gathered here develops his own idiosyncratic departure from the postmodern experimental and generic heritage, and with the exception of Moore and Goldsmith, none acknowledges his debt to Joyce beyond its expected "user" value. They draw upon his successors (Levé on Perec, Home on Quin, Moore on Sinclair), and so the Joycean heritage is already refracted and hybridised by the reworking of these intermediaries, an increasingly faraway vanishing point, if far from vanished yet.

CONCLUSION:

JOYCE THE POST-

> It is very late, it is always too late with Joyce.
> Jacques Derrida, "Two Words for Joyce" (1982)

The previous seven chapters have examined the development of post-war experimental fiction in France, Britain, and the United States, surveying—in the rough timeframe of 1960–2000—the oeuvre of over three dozen writers who, each in their unique mode, departed from the Joycean revolution of the word, with a post-2000 coda in Chapter 8. This revolution of the word has been characterised in the book's introduction as informed by five crucial "effects" of Joyce's writing: its parallactic treatment of narrative perspectives, its metempsychosis of style, its exploration of concrete writing, its subversion of "literature" by way of plagiarism, and its project of neologising the logos. It remains for the book's Conclusion to attempt to "make sense" of this vast genealogy, to construe a Joycean postmodernity (consubstantial with the Joycean avant-garde of the Introduction), to eke out some of the micro-constellations and synergies implicit within it, and draw some macro-conclusions for the study of literary history and influence.

1. "ÉCRIRE SON NOM COMME UN *MEANDERTALE*": COUNTERSIGNING JOYCE'S SIGNATURE

An apt way of taking stock of the active transformation of Joyce's legacy might take place in terms of the metaphor of "counter-signing" Joyce's signature as developed by one of his most sophisticated philosophical investigators, Jacques Derrida, who primarily applied it to the task of the critic in responding to the literary work.

Derrida's recourse to an analogy with a document that is signed by one and then countersigned by another individual ties in with his well-known theorisation of the paradoxical functioning of the linguistic sign as both a singularity and an iteration. Signatures are paradoxical in that they testify to the presence of their signatories in the act of writing, yet in order to remain recognisable they need to function independently of them, in their absence. Now, a "signature" of a "text" is irreducible for Derrida to the name of its "author" and much less so to their psychology or to signing a proper name. A signature is a matter of the unique concatenation of traces that make it up, traces that are themselves the effects of repetition and which, in turn, invite their own iteration(s).[1] Thus, a countersignature affirms that the first signature is indeed the signature it claims to be, underwrites it, and assumes responsibility for its promise. To hear Derrida's commentator John D. Caputo tell it, "texts, if there is anything to them, elicit, call for, and provoke other texts—responses, commentaries, interpretations, controversies, imitations, forgeries, plagiarisms, translations, transformations, bald misinterpretations, creative misunderstandings, etc."[2] Part of the signature's very structure is to solicit countersignatures, which name what is unique about it by signing onto the text.

Similarly, the literary work is singular only by virtue of its exploitation and repetition of existing shared codes, as is the critic's or writer's response to another writer's signature. But the countersignature must be different from the signature; one cannot countersign one's own signature, or attempt to copy the signature to be countersigned. The countersignature is just as much the mark of one's own uniqueness, and similarly the response to the literary work must mark its distance from the work as well as its affirmation of it. In conversation with Derek Attridge, Derrida spoke of this process as of a duel of singularities:

> a duel of writing and reading, in the course of which a counter-signature comes both to confirm, repeat and respect the signature of the other, of the "original" work, and to lead it off elsewhere, so running the risk of betraying it, having to betray it in a certain way so as to re-spect it, through the invention of another signature just as singular. Thus redefined, the concept of the countersignature gathers up the whole paradox: you have to give yourself over singularly to singularity, but singularity itself then does have to share itself out and so compromise itself.[3]

Two years after his interview with Attridge, at the Villanova University Roundtable in 1994, Derrida identified Joyce's signature as

> the most gigantic attempt to gather in a single work, that is, in the singularity of a work which is irreplaceable [...] the presumed totality, not only of one culture but of a number of cultures, a number of languages, literatures, and religions. This impossible task is, at the same time and in an exemplary way, both new in its modern form and very classical in its philosophical form. [...] This is made possible only by loading every sen-

---

1   Cf., e.g., Jacques Derrida, *Points de suspension: Entretiens*, ed. Elisabeth Weber (Paris: Galilée, 1992) 365. English: *Points... Interviews, 1974–94*, ed. Elisabeth Weber, trans. Peggy Kamuf et al. (Stanford: Stanford University Press, 1995) 354–5.
2   John D. Caputo, *Deconstruction in a Nutshell: A Conversation with Jacques Derrida* (Fordham: Fordham University Press, 1997) 189.
3   Jacques Derrida, "'This Strange Institution Called Literature': An Interview with Jacques Derrida," *Acts of Literature*, ed. Derek Attridge (New York: Routledge, 1992) 69.

tence, every word, with a maximum of equivocalities, virtual associations, by making this organic and linguistic totality as rich as possible.[4]

Derrida's questioner and commentator at Villanova, Caputo restates the critical double-bind identified in the countersigning operation, and the peculiarity of countersigning Joyce's signature, as follows:

> Will it endow itself with a kind of omnipotence such that no one, no commentator to come, can ever get the best of, ever circumscribe and circumnavigate 'James Joyce'? Or will this signature invite invention, novelty, will it give itself up to innumerable, incalculable innovations to come? [...] On the one hand, we must write, we must sign, we must bring about new events with untranslatable marks – and this is the frantic call, the distress of a signature that is asking for a yes from the other, the pleading injunction for a counter-signature; but on the other hand, the singular novelty of any other yes, of any other signature, finds itself already programophoned in the Joycean corpus.[5]

And yet, as Derrida pointed out in his seminal plenary talk at the 1984 Frankfurt Symposium, any such "programophoned," i.e., programmatically pre-recorded "yes," however self-enclosing,

> demands a priori its own repetition, its own memorizing, demands that a yes to the yes inhabit the arrival of the "first" yes, which is never therefore simply originary. We cannot say yes without promise to confirm it and to remember it, to keep it safe, countersigned in another yes without promise and memory, without the promise of memory.[6]

So, then, Derrida asks whether we can take account of the "yes" in Joyce's *Ulysses* and *Finnegans Wake*, of the "yes" in Joyce's "signature." The idea in reading Joyce's texts (and ultimately, in reading any and all texts, but Joyce is Derrida's pre-eminent example) is to ward off, to prevent "totalization, and the closing of the circle, and the return of Ulysses, and the self-sending of some indivisible signature."[7] In Derrida's conclusion, Joyce's signature is, in a nutshell, incalculable and not to be shut-down. That is because it is always-already directed to an "other," a direction which severs the signature in its very midst, "sending it off in innumerable directions, opening it up to multiple repetitions, allowing a self-transforming tradition to graft itself upon it, permitting, soliciting innumerable counter-signatures."[8]

---

4   Caputo, *Deconstruction in a Nutshell*, 25.
5   Ibid, 190.
6   Jacques Derrida, "*Ulysses* Gramophone: Hear say yes in Joyce," *James Joyce – The Augmented Ninth*, ed. Bernard Benstock (New York: Syracuse University Press, 1988) 68.
7   Caputo, *Deconstruction in a Nutshell*, 197.
8   Ibid, 197–8.

With regards to the two crucial metaphors identified by Derrida that govern the relationship between Joyce and the tradition in his wake, i.e., of the countersigning of signature and of "saying yes" to the other, what has been rather hazily termed a Joycean tradition throughout this book is not—though it would be poetically just—some kind of orthodoxy, school or programme, but an ensemble of "textual links" that constitute "countersignatures" to Joyce's signature, the many "ways of signing on to"[9] his texts.

2. "RITUALS ORIGINATING IN PIETY": CONSTRUCTING A JOYCEAN POSTMODERNISM

This book undertook the task set by Ellmann "to become Joyce's contemporary" by gathering an ensemble of creative "countersignatures" that sought to sign onto, confirm, underscore, encircle, or overwrite his signature, thereby also creating a genealogy of post-war Joycean avant-garde. With reference to Jolas' *transition*, this avant-garde was conceived of as a "documentary organ" of the effects of Joyce's materialist poetics as practiced in *Ulysses* and *Finnegans Wake*. Thus, the present project has been marked by the peculiar double temporality of the "future anterior": Joyce's avant-gardism, nonprogrammatic and idiosyncratic, is "what will have been done" with/about it in the future by his contemporaries.

It is postmodernity itself, in one of its inaugural formalisations of Jean-François Lyotard's *The Postmodern Condition: A Report on Knowledge*, that is based within a "future/anterior" temporality similar to that of the present construction of the Joycean avant-garde and its aftereffects:

> A postmodern artist or writer is in the position of a philosopher: the text he writes, the work he produces are not in principle governed by pre-established rules, and they cannot be judged according to a determining judgement, by applying familiar categories to the text or to the work. Those rules and categories are what the work of art itself is looking for. The artist and writer, then, are working without rules in order to formulate the rules of what *will have been done*. [...] *Post modern* would have to be understood according to the paradox of the future (*post*) anterior (*modo*).[10]

Lyotard's further conceptualisation of this paradoxical temporality poses a challenge to the whole notion of post/modernist sequentiality: "a work can only become modern if it is first post-modern. Postmodernism thus under-

---

9   Ibid, 189.
10   Jean-François Lyotard, *The Postmodern Condition: A Report on Knowledge*, trans. Geoff Bennington & Brian Massumi (Manchester: Manchester University Press, 1991) 81.

stood is not modernism at its end but in the nascent state, and this state is constant."[11] Insofar as the postmodern and modern co-exist simultaneously in any culture at any time, their difference is not temporal, but conceptual. At this point Lyotard resorts to the notion of the sublime, marking both the modern and the postmodern as different from the realist mimesis whose task is to depict the world from a viewpoint that would "give it a recognisable meaning" in order for its audience to "decode images and sequences rapidly" and thereby "protect [their] consciousness from doubt."[12]

The sublime, characterised as a disturbance of everyday sense-making (thus strongly reminiscent of Poggioli's notion of the avant-garde as "cathartic and therapeutic" disruption), consists in "presenting the existence of something unpresentable. Showing that there is something we can conceive of which we can neither see nor show."[13] The difference, then, between the modern and the postmodern, for Lyotard, lies in their different deployment of this unpresentable sublime: in the modern, the unpresentable is "invoked only as absent content, while the form, thanks to its recognisable consistency, continues to offer the reader material for consolation or pleasure." The postmodern, in contrast,

would be that which, in the modern, puts forward the unpresentable in presentation itself; that which denies itself the solace of good forms, the consensus of taste which would make it possible to share collectively the nostalgia for the unattainable; that which searches for new presentations, not in order to enjoy them but in order to impart a stronger sense of the unpresentable.[14]

Remarkably, when providing two contrastive examples, Lyotard pits against the modernist Proust and his *À la Recherche du temps perdu* none other than Joyce's *Ulysses* and *Finnegans Wake* with their deployment of allusions, intertexts, puns, and distorted language with which they disrupt conventional perception about what a novel—or any text, for that matter—should be and do:

Joyce allows the unpresentable to become perceptible in his writing itself, in the signifier. The whole range of available narrative and even stylistic operators is put into play without concern for the unity of the whole, and new operators are tried. The grammar and vocabulary of literary language are no longer accepted as given; rather, they appear as academic forms, as rituals originating in piety [...] which prevent the unpresentable from being put forward.[15]

11   Lyotard, *The Postmodern Condition*, 79.
12   Ibid, 70.
13   Ibid, 74.
14   Ibid, 81.
15   Ibid, 80–1.

Thus, inherent to one of postmodernism's canonical formulations is a challenge to its application as a period-marker, to its oppositionality vis-à-vis modernism, or even its sequential "post-" ness. Still, this challenge entailed in Lyotard's argument—put forth as early as 1979—did not prevent two other highly influential conceptualisations of the postmodern from subscribing to the periodising impetus.

Ihab Hassan's 1982 revision of his *Dismemberment of Orpheus* includes the notorious list of binary oppositions in which to capture the modern/postmodern divide, e.g., form (conjunctive, closed) vs. antiform (disjunctive, open); purpose vs. play; design vs. chance; hierarchy vs. anarchy; presence vs. absence; metaphor vs. metonymy; metaphysics vs. irony; etc., where the (inferior modernist) former is evidently supplanted and revised by the (superior postmodernist) latter.[16] Brian McHale's *Postmodernist Fiction* (1987) argues that the move from modernist to postmodernist fiction entails a shift from a focus on epistemological issues to an exploration of ontological questions. Whereas the modern is concerned with questions of truth, knowledge, and interpretation, the postmodern interrogates the following: "What is a world? What kinds of world are there, how are they constituted, and how do they differ? What happens when different kinds of world are placed in confrontation, or when boundaries between worlds are isolated?"[17] Again, a clear progression from the former to the latter is implied, even though no definite lines of division are (or indeed can be) drawn.

The particular interest in exposing these arguments here lies in how both Hassan and McHale, when dealing with Joyce's work, enlist his *Ulysses* (McHale) and *Finnegans Wake* (Hassan) for their postmodernist cause. Heyward Ehrlich's edited volume *Light Rays: James Joyce and Modernism* features Hassan's "*Finnegans Wake* and the Postmodern Imagination," which addresses the crucial question, "How does *Finnegans Wake* accord with, how does it make itself available to, the postmodern imagination?," bespeaking the conviction that the book "stands as a monstrous prophecy that we have begun to discover [...] but have not yet decided how to heed."[18] Hassan offers seven perspectives on this central question, each of which is punctuated by a "Counterpoint" composed of "postmodern rumours and random reflections."

---

16   Even though even Hassan himself is careful to voice a caveat: "Yet the dichotomies this table represents remain insecure, equivocal. For differences shift, defer. even collapse; concepts in one vertical column are not all equivalent; and inversions and exceptions, in both modernism and postmodernism, abound" (Ihab Hassan, *The Dismemberment of Orpheus: Toward a Postmodern Literature*, 2nd edition [New York: Oxford University Press, 1982], 269).

17   Brian McHale, *Postmodernist Fiction* (London: Methuen, 1987) 10.

18   Ihab Hassan, "*Finnegans Wake* and the Postmodern Imagination," *Light Rays: James Joyce and Modernism*, ed. Heyward Ehrlich (New York: New Horizon Press Publishers, 1984) 93.

The first, "A Death Book and Book of Life," broaches the issue of "the secret threat of *Finnegans Wake*: "Is *Finnegans Wake* outside literature? Or is it pointing the way for literature to go beyond itself? Or, again, is it a prophecy of the end of literature as we have come to know it?" And his answer is a peremptory yes: "That is why I call *Finnegans Wake* not only a death book but also a book of life, not simply an end but a progress as well."[19] A strangely displaced type of rumination, as late as mid-1980s and especially in a volume containing the work of John Cage or Pierre Boulez. The third perspective, "Dream & Play (And Later Structure)," discusses the contradictions inherent to "the disorder of dreams, the purposelessness of play, the cunning of structure," all contradictions on which "*Finnegans Wake* balances itself," and which are resolved in Hassan's conclusion that the "dream element" in the *Wake* is simply the author's freedom "to alter language and reality."[20] The fourth perspective, "Structure," notes with palpable irony that "all good structuralists go to *Finnegans Wake* on their way to heaven, and that is perhaps why they are so long in reaching their destination," for *Finnegans Wake*, however meticulously structured, is also "aware of the more obscure need to de-structure itself."[21] The fifth and sixth perspectives have to do with "Eroticism" and "The Language of Babel," respectively, and in a "Counterpoint" to the latter, Joyce's "revolution of language" as an exploration of the linguistic autonomy and materiality resurfaces, this time only re-dubbed postmodernist: "The postmodern endeavour in literature acknowledges that words have severed themselves from things, that language can now only refer to language. And what book, or rather what language, calls attention to itself as language, as ineluctably verbal and quite finally so, more than *Finnegans Wake*?"[22] In the seventh and last section, Hassan effectively disproves his construction of a postmodernist *Wake* by regarding it as aspiring "to the condition of a universal consciousness," the strategies deployed in the service of this goal being "as numerous as they have grown familiar." This recourse to the *Wake*'s modernist impulse is further strengthened in how, for Hassan, "the totality of the book, its effort toward a universal consciousness, fails to parody or subvert itself, fails to ironize itself."[23] The *Wake*, then, seems to subvert not only Hassan's sense of a postmodernist "post-ness" vis-à-vis modernism (published as the apex of the modernist period by one of its supposed grandmasters), but also effectively disprove some of his binary oppositions that purport to define the postmodernist in opposition to the modernist.

---

19   Hassan, "*Finnegans Wake* and the Postmodern Imagination," 95.
20   Ibid, 99.
21   Ibid, 100–1.
22   Ibid, 105.
23   Ibid, 107.

McHale's *Constructing Postmodernism* devotes an entire chapter to "The Case of *Ulysses*" and commences by observing that in spite of its traditional alignment with High Modernism, *Ulysses* "has lately entered upon a strange second career as a *postmodernist* text."[24] This is due to how it is composed of "two differentiable texts placed side by side, one of them the hallmark of High Modernism, the other something else," a something else that has recently been called "postmodernism." The relation between these two, for McHale, is "one of *excess* and *parody*: the poetics of the postmodernist chapters *exceed* the modernist poetics of the 'normal' chapters, and the postmodernist chapters *parody* modernist poetics."[25] McHale proceeds with a discussion of these two *halves*, one after the other. He examines the "modernist *Ulysses*" by means of two formal methodological sub-categories—*mobile consciousness* and *parallax*—with McHale's "other, postmodernist" *Ulysses* transforming these into the categories of the *mobile world* and *discursive parallax*, generating a postmodernist undecidability based on how "a discourse implies a world," encoding a particular version of reality, and Joyce's multiple discursive versions of reality end up inevitably "mutually incompatible, incommensurable."[26] Instead of finding fault with the oppositionality between the modern and the postmodern and striving to reconcile them, McHale resorts to other critics' re-conceptualisations of the notion of modernism that would allow him to accommodate its supposed other, although the problem identified here has clearly more to do with critical terminology and reading methods rather than with anything "intrinsic" to Joyce's text. McHale refers to Helmut Lethen's *Modernism Cut in Half*, which argues against the officially presented High Modernism of writers like Thomas Mann, which he terms "conservative" in that it excludes its avant-garde, and consequently projects it onto postmodernism.

In this context, Lyotard's contention that postmodernism presents modernism in its nascent state, and therefore *precedes* modernism, resonates again: postmodernism "thus precedes the consolidation of modernism—it is modernism with the anomalous avant-garde still left in." This process, as Lyotard remarks, is constant; McHale argues that what Lyotard means by this is, in effect, "not the particular history of the phases of the twentieth century but a general historical principle whereby each successive cultural phase recuperates what has been excluded and 'left over' from the preceding phase and bases its 'new' poetics on that leftover."[27] Thus, ironically enough, the most conclusive point McHale's book seems to make about Joyce vis-à-vis postmodernism is its very title: that postmodernism is a *construct*, a notion

---

24 Brian McHale, *Constructing Postmodernism* (London/New York: Routledge, 1992) 42.
25 McHale, *Constructing Postmodernism*, 43, 44.
26 Ibid, 54.
27 Ibid, 56.

used as a shorthand to denote both a period and aesthetics – McHale's exemplary authors include Pynchon and Brooke-Rose, to whom he devotes large sections of his study, but also—of the authors covered here—Acker, Barth, Burroughs, Federman, Gray, Sorrentino, Sukenick, and many others.

3. THE JOYCEAN ANTI-POSTMODERNISTS

Thus, not "governed by pre-established rules," but writing texts whose "rules and categories are what the work of art itself is looking for," the writers presented in this genealogy have all expressed various degrees of sceptical, if not outright hostile, attitudes towards the postmodern label.

Anthony Burgess never tired of stressing the liveliness of Joyce's heritage for the literature of his day: "We should all now be writing novels like *Finnegans Wake*, not necessarily so obscure or so large, but starting on the way Joyce has shown in exploring the resources of the language," he observed in 1964.[28] Many years later, his view was quite the same: "We've got a hell of a long way to go with modernism. Some people think *Finnegans Wake* is the end of modernism [... but] I think we're still in a modernist phase."[29]

A whole section of Christine Brooke-Rose's *A Rhetoric of the Unreal* presents her sceptical views on postmodernity that are largely dissident from those prevalent within the academia. Both terms, i.e., "modern" and "postmodern," are found "peculiarly unimaginative for a criticism that purports to deal with phenomena of which the most striking feature is imagination," this for three reasons: "They are purely historical, period words, and in that sense traditional"; second, "they are self-cancelling terms, and this may be particularly apt for an art continually described as self-cancelling"; and finally, "by way of corollary, the terms are simply lazy, inadequate." A consequent problem arises, then, with any attempt at defining the notions in terms of canon:

> [If] we are going to put D. H. Lawrence [...] and Hemingway and Proust and Kafka and Pound and Yeats and Eliot and Faulkner and Mann and Gide and Musil and Stevens and Virginia Woolf and Joyce etc. into the same modernist ragbag, the term becomes meaningless except as a purely period term, itself obsolescent since modern by definition means now. (*RU*, 344)

The postmodernist label, to Brooke-Rose's mind, suffers from a similar overinclusive "ragbaggage." Ihab Hassan is critiqued by Brooke-Rose as prone to

28   Anthony Burgess, "Speaking of Writing—VIII," *Times* (16 January, 1964): 13.
29   Samuel Coale, "An Interview with Anthony Burgess," *Modern Fiction Studies* 27 (Autumn, 1981): 444.

sweeping generalisations even when focused on the postmodernity of a single text—the *Wake*:

> Hassan does give us some more specific "modern forms" arising, directly or indirectly, out of Joyce's *Finnegans Wake*, the structure of which is "both structurally over-determined and semantically under-determined," but with coincidence as structural principle (identity as accident, recurrence and divergence), as well as the gratuitousness of every creative act. (*RU*, 349)

As Alasdair Gray, another frequent exemplar of Hassan's or McHale's postmodernist accounts, himself averred in an interview: "I have never found a definition of postmodernism that gives me a distinct idea of it. If the main characteristic is an author who describes himself as a character in his work, then Dante, Chaucer, Langland, and Wordsworth are as postmodern as James Joyce, who is merely modern."[30] John Barth's 1980 essay, "Literature of Replenishment," was written as "a companion and corrective" to his 1967 "Literature of Exhaustion." Its most striking difference is its engagement with critical theorisations of so-called postmodernism, a term which Barth finds useless and subjects to mockery, as discussed in Chapter III.[31] There is, to Barth's mind, a certain inferiority of postmodernism vis-à-vis modernism implied in the "post-," which in turn calls for a (re)definition of modernism itself, since the "post-"ness implies that modernism is over and consummated and, as such, estimable. Barth concedes that the "adversary reaction called modernist art," aimed against "the rigidities and other limitations of nineteenth-century bourgeois realism," is one that nowadays has nothing to react against as "these nineteenth-century rigidities are virtually no more." As such, "it *belongs* to the first half of our century" and "the present reaction against it is perfectly understandable," both "because the modernist coinages are by now more or less debased common currency and because we really don't *need* more *Finnegans Wake* and *Pisan Cantos*, each with its staff of tenured professors to explain it to us."[32] Finally, as Donald Barthelme has been seen to argue, with Joyce "fiction altered its placement in the world in a movement so radical that its consequences have yet to be assimilated." Departing from the well-known dictum of Beckett's essay on the "Work in Progress," Bar-

---

30   Mark Axelrod, "An Epistolary Interview, Mostly with Alasdair Gray," *Review of Contemporary Fiction* 15.2 (Summer 1995): 113.

31   "While some of the writers labeled as postmodernists, myself included, may happen to take the label with some seriousness, a principal activity of postmodernist critics [...], writing in postmodernist journal or speaking at postmodernist symposia, consists in disagreeing about what postmodernism is or ought to be, and thus about who should be admitted to the club—or clubbed into admission" (John Barth, *The Friday Book – Essays and Other Nonfiction* [New York: G. P. Putnam's Sons, 1984] 194).

32   Barth, *The Friday Book*, 202.

thelme notes that the consequences of creating literary "objects" as "worlds" in themselves present a "stunning strategic gain for the writer. He has in fact removed himself from the work, just as Joyce instructed him to do."[33]

To these writers' theoretical concerns can be added many other examples of so-called postmodernist practice aligning itself, in a Lyotardian fashion, with some quintessentially modernist/avant-gardist projects. To take just the one example of the collage: speaking of Brion Gysin's discovery and his own application of the cut-up method, Burroughs notes how the modernist heritage present in Eliot's phrase, "Who is the third who walks always beside you?," was adopted by himself and Gysin "to designate the collaborative consciousness which could be generated by the cut-up method: a third mind free of the restrictions of context, culture, and subjectivity."[34] In many respects Burroughs' heir, Iain Sinclair states (some forty years later) that his use of Alfred Watkins' psycho-geographical concept is a means to an aesthetic end steeped in modernist poetics of juxtaposition and collage.[35]

On top of all the previous are all three French post-war avant-gardes in their entirety. The New Novelists, the Oulipians, and the *Tel Quelians* all challenge the accepted division of 20th-century literature into modernist and postmodernist periods (partly of course because French literary history does know the modernist label as such), sometimes seeming to unite them, sometimes seen as standing between them, but mostly simply bypassing the division altogether. Which is also the reason why Robbe-Grillet or Butor or Queneau or Sollers left no explicit address of these questions, unlike their Anglo-American contemporaries.

4. "HIS PRODUCERS ARE THEY NOT HIS CONSUMERS?" (FW 497.1–2) REVISI(TI)NG THE JOYCEAN TRADITION

"Tradition," "genealogy," "documentary organ," "ensemble of signatures"— the eight decades of writing mapped here have obviously to do with history, which should not be taken for granted as self-evident. Two important points emerge in Dominic LaCapra's *Rethinking Intellectual History: Text, Context, and*

---

33   Donald Barthelme, *Not-Knowing: The Essays and Interviews of Donald Barthelme*, ed. Kim Her-zinger, intro. John Barth (New York: Random House, 1997) 4.
34   Qtd. in Robin Lydenberg, *Word Cultures* (Urbana/Chicago: University of Illinois Press, 1987) 44–5.
35   "All of it to be digested, absorbed, fed into the great work. Wasn't that the essence of the mod-ernist contract? Multi-voiced lyric seizures countered by drifts of unadorned fact, naked source material spliced into domesticated trivia, anecdotes, borrowings, found footage. Redundant. As much use as a whale carved from margarine, unless there is intervention by that other; unless some unpredicted element takes control, overrides the pre-planned structure, tells you what you don't know" (Iain Sinclair, *Landor's Tower: or The Imaginary Conversations* [London: Granta Books, 2002] 31).

Language that are relevant for the conception of the Joycean tradition charted in this book. LaCapra defines a text in a way which is suggestive of both
the contemporaneity of Joyce's writing à la Ellmann, and the solicitations of
countersigning the Joycean signature à la Derrida:

> What is meant by the term "text"? It may initially be seen as a situated use of language
> marked by a tense interaction between mutually implicated yet at times contestatory
> tendencies. On this view, the very opposition between what is inside and what is outside
> texts is rendered problematic, and nothing is seen as being purely and simply inside or
> outside texts. Indeed the problem becomes one of rethinking the concepts of "inside"
> and "outside" in relation to processes of interaction between language and the world.[36]

As detailed in the sections of the Introduction devoted to Joyce's materialist
poetics, this breakdown between inside and outside, the blurring of boundaries between fact/fiction, history/poetics, language/consciousness, is at the
heart of Joyce's project, always intent on demonstrating the confluences of
these binaries which inhere in all acts of language .

The first of LaCapra's notions is that of history itself seen as a process
of "iteration with alteration—a process for which language provides one
important model,"[37] which quite appositely describes both the model of the
recursive Viconian history as literalised in the *Wake* and the genealogy of
creative "iterations with alterations" forming the genealogy traced in this
book. Language is at once historical (forming part of history itself) and his-
tory-forming (the means by which history takes place). Every telling changes
both the teller and what they tell: or as Joyce "says" in the recording of his
ALP passage, "Well, you know or don't you kennet or haven't I told you every
telling has a taling and that's the he and the she of it" (*FW* 213.11–2). But it
is these various tellings and talings that constitute a history of the Joycean
avant-garde which is also at once the promise of Joycean postmodernity—the
future anterior of "what will have happened." The countersignatures of this
genealogy are re-enactments, repetitions with variations, and together they
form a protean, metempsychotic involution of the narrative process which is
both the present actuality of *Ulysses* and the *Wake* and their future promise.
This involution, as we have seen throughout, has also to do with postmodernity's hesitant embrace of the burden of its modernist influence.

The other issue is LaCapra's unanswered question about the evaluation
of greatness: "Is the judgment of greatness at times related to the sense that
certain works both reinforce tradition and subvert it, perhaps indicating

---

36 Dominick LaCapra, *Rethinking Intellectual History: Text, Context, and Language* (Ithaca: Cornell
    University Press, 1983) 26.
37 LaCapra, *Rethinking Intellectual History*, 336.

the need for newer traditions that are more open to disconcerting modes of questioning and better able to withstand the recurrent threat of collapse?" LaCapra's questioning continues:

> Do certain works themselves both try to confirm or establish something—a value, a pattern of coherence, a system, a genre—and call it into question? Is there something sensed in judgments that may not be said in reductive interpretations that make certain works all too familiar? Are processes of contestation often or typically more powerful in certain kinds of texts—for example, literary or poetic texts—in comparison with philosophical or historical ones? How watertight are these higher-order forms of classification in relation to the actual use(s) of language in texts? What does a less reductive, normalizing, or harmonizing mode of interpretation require of the reader?[38]

These questions of LaCapra's remain rhetorical and unanswered, and his referential framework is Heideggerian and Derridean, but the extent to which his notion of self-questioning literary establishments of values and systems is applicable to Joyce, and even more so, to Lyotard's notion of *post-modo*, is remarkable. This "inner contestation" in which a literary text consistently invokes its past models, only to subject them to alienation, subversion, and "desacralisation," lies at the heart both of Joyce's treatment of all his crucial avant-texts—the Bible, Homer, Shakespeare, Vico, *Don Juan*, *Faust*, Flaubert, Carroll, et al.—and of the various treatments visited upon him by his *post--modo* followers.

"Contestation" is also a crucial word for understanding the tenor of the literary revolution that was—in all three national genealogies mapped here—the 1960s. For unlike "history" as such, "literary history" never happens "of itself," but always as a result of effort, of struggle, of work. As Robert Buckeye reminisced in his pioneering 2013 book-length study on Ann Quin,

> [s]ome writers felt that their writing had not only to reflect the times, but also, in some way, lead them. The business of literature could not be conducted as it had been before. These writers dismissed traditional methods and ignored mainstream venues for new ways in which to write and alternative sites in which to situate their writing—bars were not uncommon. Little mags far from New York, London or Paris proliferated.[39]

And, in an uncanny echo of Lyotard, Buckeye also voices the chief pitfall of taking stock of literary history, a paradox that has underwritten the genea-

---

38 Ibid, 29.
39 Robert Buckeye, *Re: Quin* (Champaign/London/Dublin: Dalkey Archive Press, 2013) 8.

logy in this book: "We could not know the beginning before we knew the end."[40]

That something changed about the "business of literature" in Joyce's 20s and 30s, and then again in the post-Joycean 60s and 70s, is evident. Another way of making sense of what happened in the 1960s is via the situationist maxim from 1963, that "the moment of real poetry brings all the unsettled debts of history back into play," again applicable both to the high modernism of Joyce and Eliot (according to whose famous adage, "great poets steal") and to the *post-modo* replications thereof. The situationist quote prefaces Greil Marcus' *Lipstick Traces: A Secret History of the Twentieth Century*, with which—given that Marcus' book devotes itself to the transformation of British rock'n'roll through the 1976 intervention of "Anarchy in the UK" by the Sex Pistols, whose punk music is seen as an offshoot of situationism, which in turn had been informed by lettrism-surrealism-Dadaism—this book might share more than is immediately evident. Consider Marcus' opening ruminations on "Anarchy in the UK" as "a denial of all social facts":

> It is a joke—and yet the voice that carries it remains something new in rock 'n' roll, which is to say something new in post-war popular culture: a voice that denied all social facts, and in that denial affirmed that everything was possible. It remains new because rock 'n' roll has not caught up with it. Nothing like it had been heard in rock 'n' roll before, and nothing like it has been heard since—though, for a time, once heard, that voice seemed available to anyone with the nerve to use it. For a time, as if by magic [...] that voice worked as a new kind of free speech. In countless new throats it said countless new things.[41]

Compare this to all the numerous critical detractions of Joyce's "Work in Progress" as a colossal joke, to Jolas' / Beckett's insistence on its seriousness and the world's perceived failings in "catching up with it," and review the fifty "new throats" assembled here, through which the Joycean avant-garde has kept saying "countless new things"; the resemblance between the effects of Joyce's *Finnegans Wake* and the Sex Pistols protest-song is uncanny. Dealing with matters of history, genealogy, and influence, one is necessarily faced with the temptation to pinpoint a foundational moment, to pin down the key "event," as is Marcus:

> Is it a mistake to confuse the Sex Pistols' moment with a major event in history—and what is history anyway? Is history simply a matter of events that leave behind those

---

40   Buckeye, *Re: Quin*, 11.
41   Greil Marcus, *Lipstick Traces: A Secret History of the Twentieth Century* (first published 1989; London: Faber and Faber, 2001) 2.

things that can be weighed and measured—new institutions, new maps, new rulers, new winners and losers—or is it also the result of moments that seem to leave nothing behind, nothing but the mystery of spectral connections between people long separated by place and time, but somehow speaking the same language?[42]

Marcus' history as "the result of moments that seem to leave nothing behind" is as good a variation of Poggioli's "nihilist" theme in the avant-garde as any, and Marcus' "connections between people long separated by place and time" uncannily echo Jolas' conception of *transition* as "workshop of the intercontinental spirit."

Since history depends on it, this is perhaps an opportune moment for one last revisitation of Jolas' / Joyce's avant-garde project as seen by an eyewitness. Let us recall Stuart Gilbert's reminiscence of his sense of wonder upon opening—one "spring afternoon in Rue de l'Odéon"—the inaugural issue of *transition* magazine and finding there the excerpt from Joyce's "A Work in Progress" mysteriously beginning mid-sentence in lowercase, "riverrun brings us back to Howth Castle & Environs. Sir Tristram, violer d'amores, fr'over the short sea, had passencore re-arrived from North Armorica..."[43] Gilbert's immediate reaction is to emphasise the psycho-political dimension of *transition*'s poetics as informed in the *Wake*: a critique of "the true origin of that war [i.e., World War I]" as an excess of "the death-instinct or, crudely speaking, Original Sin," and thus to connect *transition* with Dada, which is to say,

its particular discovery: that of the futility of all doctrines and advertised ideals. [...] Under farcical pretensions Dada followed a system of thought as plausible as Descartes', and its antithesis. *Non* cogito, ergo sum. In fact, Dadaism was quite the most *sympathique* of the *isms* I have encountered during a long residence in Paris. Surréalisme, which grew out of Dada, was more doctrinary; perhaps its most important feature was the advocacy of a deliberate, total self-surrender of the artist to his subliminal self, and the practice of automatic writing.[44]

So, after all, even a Joycean Dada and surrealism, against all odds. Marcus quotes Henri Lefebvre's famous pronouncement that "the meaning of modernity" is that it "carries within itself, from the beginning, a radical negation—Dada, this event which took place in a Zurich cafe."[45] The consubstantial Joycean avant-gardism and postmodernity mapped here is also an event of radical negation, one that took place in a Paris magazine and shook the world of letters.

---

42   Marcus, *Lipstick Traces*, 4.
43   Stuart Gilbert, "*transition* Days," *Transition Workshop*, ed. Eugene Jolas (New York: The Vanguard Press, 1949) 19.
44   Gilbert, "*transition* Days," 20–1.
45   Qtd in Marcus, *Lipstick Traces*, 21.

Again compare (as there is no contrast) this with Marcus' musings on the effects of punk music, its aesthetic irreducibility, its activist sense of necessity, its anti-establishment sentiments, and the tradition in its wake:

> listening to this relatively small body of work [...] I feel a sense of awe at how fine the music was: how irreducible it remains. What remains irreducible about this music is its desire to change the world. The desire is patent and simple, but it inscribes a story that is infinitely complex [...]. The desire begins with the demand to live not as an object but as a subject of history—to live as if something actually depended on one's actions—and that demand opens onto a free street.
> Damning God and the state, work and leisure, home and family, sex and play, the audience and itself, the music briefly made it possible to experience all those things as if they were not natural facts but ideological constructs.[46]

To a writer, the demand of living as "a subject" of history, not as its object, of living "as though something actually depended" on it, means first and foremost, to "write as though it matters," as per B. S. Johnson's 1973 maxim. And to do that requires first and foremost not to take "literature" and one's place within it for granted, but to fight for its future, which is the only way of claiming it for oneself in the present, as yesterday's wars have already been waged. Just as Marcus', this book too is about a (r)evolution of one conversation, with its task being "to lead speakers and listeners unaware of each other's existence to talk to one another," and to "maintain the ability to be surprised at how the conversation goes, and to communicate that sense of surprise to other people."[47] What kind of conversation has been had among the fifty post-Joycean writers in France, Britain, and the States, can be traced by reverting to its beginning.

5. GENEALOGIES OF PARALLAX, METEMPSYCHOSIS, TRACE, FORGERY, AND NEOLOGISM

Hence, the argument concludes on a paradox: it has applied a chronological approach to what essentially is posited as a non-linear cycle of returns, a "documentary archive" of the effects of Joyce's materialist poetics in post--war Anglo- and Francophone writing. Perhaps one only needs to expand onto a planetary level in order to realise the paradox as illusory: whereas on Earth, "revolution" signifies progress, with stars and planets it denotes turning and returning. Be that as it may, the rationale behind the chronological

---

46   Marcus, *Lipstick Traces*, 5.
47   Ibid, 21.

genealogy was to bring home the point about the lasting importance of these effects, reverberating in post-war experimental fiction well beyond 2000. The chronological approach, to be sure, is not without its pitfalls (the teleological fallacy, for example) and its inelegancies. There were many other possible modes of ordering, across individual chapters, concept- or theme-based. For instance, the pentad of the crucial Joyce-effects identified in the Introduction could have yielded the following micro-genealogies:

1) narrative parallax: most of the New Novel, esp. Nathalie Sarraute, Alain Robbe-Grillet and Claude Mauriac; Raymond Queneau and Georges Perec; from Angela Carter and Jeanette Winterson to David Mitchell; from William Gaddis and John Barth to David Foster Wallace;
2) stylistic metempsychosis: from Claude Simon to Hélène Cixous and Jacques Roubaud; the late Ann Quin, J.G. Ballard, and most of Iain Sinclair; from Thomas Pynchon and Harry Mathews to Ronald Sukenick and Ishmael Reed;
3) concrete writing: from Michel Butor to Maurice Roche; from B. S. Johnson to Alasdair Gray to Steven Hall; from William Gass to Raymond Federman to Mark Danielewski;
4) forgery of fiction: most of Oulipo and Édouard Levé; from William Burroughs and Kathy Acker to Kenneth Goldsmith and Mark Amerika; from the early Christine Brooke-Rose and Alan Burns to Stewart Home;
5) neologising the logos: from Robert Pinget to Philippe Sollers; from Anthony Burgess and Brigid Brophy via Brian Aldiss to Alan Moore; from Donald Barthelme and Walter Abish to Joshua Cohen.

Of course, this exercise in pigeonholing is an approximate one—more of degree than of kind—as many writers would easily fit more than just the one category they are assigned here. In fact, such complexly Joycean experimenters as Barthelme, Brooke-Rose, Burgess, Butor, Gass, Goldsmith, Johnson, Perec, Queneau, Sollers, Sukenick, and Sinclair—to pick just a dozen—have an oeuvre so protean as to partially fit the bill on all five counts.

Were one to pair up, in a quasi-Hassanian fashion, writers according to whether their Joyce is the author of *Ulysses* or the *Wake*, one could point out to some of their crucial differences. The *Ulysses* vs. *Finnegans Wake* dichotomy is reflected in the pentad already, the first two elements falling mainly within the compass of effects launched in *Ulysses,* elements four and five being in the *Wake*'s jurisdiction, with the central one appropriately positioned halfway. This binary would rewrite the genealogy as a series of such contrastive pairings as Robbe-Grillet vs. Butor, Johnson vs. Brophy, Pynchon vs. Barthelme, Perec vs. Queneau, Sinclair vs. Moore, Mathews vs. Sukenick, Roche vs. Sollers, Ballard vs. Aldiss, Foster Wallace vs. Cohen, etc.

Still other possible categorisations would present themselves were the focus to fall on the personality of the authors, for "experiment" is related to "experience" not only in terms of etymology. One could draw lines of development in terms of (feminist) fiction written by women (from Sarraute to Cixous; from Brooke-Rose, Brophy, and Quin to Carter, Winterson, and Acker); in terms of post-colonial experimentalism and fiction dealing with post-national politics (from Brophy to Gray; from Simon to Cixous; from Reed to Cohen); one could single out believers turned heretics (Burgess and Quin, Sorrentino and Butor) or heretics turned believers (Sollers only, really); one could examine the sociological binary of writers-exiles (e.g., Brooke-Rose, Burroughs, Gaddis, Butor) vs. writers-regionalists (e.g., Mauriac, Gray, Barth, and Moore), writers-public figures (e.g., Robbe-Grillet, Johnson, Burroughs again, and Cixous) vs. writers-recluses (e.g., Quin, Pynchon, Gaddis, and Pinget), again merely to point out that these are individual articulations of a dialectical movement thematised and synthesised to a paradigmatic degree in the consubstantial life and work of James Joyce.

It should not go without saying that the national division—into fiction "in" France, the UK, and USA—is as artificial as any, and always rather absurd in the radically international and transcultural enterprise called experimental fiction, especially one that takes its cue from a cosmopolitan like Joyce. It is the teller's hope that the tale told here has managed to bring into relief as many parallels and similarities as differences and specificities among the three cultural spaces, its comparative focus always on the lookout for cross-national ties among these writers and groups (Federman in the U.S., Mathews in the Oulipo, Brooke-Rose at Paris-Vincennes, Burroughs in Paris and London, Butor in Manchester), or even more relevantly perhaps, on affinities in terms of their practice of fiction. And so this gallery features the portraits of Aldiss and Ballard as heirs to the *nouveau roman* and Burroughs; Brooke-Rose as author of syntactic lipograms à la Oulipo; Federman as affiliated with the *Tel Quel*; Cixous identifying Heppenstall as the first *nouveau romancier*; Perec's *La Disparition* as inspired by Wright's *Gadsby*, etc.

Were one indeed to attempt any of the above, one would easily have teased out meaningful lines of connection that fall by the wayside of a merely chronological arrangement. The rationale, ultimately, behind deploying the chronological arrangement is that it contains—however implicitly or potentially—all of the above, and hides nothing, since "time" (to quote Robbe-Grillet quoting Sophocles) "sees all" and shall "[find] you out against your will."

6. "ONE MORE UNLOOKEDFOR CONCLUSION LEAPED AT" (*FW* 108.32): JOYCE'S BAROQUE ERROR

To conclude purely negatively from the positive absence of political odia and monetary requests that its page cannot ever have been a penproduct of a man or woman of that period or those parts is only one more unlookedfor conclusion leaped at, being tantamount to inferring from the nonpresence of inverted commas (sometimes called quotation marks) on any page that its author was always constitutionally incapable of misappropriating the spoken words of others.   (*FW* 108.29–36)

Behind some of the many possible mappings of the vast territory of post-Joycean literary experiment in France, Britain, and America, there also hovers the more fundamental question of the "intensity" and "productivity" of the "post-Joycean" status itself, which of course is never as uniform as the grouping of all these disparate writers under one rubric might suggest.

To be sure, the writers whose works were substantially (in)formed by their dialogue with Joyce are legion. To name but five of each of the three groups, these would include Butor, Cixous, Mauriac, Queneau, and Sollers (in France); Burgess, Brophy, Johnson, Moore, and Sinclair (in Britain); and Barth, Danielewski, Gass, Sukenick, and Sorrentino (in the USA). In other cases, the adjective "post-Joycean" forms a more accidental part of their broader "avant-garde" (Burroughs, Gray, Robbe-Grillet) or specifically "fringe" status (Acker's cyberpunk, Ballard's new-wave sci-fi, Levé's conceptualism). Whether the five Joyce-effects stretch beyond mere methodological "fiction" that governs the mapping of the vast terrain of post-war avant-garde or not, what is ultimately at stake is their effectivity for the future. In other words, if the current compendium has paid critical attention not only to voices substantially Joycean, but also to some more accidentally so, it was for the sake of capturing the polyphony of literary voices post-WW2. For as the introduction hoped to make clear, unlike the sort of evolutionary organicist tradition of the past into which the present grows (à la T.S. Eliot), the Joycean "tradition" is less determined by the supposed "greatness" of the past than by its orientation towards the future, its openness to further development and solicitation of a "perpetuation of creation."

And so, in order to conclude, *il faut reculer pour mieux sauter*: The revolutionary year of 1968 saw Philippe Sollers publish not only *Nombres*—his first truly experimental work of fiction—but also his book of essays, *Writing and the Experience of Limits*. In an essay that concludes the collection, "The Novel and the Experience of Limits," Sollers writes: "LET'S ADMIT IT—the novel has become the subject for polite conversation."[48] In his critique of the

---

48   Philippe Sollers, *Writing and the Experience of Limits*, ed. David Hayman, trans. Philip Barnard
      & David Hayman (New York: Columbia University Press, 1983) 185.

normalisation of literary modernity, Sollers invokes the "Trinitarian gospel" of Proust, Joyce, Kafka, in whose wake the contemporary novel is deemed to follow its pious procession. "Dialectical necessity," he writes,

> would have the new novelists complete what was present in germ in these three authors whose revolutionary genius everyone agrees to recognise. Other names may be summoned in support; nevertheless, what matters is to know how to isolate a linear evolution that makes the advances associated with these three names a guarantee for the elevation of the contemporary novelist—an elevation that, despite a few temporary obstacles, is quickly displayed in the by now infallible museum of cultural values.[49]

Sollers' criticism is clearly not levied against Proust, Joyce, or Kafka but rather against the shrines of literary prestige consecrated to their names, where critics in their Sunday best can come pay their Christian duty, all the better to ready themselves for the weekday, when it is "business as usual":

> the Balzacian novel appears in ever greater quantities, the humanists are no less humanistic, young humanists are always at hand to take over—and the moderns, since the exception they represent only confirms the rule, waste no time in revealing that their hidden desire was always to attain the modest recognition that they were modern at the right moment. Who can blame them for that? No one.[50]

In these "museums of cultural values," even terms like "avant-garde" and "experiment" come to be invested as signifiers without meaning—which by some "dialectical" impetus convey the idea of an experiment by way of conserving the status quo. "Avant-garde," as Sollers notes, "already contains the word garde. Strange combat, strange complicity."[51]

The rest of Sollers' essay consists in the unmasking of the many illusions surrounding the "progressiveness" of as "reactionary" a genre as the bourgeois novel, to whose desacralising and critique each of the Holy Trinity had devoted his writing. Having discussed Proust's critique of aestheticism, Sollers turns to Joyce whose "limit attained by *Finnegans Wake* is crucial" in that it turns "the reader" into "the act of deciphering that which will never be total and definitive."[52] Sollers speaks of the *Wake* as of a "nocturnal unknotting" of tongues, which thus describes a universal condition: "we are nothing other

---

49   Sollers, *Writing and the Experience of Limits*, 186.
50   Ibid.
51   Ibid.
52   Ibid, 197.

than this nocturnal and diurnal movement of the legible and illegible, in us, outside us—and this is precisely what we would rather not know." And yet:

> We prefer to think Joyce committed a baroque error; we speak calmly of Mallarmé's "failure"; we insinuate that Roussel pushed the joke a little too far, that Kafka liked his illness, that Lautréamont was mad, that Artaud should have been kept locked up, that Nerval or Nietzsche merely lost control in a situation anyone could have avoided— it's a matter of common sense. Or else these writers' existence is romanticized, even though they had absolutely no desire to be "writers" in the accepted sense of that word, even though they themselves repeatedly emphasized their impersonality.[53]

In a final self-reflexive description, this study hopes to have dissected the "strange combat" of Sollers' polemics, one which turns Joyce the obscure exile—whose *Ulysses* and especially *Finnegans Wake* were lambasted by the many fathers of the literary church as "heresies" and "failures"—into the new prophet of a new apostatic dogma, of the Church of Joyce. "In tandem with this apotheosis," as Louis Armand has recently argued,

> the Joyce "brand" has come increasingly to stand for, and to be an active and substantial agent within, a dominant post-War cultural capitalism. In effect, we might say that Adorno's "culture industry" is the neo-avant-garde whose predominance Peter Bürger so strenuously lamented, while "Joyce" has duly been erected as one of that industry's temporal idols (and sub-franchised to a whole array of "post-literatures") [...]. This state of affairs has come about precisely by way of the implied interdiction that insists we learn to become "Joyce's contemporaries" without Joyce ever being permitted to be claimed as ours.[54]

In a sense, as per Armand, this book has stood Richard Ellmann's opening premise—the pedagogical project of "learning to become Joyce's contemporary"—on its head, in order to examine how Joyce can be (has been) made contemporary to those avant-gardists who soldier on, fighting the wars of the "post-war" world, the "strange combat" of literary experimentalism in the age of late capitalism. That late capitalism whose masterstroke, as per Francis Fukuyama, is the kind of *laissez-faire* postmodernism of simulacrum and pastiche that so many of the experimentalists gathered here deplore. In another sense, this book also subverts David Hayman's project in "The Wake of the *Wake*," one of pinning down a Joycean "afterlife." Nowhere has the case been made, à la Hayman, that for "writers of 'experimental' fiction

---

53   Ibid.
54   Louis Armand, "'He Proves by Algebra': James Joyce's Post-Literary Incest Machines," *Journal of Modern Literature* 44.3 (Spring 2021): 64.

[...] Joyce's *Wake must be* a prime exemplar,"[55] presumably in order to be duly revered through emulation. Critiquing this kind of pedantry inherent in the dogma of the Joycean cultural industry, Armand's meditation on the status of so-called experiment in the wake of the *Wake*, warns against precisely the messianism implied in it:

> Eighty years after the publication of the *Wake*, what future is there for socalled "experimental" writing? And what place does Joyce hold in that future? Which is to say, a future as perceived from the vantage of Ellmann and Hayman, arraigned in full view of that looking-glass of its own effecting, with its spectres dutifully gathered behind it. A very "Joycean" vantage. [...] This is the risk of any messianism. In the case of Joyce there has been the tendency to conflate in him the messianism of avantgardes in general, so that in his neo-manifestations Joyce has frequently become the paradigm of a certain post-literary avant-gardism itself, married to precisely that kind of textual paternalism Joyce himself did so much to disrupt. Which is to say, of that curious paradox arising from an impatience with the past and an Oedipal attachment to its own belatedness.[56]

Were this book merely an exercise in "Joycean" scholarship projecting its self--image onto the "future of the novel," or in literary accountancy à la Hayman, it would be next to meaningless; to come back to Beckett: "literary criticism is not bookkeeping."[57]

This book has instead aimed to show that there was a great number of writers of the perfectly experimental ilk whose relation toward the *Wake* was problematic at best. To take just the five prominent members of the "Big B" club: on the matter of the *Wake*'s exemplary character, Ballard was openly hostile, Barth elusive, Brooke-Rose dismissive, Burroughs explicitly critical, and (B. S.) Johnson evasive. The present genealogy has also included writers who kept largely silent on the subject of a specifically Joycean "indebtedness" (an economic metaphor so popular with post-Joycean criticism)—like Simon, Pinget, Quin, Aldiss, Pynchon, Federman; writers who even were explicitly opposed to him and found critical "comparisons" with Joyce detrimental to the appreciation of their work—fewer, but still: Ballard, Gaddis, Roubaud; writers who contrariwise fashioned themselves as Joycean writers and consequently paled in comparison, suffering derogatory reductions of their work—Burgess, Johnson to some extent, Barth and Sukenick, Sollers and Cixous; and writers for whom being "Joycean" meant "to do unto him as he had

---

55 David Hayman, "Some writers in the wake of the *Wake*," *TriQuarterly* 38 (Winter 1977): 1, emphasis mine.

56 Armand, "He Proves by Algebra," 64.

57 Samuel Beckett, "Dante...Bruno. Vico..Joyce," *Our Exagmination Round His Factification for Incamination of Work in Progress: A Symposium*, ed. Samuel Beckett (New York: New Directions, 1929) 19.

done to others," and to mock/parody him (Butor, Brooke-Rose, Sorrentino, et al.). There is not one "correct" way of being "Joycean," and much less so, of being "experimental."

So, the project of constructing a genealogy of post-Joycean experimentation here has not been a pedagogical one—of "educating" the lesser mortals and "converting" them to the one true faith—neither was it an exercise in nostalgia. It has not supposed that all "experimental" fiction in the wake of the *Wake* is merely a kind of "neo" (à la Bürger), nor was it asking, like Robert Hughes in the opening of his seminal *The Shock of the New*, "What has our culture lost in 1980 that the avant-garde had in 1890?"[58] Instead of inquiring into what the Joycean avant-garde might still have had that post-WWII literary experiment lost, the question asked of the material gathered here was the more positive one of examining its gains. In that respect, unlike Ellmann's or Hayman's, this book has striven to construe its Joycean tradition as a "description of effects" rather than a "prescription of dogmas." This book's inquiry was undertaken primarily by directing interest towards that vital element in the work of Joyce that infuses (and is infused by) a spirit of experimentation. Experimentation not as vogue, affect, or doctrine, but as existential necessity: the condition, as per Dewey, of experience. What Donald Theall has called "the Joyce Era" extends in this book beyond a temporal placement, to encompass an experimental temper. "Joycean" not in any formal sense, but in the intuitive praxis of the "revolution of the word." Which is also the spirit in which the authors covered here revisited Joyce, lest they were to be reduced to a slavish imitation of a critical stance. As in Jolas' and Sollers', a polemic has resided at the heart of this project. As much as it has aimed for a "compendium" recuperating the frequently marginalised writing of the last eighty years, it has disavowed the logic of the paradigm that would make of this compendium a "linear evolution," or even an "anti-canon."

To various degrees and in varying kinds, the fifty writers included here are contemporaries of Joyce, or in other words, theirs is a contemporary writing. Not of some "Joycean" dogma or afterlife eternal, but of a materiality in and of language; hence the five axioms on which the genealogy is based: "parallax of structure," "metempsychosis of style," "concrete writing," "forgery of fiction," and "neologising the logos." Hence also the insistence that despite its chronological presentation, the genealogy is understood as a non-linear cycle of returns, a "documentary archive" of the effects of Joyce's materialist poetics. The ultimate benefit of the simple chronological arrangement consists in how it allows for the least amount of distraction (conceptual, biographical, ideological, or other) from what ultimately matters most: the writing itself. What the Joycean avant-garde was built upon, and what its effects will have

58   Robert Hughes, *The Shock of the New* (New York: Knopf, 1991) 1.

resonated through. What was in its beginning, what was with Joyce, what was Joyce: the revolution of the word.

London-Paris-Prague
2014–2021

CHAPTER-BY-CHAPTER BIBLIOGRAPHY

WORKS BY JAMES JOYCE

D	*Dubliners* (ed. Margot Norris, New York: Norton & Co., 2006)
FW	*Finnegans Wake* (New York: Viking Press, 1959)
P	*A Portrait of the Artist as a Young Man,* ed. Jerri Johnson (Oxford: Oxford University Press, 2000)
SH	*Stephen Hero* (New York: New Directions, 1963)
U	*Ulysses,* ed. Hans Walter Gabler (New York: Garland, 1984)
JJ	Richard Ellmann, *James Joyce* (Revised Edition, Oxford: Oxford University Press, 1982).
L I, II, III	*The Letters of James Joyce I, II, III*, eds. Stuart Gilbert & Richard Ellmann (New York: Viking Press, 1966)

INTRODUCTION

ADAMS, Robert Martin. *Afterjoyce* (New York: Oxford University Press, 1977).

ATTRIDGE, Derek, ed. *Acts of Literature* (New York: Routledge, 1992).

ATTRIDGE, Derek, ed. *Cambridge Companion to James Joyce* (Cambridge: Cambridge University Press, 2004).

BAZARNIK, Katarzyna. *Joyce & Liberature* (Prague: Litteraria Pragensia Books, 2011).

BECKETT, Samuel, ed. *Our Exagmination Round His Factification for Incamination of Work in Progress: A Symposium* (New York: New Directions, 1929).

BLOOM, Harold. *The Western Canon—The Books and School of the Ages* (New York: Harcourt, 1994).

boundary 2, 1.1 (Autumn 1972).

BUDGEN, Frank. *James Joyce and the Making of Ulysses* (London: Oxford University Press, 1972).

BÜRGER, Peter. *Theory of the Avant-Garde*, trans. Michael Shaw (Minneapolis: Minneapolis University Press, 1984).

DEWEY, John. *Experience and Nature* (La Salle: Open Court, 1925).

GIFFORD, Don. *Ulysses Annotated—Notes for James Joyce's Ulysses* (University of California Press, 2008).

ELIOT, Thomas Stearns. *Selected Prose of T. S. Eliot*, ed. Frank Kermode (London: Harvest, 1975).

FITCH, Noel Riley (ed). *In transition: A Paris Anthology - Writing and Art from transition Magazine 1927–30* (New York: Doubleday, 1990).

HAYMAN, David & ANDERSON, Elliott, eds. *In the Wake of the Wake* (Madison: University of Wisconsin Press, 1978).

JOLAS, Eugène, ed. *Transition Workshop* (New York: The Vanguard Press, 1949).

KAUFMANN, Michael. *Textual Bodies: Modernism, Postmodernism, and Print* (London/Toronto: Associated University Press, 1994).

KENNER, Hugh. *A Colder Eye - The Modern Irish Writers* (London: Allen Lane, 1983).

The Kenyon Review X.3 (Summer 1948).

LEVIN, Harry. *James Joyce—A Critical Introduction* (1941), A Revised Edition (New York: New Directions, 1960).

LEVITT, Morton P. *Modernist Survivors* (Columbus: Ohio State University Press, 1987).

LUKÁCS, Georg. *The Theory of the Novel*, trans. Anna Bostock (orig. 1920; Cambridge: MIT, 1971).

McMILLAN, Dougald. *Transition 1927-38: The History of a Literary Era* (New York: George Bra-ziller, 1976).

MITCHELL, W.J.T. "Realism, Irrealism, and Ideology: A Critique of Nelson Goodman," *Journal of Aesthetic Education,* 25.1 (Spring 1991).

POGGIOLI, Renato. *The Theory of the Avant-Garde,* trans. Gerald Fitzgerald (Cambridge, Mass.: Harvard University Press, 1968).

SPURR, David. "Fatal Signatures: Forgery and Colonization in *Finnegans Wake,*" *European Joyce Studies, Vol. 8: Joyce – Feminism/Post/ Colonialism*, ed. Ellen Carol Jones (Amsterdam: Rodopi, 1998).

THEALL, Donald F. *Beyond the Word: Reconstructing Sense in the Joyce Era of Technology, Culture and Communication* (Toronto: University of Toronto Press, 1995).

WAUGH, Patricia, ed. *Revolutions of the Word: Intellectual Contexts for the Study of Modern Litera-ture* (London/New York: Arnold, 1997).

WERNER, Craig Hansen. *Paradoxical Resolutions* (Urbana/Chicago/London: University of Illi-nois Press, 1982).

1. CHAPTER ONE: JOYCE AND THE NEW NOVEL (1947-67)

BABCOCK, Arthur E. *The New Novel in France – Theory and Practice of the Nouveau Roman* (Lon-don: Prentice Hall International, University of Southern California, 1997).

HEATH, Stephen. *The Nouveau Roman: A Study in the Practice of Writing* (London: Elek Books, 1972).

LEHMAN, John. *I Am My Brother* (London: Longman, 1960).

MARKUS, Radvan, et al. (ed.) *Tradition and Modernity – New Essays in Irish Studies* (Prague: Char-les University, 2014).

MERCIER, Vivian. *The New Novel: From Queneau To Pinget* (New York: Farrar, Strauss & Giroux, 1971).

SAGE, Laurent Le, ed. *The French New Novel: An Introduction and a Sampler* (University Park: Pennsylvania State University Press, 1962).

STOLTZFUS, Ben. *Alain Robbe-Grillet – The Body of the Text* (London/New Jersey: Associated Uni-versity Press, 1985).

STURROCK, John. *The French New Novel* (London: Oxford University Press, 1969).

1.1 Nathalie Sarraute

AG   *The Age of Suspicion*, trans. Maria Jolas (New York: G. Braziller, 1963)
ES   *L'Ère du soupçon* (Paris: Gallimard, 1956)
PI   *Portrait d'un inconnu* (Paris: Gallimard, 1948)
T   *Tropismes* (Paris: Denoël, 1939)
Tr   *Tropisms*, trans. Maria Jolas (orig. 1963; New York: New Directions, 2015)

BARBOUR, Sarah. *Nathalie Sarraute and the Feminist Reader – Identities in Process*_(London/To-ronto: Associated University Press, 1993).

Contemporary Literature (Spring 1973).

MINOGUE, Valerie. *Nathalie Sarraute and the War of the Words: A Study of Five Novels* (Edinburgh: Edinburgh University Press, 1981).

O'BEIRNE, Emer. *Reading Nathalie Sarraute – Dialogue and Distance* (Oxford/New York: Oxford University Press, 1999).

The Paris Review 114 (Spring 1990).

1.2 Alain Robbe-Grillet

FNN *For a New Novel*, trans. Richard Howard (New York: Grove Press, 1965)

LJ   *La Jalousie* (Paris: Éditions Minuit, 1957)
LV   *Le Voyageur – textes, causeries et entretiens (1947–2001)* (Paris: Christian Bourgois, 2001)
PNR   *Pour un nouveau roman* (Paris: Les Éditions Minuit, 1961)
PVE   *Préface à une vie d'écrivain* (Paris: Seuil, 2005)
TN   *Two Novels*, trans. Richard Howard (New York: Grove Press, 1965)

BUTLER, Christopher. *After the Wake: An Essay on the Contemporary Avant-Garde* (Oxford: Clarendon Press, 1980).
MORRISSETTE, Bruce. *The Novels of Robbe-Grillet* (Ithaca/London: Cornell University Press, 1975).
SAVAGE BROSMAN, Catharine, ed. *Dictionary of Literary Biography, Volume 83: French Novelists Since 1960* (Tulane University, Detroit: The Gale Group, 1989).
STOLTZFUS, Ben. *Alain Robbe-Grillet – the Body of the Text* (London/New Jersey: Associated University Press, 1985).
SZANTO, George H. *Narrative Consciousness: Structure and Perception in the Fiction of Kafka, Beckett, and Robbe-Grillet* (Austin: University of Texas Press, 1972).

1.3 Claude Simon
BP   *La Bataille de Pharsale* (Paris: Éditions de Minuit, 1969)
H   *Histoire* (Paris: Éditions de Minuit, 1967)
RF   *La Route des Flanders* (Paris: Éditions de Minuit, 1960)
T *Triptyque* (Paris: Éditions de Minuit, 1973)

BIRN, Randi & GOULD, Karen, eds. *Orion Blinded – Essays on Claude Simon* (Lewisburg: Bucknell University Press, 1981).
BRITTON, Celia, ed. *Claude Simon* (London/New York: Longman, 1993).
CALLE-GRUBER, Mireille. *Claude Simon : une vie à écrire* (Paris : Éditions du Seuil, 2011).
DUNCAN, Alastair. *Claude Simon: Adventures in Words* (Manchester/New York: Manchester University Press, 1994).
GRIVEL, Charles, ed. *Écriture de la religion, écriture du roman* (Lille: Presses de Lille, 1979).
LOUBÈRE, J. A. E. *The Novels of Claude Simon* (Ithaca/London: Cornell University Press, 1975).
ORR, Mary. *Claude Simon – The Intertextual Dimension* (Glasgow: University of Glasgow, 1993).
Review of Contemporary Fiction 5.1 (Spring 1985).
SAVAGE BROSMAN, Catharine, ed. *Dictionary of Literary Biography, Volume 332: Nobel Prize Laureates in Literature, Part 4: Quasimodo-Yeats* (Tulane University, Detroit: The Gale Group, 2007).

1.4 Robert Pinget
CD   *Clope au dossier* (Paris: Éditions Minuit, 1961)
GF   *Graal Flibuste* (Paris: Éditions Minuit, 1956)
GrFl   *Graal Flibuste*, trans. Anna Fitzgerald (London/Dublin: Dalkey Archive Press, 2014)
I   *L'Inquisitoire* (Paris: Éditions Minuit, 1962); *The Inquisitory*, trans. Donald Watson (London/Dublin: Dalkey Archive Press, 2003)
LF   *Le Fiston* (Paris: Éditions Minuit, 1959)
R&B   *Le renard et la boussole* (Paris: Éditions Minuit, 1963)
T   *Trio—Between Fantoine and Agapa, That Voice, Passacaglia*, trans. Barbara Wright (orig. 1978 & 1982; Normal/London: Dalkey Archive Press, 2005)

HENKELS, Robert M. *Robert Pinget – The Novel as Quest* (The University of Alabama Press, 1979).
SAVAGE BROSMAN, Catharine, ed. *Dictionary of Literary Biography, Volume 83: French Novelists Since 1960* (Tulane University, Detroit: The Gale Group, 1989).
Review of Contemporary Fiction 3.2 (Summer 1983).
Robert Pinget à la lettre – Entretiens avec Madeleine Renouard (Paris: Belfond, 1993).

1.5 Claude Mauriac

A   *L'Agrandissement* (Paris: Albin Michel, 1963)
AC   *L'Alittérature contemporaine* (Paris: Albin Michel, 1958)
DLAL   *De la littérature à l'alittérature* (Paris: Bernard Grasset, 1969)
LDV   *Le Dîner en ville* (Paris: Albin Michel, 1959)
MSCH   *La Marquise sortit à cinq heures* (Paris: Albin Michel, 1961)
LTI   *Le Temps immobile, Vol. 1* (Paris: Grasset, 1974)
O   *L'Oubli* (Paris: Grasset, 1970)
TFSF   *Toutes les femmes sont fatales* (Paris: Albin Michel, 1957)

ROUDIEZ, Leon S. *French Fiction Today: A New Direction* (New Brunswick: Rutgers University Press, 1972).

1.6 Michel Butor

D   *Degrés* (Paris: Gallimard, 1960)
ET   *L'Emploi du temps* (Paris: Éditions Minuit, 1956)
M   *La Modification* (Paris: Éditions Minuit, 1957)
MO   *Mobile* (Paris: Gallimard, 1962)
P   *Portrait d'artiste en jeune singe* (Paris: Gallimard, 1967)
PM   *Passage de Milan* (Paris: Éditions Minuit, 1954)
R1   *Répertoire 1* (Paris: Éditions Minuit, 1960)
RA   *Réseau aérien* (Paris: Gallimard, 1962)

Michel Butor – Entretiens: Quarante ans de vie littéraire, Vol. 1–3 (Paris: Éditions Joseph K., 1996).
Michel Butor – Rencontre avec Roger-Michel Allemand (Paris: Argol, 2009).
LYDON, Mary. *Perpetuum Mobile – A Study of the Novels and Aesthetics of Michel Butor* (Edmonton: The University of Alberta Press, 1980).
McWILLIAMS, Dean. *The Narratives of Michel Butor: The Writer as Janus* (Columbus: Ohio University Press, 1978).
SPENCER, Michael. *Michel Butor* (New York: Twayne Publishers, 1974).
WAELTI-WALTERS, Jennifer. *Michel Butor – A Study of His View of the World and a Panorama of His Work 1954-1974* (Victoria: Sono Nis Press, 1977).

2. CHAPTER TWO: JOYCE IN BRITAIN, 1955–75

BERGONZI, Bernard. *The Situation of the Novel* (London: MacMillan, 1970/1979).
BRADBURY, Malcolm. *No, not Bloomsbury* (London: André Deutsch, 1987).
BRADBURY, Malcolm. *Possibilities* (Oxford: Oxford University Press, 1973).
BOOTH, Francis. *Among Those Left—The British Experimental Novel 1940-1980* (self-published, 2012).
BUCKNELL, G. J. *Rayner Heppenstall – A Critical Study* (London: Champaign, 2007).
CASERIO, Robert L., ed. *The Cambridge Companion to Twentieth-Century British Novel* (Cambridge: Cambridge University Press, 2009).
JOHNSON, B. S. *Aren't You Rather Young to Be Writing Your Memoirs?* (London: Hutchinson & Co., 1973).
Le Monde 6959.viia (18 May 1967).
RABINOVITZ, Rubin. *The Reaction against Experiment in the English Novel 1950-1960* (New York: Columbia University Press, 1967).
SINFIELD, Alan, ed. *Society and Literature 1945-1970*, ed. (London: Methuen & Co., 1983).
STEVENSON, Randall. *The Last of England?* (Oxford: Oxford University Press, 2004).
SUTHERLAND, J.A. *Fiction and the Fiction Industry* (London: Athlone, 1978).

2.1 Anthony Burgess
CO   *A Clockwork Orange* (London/New York: Norton Critical Edition, 2010)
J   *Joysprick* (London: André Deutsch Ltd., 1973)
MF   *MF* (New York: Alfred A. Knopf, 1971)
NLS   *Nothing Like the Sun* (London: Ballantine Books, 1965)
NS   *Napoleon Symphony* (New York: Alfred A. Knopf, 1974)
RJ   *ReJoyce* (New York: Ballantine Books, 1966)

AGGELER, Geoffrey. *Anthony Burgess – The Artist as Novelist* (University of Alabama Press, 1979).
AGGELER, Geoffrey, ed. *Critical Essays on Anthony Burgess* (Boston: G. K. Hall & Co., 1986).
COWLEY, Malcolm, ed. *Writers at Work: Paris Review Interviews* (New York: Viking, 1976).
ROUGHLEY, Alan R., ed. *Anthony Burgess and Modernity* (Manchester: Manchester University Press, 2008).
McCORMACK, Thomas, ed. *Afterwords* (London: Harper & Row, 1968).
Modern Fiction Studies 27 (Autumn 1981).

2.2 B. S. Johnson
AA   *Albert Angelo* (London: Constable, 1964)
ARY   *Aren't You Rather Young to Be Writing Your Memoirs?* (London: Hutchinson & Co., 1973)
CM   *Christie Malry's Own Double-Entry* (London: Collins, 1973)
HMN   *House Mother Normal* (London: Collins, 1971)
ST   *See the Old Lady Decently* (London: Hutchinson, 1975)
T   *Trawl* (London: Collins, 1968)

COE, Jonathan. *Like a Fiery Elephant* (London: Picador, 2004).
CONTE, Joseph M. *Design and Debris: A Chaotics of Postmodern American Fiction* (Tuscaloosa: University of Alabama Press, 2002).
HEAD, Dominic. *The Cambridge Introduction to Modern British Fiction, 1950–2000* (Cambridge: Cambridge University Press, 2002).
Review of Contemporary Fiction 5.2 (Summer 1985).
TEW, Philip. *B. S. Johnson – A Critical Reading* (Manchester, New York: Manchester University Press, 2001).

2.3 Alan Burns
B *Babel* (London: Calder & Boyars, 1969)

BURNS, Alan & SUGNET, Charles, eds. *Imagination on Trial* (London: Allison & Busby, 1981).
GORDON, Giles, ed. *Beyond the Words* (London: Hutchinson, 1975).
Review of Contemporary Fiction 17.2 (Summer 1997).

2.4 Brigid Brophy
IT   *In Transit* (London: MacDonald, 1969)

Contemporary Literature 17 (Spring 1976).
LAWRENCE, Karen. *Penelope Voyages: Women and Travel in the British Literary Tradition* (Ithaca/London: Cornell University Press, 1994).
LAWRENCE, Karen, ed. *Transcultural Joyce* (Cambridge: Cambridge University Press, 1998).
London Review of Books 2.3 (21 February 1980).
Review of Contemporary Fiction 15.3 (Fall 1995).
The Listener (25 September 1969).

2.5 Ann Quin

B   *Berg* (Chicago: Dalkey Archive, 2001)
P   *Passages* (Chicago: Dalkey Archive, 2003)
Th   *Three* (Chicago: Dalkey Archive, 2001)
Tr   *Tripticks* (Chicago: Dalkey Archive, 2002)

BROOKE-ROSE, Christine. *Stories, Theories and Things* (Cambridge: Cambridge University Press, 1991).
FRIEDMAN, Ellen G. & FUCHS, Miriam, eds. *Breaking the Sequence – Women's Experimental Fiction* (Princeton: Princeton University Press, 1989).
MOSELEY, Merritt, ed. *Dictionary of Literary Biography, Volume 231: British Novelists Since 1960* (The Gale Group: 2000).
Hungarian Journal of English and American Studies 5.2 (1999).
Liberated Arts 1.1 (2015).
Times Literary Supplement (25 June 1964; 2 June 1966).

2.6 Christine Brooke-Rose (I)

B   *Between* (Manchester: Carcanet Press, 1986)
O   *Out* (Manchester: Carcanet Press, 1986)
S   *Such* (Manchester: Carcanet Press, 1986)
T   *Thru* (Manchester: Carcanet Press, 1986)

BIRCH, Sarah. *Christine Brooke-Rose and Contemporary Fiction* (Oxford: Clarendon Press, 1994).
BRADBURY, Malcolm. *No, not Bloomsbury* (London: André Deutsch, 1987).
BROOKE-ROSE, Christine. *Stories, Theories and Things* (Cambridge: Cambridge University Press, 1991).
FRIEDMAN, Ellen G. & MARTIN, Richard, eds. *Utterly Other Discourse: the Texts of Christine Brooke-Rose* (Chicago: Dalkey Archive Press, 1995).
LAWRENCE, Karen. *Techniques for Living: Fiction and Theory in the Work of Christine Brooke-Rose* (Columbus: The Ohio State University Press, 2010).
Review of Contemporary Fiction 9.3 (Fall 1989).
SHAFFER, E. S., ed. *Comparative Criticism,* Volume 10 (Cambridge: Cambridge University Press, 1988).
WAUGH, Patricia. *Metafiction: The Theory and Practice of Conscious Fiction* (London: Methuen, 1984).

3. CHAPTER THREE: THE AMERICAN LITERARY EXPERIMENT, 1953–1973

ALLEN, Walter. *Tradition and Dream* (London: Dent, 1966).
BELLAMY, Joe David, ed. *The New Fiction – Interviews with Innovative American Writers* (Urbana, Chicago, London: University of Illinois Press, 1974).
BERGONZI, Bernard. *The Situation of the Novel* (London: Macmillan, 1970/1979).
GEDIN, Per. *Literature in the Market Place* (London 1977).
GRANTA 1 (Spring 1979).
LAWRENCE, Karen, ed. *Transcultural Joyce* (Cambridge: Cambridge University Press, 1998).
NOVILLO-CORVALÁN, Patricia. *Borges and Joyce – An Infinite Conversation* (Leeds: Maney Publishing, 2011).
SUKENICK, Ronald. *In Form: Digressions on the Act of Fiction* (Carbondale/Edwardsville: Southern Illinois University Press, 1985).
TANNER, Tony. *City of Words – American Fiction 1950–1970* (London: Jonathan Cape, 1971).
Wisconsin Studies in Contemporary Literature (Summer 1965).

3.1 William S. Burroughs

NE   *Nova Express* (London: Jonathan Cape, 1966)
Q   *Queer* (London/New York: Penguin, 1985)
TTTE   *The Ticket that Exploded* (Paris: Olympia Press, 1962)
WL   *The Western Lands* (New York: Viking Press, 1987)

BURROUGHS, William. *Burroughs Live: The Collected Interviews of William S. Burroughs 1960–1997* (Los Angeles/New York: Semiotext(e), 2001).
HARRIS, Oliver. *William Burroughs and the Secret of Fascination* (Carbondale/Edwardsville: Southern Illinois University Press, 2003).
LYDENBERG, Robin. *Word Cultures – Radical Theory and Practice in William S. Burroughs' Fiction* (Urbana/Chicago: University of Illinois Press, 1987).
MENGHAM, Rod, ed. *An Introduction to Contemporary Fiction* (Cambridge: Polity Press, 1999).
MILES, Barry. *William Burroughs: El Hombre Invisible* (New York: Hyperion, 1994).
MOTTRAM, Eric. *William Burroughs – The Algebra of Need* (London: Marion Boyars Ltd, 1977).
MURPHY, Timothy S. *Wising Up the Marks – The Amodern William Burroughs* (Berkeley/Los Angeles: University of California Press, 1997).
NORSE, Harold. *The Beat Hotel* (San Diego: Atticus Press, 1983).

3.2 William Gaddis

AA   *Agapē Agape* (New York: Viking, 2002)
J R   *J R* (New York: Alfred Knopf, 1975)
TR   *The Recognitions* (New York: Harcourt Brace & Co., 1955)

ALBERTS, Crystal, LEISE, Christopher, & VANWESENBEECK, Birger, eds. *William Gaddis, "The Last of Something": Critical Essays* (London: McFarland & Co., 2010).
MOORE, Stephen. *William Gaddis* (Boston: G. K. Hall & Co., 1989).
Letters of William Gaddis, ed. Stephen Moore (Champaign/London/Dublin: Dalkey Archive Press, 2013)
New York Times Book Review (14 July 1974).
Saturday Review (4 October 1975).
The Paris Review Interviews II (London: Picador, 2007).
Wisconsin Studies in Comparative Literature 6.2 (Summer 1965).
WOLFE, Peter. *A Vision of His Own – The Mind and Art of William Gaddis* (Madison, London: Associated University Press, 1997).

3.3 John Barth

FB   *The Friday Book – Essays and Other Nonfiction* (New York: G. P. Putnam's Sons, 1984)
L   *LETTERS* (New York: Fawcett Columbine, 1979)
LF   *Lost in the Funhouse* (New York: Doubleday, 1968)

Critique 37.4 (Summer 1996).
ROEMER, Marjorie Godlin. "The Paradigmatic Mind: John Barth's *Letters*," *Twentieth Century Literature* (33.1, Spring 1987).
SAFER, Elaine B. *The Contemporary American Comic Epic: The Novels of Barth, Pynchon, Gaddis, and Kesey* (Detroit: Wayne State University Press, 1988).
Twentieth Century Literature (April 1973).

3.4 William H. Gass

FF   *Finding a Form* (New York: Alfred Knopf, 1996)
FFL   *Fiction and the Figures of Life* (New York: Alfred Knopf, 1971)
TT   *The Tunnel* (New York: Alfred Knopf, 1995)

WMLF   *Willie Masters' Lonesome Wife* (New York: Alfred Knopf, 1971)
WWW   *The World Within the Word* (New York: Alfred Knopf, 1978)

Conversations with William H. Gass, ed. Theodore G. Ammon (Jackson: University of Mississippi Press, 2003).
McCAFFERY, Larry. *The Metafictional Muse: The Works of Robert Coover, Donald Barthelme, and William H. Gass* (Pittsburgh: University of Pittsburgh Press, 1982).

3.5 Donald Barthelme
CL   *City Life* (New York: Farrar, Strauss & Giroux, 1970)
DF   *The Dead Father* (New York: Farrar, Strauss & Giroux, 1975)
N-K   *Not-Knowing: The Essays and Interviews of Donald Barthelme*, ed. Kim Herzinger, introduction John Barth (New York: Random House, 1997)
SW   *Snow White* (New York: Touchstone, 1967)

D'HAEN, Theo & BERTENS, Hans, eds. *Narrative Turns and Minor Genres in Postmodernism* (Amsterdam: Rodopi, 1995).
HUDGENS, Michael Thomas. *Donald Barthelme – Postmodernist American Writer* (Lewiston: The Edwin Mellen Press, 2001).
PATTESON, Richard F., ed. *Critical Essays on Donald Barthelme* (New York: G. K. Hall & Co., 1992).
WALSH, Richard. *Novel Arguments. Reading Innovative American Fiction* (Cambridge: Cambridge University Press, 1995).

3.6 Thomas Pynchon
GR   *Gravity's Rainbow* (New York: Viking Press, 1973)
M&D   *Mason&Dixon* (New York: Henry Holt & Co., 1997)
SL   *Slow Learner* (New York: Little & Brown, 1984)
V   *V.* (Philadelphia: Lippincott, 1963)

BLOOM, Harold, ed. *Thomas Pynchon* (Philadelphia: Chelsea House Publishers, 2003).
Comparative Literature Studies 26 (March 1979).
COWART, David. *Thomas Pynchon – The Art of Allusion* (Carbondale/Edwardsville: Southern Illinois University Press, 1980).
DUGDALE, John. *Thomas Pynchon: Allusive Parables of Power* (London: MacMillan, 1990).
HOHNMANN, Charles. *Thomas Pynchon's Gravity's Rainbow* (New York, Bern, Frankfurt: Peter Lang Publishing, 1986).
LEVINE, George & LEVERENZ, David, eds. *Mindful Pleasures: Essays on Thomas Pynchon* (Boston: Little, Brown, 1976).
MOORE, Thomas. *The Style of Connectedness: Gravity's Rainbow and Thomas Pynchon* (Columbia: University of Missouri Press, 1987).
NEWMAN, Robert D. *Understanding Thomas Pynchon* (Columbia: University of South Carolina Press, 1986).
SEED, David. *The Fictional Labyrinths of Thomas Pynchon* (London: Macmillan, 1988).
STONEHILL, Brian. *The Self-Conscious Novel: Artifice in Fiction from Joyce to Pynchon* (Philadelphia: University of Pennsylvania Press, 1988).
Southwest Review 83.4 (1998).
The New Republic 203.2-3 (July 9-16 1990).

4. CHAPTER FOUR: JOYCEAN OULIPO, OULIPIAN JOYCE

4.1 The Joys of Constraint and Potential

KENNER, Hugh. *Flaubert, Joyce and Beckett: The Stoic Comedians* (Boston: Beacon Press, 1962).
KENNER, Hugh. *A Colder Eye – The Modern Irish Writers* (London: Allen Lane, 1983).

MATHEWS, Harry & BROTCHIE Alastair, eds. *Oulipo Compendium* (London: Atlas Press, 1998).
Oulipo – La Littérature potentielle: créations, re-créations, recreations (Paris: Gallimard, 1973).
SAUSSURE, Ferdinand de. *The Third Course of Lectures in General Linguistics (1910–1911)*, trans. & ed. E. Komatsu & R. Harris (Oxford: Pergamon, 1993).
TELLIER, Hervé le. *Esthétique de l'Oulipo* (Bordeaux: Le Castor Astral, 2006).
WARDRIP-FRUIN, Noah & MONTFORT, Nick, eds. *The New Media Reader* (Cambridge/London: The MIT Press, 2003).
Wisconsin Studies in Comparative Literature 6.2 (Summer 1965).

4.2 Raymond Queneau

BCL	*Bâtons, chiffres, lettres* (Paris: Gallimard, 1965)
EdS	*Exercises de style* (Paris: Gallimard, 1947)
EiS	*Exercises in Style*, trans. Barbara Wright (New York: New Directions, 1985)
LC	*Le chiendent* (Paris: Gallimard, 1933)
LD	*Last Days*, trans. Barbara Wright (Normal, IL: Dalkey Archive Press, 1990)
LDJ	*Les derniers jours* (Paris: Gallimard, 1936)
OCSM	*Les Oeuvres completes de Sally Mara* (Paris: Gallimard, 1962)
OETT	*On est toujours trop bon avec les femmes* (Paris: Scorpion, 1947)
RQ	*Oeuvres completes*, ed. Pléiade (Paris: Gallimard, 2002)
WATW	*We Always Treat Women Too Well*, trans. Barbara Wright (orig. 1981; Richmond: Alma Books, 2015)

BERGHEAUD, Lise. *Queneau et les formes intranquilles de la modernité* (Paris: Éditions Champion, 2010).
LEROUX, Jean-François, ed. *Dictionary of Literary Biography, Volume 258: Modern French Poets* (University of Ottawa: The Gale Group, 2002).
QUENEAU, Raymond. *Entretiens avec Georges Charbonnier* (Paris: Gallimard, 1962).
SIMONET, Claude. *Queneau déchiffré* (Paris: René Juillard, 1962).
Yale French Studies 8 (1951).

4.3 Georges Perec

LD	*La Disparition* (Paris: Denoel, 1969)
LUM	*Life: A User's Manual*, trans. David Bellos (Boston: David Godine, 2008)
LVME	*La vie mode d'emploi* (Paris: Hachette, 1979)
P/C	*Penser/Classer* (Paris: Hachette, 1985)
V	*A Void*, trans. Gilbert Adair (London: Harvill, 1994)

L'Arc 76 (1979).
Atlas de littérature potentielle (Paris: Gallimard, 1981).
BERTELLI, Dominique & RIBIÈRE, Mireille, eds. *Georges Perec – Entretiens et conférences, Volumes I-III* (Paris: Joseph K., 2003).
Cahier des Charges, eds. Hans Hartje, Bernard Magné, and Jacques Neefs (Paris: CNRS Éditions, 1993).
GASCOIGNE, David. *The Games of Fiction – Georges Perec and Modern French Ludic Narrative* (Oxford: Peter Lang, 2006).
LAWRENCE, Karen, ed. *Transcultural Joyce* (Cambridge: Cambridge University Press, 1998).
MOTTE, Warren F., Jr. *The Poetics of Experiment – A Study of the Work of Georges Perec* (Lexington: French Forum Publishers, 1984).
SCHWARTZ, Paul. *Georges Perec – Traces of his Passage* (Birmingham, Alabama: Summa Publications, 1988).
The Yearbook of English Studies – Anglo-French Literary Relations, Special Number 15 (1982).
WRIGHT, Ernest Vincent. *Gatsby,* (New York: Ramble House Edition, 1939).

4.4 Jacques Roubaud

Journal of Modern Literature 34.3 (Spring 2011).

MONTEMONT, Véronique. *Jacques Roubaud, l'amour du nombre* (Lille: Presses Universitaires du Septentrion, 2004).

POUCEL, Jean-Jacques F. *Jacques Roubaud and the Invention of Memory* (Chapel Hill: University of North Carolina Press, 2006).

TAYLOR, John, ed. *Paths to Contemporary French Literature*, Vol. 2 (New Brunswick, New Jersey: Transaction Publishers, 2009).

4.5 Harry Mathews

C   *The Conversions* (Chicago: Dalkey Archive, 1997)

CPM   *The Case of the Persevering Maltese* (Champaign/London: Dalkey Archive Press, 2003)

J   *The Journalist* (Boston: David Godine, 1994)

O   *The Sinking of the Odradek Stadion and Other Novels* (London: Harper & Row, 1985)

T   *Tlooth* (Chicago: Dalkey Archive, 1998)

Chicago Review 43.2 (Spring 1997).

CONTE, Joseph M. *Design and Debris: A Chaotics of Postmodern American Fiction* (Tuscaloosa: University of Alabama Press, 2002).

LEAMON, Warren. *Harry Mathews* (New York: Twayne Publishers, 1993).

L'Esprit Créateur 7.2 (Summer 1967).

MATTHEWS, Harry. *The Case of the Persevering Maltese – Collected Essays* (Champaign/London: Dalkey Archive Press, 2003).

Review of Contemporary Fiction 7.3 (Fall 1987).

5. CHAPTER FIVE: EXPERIMENT IN BRITISH FICTION (1975–2005)

BENTLEY, Nick, ed. *British Fiction of the 1990s* (Oxford: Routledge, 2005).

BERGER, John. "Lost Prophets," *New Society* (6 March, 1975).

BOOTH, Francis. *Among Those Left—The British Experimental Novel 1940-1980* (self-published, 2012).

BURGESS, Anthony. *Ninety-Nine Novels: The Best In English Since 1939 / A Personal Choice By Anthony Burgess* (London: Allison & Busby, 1984).

The End of the English Novel, GRANTA 3 (Spring 1980).

LODGE, David. *The Novelist at the Crossroads* (New York: Cornell University Press, 1971).

Prospect Magazine 22 (August 1997).

SCOTT, Jeremy. *The Demotic Voice in Contemporary British Fiction* (New York: Palgrave MacMillan, 2009).

TAYLOR, D. J. *A Vain Conceit* (London: Bloomsbury Publishing, 1989).

5.0 Christine Brooke-Rose (II)

A   *Amalgamemnon* (Manchester: Carcanet Press, 1984; Chicago: Dalkey Archive, 1994)

GM   *A Grammar of Metaphor* (London: Secker & Warburg, 1958)

I A   *Invisible Author* (Columbus: Ohio State University Press, 2002)

LEO   *Life, End Of* (Manchester: Carcanet Press, 2006)

N   *Next* (Manchester: Carcanet Press, 1998)

RU   *A Rhetoric of the Unreal: Studies in Narrative and Structure* (Cambridge: Cambridge University Press, 1981)

S   *Subscript* (Manchester: Carcanet Press, 1999)

STT   *Stories, Theories and Things* (Cambridge: Cambridge University Press, 1991)

T   *Textermination* (Manchester: Carcanet Press, 1991)

V   *Verbivore* (Manchester: Carcanet Press, 1990)

X   *Xorandor* (Manchester: Carcanet Press, 1986)

MENGHAM, Rod, ed. *An Introduction to Contemporary Fiction* (Cambridge: Polity Press, 1999). *Review of Contemporary Fiction* 19.2 (Summer 1999).

5.1 Bryan W. Aldiss
BH   *Barefoot in the Head: A European Fantasia* (London: Faber and Faber, 1969)

ALDISS, Brian W. & HARRISON, Harry, eds. *Hell's Cartographers: Sounding Brass Tinkling Cymbal – My Affair with Science Fiction* (London: Orbit Books, 1976).
HENIGHAN, Tom. *Brian W. Aldiss* (New York: Twayne Publishers, 1999).
HALIO, Jay L., ed. *Dictionary of Literary Biography, Volume 14: British Novelists Since 1960* (A Bruccoli Clark Layman Book: Gale Research, 1982).

5.2 J.G. Ballard
AE   *The Atrocity Exhibition* (London: Jonathan Cape, 1970)
C   *Crash* (London: Jonathan Cape, 1973)

BAXTER, John. *The Inner Man – The Life of J. G. Ballard* (London: Weidenfeld & Nicolson, 2011).
BROWN, Richard et al. (eds.) *J.G. Ballard—Landscapes of Tomorrow* (Leiden: Brill, 2016).
DELVILLE, Michel. *J. G. Ballard* (Plymouth: Northcote House Publishers, 1998).

5.3 Angela Carter
ED   *Expletives Deleted* (London: Chatto & Windus, 1992)
NS   *Nothing Sacred: Selected Writings* (London: Virago, 1982)
PNE   *The Passion of New Eve* (London: Victor Golancz, 1977)

MOSELEY, Merritt, ed. *Dictionary of Literary Biography, Volume 207: British Novelists since 1960* (A Bruccoli Clark Layman Book, Gale Group, 1999).
WANDOR, Michelene, ed. *Gender and Writing* (London: Pandora, 1983).

5.4 Jeanette Winterson
AO   *Art Objects – Essays on Ecstasy and Effrontery* (London: Jonathan Cape, 1995)
P   *The Passion* (New York: Grove Press, 1987)
PB   *The.Power.Book* (London: Vintage, 2001)

GRICE, Helena & WOODS, Tim, eds. *I'm Telling You Stories: Jeanette Winterston and the Politics of Reading; Postmodern Studies 25* (Amsterdam/Atlanta, GA: Rodopi, 1998).
ONEGA, Susana. *Jeanette Winterson* (Manchester: Manchester University Press, 2006).
REYNOLDS, Margaret & NOAKES, Jonathan, eds. *Jeanette Winterson: The Essential Guide* (London: Vintage, 2003).

5.5 Alisdair Gray
J   *1982 Janine* (Edinburgh: Canongate, 2003)
L   *Lanark: A Life in Four Books* (Edinburgh: Canongate Books Ltd., 1981)

BERNSTEIN, Stephen. *Alasdair Gray* (Lewisburg: Bucknell University Press, 1999).
CRAIG, Cairns. *The Modern Scottish Novel: Narrative and the National Imagination* (Edinburgh University Press, 1999).
CRAWFORD, Robert & NAIRN, Thom, eds. *The Arts of Alasdair Gray* (Edinburgh: Edinburgh University Press, 1991).
Edinburgh Review 74 (1986).
LEE, Alison. *Realism and Power: British Postmodern Fiction* (London: Routledge, 1990).
Review of Contemporary Fiction 15.2 (Summer 1995).
WHITE, Glyn. *Reading the Graphic Surface* (Manchester: Manchester University Press, 2005).

5.6 Iain Sinclair

EO   *Edge of the Orison: In the Traces of John Clare's Journey Out Of Essex* (London: Penguin Group, 2005)

LH   *Lud Heat and Suicide Bridge* (London: Random House; New York: Vintage, 1995)

LOT   *Lights Out for the Territory* (London: Granta Books, 1997)

LT   *Landor's Tower: or The Imaginary Conversations* (London: Granta Books, 2002)

V   *The Verbals: Iain Sinclair in Conversation with Kevin Jackson* (Tonbridge, Kent: Worple Press, 2003).

BOND, Robert & BAVIDGE, Jenny, eds. *The Work of Iain Sinclair* (Cambridge Scholars Publishing, 2007).

WOLFREYS, Julian. *Writing London* (New York/London: Palgrave MacMillan, 2004).

6. CHAPTER SIX: JOYCEAN AVANT-GARDE IN U.S. FICTION, 1973–1997

KENNEDY, Paul. *The Rise and Fall of the Great Powers* (New York: Random House, 1987).

KLINKOWITZ, Jerome. *Literary Disruptions – The Making of a Post-Contemporary American Fiction* (2ⁿᵈ edition, Urbana Chicago London: University of Illinois Press, 1980).

MILLARD, Kenneth. *Contemporary American Fiction – An Introduction to American Fiction since 1970* (Oxford: Oxford University Press, 2000).

6.0 Language poetry

IAT   *In the American Tree*: *Language, Realism, Poetry*, ed. Ron Silliman (Orono: National Poetry Foundation, University of Maine Press, 1986)

LB   *The L=A=N=G=U=A=G=E Book*, eds. Bruce Andrews & Charles Bernstein (Southern Illinois University Press, 1984)

PERLOFF, Marjorie. *The Dance of the Intellect: Studies in the Poetry of the Pound Tradition* (Evanston: Northwestern University Press, 1985).

6.1 Raymond Federman

C   *Critifiction: Postmodern Essays* (Albany: SUNY Press, 1993)

DN   *Double or Nothing Double or Nothing* (Chicago: The Swallow Press, 1971)

JC   *Journey To Chaos – Samuel Beckett's Early Fiction* (Berkeley/Los Angeles: University of California Press, 1965)

TILI   *Take It or Leave It* (New York: The Fiction Collective, 1976)

S   *Surfiction: Fiction Now and Tomorrow*, ed. Raymond Federman (1975; 2ⁿᵈ edition, enlarged, Chicago: Swallow Press, 1981)

VC   *The Voice in the Closet* (New York: Coda Press, 1979)

WMC   *To Whom It May Concern* (New York: Fiction Collective Two, 1990)

CORNIS-POPE, Marcel. *Narrative Innovation and Cultural Rewriting in the Cold War and After* (New York: Palgrave, 2001).

KUTNIK, Jerzy. *The Novel as Performance: The Fiction of Ronald Sukenick and Raymond Federman* (Carbondale/Edwardsville: Southern Illinois University Press, 1986).

Di LEO, Jeffrey R., ed. *Federman's Fictions – Innovation, Theory, Holocaust* (Albany: SUNY Press, 2011).

Style 28.3 (Fall 1994).

6.2 Ronald Sukenick

98.6   *98.6*

C   *Critifiction: Postmodern Essays* (Albany: SUNY Press, 1993)

IF	*In Form: Digressions on the Act of Fiction* (Carbondale/Edwardsville: Southern Illinois University Press, 1985).
LT	*Long Talking Bad Condition Blues* (New York: Coda Press, FC2, 1979)
MM	*Mosaic Man* (Normal, IL: Illinois University Press, 1999)
N	*Narralogues – Truth in Fiction* (Albany: SUNY Press, 2000)
O	*Out* (Chicago: The Swallow Press, 1973)
Up	*Up* (Michigan: Dial Press, 1968)

CORNIS-POPE, Marcel. *Narrative Innovation and Cultural Rewriting in the Cold War and After* (New York: Palgrave, 2001).

KUTNIK, Jerzy. *The Novel as Performance: The Fiction of Ronald Sukenick and Raymond Federman* (Carbondale/Edwardsville: Southern Illinois University Press, 1986).

ROBERSON, Matthew, ed. *Musing the Mosaic: Approaches to Ronald Sukenick* (New York: SUNY Press, 2003).

6.3 Walter Abish

AA	*Alphabetical Africa* (New York: New Directions, 1974)

BUFORD, William & BOLLA, Pete, eds. *GRANTA – New American Writing* (Spring 1979).

Conradiana 22.2 (Summer 1990).

CONTE, Joseph M. *Design and Debris: A Chaotics of Postmodern American Fiction* (Tuscaloosa: University of Alabama Press, 2002).

Critique 33.2 (Winter 1992).

ORBÁN, Katalin. *Ethical Diversions – The Post-Holocaust Narratives of Pynchon, Abish, DeLillo and Spiegelman* (New York/London: Routledge, 2005).

6.4 Ishmael Reed

MJ	*Mumbo-Jumbo: A Novel* (New York: Doubleday, 1972)

MARTIN, Reginald. *Ishmael Reed & the New Black Aesthetic Critics* (London: MacMillan Press, 1988).

McGEE, Patrick. *Ishmael Reed and the Ends of Race* (New York: St Martin's Press, 1997).

The Paris Review 128 (Winter 2016).

WILLIAMS, Dana A., ed. *African American Humor, Irony and Satire: Ishmael Reed, Satirically Speaking* (Newcastle: Cambridge Scholars Publishing, 2007).

6.5 Kathy Acker

DQ	*Don Quijote* (New York: Grove Press, 1986)
EA	*Essential Acker – The Selected Writings of Kathy Acker,* eds. Amy Scholder & Dennis Cooper (New York: Grove Press, 2002)
ES	*The Empire of the Senseless* (New York: Grove Press, 1988)
LM	*Literal Madness – Three Novels: Kathy Goes to Haiti, My Death My Life by Pier Paolo Pasolini, Florida* (New York: Grove Press, 1994)

CONTE, Joseph M. *Design and Debris: A Chaotics of Postmodern American Fiction* (Tuscaloosa: University of Alabama Press, 2002).

DEW, Spencer. *LEARNING FOR REVOLUTION* (San Diego: Hyperbole Books, San Diego University Press, 2011).

PITCHFORD, Nicola. *Tactical Readings: Feminist Postmodernism in the Novels of Kathy Acker and Angela Carter* (London: Associated University Press, 2002).

SCHOLDER, Amy, HARRYMAN, Carla, & RONELL, Avital, eds. *Lust for Life: On the Writings of Kathy Acker* (London/New York: Verso, 2006).

6.6 Gilbert Sorrentino

MS   *Mulligan Stew* (New York: Grove Press, 1979)
PL   *Pack of Lies* (Normal: Dalkey Archive Press, 1989)
SH   *Splendide-Hôtel* (New York: New Directions, 1973; Dalkey Archive, 2ⁿᵈ edition, 2001)

ARMAND, Louis, ed. *Hidden Agendas* (Prague: Litteraria Pragensia Books, 2010).
MACKEY, Louis. *Fact, Fiction, and Representation in Four Novels by Gilbert Sorrentino* (Columbia: Camden House, 1997).
McPHERON, William. *Gilbert Sorrentino: A Descriptive Bibliography* (Chicago: Dalkey Archive, 1991).

7. CHAPTER SEVEN: JOYCE AS SUCH / A TEL QUEL JOYCE

7.1 Tel Quel's "Enigmatic Reserve"
TQ   *Tel Quel* (Paris: Éditions du Seuil)

De Tel Quel à L'infini: l'avant-garde et après? Colloques de Londres et de Paris – mars 1995 (Nantes : Éditions Pleins Feux, 1999).
FFRENCH, Patrick. *The Time of Theory: A History of Tel Quel (1960–1983)* (Oxford: Clarendon Press, 1995).
FFRENCH, Patrick & LACK, Roland-François, eds. *The Tel Quel Reader* (London/New York: Routledge, 1998).
FOREST, Philippe. *Histoire de Tel Quel, 1960–1982* (Paris: Seuil, 1995).
FOREST, Philippe. *De Tel Quel à L'infini – nouveaux essais : Allaphbed 2* (Nantes : Éditions Cécile Defaut, 2006).
KAUPPI, Niiko. *The Making of an Avant-Garde: Tel Quel* (Berlin/New York: Mouton de Gruyter, 1994).

7.2 Jean-Louis Houdebine
EL   *Excès de langages* (Paris: Éditions Denoel, 1984)

7.3 Maurice Roche
Ci   *Circus* (Paris: Seuil, 1972)
Co   *Compact* (Paris: Seuil, 1966)
Cx   *Codex* (Paris: Seuil, 1974)

SHERZER, Dina. *Representation in Contemporary French Fiction* (Lincoln/London: University of Nebraska Press, 1986).
PIERSSENS, Michel. *Maurice Roche* (Amsterdam-Atlanta: Rodopi, 1989).

7.4 Hélène Cixous
D   *Dedans* (Paris: Grasset, 1969)
HCR   *The Hélène Cixous Reader*, ed. Susan Sellers (London: Routledge, 1994)
I   *Inside*, trans. Carol Barko (New York: Schocken Books, 1986)
PP   *Prénoms de personne* (Paris: Éditions du Seuil, 1974)
RM   *Le Rire de la méduse* (Paris: Galilée, 2010)
R   *Readings: The Poetics of Blanchot, Joyce, Kafka, Kleist, Lispector, and Tsvetayeva*, ed. & trans. Verena Andermatt Conley (Minneapolis: University of Minnesota Press, 1991)
S   *Souffles* (Paris: Des Femmes, 1975)

BLYTH, Ian & SELLERS, Susan, eds. *Hélène Cixous: Live Theory* (New York/London: Continuum, 2004).
CONLEY, Verena Andermatt. *Hélène Cixous: Writing the Feminine* (Lincoln/London: University of Nebraska Press, 1984).

SHIACH, Morag. *Hélène Cixous – The Politics Of Writing* (Routledge: London and New York, 1991).
PENROD, Lynn Kettler. *Hélène Cixous* (New York: Twayne Publishers, 1996).
WILCOX, Helen, McWATERS, Keith, THOMPSON, Ann & WILLIAMS, Linda R., eds. *The Body and the Text: Hélène Cixous, Reading and Teaching* (New York/London: Harvester & Wheatsheaf, 1990).

7.5 Philippe Sollers
H   *H* (Paris: Éditions du Seuil, 1973)
HE   *H*, trans. Veronika Stankovianska & David Vichnar (London: Equus Press, 2015)
L   *Lois* (Paris: Collection "Tel Quel" aux Éditions du Seuil, 1972)
N   *Nombres* (Paris: Éditions du Seuil, 1968)
P   *Paradis* (Paris: Collection "Tel Quel" aux Éditions du Seuil, 1981)
PII   *Paradis II* (Paris: Gallimard, 1986)
PJ   *Portrait du joueur* (Paris: Gallimard, 1987)

BARTHES, Roland. *Writer Sollers*, trans. Philip Thody (Minneapolis: University of Minnesota Press, 1987).
CLARK, Hilary. *The Fictional Encyclopaedia – Joyce, Pound, Sollers* (New York/London: Garland Publishing, 1990).
CHAMPAGNE, Roland A. *Philippe Sollers* (Amsterdam/Atlanta: Rodopi, 1996).
FOREST, Philippe. *Philippe Sollers* (Paris: Seuil, 1992).
POLLARD, Malcolm Charles. *The Novels of Philippe Sollers: Narrative and the Visual* (Amsterdam / Atlanta: Rodopi, 1994).

8. CHAPTER EIGHT: JOYCE POST-2000

BESSIERE, Jean. *Qu'est-il arrive aux écrivains français ? D'Alain Robbe-Grillet à Jonathan Littell* (Loveral: Éditions Labor, 2006).
KEMP, Simon. *French Fiction into the Twenty-first Century: The Return to the Story* (Cardiff: University of Wales Press, 2010).
TAYLOR, John. *Paths to Contemporary French Literature*, Vol. 1 (New Brunswick, New Jersey: Transaction Publishers, 2004).

Amerika, Mark
MD   *Meta/Data: A Digital Poetics* (Cambridge/London: MIT Press, 2007)
RB   *RemixtheBook* (Minneapolis/London: University of Minnesota Press, 2011)

AMERIKA, Mark & SUKENICK, Ronald, eds. *Degenerative Prose* (CF2, Illinois University Press: 1995).

Cohen, Joshua
BN   *Book of Numbers* (London: Vintage, 2015)
W   *Witz* (Dublin / London: Dalkey Archive Press, 2010)

VICHNAR, David & PEK, Olga eds. *Terrain—Essays on the New Poetics* (Prague: Litteraria Pragensia Books, 2014).
Ploughshares 42.1 (Spring 2016).

Danielewski, Mark Z.
HL   *House of Leaves* (London: Anchor, 2000)
OR   *Only Revolutions* (New York: Pantheon Books, 2006)

BRAY, Joe & GIBBONS, Alison, eds. *Mark Z. Danielewski* (Manchester/New York: Manchester University Press, 2011).

PÖHLMANN, Sascha ed. *Revolutionary Leaves: The Fiction of Mark Z. Danielewski* (Cambridge: Cambridge Scholars Publishing, 2012).
Contemporary Literature 45.4 (2004).
Studies in American Fiction 34.1 (Spring 2006).
Studies in Contemporary Fiction 50.1 (Fall 2008).

Foster Wallace, David
IJ *Infinite Jest* (New York: Little, Brown, 1996)

BURN, Stephen. *David Foster Wallace's Infinite Jest – A Reader's Guide* (London/New York: Continuum, 2003).
BOSWELL, Marshall. *Understanding David Foster Wallace* (Columbia: University of South California Press, 2003).
DOWLING, William & BELL, Robert. *A Reader's Companion to Infinite Jest* (New York: Xlibris, 2005).
New England Review, 36.2 (2015).
New York Review of Books, 47.2 (Feb 10, 2000).
Review of Contemporary Fiction 13.2 (Summer 1993).

Goldsmith, Kenneth
D   *Day* (Berkeley: The Figures, 2003)
F   *Fidget* (Toronto: Coach House Books, 2000)
HC   *Head Citations* (Great Barrington: The Figures, 2002)
UW   *Uncreative Writing – Managing Language in the Digital Age* (New York: Columbia University Press, 2011)

GOLDSMITH, Kenneth & DWORKIN, Craig, eds. *Against Expression: An Anthology of Conceptual Writing*, (Evanston, IL: Northwestern University Press, 2011).

Hall, Steven
RST   *The Raw Shark Texts* (Edinburgh: Canongate Books, 2007)

Contemporary Literature 52.2 (Summer 2011).
HAYLES, N. Katherine. *How We Think: Digital Media and Contemporary Technogenesis* (Chicago/London: University of Chicago Press, 2012).

Home, Stewart
69T   *69 Things to Do with a Dead Princess* (London: Cannongate, 2002)
AC   *The Assault on Culture: Utopian Currents from Lettrisme to Class War* (London: A.K. Press 1988)

London Review of Books 16.12 (June 1994).

Levé, Édouard
W   *Works*, trans. Jan Steyn (Dublin/London: Dalkey Archive Press, 2014)
N   *Newspaper*, trans. Jan Steyn & Caite Dolan-Leach (Dublin/London: Dalkey Archive Press, 2015)
AE   *Autoportrait*, trans. Lorin Stein (Dublin/London: Dalkey Archive Press, 2012)
SE   *Suicide*, trans. Jan Steyn (Dublin/London: Dalkey Archive Press, 2011)

ESPOSITO, Scott & ELKIN, Lauren. *The End of Oulipo? An Attempt to Exhaust a Movement* (Winchester / Washington: Zero Books, 2013).

Mitchell, David
CA   *Cloud Atlas* (London: Sceptre, 2004)
G   *Ghostwritten* (New York: Vintage, 1999)

Commentary 130.4 (November 2010).
London Review of Books 28. 9 (11 May 2006).
Modern Fiction Studies 58.3 (Fall 2012).
Modern Language Studies 40.2 (Winter 2011).
SubStance 44.1 (2015).

Moore, Alan
J   *Jerusalem* (New York/London: Norton & Co., 2016)
VF   *Voice of the Fire* (London: Victor Gollancz, 1996)

CONCLUSION: JOYCE THE POST-

ARMAND, Louis. *The Organ Grinder's Monkey – Culture After the Avant-Garde* (Prague: Litteraria Pragensia, 2013).
ARMAND, Louis. "'He Proves by Algebra': James Joyce's Post-Literary Incest Machines," *Journal of Modern Literature* 44.3 (Spring 2021), pp. 63–75.
BENSTOCK, Bernard, ed. *James Joyce – The Augmented Ninth* (New York: Syracuse University Press, 1988).
BUCKEYE, Robert. *Re: Quin* (Champaign/London/Dublin: Dalkey Archive Press, 2013).
Caputo, John D. *Deconstruction in a Nutshell: A Conversation with Jacques Derrida* (Fordham: Fordham University Press, 1997).
DERRIDA, Jacques. *Acts of Literature*, ed. Derek Attridge (New York: Routledge, 1992).
EHRLICH, Heyward, ed. *Light Rays: James Joyce and Modernism* (New York: New Horizon Press Publishers, 1984).
HASSAN, Ihab. *The Dismemberment of Orpheus: Toward a Postmodern Literature*, 2nd edition (New York: Oxford University Press, 1982).
LaCAPRA, Dominick. *Rethinking Intellectual History: Text, Context, and Language* (Ithaca: Cornell University Press, 1983).
LYOTARD, Jean-François. *The Postmodern Condition: A Report on Knowledge*, trans. Geoff Bennington & Brian Massumi (Manchester: Manchester University Press, 1991).
McHALE, Brian. *Constructing Postmodernism* (London/New York: Routledge, 1992).
SOLLERS, Philippe. *Writing and the Experience of Limits*, ed. David Hayman, trans. Philip Barnard & David Hayman (New York: Columbia University Press, 1983).

INDEX